CHILTON BOOK COMPANY
REPAIR & TUNE-UP GUIDE

BUICK/OLDSMOBILE PONTIAC 1975-90

All U.S. and Canadian models of full-size, rear wheel drive
BUICK Electra, LeSabre, Regal, Estate Wagon • OLDSMOBILE
Delta 88, Ninety-Eight, Custom Cruiser, Estate Wagon •
PONTIAC Bonneville, Catalina, Grand Ville, Parisienne, Safari Wagon

President GARY R. INGERSOLL
Senior Vice President, Book Publishing and Research RONALD A. HOXTER
Publisher KERRY A. FREEMAN, S.A.E.
Editor-in-Chief DEAN F. MORGANTINI, S.A.E.
Senior Editor RICHARD J. RIVELE, S.A.E.
Editor JAMES B. STEELE

CHILTON BOOK COMPANY
Radnor, Pennsylvania
19089

CONTENTS

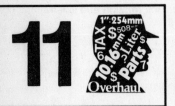

SAFETY NOTICE

Proper service and repair procedures are vital to the safe, reliable operation of all motor vehicles, as well as the personal safety of those performing repairs. This book outlines procedures for servicing and repairing vehicles using safe, effective methods. The procedures contain many NOTES, CAUTIONS and WARNINGS which should be followed along with standard safety procedures to eliminate the possibility of personal injury or improper service which could damage the vehicle or compromise its safety.

It is important to note that repair procedures and techniques, tools and parts for servicing motor vehicles, as well as the skill and experience of the individual performing the work vary widely. It is not possible to anticipate all of the conceivable ways or conditions under which vehicles may be serviced, or to provide cautions as to all of the possible hazards that may result. Standard and accepted safety precautions and equipment should be used during cutting, grinding, chiseling, prying, or any other process that can cause material removal or projectiles.

Some procedures require the use of tools specially designed for a specific purpose. Before substituting another tool or procedure, you must be completely satisfied that neither your personal safety, nor the performance of the vehicle will be endangered.

Although the information in this guide is based on industry sources and is as complete as possible at the time of publication, the possibility exists that the manufacturer made later changes which could not be included here. While striving for total accuracy, Chilton Book Company cannot assume responsibility for any errors, changes, or omissions that may occur in the compilation of this data.

PART NUMBERS

Part numbers listed in this reference are not recommendations by Chilton for any product by brand name. They are references that can be used with interchange manuals and aftermarket supplier catalogs to locate each brand supplier's discrete part number.

SPECIAL TOOLS

Special tools are recommended by the vehicle manufacturer to perform their specific job. Use has been kept to a minimum, but where absolutely necessary, they are referred to in the text by the part number of the tool manufacturer. These tools can be purchased, under the appropriate part number, from your General Motors dealer or an equivalent tool can be purchased locally from a tool supplier or parts outlet. Before substituting any tool for the one recommended, read the SAFETY NOTICE at the top of this page.

ACKNOWLEDGMENTS

The Chilton Book Company expresses appreciation to the Buick Division, Oldsmobile Division, and Pontiac Division of the General Motors Corporation for the technical information and illustrations contained within this manual.

Manufactured in the United States of America
34567890   987654321

Chilton's Repair Manual: Buick/Oldsmobile/Pontiac 1975–90
ISBN 0-8019-8039-9 pbk.
Library of Congress Catalog Card No.

General Information and Maintenance

HOW TO USE THIS BOOK

Chilton's Repair Manual for Buick, Oldsmobile and Pontiac full-sized cars is intended to help you with the care and maintenance of your car and save you money on its upkeep.

The first two chapters will be the most used, since they contain maintenance and tune-up information and procedures. Studies have shown that a properly tuned and maintained car can get at least 10% better gas mileage (which translates into lower operating costs) and periodic maintenance will catch minor problems before they turn into major repair bills. The other chapters deal with the more complex systems of your car. Operating systems from engine through brakes are covered to the extent that the average do-it-yourselfer becomes mechanically involved. This book will not explain such things as rebuilding the differential for the simple reason that the expertise required and the investment in special tools make this task impractical and uneconomical. It will give you the detailed instructions to help you change your own brake pads and shoes, tune-up the engine, replace spark plugs and filters, and do many more jobs that will save you money, give you personal satisfaction and help you avoid expensive problems.

A secondary purpose of this book is a reference guide for owners who want to understand their car and/or their mechanics better. In this case, no tools at all are required. Knowing just what a particular repair job requires in parts and labor time will allow you to evaluate whether or not you're getting a fair price quote and help decipher itemized bills from a repair shop.

Before attempting any repairs or service on your car, read through the entire procedure outlined in the appropriate chapter. This will give you the overall view of what tools and supplies will be required. There is nothing more frustrating than having to walk to the bus stop on Monday morning because you were short one gasket on Sunday afternoon. So read ahead and plan ahead. Each operation should be approached logically and all procedures thoroughly understood before attempting any work. Some special tools that may be required can often be rented from local automotive jobbers or places specializing in renting tools and equipment. Check the yellow pages of your phone book.

All chapters contain adjustments, maintenance, removal and installation procedures, and overhaul procedures. When overhaul is not considered practical, we tell you how to remove the failed part and then how to install the new or rebuilt replacement. In this way, you at least save the labor costs. Backyard overhaul of some components (such as the alternator or water pump) is just not practical, but the removal and installation procedure is often simple and well within the capabilities of the average car owner.

There are a few basic mechanic's rules that should be followed when working on any vehicle:

1. Left side of the vehicle means the driver's side; right side is the passenger's side.

2. Most screws, bolts, and nuts are right handed; they are tightened by turning clockwise and removed by turning counterclockwise.

3. Never crawl under a vehicle supported only by a jack. Jack up the vehicle, then support it with jackstands!

4. Never smoke or position an exposed flame near the battery or any part of the fuel system;

5. THINK AHEAD, TAKE YOUR TIME, AND USE COMMON SENSE DURING ALL OPERATIONS.

Safety is always the most important rule. Constantly be aware of the dangers involved in working on or around an automobile and take proper precautions to avoid the risk of personal injury or damage to the vehicle. See the section in this chapter, Servicing Your Vehicle Safely, and the SAFETY NOTICE on the acknowledgment page before attempting any service procedures and pay attention to the instructions provided. There are 3 common mistakes in mechanical work:

1. Incorrect order of assembly, disassembly or adjustment. When taking something apart or putting it together, doing things in the wrong order usually just costs you extra time; however it CAN break something. Read the entire procedure before beginning disassembly. Do everything in the order in which the instructions say you should do it, even if you can't immediately see a reason for it. When you're taking apart something that is very intricate (for example a carburetor), you might want to draw a picture of how it looks when assembled at one point in order to make sure you get everything back in its proper position. We will supply exploded views whenever possible, but sometimes the job requires more attention to detail than an illustration provides. When making adjustments (especially tune-up adjustments), do them in order. One adjustment often affects another and you cannot expect satisfactory results unless each adjustment is made only when it cannot be changed by any other.

2. Overtorquing (or undertorquing) nuts and bolts. While it is more common for overtorquing to cause damage, undertorquing can cause a fastener to vibrate loose and cause serious damage, especially when dealing with aluminum parts. Pay attention to torque specifications and utilize a torque wrench in assembly. If a torque figure is not available remember that, if you are using the right tool to do the job, you will probably not have to strain yourself to get a fastener tight enough. The pitch of most threads is so slight that the tension you put on the wrench will be multiplied many times in actual force on what you are tightening. A good example of how critical torque is can be seen in the case of spark plug installation, especially where you are putting the plug into an aluminum cylinder head. Too little torque can fail to crush the gasket, causing leakage of combustion gases and consequent overheating of the plug and engine parts. Too much torque can damage the threads or distort the plug, which changes the spark gap at the electrode. Since more and more manufacturers are using aluminum in their engine and chassis parts to save weight, a torque wrench should be in any serious do-it-yourselfer's tool box.

There are many commercial chemical products available for ensuring that fasteners won't come loose, even if they are not torqued just right (a very common brand is Loctite®). If you're worried about getting something together tight enough to hold, but loose enough to avoid mechanical damage during assembly, one of these products might offer substantial insurance. Read the label on the package and make sure the product is compatible with the materials, fluids, etc. involved before choosing one.

3. Crossthreading. This occurs when a part such as a bolt is screwed into a nut or casting at the wrong angle and forced, causing the threads to become damaged. Crossthreading is more likely to occur if access is difficult. It helps to clean and lubricate fasteners, and to start threading with the part to be installed going straight in, using your fingers. If you encounter resistance, unscrew the part and start over again at a different angle until it can be inserted and turned several times without much effort. Keep in mind that many parts, especially spark plugs, use tapered threads so that gentle turning will automatically bring the part you're threading to the proper angle if you don't force it or resist a change in angle. Don't put a wrench on the part until it's been turned in a couple of times by hand. If you suddenly encounter resistance and the part has not seated fully, don't force it. Pull it back out and make sure it's clean and threading properly.

Always take your time and be patient; once you have some experience, working on your car will become an enjoyable hobby.

TOOLS AND EQUIPMENT

Naturally, without the proper tools and equipment it is impossible to properly service your vehicle. It would be impossible to catalog each tool that you would need to perform each and every operation in this book. It would also be unwise for the amateur to rush out and buy an expensive set of tools on the theory that he may need one or more of them at sometime.

The best approach is to proceed slowly, gathering together a good quality set of those tools that are used most frequently. Don't be misled by the low cost of bargain tools. It is far better to spend a little more for better quality. Forged wrenches, 6- or 12-point sockets and fine tooth ratchets are by far preferable to their less expensive counterparts. As any good mechanic can tell you, there are few worse experiences than trying to work on a car or truck with bad tools. Your monetary savings will be far outweighed by frustration and mangled knuckles.

Begin accumulating those tools that are used most frequently; those associated with routine maintenance and tune-up.

In addition to the normal assortment of screwdrivers and pliers, you should have the following tools for routine maintenance jobs (your car uses both English and metric fasteners):

• Metric wrenches – sockets and combination open end/box end wrenches in sizes from 3mm to 19mm; and a spark plug socket ($^{13}/_{16}$ in.)

If possible, buy various length socket drive extensions. One break in this department is that the metric sockets available in the U.S. will all fit the ratchet handles and extensions you may already have (¼ in., ⅜ in., and ½ in. drive).

• Jackstands for support
• Oil filter wrench
• Oil filter spout for pouring oil
• Grease gun for chassis lubrication
• Hydrometer for checking the battery
• A container for draining oil
• Many rags for wiping up the inevitable mess

In addition to the above items there are several others that are not absolutely necessary, but handy to have around. These include absorbent gravel, a transmission fluid funnel and the usual supply of lubricants, antifreeze and fluids, although these can be purchased as needed. This is a basic list for routine maintenance, but only if your personal needs and desires can accurately determine your list of tools.

The second list of tools is for tune-ups. While the tools involved here are slightly more sophisticated, they need not be outrageously expensive. There are several inexpensive tachometer/dwell meters on the market that are every bit as good for the average mechanic as a $100.00 professional model. Just be sure that the meter scale goes to at least 1,200–1,500 rpm on the tach scale and that it works on 4-cylinder engines. A basic list of tune-up equipment could include:

1. Tach/dwell meter
2. Spark plug wrench
3. Timing light (a DC light that works from the car's battery is best, although an AC light that plugs into 110V house current will suffice at some sacrifice in brightness)
4. Wire spark plug gauge/adjusting tools
5. Set of feeler blades

In addition to these basic tools, there are several other tools and gauges you may find useful. These include:

1. A compression gauge. The screw-in type is slower to use, but eliminates the possibility of a faulty reading due to escaping pressure
2. A manifold vacuum gauge
3. A test light
4. An induction meter. This is used for determining whether or not there is current in a wire. This is handy for use if a wire is broken somewhere in a wiring harness.

As a final note, you will probably find a torque wrench necessary for all but the most basic work. There are three types of torque wrenches available: deflecting beam type, dial indicator (dial indicator) and click type. The beam and dial indicator models are perfectly adequate, although the click type models are more precise, and allow the user to reach the required torque without having to assume a sometimes awkward position in reading a scale. No matter what type of torque wrench you purchase, have it calibrated periodically to ensure accuracy.

Torque specification for each fastener will be given in the procedure in any case that a specific torque value is required. If no torque specifications are given, use the following values as a guide, based upon fastener size:

Bolts marked 6T
    6mm bolt/nut – 5–7 ft. lbs.
    8mm bolt/nut – 12–17 ft. lbs.
    10mm bolt/nut – 23–34 ft. lbs.
    12mm bolt/nut – 41–59 ft. lbs.
    14mm bolt/nut – 56–76 ft. lbs.

Bolts marked 8T
    6mm bolt/nut – 6–9 ft. lbs.
    8mm bolt/nut – 13–20 ft. lbs.
    10mm bolt/nut – 27–40 ft. lbs.
    12mm bolt/nut – 46–69 ft. lbs.
    14mm bolt/nut – 75–101 ft. lbs.

Special Tools

Special tools are occasionally necessary to perform a specific job or are recommended to make a job easier. Their use has been kept to a minimum. When a special tool is indicated, it will be referred to by the manufacturer's part number, and, where possible, an illustration of the tool will be provided so that an equivalent tool may be used. Special tools for GM cars can be purchased from a dealer or through:

Service Tool Division
Kent-Moore
29784 Little Mack
Roseville, MI 48066-2298

SERVICING YOUR VEHICLE SAFELY

It is virtually impossible to anticipate all of the hazards involved with automotive maintenance and service, but care and common sense will prevent most accidents.

The rules of safety for mechanics range from "don't smoke around gasoline," to "use the proper tool for the job." The trick to avoiding

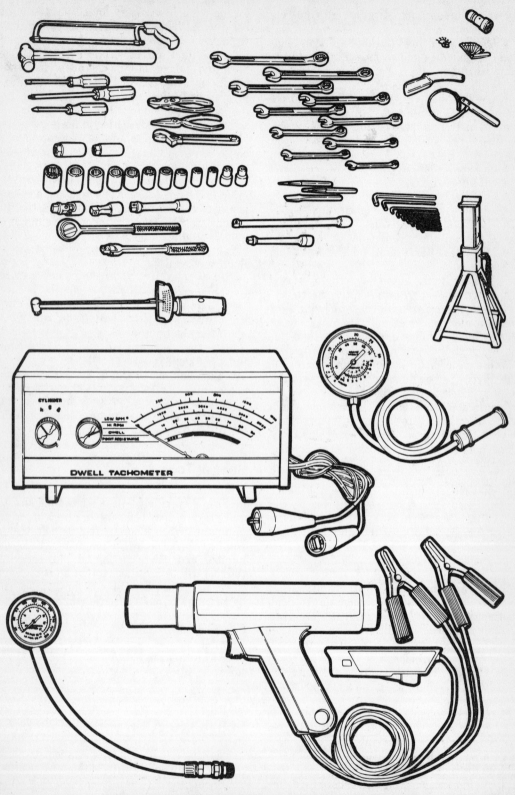

This basic collection of hand tools will handle most service needs

injuries is to develop safe work habits and take every possible precaution.

Dos

• Do keep a fire extinguisher and first aid kit within easy reach.

• Do wear safety glasses or goggles when cutting, drilling, grinding, or prying, even if you have 20-20 vision. If you wear glasses for the sake of vision, they should be made of hardened glass that can serve also as safety glasses, or wear safety goggles over your regular glasses.

• Do shield your eyes whenever you work around the battery. Batteries contain sulphuric acid. In case of contact with the eyes or skin, flush the area with water or a mixture of water and baking soda and get medical attention immediately.

• Do you safety stands for any undervehicle service. Jacks are for raising vehicles, safety stands are for making sure the vehicle stays raised until you want it to come down. Whenever the vehicle is raised, block the wheels remaining on the ground and set the parking brake.

• Do use adequate ventilation when working with any chemicals or hazardous materials. Like carbon monoxide, the asbestos dust resulting from brake lining wear can be poisonous in sufficient quantities.

• Do disconnect the negative battery cable when working on the electrical system. The secondary ignition system can contain up to 40,000 volts.

• Do follow manufacturer's directions whenever working with potentially hazardous materials. Both brake fluid and antifreeze are poisonous if taken internally.

• Do properly maintain your tools. Loose hammerheads, mushroomed punches and chisels, frayed or poorly grounded electrical cords, excessively worn screwdrivers, spread wrenches (open end), cracked sockets, slipping ratchets, or faulty droplight sockets can cause accidents.

• Likewise, keep your tools clean; a greasy wrench can slip off a bolt head, ruining the bolt and often ruining your knuckles in the process.

• Do use the proper size and type of tool for the job being done.

• Do when possible, pull on a wrench handle rather than push on it, and adjust your stance to prevent a fall.

• Do be sure that adjustable wrenches are tightly closed on the nut or bolt and pulled so that the face is on the side of the fixed jaw.

• Do select a wrench or socket that fits the nut or bolt. The wrench or socket should sit straight, not cocked.

• Do strike squarely with a hammer; avoid glancing blows.

• Do set the parking brake and block the drive wheels if the work requires the engine running.

Don'ts

• Don't run the engine in a garage or anywhere else without proper ventilation--EVER! Carbon monoxide is poisonous; it takes a long time to leave the human body and you can build up a deadly supply of it in your system by simply breathing in a little every day. You may not realize you are slowly poisoning yourself. Always use power vents, windows, fans or open the garage doors.

• Don't work around moving parts while wearing a necktie or other loose clothing. Short sleeves are much safer than long, loose sleeves; hard-toed shoes with neoprene soles protect your toes and give a better grip on slippery surfaces. Jewelry such as watches, fancy belt buckles, beads or body adornment of any kind is not safe working around a vehicle. Long hair should be tied back under a hat or cap.

• Don't use your pockets for toolboxes. A fall or bump can drive a screwdriver deep into your body. Even a wiping cloth hanging from the back pocket can wrap around a spinning shaft or fan.

• Don't smoke when working around gasoline, cleaning solvent or other flammable material.

• Don't smoke when working around the battery. When the battery is being charged, it gives off explosive hydrogen gas.

• Don't use gasoline to wash your hands; there are excellent soaps available. Gasoline may contain lead, and lead can enter the body through a cut, accumulating in the body until you are very ill. Gasoline also removes all the natural oils from the skin so that bone dry hands will suck up oil and grease.

• Don't service the air conditioning system unless you are equipped with the necessary tools and training. The refrigerant, R-12, is extremely cold when compressed, and when released into the air will instantly freeze any surface it contacts, including your eyes. Although the refrigerant is normally non-toxic, R-12 becomes a deadly poisonous gas in the presence of an open flame. One good whiff of the vapors from burning refrigerant can be fatal.

• Don't use screwdrivers for anything other than driving screws! A screwdriver used as a prying tool can snap when you least expect it, causing injuries. At the very least, you'll ruin a good screwdriver.

• Don't use a bumper jack (that little ratchet, scissors, or pantograph jack supplied with the vehicle) for anything other than changing a flat! These jacks are only intended for emergency use out on the road; they are NOT designed as a maintenance tool. If you are serious about maintaining your vehicle yourself, invest in a hydraulic floor jack of at least 1½ ton capacity, and at least two sturdy jackstand.

SERIAL NUMBER IDENTIFICATION

Vehicle Identification Number Plate

The Vehicle Identification Number (VIN) is important for ordering parts and for servicing. The VIN is a thirteen digit (1975–1980) or seventeen digit (1981 and later) sequence of numbers and letters visible on a plate fastened to the upper left instrument panel area, seen through the windshield.

NOTE: *Model years appear in the VIN as the last digit of each particular year (6 is 1976, 8 is 1978, etc.), until 1980 (which is A). This is the final year under the thirteen digit code. The seventeen digit VIN begins with 1981 (B), and continues 1982 (C), 1983 (D), etc.*

Automatic Transmission Identification

All Buick, Oldsmobile and Pontiac models covered in this guide use various GM Turbo Hydra-Matic (THM) automatic transmissions. Transmission identification numbers are found on either side of the transmission case, depend-

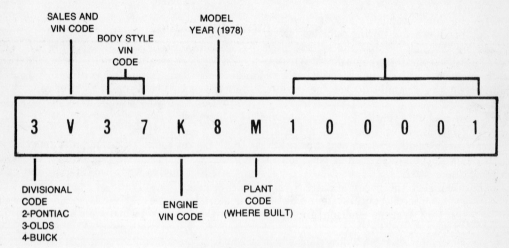

Thirteen digit VIN, 1975 to 1980

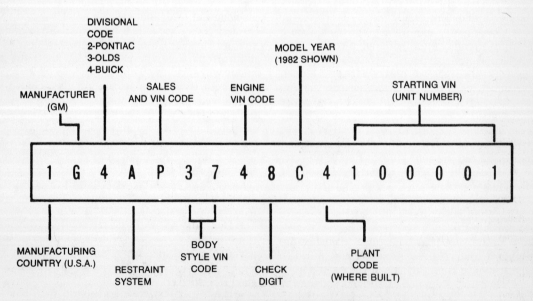

Seventeen digit VIN, 1981 and later

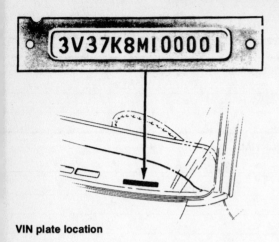

VIN plate location

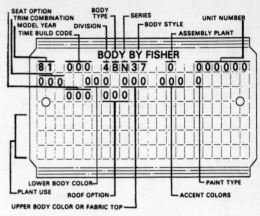

Body number plate—U.S. models

Engine Identification Codes

Engine	Eng. Mfg.	Bbl.	'75	'76	'77	'78	'79	'80	'81	'82	'83	'84–'86	'86–'87	'88–'90
						BUICK								
6-231	Buick	2			C	A,G	A	A	A	A	A	A	A	
6-231	Buick	2, 4-Turbo				3	3	3						
6-231	Buick	FI											Z	
6-252	Buick	4						4	4	4	4	4		
8-301	Pont.	2			Y	Y	Y							
8-301	Pont.	4						W						
8-305	Chev.	2				U	G							
8-307	Olds.	4							Y	Y	Y	Y	Y	Y
8-350	Olds.	4			R	R	R	R						
8-350	Chev.	4				L								
8-350	Buick	4	J	J	J	X	X	X						
8-350	Olds.	Diesel						N	N	N	N	N		
8-403	Olds.	4			K	K	K							
8-455	Buick	4	T	Y										
						OLDSMOBILE								
6-231	Buick	2			C	A	A	A	A	A	A			
6-252	Buick	4							4	4	4			
8-260	Olds.	2			F	F	F		F	8	8			
8-265	Pont.	2						S						
8-301	Pont.	2				Y								
8-307	Olds.	4							Y	Y	Y	Y	Y	Y
8-350	Olds.	4	K	R	R	R	R	R						
8-350	Chev.	4				L								
8-350	Olds.	Diesel				N	N	N	N	N	N	N		
8-400	Olds.	2	R											

Engine Identification Codes (cont.)

Engine	Eng. Mfg.	Bbl.	'75	'76	'77	'78	'79	'80	'81	'82	'83	'84–'86	'86–'87	'88–'90
OLDSMOBILE														
8-400	Olds.	4	S											
8-403	Olds.	4			K	K	K	K						
8-455	Olds.	4	T	T										
PONTIAC														
6-231	Buick	2					A	A	A	A	A	A	A	A
6-252	Buick	4								4				
8-265	Pont.	2						S	S					
8-301	Pont.	2				Y	Y							
8-301	Pont.	4				W	W	W						
8-305	Chev.	2									H	H		
8-307	Olds.	4							Y				Y	Y①
8-350	Olds.	4			R	R	R	R						
8-350	Chev.	4				L	L							
8-350	Pont.	4		P	P									
8-350	Buick	4				X	X							
8-350	Olds.	Diesel						N	N	N	N	N		
8-400	Pont.	2	R	R										
8-400	Pont.	4	S	S		Z	Z							
8-403	Olds.	4			K	K	K	K						
8-455	Pont.	4	W	W										

① Vehicle discontinued in 1990.

ing on model. Some models also have I.D. numbers stamped on the governor cover.

Buick models are equipped with the 200, 200C, 200-4R, 350, 375B and 400 transmissions. Oldsmobile uses the 200, 200C, 2004R, 250, 350, 375B and 400 and 200-4R units, and Pontiacs are equipped with the 200, 200C, 2004R, 350, 200-4R and 400 transmissions. The 375B transmission was last used in 1976, while the 200-4R was introduced in 1981.

A quick way to visually identify the transmissions is to look at the shapes of the pans. The 250, 350 and 375B have a squarish pan with the right rear corner cut off. The 200 pan is similar but more rectangular. The pan of the 400 model transmission is irregularly shaped. See Chapter 7 for pan illustrations.

The 200, 250, 350 and 375B models are also identified by their kickdown linkage, which is actuated by a cable attached to the accelerator pedal linkage. The 400 model transmission has

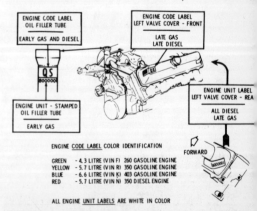

Engine number locations, engine VIN F,P,N,R,Y and K. 1975–77 Olds and Pontiac number stamped on oil filler tube

Body number plate—Canadian models

Engine VIN location, late model Olds 231 V-6

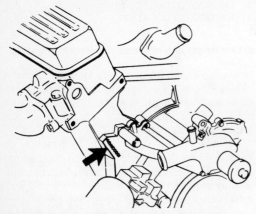

Early V6 engine number location, 1977 shown

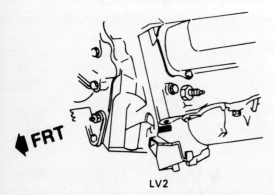

VIN location, 5.0L Olds 307 cid (VIN Y)

an electric kickdown connected to a switch on the accelerator linkage.

The 200 model transmission was first used in 1977 and is the first all metric unit built by GM in the U.S. This transmission sometimes has the word METRIC stamped on the pan. The 200-4R model is an automatic overdrive version

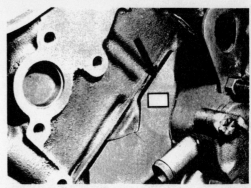

1975 Pontiac and Olds 400 V8 engine number location

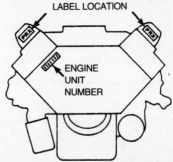

Engine VIN locations, 265, 301, 305 and 350 (L code) V8s

Turbo Hydra-Matic 350 serial number

Turbo Hydra-Matic 200, 200C, 400 serial number plate on the right side of the transmission case

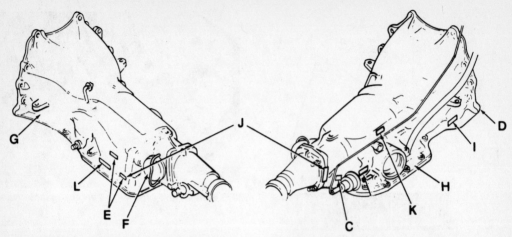

C. THM 200 AND THM 200-4R I.D. TAG LOCATION
D. THM 200 AND THM 200-4R VIN LOCATION
E. THM 200 AND THM 200-4R VIN OPTIONAL LO-
     CATIONS
F. THM 250C I.D. STAMP LOCATION
G. THM 250C VIN LOCATION

H. THM 350C STAMPED I.D. LOCATION
I. THM 350C VIN LOCATION
J. THM 350C OPTIONAL VIN LOCATIONS
K. THM 400 I.D. TAG LOCATION
L. THM 400 VIN LOCATION

Transmission I.D. location. 375B unit same as 350 except for longer output shaft and extension housing

of the 200 transmission. The 200C, 250C and 350C transmissions are similar to those given these number designations without the C except that they incorporate a lockup clutch in the torque converter.

There is little visual difference between the 350 and 375B transmissions, except that the latter has a longer output shaft and extension housing.

Drive Axle Identification

The drive axle identification is stamped on the forward portion of the housing or on a tag bolted to the rear cover.

Vehicle Emission Control Information Label

The Vehicle Emission Control Information Label is located in the engine compartment (fan shroud, radiator support, hood underside, etc.) of every vehicle produced by General Motors. The label contains important emission specifications and setting procedures, as well as a vacuum hose schematic with various emissions components identified.

When servicing your Buick, Oldsmobile or Pontiac, this label should always be checked for up-to-date information pertaining specifically to your vehicle.

NOTE: *Always follow the timing procedures on this label when adjusting ignition timing.*

ROUTINE MAINTENANCE

Air Cleaner

All engines are equipped with dry type air cleaners with replaceable air filter elements. The positive crankcase ventilation system (PCV) air filter element on gasoline engines is also found in the air filter housing (usually mounted on the inside of the housing rim). Both of these filter elements should be replaced

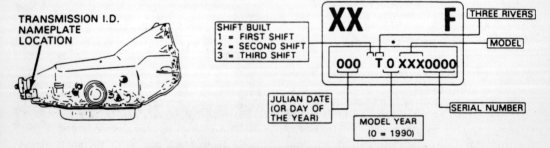

Turbo Hydra-Matic 200-4R identification location—late model

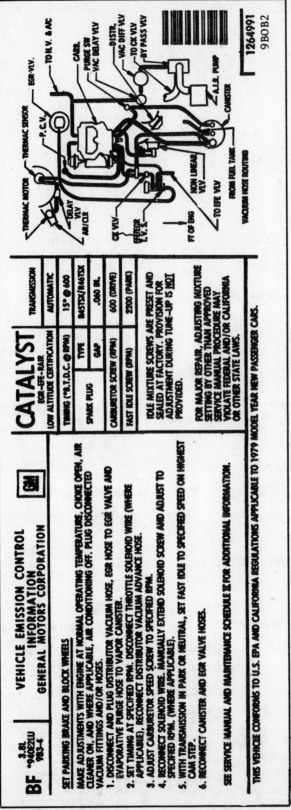

Typical emissions decal, 1979 231 V6 shown

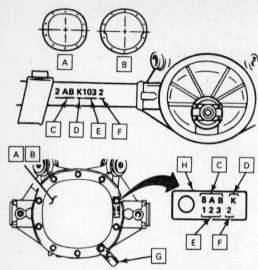

A. 7½ in. ring gear axle cover
B. 8½ in. ring gear axle cover
C. Axle code
D. Manufacturer code K— GM of Canada, St.
Catharines, code G— Saginaw, Detroit
E. Day built
F. Shift 1—day, shift 2— night
G. Limit slip tag
H. Axle code tag

Drive axle identification

Replacing the air filter

Wipe out the inside of the air cleaner assembly with a clean rag

at 30,000 mile or 1½ year intervals (36 month intervals on 1983 and later models) on all models, except in extremely dusty or smoggy conditions where replacement should be much more frequent.

NOTE: *Never remove the air cleaner from a diesel with the engine running. The intake vacuum is very great, and dirt or nearby objects (even the air cleaner wingnut!) may be sucked directly into the combustion chambers. This will almost always cause major engine damage.*

Air Cleaner Element and PCV Filter
REMOVAL AND INSTALLATION

1. Remove the wing nut(s) from the top of the air cleaner assembly and lay it aside.
2. Remove the air cleaner cover and gently lift the air cleaner element out of the housing without knocking any dirt into the carburetor.
3. Pull the PCV filter out of the retainer.
4. Wipe the inside of the air cleaner housing with a paper towel or clean rag.
5. Clean the inside of the PCV filter retainer and install a new PCV filter element.
6. Install a new air cleaner element.
7. Replace the air cleaner cover and install the wing nut(s).

Check the PCV filter in the air cleaner assembly

Fuel Filter
REMOVAL AND INSTALLATION
Gasoline Engines

The carburetor inlet fuel filter should be replaced every year or 15,000 miles or more often if necessary. This paper element filter is located behind the large fuel line inlet nut on the carburetor. Some vehicles may also have an inline fuel filter located between the fuel pump and carburetor. This filter should be changed at the same time as the inlet-type filter; in both cases filters should only be changed when the engine is cold for safety related reasons.

To replace the inlet (carburetor body) fuel filter:

Fuel filter location, gasoline engines

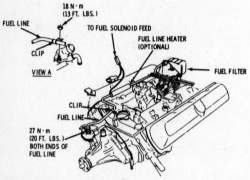

18 N·m
(13 FT. LBS.)

FUEL LINE

TO FUEL SOLENOID FEED

FUEL LINE HEATER
(OPTIONAL)

CLIP

VIEW A

FUEL FILTER

CLIP

FUEL LINE

27 N·m
(20 FT. LBS.)
BOTH ENDS OF
FUEL LINE

Diesel fuel filter and lines

1. Place some absorbent rags under the fuel fittings to catch the gasoline which will spill out when the lines are loosened.

2. Disconnect the fuel line connection at the intake fuel filter nut. Plug the opening to prevent loss of fuel.

NOTE: *Always hold the large inlet nut stationary with a wrench while loosening the fuel line flare nut using a flare nut wrench.*

3. Remove the intake fuel filter nut from the carburetor with a box wrench or socket.

4. Remove the filter element and spring.

5. The filter element can be cleaned in solvent and blown dry. However, for the low cost of a new filter it is more advisable to simply install a new element.

6. Install the element spring, then the filter element in the carburetor.

7. Install a new gasket on the intake fuel nut, then install the nut in the carburetor body and torque to 46 ft. lbs. (62 Nm).

8. Install the fuel line and torque to 22 ft. lbs. (30 Nm). Check for leaks at all fittings with the engine idling.

Some models have an inline fuel filter in addition to the inlet filter in the carburetor. This filter is cylindrical and located in the fuel line be-

tween the pump and the carburetor. It may be made of either metal or plastic.

To replace the in-line filter:

1. Place some absorbent rags under the filter, remembering that it will be full of gasoline when removed.

2. Use a pair of pliers to expand the clamp on one end of the filter, then slide the clamp down past the point to which the filter pipe extends in the rubber hose. Do the same with the other clamp.

3. Gently twist and pull the hoses free of the filter pipes. Remove and discard the old filter.

4. Install the new filter into the hoses, slide the clamps back into place, and check for leaks with the engine idling.

Diesel Engines

The diesel fuel filter is mounted on the rear of the intake manifold, and is larger than that on a gasoline engine because diesel fuel generally is "dirtier" (has more suspended particles) than gasoline.

The diesel fuel filter should be changed every 30,000 miles or two years.

To install a new filter:

1. With the engine cool, remove the air cleaner and plug the air intake, then place absorbent rags underneath the fuel line fittings at the filter.

2. Disconnect the fuel lines from the filter.

3. Unbolt the filter from its bracket.

4. Install the new filter. Connect the fuel lines to the filter but tighten them only finger tight. Note that the two lines are of different sizes so that the filter cannot be installed in the wrong position. Install and tighten the wingnut and then torque the larger fuel line to 20 ft.lbs. (27 Nm) and the smaller one to 13 ft.lbs. (18 Nm). Start the engine and check for leaks. Run the engine for about two minutes, then shut the engine off for the same amount of time to allow any trapped air in the injection system to bleed off.

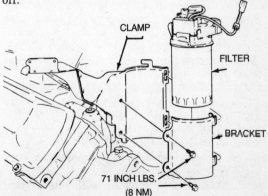

CLAMP

FILTER

BRACKET

71 INCH LBS.
(8 NM)

Diesel fuel filter

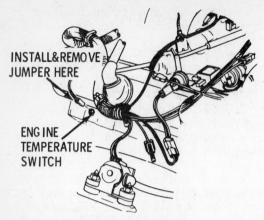

INSTALL&REMOVE JUMPER HERE

ENGINE TEMPERATURE SWITCH

H.P.C.A. solenoid activation, diesels

The GM diesel vehicles also have a fuel filter inside the fuel tank which is maintenance free. NOTE: *If the filter element ever becomes clogged, the engine will stop. This stoppage is usually preceded by a hesitation or sluggish running. General Motors recommends that after changing the diesel fuel filter, the Housing Pressure Cold Advance be activated manually, if the engine temperature is above 125°F (52°C). Activating the H.P.C.A. will reduce engine cranking time.*

To activate the H.P.C.A. solenoid, disconnect the two lead connector at the engine temperature switch and bridge the connector with a jumper. After the engine is running, remove the jumper and reconnect the connector to the engine temperature switch. When the new filter element is installed, start the engine and check for leaks.

Positive Crankcase Ventilation (PCV) Valve

TESTING

All gasoline engines covered in this guide are equipped with a closed crankcase emission control system (see Chapter 4) featuring a vacuum operated Positive Crankcase Ventilation valve (PCV). A faulty PCV valve or clogged hoses to and from the valve can cause a rough idle, oil leaks, or excessive oil sludging. Check the system at least once a year and replace the valve at least every 30 months or 30,000 miles. A general test is to remove the PCV valve from the valve cover and shake it. If a rattle is heard, the valve is usually OK.

A more positive test is:

1. Remove the PCV valve from the rocker arm cover or intake manifold.

2. Connect a tachometer to the engine and run the engine at idle.

3. Check the tachometer reading, then place

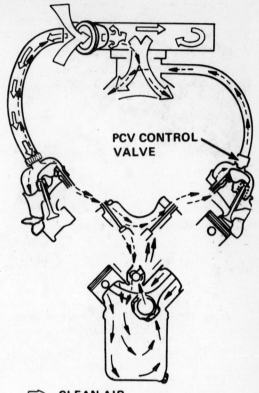

PCV CONTROL VALVE

⇨ **CLEAN AIR**

➡ **VOLATILE OIL FUMES**

⇢ **MIXTURE OF AIR AND FUMES**

Typical PCV system flow

your thumb over the end of the valve. You should feel a suction.

4. Check the tachometer again. The engine speed should have dropped at least 50 rpm. It should return to a normal idle when you remove your thumb from the end of the valve.

5. If the engine does not change speed or if

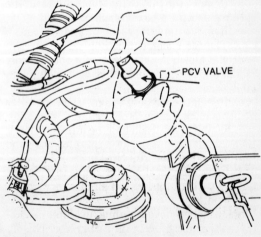

PCV VALVE

Checking the PCV valve for vacuum

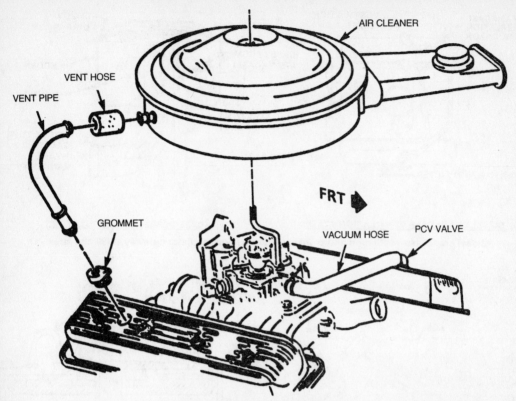

AIR CLEANER

VENT HOSE

VENT PIPE

FRT

GROMMET

VACUUM HOSE   PCV VALVE

Gasoline crankcase ventilation system

the change is less than 50 rpm, the hose is clogged or the valve defective. Check the hose first. If it is not clogged, replace the PCV valve. Test the new valve in the same way.

REMOVAL AND INSTALLATION

The large base of the PCV valve fits into the valve cover of the engine via a grommet. At the upper end there is a connection to a rubber hose. This hose feeds into the air intake system at the base of the carburetor. To replace the valve, gently pull the top out of the hose. Then, pull the base out of the grommet. Replace the PCV valve in reverse order. It is vitally important that you replace the length of hose into which the PCV top connection fits if the hose has gotten brittle, because it will seal poorly, leak, and cause engine idling problems. The same goes for the grommet in the valve cover because if this leaks, crankcase ventilation may not be complete enough, leaving the oil unnecessarily dirty.

Crankcase Depression Regulator and Flow Control Valve

REMOVAL AND INSTALLATION

8–350 Diesel Engines

The Crankcase Depression Regulator (CDR), found on 1981 and later diesels, and the flow

control valve, used from 1978 to 1980, are designed to scavenge crankcase vapors in basically the same manner as the PCV valve on gasoline engines. The valves are located either on the left rear corner of the intake manifold (CDR), or on the rear of the intake crossover pipe (flow control valve). On each system there are two ventilation filters, one per valve cover.

The filter assemblies should be cleaned every 15,000 miles by simply prying them carefully from the valve covers (without damaging the grommets underneath), and washing them out in solvent. The ventilation pipes and tubes should also be cleaned. Both the CDR and flow control valves should also be cleaned every 30,000 miles (the cover can be removed from the CDR; the flow control valve can simply be flushed with solvent). Dry each valve, filter, and hose with compressed air before installation.

NOTE: *Do not attempt to test the crankcase controls on these diesels. Instead, clean the valve cover filter assembly and vent pipes and check the vent pipes.*

Replace the breather cap assembly every 30,000 miles. Replace all rubber fittings as required every 15,000 miles.

Evaporative Canister

The evaporative canister, sometimes referred to as a charcoal canister, is mounted inside the

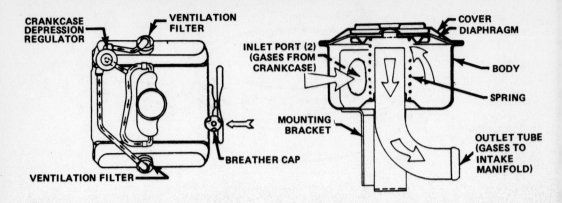

DIESEL CRANKCASE VENTILATION SYSTEM **CRANKCASE DEPRESSION REGULATOR**

Diesel crankcase ventilation and crankcase depression regulator cutaway, 1980 and later

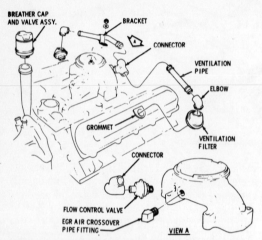

Diesel crankcase ventilation system, 1978–80

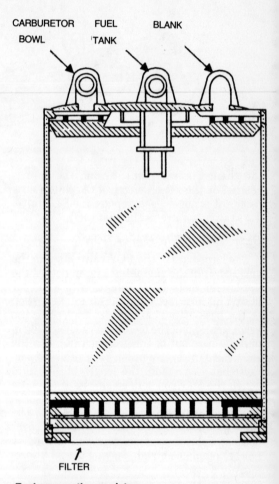

Fuel evaporation canister

engine compartment. The canister and its filter are part of the evaporative emissions system (see Chapter 4) and work to eliminate the release of unburned fuel vapor into the atmosphere. The vapor is absorbed by the carbon in the canister and stored until manifold vacuum, when the engine is running, draws the vapors into the engine for burning.

The filter in the bottom of canisters with open bottoms must be changed every two years or 24,000 miles, or more often under extremely dusty or smoggy conditions. To change the filter, proceed as follows:

1. Tag and disconnect all hoses connected to the evaporative canister.

2. Loosen the retaining clamps and then lift out the canister.

3. Grasp the filter element in the bottom of the canister with your fingers and pull it out. Replace it with a new element.

4. Replace the canister in the clamps and reconnect all hoses. If any of the hoses are brittle or cracked, replace them only with fuel-resistant replacement hose marked EVAP.

Battery

SPECIFIC GRAVITY CHECK (EXCEPT MAINTENANCE FREE BATTERIES)

Check the specific gravity of the battery (your diesel has two) at every tune-up for gasoline engines and at every oil change for diesels. It should be between 1.20 and 1.30 at room temperature.

NOTE: *See Fluid Level Checks later in this chapter for information on maintenance free batteries.*

The specific gravity is checked with a hydrometer, an inexpensive instrument available in most auto parts stores, auto departments and many hardware stores. The hydrometer looks like a turkey baster, having a rubber squeeze bulb on one end and a nozzle at the other. Insert the nozzle end into each battery cell and suck enough electrolyte (battery water) into the hydrometer to just lift the float. The specific gravity is then read by the graduations on the float. Some hydrometers are color coded, with each color signifying a certain range of specific gravity.

All cells of your battery should produce nearly equal specific gravity readings. Do not be extremely alarmed if all of your battery's cells are equally low (but check to see if your alternator belt is tight); however, it is a big difference between two or more cells that should be of concern. Generally, if after charging, the specific gravity between any two cells varies more than 50 points (0.050), the battery is bad and should be replaced.

It is not possible to check the specific gravity in this manner on sealed (maintenance free) batteries. Instead, the indicator built into the top of the case must be relied on to display any signs of battery deterioration. If the indicator is dark, the battery can be assumed to be OK. If the indicator is light, the specific gravity is low and the battery should be charged or replaced.

FILLING THE BATTERY

Batteries should be checked for proper electrolyte level at least once a month or more frequently. Keep a close eye on any cell or cells that are unusually low or seem to constantly need water. This may indicate a battery on its last legs, a leak, or a problem with the charging system.

Top up each cell to about ⅜ in. (9.5mm) above the tops of the plates. Always use distilled water (available in supermarkets or auto parts stores), because most tap water contains chemicals and minerals that may slowly damage the plates of your battery.

CLEANING CABLES AND CLAMPS

Twice a year, the battery terminal posts and the cable clamps should be cleaned. Loosen the clamp bolts (you may have to brush off any corrosion with a baking soda and water solution if they are really messy) and remove the cables, negative cable first. On batteries with posts on top, the use of a battery clamp puller is recommended. It is easy to break off a battery termi-

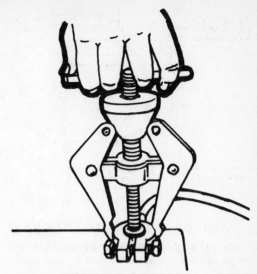

Top terminal battery clamps may be removed with this inexpensive tool

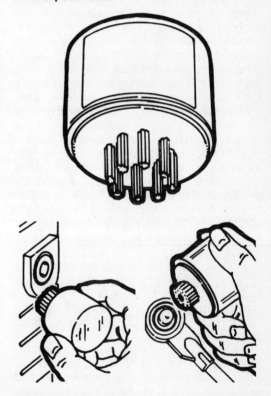

Side terminal batteries require a small stiff wire brush

nal if a clamp gets stuck without the puller. These pullers are inexpensive and available in most auto parts stores or auto departments. Side terminal battery cables are secured with a bolt.

The best tool for battery clamp and terminal maintenance is a battery terminal brush. This inexpensive tool has a female ended wire brush for cleaning terminals, and a male ended wire

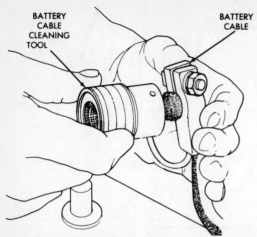

Cleaning the cable clamps. Make sure both the clamps and terminal posts are cleaned until shiny

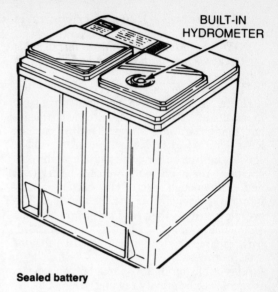

Sealed battery

brush inside for cleaning the insides of battery clamps. When using this tool, make sure you get both the terminal posts and the insides of the clamps nice and shiny. Any oxidation, corrosion or foreign material will prevent a sound electrical connection and inhibit either starting or charging. If your battery has side terminals, there is also a cleaning tool available for these.

Before installing the cables, remove the battery holddown clamp or strap and remove the battery. Inspect the battery casing for leaks or cracks (which unfortunately can only be fixed by buying a new battery). Check the battery tray, wash it off with warm soapy water, rinse and dry. Any rust on the tray should be sanded away, and the tray given at least two coats of a quality anti-rust paint. Replace the battery, and install the holddown clamp or strap, but do not overtighten.

Reinstall your clean battery cables, negative cable last. Tighten the cables on the terminal posts snugly; do not overtighten. Wipe a thin coat of petroleum jelly or grease all over the outside of the clamps. This will help to inhibit corrosion.

Finally, check the battery cables themselves. If the insulation of the cables is cracked or broken, or if the ends are frayed, replace the cable with a new cable of the same length or gauge.

CAUTION: *Batteries give off hydrogen gas, which is explosive. DO NOT SMOKE around the battery! The battery electrolyte contains sulfuric acid; if you should splash any into your eyes or skin, flush with plenty of clear water and get immediate medical help.*

CHECKING THE BATTERY SPECIFIC GRAVITY

The specific gravity of the battery should be checked at every tune-up. If the battery termi-

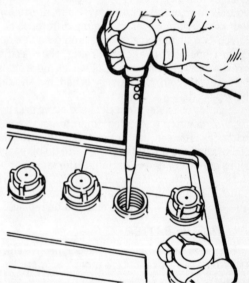

An inexpensive hydrometer will test the battery charge state

nals become corroded, they must be cleaned using a wire brush or battery cleaning tool. Clamps and terminals should be shiny for a good connection, and the clamps should be coated lightly with petroleum jelly when assembled to the terminal posts, to retard corrosion.

A trickle charger (slow charger) is recommended for battery charging. If a fast charger must be used while the battery is in the vehicle, disconnect the battery before connecting the charger.

CAUTION: *Batteries naturally give off a certain amount of explosive hydrogen gas, more so when they are being charged. Keep any flame or spark source away from batteries at all times.*

TESTING THE MAINTENANCE FREE BATTERY

All later model vehicles are equipped with maintenance free batteries, which do not require normal attention as far as fluid level checks are concerned. However, the terminals require periodic cleaning, which should be performed at least once a year.

The sealed top battery cannot be checked for charge in the normal manner, since there is no provision for access to the electrolyte. To check the condition of the battery:

1. If the indicator eye on top of the battery is dark, the battery has enough fluid. If the eye is light, the electrolyte fluid is too low and the battery must be replaced.

2. If a green dot appears in the middle of the eye, the battery is sufficiently charged. Proceed to Step 4. If no green dot is visible, charge the battery as in Step 3.

3. Charge the battery at this rate:

CAUTION: *Do not charge the battery for more than 50 amp/hours (to figure this, or course multiply the amps of the charging rate by the number of hours). If the green dot appears, or if electrolyte squirts out of the vent hole, stop the charge and proceed to Step 4.*

It may be necessary to tip the battery from side to side to get the green dot to appear after charging.

4. Connect a battery load tester and a voltmeter across the battery terminals (the battery cables should be disconnected from the battery). Apply a 300 amp load to the battery for 15 seconds to remove the surface charge. Remove the load.

5. Wait 15 seconds to allow the battery to recover. Apply the appropriate test load, as specified in the following charts:

Apply the load for 15 seconds while reading the voltage. Disconnect the load.

Charging Rate Amps	Time
75	40 min
50	1 hr
25	2 hr
10	5 hr

Temperature (°F)	Minimum Voltage
70 or above	9.6
60	9.5
50	9.4
40	9.3
30	9.1
20	8.9
10	8.7
0	8.5

Cars Up to 1983

Battery	Test Load
Y85-4	130 amps
R85-5	170 amsp
R87-5	210 amps
R89-5	230 amps

1984–85 Cars

Battery	Test Load
1981099	150
1981103	200
1981104	250
1981106	270
1981107	380
1981110	190
1981140	550
1981157	230
1981296	310

1986 Cars

Battery	Test Load
1981101	160
1981102	200
1981103	200
1981104	250
1981296	315
1981577	260
1981607	280

1987–90 Cars

Battery	Test Load
1981730	260
1981601	310
1981600	260
1981731	280
1981735	360

6. Check the results against the following chart. If the battery voltage is at or above the specified voltage for the temperature listed, the battery is good. If the voltage falls below what's listed, the battery should be replaced.

Early Fuel Evaporation System (Heat Riser)

VALVE LUBRICATION AND SYSTEM OPERATING CHECK

The EFE system uses a throttling type valve in the exhaust manifold on one side of V6 and V8 engines. The valve is actuated by a vacuum diaphragm and will quickly develop operating problems if it binds due to corrosion. The shafts

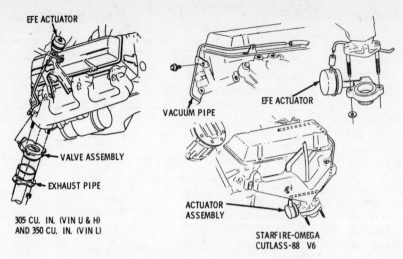

305 CU. IN. (VIN U & H)
AND 350 CU. IN. (VIN L)

STARFIRE-OMEGA
CUTLASS-88 V6

Checking the Early Fuel Evaporation System actuator

should be thoroughly soaked with a solvent designed to remove rust from heat risers every 30,000 miles.

Every 30,000 miles, apply 10 in. of vacuum to the valve from an external source, or start the engine from an overnight cold condition. The valve should close all the way. If the valve binds and cannot be unstuck through application of solvent, it should be replaced.

Belts

INSPECTION

Inspect your vehicle's drive belts every 7,500 miles or six months for evidence of wear such as cracking, fraying, and incorrect tension. Replace the belts at a maximum of 30,000 miles, even if they still look acceptable.

ADJUSTING

You can determine belt tension at a point halfway between the pulleys by pressing on the belt with moderate thumb pressure. The amount of deflection should be in proportion to the length of the belt between pulleys (measured from the center of each pulley). For example, a belt stretched 13–16 in. (330–406mm) between pulleys should deflect ½ in. (13mm) at the halfway point; a belt stretched 7–10 in. (178–254mm) should deflect ¼ in. (6.3mm), etc. If the deflection is found to be too little or too tight, an adjustment must be made.

Before adjusting any of your engine's drive belts, clean all mounting bolts on the component being adjusted and apply penetrating oil if necessary on those bolts which are hard to reach; which may be many if your vehicle has a V8 with lots of power options. Loosen the mounting and adjusting bolts of whichever component (alternator, air pump, air condition-

er compressor, power steering pump, etc.) you are adjusting. Pull outward, away from the engine, on the component until the belt seems tight. Temporarily snug up on the adjusting

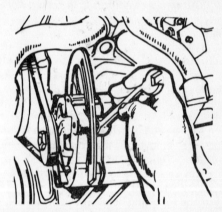

To adjust belt tension or to change belts, first loosen the component's mounting and adjusting bolts slightly

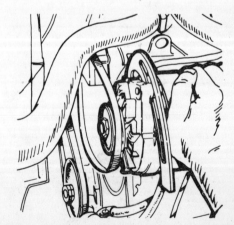

Push the component towards the engine and slip off the belt

HOW TO SPOT WORN V-BELTS

V-Belts are vital to efficient engine operation—they drive the fan, water pump and other accessories. They require little maintenance (occasional tightening) but they will not last forever. Slipping or failure of the V-belt will lead to overheating. If your V-belt looks like any of these, it should be replaced.

This belt has deep cracks, which cause it to flex. Too much flexing leads to heat build-up and premature failure. These cracks can be caused by using the belt on a pulley that is too small. Notched belts are available for small diameter pulleys.

Cracking or weathering

Oil and grease on a belt can cause the belt's rubber compounds to soften and separate from the reinforcing cords that hold the belt together. The belt will first slip, then finally fail altogether.

Softening (grease and oil)

Glazing is caused by a belt that is slipping. A slipping belt can cause a run-down battery, erratic power steering, overheating or poor accessory performance. The more the belt slips, the more glazing will be built up on the surface of the belt. The more the belt is glazed, the more it will slip. If the glazing is light, tighten the belt.

Glazing

The cover of this belt is worn off and is peeling away. The reinforcing cords will begin to wear and the belt will shortly break. When the belt cover wears in spots or has a rough jagged appearance, check the pulley grooves for roughness.

Worn cover

This belt is on the verge of breaking and leaving you stranded. The layers of the belt are separating and the reinforcing cords are exposed. It's just a matter of time before it breaks completely.

Separation

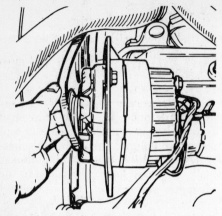

Slip the new belt over the pulley

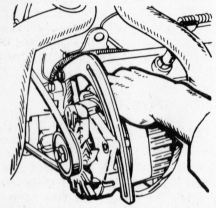

Pull outward on the component and tighten the mounting bolts

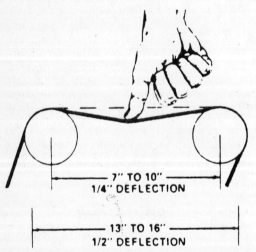

A belt gauge is recommended, but you can check belt tension with thumb pressure

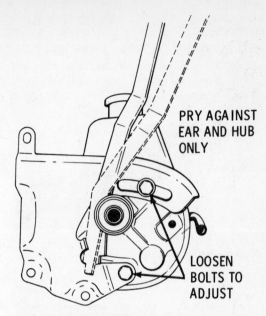

PRY AGAINST EAR AND HUB ONLY

LOOSEN BOLTS TO ADJUST

PULLEY REMOVED FOR PHOTO PURPOSE

Power steering pump belt adjustment

dowel rod works fine. Excessive force on any of the component housings (which are usually aluminum) will damage the housings.

REMOVAL AND INSTALLATION

To replace a belt, follow the above procedure for belt adjustment to the point of loosening the adjusting bolt. Push the component in towards the engine; this should give enough slack in the belt to remove it from the pulleys. Tighten the new belt in the normal manner.

Hoses

Hoses are frequently overlooked in normal maintenance. Both upper and lower radiator hoses and all heater hoses should be checked for deterioration, leaks and loose hose clamps at every tune-up. Check the hoses by feel; they should be pliable. Any hose that feels hard or brittle should be replaced as soon as possible; in any case, replace radiator hoses as necessary every two years or 30,000 miles.

REMOVAL AND INSTALLATION

1. Drain the radiator as detailed later in this chapter.

CAUTION: *When draining the coolant, keep in mind that cats and dogs are attracted by the ethylene glycol antifreeze, and are quite likely to drink any that is left in an uncovered container or in puddles on the ground. This will prove fatal in sufficient quantity. Always drain the coolant into a sealable container.*

bolt and check belt deflection; if it is OK, tighten the mounting bolts and adjusting bolt.

NOTE: *Avoid using a metal pry bar when adjusting belt tension of any component; a sawed-off broom handle or large wooden*

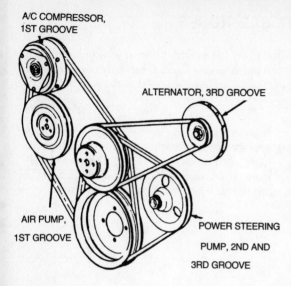

A/C COMPRESSOR, 1ST GROOVE

ALTERNATOR, 3RD GROOVE

AIR PUMP, 1ST GROOVE

POWER STEERING PUMP, 2ND AND 3RD GROOVE

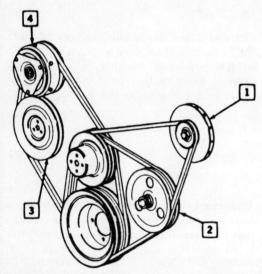

V-belt routing—late model 5.0L (VIN Y) standard and heavy duty cooling system

Coolant should be reused unless it is contaminated or several years old.

2. Loosen the hose clamps at each end of the hose to be removed.

3. Working the hose back and forth, slide it off its connection and then install a new hose if necessary.

4. Position the hose clamps at least ¾ in. (19mm) from the end of the hose and tighten them.

NOTE: *Old hoses have a tendency to remain stuck to the outlets after the hose clamps are loosened. If this is the case, slice the ends of the old hose with a utility knife or single-edged razor blade. Always make sure that the hose clamps are beyond the bead and placed in the center of the clamping surface before tightening them.*

Air Conditioning
SAFETY PRECAUTIONS

There are two particular hazards associated with air conditioning systems and they both relate to the refrigerant gas.

First, the refrigerant gas (R-12) is an extremely cold substance. When exposed to air, it will instantly freeze any surface it comes in contact with, including your eyes. The other hazard relates to fire. Although normally nontoxic, the R-12 gas becomes highly poisonous in the presence of an open flame. One good whiff of the vapor formed by burning R-12 can be fatal. Keep all forms of fire (including cigarettes) well clear of the air conditioning system.

All major repair work to the air conditioning system should be left to a professional air conditioning mechanic. DO NOT, Under any circumstances, attempt to loosen or tighten any fitting, or perform any work other than what is outlined here.

CHECKING FOR OIL LEAKS

Refrigerant leaks show up as oily areas on the various components because the compressor oil is transported around the entire system along with the refrigerant. Look for oil spots on all the hoses and lines, and especially on the hose and tubing connections. If there are oily deposits, the system may have a leak, and you should have it checked by a qualified air conditioning technician.

Because all atmospheric air contains at least some moisture, water will enter the system and mix with the R-12 and the oil. Trace amounts of moisture will cause sludging of the oil, and corrosion of the system. Saturation and clogging of the accumulator-drier, and freezing of the orifice will eventually result. As air fills the system to a greater and greater extend, it will interfere more and more with the normal flows of refrigerant and heat.

NOTE: *A small area of oil on the front of the compressor is normal and no cause for alarm.*

CHECK THE COMPRESSOR BELT

Refer to the section above on Drive Belts.

KEEP THE CONDENSER CLEAN

Periodically inspect the front of the condenser for bent fins or foreign material (dirt, bugs, leaves, etc.). If any cooling fins are bent, straighten them carefully with needlenosed pliers. You can remove any debris with a stiff bristle brush or hose.

HOW TO SPOT BAD HOSES

Both the upper and lower radiator hoses are called upon to perform difficult jobs in an inhospitable environment. They are subject to nearly 18 psi at under hood temperatures often over 280°F., and must circulate nearly 7500 gallons of coolant an hour—3 good reasons to have good hoses.

A good test for any hose is to feel it for soft or spongy spots. Frequently these will appear as swollen areas of the hose. The most likely cause is oil soaking. This hose could burst at any time, when hot or under pressure.

Swollen hose

Cracked hoses can usually be seen but feel the hoses to be sure they have not hardened; a prime cause of cracking. This hose has cracked down to the reinforcing cords and could split at any of the cracks.

Cracked hose

Weakened clamps frequently are the cause of hose and cooling system failure. The connection between the pipe and hose has deteriorated enough to allow coolant to escape when the engine is hot.

Frayed hose end (due to weak clamp)

Debris, rust and scale in the cooling system can cause the inside of a hose to weaken. This can usually be felt on the outside of the hose as soft or thinner areas.

Debris in cooling system

JUMP STARTING A DEAD BATTERY

The chemical reaction in a battery produces explosive hydrogen gas. This is the safe way to jump start a dead battery, reducing the chances of an accidental spark that could cause an explosion.

Jump Starting Precautions

1. Be sure both batteries are of the same voltage.
2. Be sure both batteries are of the same polarity (have the same grounded terminal).
3. Be sure the vehicles are not touching.
4. Be sure the vent cap holes are not obstructed.
5. Do not smoke or allow sparks around the battery.
6. In cold weather, check for frozen electrolyte in the battery.
7. Do not allow electrolyte on your skin or clothing.
8. Be sure the electrolyte is not frozen.

Jump Starting Procedure

1. Determine voltages of the two batteries; they must be the same.
2. Bring the starting vehicle close (they must not touch) so that the batteries can be reached easily.
3. Turn off all accessories and both engines. Put both cars in Neutral or Park and set the handbrake.
4. Cover the cell caps with a rag—do not cover terminals.
5. If the terminals on the run-down battery are heavily corroded, clean them.
6. Identify the positive and negative posts on both batteries and connect the cables in the order shown.
7. Start the engine of the starting vehicle and run it at fast idle. Try to start the car with the dead battery. Crank it for no more than 10 seconds at a time and let it cool off for 20 seconds in between tries.
8. If it doesn't start in 3 tries, there is something else wrong.
9. Disconnect the cables in the reverse order.
10. Replace the cell covers and dispose of the rags.

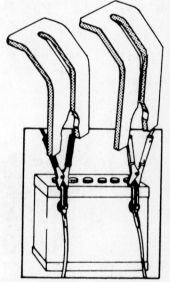

Side terminal batteries occasionally pose a problem when connecting jumper cables. There frequently isn't enough room to clamp the cables without touching sheet metal. Side terminal adaptors are available to alleviate this problem and should be removed after use.

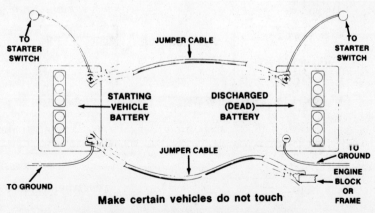

TO STARTER SWITCH

JUMPER CABLE

TO STARTER SWITCH

STARTING VEHICLE BATTERY

DISCHARGED (DEAD) BATTERY

JUMPER CABLE

TO GROUND

TO GROUND

ENGINE BLOCK OR FRAME

Make certain vehicles do not touch

This hook-up for negative ground cars only

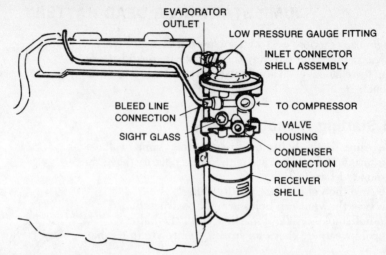

EVAPORATOR
OUTLET

LOW PRESSURE GAUGE FITTING

INLET CONNECTOR
SHELL ASSEMBLY

BLEED LINE
CONNECTION

TO COMPRESSOR

SIGHT GLASS

VALVE
HOUSING

CONDENSER
CONNECTION

RECEIVER
SHELL

Air conditioning VIR assembly showing sight glass and connections

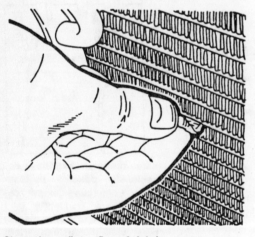

Clean the radiator fins of debris

ADDITIONAL PREVENTIVE MAINTENANCE CHECKS

Antifreeze

In order to prevent heater core freeze-up during air conditioner operation, it is necessary to maintain permanent type antifreeze protection of $+15°F$ ($-9°C$) or lower. A reading of $-15°F$ ($-26°C$) is ideal since this protection also supplies sufficient corrosion inhibitors for the protection of the engine cooling system.

WARNING: *Do not use antifreeze longer than specified by the manufacturer.*

Radiator Cap

For efficient operation of an air conditioned vehicle's cooling system, the radiator cap should have a holding pressure which meets

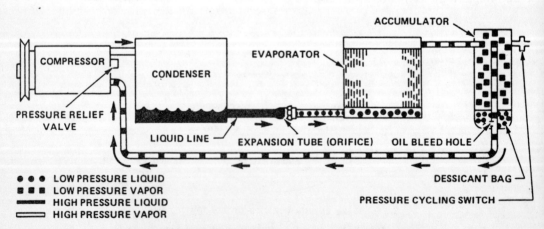

COMPRESSOR

CONDENSER

EVAPORATOR

ACCUMULATOR

PRESSURE RELIEF
VALVE

LIQUID LINE

EXPANSION TUBE (ORIFICE)

OIL BLEED HOLE

DESSICANT BAG

PRESSURE CYCLING SWITCH

● ● ● LOW PRESSURE LIQUID
■ ■ ■ LOW PRESSURE VAPOR
▬▬▬ HIGH PRESSURE LIQUID
⬒⬒⬒ HIGH PRESSURE VAPOR

Cycling clutch orifice tube (CCOT) system components—1978–90

manufacturer's specifications. A cap which fails to hold these pressure should be replaced.

Condenser

Any obstruction of or damage to the condenser configuration will restrict the air flow which is essential to its efficient operation. It is therefore, a good rule to keep this unit clean and in proper physical shape.

NOTE: *Bug screens are regarded as obstructions.*

Condensation Drain Tube

This single molded drain tube expels the condensation, which accumulates on the bottom of the evaporator housing, into the engine compartment.

If this tube is obstructed, the air conditioning performance can be restricted and condensation buildup can spill over onto the vehicle's floor.

OPERATE THE AIR CONDITIONING SYSTEM PERIODICALLY

A lot of air conditioning problems can be avoided by simply running the air conditioner at least once a week, regardless of the season. Let the system run for at least 5 minutes (even in the winter) and you'll keep the internal parts well lubricated as well as preventing the hoses from hardening.

REFRIGERANT LEVEL CHECK

There are two ways to check refrigerant level, depending on the model year of your vehicle.

NOTE: *If your vehicle is equipped with an aftermarket (non GM) air conditioner, the following checks may not apply. Contact the manufacturer for instructions on system checks.*

With Sight Glass, 1975–77

The sight glass, for checking the refrigerant charge, is located on top of the VIR (valves-in-receiver). The VIR looks like a small fire extinguisher and is located on the front of the engine compartment, usually on the left side of the radiator or at the heater plenum at the firewall.

This test is most effective if the outside air temperature is warm (70°F [21°C] or above).

1. Place the transmission in **PARK**, and apply the parking brake.

2. Have a helper control the accelerator pedal and run the engine to 1500 rpm (fast idle).

3. Set the air conditioner controls on the instrument panel for maximum cold with the blower on HIGH.

4. Look at the sight glass on top of the VIR. (You'll probably have to wipe it clean first). If a steady stream of bubbles is present in the sight glass, the system is low on charge. There is a good chance the system has a leak.

5. If no bubbles are present, the system is either full charged or completely empty. Feel the high and low pressure lines at the compressor; if no appreciable temperature difference is felt, the system is empty or nearly so.

6. If one hose is warm (high pressure) and the other is cold (low pressure), the system may be OK. However, you are probably making these tests because there is something wrong with your air conditioner, so proceed to the next step.

7. Have your helper turn the fan control on and off to operate the compressor clutch. Watch the sight glass.

8. If bubbles appear when the clutch is disengaged and disappear when it is engaged, the system is properly charged.

9. If the refrigerant takes more than 45 seconds to bubble when the clutch is disengaged, the system is more than likely overcharged. This condition will usually result in poor air conditioner operation (poor cooling) at low speeds.

10. Finally, check for oil streaks in the sight glass, which are a sign of trouble. Most of the time, if you see oil in the sight glass it will appear as a series of streaks, although occasionally it may be a solid stream of oil. In either case, it means that part of the charge has been lost.

NOTE: *If you are sure that the system has a leak, it should be repaired as soon as possible. Leaks may allow moisture into the system, causing internal rust. The system will have to be flushed, evacuated, leak tested and recharged.*

Without Sight Glass, 1978 and Later

The vehicles built in these years are not equipped with a sight glass in their Cycling Clutch Orifice Tube (CCOT) systems. On these vehicles it is necessary to feel the temperature difference in the inlet and outlet lines at the compressor to gauge the refrigerant level. Use the following procedure. A set of manifold gauges can be hocked up to read the refrigerant levels.

CAUTION: *Always wear safety goggles when working on a system to protect the eyes. If refrigerant contacts the eye, it is advisable in all cases to see a physician as soon as possible.*

1. Connect a gauge set (engine not running). The LOW side gauge hose to the suction line near the accumulator and the HIGH side gauge hose to the liquid line or muffler. The muffler is a round shaped can about three times larger than the liquid line.

Amount of refrigerant / Check item	Almost no refrigerant	Insufficient	Suitable	Too much refrigerant
Temperature of high pressure and low pressure lines.	Almost no difference between high pressure and low pressure side temperature.	High pressure side is warm and low pressure side is fairly cold.	High pressure side is hot and low pressure side is cold.	High pressure side is abnormally hot.
State in sight glass	Bubbles flow continuously. Bubbles will disappear and something like mist will flow when refrigerant is nearly gone.	The bubbles are seen at intervals of 1 - 2 seconds.	Almost transparent. Bubbles may appear when engine speed is raised and lowered. No clear difference exists between these two conditions.	No bubbles can be seen.
Pressure of system.	High pressure side is abnormally low.	Both pressure on high and low pressure sides are slightly low.	Both pressures on high and low pressure sides are normal.	Both pressures on high and low pressure sides are abnormally high.
Repair.	Stop compressor immediately and conduct an overall check.	Check for gas leakage, repair as required, replenish and charge system.		Discharge refrigerant from service valve of low pressure side.

Using a sight glass to determine the relative refrigerant charge.

RELATIVE HUMIDITY (%)	AMBIENT AIR TEMP °F	AMBIENT AIR TEMP °C	LOW SIDE kPa	LOW SIDE PSIG	ENGINE SPEED (rpm)	CENTER DUCT AIR TEMPERATURE °F	CENTER DUCT AIR TEMPERATURE °C	HIGH SIDE kPa	HIGH SIDE PSIG
20	70	21	200	29	2000	40	4	1034	150
	80	27	200	29		44	7	1310	190
	90	32	207	30		48	9	1689	245
	100	38	214	31		57	14	2103	305
30	70	21	200	29	2000	42	6	1034	150
	80	27	207	30		47	8	1413	205
	90	32	214	31		51	11	1827	265
	100	38	221	32		61	16	2241	325
40	70	21	200	29	2000	45	7	1138	165
	80	27	207	30		49	9	1482	215
	90	32	221	32		55	13	1931	280
	100	38	269	39		65	18	2379	345
50	70	21	207	30	2000	47	8	1241	180
	80	27	221	32		53	12	1620	235
	90	32	234	34		59	15	2034	295
	100	38	276	40		69	21	2413	350
60	70	21	207	30	2000	48	9	1241	180
	80	27	228	33		56	13	1655	240
	90	32	249	36		63	17	2069	300
	100	38	296	43		73	23	2482	360
70	70	21	207	30	2000	50	10	1276	185
	80	27	234	34		58	14	1689	245
	90	32	262	38		65	18	2103	305
	100	38	303	44		75	24	2517	365
80	70	21	207	30	2000	50	10	1310	190
	80	27	234	34		59	15	1724	250
	90	32	269	39		67	19	2137	310
90	70	21	207	30	2000	50	10	1379	200
	80	27	249	36		62	17	1827	265
	90	32	290	42		71	22	2275	330

A/C performance test chart

2. Close (clockwise) both gauge set valves.

3. Park the vehicle in the shade, at least 5 feet from any walls. Start the engine, set the parking brake, place the transmission in NEUTRAL and establish an idle of 1,100–2,000 rpm.

4. Run the air conditioning system for full cooling, in the **MAX or COLD** mode.

5. The low pressure gauge should read 5–20 psi; the high pressure gauge should indicate 120–180 psi. Refer to the "Air Conditioner Performance Test Chart" illustration in this section for optimum pressure and temperature specifications.

WARNING: *These pressures are the norm for an ambient temperature of 70–80°F (21–27°C). Higher air temperatures along with high humidity will cause higher system pressures. At idle speed and an ambient temperature of 110°F (43°C), the high pressure reading can exceed 300 psi.*

Under these extreme conditions, you can keep the pressures down by directing a large electric floor fan through the condenser.

TEST GAUGES

Most of the service work performed in air conditioning requires the use of a set of two gauges, one for the high (head) pressure side of the system, the other for the low (suction) side.

The low side gauge records both pressure and vacuum. Vacuum readings are calibrated from 0 to 30 inches Hg and the pressure graduations read from 0 to no less than 60 psi.

The high side gauge measures pressure from 0 to at least 600 psi.

Both gauges are threaded into a manifold that contains two hand shut-off valves. Proper manipulation of these valves and the use of the attached test hoses allow the user to perform the following services:

1. Test high and low side pressures.

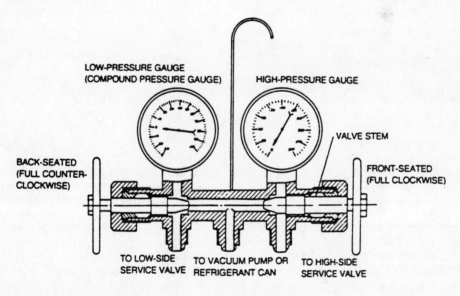

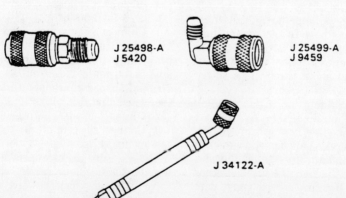

Manifold gauge set and low side adapters

2. Remove air, moisture, and contaminated refrigerant.

3. Purge the system of refrigerant.

4. Charge the system with refrigerant.

The manifold valves are designed so that they have no direct effect on gauge readings, but serve only to provide for, or cut off, flow of refrigerant through the manifold. During all testing and hook-up operations, the valves are kept in a close position to avoid disturbing the refrigeration system. The valves are opened only to purge the system or refrigerant or to charge it.

DISCHARGING THE SYSTEM

CAUTION: *Always wear safety goggles when working on a system to protect the eyes. If refrigerant contacts the eye, it is advisable in all cases to see a physician as soon as possible.*

1. Remove the caps from the high and low pressure charging valves in the high and low pressure lines.

2. Turn both manifold gauge set hand valves to the fully closed (clockwise) position.

3. Connect a gauge set (engine not running). The LOW side gauge hose to the suction line near the accumulator and the HIGH side gauge hose to the liquid line or muffler. The muffler is a round shaped can about three times larger than the liquid line.

4. Place the end of the center hose away from you and the vehicle and into a suitable container.

5. Open the low pressure gauge valve slightly and allow the system pressure to bleed off.

6. When the system is just about empty, open the high pressure valve very slowly to avoid losing an excessive amount of refrigerant oil. Allow any remaining refrigerant to escape.

EVACUATING THE SYSTEM

NOTE: *This procedure requires the use of a vacuum pump.*

1. Connect a gauge set (engine not running). The LOW side gauge hose to the suction line near the accumulator and the HIGH side gauge hose to the liquid line or muffler. The muffler is a round shaped can about three times larger than the liquid line.

2. Discharge the system.

3. On 1983 and later models, make sure that the low pressure gauge set hose is connected to the low pressure service gauge port on the top center of the accumulator/drier assembly or in the suction line and the high pressure hose connected to the high pressure service gauge port on the compressor discharge (liquid) line.

4. Connect the center service hose to the inlet fitting of the vacuum pump.

5. Turn both gauge set valves to the wide open position.

6. Start the pump and note the low side gauge reading.

7. Operate the pump until the low pressure gauge reads 25–30 inch Hg. Continue running the vacuum pump for 10 minutes more. If you have replaced some component in the system, run the pump for an additional 20–30 minutes.

8. Leak test the system. Close both gauge set valves. Turn off the pump. The needle should remain stationary at the point at which the pump was turned off. If the needle drops to zero rapidly, there is a leak in the system which must be repaired.

LEAK TESTING

Some leak tests can be performed with a soapy water solution. There must be at least a ½ lb. charge in the system for a leak to be detected. The most extensive leak tests are performed with either a Halide flame type leak tester or the more preferable electronic leak tester.

In either case, the equipment is expensive, and, the use of a Halide flame detector can be **extremely** hazardous!

CHARGING THE SYSTEM (MAXIMUM R–12 CHARGE)

CAUTION: *NEVER OPEN THE HIGH PRESSURE SIDE WITH A CAN OF REFRIGERANT CONNECTED TO THE SYSTEM! OPENING THE HIGH PRESSURE SIDE WILL OVERPRESSURIZE THE CAN, CAUSING IT TO EXPLODE! Always wear safety goggles when working on a system to protect the eyes. If refrigerant contacts the eye, it is advisable in all cases to see a physician as soon as possible.*

Refrigerant 12 Capacities:
- 1968–72 3.00 lbs.
- 1973–77 3.75 lbs.
- 1978–90 3.50 lbs.

1. Connect a gauge set (engine not running). The LOW side gauge hose to the suction line near the accumulator and the HIGH side gauge hose to the liquid line or muffler. The muffler is a round shaped can about three times larger than the liquid line.

2. Close (clockwise) both gauge set valves.

3. Connect the center hose to the refrigerant can opener valve.

4. Make sure the can opener valve is closed, that is, the needle is raised, and connect the valve to the can. Open the valve, puncturing the can with the needle.

5. Loosen the center hose fitting at the pressure gauge, allowing refrigerant to purge the

hose of air. When the air is bled, tighten the fitting.

CAUTION: *IF THE LOW PRESSURE GAUGE SET HOSE IS NOT CONNECTED TO THE ACCUMULATOR/DRIER, KEEP THE CAN IN AN UPRIGHT POSITION!*

6. Disconnect the wire harness snap-lock connector from the clutch cycling pressure switch and install a jumper wire across the two terminals of the connector.

7. Open the low side gauge set valve and the can valve.

8. Allow refrigerant to be drawn into the system.

9. When no more refrigerant is drawn into the system, close both gauge valves, start the engine and run it at about 2,000 rpm. Turn on the system and operate it at the full high position. The compressor will operate and pull refrigerant gas into the system.

NOTE: *To help speed the process, the can may be placed, upright, in a pan of warm water, not exceeding 125°F (52°C).*

10. If more than one can of refrigerant is needed, close the can valve and gauge set low side valve when the can is empty and connect a new can to the opener. Repeat the charging process until the sight glass (if equipped) indicates a full charge. The frost line on the outside of the can will indicate what portion of the can has been used.

CAUTION: *NEVER ALLOW THE HIGH PRESSURE SIDE READING TO EXCEED 280 psi!*

11. When the charging process has been completed, close the gauge set valve and can valve. Remove the jumper wire and reconnect the cycling clutch wire. Run the system for at least five minutes to allow it to normalize. Low pressure side reading should be 4–25 psi; high pressure reading should be 120–210 psi at an ambient temperature of 70–90°F (21–32°C). Refer to the "Air Conditioner Performance Test Chart" in this chapter.

12. Turn the engine OFF before removing the manifold gauges.

13. Loosen both service hoses at the gauges to allow any refrigerant to escape. Remove the gauge set and install the dust caps on the service valves.

NOTE: *Multi-can dispensers are available which allow a simultaneous hook-up of up to four 14 oz. cans of R-12.*

CAUTION: *The maximum charge for these systems the CCOT system is 3.50 lbs. Never exceed the recommended maximum charge for the system!*

REFRIGERANT OIL CAPACITIES

The R-4 compressor system requires a total of **8 fluid ounces (240ml)** of 525 viscosity refrigerant oil.

New oil quantities must be added to the system during component replacement and excessive leaks. Refer to the following for specific oil quantities.

1. No signs of excessive oil leaks, add:
   a. COMPRESSOR – remove, drain oil,

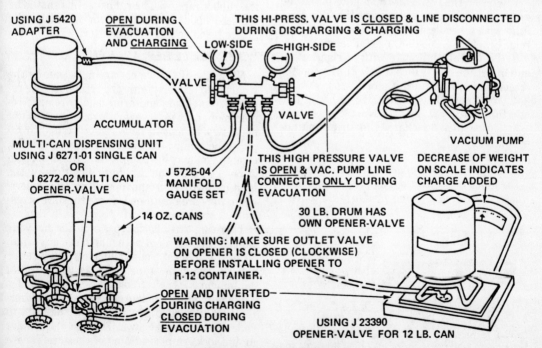

USING J 5420 ADAPTER

OPEN DURING EVACUATION AND CHARGING

THIS HI-PRESS. VALVE IS <u>CLOSED</u> & LINE DISCONNECTED DURING DISCHARGING & CHARGING

LOW-SIDE

HIGH-SIDE

VALVE

VALVE

ACCUMULATOR

MULTI-CAN DISPENSING UNIT USING J 6271-01 SINGLE CAN OR J 6272-02 MULTI CAN OPENER-VALVE

J 5725-04 MANIFOLD GAUGE SET

14 OZ. CANS

THIS HIGH PRESSURE VALVE IS <u>OPEN</u> & VAC. PUMP LINE CONNECTED <u>ONLY</u> DURING EVACUATION

30 LB. DRUM HAS OWN OPENER-VALVE

VACUUM PUMP

DECREASE OF WEIGHT ON SCALE INDICATES CHARGE ADDED

WARNING: MAKE SURE OUTLET VALVE ON OPENER IS CLOSED (CLOCKWISE) BEFORE INSTALLING OPENER TO R-12 CONTAINER.

<u>OPEN</u> AND INVERTED DURING CHARGING <u>CLOSED</u> DURING EVACUATION

USING J 23390 OPENER-VALVE FOR 12 LB. CAN

A/C system service procedures

measure if less than 1 oz. (30ml) - add 2 oz. (60ml). If the measurement is more, add the same amount of new oil.

   b. EVAPORATOR – add 3 oz. (90ml).

   c. CONDENSER – add 1 oz. (30ml).

   d. ACCUMULATOR – add 3.5 oz. (105ml).

   e. MUFFLER – add 0.5 oz. (15ml).

2. Refrigerant oil leak due to a large leak, add:

   a. When the defective component has been replaced and the lead has been repaired, add 3 oz. (90ml) plus the required amount of oil for the particular component as previously outlined.

   b. Up to 4 oz. (120ml) of oil can collect in the compressor crankcase. When replacing the compressor, drain the oil from the drain plug and measure the amount. New replacement compressors will be shipped with about 8 oz. (240ml) of oil. Drain the oil from the new compressor and add the same amount as drained from the old one.

Orifice Tube Service

The orifice tube can be cleaned with solvent and compressed air. Replace the tube if the plastic frame is broken, brass orifice tube is damaged or plugged, screen material is torn and screen is plugged with fine gritty material.

REMOVAL AND INSTALLATION

1. Discharge the air conditioner as previously outlined in this section.

2. Loosen the fitting at the liquid line to the evaporator inlet pipe and remove the tube carefully with a needle nosed pliers or orifice tube removing tool J–26549–C or equivalent.

3. **To install:** lubricate with refrigerant oil and insert the new orifice tube with the shorter screen end in first until it stops.

4. With new O-rings, install the liquid line and torque to 11 ft. lbs. (17 Nm).

5. Evacuate and recharge the Air Conditioner system.

NOTE: *If the orifice tube can not be removed easily because of impacted residue, perform the following: Clean out as much residue as possible. Carefully apply heat to the area with*

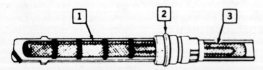

1. Long screen end (inlet)
2. O-ring
3. Short screen end (outlet)

Orifice (expansion) tube—install with the shorter screen end in the evaporator inlet pipe (towards the evaporator) use a new O-ring

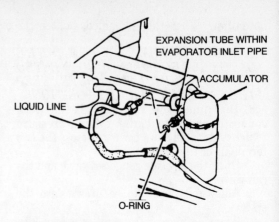

EXPANSION TUBE WITHIN EVAPORATOR INLET PIPE

ACCUMULATOR

LIQUID LINE

O-RING

Orifice tube location

a heat gun or hair dryer ¼ inch from the dimples on the inlet pipe. Using the orifice removing tool J–26549–C, carefully turn with a push-pull motion to loosen the impacted tube. Swab the inside of the inlet pipe with R-11 or equivalent to remove any residue. Flush the system with air conditioner flush only. Install the new orifice tube as previously outlined.

Windshield Wipers

Intense heat from the sun, snow and ice, road oils, and the chemicals used in windshield washer solvent combine to deteriorate the rubber wiper blades of your windshield wipers. If you live in a big city, smog will also deteriorate the rubber rapidly. The rubber refills should be replaced about twice a year or whenever the blades begin to streak or chatter.

WIPER REFILL REPLACEMENT

Normally, if the wipers are not cleaning the windshield properly, only the refill has to be replaced. The blade and arm usually require replacement only in the event of damage. It is not necessary (except in new Tridon refills) to remove the arm or the blade to replace the refill, though you may have to position the arm higher on the glass. You can do this by turning the ignition switch on and operating the wipers, when they are positioned where they are accessible, turn the switch off.

There are three basic types of refills and your Buick, Olds or Pontiac could have any kind, since aftermarket blades and arms may not use exactly the same type refill as the original equipment.

Some types, such as Anco use a release button that is pushed down to allow the refill to slide out of the yoke jaws. The new refill slides in and locks in place. Some of these refills are removed by locating where the metal backing

Troubleshooting Basic Air Conditioning Problems

Problem	Cause	Solution
There's little or no air coming from the vents (and you're sure it's on)	• The A/C fuse is blown • Broken or loose wires or connections • The on/off switch is defective	• Check and/or replace fuse • Check and/or repair connections • Replace switch
The air coming from the vents is not cool enough	• Windows and air vent wings open • The compressor belt is slipping • Heater is on • Condenser is clogged with debris • Refrigerant has escaped through a leak in the system • Receiver/drier is plugged	• Close windows and vent wings • Tighten or replace compressor belt • Shut heater off • Clean the condenser • Check system • Service system
The air has an odor	• Vacuum system is disrupted • Odor producing substances on the evaporator case • Condensation has collected in the bottom of the evaporator housing	• Have the system checked/repaired • Clean the evaporator case • Clean the evaporator housing drains
System is noisy or vibrating	• Compressor belt or mountings loose • Air in the system	• Tighten or replace belt; tighten mounting bolts • Have the system serviced

Sight glass condition
  Constant bubbles, foam or oil streaks
  Clear sight glass, but no cold air
  Clear sight glass, but air is cold
  Clouded with milky fluid
	
	• Undercharged system
	
	• No refrigerant at all
	• System is OK
	• Receiver drier is leaking dessicant
		
		• Charge the system
		
		• Check and charge the system
		
		• Have system checked

Large difference in temperature of lines	• System undercharged	• Charge and leak test the system
Compressor noise	• Broken valves • Overcharged • Incorrect oil level • Piston slap • Broken rings • Drive belt pulley bolts are loose	• Replace the valve plate • Discharge, evacuate and install the correct charge • Isolate the compressor and check the oil level. Correct as necessary. • Replace the compressor • Replace the compressor • Tighten with the correct torque specification
Excessive vibration	• Incorrect belt tension • Clutch loose • Overcharged • Pulley is misaligned	• Adjust the belt tension • Tighten the clutch • Discharge, evacuate and install the correct charge • Align the pulley
Condensation dripping in the passenger compartment	• Drain hose plugged or improperly positioned • Insulation removed or improperly installed	• Clean the drain hose and check for proper installation • Replace the insulation on the expansion valve and hoses
Frozen evaporator coil	• Faulty thermostat • Thermostat capillary tube improperly installed • Thermostat not adjusted properly	• Replace the thermostat • Install the capillary tube correctly • Adjust the thermostat
Low side low—high side low	• System refrigerant is low • Expansion valve is restricted	• Evacuate, leak test and charge the system • Replace the expansion valve
Low side high—high side low	• Internal leak in the compressor—worn	• Remove the compressor cylinder head and inspect the compressor. Replace the valve plate assembly if necessary. If the compressor pistons, rings or

Troubleshooting Basic Air Conditioning Problems (cont.)

Problem	Cause	Solution
Low side high—high side low (cont.)		cylinders are excessively worn or scored replace the compressor
	• Cylinder head gasket is leaking	• Install a replacement cylinder head gasket
	• Expansion valve is defective	• Replace the expansion valve
	• Drive belt slipping	• Adjust the belt tension
Low side high—high side high	• Condenser fins obstructed	• Clean the condenser fins
	• Air in the system	• Evacuate, leak test and charge the system
	• Expansion valve is defective	• Replace the expansion valve
	• Loose or worn fan belts	• Adjust or replace the belts as necessary
Low side low—high side high	• Expansion valve is defective	• Replace the expansion valve
	• Restriction in the refrigerant hose	• Check the hose for kinks—replace if necessary
	• Restriction in the receiver/drier	• Replace the receiver/drier
	• Restriction in the condenser	• Replace the condenser
Low side and high side normal (inadequate cooling)	• Air in the system	• Evacuate, leak test and charge the system
	• Moisture in the system	• Evacuate, leak test and charge the system

strip or the refill is wider. Insert a small prybar between the frame and metal backing strip. Press down to release the refill from the retaining tab.

Another type, such as Trico, is unlocked at one end by squeezing two metal tabs, and then sliding the refill out of the frame jaws. When the new refill is installed, the tabs will click into place, locking the refill.

The third, or polycarbonate type is held in place by a locking lever that is pushed downward and out of the groove in the arm to free the refill. When the new refill is installed, it will lock in place automatically.

Regardless of the type of refill used, make sure that all of the frame jaws are engaged as the refill is pushed into place and locked. The metal blade holder and frame will scratch the glass if allowed to touch it.

Tires

Tire inflation is probably the most ignored area of auto maintenance. Gasoline mileage can drop as much as 0.8% for every 1 pound per square inch (psi) of under inflation. Proper tire inflation is also a very important factor in the handling and safety of the vehicle. Tire life is also affected by air pressure.

Tires should be checked weekly for proper air pressure. A chart, located either in the glove compartment or on the driver's or passenger's door, gives the recommended inflation pressures for your vehicle depending on type of tires used (radial or bias-ply) and whether the vehicle is loaded or unloaded.

Tire pressures should be checked before driving when the tires are still cool. Every 10° rise (or drop) in tire temperature means a difference of 1 psi, which explains why your vehicle's tires look low on a cold morning. Two items should be a permanent fixture in every vehicle's glove compartment; a tire pressure gauge and a tread depth gauge. Never trust the gauge that is built into service station air pumps; they are notoriously inaccurate.

CAUTION: *Never counteract excessive pressure build-up in a hot tire by bleeding off air pressure (letting some air out). This will only further raise the tire operating temperature. It is best under these circumstances to let the tire cool the next time you stop, then bleed off the pressure.*

Before starting on a long trip with lots of luggage, add about 2–4 psi to the tires to make them run cooler, but never exceed the maxi-

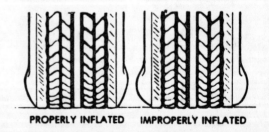

PROPERLY INFLATED   IMPROPERLY INFLATED

RADIAL TIRE   211344

All radials have a slight "bulge" when properly inflated

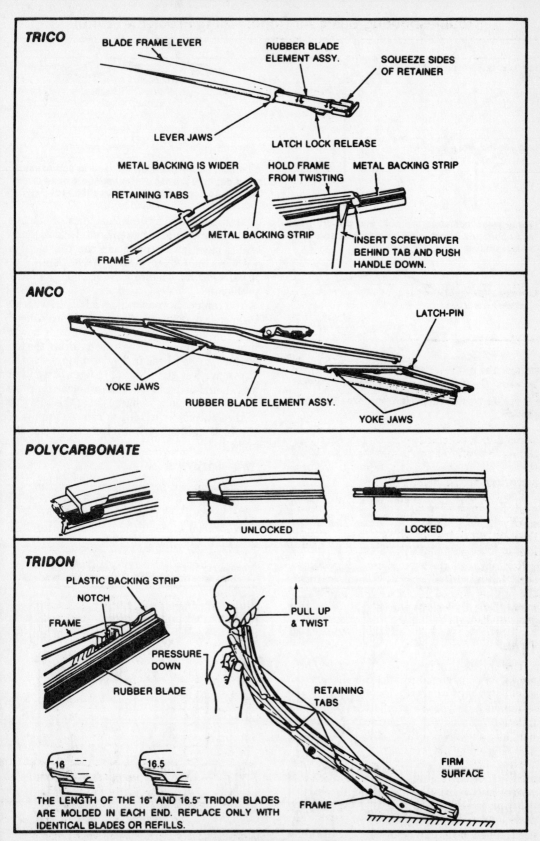

TRICO

BLADE FRAME LEVER

RUBBER BLADE ELEMENT ASSY.

SQUEEZE SIDES OF RETAINER

LEVER JAWS

LATCH LOCK RELEASE

METAL BACKING IS WIDER

HOLD FRAME FROM TWISTING

METAL BACKING STRIP

RETAINING TABS

METAL BACKING STRIP

FRAME

INSERT SCREWDRIVER BEHIND TAB AND PUSH HANDLE DOWN.

ANCO

YOKE JAWS

LATCH-PIN

RUBBER BLADE ELEMENT ASSY.

YOKE JAWS

POLYCARBONATE

UNLOCKED

LOCKED

TRIDON

PLASTIC BACKING STRIP

NOTCH

FRAME

PULL UP & TWIST

PRESSURE DOWN

RUBBER BLADE

RETAINING TABS

16   16.5

FIRM SURFACE

THE LENGTH OF THE 16" AND 16.5" TRIDON BLADES ARE MOLDED IN EACH END. REPLACE ONLY WITH IDENTICAL BLADES OR REFILLS.

FRAME

Popular styles of wiper refills

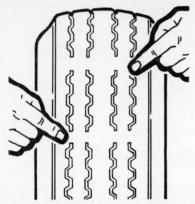

Tread wear indicators are built into the tire tread and appear as ½ inch wide bands when ¹/₁₆ inch of tread remains

Check the tire tread depth with an inexpensive depth gauge

mum inflation pressure marked on the side of the tire.

TREAD DEPTH

ll tires made since 1968 have 8 built-in tread wear indicator bars that show up as ½ in. (13mm) wide smooth bands across the tire when $\frac{1}{16}$ in. (1.6mm) of tread remains. The ap-

A Lincoln penny can also be used to approximate tread depth. If the top of Honest Abe's head is visible in 2 adjacent grooves, replace the tire

pearance of these tread wear indicators means that the tires should be replaced. In fact, many states have laws prohibiting the use of tires with less than $\frac{1}{16}$ in. (1.6mm) tread depth. Unusual wear may indicate front end alignment problems.

You can check your own tread depth with an inexpensive gauge or by using a Lincoln head penny. Slip the Lincoln penny, upside-down, into several tread grooves. If you can see the top of Honest Abe's head in 2 adjacent grooves, the tires have less than $\frac{1}{16}$ in. (1.6mm) tread left and should be replaced. You can measure snow tires in the same manner by using the tails side of the Lincoln penny. If you can see the top of the Lincoln Memorial, it's time to replace the snow tire.

TIRE ROTATION

Tire wear can be equalized by switching the position of the tires about every 6,000 miles (see the accompanying diagram). Including a conventional spare in the rotation pattern can give up to 20% more tire life.

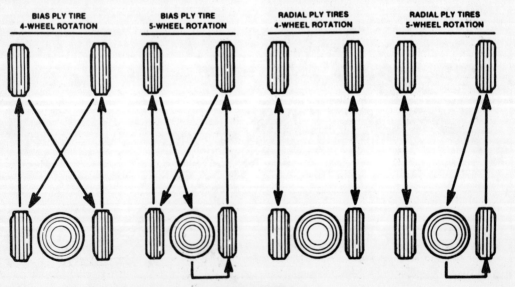

Tire rotation patterns

Troubleshooting Basic Wheel Problems

Problem	Cause	Solution
The car's front end vibrates at high speed	• The wheels are out of balance • Wheels are out of alignment	• Have wheels balanced • Have wheel alignment checked/adjusted
Car pulls to either side	• Wheels are out of alignment • Unequal tire pressure • Different size tires or wheels	• Have wheel alignment checked/adjusted • Check/adjust tire pressure • Change tires or wheels to same size
The car's wheel(s) wobbles	• Loose wheel lug nuts • Wheels out of balance • Damaged wheel • Wheels are out of alignment • Worn or damaged ball joint • Excessive play in the steering linkage (usually due to worn parts) • Defective shock absorber	• Tighten wheel lug nuts • Have tires balanced • Raise car and spin the wheel. If the wheel is bent, it should be replaced • Have wheel alignment checked/adjusted • Check ball joints • Check steering linkage • Check shock absorbers
Tires wear unevenly or prematurely	• Incorrect wheel size • Wheels are out of balance • Wheels are out of alignment	• Check if wheel and tire size are compatible • Have wheels balanced • Have wheel alignment checked/adjusted

CAUTION: *Do not include the new Space Saver® or temporary spare tires in the rotation pattern. These tires are designed ONLY to get you to the next service facility after a flat tire; they are NOT designed for high speed or extended driving.*

There are certain exceptions to tire rotation, however. Studded snow tires should not be rotated, and radials should be kept on the same side of the vehicle, maintaining the same direction of rotation. The belts on radial tires get set in a pattern after they accumulate mileage, and if the direction of rotation is reversed, it can cause a rough ride, vibration and possible ill handling.

TIRE STORAGE

Store tires at a proper inflation pressures if they are mounted on wheels. Mark radial and studded snow tires with an arrow showing direction of rotation so they can be mounted the same way. All tires should be kept in a cool, dry place. If tires are stored in the garage or basement, do not let them stand on a concrete floor; lay them down on strips of wood.

Troubleshooting Basic Tire Problems

Problem	Cause	Solution
The car's front end vibrates at high speeds and the steering wheel shakes	• Wheels out of balance • Front end needs aligning	• Have wheels balanced • Have front end alignment checked
The car pulls to one side while cruising	• Unequal tire pressure (car will usually pull to the low side) • Mismatched tires • Front end needs aligning	• Check/adjust tire pressure • Be sure tires are of the same type and size • Have front end alignment checked
Abnormal, excessive or uneven tire wear See "How to Read Tire Wear"	• Infrequent tire rotation • Improper tire pressure • Sudden stops/starts or high speed on curves	• Rotate tires more frequently to equalize wear • Check/adjust pressure • Correct driving habits
Tire squeals	• Improper tire pressure • Front end needs aligning	• Check/adjust tire pressure • Have front end alignment checked

Tire Size Comparison Chart

"Letter" sizes			Inch Sizes	Metric-inch Sizes		
"60 Series"	"70 Series"	"78 Series"	1965–77	"60 Series"	"70 Series"	"80 Series"
			5.50-12, 5.60-12	165/60-12	165/70-12	155-12
		Y78-12	6.00-12			
		W78-13	5.20-13	165/60-13	145/70-13	135-13
		Y78-13	5.60-13	175/60-13	155/70-13	145-13
			6.15-13	185/60-13	165/70-13	155-13, P155/80-13
A60-13	A70-13	A78-13	6.40-13	195/60-13	175/70-13	165-13
B60-13	B70-13	B78-13	6.70-13	205/60-13	185/70-13	175-13
			6.90-13			
C60-13	C70-13	C78-13	7.00-13	215/60-13	195/70-13	185-13
D60-13	D70-13	D78-13	7.25-13			
E60-13	E70-13	E78-13	7.75-13			195-13
			5.20-14	165/60-14	145/70-14	135-14
			5.60-14	175/60-14	155/70-14	145-14
			5.90-14			
A60-14	A70-14	A78-14	6.15-14	185/60-14	165/70-14	155-14
	B70-14	B78-14	6.45-14	195/60-14	175/70-14	165-14
	C70-14	C78-14	6.95-14	205/60-14	185/70-14	175-14
D60-14	D70-14	D78-14				
E60-14	E70-14	E78-14	7.35-14	215/60-14	195/70-14	185-14
F60-14	F70-14	F78-14, F83-14	7.75-14	225/60-14	200/70-14	195-14
G60-14	G70-14	G77-14, G78-14	8.25-14	235/60-14	205/70-14	205-14
H60-14	H70-14	H78-14	8.55-14	245/60-14	215/70-14	215-14
J60-14	J70-14	J78-14	8.85-14	255/60-14	225/70-14	225-14
L60-14	L70-14		9.15-14	265/60-14	235/70-14	
	A70-15	A78-15	5.60-15	185/60-15	165/70-15	155-15
B60-15	B70-15	B78-15	6.35-15	195/60-15	175/70-15	165-15
C60-15	C70-15	C78-15	6.85-15	205/60-15	185/70-15	175-15
	D70-15	D78-15				
E60-15	E70-15	E78-15	7.35-15	215/60-15	195/70-15	185-15
F60-15	F70-15	F78-15	7.75-15	225/60-15	205/70-15	195-15
G60-15	G70-15	G78-15	8.15-15/8.25-15	235/60-15	215/70-15	205-15
H60-15	H70-15	H78-15	8.45-15/8.55-15	245/60-15	225/70-15	215-15
J60-15	J70-15	J78-15	8.85-15/8.90-15	255/60-15	235/70-15	225-15
	K70-15		9.00-15	265/60-15	245/70-15	230-15
L60-15	L70-15	L78-15, L84-15	9.15-15			235-15
	M70-15	M78-15				255-15
		N78-15				

Note: Every size tire is not listed and many size comparisons are approximate, based on load ratings. Wider tires than those supplied new with the vehicle, should always be checked for clearance.

BUYING NEW TIRES

When buying new tires, give some though to the following points, especially if you are considering a switch to larger tires or a different profile series:

1. All four tires must be of the same construction type. This rule cannot be violated. Radial, bias, and bias belted tires must not be mixed.

2. The wheels should be the correct width for the tire. Tire dealers have charts of tire and rim compatibility. A mismatch will cause sloppy handling and rapid tire wear. The tread width should match the rim width (inside bead to inside bead) within an inch. For radial tires. the rim width should be 80% or less of the tire (not tread) width.

3. The height (mounted diameter) of the new tires can change speedometer accuracy, engine speed at a given road speed, fuel mileage, acceleration, and ground clearance. Tire manufacturers furnish full measurement specifications.

4. The spare tire should be usable, at least for short distance and low speed operation, with the new tires.

5. There should not be any body interference when loaded, on bumps or in turns.

Care For Aluminum Wheels

Aluminum wheels should be cleaned and waxed regularly. Do not use abrasive cleaners because they may damage the protective coating.

FLUIDS AND LUBRICANTS

Fuel and Engine Oil Recommendations

ENGINE OIL

When adding oil to the crankcase or changing the oil or filter, it is important that oil of an equal quality to original equipment be used in your vehicle. The use of inferior oils may void the warranty, damage your engine, or both.

The SAE (Society of Automotive Engineers) grade number of oil indicates the viscosity of the oil (its ability to lubricate at a given temperature). The lower the SAE number, the lighter the oil; the lower the viscosity, the easier it is to crank the engine in cold weather but the less the oil will lubricate and protect the engine at high temperatures. This number is marked on every oil container.

Oil viscosities should be chosen from those oils recommended for the lowest anticipated temperatures during the oil change interval. Multigrade oils have been developed because of the need for an oil that embodies both good lubrication at high temperatures and easy cranking in cold weather. All oils are thick at low temperatures and thin out as the temperature rises. Basically, a multigrade oil is thinner at lower temperatures and thicker at high temperatures relative to straight weight oils. For example, a 10W–40 oil (the W stands for winter) exhibits the characteristics of a 10 weight (SAE 10) oil when the vehicle is first started and the oil is cold. Its lighter weight allows it to travel to the lubricating surfaces quicker and offer less

resistance to starter motor cranking than, say, a straight 30 weight (SAE 30) oil. But after the engine reaches operating temperature, the 10W–40 oil begins acting like straight 40 weight (SAE 40) oil, its heavier weight providing greater lubrication with less chance of foaming than a straight 30 weight oil would *at that temperature*.

After extensive testing of 10W–40 oils, General Motors recently concluded that they should be replaced by oils that offer less of a viscosity range. Note that 10W–30 or 15W–40 oils are preferred for use by GM on 1984 and later models, as shown in the viscosity chart that accompanies this section of this book.

NOTE: *Single grade (straight weight) oils such as SAE 30 are more satisfactory than multi-viscosity oils for highway driving in diesel engines.*

The API (American Petroleum Institute) designation, also found on the oil container, indicates the classification of engine oil used under certain given operating conditions. Only oils designated for use Service **SE**, or **SF** heavy duty detergent should be used in your Buick, Olds or Pontiac. For 1984 and later models, only **SF** oils are approved by GM. Oils of the SE and SF type perform many functions inside the engine besides their basic function of lubrication. Through a balanced system of metallic detergents and polymeric dispersants, the oil prevents high and low temperature deposits and also keeps sludge and dirt particles in suspension. Acids, particularly sulphuric acid, as well as other by-products of engine combustion are neutralized by the oil. If these acids are allowed

Recommended Lubricants

Item	Lubricant
Engine Oil	API "SE" or "SF" ①
Automatic Transmission	DEXRON® II ATF
Rear Axle-Standard	SAE 80W GL-5 or SAE 80W/90 GL-5
Positraction/Limited Slip	GM Part #1052271 or 1052272
Power Steering Reservoir	DEXRON® ATF—1975–76 Power Steering Fluid—1977 and later
Brake Fluid	DOT 3
Antifreeze	Ethlyene Glycol—GM spec. 1825M
Front Wheel Bearings	GM Wheel Bearing Grease
Clutch Linkage	Engine Oil
Hood and Door Hinges	Engine Oil
Chassis Lubrication	NLGI #1 or NLGI #2
Lock Cylinders	WD-40 or Powdered Graphite

① On 1984 and later models, use SF/CD or SF/CC

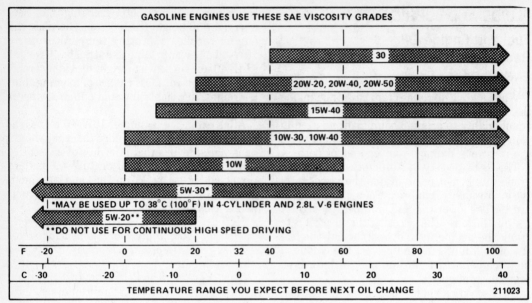

Gasoline engine oil viscosity chart

to concentrate, they can cause corrosion and rapid wear of the internal engine parts.

CAUTION: *Non-detergent or straight mineral oils should not be used in your GM engine.*

DIESEL ENGINE OIL

Diesel engines require different engine oil from those used in gasoline engines. Besides doing the things gasoline engine oil does, diesel oil must also deal with increased engine heat and the diesel blow-by gases, which create sulphuric acid, a highly corrosive compound.

Under the American Petroleum Institute (API) classifications, gasoline engine oil codes begin with an **S**, and diesel engine oil codes begin with a **C**. This first letter designation is followed by a second letter code which explains what type of service (heavy, moderate, light) the oil is meant for. For example, the top of a typical oil can will include: **API SERVICES SC, SD, SE, CA, CB, CC**. This means the oil in the can is a good, moderate duty engine oil when used in a diesel engine.

It should be noted here that the further down the alphabet the second letter of the API classification is, the greater the oil's protective qualities are (CD is the severest duty diesel engine oil, CA is the lightest duty oil, etc.) The same is true for gasoline engine oil classifications (SF is the severest duty gasoline engine oil, SA is the lightest duty oil, etc.).

Many diesel manufacturers recommend an oil with both gasoline and diesel engine API classifications. Consult the owner's manual for specifications.

The top of the oil can will also contain an SAE (Society of Automotive Engineers) designation, which gives the oil's viscosity. A typical designation will be: SAE 10W-30, which means the oil is a winter viscosity oil, meaning it will flow and give protection at low temperatures.

On the diesel engine, oil viscosity is critical, because the diesel is much harder to start (due to its higher compression) than a gasoline engine. Obviously, if you fill the crankcase with a very heavy oil during the winter (SAE 20W-50, for example) the starter is going to require a lot of current from the battery to turn the engine. And, since batteries don't function well in cold weather in the first place, you may find yourself stranded some morning. Consult the owner's manual for recommended oil specifications for the climate you live in.

Revised oil viscosity chart for 1984 and later vehicles, showing GM's revised findings and preference for 10W–30 oils

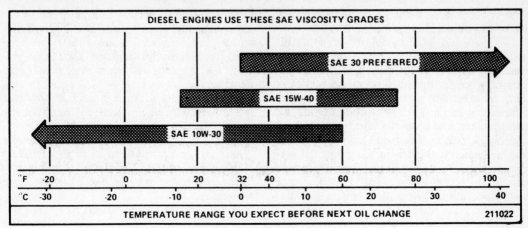

Diesel oil viscosity chart

SYNTHETIC OIL

There are excellent synthetic and fuel efficient oils available that, under the right circumstances, can help provide better fuel mileage and better engine protection. However, these advantages come at a price, which can be three or four times the price per quart of conventional motor oils.

Before pouring any synthetic oils into your vehicle's engine, you should consider the condition of the engine and the type of driving you do. Also, check the vehicle's warranty conditions regarding the use of synthetics.

Generally, it is best to avoid the use of snythetic oil in both brand new and older, high mileage engines. New engines require a proper break-in, and the synthetics are so slippery that they can prevent this; most manufacturers recommend that you wait at least 5,000 miles before switching to a synthetic oil. Conversely, older engines are looser and tend to use more oil; synthetics will slip past worn parts more readily than regular oil, and will be used up faster. If your vehicle already leaks and/or uses oil (due to worn parts and bad seals or gaskets), it will leak and use more with a slippery synthetic inside.

Consider your type of driving. If most of your accumulated mileage is on the highway at higher, steadier speeds, a synthetic oil will reduce friction and probably help delivery better fuel mileage. Under such ideal highway conditions, the oil change interval can be extended, as long as the oil filter will operate effectively for the extended life of the oil. If the filter can't do its job for this extended period, dirt and sludge will build up in your engine's crankcase, sump, oil pump and lines, no matter what type of oil is used. If using synthetic oil in this manner, you should continue to change the oil filter at the recommended intervals.

Vehicles used under harder, stop-and-go, short hop circumstances should always be serviced more frequently and for these vehicles synthetic oil may not be a wise investment. Because of the necessary shorter change interval needed for this type of driving, you cannot take advantage of the long recommended change interval of most synthetic oils.

Finally, most synthetic oils are not compatible with conventional oils and cannot be added to them. This means you should always carry a couple of quarts of synthetic oil with you while on a long trip, as not all service stations carry this oil.

FUEL

Gasoline

It is important you you use fuel of the proper octane rating in your vehicle. Octane rating is based on the quantity of anti-knock compounds added to the fuel and it determines the speed at which the gasoline will burn. The lower the octane, the faster the gas burns. The higher the octane, the slower the fuel burns and a greater percentage of compounds in the fuel prevent

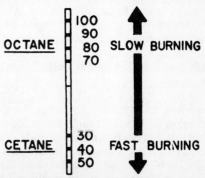

Diesel engine fuel cetane versus gasoline engine octane ratings. The higher the cetane number, the faster the fuel burns

spark ping (knock), detonation and preignition, and postignition (dieseling).

All 1975 and later models covered in this guide will perform happily on unleaded regular gasoline. Owners of turbocharged Buick vehicles may opt for unleaded premium fuel of at least 91 octane to protect against detonation. Since many factors such as altitude, terrain, air temperature, and humidity affect operating efficiency, knocking may result even though the recommended fuel grade is being used. If persistent knocking occurs, it may be necessary to switch to a higher grade of fuel. Continuous or heavy knocking may result in engine damage.

NOTE: *Your engine's fuel requirement can change with time, mainly due to carbon buildup, which will in turn change the compression ratio. If your engine pings, knocks, or diesels (runs with the ignition off) switch to a higher grade of fuel. Sometimes just changing brands will cure the problem. If it becomes necessary to retard the timing from the specifications, don't change it more than a few degrees. Retarded timing will reduce power output and fuel mileage, in addition to making the engine run hotter.*

Diesel Fuel

Fuel makers produce two grades of diesel fuel, No. 1 and No. 2, for use in automotive diesel engines. Generally speaking, No. 2 fuel is recommended over No. 1 for driving in temperatures above 20°F (−7°C). In fact, in many areas, No. 2 diesel is the only fuel available. By comparison, No. 2 diesel fuel is less volatile than No. 1 fuel, and gives better fuel economy. No. 2 fuel is also a better injection pump lubricant.

Two important characteristics of diesel fuel are its cetane number and its viscosity.

The cetane number of a diesel fuel refers to the ease with which a diesel fuel ignites. High cetane numbers mean that the fuel will ignite with relative ease so that it ignites well in an engine being cranked at low temperatures. Naturally, the lower the cetane number, the higher the temperature must be to ignite the fuel. Most commercial fuels have cetane numbers that range from 35 to 65. No. 1 diesel fuel generally has a higher cetane rating than No. 2 fuel.

Viscosity is the ability of a liquid, in this case diesel fuel, to flow. Using straight No. 2 diesel fuel below 20°F (−7°C) can cause problems, because this fuel tends to become cloudy, meaning wax crystals begin forming in the fuel. 20°F (−7°C) is often called the cloud point for No. 2 fuel. In extreme cold weather, No. 2 fuel can stop flowing altogether. In either case, fuel flow is restricted, which can result in a no start condition or poor engine performance. Fuel manu-

facturers often winterize No. 2 diesel fuel by using various fuel additives and blends (No. 1 diesel fuel, kerosene, etc.) to lower its winter time viscosity. Generally speaking, though, No. 1 diesel fuel is more satisfactory in extremely cold weather.

NOTE: *No. 1 and No. 2 diesel fuels will mix and burn with no ill effects, although the engine manufacturer will undoubtedly recommend one or the other. Consult the owner's manual for information.*

Depending on local climate, most fuel manufacturers make winterized No. 2 fuel available seasonally.

Many automobile manufacturers (Oldsmobile, for example) publish pamphlets giving the locations of diesel fuel stations nationwide. Contact the local dealer for information.

Do not substitute home heating oil for automotive diesel fuel. While basic characteristics of these oils are similar, the heating oil is not capable of meeting diesel cetane ratings. This means that using it might offer not only hard starting but engine knock; even under warm operating conditions. This could result in unnecessary engine wear or damage.

Further, furnace oil is not blended for operation at colder temperatures as most heating oil filters are located indoors. It could easily clog fuel filters with wax.

The equipment used in burning furnace oil does not contain the extremely fine machined surfaces or extremely tiny nozzle openings used in a diesel engine fuel system. Very small amounts of dirt and abrasives that will pass right through a heating oil fuel system could play havoc with your diesel's injection system. Finally, minimum standards regarding sulphur and ash that help keep deposits out of your diesel engine and minimize corrosion may not be met by furnace oil.

One more word on diesel fuels. Don't thin diesel fuel with gasoline. The result is the most highly explosive mixture possible in your fuel tank and unwarranted danger. Fuel thinned with gasoline may not adequately lubricate the injection system, leading to premature pump and nozzle failure and need for an expensive overhaul. Cetane rating will also be effected in an undesirable way.

It's best to buy No. 1 or blended No. 2 fuel for wintertime use. If you must use some means to keep No. 2 fuel from waxing, blend it with No. 1 or use a quality anti-waxing agent.

Engine
OIL LEVEL CHECK

Every time you stop for fuel, check the engine oil as follows:

1. Make sure the vehicle is parked on level ground.

2. When checking the oil level it is best for the engine to be at normal operating temperature, although checking the oil immediately after stopping will lead to a false reading. Wait a few minutes after turning off the engine to allow the oil to drain back into the crankcase.

3. Open the hood and locate the dipstick which will be on either the right or left side depending upon your particular engine. Pull the dipstick from its tube, wipe it clean and then reinsert it.

4. Pull the dipstick out again and, holding it horizontally, read the oil level. The oil should be between the FULL and ADD marks on the dipstick. If the oil is below the ADD mark, add oil of the proper viscosity through the capped opening in the top of the cylinder head cover. See the Oil and Fuel Recommendations chart in this chapter for the proper viscosity and rating of oil to use.

5. Replace the dipstick and check the oil level again after adding any oil. Be careful not to overfill the crankcase. Approximately one quart

of oil will raise the level from the ADD mark to the FULL mark. Excess oil will generally be consumed at a faster rate.

OIL AND FILTER CHANGE

The oil in the engine of your Buick, Olds or Pontiac should be changed every six months or 7,500 miles, whichever comes first (except turbo V6 and diesels). If you live in an extremely dusty or smoggy area, or drive for moderately short distances in cold weather (less than four miles with the temperature below freezing), change your vehicle's oil more frequently. The oil should be changed every 3,000 miles or four months under these conditions. A new filter should be installed with every oil change, and the used oil put into a suitable container and taken to a collection or reclamation point for recycling (many garages and gas stations have storage tanks for this purpose).

NOTE: *GM recommends that the filter be*

Checking the engine oil level with the dipstick

The oil level should show between the "ADD" and "FULL" marks on the dipstick

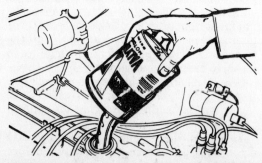

Add oil through the capped opening in the valve cover

Drain plug on bottom of engine oil pan

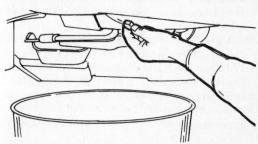

Keep an inward pressure on the plug as you unscrew it, so the oil won't escape until you pull the plug away

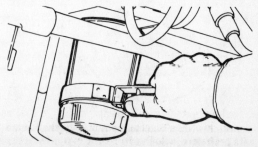

Use a strap wrench to remove the oil filter

changed every other oil change, unless the vehicle is driven under those conditions requiring more frequent changes or those in which the time limit expires before the mileage limit. Our recommendation is that, regardless of the interval, the filter should be changed at every oil change. This offers excellent protection against a situation in which the filter becomes clogged, bypassing dirty oil directly to the engine's wearing parts. It also permits a more complete removal of dirty oil from the engine's filter and oil galleries, which hold a quart or more of contaminated fluid. Change the oil in turbocharged vehicles every 3,000 miles; change the oil in diesel vehicles every 5,000 miles. On diesels, if you are towing a trailer, it is dusty, or you are driving trips of four miles or less in below freezing temperatures, change the oil every 2,500 miles or three months, whichever comes first.

The oil should always be changed while hot, so the dirt and particles will still be suspended in the oil when it drains out of the engine. To change the oil and filter:

1. Run the engine until it reaches normal operating temperature.

2. Put the transmission in **PARK**, set the parking brake and jack up the front of the vehicle. Support the front end with jackstands.

3. Slide a drain pan of at least 6 quarts capacity under the engine oil pan.

4. Loosen the drain plug. Turn the plug out slowly by hand, keeping an inward pressure on the plug as you unscrew it so the hot oil will not escape until the plug is completely removed.

CAUTION: *When you are ready to release the plug, pull it away from the drain hole quickly, to avoid being burned by the hot oil.*

5. Allow the oil to drain completely and then install the drain plug. DO NOT OVERTIGHTEN the plug, or you will strip the threads in the drain hole and you'll have to buy a new pan or an over-sized replacement plug. A suitable torque is 20 ft. lbs. (41 Nm).

6. Using an oil filter strap wrench, remove

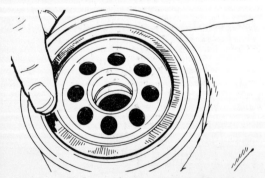

Apply a light coat of oil to the rubber gasket on the oil filter before installing it

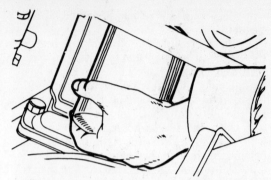

Install the new filter by hand only; DO NOT use the strap wrench

the oil filter. Keep in mind that it's holding about a quart of dirty, hot oil.

7. As soon as you remove the oil filter, hold it upright until you can empty it into the drain pan. Dispose of the filter.

CAUTION: *Prolonged and repeated skin contact with used engine oil, with no effort to remove the oil, may be harmful. Follow these simple precautions when handling used motor oil.*

1. Avoid prolonged skin contact with used motor oil.

2. Remove oil from skin by washing thoroughly with soap and water or waterless hand cleaner. Do not use gasoline, thinners or solvents.

8. Using a clean rag, wipe off the filter mounting adaptor on the engine block. Be sure that the rag does not leave any lint which could clog an oil passage.

9. Wipe a coating of clean engine oil on the rubber gasket of the new filter. Spin it onto the engine by hand. DO NOT use the strap wrench. When the gasket starts to snug up against the adaptor surface, give it another ½-¾ turn by hand (check the instructions provided by the filter manufacturer). Don't turn it any more, or you'll squash the gasket and the filter will leak.

10. Refill the engine with the correct amount of fresh oil through the valve cover cap, or breather tube (diesels). See the Capacities chart in this chapter.

11. Check the oil level on the dipstick. It is normal for the oil level to be slightly above the full mark right after an oil change because the filter and engine oil passages are dry. Start the engine and allow it to idle for a few minutes to fill these passages and the filter.

CAUTION: *Do not run the engine above idle speed until the oil pressure light (usually red) goes out, indicating the engine has built up oil pressure.*

12. Shut off the engine and allow the oil to drain back down for a few minutes before checking the dipstick again. Add more oil, if

necessary. Check for oil leaks around the filter and drain plug.

Automatic Transmission

FLUID RECOMMENDATIONS

NOTE: *Always use DEXRON®II ATF. The use of ATF Type F or any other fluid will cause severe damage to the transmission.*

There are two basic different types of automatic transmission fluid. They have radically different viscosities, meaning that they will behave quite differently as to both clutch operation and seal efficiency, both critical aspects of automatic transmission operation. The Type F fluid is used only in certain transmissions used in Ford Motor Co. products. Using it in a General Motors Corp. automatic transmission will produce disastrous results, including leaks and rough shifting.

The fluid used in G.M. units, as well as many other products, was originally known as Type A. An additive package that met Type A viscosity requirements but also included appropriate resistance to breakdown at high temperatures and leakage was developed and named Dexron®. It incorporated a rare type of whale oil that became unavailable in 1973. A new designation, Dexron®II was developed to replace the original Dexron®, utilizing soybean oil rather than whale oil. Dexron®II meets all the basic standards for what had been Dexron® and Type A.

It is vitally important to understand that, while some older G.M. vehicles might have been able to use one of the earlier designations, all the models covered in this book should use only Dexron®II. In case you should run into remaining supplies of either Dexron® or Type A fluid, it is important to understand that:

1. Only Dexron®II should be used in the models covered by this book.

2. You must not allow yourself to be sold on the use of the wrong designation, merely because the fluid is of the same basic type. The wrong fluid could work for some time without producing problems, and then create them many miles later.

LEVEL CHECK

Check the automatic transmission fluid level at least every 7,500 miles. The dipstick can be found in the rear of the engine compartment. The fluid level should be checked only when the transmission is hot (normal operating temperature). The transmission is considered hot after about 20 miles of highway driving.

1. Park the vehicle on a level surface with the engine idling. Shift the transmission into **NEUTRAL** and set the parking brake.

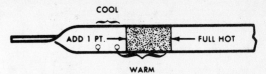

On the automatic transmission dipstick, the proper level is within the shaded marks

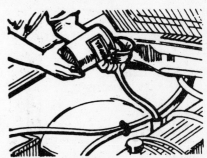

Add automatic transmission fluid through the transmission dipstick tube

2. Remove the dipstick, wipe it clean and then reinsert it firmly. Be sure that it has been pushed all the way in. Remove the dipstick again and check the fluid level while holding it horizontally. With the engine running, the fluid level should be between the second notch and the FULL HOT line. If the fluid must be checked when it is cool, the level should be between the first and second notches.

3. If the fluid level is below the second notch (engine hot) or the first notch (engine cold), add DEXRON®II automatic transmission fluid through the dipstick tube. This is easily done with the aid of a funnel. Check the level often as you are filling the transmission. Be extremely careful not to overfill it. Overfilling will cause slippage, seal damage and overheating. Approximately one pint of ATF will raise the fluid level from one notch/line to the other.

The fluid on the dipstick should always be a bright red color. If it is discolored (brown or black), or smells burnt, serious transmission troubles, probably due to overheating, should be suspected. The transmission should be inspected by a qualified technician to locate the cause of the burnt fluid.

DRAIN, REFILL, AND FILTER CHANGE

The four types of pan gaskets on the automatic transmissions covered here are pictured for ready identification.

The fluid should be changed with the transmission warm. A 20 minute drive at highway speeds should accomplish this.

1. Raise and support the vehicle with jackstands, preferably in a level attitude.

2. The support crossmember may have to be removed on some models. Support the trans-

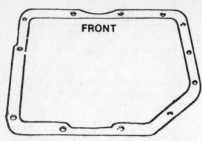

Turbo Hydra-Matic 250, 350, 375B pan shape

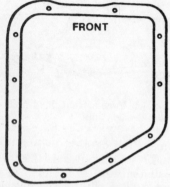

Turbo Hydra-Matic 200 pan shape

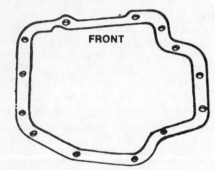

Turbo Hydra-Matic 400 pan shape

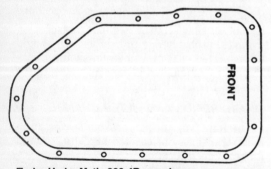

Turbo Hydra-Matic 200-4R pan shape

4. Pry the pan loose and let it drain.

5. Remove the pan and gasket. Clean the pan thoroughly with solvent and air dry it. Be very careful not to get any lint from rags in the pan.

NOTE: *It is normal to find a SMALL amount of metal shavings in the pan. An excessive amount of metal shavings indicates transmission damage which must be handled by a professional automatic transmission mechanic.*

6. Remove the strainer-to-valve body screws, the strainer, and the gasket. Most 350 transmissions will have a throw-away filter instead of a strainer. On the 400 and 200-4R transmission, remove the filter retaining bolt, filter, and intake pipe O-ring.

7. If there is a strainer, clean it in solvent and air dry.

8. Install the new filter or cleaned strainer with a new gasket. Tighten the screws to 12 ft. lbs. (16 Nm). On the 400, install a new intake pipe O-ring and a new filter, tightening the retaining bolt to 120 inch lbs. (14 Nm).

NOTE: *While the transmission pan is removed, you may want to install an after market oil pan drain plug kit, available at a local*

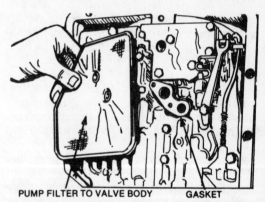

PUMP FILTER TO VALVE BODY   GASKET

Removing the filter and gasket on a Turbo Hydra-Matic 200, 350 or 375B

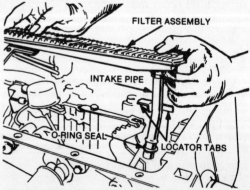

FILTER ASSEMBLY

INTAKE PIPE

O-RING SEAL   LOCATOR TABS

Removing the filter, intake pipe and O-ring on Turbo Hydra-Matic 400

mission with a transmission jack or equivalent before removing the crossmember.

3. Place a large pan under the transmission pan. Remove all the front and side pan bolts. Loosen the rear bolts about four turns.

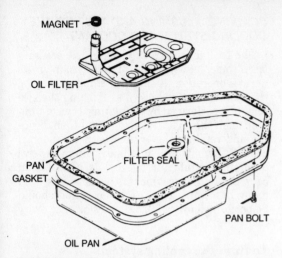

Transmission pan, gasket and filter assembly—Turbo Hydra-Matic 200-4R

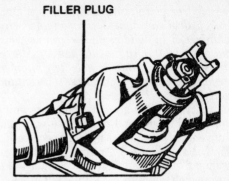

Remove the filler plug to check the lubricant level in the rear axle

parts distributor or transmission repair shop. This will make future fluid changes easier.

9. Install the pan with a new gasket. Tighten the bolts evenly to 97 inch. lbs. (11 Nm). Do NOT overtighten, gasket may break causing a leak.

10. Lower the vehicle enough to add the proper amount of DEXRON®II automatic transmission fluid through the dipstick tube.

11. Start the engine in Park and let it idle. Do not race the engine. Shift into each shift lever position, shift back into Park, and check the fluid level on the dipstick. The level should be ¼ in. (6.3mm) below ADD. Be very careful not to overfill. Recheck the level after the vehicle has been driven long enough to thoroughly warm up the transmission. Add fluid as necessary. The level should then be at FULL when the transmission is at normal operating temperature.

Rear Axle

FLUID RECOMMENDATIONS

Most gear oils come in a plastic squeeze bottle with a nozzle end, which makes adding lubricant simple. You can also use a common turkey baster for this job. Use only standard GL-5 hypoid-type gear oil--SAE 80W or SAE 80W/90.

NOTE: *On all models equipped with a positraction/limited slip differential, GM recommends that you use only special GM lubricant available at your local Buick, Oldsmobile or Pontiac parts department. Also, the standard GL-5 fluid with an limit slip additive can be used.*

LEVEL CHECK

The oil in the differential should be checked at least every 7,500 miles.

1. Park the vehicle on a level surface and remove the filler plug from the front side of the differential.

2. If the oil begins to trickle out of the hole when the plug is removed, the differential is full. If no lubricant trickles out, carefully insert your finger (watch out for sharp threads) into the hole and check that the oil is up to the bottom edge of the filler hole.

3. If not, add oil through the hole until the level is at the edge of the hole. Torque the fill plug to 29 ft. lbs. (39 Nm).

DRAIN AND REFILL

There is no recommended change interval for the rear axle lubricant, but it is always a good idea to change the lube if you have purchased the vehicle used or if it has been driven in water high enough to reach the axle.

1. Park the vehicle on a level surface and set the parking brake.

2. Remove the rear axle filler plug on the front side of the differential housing.

3. Place a large drain pan underneath the rear axle.

4. Unscrew the retaining bolts and remove the rear axle cover. The axle lubricant will now be able to drain into the container.

5. Clean all gasket mating surfaces. Using a new cover gasket and sealant, install the axle cover. Tighten the retaining bolts in a crisscross pattern to 22 ft. lbs. (30 Nm).

6. Refill the axle with the proper quantity (see Capacities chart in this chapter) of SAE 80W, SAE 80W-90 GL-5 or limited slip gear lubricant. Replace the filler plug and torque to 29 ft. lbs. (39 Nm), take the vehicle for a short ride and check for any leaks around the plug or rear cover.

Cooling System

FLUID RECOMMENDATIONS

CAUTION: *When draining the coolant, keep in mind that cats and dogs are attracted by the ethylene glycol antifreeze, and are quite likely to drink any that is left in an uncovered container or in puddles on the ground. This will prove fatal in sufficient quantity. Always drain the coolant into a sealable container. Coolant should be reused unless it is contaminated or several years old.*

A quality, ethylene glycol coolant containing corrosion inhibitors and compatible with aluminum engine parts, meeting GM Specification 1825-M should be used. Antifreeze concentration should be high enough to maintain freezing protection down to $-34°F$ ($-37°C$).

LEVEL CHECK

It's a good idea to check the coolant level every time you stop for fuel. If the engine is hot, let it cool for a few minutes and then check the level following the procedure given earlier in this chapter.

It is best to check the coolant level when the engine and radiator are cool. Buick, Oldsmobile and Pontiac vehicles covered in this guide are equipped with coolant recovery tanks connected by hoses to the radiator and mounted on the inner fender skirt. If the coolant level is at or near the FULL COLD (engine cold) or the FULL HOT (engine hot) lines on the tank, the level is satisfactory.

Check the freezing protection rating at least twice a year, preferably in mid-fall and mid-spring. This can be done with an antifreeze tester, the use of which is detailed in Step 11 under Cooling System in this chapter.

CAUTION: *Never add coolant to a hot engine. Stop the engine and allow it to cool. Then, start it to circulate coolant uniformly through the block and add coolant slowly as the engine idles. Otherwise you risk cracking the block. The coolant recovery tank is the only accurate place to check the coolant level; however, coolant can be added to either the tank or directly to the radiator. NEVER REMOVE THE RADIATOR CAP UNTIL THE ENGINE HAS HAD AMPLE TIME TO COOL TO BELOW OPERATING TEMPERATURE.*

If you find the coolant level low, add a 50/50 mixture of ethylene glycol based antifreeze and clean water. Do not add straight water unless you are out on the road and in emergency circumstances; if this is the case, drain the radiator and replenish the cooling system with an ethylene glycol mix at the next opportunity. Modern ethylene glycol antifreezes are special blends of anti-corrosive additives and lubricants that help keep the cooling system clean and help lubricate the water pump seal, which is why they are recommended by the manufacturers.

DRAINING, FLUSHING AND TESTING THE COOLING SYSTEM AND COOLANT

The cooling system in your vehicle accumulates some internal rust and corrosion in its normal operation. A simple method of keeping the system clean is known as flushing the system. It is performed by circulating a can of radiator flush through the system, and then draining and refilling the system with the normal coolant. Radiator flush is marketed by several different manufacturers, and is available in cans at auto departments, parts stores, and many hardware stores. This operation should be performed every 30,000 miles or once every two years.

To flush the cooling system:

1. Drain the existing antifreeze and coolant. Open the radiator and engine drain petcocks (located near the bottom of the radiator and on the side of the engine block, down low, respectively), or disconnect the bottom radiator hose at the radiator outlet.

NOTE: *Before opening the radiator petcock, spray it with some penetrating oil.*

CAUTION: *Be aware that if the engine has been run up to operating temperature, the coolant emptied will be HOT.*

2. Close the petcock or reconnect the lower hose and fill the system with water; hot water, if possible, if the engine has been run. Fill slowly with the engine idling.

3. Add a can of quality radiator flush to the radiator, following any special instructions on the can.

4. Idle the engine as long as specified on the can of flush, or until the upper radiator hose gets hot.

5. Drain the system again. There should be

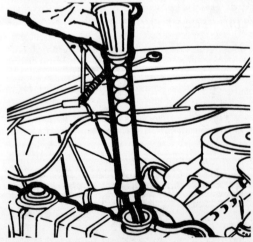

Check anti-freeze protection with an inexpensive tester

Some radiator caps have pressure release levers

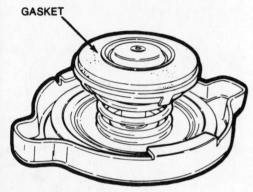

GASKET

Check the cap for wear or cracks

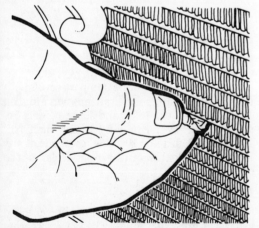

Keep the radiator fins clear of dirt and bugs for maximum cooling

quite a bit of scale and rust in the drained water.

6. Repeat the rinsing process until the drained water is almost completely clear.

7. Close all petcocks and connect all hoses.

8. Flush the coolant recovery reservoir with water and leave empty.

9. Determine the capacity of your vehicle's cooling system (see Capacities specifications in this guide). Add a 50/50 mix of ethylene glycol antifreeze and water to provide the desired protection.

10. Run the engine to operating temperature, then stop the engine and check for leaks. Check the coolant level and top up if necessary.

11. Check the protection level of your antifreeze mix with an antifreeze tester (a small, inexpensive syringe-type device available at any auto parts store). The tester has five or six small colored balls inside, each of which signify a certain temperature rating. Insert the tester in the recovery tank and suck just enough coolant into the syringe to float as many individual balls as you can (without sucking in too much coolant and floating all the balls at once). A table supplied with the tester will explain how many floating balls equal protection down to a certain temperature. Three floating balls might mean the coolant will protect your engine down to 5°F (-15°C), for example.

CHECK THE RADIATOR CAP

CAUTION: *Never remove the radiator cap until the engine has cooled down well below operating temperature. Otherwise, you can be burned by escaping hot water and steam. Read the following paragraphs carefully for additional instructions.*

When you do remove the cap, cover it with a heavy rag to protect yourself and turn it slowly until it reaches the first stop. If the cap is working right, any pressure that is in the system will be released and you'll hear escaping steam or air pressure. Also, the cap will feel just slightly loose; you'll be able to move it up and down slightly.

If you don't hear any escaping pressure and the engine is warm at all, it's best to wait until it cools. This is because the cap gasket can get wedged between the metal backing and the filler neck of the radiator, sealing pressure in right through the point in loosening the cap where the cap will be blown upward by escaping pressure.

Note that engines that are overheating due to rust in the cooling system are far more prone to danger than engines that are running cool. They should be treated after until the block is cool to the touch.

After you remove the cap, make sure the gasket is no larger than the metal backing. If it has swelled and overlaps the edge, do not re-use it. Caps incorporating a manual pressure release are available and this is an excellent safety feature, although any cap that is regularly inspected and found to be in good mechanical condition is safe. No cap is safe if it is removed with the engine at or above normal operating temperature or (in the case of standard caps) without turning it cautiously to the first detent to release pressure. Anytime you check the coolant level, check the radiator cap as well. A worn or cracked gasket can mean improper sealing, which can cause lost coolant, lost pressure, and engine overheating (the cooling system is pressurized and the radiator cap has a pressure rating above the pressure of the system).

A worn cap should be replaced with a new one. Make sure the new cap has the proper pressure rating for your vehicle's system; this is usually marked on the standard factory cap. Never buy a cap having a rating less than the pressure of your vehicle's system.

CLEAN THE RADIATOR OF DEBRIS

The efficiency of the radiator can be seriously impaired by blockage of the radiator fins. Leaves, insects, road dirt, paper. All are common obstacles to fresh air entering your radiator and doing its job.

Large pieces of debris, leaves and large insects can be removed from the fins by hand. The smaller pieces can be washed out with water pressure from a garden hose. This is often a neglected area of auto maintenance, so do a thorough job.

Bent radiator fins can be straightened carefully with a pair of needlenosed pliers. The fins are soft, so don't wiggle them; move them once.

Brake Master Cylinder

FLUID RECOMMENDATIONS

When making additions of brake fluid, use only fresh, uncontaminated brake fluid which meets or exceeds DOT 3 standards (as stated on the container).

LEVEL CHECK

The brake master cylinder is located under the hood, in the left rear section of the engine compartment. It is divided into two sections

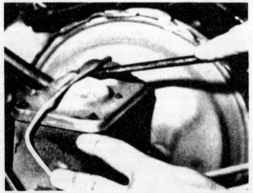

Pry off the retaining clip to check the master cylinder—early model

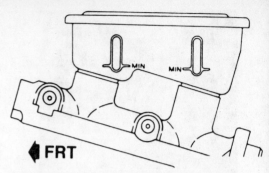

Fluid level—late model plastic reservoir

(reservoirs) and the fluid must be kept within ¼ in. (6.3mm) of the top edge of both reservoirs. The level should be checked at least every 7,500 miles.

NOTE: *Any sudden decrease in the level of fluid indicates a possible leak in the system and should be checked out immediately.*

To check the fluid level, simply pry off the retaining bail and then lift off the top cover of the master cylinder. Be careful not to spill any brake fluid on painted surfaces, as it eats paint. Do not allow the brake fluid container or the master cylinder reservoir to remain open any longer than necessary; brake fluid absorbs moisture from the air, reducing its effectiveness and causing corrosion in the lines.

NOTE: *The reservoir cover on some later models may be without a retaining bail. If so, simply pry the cover off with your fingers.*

Power Steering Pump

FLUID RECOMMENDATIONS

If the level is low, fill the pump reservoir with DEXRON®II Automatic Transmission Fluid on 1975–76 vehicles. 1977 and later models require GM Power Steering Fluid, part No. 1052271, 1050017 or 1052884, available at any Buick, Olds, Pontiac or Chevrolet dealer, or the equivalent.

LEVEL CHECK

Power steering fluid level should be checked at least every 7,500 miles. The power steering pump is belt driven and has the dipstick built into the filler cap. To prevent possible overfilling, check the fluid level only when the fluid has warmed up to operating temperature and with the front wheels turned straight ahead. Fill the reservoir until the fluid level measures FULL on the reservoir dipstick. When the fluid level is low, there is usually a moaning sound coming from the pump as the front wheels are turned, especially when standing still or parking. The steering wheel will also be difficult to turn when fluid level in the pump reservoir gets low.

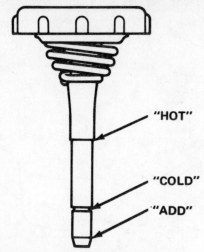

Power steering pump dipstick/filler cap

"HOT"

"COLD"

"ADD"

NOTE: *When adding water to a battery in freezing weather, the vehicle should be driven immediately for a few miles so that the water and electrolyte mix. Otherwise, the battery may freeze.*

Battery

Check the battery fluid level (except in maintenance free batteries) in each cell at least once a month, more often during extreme weather (mid-summer and mid-winter) and extended periods of travel. The electrolyte (water) level should be about ⅜ in. (9.5mm) above the plates as you look down into each cell. Filling each cell to the bottom of the cell ring is satisfactory.

Some battery makes are equipped with an eye in the cap of one cell. If this eye glows or has an amber color, the level is low and only distilled water should be added. If the eye has a dark appearance, the battery electrolyte level is high enough. It is also wise to check each cell individually on these eye type batteries.

Distilled water is the only fluid you should add to your vehicle's battery. It is widely available in supermarkets and auto stores. Tap water in most areas of the U.S. contains chemicals and minerals that are harmful in the long run to battery plates.

OVERFLOW   CORRECT   SHORTAGE

INDICATOR

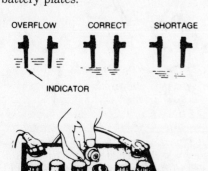

Add battery water until it is level with the bottoms of the filler holes

Chassis Greasing
FRONT SUSPENSION

Every year or 7,500 miles the front suspension ball joints, both upper and lower on each side of the vehicle, must be greased. Most vehicles covered in this guide should be equipped with grease nipples on the ball joints, although some may have plugs which must be removed and nipples installed.

Raise the front end of the vehicle and safely support it with jackstands. Block the rear wheels and firmly apply the parking brake. If the vehicle has been parked in temperatures below 20°F (−7°C) for any length of time, park it in a heated garage for an hour or so until the ball joints loosen up enough to accept the grease.

Depending on which front wheel you work on first, turn the wheel and tire outward, either full lock right or full lock left. You now have the ends of the upper and lower suspension control arms in front of you; the grease nipples are visible pointing up (top ball joint) and down (lower ball joint) through the end of each control arm. If the nipples are not accessible enough, remove the wheel and tire. Wipe all dirt and crud from the nipples or from around the plugs (if installed). If plugs are on the vehicle, remove them and install grease nipples in the holes (nipples are available in various thread sizes at most auto parts stores). Using a hand operated, low pressure grease gun loaded with a quality chassis grease, grease the ball joint only until the rubber joint boot begins to swell out.

NOTE: *Do not pump so much grease into the ball joint that excess grease squeezes out of the rubber boot. This destroys the watertight seal.*

STEERING LINKAGE

The steering linkage should be greased at the same interval as the ball joints. Grease nipples are installed on the steering tie rod ends on most models. Wipe all dirt and crud from around the nipples at each tie rod end. Using a hand operated, low pressure grease gun loaded with a suitable chassis grease, grease the linkage until the old grease begins to squeeze out around the tie rod ends. Wipe off the nipples and any excess grease. Also grease the nipples on the steering idler arms.

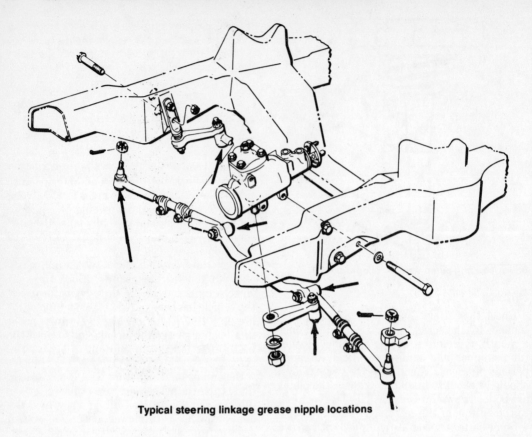

Typical steering linkage grease nipple locations

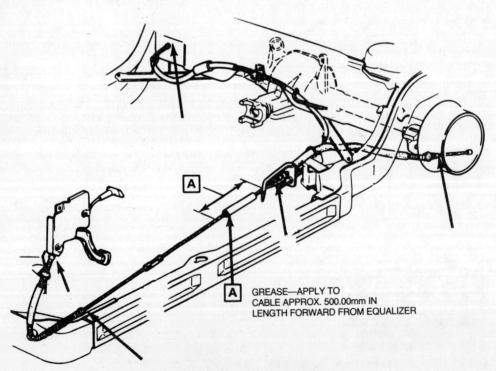

A

A

GREASE—APPLY TO
CABLE APPROX. 500.00mm IN
LENGTH FORWARD FROM EQUALIZER

Parking brake cable grease points

PARKING BRAKE LINKAGE

Use chassis grease on the parking brake cable where it contacts the cable guides, levers and linkage.

AUTOMATIC TRANSMISSION LINKAGE

Apply a small amount of clean engine oil to the kickdown and shift linkage points at 7,500 mile intervals.

Body Lubrication

HOOD LATCH AND HINGES

Clean the latch surfaces and apply clean engine oil to the latch pilot bolts and the spring anchor. Also lubricate the hood hinges with engine oil. Use a chassis grease to lubricate all the pivot points in the latch release mechanism.

DOOR HINGES

The gas tank filler door, vehicle doors, and trunk lid hinges should be wiped clean and lubricated with clean engine oil once a year. Use engine oil to lubricate the trunk lock mechanism and the lock bolt striker. The door lock cylinders and latch mechanisms should be lubricated periodically with a few drops of graphite lock lubricant or a few shots of silicone spray.

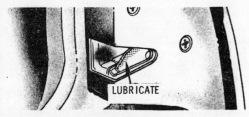

Use graphite lube on the door lock fork bolts

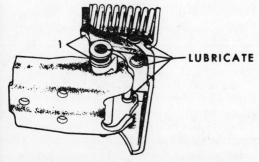

Front door hinge lubrication; use a spray lube

Wheel Bearings

Properly adjusted bearings have a slightly loose feeling. Wheel bearings must never be preloaded. Preloading will damage the bearings and eventually the spindles. If the bearings are too loose, they should be cleaned, inspected, and then adjusted.

Hold the tire at the top and bottom and move the wheel in and out of the spindle. If the movement is greater than 0.005 in. (0.127mm), the bearings are too loose.

ADJUSTMENT

1. Raise and support the vehicle by the lower control arm with jackstands.
2. Remove the hub cap, then remove the dust cap from the hub.
3. Remove the cotter pin and loosen the spindle nut.
4. Spin the wheel forward by hand. Tighten the nut until snug (about 12 ft. lbs. (16 Nm) to fully seat the bearings.
5. Back off the nut ¼–½ turn until it is just loose, then tighten it finger-tight.
6. Loosen the nut until either hole in the spindle lines up with a slot in the nut and then insert the cotter pin. This may appear to be too loose, but it is the correct adjustment. The spindle nut should not be even finger tight.
7. Proper adjustment creates 0.001–0.005 in. (0.025–0.127mm) of end play.

REMOVAL AND INSTALLATION

CAUTION: *Some brake pads contain asbestos, which has been determined to be a cancer causing agent. Never clean the brake surfaces with compressed air! Avoid inhaling any dust from any brake surface! When cleaning brake surfaces, use a commercially available brake cleaning fluid.*

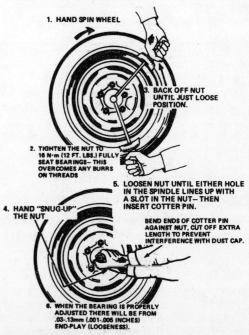

Wheel bearing adjustment

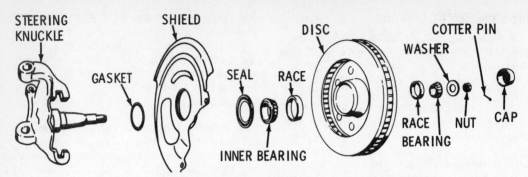

Exploded view of knuckle and hub assembly showing wheel bearings

1. Raise the vehicle and support with jackstands. Remove the wheel, caliper, hub and disc assembly.

2. Remove the outer roller bearing assembly from the hub. The inner bearing assembly can be removed after prying out the inner seal. Discard the seal.

3. Wash all parts in solvent and check for excessive wear or damage.

To install:

4. To replace the outer or inner race, knock out the old race with a hammer and brass drift. New races must be installed squarely and evenly to avoid damage.

WARNING: *Never use old bearing parts with new parts. If the old bearing is damaged, the entire bearing assembly will have to be replaced including the outer race.*

5. Pack the bearings with a high melting point bearing lubricant.

6. Lightly grease the spindle and the inside of the hub.

7. Place the inner bearing in the hub race and install a new grease seal.

8. Carefully install the hub and disc assembly.

9. Install the outer wheel bearing.

10. Install the washer and nut and adjust the bearings according to the procedure outlined above.

11. Install the caliper and torque the mounting bolts to 35 ft. lbs. (48 Nm).

12. Install the dust cap, wheel and tire assembly, then lower the vehicle to the ground.

PACKING

Clean the wheel bearings thoroughly with solvent and check their condition before installation.

CAUTION: *If using compressed air to dry the bearings, do NOT allow the bearing to turn without lubrication.*

Apply a sizable dab of lubricant to the palm of one hand. Using your other hand, work the bearing into the lubricant so that the grease is pushed through the rollers and out the other

side. Keep rotating the bearing while continuing to push the lubricant through it.

TRAILER TOWING

Your vehicle is designed and intended to be used mainly to carry people. Towing a trailer will affect handling, durability and economy. Your safety and satisfaction depend upon proper use of correct equipment. Also, you should avoid overloads and other abusive use.

Factory trailer towing packages are available on most vehicles. However, if you are installing a trailer hitch and wiring on your vehicle, there are a few thing that you ought to know.

Information on trailer towing, special equipment and optional equipment is available at your local dealership. You can write to Oldsmobile Customer Service Department, P.O. Box 30095, Lansing, MI 48909 or Pontiac Customer Service Department, One Pontiac Plaza, Pontiac, Michigan 48053. In Canada, General Motors of Canada Limited, Customer Service Department, Oshawa, Ontario L1J 5Z6.

Trailer Weight

Trailer weight is the first, and most important, factor in determining whether or not your vehicle is suitable for towing the trailer you have in mind. The horsepower-to-weight ratio should be calculated. The basic standard is a ratio of 35:1. That is, 35 pounds of GVW (gross vehicle weight) for every horsepower.

To calculate this ratio, multiply you engine's rated horsepower by 35, then subtract the weight of the vehicle, including passengers and luggage. The resulting figure is the ideal maximum trailer weight that you can tow. One point to consider: a numerically higher axle ratio can offset what appears to be a low trailer weight. If the weight of the trailer that you have in mind is somewhat higher than the weight you just calculated, you might consider changing your rear axle ratio to compensate.

Hitch Weight

There are three kinds of hitches: bumper mounted, frame mounted, and load equalizing.

Bumper mounted hitches are those which attach solely to the vehicle's bumper. Many states prohibit towing with this type of hitch, when it attaches to the vehicle's stock bumper, since it subjects the bumper to stresses for which it was not designed. Aftermarket rear step bumpers, designed for trailer towing, are acceptable for use with bumper mounted hitches.

CAUTION: *Do NOT attach any hitch to the bumper bar on the vehicle. A hitch attachment may be made through the bumper mounting locations, but only if an additional attachment is also made.*

Frame mounted hitches can be of the type which bolts to two or more points on the frame, plus the bumper, or just to several points on the frame. Frame mounted hitches can also be of the tongue type, for Class I towing, or, of the receiver type, for classes II and III.

Load equalizing hitches are usually used for large trailers. Most equalizing hitches are welded in place and use equalizing bars and chains to level the vehicle after the trailer is hooked up.

The bolt-on hitches are the most common, since they are relatively easy to install.

Check the gross weight rating of your trailer. Tongue weight is usually figured as 10% of gross trailer weight. Therefore, a trailer with a maximum gross weight of 2,000 lbs. will have a maximum tongue weight of 200 lbs. Class I trailers fall into this category. Class II trailers are those with a gross weight rating of 2,000–3,500 lbs., while Class III trailers fall into the 3,500–6,000 lbs. category. Class IV trailers are those over 6,000 lbs. and are for use with fifth wheel trucks, only.

When you have determined the hitch that you'll need, follow the manufacturer's installation instructions, exactly, especially when it comes to fastener torques. The hitch will subjected to a lot of stress and good hitches come with hardened bolts. Never substitute an inferior bolt for a hardened bolt.

More frequent service is required when using your vehicle to pull a trailer. The automatic transmission fluid, engine oil/filter and rear axle lubricant change requirements for change. Change the engine oil/filter every 3,000 miles (5,000 km), transmission and rear axle fluid every 15,000 miles (25,000 km).

Wiring

Wiring the vehicle for towing is fairly easy. There are a number of good wiring kits available and these should be used, rather than trying to design your own. All trailers will need brake lights and turn signals as well as tail lights and side marker lights. Most states require extra marker lights for overly wide trailers. Also, most states have recently required back-up lights for trailers, and most trailer manufacturers have been building trailers with back-up lights for several years.

Additionally, some Class I, most Class II and just about all Class III trailers will have electric brakes.

Add to this number an accessories wire, to operate trailer internal equipment or to charge the trailer's battery, and you can have as many as seven wires in the harness.

Determine the equipment on your trailer and buy the wiring kit necessary. The kit will contain all the wires needed, plus a plug adapter set which included the female plug, mounted on the bumper or hitch, and the male plug, wired into, or plugged into the trailer harness.

When installing the kit, follow the manufacturer's instructions. The color coding of the wires is standard throughout the industry.

One point to note, some domestic vehicles, and most imported vehicles, have separate turn signals. On most domestic vehicles, the brake lights and rear turn signals operate with the same bulb. For those vehicles with separate turn signals, you can purchase an isolation unit so that the brake lights won't blink whenever the turn signals are operated, or, you can go to your local electronics supply house and buy four diodes to wire in series with the brake and turn signal bulbs. Diodes will isolate the brake and turn signals. The choice is yours. The isolation units are simple and quick to install, but far more expensive than the diodes. The diodes, however, require more work to install properly, since they require the cutting of each bulb's wire and soldering in place of the diode.

One final point, the best kits are those with a spring loaded cover on the vehicle mounted socket. This cover prevents dirt and moisture from corroding the terminals. Never let the vehicle socket hang loosely. Always mount it securely to the bumper or hitch.

PUSHING AND TOWING

All Buick, Oldsmobile and Pontiac models covered in this guide are equipped with automatic transmissions and thus cannot be push started. The vehicle can be towed, however, with the transmission in Neutral as long as the speed does not exceed 35 mph and the distance does not exceed 15 miles. If the above speeds and distances must be exceeded, the vehicle's

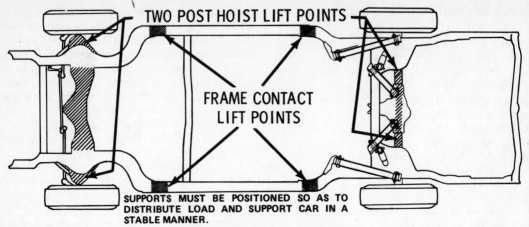

TWO POST HOIST LIFT POINTS

FRAME CONTACT LIFT POINTS

SUPPORTS MUST BE POSITIONED SO AS TO DISTRIBUTE LOAD AND SUPPORT CAR IN A STABLE MANNER.

Vehicle lift points; all cars similar

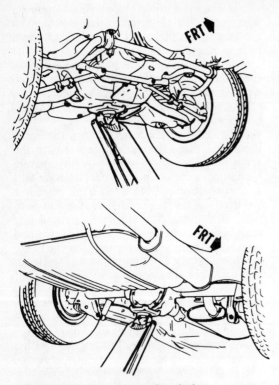

Vehicle lifting points using a floor jack

driveshaft must be disconnected first, or the rear wheels raised. The tow truck operator typically has a special dolly for this purpose. Towing with the rear wheels raised also requires the steering wheels to be locked in the straight ahead position (do not rely on the steering column lock for this purpose).

JUMP STARTING

Jump Starting A Dual Battery Diesel

All GM 350 V8 diesels are equipped with two 12 volt batteries. The batteries are connected in parallel circuit (positive terminal to positive terminal, negative terminal to negative terminal). Hooking the batteries up in parallel circuit increases battery cranking power without increasing total battery voltage output (12 volts). On the other hand, hooking two 12 volt batteries up in a series circuit (positive terminal to negative terminal, positive terminal to negative terminal) increases total battery output to 24 volts (12 volts + 12 volts).

CAUTION: *NEVER hook the batteries up in a series circuit or the entire electrical system will be severely damaged. This may even start a fire!*

In the event that a dual battery diesel must be jump started, use the following procedure.

1. Open the hood and locate the batteries. On GM diesels, the manufacturer usually suggests using the battery on the driver's side of the vehicle to make the connection.

2. Position the donor vehicle so that the jumper cables will reach from its battery (must be 12 volt, negative ground) to the appropriate battery in the diesel. Do not allow the vehicles to touch.

3. Shut off all electrical equipment on both vehicles. Turn off the engine of the donor vehicle, set the parking brakes on both vehicles and block the wheels. Also, make sure both vehicles are in **NEUTRAL** (manual transmission models) or **PARK** (automatic transmission models).

4. Using the jumper cables, connect the positive (+) terminal of the donor vehicle battery to the positive terminal of one (not both) of the diesel batteries.

5. Using the second jumper cable, connect the negative (−) terminal of the donor battery to a solid, stationary, metallic point on the diesel (alternator bracket, engine block, etc.). Be very careful to keep the jumper cables away

from moving parts (cooling fan, alternator belt, etc.) on both vehicles.

6. Start the engine of the donor vehicle and run it at moderate speed.

7. Start the engine of the diesel.

8. When the diesel starts, disconnect the battery cables in the reverse order of attachment.

JACKING

All models covered in this guide are equipped from the factory with a ratchet-type bumper jack. This jack was only designed to aid tire changing in emergency situations; it was NOT designed as a maintenance tool. Never get under the vehicle when it is supported by only a jack.

NOTE: *A sturdy set of jackstands (at least two) and a hydraulic floor jack of at least 1½ ton capacity are two of the best investments you can make if you are serious about maintaining your own vehicle. The added safety and utility of a hydraulic floor jack makes this tool pay for itself many times over through the years.*

Drive-on ramps are also commercially available; they raise the front end of the vehicle up about 10–12 in. (254–305mm). Make sure yours are of all-welded construction and made from strong, square tubing. You must make sure the rear wheels are blocked when using ramps.

CAUTION: *NEVER Use concrete cinder blocks for supporting any type of vehicle. Their use can be extremely dangerous, as they easily break if the load is not perfectly distributed.*

Regardless of the method of jacking or hoisting the vehicle, there are only certain areas of the undercarriage and suspension you can safely use to support the vehicle. Some models are equipped with slots in the bumpers, into which the bumper jack engages for changing tires. See the accompanying illustration, and make sure that only the shaded areas are used. Also, be especially careful not to damage the catalytic converter when jacking or supporting the vehicle.

Gasoline-Engined Cars Maintenance Intervals 1975–76

Interval At Which Services Are To Be Performed	Service
LUBRICATION AND GENERAL MAINTENANCE	
Every 6 months or 7,500 miles	*CHASSIS-Lubricate ●*FLUID LEVELS-Check *ENGINE OIL-Change
At first oil change-then every 2nd	*ENGINE OIL FILTER-Replace (V-6 Replace each oil change)
See Explanation of Maintenance Schedule	TIRES-Rotate DIFFERENTIAL or TORONADO FINAL DRIVE
Every 12 months	AIR CONDITIONING SYSTEM-Check charge & hose condition. TEMPMATIC AIR FILTER-Replace every other year.
Every 12 months or 15,000 miles	*COOLING SYSTEM-See Explanation of Maintenance Schedule
Every 30,000 miles	WHEEL BEARINGS-(Toronado rear)-Clean and repack WHEEL BEARINGS-Clean & repack (except Toronado) FINAL DRIVE AXLE BOOTS & OUTPUT SHAFT SEAL-Check Cond. *AUTOMATIC TRANS.-Change fluid and service filter MANUAL STEERING GEAR-Check seals CLUTCH CROSS SHAFT-Lubricate
SAFETY MAINTENANCE	
Every 6 months or 7,500 miles	TIRES AND WHEELS-Check condition *EXHAUST SYSTEM-Check condition of system *DRIVE BELTS-Ck. cond. & adjustment. Replace every 30,000 miles FRONT AND REAR SUSPENSION & STEERING SYSTEM-Ck. cond. BRAKES AND POWER STEERING-Check all lines and hoses

Gasoline-Engined Cars Maintenance Intervals
1975–76

Interval At Which Services Are To Be Performed	Service
SAFETY MAINTENANCE	
Every 12 months or 15,000 miles	DRUM BRAKES AND PARKING BRAKE-Check condition of linings; adjust parking brake THROTTLE LINKAGE-Check operation and condition UNDERBODY-Flush and check condition BUMPERS-Check condition
EMISSION CONTROL MAINTENANCE	
At 1st 6 months or 7,500 miles-then at 18 month/22,500 mile Intervals Thereafter	THERMOSTATICALLY CONTROLLED AIR CLEANER-Check operation CARBURETOR CHOKE-Check operation ENGINE IDLE SPEED ADJUSTMENT EFE VALVE-Check operation CARBURETOR-Torque attaching bolts or nuts to manifold
Every 12 months or 15,000 miles	CARBURETOR FUEL INLET FILTER-Replace VACUUM ADVANCE SYSTEM AND HOSES-Check oper. PCV SYSTEMS-See Explanation of Maintenance Schedule
Every 18 months or 22,500 miles	IDLE STOP SOLENOID OR DASHPOT-Check operation SPARK PLUG AND IGNITION COIL WIRES-Inspect and clean
Every 22,500 miles	SPARK PLUGS-Replace ENGINE TIMING ADJUSTMENT & DISTRIBUTOR CHECK
Every 24 months or 30,000 miles	ECS SYSTEM-See Explanation of Maintenance Schedule FUEL CAP, TANK AND LINES-Check condition
Every 30,000 miles	AIR CLEANER ELEMENT-Replace

* Also Required Emission Control Maintenance
● Also a Safety Service

1977 and Later

When to Perform Services (Months or Miles, Whichever Occurs First)	Services
LUBRICATION AND GENERAL MAINTENANCE	
Every 12 months or 7,500 miles (12 000 km)	●CHASSIS-Lubricate ●FLUID LEVELS-Check CLUTCH PEDAL FREE TRAVEL-Check/Adjust
See Explanation of Maintenance Schedule	*ENGINE OIL-Change *ENGINE OIL FILTER-Replace TIRES-Rotation (Radial Tires) REAR AXLE OR FINAL DRIVE-Check lube
Every 12 months or 15,000 miles (24 000 km)	*COOLING SYSTEM-See Explanation of Maintenance Schedule
Every 30,000 miles (48 000 km)	WHEEL BEARINGS-Repack FINAL DRIVE BOOTS AND SEALS (Toronado)-Check condition CLUTCH CROSS SHAFT-Lubricate
See Explanation	AUTOMATIC TRANSMISSION-Change fluid and service filter

Gasoline-Engined Cars Maintenance Intervals
1977 and Later

When to Perform Services (Months or Miles, Whichever Occurs First)	Services
SAFETY MAINTENANCE	
Every 12 months or 7,500 miles (12 000 km)	TIRES, WHEELS AND DISC BRAKES-Check condition *EXHAUST SYSTEM-Check condition SUSPENSION & STEERING SYSTEM-Check condition BRAKES AND POWER STEERING-Check all lines and hoses
Every 12 months or 15,000 miles (24 000 km)	*DRIVE BELTS-Check condition and adjustment (1) DRUM BRAKES AND PARKING BRAKE-Check condition of linings; adjust parking brake THROTTLE LINKAGE-Check operation and condition BUMPERS-Check condition *FUEL CAP, TANK AND LINES-Check
EMISSION CONTROL MAINTENANCE	
At first 6 Months or 7,500 Miles (12 000 km)–Then at 24-Month/ 30,000 Mile (48 000 km) Intervals as Indicated in Log, Except Choke Which Requires Service at 45,000 Miles (72 000 km)	CARBURETOR CHOKE & HOSES-Check (2) ENGINE IDLE SPEED-Check adjustment (2) EFE SYSTEM-Check operation (If so equipped) CARBURETOR-Torque attaching bolts or nuts to manifold (2)
Every 30,000 miles (48 000 km)	THERMOSTATICALLY CONTROLLED AIR CLEANER-Check operation VACUUM ADVANCE SYSTEM AND HOSES-Check (3) SPARK PLUG WIRES-Check IDLE STOP SOLENOID AND/OR DASH POT OR ISC-Check operation SPARK PLUGS-Replace (2) ENGINE TIMING ADJUSTMENT AND DISTRIBUTOR-Check AIR CLEANER AND PCV FILTER ELEMENT-Replace (2) PCV VALVE-Replace EGR VALVE-Service

● Also a Safety Service
* Also an Emission Control Service
(1) In California, a separately driven air pump belt check is recommended but not required at 15,000 miles (24 000 km) and 45,000 miles (72 000 km).
(2) Only these emission control maintenance items are considered to be required maintenance as defined by the California Air Resources Board (ARB) regulation and are, according to such regulation, the minimum maintenance an owner in California must perform to fulfill the minimum requirements of the emission warranty. All other emission maintenance items are recommended maintenance as defined by such regulation. General Motors urges that all emission control maintenance items be performed.
(3) Not applicable on vehicles equipped with electronic spark timing (EST).

Diesel Maintenance Intervals

When to Perform Services (Months or Miles, Whichever Occurs First)	Services
LUBRICATION AND GENERAL MAINTENANCE	
Every 5,000 Miles (8 000 km)	*ENGINE OIL-Change *OIL FILTER-Change ●CHASSIS-Lubricate ●FLUID LEVELS-Check
See Explanation	TIRES-Rotation REAR AXLE OR FINAL DRIVE-Check lube

Diesel Maintenance Intervals (cont.)

When to Perform Services (Months or Miles, Whichever Occurs First)	Services
Every 12 months or 15,000 miles (24 000 km)	*COOLING SYSTEM-Check *CRANKCASE VENTILATION-Service
Every 30,000 miles (48 000 km)	WHEEL BEARINGS-Repack FINAL DRIVE BOOTS AND SEALS-Check
See Explanation	AUTOMATIC TRANSMISSION-Change fluid and filter
SAFETY MAINTENANCE	
At first 5,000 miles (8 000 km) Then at 15,000/30,000/45,000 miles	*EXHAUST SYSTEM-Check condition
Every 12 months or 10,000 miles (16 000 km)	TIRES, WHEEL AND DISC BRAKE-Check SUSPENSION AND STEERING-Check BRAKES AND POWER STEERING-Check
Every 5,000 Miles (8 000 km)	*DRIVE BELTS-Check condition and adjustment
Every 12 months or 15,000 miles (24 000 km)	DRUM BRAKES AND PARKING BRAKE-Check THROTTLE LINKAGE-Check operation BUMPERS-Check condition
EMISSION CONTROL MAINTENANCE	
At first 5,000 miles (8 000 km) Then at 15,000/30,000/45,000 miles	EXHAUST PRESSURE REGULATOR VALVE
At first 5,000 miles (8 000 km) Then at 30,000 miles (48 000 km)	ENGINE IDLE SPEED-Adjust
Every 30,000 miles (48 000 km)	AIR CLEANER-Replace FUEL FILTER-Replace

● Also a Safety Service
* Also on Emission Control Service

Capacities

Year	Engine No. Cyl Displacement (Cu. In.)	Engine Crankcase Add 1 Qt For New Filter*	Transmission (Pts To Refill After Draining) Automatic	Drive Axle (pts)	Fuel Tank (gals)	Cooling System (qts) With Heater	Cooling System (qts) With A/C	Heavy Duty Cooling
OLDSMOBILE 88, 98, WAGONS								
'75	8-350	4	6	5.4①	26②	20	22.5	22.5
	8-400	5	6	5.4①	26②	21	21.5	23.5
	8-455	4	6	5.4①	26②	21	21.5	23.5
'76	8-350	4	6	5.4①	26②	20	22.5	22.5
	8-400	5	6	5.4①	26②	21	21.5	23.5
	8-455	4	6	5.4①	26②	21	21.5	23.5
'77	6-231	4	6	4.25	21	12.7	12.8	—
	8-260	4	6	4.25	21	16.9	17.0	—
	8-350 Chev.	4	6	4.25	21	16.0	16.7	—
	8-350 Olds. 88	4	6	4.25	21	14.6	15.3	—

Capacities (cont.)

Year	Engine No. Cyl Displacement (Cu. In.)	Engine Crankcase Add 1 Qt For New Filter*	Transmission (Pts To Refill After Draining) Automatic	Drive Axle (pts)	Fuel Tank (gals)	Cooling System (qts) With Heater	With A/C	Heavy Duty Cooling
			OLDSMOBILE 88, 98, WAGONS (cont.)					
'77 (cont.)	8-350 Olds. 98	4	6	4.25	24.5	14.6	15.3	—
	8-403	4	6	4.25	24.5	15.7	16.4	—
'78	6-231	4	6	③	25.25	12.25	12.25	12.25
	8-260	4	6	③	22.25④	16.25	16.25	16.75
	8-350	4	6	③	22.25④	14.5	14.5	15.5
	8-350 Diesel	7⑤	6	③	22.0	18.0	18.0	18.0
	8-403	4	6	③	⑥	15.75	16.5	16.5
'79	6-231	4	6	4.25	25.0⑦	13.3	13.3	—
	8-260	4	6	4.25	25.0⑦	16.25	16.25	16.5
	8-301	4⑧	6	4.25	25.0⑦	20	20	21
	8-350	4	6	4.25	25.0⑦	14.5	14.5	15.5
	8-350 Diesel	7⑤	6	4.25	27	18.0	18	—
	8-403	4	6	4.25	25.0⑦	15.75	16.4	16.25
'80	6-231	4	6	③	20.75	13.0	13.0	—
	8-265	4⑧	6	③	25⑦	19	19.75	19.75
	8-307	4	6	③	25⑦	15.5	15.25	16.25
	8-350	4	6	③	25	14.5	14.5	15.5
	8-350 Diesel	7⑤	6	③	27④	18.0	18.0	18.0
'81	6-231	4	6	4	25	13	13	—
	6-252	4	6	4	25	12.8	12.8	12.8
	8-260	4	6	4	25④	15.9	15.5	16.5
	8-307	4	6	4	25④	15.6	15.3	16.2
	8-350 Diesel	7⑤	6	4	27④	18.0	18.0	18.0
'82	6-231	4	6	4	25	13.0	13.0	—
	6-252	4	6	4	25	12.8	12.8	12.8
	8-260	4	6	4	25	16.5	16.2	17.2
	8-307	4	6	4	25	16.2	16.1	16.1
	8-350 Diesel	7⑤	6	4	27④	18.0	18.0	18.0
'83	6-231	4	6	4	25	13.7	13.7	—
	6-252	4	6	4	25	13.7	13.7	13.7
	8-260	4	6	4	25	16	16.5	16.5
	6-260 Diesel	6⑤	6	4	26④	14.5	15.3	15.3
	8-307	4	6	4	25	16.2	16.2	16.1
	8-350 Diesel	7⑤	6	4	27④	18.3	18.3	18.0
'84–'85	6-231	4	7⑲	4.25⑳	25	13	13	—
	8-307	4	7㉑	4.25⑳	25㉓	25.5	15.25	16
	8-350 Diesel	6	7㉑	4.25⑳	27㉓	18.25	18	18
'86–'87	8-306	4	7	4.25⑳	22	—	15.3	—

Capacities (cont.)

Year	Engine No. Cyl Displacement (Cu. In.)	Engine Crankcase Add 1 Qt For New Filter*	Transmission (Pts To Refill After Draining) Automatic	Drive Axle (pts)	Fuel Tank (gals)	Cooling System (qts)		Heavy Duty Cooling
						With Heater	With A/C	
			OLDSMOBILE 88, 98, WAGONS (cont.)					
'86–'87	8-307	4	7	4.25 ⑳	22	—	15.3	—
'88	8-307 Wagon	4	7	㉔	22	—	15.3	16.0
'89	8-307 Wagon	4	7	㉔	22	17.0	17.0	17.6
'90	8-307 Wagon	4	7	㉔	22	15.9	15.9	16.4
			BUICK LE SABRE, ELECTRA, WAGONS					
'75	8-350	4	6	4.25	18.5	12.7	12.7	—
	8-455	4	7	5.4	26.0	16.9	17.2	—
'76	8-350	4	6	4.25	26.0	16.9	17.2	—
	8-455	4	7	5.4	26.0	16.9	17.2	—
'77	6-231	4	6	4.25	26.0	16.9	17.2	—
	8-301	5.5	6	4.25	21.0	18.3	19.1	—
	8-350 Buick, Olds.	4	6	4.25	21.0	14.6	15.4	—
	8-403	4	7	4.25	21.0 ⑨	15.7	16.6	—
'78	6-231	4	⑩	③	21.0	12.9	12.9	12.9
	8-301	5	⑩	③	21.0 ⑪	20.9	20.9	21.6
	8-305	4	⑩	③	21.0 ⑪	16.6	16.7	16.7
	8-350 Buick	5	⑩	③	25.3 ②	14.1	14.1	14.9
	8-350 Chev.	4	⑩	③	21.0 ⑪	16.6	16.7	18.0
	8-350 Olds.	4	⑩	③	21.0 ②⑫	14.6	14.5	15.4
	8-403	4	⑩	③	25.3 ②⑫	15.7	16.6	16.6
'79	6-231 ⑪	4	⑩	③	21.0	12.9	12.9	12.9
	8-301 ⑪	4	⑩	③	21.0	20.9	20.9	20.9
	8-305 ⑪	4	⑩	③	21.0	20.9	20.9	20.9
	8-350 Buick ⑪	4	⑩	③	21.0	14.1	14.1	14.9
	8-350 Buick ⑬	4	⑩	③	25.3	14.6	14.5	15.4
	8-350 Olds. ⑪	4	⑩	③	21.0	14.6	14.5	15.4
	8-403 ⑪	4	⑩	③	21.0	15.7	16.6	16.6
	8-403 ⑬	4	⑩	③	25.3	15.7	16.6	16.6
'80	6-231 ⑪	4	⑩	③	25.0 ⑪	13.0	13.0	13.0
	6-252	4	⑩	③	25.0	13.0	13.0	13.0
	8-301 ⑪	4	⑩	③	25.0 ⑪	18.9	18.9	18.9
	8-350 Buick ⑪⑬	4	⑩	③	25.0 ⑪	14.3	14.2	14.7
	8-350 Olds. ⑪⑬	4	⑩	③	25.0	—	14.5	15.2
	8-350 Diesel	7 ⑤	⑩	③	23.0 ⑭	18.3	18.0	18.0
'81	6-231 ⑪	4	⑩	③	25.0 ⑪	13.0	13.0	13.0
	6-252	4	⑩	③	25.0	13.0	13.0	13.0
	8-301 ⑪	4	⑩	③	25.0 ⑪	18.9	18.9	18.9
	8-307	4	⑩	③	25.0 ⑪	15.6	16.3	16.0

Capacities (cont.)

Year	Engine No. Cyl Displacement (Cu. In.)	Engine Crankcase Add 1 Qt For New Filter *	Transmission (Pts To Refill After Draining) Automatic	Drive Axle (pts)	Fuel Tank (gals)	Cooling System (qts) With Heater	Cooling System (qts) With A/C	Heavy Duty Cooling
BUICK LE SABRE, ELECTRA, WAGONS (cont.)								
'81	8-350 Buick ⑪⑬	4	⑩	③	25.0 ⑪	14.3	14.2	14.7
	8-350 Olds. ⑪⑬	4	⑩	③	25.0	—	14.5	15.2
	8-350 Diesel	7 ⑤	⑩	③	23.0	18.3	18.0	18.0
'82	6-231, 6-252	4	⑩	③	25.0	13.0	13.0	13.0
	8-307	4	⑩	③	25.0	15.4	16.2	16.2
	8-350 Diesel	7 ⑤	⑩	③	23.0 ⑭	18.3	18.0	18.0
'83	6-231, 6-252	4	⑩	③	25.0	13.0	13.1	13.1
	8-307	4	⑩	③	25.0	15.4	16.2	16.2
	8-350 Diesel	7 ⑤	⑩	③	23.0 ⑭	18.3	18.0	18.0
1984	6-231	4	㉓	㉔	㉕	13	13	13
	6-252	4	㉓	㉔	㉕	13	13	13
	8-307	4	㉓	㉔	㉕	15.4	16	16
	8-350 Diesel	6.5	㉓	㉔	㉕	18.3	17.9	17.9
1985	6-231	4	㉝	㉔	㉞	13.0	13.0	—
	6-231 Turbo	4	㉝	㉔	㉞	13.0	13.0	13.0
	8-307	4	㉝	㉔	㉞	15.4	16.0	16.0
	8-350 Diesel	6.5	㉝	㉔	㉞	18.3	17.9	17.9
1986	6-231	4	7	㉔	18.1 ㊱	12.9	13.0	13.5
	6-231 ㉟	5	7	㉔	18.1	13.0	13.0	13.5
	8-307	4	7	㉔	18.1	14.9	15.6	15.5
	8-307 Wagon	4	7	㉔	22	15.4	16.0	16.0
1987	8-307 Wagon	4	7	㉔	22	15.4	16.0	16.0
1988	8-307 Wagon	4	10.1	4.25	22	15.0	15.0	16.0
1989	8-307 Wagon	4	7	㉔	22	17.0	17.0	17.6
1990	8-307 Wagon	4	7	㉔	22	15.9	15.9	16.4
PONTIAC BONNEVILLE, CATALINA, WAGON								
'75	8-400	5	7.5	5.5	25.8 ②	18.6	19.8	19.8
	8-455	5	7.5	5.5	25.8 ②	18.0	18.4	18.4
'76	8-350 Pont.	5	6	3.5	20	19.8	21.0	—
	8-400	5	7.5	5.5	25.8 ②	21.6	22.4	—
	8-403	4	7.5	4.25	24.5	16.1	16.1	—
	8-455	5	7.5	5.5	25.8 ②	18.0	18.4	18.4
'77	8-350 Olds.	4	6	3.5	20	15.1	15.1	—
	8-350 Pont.	5	6	3.5	20	19.8	21.0	—
	8-403	4	7.5	4.25	24.5	16.1	16.1	16.1
'78	6-231	4	⑮	③	21	14.2	14.1	14.1
	8-301	5	⑮	③	21	20.2	20.1	20.8
	8-350 Buick	5	7.5	③	22	18.6	19.1	19.1

Capacities (cont.)

Year	Engine No. Cyl Displacement (Cu. In.)	Engine Crankcase Add 1 Qt For New Filter*	Transmission (Pts To Refill After Draining) Automatic	Drive Axle (pts)	Fuel Tank (gals)	Cooling System (qts) With Heater	With A/C	Heavy Duty Cooling
			PONTIAC BONNEVILLE, CATALINA, WAGON (cont.)					
'78	8-350 Chev.	4	⑩	③	21	16.5	16.7	16.7
	8-350 Olds.	4	7.5	③	21	16.5	16.5	16.4
	8-400	5	7.5	③	21	26.3	20.3	20.3
	8-403	4	7.5	③	21	17.7	23.0	23.0
'79	6-231	4	6	3.5	21	13.9	13.9	13.9
	8-301	4	6	3.5 ⑯	21	20.2	20.1	20.9
	8-350 Chev.	4	⑩	③	㉑	16.5	16.7	16.7
	8-350 Olds.	4	6	3.5 ⑯	21	16.5	16.4	17.1
	8-350 Buick	4	6	3.5 ⑯	21	16.6	18.6	16.6
	8-403	4	6	3.5 ⑯	21	17.7	23.0	18.5
'80	6-231	4	8	3.5	21	12.6	12.6	—
	8-265	4	8	3.4	20.7	20	20	20
	8-301	4	6	3.4	20.7	20	20	20
	8-350 Olds.	4	6	3.5 ⑮	21	16.5	16.4	17.1
	8-350 Diesel	7 ⑤	⑩	③	23.0	—	17.0	17.0
'81	6-231	4	8	3.4	20.7	—	17.0	17.0
	8-265	4	8	3.4	25.0	20	20	20
	8-307	4	8	3.4	25.0	14.9	15.6	15.6
	8-350 Diesel	7 ⑤	⑩	3.5 ⑮	23.0	—	17.0	17.0
'82	6-231	4	8	3.4	18.1	—	17.0	17.0
	6-252	4	⑰	3.5	18.1	13.0	13.1	13.1
	8-350 Diesel	7 ⑤	⑰	3.5	19.8 ⑱	17.3	17.3	17.3
'83	6-231	4	8	3.4	18.1	—	17.0	17.0
	8-305	4	⑰	3.5	18.1	15.0	15.1	15.1
	8-350 Diesel	7 ⑤	⑰	3.5	19.8 ⑱	17.3	17.3	17.3
'84	6-231	4	㉖	㉗	17.5 ㉗	12.9	12.9	12.9
	8-305	4	㉖	㉗	17.5 ㉘	15.3	16.1	16.1
	8-350 Diesel	6.5	㉖	㉗	19.8 ㉘	17.2	17.2	17.2
'85	6-231	4	8.5	3.5	㉙	12.2 ㉚	12.2 ㉚	12.6
	8-305	4	9.9	3.5	㉙	15.0 ㉚	15.0 ㉚	16.1
'86	8-350 Diesel	6	10.1	3.5	㉙	18.0 ㉚	18.0 ㉚	—
	8-231	4	㉛	㉔	㉙	12.2 ㉜	12.0 ㉜	12.6 ㉜
	8-305	4	㉛	㉒	㉙	15.0 ㉜	15.0 ㉜	—㉜
'87	8-305	4	10	㉔	22	—	15.0	16.0
'88	8-307 Wagon	4	10.1	4.25	22	—	15.0	16.0
'89	8-307 Wagon	4	7	㉔	22	17.1	17.1	17.6

Capacities (cont.)

Year	Engine No. Cyl Displacement (Cu. In.)	Engine Crankcase Add 1 Qt For New Filter*	Transmission (Pts To Refill After Draining) Automatic	Drive Axle (pts)	Fuel Tank (gals)	Cooling System (qts)		Heavy Duty Cooling
						With Heater	With A/C	

① 10 and 12 bolt covers
② 22 on station wagons
③ 7.5 inch ring gear (10 bolt cover): 3.5
   8.5 and 8.75 inch ring gear (10 bolt cover): 4.25
   8.75 inch Buick and Pontiac: 5.4
④ 22.5 gal on station wagon
⑤ Includes mandatory filter change
⑥ 88 sedan and Calif. coupe: 21.0
   All others 25.25
⑦ Royale, Royale Brougham Coupe and Sedan: 20.75
⑧ 4 qts also with filter change
⑨ Electra 24.5, Estate Wagon 22
⑩ THM 200 and 200R-4: 7 pts.; THM 250C: 8 pts.;
   THM 350C: 6.3 pts.
⑪ Le Sabre
⑫ Electra 25.3
⑬ Electra
⑭ Wagon 27
⑮ THM 200: 6.0
   THM 350: 7.5

⑯ Wagon: 4.25
⑰ THM 250C: 5.5
   THM 350C: 6.3
⑱ Wagon 18.2
⑲ Applies to 200C automatic. 250C—8.0. In 1985, the capacity for the 200C become 8½ pts.
⑳ Applies to 8½ in. ring gear axle. With 7½ in. ring gear axle, capacity is 3.5.
㉑ Applies to 1984. 1985 models hold 8.4 pts. with the 200C transmission and 10.5 pts. with the 200-4R transmission.
㉒ Applies to sedans, Wagon—22
㉓ 200C—7;
   200-4R—7;
   250C—8
㉔ 7½ in. ring gear—3.5
   8½ in. ring gear—4.25
   8¾ in. ring gear—5.3
㉕ Sedan with gas engine—25
   Wagons—22
   Sedan with diesel—26

Tune-Up and Performance Maintenance

T2

TUNE-UP PROCEDURES

The tune-up is a routine maintenance procedure which is essential for the efficient and economical operation of your vehicle's engine. Regular tune-ups will also help prolong the life of the engine.

The interval between tune-ups is a variable factor which depends upon the way you drive your vehicle, the conditions under which you drive it (city versus highway, weather, etc.), and the type of engine installed. A complete tune-up should be performed on your Buick, Olds or Pontiac at least every 15,000 miles or one year, whichever comes first. 1981–83 vehicles have an increased tune-up interval of 25,000 miles. On 1984 and later models, it is 30,000 miles.

This interval should be halved if the vehicle is operated under severe conditions such as trailer towing, prolonged idling (a common occurrence in the city), start and stop driving, or if starting and running problems are noticed. It is assumed here that the routine maintenance described in Chapter 1 has been followed, as this goes hand-in-hand with the recommended tune-up procedures. The end result of a tune-up can only be the sum of all the various steps, so every step applicable to the tune-up should be followed.

NOTE: *If the specifications on the underhood sticker in the engine compartment of your vehicle disagree with the Tune-Up Specifications chart in this chapter, the figures on the sticker must be used. The sticker often reflects changes made during the production run, or displays specifications that apply only to your particular engine.*

The replaceable parts involved in a tune-up include the spark plugs, air filter, distributor cap, rotor, and the spark plug wires. In addition to these parts and the adjustments involved in properly installing them, there are several adjustments of other parts involved in completing the job. These include carburetor idle speed and air/fuel mixture, ignition timing, and valve clearance adjustments.

This chapter gives specific procedures on how to tune-up your Buick, Pontiac or Oldsmobile, and is intended to be as complete and basic as possible.

CAUTION: *When working with a running engine, make sure that there is proper ventilation. Also make sure that the transmission is in Neutral (unless otherwise specified) and the parking brake is fully applied. Always keep hands, clothing and tools well clear of the hot exhaust manifolds and radiator and especially the belts and fan. Remove any wrist or long neck jewelry or ties before beginning any job, and tuck long hair under a cap. When the engine is running, do not grasp ignition wires, distributor cap or coil wires as a shock in excess of 50,000 volts may result. Whenever working around the distributor, make sure the ignition is OFF.*

Diesel Engine Precautions

1. Never run the engine with the air cleaner removed; if anything is sucked into the inlet manifold it will go straight to the combustion chambers, or jam behind a valve.
2. Never wash a diesel engine: the reaction of a warm fuel injection pump to cold (or even warm) water can ruin the pump.
3. Never operate a diesel engine with one or more fuel injectors removed unless fully familiar with injector testing procedures: some diesel injection pumps spray fuel at up to 1400 psi; enough pressure to allow the fuel to penetrate your skin!
4. NEVER skip engine oil and filter changes.
5. Strictly follow the manufacturer's oil and fuel recommendations as given in the owner's manual.
6. Do not use home heating oil as fuel for your diesel unless it's a dire emergency.

Gasoline Engine Tune-Up Specifications

(When analyzing compression test results, look for uniformity among cylinders rather than specific pressures)

OLDSMOBILE 88, 98, WAGONS

Year	Engine V.I.N. Code	Engine Type (No. of cyl- C.I.D.)	Engine Manufacturer	Spark Plugs Orig. Type	Gap (in.)	Distributor Point Dwell (deg.)	Point Gap (in.)	Ignition Timing (deg. B.T.D.C.) Automatic Transmission	Intake Valve Opens (°B.T.D.C.)	Fuel Pump Pressure (psi)	Idle Speed (rpm) Automatic Transmission
'75	K	8-350	Olds.	R45SX	.080	Electronic		20B @ 1100	16	5½–6½	650/550
	R,S	8-400	Olds.	R45TSX	.060	Electronic		16B	20	5½–6½	650
	T	8-455	Olds.	R46SX	.080	Electronic		16B @ 1100	20	5½–6½	650/550
'76	R	8-350	Olds.	R45SX	.080	Electronic		20B	16	5½–6½	650 ⊤/550(600)
	K	8-403	Olds.	R46SZ	.060	Electronic		20B @ 1100	16	5½–6½	650/550 [700/600]
	T	8-455	Olds.	R46SX	.080	Electronic		16B ②	20	5½–6½	650 ⊤/550(600)
'77	C	6-231	Buick	R46TSX	.060 ③	Electronic		12B	17	6–7	670/600
	F	8-260	Olds.	R46SZ	.060	Electronic		16B @ 1100	14	6–7	650/550
	L	8-350	Chev.	R45TS	.045	Electronic		8B	28	7–9	650/500
	R	8-350	Olds.	R46SZ	.060	Electronic		20B ② @ 1100	16	6–7	650/550 [700/600]
	K	8-403	Olds.	R46SZ	.060	Electronic		20B @ 1100	16	6–7	650/550 [700/600]
'78	A	6-231	Buick	R46TSX	.060	Electronic		15B	17	5.5–6.5	600
	F	8-260	Olds.	R46SZ	.060	Electronic		18B @ 1100	14	5.5–6.5	550
	R	8-350	Olds.	R46SZ	.060	Electronic		20B @ 1100	16	5.5–6.5	650[700]
	K	8-403	Olds.	R46SZ	.060	Electronic		18B ④ @ 1100	16	5.5–6.5	550[600]
'79	A	6-231	Buick	R46TSZ	.060	Electronic		12B	16	5.5–6.5	550
	F	8-260	Olds.	R46SZ	.060	Electronic		18B @ 1100	14	5.5–6.5	550
	Y	8-301	Pont.	R46TSX	.060	Electronic		12B	16	5.5–6.5	650(500)
	R	8-350	Olds.	R46SZ	.060	Electronic		20B @ 1100	16	5.5–6.5	550

Gasoline Engine Tune-Up Specifications (cont.)

(When analyzing compression test results, look for uniformity among cylinders rather than specific pressures)

OLDSMOBILE 88, 98, WAGONS

Year	Engine V.I.N. Code	Engine Type (No. of cyl- C.I.D.)	Engine Manufacturer	Spark Plugs Orig. Type	Gap (in.)	Distributor Point Dwell (deg.)	Point Gap (in.)	Ignition Timing (deg. B.T.D.C.) Automatic Transmission	Intake Valve Opens (°B.T.D.C.)	Fuel Pump Pressure (psi)	Idle Speed (rpm) Automatic Transmission
'79	K	8-403	Olds.	R46SZ	.060	Electronic		24B(20B) @ 1100	16	5.5–6.5	550
'80	A	6-231	Buick	R45TS [5]	.040 [6]	Electronic		15B	16	3–4.5	670/550 [7]
	S	8-265	Pont.	R45TSZ	.060	Electronic		10B	27	7–8½	650/550
	Y	8-307	Olds.	R46SX	.080	Electronic		20B	20	5.5–6.5	600/500
	R	8-350	Olds.	R46SX	.080	Electronic		18B	15	5.5–6.5	600(650)/600(550)
'81	A	6-231	Buick	R45TSX	.080	Electronic		[8]	16	4.25–5.75	[8]
	4	6-252	Buick	R45TSX	.080	Electronic		[8]	16	4.25–5.75	[8]
	F	8-260	Olds.	R46SX	.080	Electronic		18B	14	5.5–6.5	[8]
	Y	8-307	Olds.	R46SX	.080	Electronic		15B	20	6–7.5	[8]
'82	A	6-231	Buick	R45TS	.040	Electronic		[8]	16	4.25–5.75	[8]
	4	6-252	Buick	R45TS8	.080	Electronic		[8]	16	4.25–5.75	[8]
	8	8-260	Olds.	R46SX	.080	Electronic		[8]	14	5.5–6.5	[8]
	Y	8-307	Olds.	R46SX	.080	Electronic		[8]	—	6–7.5	[8]
'83	A	6-231	Buick	R45TS	.040	Electronic		[8]	16	4.25–5.75	[8]
	4	6-252	Buick	R45TS8	.080	Electronic		[8]	16	4.25–5.75	[8]
	8	8-260	Olds.	R46SX	.080	Electronic		[8]	14	5.5–6.5	[8]
	Y	8-307	Olds.	R46SX	.080	Electronic		[8]	—	6–7.5	[8]
'84	A	6-231	Buick	R45TSX	.060	Electronic		15B	N.A.	5.5–6.5	450/1000 [18]
	Y	8-307	Olds.	R46SX [19]	.080 [19]	Electronic		20B @ 1100	N.A.	5.5–6.5	500/575 [18]
'85	Y	8-307	Olds.	FR3LS6	.060	Electronic		20B @ 1100	N.A.	5.5–6.5	450/700 [19]

Year	Code	Engine	Make	Spark Plug	Gap	Ignition	Timing		Pressure	RPM
'86	Y	8-307	Olds.	FR3LS6	.060	Electronic	20B	N.A.	6-7.5	⑧
'87	Y	8-307	Olds.	FR3CLS6	.060	Electronic	20B	N.A.	5.5-6.5	⑧
'88	Y	8-307	Olds.	FR3LS6	.060	Electronic	⑧	N.A.	5.5-6.5	⑧
'89	Y	8-307	Olds.	FR3LS6	.060	Electronic	⑧	N.A.	5.5-6.5	450/475 ⑱
'90	Y	8-307	Olds.	FR3LS6	.060	Electronic	⑧	N.A.	5.5-6.5	450/475 ⑱

BUICK LE SABRE, ELECTRA, WAGONS

Year	Code	Engine	Make	Spark Plug	Gap	Ignition	Timing		Pressure	RPM
'75	J	8-350	Buick	R45TSX	.060	Electronic	12B	19	4.25-5.75	600
	T	8-455	Buick	R45TSX	.060	Electronic	12B	10	7.5-9	600
'76	J	8-350	Buick	R45TSX	.060	Electronic	12B	13.5	5-6.5	600
	Y	8-455	Buick	R45TSX	.060	Electronic	12B	10	7.5-9	600
'77	C	6-231	Buick	R46TS or R46TSX	.040 .060	Electronic	12B	17	4.25-5.75	600
	Y	8-301	Pont.	R46TSX	.060	Electronic	12B	27	7-8.5	650/550
	R	8-350	Olds.	R46SZ	.060	Electronic	20B @ 1100 ⑨	16	5.5-6.5	650/550 [650/600]
	J	8-350	Buick	R46TS or R46TSX	.040 .060	Electronic	12B	13.5	7.5-9	600
	K	8-403	Olds.	R46SX	.060	Electronic	24B(20B)[20B] @ 1100	16	6-7.5	650/550 [650/600]
'78	A	6-231	Buick	R46TSX	.060	Electronic	15B	17	4.5-5.5	670/600
	G	6-231	Buick	R44TSX	.060	Electronic	15B @ 600	17	4.5-5.5	650
	3	6-231 Turbo	Buick	R44TSX	.060	Electronic	15B @ 600	17	4.5-5.5	650
	Y	8-301	Pont.	R46TSX	.060	Electronic	12B @ 550	27	7-8.5	650/550
	U	8-305	Chev.	R45TS	.045	Electronic	4B @ 500 (6B @ 500) [8B @600]	28	7.5-9	600/500 (650/500) [700/600]
	R	8-350	Olds.	R46SZ	.060	Electronic	20B @ 1100	16	5.5-6.5	650/550 [700/600]
	L	8-350	Chev	R45TS	.045	Electronic	8B @ 500 [8B @ 600]	28	7.5-9	600/500 [650/600]

Gasoline Engine Tune-Up Specifications (cont.)

(When analyzing compression test results, look for uniformity among cylinders rather than specific pressures)

BUICK LE SABRE, ELECTRA, WAGONS

Year	Engine V.I.N. Code	Engine Type (No. of cyl-C.I.D.)	Engine Manufacturer	Spark Plugs Orig. Type	Gap (in.)	Distributor Point Dwell (deg.)	Point Gap (in.)	Ignition Timing (deg. B.T.D.C.) Automatic Transmission	Intake Valve Opens (°B.T.D.C.)	Fuel Pump Pressure (psi)	Idle Speed (rpm) Automatic Transmission
	X	8-350	Buick	R46TSX	.060	Electronic		15B @ 600	16	7.5-9	550
	K	8-403	Olds.	R46SZ	.060	Electronic		20B @ 1100	16	5.5-6.5	650/550 [700/600]
'79	A	6-231	Buick	R45TSX or R46TSX	.060 .060	Electronic		15B @ 800	16	4.25-5.75	670/550 (600) [600]
	3	6-231 Turbo	Buick	R44TSX	.060	Electronic		15B	16	4.25-5.75	650
	Y	8-301	Pont.	R46TSX	.060	Electronic		12B @ 550	27	7-8.5	650/550
	G	8-305	Chev.	R45TS	.045	Electronic		4B @ 600	28	7.5-9	[10]
	R	8-350	Olds.	R46SZ	.060	Electronic		20B @ 1100	16	6-7.5	650/550 (600/500) [700/600]
	X	8-350	Buick	R45TSX or R46TSX	.060 .060	Electronic		15B	13.5	6	550
	K	8-403	Olds.	R46SZ	.060	Electronic		20B @ 1100	16	6-7.5	650/550 (600/500) [700/600]
'80	A	6-231	Buick	R45TSX	.060	Electronic		15B @ 550	16	5.5-6.5	670/550 [11] (620/650) [12] 550 [13]
	3	6-231	Buick	R45TS	.040	Electronic		15B @ 650	16	5.5-6.5	650
	4	6-252	Buick	R45TSX	.060	Electronic		15B @ 550	16	5.5-6.5	680/550 [14] 550 [13]
	W	8-301	Pont.	R45TSX	.060	Electronic		12B @ 500	27	7-8.5	650/500 [14] 550 [13]

R	8-350	Olds.	R46SX or R47SX	.080 / .080	Electronic	18B @ 1100	16	5.5-6.5	650/550
X	8-350	Buick	R45TSX	.060	Electronic	15B @ 550	13.5	6-7.5	550
'81									
A	6-231	Buick	R45TS8	.080	Electronic	[15]	16	5.5-6.5	[15]
4	6-252	Buick	R45TS8	.080	Electronic	[15]	16	5.5-6.5	[15]
Y	8-307	Olds.	R45TS4	.060	Electronic	[15]	20	5.5-6.5	[15]
'82–'83									
A	6-231	Buick	R45TS8	.080	Electronic	[15]	16	5.5-6.5	[15]
4	6-252	Buick	R45TS8	.080	Electronic	[15]	16	5.5-6.5	[15]
Y	8-307	Olds.	R46SX	.080	Electronic	[15]	20	5.5-6.5	[15]
'84–'85									
A	6-231	Buick	R45TS8	[8]	Electronic	[8]	N.A.	4.3-5.8	450/1000 [18]
4	6-252	Buick	R45TS8	[8]	Electronic	[8]	N.A.	N.A.	450/900 [18]
Y	8-307	Olds.	R46SX	[8]	Electronic	[8]	N.A.	6.0-7.5	500/725 [18]
'86–'87									
A	6-231	Buick	[8]	[8]	Electronic	[8]	[8]	5.5-6.5	[8]
7	6-231	Buick	[8]	[8]	Electronic	[8]	[8]	37-43	[8]
Y	8-307	Olds.	FR3LS6	.060	Electronic	[8]	[8]	5.5-6.5	[8]
'88									
Y	8-307	Olds.	FR3LS6	.060	Electronic	[8]	[8]	5.5-6.5	[8]
'89									
Y	8-307	Olds.	FR3LS6	.060	Electronic	[8]	N.A.	5.5-6.5	450/475 [18]
'90									
Y	8-307	Olds.	FR3LS6	.060	Electronic	[8]	N.A.	5.5-6.5	450/475 [18]
PONTIAC BONNEVILLE, CATALINA, WAGONS									
'75									
R	8-400	Pont.	R46TSX	.060	Electronic	16B	22	7-8.5	650
S	8-400	Pont.	R45TSX	.060	Electronic	16B(12B)	30	5-6.5	650
W	8-455	Pont.	R45TSX	.060	Electronic	16B(10B)	23	5-6.5	650(625)
'76									
P	8-350	Pont.	R46TSX	.060	Electronic	16B	26	7-8.5	600
R	8-400	Pont.	R45TSX	.060	Electronic	16B	30	7-8.5	575
S	8-400	Pont.	R45TSX	.060	Electronic	16B(12B)	30	5-6.5	650
K	8-403	Olds.	R46SZ	.080	Electronic	20B @ 1100	16	5.5-6.5	600
W	8-455	Pont.	R45TSX	.060	Electronic	16B	33	7-8.5	550(600)

Gasoline Engine Tune-Up Specifications (cont.)

(When analyzing compression test results, look for uniformity among cylinders rather than specific pressures)

PONTIAC BONNEVILLE, CATALINA, WAGONS

Year	Engine V.I.N. Code	Engine Type (No. of cyl— C.I.D.)	Engine Manufacturer	Spark Plugs Orig. Type	Gap (in.)	Distributor Point Dwell (deg.)	Point Gap (in.)	Ignition Timing (deg. B.T.D.C.) Automatic Transmission	Intake Valve Opens (°B.T.D.C.)	Fuel Pump Pressure (psi)	Idle Speed (rpm) Automatic Transmission
'77	R	8-350	Olds.	R46SX R46SZ	.080	Electronic		20B @ 1100	16	5.5-6.5	600,550 ⑧
	P	8-350	Pont.	R45TSX	.060	Electronic		16B	29	7-8.5	575,600 ⑧
	K	8-403	Olds.	R46SX or R46SZ	.080	Electronic		20B @ 1100	16	6-7.5	600,550 ⑧
'78	A	6-231	Buick	R46TSX	.060	Electronic		15B	17	4.5-5.75	600
	Y	8-301	Pont.	R46TSX	.060	Electronic		12B	27	7-8.5	550
	W	8-301	Pont.	R45TSX	.060	Electronic		12B	27	7-8.5	550
	R	8-350	Olds.	R46SZ	.060	Electronic		20B @ 1100	17	5.5-6.5	550
	L	8-350	Chev.	R45TS	.045	Electronic		8B @ 500 [8B @ 600]	28	7.5-9	600/500 [650/600]
	X	8-350	Buick	R45TSX	.060	Electronic		15B	16	4.5-5.5	550
	Z	8-400	Pont.	R45TSX	.060	Electronic		16B	29	7-8.5	575
	K	8-403	Olds.	R46SZ	.060	Electronic		20B @ 1100	16	6-7.5	600(550)
'79	A	6-231	Buick	R46TSX	.060	Electronic		15B	16	4.5-5.5	600
	Y	8-301	Pont.	R46TSX	.060	Electronic		12B	16	7-8.5	650
	W	8-301	Pont.	R45TSX	.060	Electronic		12B	16 ⑯	7-8.5	500(650)
	R	8-350	Olds.	R46SZ	.060	Electronic		20B @ 1100	16	5.5-6.5	550
	L	8-350	Chev.	R45TS	.060	Electronic		8B @ 500 [8B @ 600]	28	7.5-9	650/550 [700/600]
	X	8-350	Buick	R46TSX	.060	Electronic		15B	16	4.5-5.5	550
	Z	8-400	Pont.	R45TSX	.060	Electronic		16B	29	7-8.5	575

Year	Code	Engine	Mfr.	Spark Plug	Gap	Ignition	Timing (18B(20B) @ 1100)		Gap	Idle Speed
'80	K	8-403	Olds.	R46SZ	.060	Electronic	18B(20B) @ 1100	16	5.5–6.5	500(500)
	A	6-231	Buick	R45TSX⑰	.060⑰	Electronic	15B	16	3–4.5	620/550
	S	8-265	Pont.	R45TSX	.060	Electronic	10B	27	7–8.5	650/550
	W	8-301	Pont.	R45TSX	.060	Electronic	12B	16	7–8.5	650/500
	R	8-350	Olds.	R43TS	.045	Electronic	6B	28	7.5–9	650/550
'81	A	6-231	Buick	R45TS8	.080	Electronic	⑧	16	4.25–5.75	⑧
	S	8-265	Pont.	R45TSX	.060	Electronic	12B	16	7–8.5	⑧
	Y	8-307	Olds.	R46SX	.080	Electronic	15B	14	5.5–6.5	⑧
'82	A	6-231	Buick	R45TS8	.080	Electronic	15B	16	4.25–5.75	⑧
	4	6-252	Buick	R45TS8	.080	Electronic	15B	16	4.25–5.75	⑧
'83	A	6-231	Buick	R45TS8	.080	Electronic	15B	16	4.25–5.75	⑧
	H	8-305	Chev.	R45TS	.045	Electronic	⑧	N.A.	7.5–9	⑧
'84–'85	A	6-231	Buick	⑧	⑧	Electronic	⑧	N.A.	N.A.	450/900 ⑲
	H	8-305	Chev.	⑧	⑧	Electronic	⑧	N.A.	N.A.	⑧
'86	A	6-231	Buick	R45TSX	.045	Electronic	⑧	N.A.	5.5–6.5	450/900 ⑲㉑
	H	8-305	Chev.	R45TS	.045	Electronic	⑧	N.A.	5.5–6.5	450/700 ⑲
'87	Y	8-307	Olds.	FR3LS6	.060	Electronic	20B	N.A.	5.5–6.5	⑧
'88	Y	8-307	Olds.	FR3LS6	.060	Electronic	⑧	N.A.	5.5–6.5	⑧
'89	Y	8-307	Olds.	FR3LS6	.060	Electronic	⑧	N.A.	5.5–6.5	450/475 ⑱

NOTE: The underhood specifications sticker often reflects tune-up specification changes made in production. Sticker figures must be used if they disagree with those in this chart.

Part numbers in this chart are not recommendations by Chilton for any product or brand name.

Figures in parentheses ( ) indicates a special figure for California models; figure in brackets [ ] indicates a special figure for high-altitude models.

Where two idle speed figures appear separated by a slash, the first is idle speed with solenoid energized, the second is idle speed with solenoid disconnected.

① A/C on and A/C compressor clutch wires disconnected
② 18B with 2.4:1 axle ratio in 98
③ .040 with R46TS
④ 88 station wagon: 20B @ 1100
⑤ With C-4 ignition: R45TSX
⑥ With C-4 ignition: .060

Gasoline Engine Tune-Up Specifications

(When analyzing compression test results, look for uniformity among cylinders rather than specific pressures)

| Year | Engine V.I.N. Code | Engine Type (No. of cyl. C.I.D.) | Engine Manufacturer | Spark Plugs | | Distributor | | Ignition Timing (deg. B.T.D.C.) | Intake Valve Opens (°B.T.D.C.) | Fuel Pump Pressure (psi) | Idle Speed (rpm) |
				Orig. Type	Gap (in.)	Point Dwell (deg.)	Point Gap (in.)	Automatic Transmission			Automatic Transmission

⑦ With C-4 ignition: 620/550

⑧ See underhood sticker

⑨ Except Calif. Le Sabre coupes and sedans, which should be set at 18B @ 1100

⑩ With solenoid energized, set solenoid screw to 600 rpm; with solenoid de-energized, set the carburetor screw to 550 rpm for models with A/C, 500 for models without A/C.

⑪ With A/C, 49 states only

⑫ With A/C, Calif. models only

⑬ All models without A/C

⑭ All models with A/C

⑮ On vehicles equipped with computerized emissions systems (which have no distributor vacuum advance unit) with idle speed and ignition timing are controlled by the emissions computer. These adjustments should be performed professionally on models so equipped.

⑯ High performance—27

⑰ Low altitude without C-4 ignition: R45TS, gap .040

⑱ Refers to minimum authority and maximum authority adjustments. See text.

⑲ 1985 models only use FR3LS6 plugs gapped at .060 in.

⑳ 1985 spec's only—6.0—7.5

㉑ Applies to '86 only. '87 figures are 450/1000.

Troubleshooting Engine Performance

Problem	Cause	Solution
Hard starting (engine cranks normally)	· Binding linkage, choke valve or choke piston	· Repair as necessary
	· Restricted choke vacuum diaphragm	· Clean passages
	· Improper fuel level	· Adjust float level
	· Dirty, worn or faulty needle valve and seat	· Repair as necessary
	· Float sticking	· Repair as necessary
	· Faulty fuel pump	· Replace fuel pump
	· Incorrect choke cover adjustment	· Adjust choke cover
	· Inadequate choke unloader adjustment	· Adjust choke unloader
	· Faulty ignition coil	· Test and replace as necessary
	· Improper spark plug gap	· Adjust gap
	· Incorrect ignition timing	· Adjust timing
	· Incorrect valve timing	· Check valve timing; repair as necessary
Rough idle or stalling	· Incorrect curb or fast idle speed	· Adjust curb or fast idle speed
	· Incorrect ignition timing	· Adjust timing to specification
	· Improper feedback system operation	· Refer to Chapter 4
	· Improper fast idle cam adjustment	· Adjust fast idle cam
	· Faulty EGR valve operation	· Test EGR system and replace as necessary
	· Faulty PCV valve air flow	· Test PCV valve and replace as necessary
	· Choke binding	· Locate and eliminate binding condition
	· Faulty TAC vacuum motor or valve	· Repair as necessary
	· Air leak into manifold vacuum	· Inspect manifold vacuum connections and repair as necessary
	· Improper fuel level	· Adjust fuel level
	· Faulty distributor rotor or cap	· Replace rotor or cap
	· Improperly seated valves	· Test cylinder compression, repair as necessary
	· Incorrect ignition wiring	· Inspect wiring and correct as necessary
	· Faulty ignition coil	· Test coil and replace as necessary
	· Restricted air vent or idle passages	· Clean passages
	· Restricted air cleaner	· Clean or replace air cleaner filler element
	· Faulty choke vacuum diaphragm	· Repair as necessary
Faulty low-speed operation	· Restricted idle transfer slots	· Clean transfer slots
	· Restricted idle air vents and passages	· Clean air vents and passages
	· Restricted air cleaner	· Clean or replace air cleaner filter element
	· Improper fuel level	· Adjust fuel level
	· Faulty spark plugs	· Clean or replace spark plugs
	· Dirty, corroded, or loose ignition secondary circuit wire connections	· Clean or tighten secondary circuit wire connections
	· Improper feedback system operation	· Refer to Chapter 4
	· Faulty ignition coil high voltage wire	· Replace ignition coil high voltage wire
	· Faulty distributor cap	· Replace cap
Faulty acceleration	· Improper accelerator pump stroke	· Adjust accelerator pump stroke
	· Incorrect ignition timing	· Adjust timing
	· Inoperative pump discharge check ball or needle	· Clean or replace as necessary
	· Worn or damaged pump diaphragm or piston	· Replace diaphragm or piston

Troubleshooting Engine Performance (cont.)

Problem	Cause	Solution
Faulty acceleration (cont.)	• Leaking carburetor main body cover gasket	• Replace gasket
	• Engine cold and choke set too lean	• Adjust choke cover
	• Improper metering rod adjustment (BBD Model carburetor)	• Adjust metering rod
	• Faulty spark plug(s)	• Clean or replace spark plug(s)
	• Improperly seated valves	• Test cylinder compression, repair as necessary
	• Faulty ignition coil	• Test coil and replace as necessary
	• Improper feedback system operation	• Refer to Chapter 4
Faulty high speed operation	• Incorrect ignition timing	• Adjust timing
	• Faulty distributor centrifugal advance mechanism	• Check centrifugal advance mechanism and repair as necessary
	• Faulty distributor vacuum advance mechanism	• Check vacuum advance mechanism and repair as necessary
	• Low fuel pump volume	• Replace fuel pump
	• Wrong spark plug air gap or wrong plug	• Adjust air gap or install correct plug
	• Faulty choke operation	• Adjust choke cover
	• Partially restricted exhaust manifold, exhaust pipe, catalytic converter, muffler, or tailpipe	• Eliminate restriction
	• Restricted vacuum passages	• Clean passages
	• Improper size or restricted main jet	• Clean or replace as necessary
	• Restricted air cleaner	• Clean or replace filter element as necessary
	• Faulty distributor rotor or cap	• Replace rotor or cap
	• Faulty ignition coil	• Test coil and replace as necessary
	• Improperly seated valve(s)	• Test cylinder compression, repair as necessary
	• Faulty valve spring(s)	• Inspect and test valve spring tension, replace as necessary
	• Incorrect valve timing	• Check valve timing and repair as necessary
	• Intake manifold restricted	• Remove restriction or replace manifold
	• Worn distributor shaft	• Replace shaft
	• Improper feedback system operation	• Refer to Chapter 4
Misfire at all speeds	• Faulty spark plug(s)	• Clean or replace spark plug(s)
	• Faulty spark plug wire(s)	• Replace as necessary
	• Faulty distributor cap or rotor	• Replace cap or rotor
	• Faulty ignition coil	• Test coil and replace as necessary
	• Primary ignition circuit shorted or open intermittently	• Troubleshoot primary circuit and repair as necessary
	• Improperly seated valve(s)	• Test cylinder compression, repair as necessary
	• Faulty hydraulic tappet(s)	• Clean or replace tappet(s)
	• Improper feedback system operation	• Refer to Chapter 4
	• Faulty valve spring(s)	• Inspect and test valve spring tension, repair as necessary
	• Worn camshaft lobes	• Replace camshaft
	• Air leak into manifold	• Check manifold vacuum and repair as necessary
	• Improper carburetor adjustment	• Adjust carburetor
	• Fuel pump volume or pressure low	• Replace fuel pump
	• Blown cylinder head gasket	• Replace gasket
	• Intake or exhaust manifold passage(s) restricted	• Pass chain through passage(s) and repair as necessary
	• Incorrect trigger wheel installed in distributor	• Install correct trigger wheel

Troubleshooting Engine Performance (cont.)

Problem	Cause	Solution
Power not up to normal	• Incorrect ignition timing	• Adjust timing
	• Faulty distributor rotor	• Replace rotor
	• Trigger wheel loose on shaft	• Reposition or replace trigger wheel
	• Incorrect spark plug gap	• Adjust gap
	• Faulty fuel pump	• Replace fuel pump
	• Incorrect valve timing	• Check valve timing and repair as necessary
	• Faulty ignition coil	• Test coil and replace as necessary
	• Faulty ignition wires	• Test wires and replace as necessary
	• Improperly seated valves	• Test cylinder compression and repair as necessary
	• Blown cylinder head gasket	• Replace gasket
	• Leaking piston rings	• Test compression and repair as necessary
	• Worn distributor shaft	• Replace shaft
	• Improper feedback system operation	• Refer to Chapter 4
Intake backfire	• Improper ignition timing	• Adjust timing
	• Faulty accelerator pump discharge	• Repair as necessary
	• Defective EGR CTO valve	• Replace EGR CTO valve
	• Defective TAC vacuum motor or valve	• Repair as necessary
	• Lean air/fuel mixture	• Check float level or manifold vacuum for air leak. Remove sediment from bowl
Exhaust backfire	• Air leak into manifold vacuum	• Check manifold vacuum and repair as necessary
	• Faulty air injection diverter valve	• Test diverter valve and replace as necessary
	• Exhaust leak	• Locate and eliminate leak
Ping or spark knock	• Incorrect ignition timing	• Adjust timing
	• Distributor centrifugal or vacuum advance malfunction	• Inspect advance mechanism and repair as necessary
	• Excessive combustion chamber deposits	• Remove with combustion chamber cleaner
	• Air leak into manifold vacuum	• Check manifold vacuum and repair as necessary
	• Excessively high compression	• Test compression and repair as necessary
	• Fuel octane rating excessively low	• Try alternate fuel source
	• Sharp edges in combustion chamber	• Grind smooth
	• EGR valve not functioning properly	• Test EGR system and replace as necessary
Surging (at cruising to top speeds)	• Low carburetor fuel level	• Adjust fuel level
	• Low fuel pump pressure or volume	• Replace fuel pump
	• Metering rod(s) not adjusted properly (BBD Model Carburetor)	• Adjust metering rod
	• Improper PCV valve air flow	• Test PCV valve and replace as necessary
	• Air leak into manifold vacuum	• Check manifold vacuum and repair as necessary
	• Incorrect spark advance	• Test and replace as necessary
	• Restricted main jet(s)	• Clean main jet(s)
	• Undersize main jet(s)	• Replace main jet(s)
	• Restricted air vents	• Clean air vents
	• Restricted fuel filter	• Replace fuel filter
	• Restricted air cleaner	• Clean or replace air cleaner filter element
	• EGR valve not functioning properly	• Test EGR system and replace as necessary
	• Improper feedback system operation	• Refer to Chapter 4

7. Do not use starting fluids in the automotive diesel engine, as it can cause severe internal engine damage.

8. Do not run a diesel engine with the Water in Fuel warning light on in the dashboard. See Chapter 5 for water purging procedure.

9. If removing water from the fuel tank yourself, use the same caution you would use when working around gasoline engine fuel components.

10. Do not allow diesel fuel to come in contact with rubber hoses or components on the engine, as it can damage them.

Spark Plugs

A typical spark plug consists of a metal shell surrounding a ceramic insulator. A metal electrode extends downward through the center of the insulator and protrudes a short distance. Located at the end of the plug and attached to the side of the outer metal shell is the side electrode. This side electrode bends in at 90° so its tip is even with, and parallel to, the tip of the center electrode. This distance between these two electrodes (measured in thousandths of an inch) is called spark plug gap. The spark plug in no way produces a spark but merely provides a gap across which the current can arc. The electronic ignition system produces approximately 50,000 volts, which travels to the distributor where it is distributed through the spark plug wires to the plugs. The current passes along the center electrode and jumps the gap to the side electrode and, in so doing, ignites the air/fuel mixture in the combustion chamber. All plugs used since 1969 have a resistor built into the center electrode to reduce interference to any nearby radio and television receivers. The resistor also cuts down on erosion of plug electrodes caused by excessively long sparking. Resistor spark plug wiring is original equipment on all models.

Spark plug life and efficiency depend upon the condition of the engine and the temperatures to which the plug is exposed. Combustion chamber temperatures are affected by many factors such as compression ratio of the engine, fuel/air mixtures, exhaust emission equipment, and the type of driving you do. Spark plugs are designed and classified by number according to the heat range at which they will operate most efficiently. The amount of heat that the plug absorbs is determined by the length of the lower insulator. The longer the insulator (it extends farther into the engine), the hotter the plug will operate; the shorter it is, the cooler it will operate. A plug that has a short path for heat transfer and remains too cool will quickly accumulate deposits of oil and carbon since it is not hot enough to burn them off. This leads to plug fouling and consequently to misfiring. A plug that has a long path for heat transfer will have no deposits but, due to the excessive heat, the electrodes will burn away quickly and, in some instances, pre-ignition may result. Pre-ignition takes place when plug tips get so hot that they glow sufficiently to ignite the fuel/air mixture before the spark does. This early ignition will usually cause a pinging (sounding much like castanets) during low speeds and heavy loads. In severe cases, the heat may become enough to start the fuel/air mixture burning throughout the combustion chamber rather than just to the front of the plug as in normal operation. At this time, the piston is rising in the cylinder making its compression stroke. The burning mass is compressed and explosion results, producing tremendous pressure. Something has to give, and it does; pistons are often damaged. Obviously, this detonation (explosion) is a destructive condition that can be avoided by installing a spark plug designed and specified for your particular engine.

A set of spark plugs usually requires replacing after 15,000 miles depending on the type of driving you do; this interval has been increased to 25,000 miles for 1981 and '82 models and 30,000 miles for 1983 and later models. The electrode on a new spark plug has a sharp edge but, with use, this edge becomes rounded by erosion causing the plug gap to increase. In normal operation, plug gap increases about 0.001 in. (0.025mm) in every 1,000–2,000 miles. As the gap increases, the plug's voltage requirement also increases. It requires a greater voltage to jump the wider gap and about two to three times as much voltage to fire a plug at high speeds and acceleration than at idle.

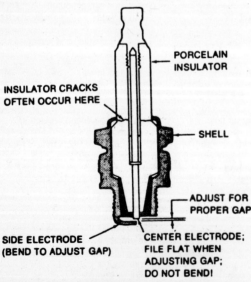

PORCELAIN INSULATOR

INSULATOR CRACKS OFTEN OCCUR HERE

SHELL

ADJUST FOR PROPER GAP

SIDE ELECTRODE (BEND TO ADJUST GAP)

CENTER ELECTRODE; FILE FLAT WHEN ADJUSTING GAP; DO NOT BEND!

Cross section of a spark plug

The higher voltage produced by the HEI (High Energy Ignition) coil is one of the primary reasons for the prolonged replacement interval for spark plugs in the 1975 and later vehicles covered in this guide. A consistently hotter spark prevents the fouling of plugs for much longer than could normally be expected; this spark is also able to jump across a larger gap more efficiently than a spark from a conventional system. However, even plugs used with the HEI system wear after time in the engine.

Worn plugs become obvious during acceleration. Voltage requirement is greatest during acceleration and a plug with an enlarged gap may require more voltage than the coil is able to produce. As a result, the engine misses and sputters until acceleration is reduced. Reducing acceleration reduces the plug's voltage requirement and the engine runs smoother. Slow, city driving is hard on plugs. The long periods of idle experienced in traffic creates an overly rich gas mixture. The engine is not running fast enough to completely burn the gas and, consequently, the plugs are fouled with gas deposits and engine idle becomes rough. In many cases, driving under the right conditions can effectively clean these fouled plugs.

NOTE: *Normal driving is assumed to be a mixture of idling, slow speed and high speed operation, with some of each making up the daily total driving. Occasional high speed*

THE SHORTER THE PATH, THE FASTER THE HEAT IS DISSIPATED AND THE COOLER THE PLUG

THE LONGER THE PATH, THE SLOWER THE HEAT IS DISSIPATED AND THE HOTTER THE PLUG

HEAVY LOADS, HIGH SPEEDS

SHORT TRIP STOP-AND-GO

SHORT Insulator Tip
Fast Heat Transfer
LOWER Heat Range
COLD PLUG

LONG Insulator Tip
Slow Heat Transfer
HIGHER Heat Range
HOT PLUG

Spark plug heat range

1 2 3 4 5
R 4 5 T S X

1 — R--INDICATES RESISTOR-TYPE PLUG.
2 — "4" INDICATES 14 mm THREADS.
3 — HEAT RANGE
4 — TS--TAPERED SEAT.
      S--EXTENDED TIP
5 — SPECIAL GAP

Spark plug type number chart, using the R45TSX as an example

driving is essential to good spark plug performance as the increased combustion heat burns away excess deposits of carbon and oxides that build up from frequent idling or stop-and-go driving.

There are several reasons why a spark plug will foul and you can usually learn which is at fault by just looking at the plug. A few of the most common reasons for plug fouling, and a description of the fouled plug's appearance, can be found in the color insert in this book.

Accelerate your vehicle to the speed where the engine begins to miss and then slow down to the point where the engine smooths out. Run at this speed for a few minutes and then accelerate again to the point of engine miss. With each repetition this engine miss should occur at increasingly higher speeds and then disappear altogether. Do not attempt to shortcut this procedure by hard acceleration; this will compound problems by fusing deposits into a hard permanent glaze. Gapping a plug too close will produce a rough idle while gapping it too wide will increase its voltage requirement and cause missing at high speeds and during acceleration.

NOTE: *Fouled spark plugs can also be caused by oil getting past the piston rings into the combustion chamber. A hotter plug may temporarily solve the problem, but in this case engine repair may be necessary.*

The type of driving you do may require a change in spark plug heat range. If the majority of your driving is done in the city and rarely at high speeds, plug fouling may necessitate changing to a plug with a heat range one number higher than that specified by the vehicle manufacturer. For example, a 1980 Buick with 231 V6 engine requires an R45TS plug. Frequent city driving may foul these plugs making engine operation rough. An R46SX is the next hottest plug in the AC heat range (the higher the AC number, the hotter the plug) and its insulator is longer than the R45TS so that it can absorb and retain more heat than the shorter R45. This hotter R46SX burns off deposits even at low city speeds but would be too hot for prolonged turnpike driving. Using this plug at high speeds would create dangerous pre-ignition. On the other hand, if the aforementioned Buick were used almost exclusively for long distance high speed driving, the specified R45TS might be too hot resulting in rapid electrode wear and dangerous pre-ignition. In this case, it might be wise to change to a colder R44. If the vehicle is used for abnormal driving (as in the examples above), or the engine has been modified for higher performance, then a change to a plug of a different heat range may be necessary. For a modified vehicle it is always wise to go to a colder plug as a protection against pre-ignition. It will require more frequent plug cleaning, but destructive detonation during acceleration will be avoided.

REMOVAL

When you're removing spark plugs, you should work on one at a time. Don't start by removing the plug wires all at once because unless you number them, they're going to get mixed up. On some models though, it will be more convenient for you to remove all the wires before you start to work on the plugs. If this is necessary, take a minute before you begin and number the wires with tape before you take them off. The time you spend here will pay off later on.

1. Twist the spark plug boot and remove the boot from the plug. You may also use a plug wire removal tool designed especially for this purpose. Do not pull on the wire itself. When the wire has been removed, take a wire brush and clean the area around the plug. Make sure that all the grime is removed so that none will enter the cylinder after the plug has been removed.

2. Remove the plug using the proper size socket, extensions, and universals as necessary. Most of the spark plugs on the engines covered in this guide take a ⅝ in. plug socket, but some may take a ¹³⁄₁₆ in. socket.

NOTE: *Allow the engine to cool completely before removing the spark plugs on engines with aluminum cylinder heads. Damage to the spark plug threads may result.*

3. If removing the plug is difficult, drip some penetrating oil on the plug threads, allow it to work, then remove the plug. Also, be sure that the socket is straight or square on the plug, es-

Remove the spark plugs with a ratchet and long extension

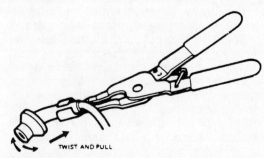

Special pliers used to remove the boots and wire from the spark plug

pecially on those hard to reach rear cylinder plugs.

INSPECTION

Check the plugs for deposits and wear. If they are not going to be replaced, clean the plugs thoroughly. Remember that any kind of deposit will decrease the efficiency of the plug. Plugs can be cleaned on a spark plug cleaning machine, which can sometimes be found in service stations, or you can do an acceptable job of cleaning with a stiff brush. If the plugs are cleaned, the electrodes must be filed flat. Use an ignition points file, not an emery board or the like, which will leave deposits. The electrodes must be filled perfectly flat with sharp edges; rounded edges reduce the spark plug voltage by as much as 50%.

Check spark plug gap before installation. The ground electrode (the L-shaped one connected to the body of the plug) must be parallel to the center electrode and the specified size wire gauge (see Tune-Up Specifications should pass through the gap with a slight drag. Always check the gap on new plugs; it usually is not set correctly at the factory. Use a spark plug gapping tool, which has wire gauges for gapping and a special bending tool for adjusting the side electrode. Do not use a flat feeler gauge when measuring the plug gap because it will give an inaccurate reading, and absolutely never bend the center electrode. Also, be careful not to bend the side electrode too far or too often; it may weaken and break off within the engine

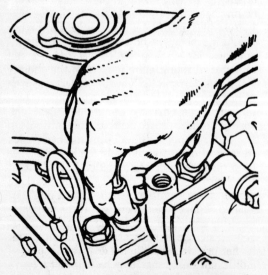

Twist and pull on the rubber boot to remove the spark plug wires; never pull on the wire itself

(causing engine damage and requiring removal of the cylinder head to retrieve it).

INSTALLATION

1. Lubricate the threads of the spark plugs with a drop of oil. Install the plugs and tighten them hand-tight. Take care not to cross-thread them.

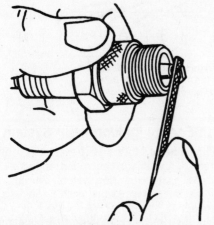

Plugs still in good condition can be filed and re-used

Always use a wire gauge to check the electrode gap

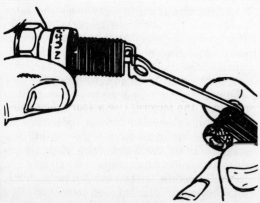

Adjust the electrode gap by bending the side electrode

HEI Plug Wire Resistance Chart

Wire Length	Minimum	Maximum
0–15 inches	3000 ohms	10,000 ohms
15–25 inches	4000 ohms	15,000 ohms
25–35 inches	6000 ohms	20,000 ohms
Over 35 inches		25,000 ohms

2. Tighten the spark plugs with the socket. Do not apply the same amount of force you would use for a bolt; just snug them in. If a torque wrench is available, tighten to 11–15 ft. lbs. (14–20 Nm).

3. Install the wires on their respective plugs. Make sure the wires are firmly connected. You will be able to feel them click into place.

CHECKING AND REPLACING SPARK PLUG WIRES

Every 10,000 miles, inspect the spark plug wires for burns, cuts, or breaks in the insulation. Check the boots and the nipples on the distributor cap. Replace any damaged wiring.

Every 30,000 miles or so, the resistance of the wires should be checked with an ohmmeter. Wires with excessive resistance will cause misfiring, and may make the engine difficult to start in damp weather. Generally, the useful life of the cables is 45,000–60,000 miles.

To check resistance, remove the distributor cap, leaving the wires in place. Connect one lead of an ohmmeter to an electrode within the cap; connect the other lead to the corresponding spark plug terminal (remove it from the spark plug for this test). Replace any wire which shows a resistance over $30,000\Omega$. Generally speaking, however, resistance should not be over $25,000\Omega$, and $30,000\Omega$ must be considered the outer limit of acceptability.

It should be remembered that resistance is also a function of length; the longer the wire, the greater the resistance. Thus, if the wires on your vehicle are longer than the factory originals, the resistance will be higher, possibly outside these limits.

When installing new wires, replace them one at a time to avoid mixups. Start by replacing the longest one first. Install the boot firmly over the spark plug. Route the wire over the same path as the original. Insert the nipple firmly onto the tower on the distributor cap, then install the cap cover and latches to secure the wires.

FIRING ORDERS

NOTE: *To avoid confusion, replace spark plug wires one at a time.*

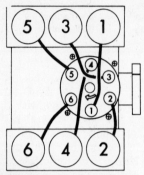

Buick-built 231, 252 V6 (3.8L, 4.2L)
Engine firing order: 1-6-5-4-3-2
Distributor rotation: clockwise
V6 harmonic balancers have two timing marks: one is 1/8 in. wide, and one is 1/16 in. wide. Use the 1/16 in. mark for timing with a hand-held light. The 1/8 in. mark is used only with a magnetic timing pick-up probe.

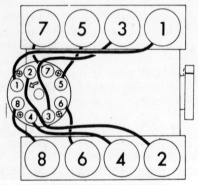

Olds-built 260, 307, 350, 400, 403, 455 V8
Pontiac-built 265, 301, 350, 400, 455 V8
Engine firing order: 1-8-4-3-6-5-7-2
Distributor rotation: counterclockwise

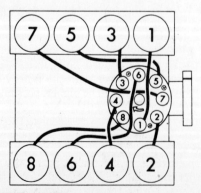

Buick-built 350 V8
Firing order: 1-8-4-3-6-5-7-2
Distributor rotation: clockwise

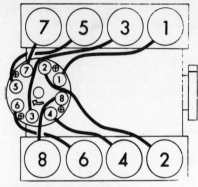

Chevrolet-built 305, 350 V8
Firing Order: 1-8-4-3-6-5-7-2
Distributor rotation: clockwise

High Energy Ignition (HEI) System

The General Motors HEI system is a pulse-triggered, transistor controlled, inductive discharge electronic ignition system. The entire ignition system is contained within the distributor cap.

The distributor, in addition to housing the mechanical and vacuum advance mechanisms (1975 through 1980), contains the ignition coil, the electronic control module, and the magnetic triggering device. The magnetic pick-up assembly contains a permanent magnet, a pole piece with internal teeth, and a pick-up coil (not to be confused with the ignition coil).

All spark timing changes in the 1981 and later distributors are done electronically by the Electronic Control Module (ECM), which monitors information from various engine sensors, computes the desired spark timing and then signals the distributor to change the timing accordingly. No vacuum or mechanical advance units are used.

In the HEI system, as in other electronic ignition systems, the breaker points have been replaced with an electronic switch, a transistor, which is located within the control module. This switching transistor performs the same function the points did in older conventional ignition systems; it simply turns coil primary current on and off at the correct time. So, electronic and conventional points-type ignition systems operate on the same basic principle.

The module which houses the switching transistor is controlled (turned on and off) by a magnetically generated impulse, induced in the pick-up coil. When the teeth of the rotating timer align with the teeth of the pole piece, the induced voltage in the pick-up coil signals the electronic module to open the coil primary circuit. The primary current then decreases, and a high voltage is induced in the ignition coil secondary windings which is then directed

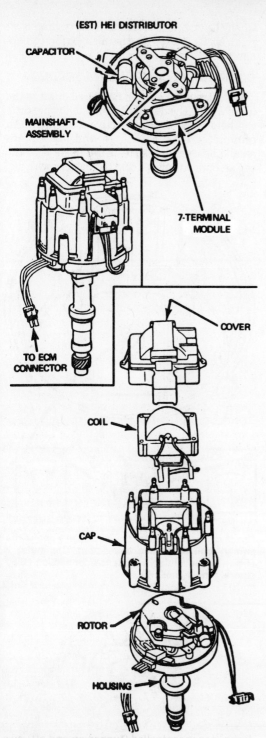

(EST) HEI DISTRIBUTOR

CAPACITOR

MAINSHAFT ASSEMBLY

7-TERMINAL MODULE

TO ECM CONNECTOR

COVER

COIL

CAP

ROTOR

HOUSING

HEI distributor, exploded view

only and has nothing to do with the ignition process. The module automatically controls the dwell period, increasing it with increasing engine speed. Since dwell is automatically controlled, it cannot be adjusted. The module itself is non-adjustable and non-repairable and must be replaced if found defective.

HEI System Testers

Instruments designed specifically for testing HEI systems are available from several tool manufacturers. Some of these will even test the module itself. However, the tests given in the following section will require only an ohmmeter and a voltmeter.

TROUBLESHOOTING THE HEI SYSTEM

The symptoms of a defective component within the HEI system are exactly the same as those you would encounter in a conventional system. Some of these symptoms are:

- Hard or No Starting
- Rough Idle
- Poor Fuel Economy
- Engine misses under load or while accelerating.

If you suspect a problem in your ignition system, there are certain preliminary checks which you should carry out before you begin to check the electronic portions of the system. First, it is extremely important to make sure the vehicle battery is in a good state of charge. A defective or poorly charged battery will cause the various components of the ignition system to read incorrectly when they are being tested. Second, make sure all wiring connections are clean and tight, not only at the battery, but also at the distributor cap, ignition coil, and at the electronic control module.

CAUTION: *The HEI ignition system can generate voltage of 30,000–50,000 volts. When testing the system, do NOT hold a spark plug wire while the engine is running or cranking. Personal injury and or damage to the ignition system may result if this caution is not followed.*

Since the only change between electronic and

through the rotor and spark plug wires to fire the spark plugs.

In essence, the pick-up coil module system simply replaces the conventional breaker points and condenser. The condenser found within the distributor is for radio suppression purposes

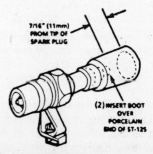

7/16" (11mm) FROM TIP OF SPARK PLUG

(2) INSERT BOOT OVER PORCELAIN END OF ST-125

HEI spark tester tool ST-125

conventional ignition systems is in the distributor component area, it is imperative to check the secondary ignition circuit first. If the secondary circuit checks out properly, then the engine condition is probably not the fault of the ignition system. To check the secondary ignition system, perform a simple spark test. Remove one of the plug wires and insert a HEI spark tester tool ST–125 or equivalent in the plug socket. Ground the spark tester to the block and crank the engine. Do NOT touch the spark plug wire while cranking. If a normal spark occurs, try each spark plug wire until a no spark condition is found. If all plug wire spark, the problem is probably not in the ignition system. Check for fuel system problems, or fouled spark plugs.

If, however, there is no spark or a weak spark, then further ignition system testing will have to be done. Troubleshooting techniques fall into two categories, depending on the nature of the problem. The categories are (1) Engine cranks, but won't start or (2) Engine runs, but runs rough or cuts out. To begin with, let's consider the first case.

Engine Fails to Start

If the engine won't start, perform a spark test as described earlier. This will narrow the problem area down considerably. If no spark occurs, check for the presence of normal battery voltage at the battery (BAT) terminal in the distributor cap. The ignition switch must be in the **ON** position for this test. Either a voltmeter or a test light may be used for this test. Connect the test light wire to ground and the probe end to the BAT terminal at the distributor. If the light comes on, you have voltage to the distributor. If the light fails to come on, this indicates an open circuit in the ignition primary wiring leading to the distributor. In this case, you will have to check wiring continuity back to the ignition switch using a test light. If there is battery voltage at the BAT terminal, but no spark at the plugs, then the problem lies within the distributor assembly. Go on to the distributor components test section.

Engine Runs, But Runs Roughly or Cuts Out

1. Make sure the plug wires are in good shape first. There should be no obvious cracks or breaks. You can check the plug wires with an ohmmeter, but do not pierce the wires with a probe. Check the chart for the correct plug wire resistance.

2. If the plug wires are OK, remove the cap assembly and check for moisture, cracks, clips, or carbon tracks, or any other high voltage leaks or failures. Replace the cap if any defects are found. Make sure the timer wheel rotates

when the engine is cranked. If everything is all right so far, go on to the distributor components test section following.

DISTRIBUTOR COMPONENTS TESTING

If the trouble has been narrowed down to the units within the distributor, the following tests can help pinpoint the defective component. An ohmmeter with both high and low ranges should be used. These tests are made with the cap assembly removed and the battery wire dis-

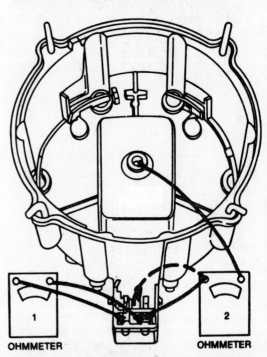

Checking the coil resistance. Ohmmeter 1 shows the primary coil resistance connection. Ohmmeter 2 shows the secondary resistance connection (1980 shown, others similar)

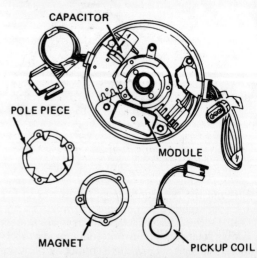

Pickup coil removed and disassembled

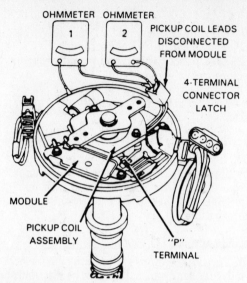

OHMMETER 1 OHMMETER 2 PICKUP COIL LEADS DISCONNECTED FROM MODULE

4-TERMINAL CONNECTOR LATCH

MODULE

PICKUP COIL ASSEMBLY

"P" TERMINAL

REMOVE ROTOR THEN REMOVE PICKUP COIL LEADS FROM MODULE.

CONNECT OHMMETER TEST 1 AND THEN TEST 2.

FLEX LEADS BY HAND TO CHECK FOR INTERMITTENT OPENS.

TEST 1 – SHOULD READ INFINITE AT ALL TIMES.
TEST 2 – SHOULD READ STEADY AT ONE VALUE WITHIN 500-1500 OHM RANGE.
NOTE: OHMMETER MAY DEFLECT IF TURNING SHAFT CAUSES TEETH TO ALIGN. THIS IS NOT A DEFECT.

Pick-up coil testing

connected. If a tachometer is connected to the TACH terminal, disconnect it before making these tests.

1. Connect an ohmmeter between the TACH and BAT terminals in the distributor cap. The primary coil resistance should be **0 or nearly 0** Ω. If not replace the coil.

2. To check the coil secondary resistance, connect an ohmmeter between the rotor button and the BAT terminal. Note the reading. Connect the ohmmeter between the rotor button and the TACH terminal. Note the reading. The resistance in both cases should be 6,000–30,000Ω. Be sure to test between the rotor button and both the BAT and TACH terminals.

3. Replace the coil only if the readings in Step 1 and Step 2 are infinite.

NOTE: *These resistance checks will not disclose shorted coil windings. This condition can only be detected with scope analysis or a suitably designed coil tester. If these instruments are unavailable, replace the coil with a known good coil as a final coil test.*

4. To test the pick-up coil, first disconnect the white and green module leads. Set the ohmmeter on the high scale and connect it between a ground and either the white or green lead.

Any resistance measurement less than infinite requires replacement of the pick-up coil.

5. Pick-up coil continuity is tested by connecting the ohmmeter (on low range) between the white and green leads. Normal resistance is 650–850Ω, or 500–1,500Ω on 1977 and later models. Move the vacuum advance arm while performing this test (early models). This will detect any break in coil continuity. Such a condition can cause intermittent misfiring. Replace the pick-up coil if the reading is outside the specified limits.

6. If no defects have been found at this time, and you still have a problem, then the module will have to be checked. If you do not have access to a module tester, the only possible alternative is a substitution test. If the module fails the substitution test, replace it.

ADJUSTMENTS

Dwell Angle

All Buick, Olds and Pontiac models covered in this guide are equipped with electronic ignition systems using the HEI (High Energy Ignition) distributors. Dwell angle is permanently set on these units, requiring no adjustment or checking. There are no ignition points or other electro-mechanical parts to service.

HEI SYSTEM MAINTENANCE

Except for periodic checks of the spark plug wires, and an occasional check of the distributor cap for cracks (see Steps 1 and 2 under Engine Runs, But Runs Rough or Cuts Out for details), no maintenance is required on the HEI System. No periodic lubrication is necessary; engine oil lubricates the lower bushing, and an oil-filled reservoir lubricates the upper bushing.

COMPONENT REPLACEMENT

Integral Ignition Coil

1. Disconnect the negative (–) battery cable.
2. Disconnect the feed and module wire terminal connectors from the distributor cap.
3. Remove the ignition set retainer.
4. Remove the 4 coil cover-to-distributor cap screws and the coil cover.
5. Using a blunt drift, press the coil wire spade terminals up out of distributor cap.
6. Lift the coil up out of the distributor cap.
7. Remove and clean the coil spring, rubber seal washer and coil cavity of the distributor cap.

To install:

8. Coat the rubber seal with a dielectric lubricant furnished in the replacement ignition coil package.
9. Install the coil spring, coil assembly and

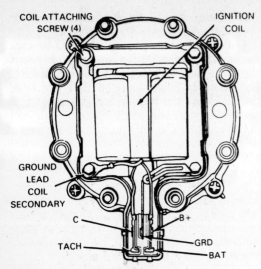

Ignition coil terminal location

press the coil terminals into the distributor cap. Refer to the coil terminal illustration for terminal location.

10. Install the coil cover and torque the attaching screws to 60 inch lbs. (6 Nm).

11. Position the spark plug wire and retainer over the correct cap terminals and engage the retainer and plug wires to the cap. Attach the distributor feed wires and negative battery cable.

Distributor Cap

1. Disconnect the negative (−) battery cable.
2. Remove the air cleaner, feed and module wire terminal connectors from the distributor cap.
3. Remove the retainer and spark plug wires from the cap.
4. Depress and release the 4 distributor cap-to-housing retainers and lift off the cap assembly.
5. Remove the four coil cover screws and cover.
6. Using a finger or a blunt drift, push the coil spade terminals up out of the distributor cap.
7. Remove all four coil screws and lift the coil, coil spring and rubber seal washer out of the cap coil cavity.
8. Using a new distributor cap, reverse the above procedures to assemble being sure to clean and lubricate the rubber seal washer with dielectric lubricant. Torque the coil cover attaching screws to 60 inch lbs. (6 Nm). Make sure the spark plug wire retainer and the four cap-to-housing retainers are fully engaged. Connect the negative battery cable.

Rotor

1. Disconnect the negative (−) battery cable and remove the air cleaner assembly.
2. Disconnect the feed and module wire connectors from the distributor.
3. Depress and release the 4 distributor cap-to-housing retainers and lift off the cap assembly.
4. Remove the two rotor attaching screws and rotor.
5. Install the rotor, make sure the square shaft tab is properly engaged with the rotor and torque the retaining screws to 60 inch lbs. (6 Nm). Reinstall the cap and connect the negative battery cable.

Vacuum Advance (1975–80)

1. Disconnect the negative battery cable and remove the air cleaner. Remove the distributor cap and rotor as previously described.
2. Disconnect the vacuum hose from the vacuum advance unit.
3. Remove the two vacuum advance retaining screws, pull the advance unit outward, rotate and disengage the operating rod from its tang.
4. Install the vacuum advance and engage the operating rod, torque the screws to 60 inch lbs. (6 Nm) and install the distributor cap.
5. Install the air cleaner and connect the negative battery cable.

Module

1. Disconnect the negative (−) battery cable. Remove the air cleaner.
2. Remove the distributor cap and rotor as previously described.
3. Disconnect the harness connector and pick-up coil spade connectors from the module. Be careful not to damage the wires when removing the connector.

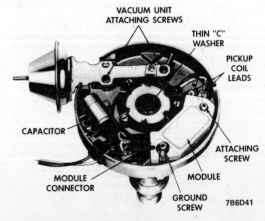

Distributor base and components

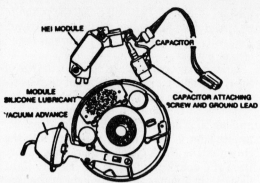

Be sure to coat the mating surfaces with silicone lubricant when replacing the H.E.I. module

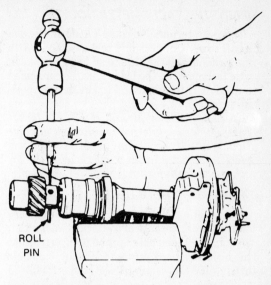

Removing distributor roll pin, gear and shaft

4. Remove the two screws and module from the distributor housing.

5. Coat the bottom of the new module with dielectric silicone lubricant supplied with the new module.

To install:

NOTE: *The silicone lubricant supplied with new modules MUST be applied, as it serves as a heat conductor and aids in module cooling. Running the engine and ignition system without the silicone lubricant is the equivalent of running the engine without antifreeze! That is, the module will cook itself without the lubricant!*

1. Install the module and torque the retaining screws to 48 inch lbs. (5 Nm).

2. Connect the module wiring harnesses and install the distributor cap.

3. Connect the negative battery cable and install the air cleaner.

Pick-up Coil

1. Disconnect the negative (–) battery cable.

2. Remove the air cleaner assembly.

3. Mark the base of the distributor and the position of the rotor-to-housing. Remove the distributor-to-engine block retainer and bolt. Make sure the distributor base is marked with a scribe or grease pen for proper timing after installation.

4. Remove the distributor cap and disconnect the cap harnesses.

5. Twist and pull upward to remove the distributor assembly from the block.

6. Mark the distributor shaft and gear so they can be reassembled in the position.

7. Drive out the roll pin with a flat punch or equivalent.

8. Remove the gear and pull the shaft out of the distributor housing.

9. Disconnect the pick-up harness.

10. Remove the three pick-up coil attaching screws and remove the magnetic shield, C washer, pick-up coil, magnet and pole piece.

To install:

1. Install the pick-up coil so wires go through the opening provided.

2. Install the magnet, pole piece and torque the three screws to 50 inch lbs. (5 Nm).

3. Clean the shaft with solvent to remove the varnish to ease installation.

4. Install the C washer, shaft, gear and tap in the roll pin. Make sure the marks are lined up. Connect the pick-up wiring harness.

5. Install the distributor into the block at the original marked position.

WARNING: *Make sure the distributor seats into the block fully. The base of the housing will stick up about ¼ of an inch until the distributor gear engages the oil pump drive. Damage to the oil pump, distributor and engine may result if the distributor is forced into position by tightening the distributor retainer bolt. If the distributor will not fully seat, grab the housing and shaft, twist and wiggle until the distributor drops into the oil pump drive. If this does not work, install a socket wrench onto the large bolt on the front of the crankshaft pulley. Turn the crankshaft in either direction until the distributor drops into the block fully.*

6. Install the distributor and retainer. Hand tighten the bolt at this time.

7. Install the distributor cap, connect the wiring harness and negative battery cable.

8. Plug all disconnected vacuum lines, install a inductive timing light and adjust the timing to specifications. Refer to the underhood sticker and timing procedures in this chapter for more information.

9. Install the air cleaner and connect the vacuum hoses.

HEI SYSTEM TACHOMETER HOOKUP

There is a terminal marked TACH on the distributor cap. Connect one tachometer lead to this terminal and the other lead to a ground. On some tachometers, the leads must be connected to the TACH terminal and to the battery positive terminal.

CAUTION: *Never ground the TACH terminal; serious module and ignition coil damage will result. If there is any doubt as to the correct tachometer hookup, check with the tachometer manufacturer.*

TACHOMETER HOOKUP--DIESEL ENGINE

A magnetic pick-up tachometer is necessary for diesel work because of the lack of an ignition system. The tachometer probe is inserted into the hole in the timing indicator (models through 1981) or timing probe holder (1982–85 models).

Ignition Timing

Ignition timing is the measurement, in degrees of crankshaft rotation, of the point at which the spark plugs fire in each of the cylinders. It is measured in degrees before or after Top Dead Center (TDC) of the compression stroke.

Because it takes a fraction of a second for the spark plug to ignite the mixture in the cylinder, the spark plug must fire a little before the piston reaches TDC. Otherwise, the mixture will not be completely ignited as the piston passes TDC and the full power of the explosion will not be used by the engine.

The timing measurement is given in degrees of crankshaft rotation before the piston reaches TDC (BTDC). If the setting for the ignition timing is 5° BTDC, the spark plug must fire 5° before each piston reaches TDC. This only holds true, however, when the engine is at idle speed.

As the engine speed increases, the pistons go faster. The spark plugs have to ignite the fuel even sooner if it is to be completely ignited when the piston reaches TDC. To do this, the distributor has two means to advance the timing of the spark as the engine speed increases. This is accomplished by centrifugal weights within the distributor, and a vacuum diaphragm mounted on the side of the distributor (early models). The later model engines are control the spark timing through the ECM (electronic control module).

If the ignition is set too far advanced (BTDC), the ignition and expansion of the fuel in the cylinder will occur too soon and cause engine ping. If the ignition spark is set too far retarded, after TDC (ATDC), the piston will have already passed TDC and started on its way down when the fuel is ignited. This will cause the piston to be forced down for only a portion of its travel. This will result in poor engine performance and lack of power.

Timing marks consist of a notch on the rim of the crankshaft pulley and a scale of degrees attached to the front of the engine. The notch corresponds to the position of the piston in the number 1 cylinder. A stroboscopic (dynamic) timing light is used, which is hooked into the circuit of the No. 1 cylinder spark plug. Every time the spark plug fires, the timing light flashes. By aiming the timing light at the timing marks, the exact position of the piston within the cylinder can be read, since the stroboscopic flash makes the mark on the pulley appear to be standing still. Proper timing is indicated when the notch is aligned with the correct number on the scale.

There are three basic types of timing lights available. The first is a simple neon bulb with two wire connections (one for the spark plug and one for the plug wire, connecting the light in series). This type of light is quite dim, and must be held closely to the marks to be seen, but it is quite inexpensive. The second type of light operates from the vehicle's battery. Two alligator clips connect to the battery terminals, while a third wire connects to the spark plug with an adapter. This type of light is more expensive, but the xenon bulb provides a nice bright flash which can even be seen in sunlight. The third type replaces the battery source with 110 volt house current. Some timing lights have other functions built into them, such as dwell meters, tachometers, or remote starting switches. These are convenient, in that they reduce the tangle of wires under the hood, but may duplicate the functions of the tools you already have.

If your vehicle has electronic ignition, you should use a timing light with an inductive pickup. This pickup simply clamps onto the No. 1 spark plug wire, eliminating the adapter. It is not susceptible to cross firing or false triggering, which may occur with a conventional light, due to the greater voltages produced by the electronic ignition.

CHECKING AND ADJUSTMENT

Non-ESC Models (Before 1980)

NOTE: *The non-ESC (electronic spark controlled) vehicles are equipped with a vacuum advance unit at the distributor.*

1. Warm the engine to normal operating temperature. Shut off the engine and connect the timing light to the No. 1 spark plug left (driver) front of engine.

NOTE: *Do NOT, Under any circumstances,*

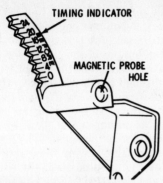

Timing indicator on Oldsmobile-built V8; others similar. Timing mark is on the harmonic balancer.

pierce a spark plug wire to hook up the light. Once the insulation is broken, voltage will jump to the nearest ground, and the spark plug will not fire properly.

2. Clean off the timing marks and mark the pulley or damper notch and the timing scale with white chalk or paint. The timing notch on the damper or pulley can be elusive. Bump the engine around with the starter or turn the crankshaft with a wrench on the front pulley bolt to get it to an accessible position.

3. Disconnect and plug the vacuum advance hose at the distributor, to prevent any distributor advance. The vacuum line is the rubber hose connected to the metal cone-shaped canister on the side of the distributor. A short screw, pencil, or a golf tee can be used to plug the hose.

NOTE: *1981 models with Electronic Spark Control have no vacuum advance, therefore you may skip the previous step, but you must disconnect the four terminal ESC connector before going on.*

4. Start the engine and adjust the idle speed to that specified in the Tune-Up Specifications chart. Some vehicles require that the timing be set with the transmission in Neutral. You can disconnect the idle solenoid, if any, to get the speed down. Otherwise, adjust the idle speed screw. This is to prevent any centrifugal advance of timing in the distributor.

On 1975-77 HEI systems, the tachometer connects to the TACH terminal on the distributor and to a ground. For 1978 and later models, all tachometer connections are to the TACH terminal. Some tachometers must connect to the TACH terminal and to the positive battery terminal. Some tachometers won't work at all with HEI. Consult the tachometer manufacturer if the instructions supplied with the unit do not give the proper connection.

CAUTION: *Never ground the HEI TACH terminal; serious system damage will result, including module burnout.*

5. Aim the timing light at the timing marks.

Be careful not to touch the fan, which may appear to be standing still. Keep your clothes and hair, and the light's wires clear of the fan, belts, and pulleys. If the pulley or damper notch is not aligned with the proper timing mark (see the Tune-Up Specifications chart), the timing will have to be adjusted.

NOTE: *TDC or Top Dead Center corresponds to 0°B, or BTDC, or Before Top Dead Center, may be shown as BEFORE; A, or ATDC, or After Top Dead Center, may be shown as AFTER.*

6. Loosen the distributor base clamp locknut. You can buy special wrenches which make this task a lot easier on V8s. Turn the distributor slowly to adjust the timing, holding it by the body and not the cap. Turn the distributor in the direction of rotor rotation (found in the Firing Order illustration) to retard, and against the direction to advance.

NOTE: *The 231 and 252 V6 engines have two timing marks on the crankshaft pulley. One timing mark is 1/8 in. (3.1mm) wide and the other, 4 in. (101mm), is 1/16 in. (1.6mm) wide. The smaller mark is used for setting the timing with a hand-held timing light. The larger mark is used with the magnetic probe and is only of use to a professional mechanic. Make sure you set the timing using the smaller mark.*

7. Tighten the locknut. Check the timing, in case the distributor moved as you tightened it.

8. Replace the distributor vacuum hose, if removed. Correct the idle speed.

9. Shut off the engine and disconnect the light.

ESC Models (After 1980)

NOTE: *ESC (electronic spark control) equipped models do not have a vacuum advance unit on the distributor. The spark is controlled by the ECM (electronic control module). ESC distributors have a four wire connector instead of a vacuum advance unit.*

1. The timing marks are the same as the non-ESC vehicles. Refer to the underhood sticker for proper timing procedures and specifications. If there is no sticker, follow these procedures to adjust ignition timing.

2. Start the engine and allow it to reach normal operating temperature.

3. If equipped, make sure the air conditioner is turned OFF.

4. Ground the Diagnostic terminal of the ALDL (assembly line diagnostic link) located under the dash panel on the left (driver) side. Using a small piece of wire, ground the A to B terminal as in the "ALDL terminal illustration in this section".

5. Using a timing light of meter, set the tim-

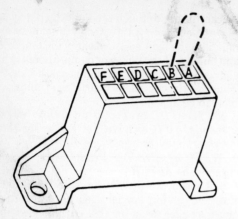

Electronic spark control equipped vehicles. Ground the A and B terminals at the ALDL link

ing at the specified RPM by loosening the distributor hold-down clamp and rotating the distributor until the specified timing is obtained at the timing marks on the crankshaft pulley.

6. Tighten the hold-down clamp and recheck the timing to ensure the distributor has not moved during this procedures.

7. With the engine RUNNING, remove the ground wire at the ALDL under the dash panel. The engine should be running so no trouble codes are stored in the ECM.

8. Make any necessary carburetor adjustments and reconnect any removed vacuum lines.

Valve Lash

All engines covered in this guide are equipped with hydraulic valve lifters. Engines so equipped operate with zero clearance in the valve train; because of this the rocker arms are non-adjustable. The hydraulic lifters themselves do not require any adjustment as part of the normal tune-up, although they occasionally become noisy (especially on high mileage engines) and need to be replaced. Hydraulic lifter service is covered in Chapter 3.

Idle Speed And Mixture Adjustment

CARBURETOR OPERATION

This section contains only carburetor adjustments as they normally apply to engine tune-ups. Descriptions of the carburetors and complete adjustment procedures can be found in Chapter 5.

When the engine in your Buick, Olds or Pontiac is running, air/fuel mixture from the carburetor is being drawn into the engine by a partial vacuum which is created by the downward movement of the pistons on the intake stroke of the 4-stroke cycle of the engine. The amount of air/fuel mixture that enters the engine is con-

trolled by throttle plates in the bottom of the carburetor. When the engine is not running, the throttle plates are closed, completely blocking off the bottom of the carburetor from the inside of the engine. The throttle plates are connected, through the throttle linkage, to the gas pedal. What you are actually doing when you depress the gas pedal is opening up the throttle plates in the carburetor to admit more of the fuel/air mixture to the engine. The further you open the throttle plates in the carburetor, the higher the engine speed becomes.

As previously stated, when the engine is not running, the throttle plates in the carburetor remain closed. When the engine is idling, it is necessary to open the throttle plates slightly. To prevent having to keep your foot on the gas pedal when the engine is idling, an an idle speed adjusting screw was added to the carburetor. This screw has the same effect as keeping your foot slightly depressed on the gas pedal. The idle speed adjusting screw contacts a lever, or, on most late model vehicles, a solenoid on the outside of the carburetor. When the screw is turned in, it opens the throttle plate or plates on the carburetor, raising the idle speed of the engine. This screw is called the curb idle adjusting screw and the procedures in this section will tell you how to adjust it.

Since it is difficult for the engine to draw the air/fuel mixture from the carburetor with the small amount of throttle plate opening that is present when the engine is idling, an idle mixture passage is provided in the carburetor. This passage delivers air/fuel mixture to the engine from a hole which is located in the bottom of the carburetor below the throttle plates. This idle mixture passage contains an adjusting screw which restricts the amount of air/fuel mixture that enters the engine at idle. The idle mixture screws are capped on late model vehicles due to emission control regulations.

ADJUSTMENTS

Idle mixture and idle speed adjustments are critical aspects of engine tune-up and exhaust emission control. It is important that all tune-up instructions be carefully followed to ensure good engine performance and minimum exhaust pollution. Through the succeeding model years covered in this guide, the different combinations of emissions systems on different engine models have resulted in a wide variety of tune-up specifications. See the Tune-Up Specifications chart at the beginning of this chapter. All models covered here have an emissions information sticker placed within easy sight in the engine compartment, giving timing, carburetor adjustment and other important tune-up information. If there is any difference between the specifications listed in this guide and those on your vehicle's emissions sticker, always follow the specs on the sticker.

The following carburetor adjustment procedures are listed by year, carburetor type, and engine displacement and code where necessary (consult the Engine Identification Code chart in this guide), as many of the carburetors covered are used simultaneously by all four GM divisions. Other carburetor adjustments and maintenance are found in Chapter 5.

NOTE: *Idle mixture screws have been preset and capped at the factory. The caps should be removed only in the case of major carburetor overhaul, or if all other possible causes of poor idle have been thoroughly checked. If you must adjust the idle mixture, have the carbon monoxide (CO) concentration checked at a professional shop equipped with a CO meter. Mixture adjustments are included only where it is possible for the owner/mechanic to perform them.*

Curb Idle

1975-76 ROCHESTER 2GC, 2BBL

1. With the engine at normal operating temperature, remove the air cleaner and disconnect the air cleaner vacuum hose at the intake manifold. Plug the fitting with a clean rag.
2. Make sure the choke plate is open and the air conditioning is off.
3. Set the parking brake and block the drive wheels.
4. Disconnect the evaporative emission hose from the air cleaner.
5. Disconnect the hose from the E.G.R. valve. Plug the hose to the carburetor with a golf tee or pencil.
6. Disconnect the distributor vacuum hose, and plug the hose to the carburetor as above.
7. Connect a tachometer to the engine.
8. With the timing properly adjusted, adjust the carburetor idle solenoid screw (with solenoid energized) so that the engine is turning 650 rpm (or the figure specified on the underhood sticker) or with the transmission in Drive. The solenoid is energized when the plunger is fully extended; open the throttle slightly for this to occur.

NOTE: *On Pontiac vehicles, disconnect the idle solenoid lead.*

CAUTION: *Any time the vehicle is tuned with the transmission in gear, you must always have a helper in the vehicle with his or her foot on the brake. The parking brake must be fully applied.*

9. Disconnect the carburetor solenoid. With the transmission again in Drive, adjust the solenoid screw so that the engine turns 550 rpm (or the figure specified on the underhood sticker).
10. Reconnect the distributor vacuum hose, evaporative emission and E.G.R. hoses. Disconnect the tachometer.

1975-76 ROCHESTER M4MC AND 4MC 4BBL

1. Run the engine to normal operating temperature. Remove the air cleaner and disconnect the air cleaner vacuum hose at the intake manifold. Plug the fitting with a clean rag.
2. Make sure the choke plate is open and the air conditioning turned off.
3. Set the parking brake and block the rear wheels. Connect a tachometer to the engine.
4. Disconnect and plug the carburetor hoses from the vapor canister and the E.G.R. valve. Plug the hoses with golf tees or pencils.
5. With the timing adjusted properly, set the slow idle screw to obtain 550 rpm (non-California 350 and 455 cu. in V8s) or 600 rpm (Calif.) in **DRIVE**. Adjust 400 V8s to 650 rpm in **DRIVE**. If the sticker specs vary from these, adjust to sticker specifications.

CAUTION: *When adjusting idle speeds with the vehicle in* **DRIVE**, *always have a helper in the vehicle with his or her foot on the brake and the parking brake fully applied.*

6. Adjust the idle speed-up solenoid on 350 and 455 V8s with air conditioning off to 650 rpm. The air conditioning compressor wires must be disconnected at the air conditioning compressor, and the transmission must be in **DRIVE**.
7. Reconnect the compressor wires and reconnect all hoses.

1977 ROCHESTER 2GC 2BBL

1. Run the engine to normal operating temperature. Block the rear wheels and firmly set the parking brake.
2. Disconnect and plug the distributor vacuum advance hose, vapor canister hose, and E.G.R. vacuum hose, using golf tees or pencils.
3. Disconnect the emission hose from the air cleaner. Keep the air cleaner connected.
4. With the timing properly adjusted and the air cleaner attached, make sure the choke plates are open and the air conditioning is off. Connect a tachometer to the engine.
5. Place the transmission in **DRIVE**. Make sure you have a helper inside the vehicle with his or her foot on the brake, and the parking brake fully applied. Adjust the idle speed screw until the engine is idling at the specified rpm (see underhood sticker or Tune-Up Specifications chart in this guide). On vehicles with an air conditioning idle solenoid (on carburetor), disconnect the air conditioner compressor clutch wire, and turn the air conditioning on. Adjust the screw on the idle solenoid so the en-

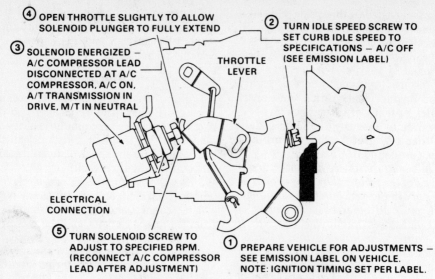

④ OPEN THROTTLE SLIGHTLY TO ALLOW SOLENOID PLUNGER TO FULLY EXTEND

③ SOLENOID ENERGIZED — A/C COMPRESSOR LEAD DISCONNECTED AT A/C COMPRESSOR, A/C ON, A/T TRANSMISSION IN DRIVE, M/T IN NEUTRAL

② TURN IDLE SPEED SCREW TO SET CURB IDLE SPEED TO SPECIFICATIONS — A/C OFF (SEE EMISSION LABEL)

THROTTLE LEVER

ELECTRICAL CONNECTION

⑤ TURN SOLENOID SCREW TO ADJUST TO SPECIFIED RPM. (RECONNECT A/C COMPRESSOR LEAD AFTER ADJUSTMENT)

① PREPARE VEHICLE FOR ADJUSTMENTS — SEE EMISSION LABEL ON VEHICLE. NOTE: IGNITION TIMING SET PER LABEL.

2GC 2-barrel slow idle adjustment, A/C equipped

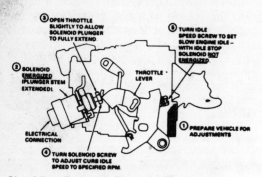

Slow idle adjustment, 2-barrel with solenoid

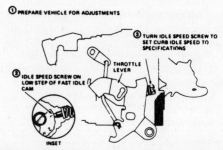

Idle speed adjustment, 1977 4-barrel without solenoid

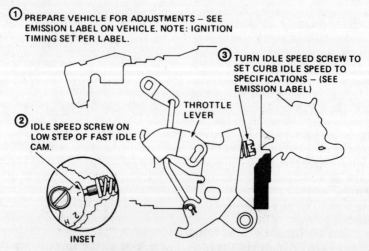

① PREPARE VEHICLE FOR ADJUSTMENTS — SEE EMISSION LABEL ON VEHICLE. NOTE: IGNITION TIMING SET PER LABEL.

③ TURN IDLE SPEED SCREW TO SET CURB IDLE SPEED TO SPECIFICATIONS — (SEE EMISSION LABEL)

THROTTLE LEVER

② IDLE SPEED SCREW ON LOW STEP OF FAST IDLE CAM.

INSET

Idle speed adjustment—2 barrel without solenoid

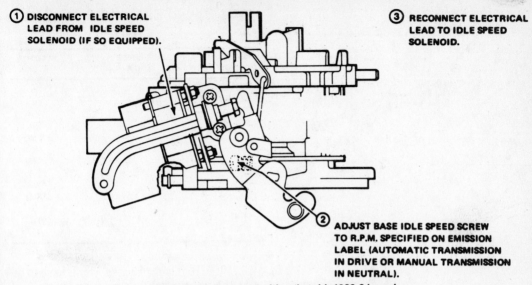

① DISCONNECT ELECTRICAL LEAD FROM IDLE SPEED SOLENOID (IF SO EQUIPPED).

③ RECONNECT ELECTRICAL LEAD TO IDLE SPEED SOLENOID.

② ADJUST BASE IDLE SPEED SCREW TO R.P.M. SPECIFIED ON EMISSION LABEL (AUTOMATIC TRANSMISSION IN DRIVE OR MANUAL TRANSMISSION IN NEUTRAL).

Idle speed adjustment with solenoid, 1980 2-barrel

gine idles at the speed specified solenoid energized idle speed.

6. Reconnect all hoses, and disconnect the tachometer.

305 V8 (WITHOUT AIR CONDITIONING) TO 1982

1. Non-air conditioned Buicks equipped with the 305 2-barrel (Chevrolet) V8 and an idle speed solenoid, place the idle speed screw on the low step of the fast idle cam.

2. Adjust the idle speed screw until the engine is turning the specified curb idle rpm.

ALL OTHER V8 AND V6, 2- AND 4-BARREL (NO AIR CONDITIONING) TO 1982

1. On non-air conditioned vehicles equipped with the idle solenoid, open the throttle (with solenoid energized) to allow the plunger to extend.

2. Adjust the solenoid screw to obtain the specified solenoid energized idle rpm.

3. Disconnect the electrical lead attached to the solenoid. With the solenoid de-energized, adjust the idle speed screw to obtain the specified curb idle rpm.

ALL AIR CONDITIONED MODELS – TO 1982

1. Adjust the idle speed screw until the engine is turning the specified curb idle rpm.

2. Disconnect the air conditioning compressor clutch lead at the compressor.

3. Turn on the air conditioning to energize the idle solenoid. Place the transmission in **DRIVE**, making sure the parking brake is firmly applied and that a helper is in the vehicle with his or her foot on the brake. Open the throttle slightly to allow the solenoid plunger to fully extend.

4. Adjust the idle solenoid screw to obtain the specified solenoid energized rpm.

5. Reconnect the air conditioning compressor clutch lead and disconnect the tachometer.

IDLE LOAD COMPENSATOR ADJUSTMENT
1983-90 MODELS WITH E4MC CARBURETOR

NOTE: *To accomplish this adjustment, you'll need not only a tachometer, but a special adjusting tool J-29607, BT-8022 or equivalent, a 3/32 in. hex key, and a spare rubber cap, drilled to accept this key.*

1. Prepare the vehicle for adjustment by following instructions on the engine compartment sticker.

2. Connect a tachometer to the distributor side of the TACH filter or other connector. Remove the air cleaner. Disconnect and plug vacuum hoses going to: the Thermal Vacuum Valve, EGR valve, the canister purge port, and the ILC (Idle Load Compensator).

3. Back out the idle stop screw on the carburetor three turns. Make sure air conditioning is OFF. Set the parking brake, put the transmission in **PARK**, and block the drive wheels.

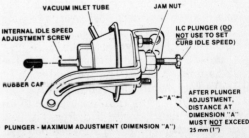

VACUUM INLET TUBE   JAM NUT

INTERNAL IDLE SPEED ADJUSTMENT SCREW

ILC PLUNGER (DO NOT USE TO SET CURB IDLE SPEED)

RUBBER CAP

AFTER PLUNGER ADJUSTMENT, DISTANCE AT DIMENSION "A" MUST NOT EXCEED 25 mm (1")

PLUNGER - MAXIMUM ADJUSTMENT (DIMENSION "A")

Adjusting the Idle Load Compensator on 1983–1990 models

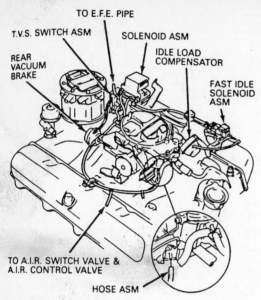

TO E.F.E. PIPE

T.V.S. SWITCH ASM

SOLENOID ASM

REAR VACUUM BRAKE

IDLE LOAD COMPENSATOR

FAST IDLE SOLENOID ASM

TO A.I.R. SWITCH VALVE & A.I.R. CONTROL VALVE

HOSE ASM

Idle load compensator vacuum components—late model

Idle Speed Control Adjustment Chart

Identification Letter	Plunger Length (in.)	Dimension "B" (in.)
NONE	9/16	7/32
NONE	41/64	5/16
X	47/64	25/64
A	49/64	27/64
Y	51/64	15/32
S	27/32	1/2
Z	7/8	35/63
G	29/32	37/64
E	1	43/64
L	13/32	3/4
J	13/16	27/32
N	1 17/64	59/64
T	1 11/32	1

4. Start the engine. If it is not hot already, idle it until it is warm (water flowing through the radiator). Hold the jam nut with a wrench while you turn the plunger as necessary to obtain 725 rpm. Make sure to hold the nut securely as, if it turns, it could damage guide tabs.

5. Now, remove the plug and reconnect the ILC vacuum hose to the ILC port. Read the idle speed on the tach. It should be 500 rpm in **DRIVE**. Have someone apply the brake pedal and put the transmission in Drive before taking your reading. If the reading meets specification, proceed to Step 11. Otherwise, proceed with the steps below.

6. Stop the engine, remove the ILC, and then plug the vacuum hose leading to it with a rubber plug.

7. Remove the rubber cap from the center outlet tube of the ILC and, if there is one, remove the metal plug from the tube. Install the ILC back onto the carburetor and re-attach any items that were detached, such as the throttle return spring. Remove the plug from the vacuum hose and reconnect the hose to the ILC.

8. Install the rubber cap through which you have drilled a hole with the hex wrench passing through the hole in the cap. Engage the wrench with the adjusting screw inside the ILC.

9. Have a helper start the engine with the brake applied and put the transmission in **DRIVE**. Then, adjust the wrench until the rpm is 500. Turn the screw counterclockwise to increase speed and clockwise to decrease it. One turn equals about 75–100 rpm. When 500 rpm is attained, remove the wrench and drilled cap. Replace the complete rubber cap.

10. If the rpm is not correct, you'll have to repeat the adjustment, allowing for the amount and direction of the discrepancy. For example, if the rpm is 450, turn the screw one half turn counterclockwise. The adjustment is not correct until the engine runs at 500 rpm with the complete rubber cap installed.

11. With the engine running and transmission in **DRIVE**, as before, measure the distance from the jam nut to the tip of the plunger (Dimension A). It must not exceed 1 in. (25.4mm).

12. Disconnect and plug the vacuum hose again. Apply a vacuum source such as a vacuum pump to the port to fully retract the plunger. Now, adjust the idle stop screw on the carburetor float bowl to give 500 rpm in **DRIVE**. Then, put the transmission in **PARK**, and turn the engine off.

13. Remove vacuum hose plugs and reconnect all hoses. Reinstall the air cleaner.

IDLE SPEED CONTROL ADJUSTMENT

NOTE: *Use on the E4ME and E2ME carburetors, this device controls idle speed electronically via the Electronic Control Module. It is factory adjusted and does not require adjustment as a matter of routine maintenance. If diagnostic work on the vehicle indicates that idle speed is not to specification, it may be adjusted. A special tool J-29607, BT-8022 or equivalent is required to make the adjustment. The plunger has an unusual head to discourage tampering. You'll also need separate tach and dwell meters.*

1. Look at the unthreaded portion of the adjustable plunger, just below the head, for a letter code. If there is a letter, note what it is for later use, and then go on to the next step. Except on the 3.8L V6 in 1986–87, if there is no letter, use the special wrench to remove the plunger by unscrewing it. Then, measure the

length (Dimension A) from the threaded end to the inner surface of the head. Note and record this dimension for later use. On the 3.8L V6 in 1986–87, use the second line of the chart, showing dimensions of $^{41}/_{64}$ in. (16mm) and $^5/_{16}$ in. (8mm).

2. Prepare the engine for adjustments as detailed on the engine compartment sticker. Connect a tachometer, using the distributor side of the tach filter, if one is used.

3. Connect a dwell meter to the mixture control solenoid (M/C) dwell lead. Set the dwell meter (or read the meter) on the six cylinder scale regardless of the type of engine.

4. Turn the A/C off.

5. Start the engine and run it until the ECM system enters closed loop operation. At this point the dwell meter reading will begin to vary, indicating that the oxygen sensor is regulating fuel flow through a solenoid in the carburetor.

6. Now, turn the ignition switch off and unplug the connector going to the ISC motor.

7. Ground the **D** terminal of the motor connection (see illustration) with a jumper wire. Then, connect another jumper wire from the battery positive terminal to the **C** connection while simultaneously applying pressure with your finger to the plunger to help it retract. If the plunger is not assisted in this way, the internals of the ISC may be damaged. Also, as soon as the plunger is retracted, remove the 12 volt jumper to prevent damage to the ISC. Make sure you make the right connections. If you were to connect across terminals **A** and **B**, this also would cause ISC damage.

8. Block drive wheels and apply the parking brake. Start the engine and run it until the dwell meter reading varies. Then, put the transmission (if it's automatic) in **DRIVE**. Make sure the carburetor is not on the fast idle cam.

9. Now, note the rpm on the tach and adjust the carburetor slow idle stop screw (minimum authority) to the lower figure shown in the

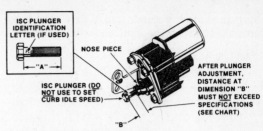

Measuring ISC plunger length "Dimension A" and maximum adjustment "Dimension B"

tune-up chart. Then, if the vehicle has an automatic, put it back in **PARK**.

10. Now, ground terminal **C** again, and jumper the 12 volt source to terminal **D** to fully extend the plunger. Leave the power connected only long enough to extend the plunger, or the ISC may be damaged. Again, make sure you are making the right connection.

11. On manual transmission vehicles:

Use the special tool to turn the plunger until the engine runs at the higher rpm (Maximum Authority) shown in the tune-up chart.

On vehicles with automatic transmissions: with the transmission in **PARK**, use the special tool to preset the plunger for 1,500 rpm. Then, set the parking brake and block the drive wheels and put the transmission in **DRIVE**. Then, use the special tool to turn the plunger to get the higher figure (Maximum Authority) shown in the tune-up chart.

For both types of transmissions, now reapply power as described in Step 10 to make sure the plunger is fully extended. Recheck the Maximum Authority rpm to make sure it is still correct. Readjust if necessary.

12. Now measure dimension **B**, as shown in the illustration. This is the distance from the back side of the plunger head to the front surface of the nose piece-the portion of the assembly the plunger fits into. This is the dimension you determined in Step 1. If the dimension should be too great, adjust the plunger with the special tool until it is within the specified limit.

13. Fully retract the plunger by jumping to connections as described in Step 7. Put the transmission in **PARK** if it's an automatic. Turn the ignition switch off. Remove all instruments and jumper wires and reconnect the ISC motor connector. On engines using the E2ME 2-barrel carburetor, an INTERMITTENT trouble code will be sent. To clear this, you must remove battery voltage from the ECM (Electronic Control Module), a metal cased box located under the dash in the passenger compartment. With the ignition off, unplug the connector to this box or pull the fuse in the fuse box which is labeled ECM. The power must be in-

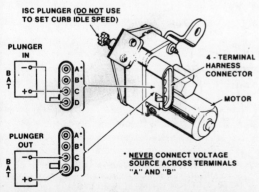

Making connections to retract and extend the plunger

terrupted for 10 seconds and **MUST ONLY** be interrupted with the ignition switch **OFF**.

Fast Idle Adjustment

NOTE: *Refer to the underhood sticker for all carburetor adjustments. If there is no sticker present, refer to the procedures and illustrations that closely resemble your fuel system. Read all procedures carefully and understand them before performing any adjustments to your vehicle.*

1975–76 2GC

NOTE: *The fast idle is present on some Oldsmobile 400 V8 engines when the slow idle is adjusted.*

1. Place the fast idle cam follower on the low step of the fast idle cam, against the shoulder of the next higher step.

2. Adjust the fast idle screw to obtain the following specified idle speeds (with transmission in **PARK**):
- 900 rpm, 350 V8 (non-Calif.)
- 1000 rpm, 350 V8 (Calif.)
- 1800 rpm, 400 V8 (where adjustable)

1975–76 AMC, M4MC

1. On 350 and 455 V8s, place the fast idle cam follower on the lowest step of the fast idle cam against the shoulder of the next highest step. Adjust the fast idle screw to 900 rpm in **PARK**.

2. On 400 cu. in. V8s, place the cam follower on the highest step of the fast idle cam. Adjust the fast idle screw until the engine is turning 800 rpm in **PARK**.

3. Reconnect all hoses and install the air cleaner. Disconnect the tach.

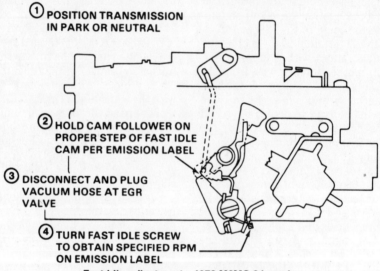

① POSITION TRANSMISSION IN PARK OR NEUTRAL

② HOLD CAM FOLLOWER ON PROPER STEP OF FAST IDLE CAM PER EMISSION LABEL

③ DISCONNECT AND PLUG VACUUM HOSE AT EGR VALVE

④ TURN FAST IDLE SCREW TO OBTAIN SPECIFIED RPM ON EMISSION LABEL

Fast idle adjustment—1978 M2MC 2-barrel

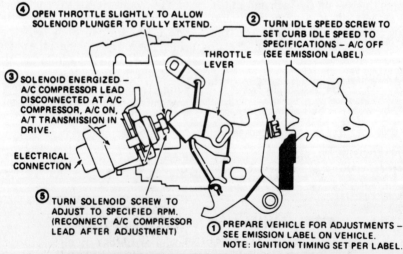

④ OPEN THROTTLE SLIGHTLY TO ALLOW SOLENOID PLUNGER TO FULLY EXTEND.

② TURN IDLE SPEED SCREW TO SET CURB IDLE SPEED TO SPECIFICATIONS – A/C OFF (SEE EMISSION LABEL)

THROTTLE LEVER

③ SOLENOID ENERGIZED – A/C COMPRESSOR LEAD DISCONNECTED AT A/C COMPRESSOR, A/C ON, A/T TRANSMISSION IN DRIVE.

ELECTRICAL CONNECTION

⑤ TURN SOLENOID SCREW TO ADJUST TO SPECIFIED RPM. (RECONNECT A/C COMPRESSOR LEAD AFTER ADJUSTMENT)

① PREPARE VEHICLE FOR ADJUSTMENTS – SEE EMISSION LABEL ON VEHICLE. NOTE: IGNITION TIMING SET PER LABEL.

1977 4-barrel idle speed adjustment, solenoid-equipped

1977 ALL MODELS

No fast idle adjustment is necessary, as the fast idle is automatically adjusted when the curb idle is set.

1978–80

NOTE: *The fast idle on all 231 V6 and some 305 V8 engines is automatically set when the curb idle adjustment is made. Refer to the emissions sticker under your vehicle's hood for this specific application.*

Prepare the engine and vehicle according to the emissions sticker before proceeding with the steps below.

BUICK V8

1. Set the cam follower on the specified step of the fast idle cam according to the emissions sticker. Disconnect the vacuum hose at the E.G.R. valve on 2-barrel models and plug this.

2. Turn the fast idle screw out until the butterfly valves in the primary throttle boxes are closed. You can see this by looking down into the carburetor; the butterfly valves are at the bottom of the bores.

3. Turn the fast idle screw in to adjust the idle speed to specifications. On 4-barrel models, turn the fast idle screw in until it just contacts the lever, then turn it in an additional three turns. Adjust to specified rpm.

PONTIAC V8

1. After making all adjustment preparations according to the emissions sticker, place the transmission in Neutral.

2. Place the cam follower on the specified step of the fast idle cam.

3. Disconnect and plug the E.G.R. vacuum hose, using a golf tee or pencil, at the E.G.R. valve.

4. Adjust the fast idle speed screw to obtain the specified rpm using a tachometer.

OLDSMOBILE V8

Since the carburetor tuning procedures vary by model and component application, the procedure given on the emissions sticker in the engine compartment should be followed.

1981–87

Carburetor adjustment procedures for 1981–87 models vary by model and component application. Follow the procedure on the underhood emissions sticker, using the diagrams included in this guide for reference. If no sticker is found, follow the procedures and illustrations that closely resemble your carburetor.

Minimum Idle Speed Adjustment

THROTTLE BODY FUEL INJECTION

This is a simple procedure, but it is never performed in routine maintenance. It is required after throttle body replacement, only. See Chapter 5 for applicable procedures.

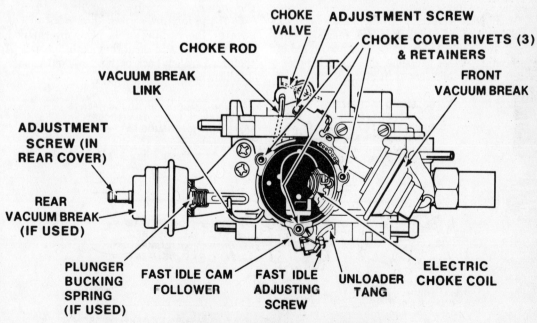

CHOKE SYSTEM - TYPICAL
(ELECTRIC CHOKE TYPE)
Locations of the choke adjustments—1984–85 2bbl carburetors. 1984–90 4bbl similar

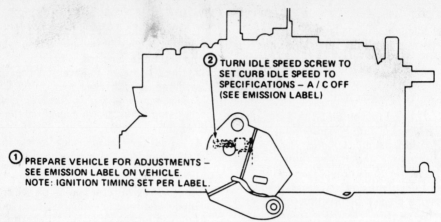

1978–83 4-barrel adjustment without solenoid

Idle Mixture Adjustment

1975–76 2GC

1. Adjust the slow idle as outlined above. Keep all hoses disconnected, and keep the tachometer connected. Make sure the parking brake is set and the drive wheels blocked.

2. Break off the mixture tabs, using care not to damage the mixture adjusting screws.

3. Turn out the mixture screws equally until the maximum idle speed is achieved. Turning the screws in richens the mixture. Reset the speed if necessary with the solenoid screw to 80 rpm above specified rpm. If the mixture screws were out of balance, lightly seat both screws then back both out 5 full turns to attain an equal adjustment point.

4. Equally lean (turn in) the mixture screws until the specified idle speed is reached. The carburetor solenoid must be energized for this procedure. Reset the slow idle speed if necessary with the air cleaner in place.

8-350 AND 455 EXCEPT CALIFORNIA

1. Run the engine to normal operating temperature. Remove the air cleaner, disconnect the vacuum hose at the intake manifold, and plug the fitting.

2. Make sure the choke plate is open and the air conditioning is off.

3. Block the rear wheels and firmly set the parking brake.

4. Disconnect the carburetor hoses from the vapor (charcoal) canister and E.G.R. valve and plug the hoses with golf tees or pencils. Leave the distributor vacuum hose connected.

5. Break off the mixture tabs from the caps, using care not to damage the screws. Connect a tachometer and an accurate vacuum gauge to the engine.

6. If the mixture screws appear out of balance or the carburetor is being overhauled, turn the screws in until they both lightly seat themselves, then back both screws out equally 3 full turns.

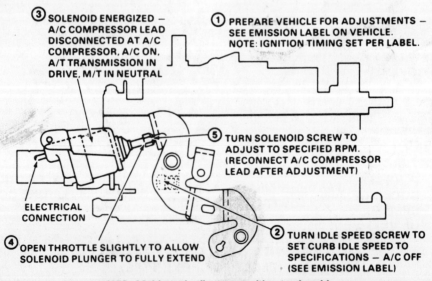

1978–83 4-barrel adjustment without solenoid

7. Equally richen (turn out) the mixture screws until maximum idle speed is achieved. Note the manifold vacuum reading.

8. With the transmission in **DRIVE**, adjust the idle speed screw until the engine is turning 580 rpm. Observe the cautions in above sections on tuning an engine while the transmission is in **DRIVE**.

9. Equally lean (turn in) the mixture screws until the idle speed is 550 rpm. Manifold vacuum should not be reduced more than 2 in.Hg from the reading obtained in step 7. If the reading is reduced more than 2 in.Hg, repeat the procedure.

10. Reconnect the canister and E.G.R. hoses, and install the air cleaner and air cleaner vacuum hoses. Disconnect the tach.

8–350 and 455 CALIFORNIA V8s

1. Follow steps 1 through 5 of the above procedure.

2. Turn in the idle mixture screws until they seat themselves lightly. Equally richen (turn out) the screws 4 full turns. Note the manifold vacuum reading.

3. With the transmission in **DRIVE** (and observing the above Cautions), adjust the idle speed screw so the engine is turning 625 rpm.

4. Equally lean (turn in) the mixture screws until the idle speed is 600 rpm. Manifold vacuum should not be reduced by more than 2 in.Hg from the reading obtained in step 2. If the reading is less than this, repeat the procedure.

5. Reconnect the distributor, canister, and E.G.R. hoses. Disconnect the vacuum gauge and tachometer.

6. Install the air cleaner and air cleaner vacuum hoses.

ROCHESTER 2GE 2BBL

NOTE: *The following mixture adjustment is for non-Calif., non-high altitude vehicles. Calif. and high altitude mixture adjustment requires propane, and should only be performed by a professional.*

1. Run the engine to normal operating temperature and turn the air conditioning off. Set the parking brake and block the rear wheels.

2. Remove the air cleaner for access to the carburetor, but leave the hoses connected. Follow instructions on the engine compartment emissions sticker in disconnecting other hoses.

3. Connect a tachometer to the engine. Disconnect the distributor vacuum advance hose and plug it with a golf tee or pencil.

4. Make sure the ignition timing is set correctly, then reconnect the vacuum advance hose.

5. Carefully break off the mixture tabs from the caps; do not damage the screws.

6. Turn in the mixture screws until they both lightly seat themselves, then back both out equally until the engine will just idle.

7. Place the transmission in **DRIVE**, making sure the parking brake is firmly applied and a helper is in the vehicle with his or her foot on the brake.

8. Back out the mixture screws ⅛ turn at a time equally, alternating from screw to screw where there are two screws, until the highest possible idle speed is obtained.

9. Adjust the idle speed screw to obtain the specified curb idle.

10. Reconnect all hoses and install the air cleaner.

260 AND 301 V8s ROCHESTER 2MC, M2MC 2-BARREL

Follow the above adjustment procedure for the 2GE 2-barrel in adjusting the 2MC/M2MC carburetors. On models with the air conditioning idle solenoid, energize the solenoid (by opening the throttle slightly so the plunger extends) until the engine is turning the specified solenoid energized rpm. Turn off the A/C and adjust the carburetor idle speed screw to the specified curb idle rpm.

ROCHESTER M4MC 4-BARREL

Follow the 1975–76 adjustments above for the 1977 M4MC carburetor. Use the idle speed specifications from the 1977 Tune-Up Specifications chart or from the underhood sticker.

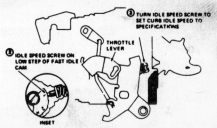

Idle speed adjustment, 1977 4-barrel without solenoid

1978–85 ALL V6 AND V8

1978–85 models require operating the engine with a special propane fuel enrichment device in order for idle mixture to be adjusted. Later models require extensive carburetor modifications to gain access to mixture adjustments and, in many cases, a number of special tools. Idle mixture on these models is constantly monitored and controlled by computer and only extreme carburetor misadjustment at the factory will necessitate service adjustment.

If your engine does not idle properly, and you have ruled out vacuum leaks and ordinary maintenance problems such as improperly adjusted ignition timing or worn spark plugs, we suggest you have idle mixture checked and adjusted by a competent professional who has the specialized tools and equipment required to do the job.

1986–90 ALL V6 AND V8

Idle mixture is not adjusted as a routine maintenance operation. While the procedure itself is simple and uses only a tachometer, it is extremely difficult to gain access to mixture needles, as tampering is discouraged. Doing so requires completely disassembling the carburetor and using a hacksaw and center punch to slot and break the throttle body casting. This is an extremely difficult procedure with a high risk of damaging expensive parts. We suggest you leave the job to a professional mechanic who routinely performs major carburetor rebuilding work.

Diesel Fuel Injection

IDLE SPEED ADJUSTMENT

All 350 V8 Diesels

A special tachometer with an RPM counter suitable for the 350 V8 diesel is necessary for this adjustment; a standard tach suitable for gasoline engines will not work.

1. Place the transmission in **PARK**, block the rear wheels and firmly set the parking brake.

2. If necessary, adjust the throttle linkage as described in Chapter 7.

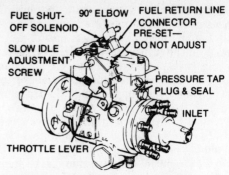

Diesel injection pump slow idle screw

3. Start the engine and allow it to warm up for 10–15 minutes.

4. Shut off the engine and remove the air cleaner.

5. Clean off any grime from the timing probe holder on the front cover; also clean off the crankshaft balancer rim.

6. Install the magnetic probe end of the tachometer fully into the timing probe holder. Complete the remaining tachometer connections according to the tach manufacturer's instructions.

7. Disconnect the two-lead connector from the generator.

8. Make sure all electrical accessories are OFF.

NOTE: *At no time should either the steering wheel or the brake pedal be touched.*

9. Start the engine and place the transmis-

Diesel Tune-Up Specifications

Year	Eng V.I.N. Code	Engine No. Cyl. Displacement (Cu. in.)	Eng. Mfg.	Fuel Pump Pressure (psi)	Compression (lbs)▲	Injection/ Ignition Timing (deg) Auto. Trans.	Intake Valve Opens (deg)	Idle Speed● (rpm)
'78	N	8-350	Olds.	5.5–6.5	275 min.	①	16	650/575
'79	N	8-350	Olds.	5.5–6.5	275 min.	①	16	650/675
'80	N	8-350	Olds.	5.5–6.5	275 min.	5B ②	16	750/600
'81	N	8-350	Olds.	5.5–6.5	275 min.	①	16	①
'82	N	8-350	Olds.	5.5–6.5	275 min.	①	16	①
'83	N	8-350	Olds.	5.5–6.5	275 min.	①	16	①
'84–'85	N	8-350	Olds.	5.5–6.5	300 min.	4A ③	N.A.	750/600

NOTE: The underhood specifications sticker often reflects changes made in production. Sticker figures must be used if they disagree with those in this chart.
① See underhood specifications sticker.
② Static
③ Injection timing @ 1250 rpm in Park
● Where two idle speed figures appear separated by a slash, the first is idle speed with solenoid energized; the second is with solenoid disconnected.
▲ The lowest cylinder reading should not be less than 70% of the highest cylinder reading on models to 1983. On 1984 and later models, the lowest cylinder reading should be 80% of the highest.

sion in **DRIVE** (after first making sure the parking brake is firmly applied).

10. Check the slow idle speed reading against the one printed on the underhood emissions sticker. Reset if necessary.

11. Unplug the connector from the fast idle cold advance (engine temperature) switch, and install a jumper wire between the connector terminals.

NOTE: *DO NOT allow the jumper to ground.*

12. Check the fast idle speed and reset if necessary according to the specification printed on the underhood emissions sticker.

13. Remove the jumper wire and reconnect it to the temperature switch.

14. Recheck the slow idle speed and reset if necessary.

15. Shut off the engine.

16. Reconnect the leads at the generator and air conditioning compressor.

17. Disconnect and remove the tachometer.

18. If the vehicle is equipped with cruise control, adjust the servo throttle rod to minimum slack, then put the clip in the first free hole closest to the bellcrank or throttle lever.

19. Install the air cleaner.

Engine and Engine Overhaul

3

ENGINE ELECTRICAL

Understanding The Engine Electrical System

The engine electrical system can be broken down into three separate and distinct systems:
1. The starting system
2. The charging system
3. The ignition system

Battery and Starting System

The battery is the first link in the chain of mechanisms which work together to provide cranking of the automobile engine. In most modern vehicles, the battery is a lead-acid electrochemical device consisting of six two-volt (2 V) subsections connected in series so the unit is capable of producing approximately 12 V of electrical pressure. Each subsection, or cell, consists of a series of positive and negative plates held a short distance apart in a solution of sulfuric acid and water. The two types of plates are of dissimilar metals. This causes a chemical reaction to be set up, and it is this reaction which produces current flow from the battery when its positive and negative terminals are connected to an electrical appliance such as a lamp or motor. The continued transfer of electrons would eventually convert the sulfuric acid in the electrolyte to water, and make the two plats identical in chemical composition. As electrical energy is removed from the battery, its voltage output tends to drop. Thus, measuring battery voltage and batter electrolyte composition are two ways of checking the ability of the unit to supply power. During the starting of the engine, electrical energy is removed from the battery. However, if the charging circuit is in good condition and the operating conditions are normal, the power removed from the battery will be replaced by the generator (or alternator) which will force electrons back through the battery, reversing the normal flow, and restoring the battery to its original chemical state.

The battery and starting motor are linked by very heavy electrical cables designed to minimize resistance to the flow of current. Generally, the major power supply cable that leaves the battery goes directly to the starter, while other electrical system needs are supplied by a smaller cable. During the starter operation, power flows from the battery to the starter and is grounded through the vehicle's frame and the battery's negative ground strap.

The starting motor is a specially designed, direct current electric motor capable of producing a very great amount of power for its size. One thing that allows the motor to produce a great deal of power is its tremendous rotating speed. It drives the engine through a tiny pinion gear (attached to the starter's armature), which drives the very large flywheel ring gear at a greatly reduced speed. Another factor allowing it to produce so much power is that only intermittent operation is required of it. Thus, little allowance for air circulation is required, and the windings can be built into a very small space.

The starter solenoid is a magnetic device which employs the small current supplied by the starting switch circuit of the ignition switch. This magnetic action moves a plunger which mechanically engages the starter and electrically closes the heavy switch which connects it to the battery. The starting switch circuit consists of the starting switch contained within the ignition switch, a transmission neutral safety switch or clutch pedal switch, and the wiring necessary to connect these with the starter solenoid or relay.

A pinion, which is a small gear, is mounted to a one-way drive clutch. This clutch is splined to the starter armature shaft. When the ignition switch is moved to the START position, the so-

Troubleshooting Basic Starting System Problems

Problem	Cause	Solution
Starter motor rotates engine slowly	• Battery charge low or battery defective	• Charge or replace battery
	• Defective circuit between battery and starter motor	• Clean and tighten, or replace cables
	• Low load current	• Bench-test starter motor. Inspect for worn brushes and weak brush springs.
	• High load current	• Bench-test starter motor. Check engine for friction, drag or coolant in cylinders. Check ring gear-to-pinion gear clearance.
Starter motor will not rotate engine	• Battery charge low or battery defective	• Charge or replace battery
	• Faulty solenoid	• Check solenoid ground. Repair or replace as necessary.
	• Damage drive pinion gear or ring gear	• Replace damaged gear(s)
	• Starter motor engagement weak	• Bench-test starter motor
	• Starter motor rotates slowly with high load current	• Inspect drive yoke pull-down and point gap, check for worn end bushings, check ring gear clearance
	• Engine seized	• Repair engine
Starter motor drive will not engage (solenoid known to be good)	• Defective contact point assembly	• Repair or replace contact point assembly
	• Inadequate contact point assembly ground	• Repair connection at ground screw
	• Defective hold-in coil	• Replace field winding assembly
Starter motor drive will not disengage	• Starter motor loose on flywheel housing	• Tighten mounting bolts
	• Worn drive end busing	• Replace bushing
	• Damaged ring gear teeth	• Replace ring gear or driveplate
	• Drive yoke return spring broken or missing	• Replace spring
Starter motor drive disengages prematurely	• Weak drive assembly thrust spring	• Replace drive mechanism
	• Hold-in coil defective	• Replace field winding assembly
Low load current	• Worn brushes	• Replace brushes
	• Weak brush springs	• Replace springs

lenoid plunger slides the pinion toward the flywheel ring gear via collar and spring. If the teeth on the pinion and flywheel match properly, the pinion will engage the flywheel immediately. If the gear teeth butt one another, the spring will be compressed and will force the gears to mesh as soon as the starter turns far enough to allow them to do so. As the solenoid plunger reaches the end of its travel, it closes the contacts that connect the battery and starter and then the engine is cranked.

As soon as the engines starts, the flywheel ring gear begins turning fast enough to drive the pinion at an extremely high rate of speed. At this point, the one-way clutch begins allowing the pinion to spin faster than the starter shaft so that the starter will not operate at excessive speed. When the ignition switch is released from the starter position, the solenoid is de-energized, and a spring contained within the solenoid assembly pulls the gear out of mesh and interrupts the current flow to the starter.

Some starters employ a separate relay, mounted away from the starter, to switch the motor and solenoid current on and off. The relay thus replaces the solenoid electrical switch, but does not eliminate the need for a solenoid mounted on the starter used to mechanically engage the starter drive gears. The relay is used to reduce the amount of current the starting switch must carry.

The Charging System

The automobile charging system provides electrical power for operation of the vehicle's ignition and starting systems and all the electrical accessories. The battery serves as an electrical surge or storage tank, storing (in chemical form) the energy originally produced by the en-

Troubleshooting Basic Charging System Problems

Problem	Cause	Solution
Noisy alternator	• Loose mountings • Loose drive pulley • Worn bearings • Brush noise • Internal circuits shorted (High pitched whine)	• Tighten mounting bolts • Tighten pulley • Replace alternator • Replace alternator • Replace alternator
Squeal when starting engine or accelerating	• Glazed or loose belt	• Replace or adjust belt
Indicator light remains on or ammeter indicates discharge (engine running)	• Broken fan belt • Broken or disconnected wires • Internal alternator problems • Defective voltage regulator	• Install belt • Repair or connect wiring • Replace alternator • Replace voltage regulator
Car light bulbs continually burn out—battery needs water continually	• Alternator/regulator overcharging	• Replace voltage regulator/alternator
Car lights flare on acceleration	• Battery low • Internal alternator/regulator problems	• Charge or replace battery • Replace alternator/regulator
Low voltage output (alternator light flickers continually or ammeter needle wanders)	• Loose or worn belt • Dirty or corroded connections • Internal alternator/regulator problems	• Replace or adjust belt • Clean or replace connections • Replace alternator or regulator

gine driven generator (alternator). The system also provides a means of regulating generator output to protect the battery from being overcharged and to avoid excessive voltage to the accessories.

The storage battery is a chemical device incorporating parallel lead plats in a tank containing a sulfuric acid-water solution. Adjacent plates are slightly dissimilar, and the chemical reaction of the two dissimilar plates produces electrical energy when the battery is connected to a load such as the starter motor. The chemical reaction is reversible, so that when the generator is producing a voltage (electrical pressure) greater than that produced by the battery, electricity is forced into the battery, and the battery is returned to its fully charged state.

The vehicle's generator is driven mechanically, through V-belts, by the engine crankshaft. It consists of two coils of fine wire, one stationary (the stator) and one movable (the rotor). The rotor may also be known as the armature, and consists of fine wire wrapped around an iron core which is mounted on a shaft. The electricity which flows through the two coils of wire (provided initially by the battery in some cases) creates an intense magnetic field around both rotor and stator, and the interaction between the two fields creates voltage, allowing the generator to power the accessories and charge the battery.

There are two types of generators; the earlier is the direct current (DC) type. The current produced by the DC generator is generated in the armature and carried off the spinning armature by stationary brushes contacting the commutator. The commutator is a series of smooth metal contact plates on the end of the armature. The commutator plates, which are separated from one another by a very short gap, are connected to the armature circuits so that current will flow in one direction only in the wires carrying the generator output. The generator stator consists of two stationary coils of wire which draw some of the output current of the generator to form a powerful magnetic field and create the interaction of fields which generates the voltage. The generator field is wired in series with the regulator.

Newer automobiles use alternating current generators or alternators because they are more efficient, can be rotated at higher speeds, and have fewer brush problems. In an alternator, the field rotates while all the current produced passes only through the stator windings. The brushes bear against continuous slip rings rather than a commutator. This causes the current produced to periodically reverse the direction of its flow. Diodes (electrical one-way switches) block the flow of current from traveling in the wrong direction. A series of diodes is wired together to permit the alternating flow of the stator to be converted to a pulsating, but unidirectional flow at the alternator output. The alternator's field is wired in series with the voltage regulator.

The regulator consists of several circuits. Each circuit had a core, or magnetic coil of wire, which operates a switch. Each switch is connected to ground through one or more resistors. The coil of wire responds directly to system voltage. When the voltage reaches the required level, the magnetic field created by the winding of wire closes the switch and inserts a resistance into the generator field circuit, thus reducing the output. The contacts of the switch cycle open and close many times each second to precisely control voltage.

While alternators are self-limiting as far as maximum current is concerned, DC generators employ a current regulating circuit which responds directly to the total amount of current flowing through the generator circuit rather than to the output voltage. The current regulator is similar to the voltage regulator except that all system current must flow through the energizing coil on its way to the various accessories.

Safety Precautions

Observing these precautions will ensure safe handling of the electrical system components, and will avoid damage to the vehicle's electrical system:

• Be absolutely sure of the polarity of a booster battery before making connections. Connect the cables positive to positive, and negative to negative. Connect positive cables first and then make the last connection to a ground on the body of the booster vehicle so that arcing cannot ignite hydrogen gas that may have accumulated near the battery. Even momentary connection of a booster battery with the polarity reserved will damage alternator diodes.

• Disconnect both vehicle battery cables before attempting to charge a battery.

• Never ground the alternator or generator output or battery terminal. Be cautious when using metal tools around a battery to avoid creating a short circuit between the terminals.

• Never ground the field circuit between the alternator and regulator.

• Never run an alternator or generator without load unless the field circuit is disconnected.

• Never attempt to polarize an alternator.

• Keep the regulator cover in place when taking voltage and current limiter readings.

• Use insulated tools when adjusting the regulator.

Ignition Coil

On all models, the ignition coil is located in the distributor cap, connecting directly to the rotor.

TESTING

Coil-in-Cap

1. Remove the distributor cap and remove the coil from it as described below.

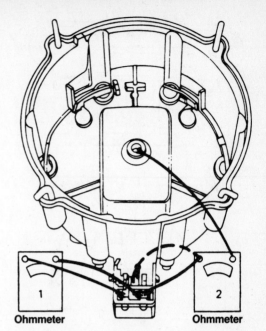

Testing the distributor-cap-mounted ignition coil

2. Connect an ohmmeter across the primary connections, as shown by the ohmmeter and wiring on the left side. The resistance should be zero or very close to zero. High resistance or infinite resistance indicates a partial or complete open circuit, and the need to replace the coil.

3. Connect the ohmmeter between the primary ground and the coil secondary connector as shown via the ohmmeter and wiring on the right side of the illustration. Set the resistance to the higher scale. Test resistance as shown by the solid wire connections and then repeat the test with the wire connected as shown by the dotted line. If both readings are infinite, the coil is bad. If both or either show continuity, the coil is okay.

Separately Mounted Coil

1. Disconnect the secondary lead and unplug the primary leads. Remove the mounting bolts and remove the coil from the engine.

2. First connect an ohmmeter, set to the high scale, as shown on the left. The resistance should be nearly infinite. If it is not, replace the coil.

3. Connect the ohmmeter as shown in the center picture. Use the low resistance scale. The reading should be very low, nearly zero. Otherwise, replace the coil.

4. Reset the ohmmeter to the high resistance scale and connect it as shown on the right. There should be obvious continuity; the ohmmeter should not read infinite. If it does replace the coil. If all three tests are passed, the coil is satisfactory.

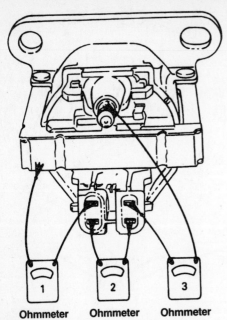

Ohmmeter   Ohmmeter   Ohmmeter

Testing the separately mounted ignition coil

REMOVAL AND INSTALLATION

1. Mark the high tension wires. Then, carefully disconnect each from the distributor cap. Squeeze the latches together and then disconnect the connector that runs from the cap to the distributor base.

2. Use a large, flat bladed prybar to first depress and then rotate the wire type latch away from the underside of the distributor on either side. Remove the cap.

3. Turn the cap upside down. Remove the four bolts from the four corners of the coil, noting the location of the secondary ground lead. Then, remove the primary wiring from the connector in the cap, noting the routing of positive and negative leads.

4. Remove the coil and wiring. Then, remove the arc seal from underneath.

5. Wipe the mounting area for the coil clean with a soft cloth. Inspect the cap for defects, especially heat or carbon tracks, and replace it if necessary.

6. Install a new coil into position, and carefully route the primary wiring positive and negative leads properly.

7. Position the coil ground wire as it was at removal and then install and snug up the four coil mounting bolts. Install the cap and wiring in reverse order.

Ignition Module

REMOVAL AND INSTALLATION

1. Mark the high tension wires. Then, carefully disconnect each from the distributor cap. Squeeze the latches together and then discon-

nect the connector that runs from the cap to the distributor base.

2. Use a large, flat bladed prybar to first depress and then rotate the wire type latch away from the underside of the distributor on either side. Remove the cap.

3. Carefully note the colors of the two leads. Mark them, if necessary. Then disconnect them.

4. Remove the two module attaching screws and pull the module upward and out, being careful not to disturb the grease, if the module may be re-used.

To install:

NOTE: *The module is mounted via a thick layer of grease. This grease is analogous to the coolant in an engine. It carries intense heat away from the module. Make sure to coat the lower surface of the module, as well as the mounting surface in the distributor with the grease included in the packed with the new module if the module is replaced. Make sure not to disturb the old grease layer on the old module if it is to be re-used. Failure to do this will cause the module to fail prematurely!*

5. Remount the module, connect the leads in the proper order, tighten the retaining screws and reinstall the distributor cap.

High Energy Ignition (HEI) Distributor

The Delco-Remy High Energy Ignition (HEI) system is a breakerless (has no ignition points), pulse triggered, transistor controlled, inductive discharge ignition system that is standard on the Buick, Olds and Pontiac vehicles covered in this guide.

There are only nine electrical connections in the system; the ignition switch feed wire and the eight spark plug leads (early models). After 1980, the EST wiring harness has to be disconnected. The coil is located in the distributor cap, connecting directly to the rotor.

The magnetic pick up assembly located inside the distributor contains a permanent magnet, a pole piece with internal teeth, and a pick up coil. When the teeth of the rotating timer core and pole piece align, an induced voltage in the pick-up coil signals the electronic module to open the coil primary circuit. As the primary current decreases, a high voltage is induced in the secondary windings of the ignition coil directing a spark through the rotor and high voltage leads to fire the spark plugs. The dwell period is automatically controlled by the electronic module and is increased with increasing engine rpm. The HEI system features, as do most electronic ignition systems, a longer spark duration which is instrumental in firing today's lean and

EGR-diluted fuel/air mixtures (a lean mixture requires a much hotter, longer duration spark to ignite it than does a rich mixture). A capacitor, which looks like the condenser in the old points-type ignition systems, is located within the HEI distributor and is used for noise (static) suppression in conjunction with the vehicle's radio. The capacitor is not a regularly replaced component.

As noted in Chapter 2, 1981 and later models continue to use the HEI distributor, although it now incorporates an Electronic Spark Timing system (for more information on EST, please refer to Chapter 4). With the EST system, all spark timing changes are performed electronically by the Electronic Control Module (ECM) which monitors information from various engine sensors, computes the desired spark timing and then signals the distributor to change the timing accordingly. Because all timing changes are controlled electronically, no vacuum or mechanical advance systems are used.

REMOVAL AND INSTALLATION

Engine Not Disturbed

NOTE: *Do not rotate the engine while the distributor is out in order to make installing it simpler and easier. If the engine is inadvertently disturbed while the distributor is out, see the procedure below.*

1. Disconnect the ground cable from the battery. On 1984 and later models, disconnect the ignition switch battery feed wire and, if the vehicle is equipped with a tach, the tachometer lead from the cap.

2. Tag and disconnect the feed and module terminal connectors from the distributor cap. DO NOT use a screwdriver to release the terminal connectors.

3. On 1975–80 models, disconnect the hose at the vacuum advance unit.

4. Depress and release the 4 distributor cap-to-housing retainers and lift off the cap assembly.

5. Using a magic marker, make locating marks on the rotor and module and on the distributor housing and engine to simplify installation. Mark the rotor-to-housing and housing-to-engine block positions.

NOTE: *The distributor must be installed with the rotor and housing in the correct position.*

6. Loosen and remove the distributor clamp and bolt. Carefully lift the distributor just until the point where the rotor stops rotating. Be careful not to disturb the position of the rotor. Now, again mark the relative positions of the rotor-to-distributor housing. The rotor must be aligned with this position before you engage

distributor and camshaft drive gears during installation.

To install:

7. With a new O-ring on the distributor housing and the second mark on the rotor aligned with the mark on the module, install the distributor, taking care to align the mark on the housing with the one on the engine. It may be necessary to lift the distributor and turn the rotor slightly to align the gears and the oil pump driveshaft.

WARNING: *Make sure the distributor seats into the block fully. The base of the housing will stick up about ¼ in. until the distributor gear engages the oil pump drive. Damage to the oil pump, distributor and engine may result if the distributor is forced into position by tightening the distributor clamp bolt. If the distributor will not fully seat, grab the housing and shaft, twist and wiggle until the distributor drops into the oil pump drive. If this does not work, install a socket wrench onto the large bolt on the front of the crankshaft pulley. Turn the crankshaft in either direction until the distributor drops into the block fully.*

8. With the respective marks aligned, install the clamp and the bolt finger-tight.

9. Install and secure the distributor cap.

10. Connect the feed and module connectors to the distributor cap. Reconnect the ignition switch battery feed wire and tach connector where necessary.

11. Connect a timing light to the engine and plug the vacuum hose, if so equipped.

12. Connect the ground cable to the battery.

13. Start the engine and set the timing to specifications.

14. Turn the engine off and torque the distributor clamp bolt to 15 ft. lbs. (20 Nm). Disconnect the timing light and unplug and disconnect the hose to the vacuum advance.

Engine Disturbed

CAUTION: *The engine MUST be completely cooled down before performing this procedure. A hot engine may cause burns and personal injury.*

1. Disconnect the negative (−) battery cable.

2. Remove the No. 1 cylinder spark plug. Turn the engine using a socket wrench on the large bolt on the front of the crankshaft pulley. Place a finger near the No. 1 spark plug hole and turn the crankshaft until the piston reaches Top Dead Center. As the engine approaches Top Center, you will feel air being expelled by the No. 1 cylinder. If the crankshaft timing indicator says Top Center has been reached but the other condition is not being met, turn the engine another full turn (360°).

Once the engine's position is correct, replace the spark plug. Line the mark on the crankshaft damper with the 0° mark on the timing indicator.

NOTE: *When the timing marks are lined up at 0°, the No. 1 piston can be either on the exhaust stroke or the compression stroke. This is why air has to be felt being forced out of the spark plug hole during the compression stroke. The timing will be incorrect if the distributor is installed during the exhaust stroke.*

3. Using the firing order illustration if necessary, find No. 1 cylinder on the distributor cap. Turn the rotor until the rotor contact is approximately aligned with the wire going to No. 1 cylinder, as if the distributor had just fired No. 1 cylinder. Install the distributor as described above, turning the rotor slightly to mesh the gear teeth and oil pump driveshaft so that the rotor comes out in the proper position. Make sure the distributor is fully seated in the block before tightening the hold-down clamp.

Alternator

The alternating current generator (alternator) supplies a continuous output of electrical energy at all engine speeds. The belt-driven alternator generates electrical energy and recharges the battery by supplying it with electrical current. The alternator consists of four main assemblies; two end frame assemblies, a stator assembly, and a rotor assembly. The rotor assembly is supported in the drive end frame by a ball bearing and at the other end by a roller bearing. These bearings are permanent-

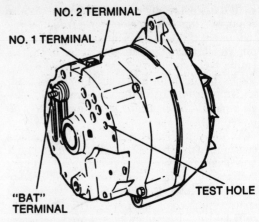

Typical generator

ly lubricated and require no maintenance. There are six diodes in the end frame assembly. These diodes are electrical check valves that also change the alternating current developed within the stator windings to direct current (DC) at the output (BAT) terminal. Three of these diodes are negative and are mounted flush with the end frame while the other three are positive and are mounted into a component called a heat sink (which serves as a reservoir for excess heat, thus protecting the alternator). The positive diodes are easily identified as the ones within small cavities or depressions.

No periodic adjustments or maintenance of any kind, except for regular belt adjustments, are required on the entire alternator assembly. Alternator output in amps, is sometimes stamped on the case of each unit, near the

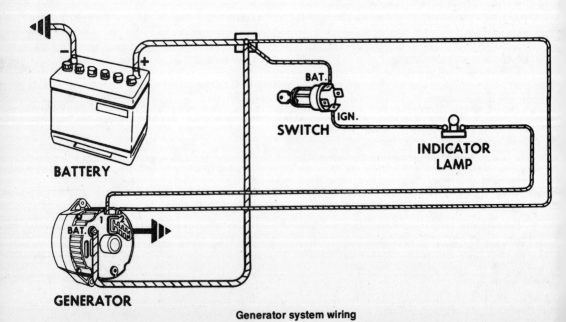

Generator system wiring

Alternator Output Specifications

Year	Part No.	Field Current @ 12V	Output (amps)	Volts @ 75°F
		BUICK		
1975	1102389	4–4.5	42	13.6–14.2
	1102391	4–4.5	61	13.6–14.2
	1102939	4–4.5	63	13.6–14.2
1976	1102389	4–4.5	42	13.6–14.2
	1102391	4–4.5	61	13.6–14.2
	1102939	4–4.5	63	13.6–14.2
1977	1102485	4–4.5	42	13.6–14.2
	1102486	4–4.5	61	13.6–14.2
	1102854	4–4.5	63	13.6–14.2
1978	1102841	4–4.5	42	13.6–14.2
	1102391	4–4.5	61	13.6–14.2
1979	1102389	4–4.5	42	13.9–14.5
	1102392	4–4.5	63	13.9–14.5
	1102842	4–4.5	63	13.9–14.5
1980	1103043	4–4.5	42	13.9–14.5
	1103085	4–4.5	55	13.9–14.5
	1103111	4–4.5	63	13.9–14.5
	1103121	4–4.5	63	13.9–14.5
	1101066	4–4.5	70	13.9–14.5
1981	1100164	4–4.5	55	13.9–14.5
	1100156	4–4.5	55	13.9–14.5
	1100121	4–4.5	63	13.9–14.5
	1101037	4–4.5	70	13.9–14.5
1982–83	1101037	—	70	—
	1100121	—	60	—
	1100121	—	63	—
1984	1100239	—	56	—
	1105564	—	66	—
	1105566	—	66	—
	1105250	—	70	—
	1100200	—	78	—
	1100260	—	78	—
	1105567	—	78	—
	1105565	—	78	—
	1105443	—	94	—
	1105493	—	94	—
1985	—	—	56	—
	—	—	66	—

Alternator Output Specifications (cont.)

Year	Part No.	Field Current @ 12V	Output (amps)	Volts @ 75°F
		BUICK		
1985	—	—	78	—
	—	—	94	—
1986–87	1100239	—	55	—
	1105197	—	70	—
	1100200	—	78	—
	1105565	—	78	—
1988–90	1101229	4–4.5	85	13.5–16.0
	1101253	—	85	13.5–16.0
	1101254	—	120	—
	1101454	—	120	—
		OLDSMOBILE		
1975	1102483	4–4.5	37	13.6–14.2
	1102488	4–4.5	57	13.6–14.2
	1102550	4–4.5	63	13.6–14.2
1976	1102841	4–4.5	42	13.6–14.2
	1102843	4–4.5	61	13.6–14.2
	1102842	4–4.5	63	13.6–14.2
	1102844	4–4.5	63	13.6–14.2
1977	1102841	4–4.5	42	13.6–14.2
	1102843	4–4.5	61	13.6–14.2
	1102844	4–4.5	63	13.6–14.2
	1102842	4–4.5	63	13.6–14.2
1978–'79	1102841	4–4.5	42	13.9–14.5 ①
	1102479	4–4.5	55	13.9–14.5 ①
	1102843	4–4.5	61	13.9–14.5 ①
	1102844	4–4.5	63	13.9–14.5 ①
	1102842	4–4.5	63	13.9–14.5 ①
	1101016	4–4.5	80	13.9–14.5 ①
1980	1103043	4–4.5	42	13.9–14.5
	1103085	4–4.5	55	13.9–14.5
	1103111	4–4.5	63	13.9–14.5
	1103121	4–4.5	63	13.9–14.5
	1101066	4–4.5	70	13.9–14.5
1981	1100164	4–4.5	55	13.9–14.5
	1100156	4–4.5	55	13.9–14.5
	1100121	4–4.5	63	13.9–14.5
	1101037	4–4.5	70	13.0–14.5

Alternator Output Specifications (cont.)

Year	Alternator Part No.	Field Current @ 12V	Output (amps)	Regulator Volts @ 75°F
OLDSMOBILE				
1982	1100110-NL	—	42	—
	1101037-ZU	—	70	—
	1101088-AX	—	70	—
	1101045-FZ	—	85	—
	1101084-NU	—	85	—
	1100164-FM	—	55	—
	1100121-HT	—	63	—
	1100156-AY	—	55	—
1983	1100230	—	42	—
	1100239	—	55	—
	1100100	—	78	—
	1100260	—	78	—
	1105343	—	85	—
	1105198	—	85	—
	1100300	—	63	—
	1105022	—	78	—
	1100247	—	63	—
1984–85	1100239	—	55	—
	1100260	—	78	—
	1105564	—	66	—
	1105565	—	78	—
	1105566	—	66	—
	1105567	—	78	—
1986–87	1105565	—	78	—
1988–90	1101229	4–4.5	85	13.5–16.0
	1101253	—	85	13.5–16.0
	1101254	—	100	—
	1101454	—	120	—
PONTIAC				
1975	1102481	4–4.5	37	13.6–14.2
	1102482	4–4.5	55	13.6–14.2
	1101027	4–4.5	80	13.6–14.2
1976	1102481	4–4.5	37	13.6–14.2
	1102482	4–4.5	55	13.6–14.2
	1102486	4–4.5	61	13.6–14.2
	1102384	4–4.5	37	13.6–14.2
	1102385	4–4.5	55	13.6–14.2
	1101027	4–4.5	80	13.6–14.2

Alternator Output Specifications (cont.)

Year	Alternator Part No.	Field Current @ 12V	Output (amps)	Regulator Volts @ 75°F
PONTIAC				
1977	1102841	4–4.5	42	13.6–14.2
	1102906	4–4.5	61	13.6–14.2
	1102842	4–4.5	63	13.6–14.2
	1102485	4–4.5	42	13.6–14.2
	1102486	4–4.5	61	13.6–14.2
	1102854	4–4.5	63	13.6–14.2
	1102843	4–4.5	61	13.6–14.2
	1101016	4–4.5	80	13.6–14.2
1978	1102485	4–4.5	42	13.6–14.2
	1102841	4–4.5	42	13.6–14.2
	1102389	4–4.5	42	13.6–14.2
	1102906	4–4.5	61	13.6–14.2
	1102391	4–4.5	61	13.6–14.2
	1102843	4–4.5	61	13.6–14.2
	1102892	4–4.5	63	13.6–14.2
	1102844	4–4.5	63	13.6–14.2
	1101016	4–4.5	80	13.6–14.2
1979	1103033	4–4.5	42	13.9–14.5
	1103055	4–4.5	42	13.9–14.5
	1102389	4–4.5	42	13.9–14.5
	1103056	4–4.5	63	13.9–14.5
	1103058	4–4.5	63	13.9–14.5
	1102392	4–4.5	63	13.9–14.5
	1103076	4–4.5	63	13.9–14.5
	1102842	4–4.5	63	13.9–14.5
	1101016	4–4.5	80	13.9–14.5
1980	1103043	4–4.5	42	13.5–16
	②	4–4.5	63	13.5–16
	②	4–4.5	63	13.5–16
	②	4–4.5	70	13.5–16
1981	1103088	4–4.5	55	14.7
	1103091	4–4.5	63	14.7
	1101037	4–4.5	70	14.7
	1101038	4–4.5	70	14.7
1982–83	—	—	55	—
	—	—	63	—
	—	—	70	—
1984–85	—	—	42	—

Alternator Output Specifications (cont.)

Year	Alternator Part No.	Alternator Field Current @ 12V	Alternator Output (amps)	Regulator Volts @ 75°F
PONTIAC				
—	—	—	56	—
—	—	—	66	—
—	—	—	70	—
—	—	—	78	—
—	—	—	85	—
—	—	—	94	—
1986–87	1100239	—	55	—
	1105197	—	70	—
	1100200	—	78	—
	1105565	—	78	—
1988–90	1101229	4–4.5	85	13.5–16.0
	1101253	—	85	13.5–16.0
	1101254	—	100	—
	1101454	—	120	—

NOTE: All alternators made by Delco-Remy Regulators are integral with alternator unit
① 1978 13.6–14.2
② Not available

mounting hole. Output ratings of the alternators fitted to engines covered here are 37, 42, 55, 57, 61, 63, 70 and 80 amps. Regulator voltages range between 13.6 and 16 volts at 75°.

Alternator

ALTERNATOR PRECAUTIONS

WARNING: *To prevent serious damage to the alternator and the rest of the charging system, the following precautions must be observed:*

1. When installing a battery, make sure that the positive cable is connected to the positive terminal and the negative to the negative.

2. When jump-starting the vehicle with another battery, make sure that like terminals are connected. This also applies when using a battery charger.

3. Never operate the alternator with the battery disconnected or otherwise on an uncontrolled open circuit. Double-check to see that all connections are tight.

4. Do not short across or ground any alternator or regulator terminals.

5. Do not try to polarize the alternator.

6. Do not apply full battery voltage to the field (brown) connector.

7. Always disconnect the battery ground cable before disconnecting the alternator lead.

REMOVAL

1. Disconnect the battery ground cable to prevent diode damage.

2. Tag and disconnect the alternator wiring.

3. Remove the alternator brace bolt. If the vehicle is equipped with power steering, loosen the pump brace and mount nuts. Detach the drive belt(s).

4. Support the alternator and remove the mount bolt(s). Remove the unit from the vehicle.

INSTALLATION AND BELT ADJUSTMENT

To install, position the alternator into the mounting brackets and hand tighten the mounting bolts. Alternator belt tension is quite critical. A belt that is too tight may cause alternator bearing failure; one that is too loose will cause a gradual battery discharge as well as belt wear. For details on correct belt adjustment, see "Drive Belts" in Chapter 1.

NOTE: *When adjusting alternator belt tension, apply pressure at the center of the alternator unit, NEVER against either end frame.*

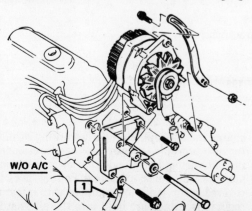

W/O A/C

1

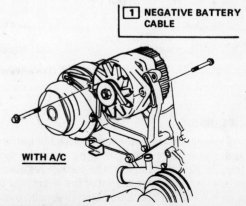

1 NEGATIVE BATTERY CABLE

WITH A/C

Alternator mounting—early model V8 engines

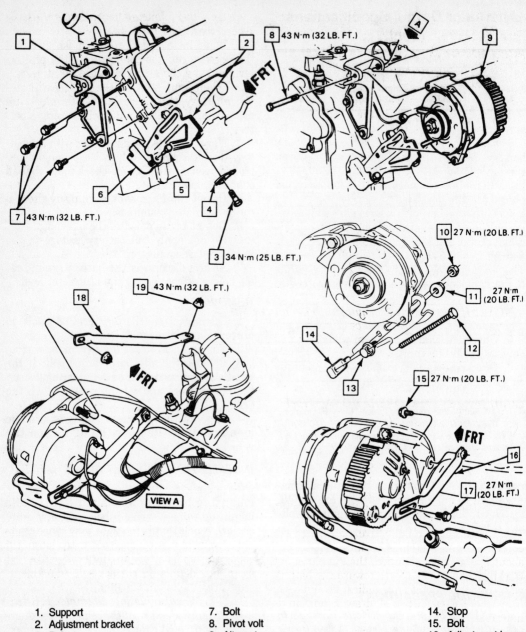

1. Support
2. Adjustment bracket
3. Bolt
4. Bend lock tab around bolt head
5. Bolt
6. Power steering pump bracket
7. Bolt
8. Pivot volt
9. Alternator
10. Nut
11. Nut
12. Belt tension adjustment bolt
13. Adjuster
14. Stop
15. Bolt
16. Adjustment brace
17. Bolt
18. Brace
19. Nut

Alternator mounting—late model Olds 307 (VIN Y)

Regulator

The voltage regulator works with the battery and alternator to comprise the charging system. As its name implies, the voltage regulator regulates the voltage output of the alternator to a safe level (so the alternator does not over-charge the battery). A properly working regulator also prevents excessive voltage from burning out wiring, bulbs and other electrical components. All Buick, Olds and Pontiac models covered in this guide are equipped with integral regulators, which are built into the alternator case. The regulators are solid state and require no maintenance or adjustment.

PRELIMINARY CHARGING SYSTEM TESTS

1. If you suspect a defect in your charging system, first perform these general checks before going on to more specific tests.

2. Check the condition of the alternator belt and tighten if necessary.

3. Clean the battery cable connections at the battery. Make sure the connections between the battery wires and the battery clamps are good. Reconnect the negative terminal only and proceed to the next step.

4. With the key off, insert a test light between the positive terminal on the battery terminal clamp. If the test light comes on, there is a short in the electrical system of the vehicle. The short must be repaired before proceeding. If the light does not come on, then proceed to the next step.

NOTE: *If the vehicle is equipped with an electric clock, the clock must be disconnected.*

5. Check the charging system wiring for any obvious breaks or shorts.

6. Check the battery to make sure it is fully charged and in good condition.

CHARGING SYSTEM OPERATIONAL TEST

NOTE: *You will need a current indicator to perform this test. If the current indicator is to give an accurate reading, the battery cables must be the same gauge and length as the original equipment.*

1. With the engine running and all electrical systems turned off, place a current indicator over the positive battery cable.

2. If a charge of roughly five amps is recorded, the charging system is working. If a draw of about five amps is recorded, the system is not working. The needle moves toward the battery when a charge condition is indicated, and away from the battery when a draw condition is indicated.

3. If a draw is indicated, proceed with further testing. If an excessive charge (10–15 amps) is indicated, the regulator may be at fault.

OUTPUT TEST

1975–87 SI Series

1. You will need an ammeter for this test.

2. Disconnect the battery ground cable.

3. Disconnect the wire from the battery terminal on the alternator.

4. Connect the ammeter negative lead to the battery terminal wire removed in step three, and connect the ammeter positive lead to the battery terminal on the alternator.

5. Reconnect the battery ground cable and

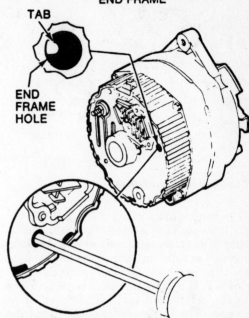

INSERT SCREWDRIVER
GROUND TAB TO
END FRAME

TAB

END
FRAME
HOLE

SI series alternator test hole

turn on all electrical accessories. If the battery is fully charged, disconnect the coil wire and bump the starter a few times to partially discharge it.

6. Start the engine and run it until you obtain a maximum current reading on the ammeter.

7. If the current is within ten amps of the rated output of the alternator, the alternator is working properly. If the current is not within ten amps, insert a probe into the test hole in the end frame of the alternator and ground the tab in the test hole against the side of the hole.

NOTE: *The 1975–87 SI series alternator is equipped with the test hole, whereas the 1987–present CS series alternator is not equipped with a test hole.*

8. If the current is now within ten amps of the rated output, remove the alternator and have the voltage regulator replaced. If it is still below ten amps of rated output, have the alternator repaired. See the alternator and regulator output chart in this chapter.

1987–90 CS Series

The CS series alternator comes in a variety of sizes as does the SI series. The most used sizes are the 130 and 144. These numbers represent the outside diameter of the stator laminations in millimeters. The main difference between the CS and SI series is the newly designed voltage regulator and the absence of a diode trio.

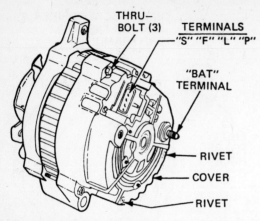

CS series alternator—1987–90

The remaining components are basic to the earlier SI models. The CS series may have a combination of a four terminal connector at the alternator. All or only two connections may be used depending on the vehicle. The terminals are labeled S, F, L, P. The P terminal is connected to the stator and a diesel tachometer, if so equipped. The L terminal is connected to the charge indicator bulb. The F terminal is connected internally to the field positive and may be used as a fault indicator. The S terminal may be connected to a external voltage source, such as battery voltage. The P, F and S terminals are optional.

1. Check all preliminary charging system tests before continuing.

2. With the ignition switch ON and the engine NOT running, the alternator lamp should be ON. If not, check for an open circuit between the grounding lead and ignition switch. Check for a burned out bulb.

3. With the engine RUNNING at moderate speed, the lamp should be OFF. If not, turn OFF the engine and disconnect the harness connector at the alternator. Start the engine and check the lamp. If the lamp goes OFF, repair or replace the alternator. If the lamp stays ON, check for a grounded L terminal wire in the harness.

4. Is the battery undercharged or overcharged?

a. Disconnect the wiring harness connector from the alternator.

b. With ignition switch ON, engine NOT running, connect a voltmeter from ground to the L terminal. A zero reading indicates an open circuit between the terminal and battery.

c. Reconnect the harness connector and run the engine at moderate speed. Measure the voltage across the battery. If it is above 16V, repair or replace the alternator.

d. Turn on all accessories, load the battery with a carbon pile to obtain maximum amperage. Maintain voltage at 13V or greater. If the amperage is within 15 amps of rated output, the alternator is OK. If NOT within 15 amps, replace or repair the alternator.

Battery

REMOVAL AND INSTALLATION

CAUTION: *When working on the battery, be careful at all times to keep metal wrenches from connecting across the battery terminal posts.*

1. Use a wrench to loosen the through-bolt for the terminal. If necessary, use a prybar carefully to spread the terminal halves apart. Disconnect the negative terminal. Then, repeat the process to disconnect the positive terminal.

2. Remove the retainer screw from the retaining block located behind the battery. Remove the retainer.

3. Carefully lift the battery out of the engine compartment using a battery lifting strap or equivalent.

4. Thoroughly clean the entire battery box area. Use a mild solution of baking soda and water to cut through the corrosion. This is done because the battery retains its charge better in a clean environment.

5. Replace the battery with one having an equal or higher rating in amp/hours. Note that the older a vehicle is, the more likely it is to benefit from an increase in battery capacity due to increased resistance in the wiring.

6. Replace the battery in exact reverse order, making sure it is securely mounted before starting to connect the wiring. Make sure the battery terminals are clean, using a special brush designed for that purpose, if necessary.

7. Connect the positive terminal first, and then the negative, tightening them securely. Coat the terminals with petroleum jelly to protect them from corrosion.

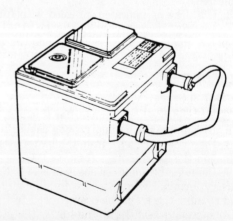

Battery lifting strap—top terminal strap similar

Starter

REMOVAL AND INSTALLATION

Except Below

NOTE: *The starters on some engines require the addition of shims to provide proper clearance between the starter pinion gear and the flywheel. These shims are available in 0.015 in. (0.4mm) sizes from Buick, Oldsmobile and Pontiac dealers. Flat washers can be used if shims are unavailable.*

1. **Important**, disconnect the negative battery cable.

2. Raise the vehicle to a convenient working height and safely support it with jackstands.

3. Disconnect all wiring from the starter solenoid. Replace each nut as the connector is removed, as thread sizes differ from connector to connector. Tag the wires for later connection.

4. Remove the flywheel housing cover. On automatic transmission V6s, disconnect the oil cooler lines at the transmission.

Chilton Time Saver: *Starter removal on certain models may necessitate the removal of the frame support. This support runs from the corner of the frame to the front crossmember. To remove:*

a. Loosen the mounting bolt that attaches the support to the corner of the frame.

b. Loosen and remove the mounting bolt that attaches the support to the front crossmember and then swing the support out of the way.

c. Install the crossmember and mounting bolts. Torque the bolts to 80 ft. lbs. (109 Nm).

5. Remove the front bracket from the starter and the two mounting bolts. On engines with a starter solenoid heat shield, remove the front bracket upper bolt and detach the bracket from the starter.

6. Remove the front bracket bolt or nut. Lower the starter front end first, then remove the unit from the vehicle.

7. Installation is the reverse of removal. Make sure that any shims removed are replaced (see shimming procedure below). Torque the two mounting bolts to 25–35 ft. lbs. (34–48 Nm). Connect the starter wires and install heat shields if removed.

1984–87 Olds V6

1. Disconnect the negative battery cable. Raise the vehicle and support with jackstands.

2. Remove the exhaust crossover pipe.

3. Disconnect the oil cooler lines at the transmission on vehicles equipped with automatics. Remove the lower flywheel cover.

4. Place an object under the starter that will support it 6–8 in. (152–203mm) below its nor-

mal position. Then, remove the mounting bolts and lower the starter onto the support.

5. Label and then disconnect wiring. Do not mix up mounting nuts for the wiring, as different thread types may be used on the different connectors.

To install:

1. Position the starter into the mounting area.

2. Install the mounting bolts and torque to 35 ft. lbs. (47 Nm).

3. Install the heat shield, connect the starter terminals and negative battery cable.

4. Start the engine and check for proper operation.

1984–87 Olds V8

1. Disconnect the negative battery cable. Raise the vehicle and support it securely with jackstands.

2. Remove the bolts that attach the upper starter support. Remove the heat shield.

3. Remove the flywheel housing cover. Place an object under the starter that will support it 6–8 in. (152–203mm) under its normal position. Then, remove the two forward starter mounting bolts and lower the starter onto the support. Label and then disconnect the wiring. Keep attaching nuts in order, as different types of thread may be used on the wiring connectors.

To install:

1. Raise the starter motor into position and support below the mounting area.

2. Connect the starter harness to the same terminal as removed.

3. Install the starter and mounting bolts. Torque the mounting bolts to 35 ft. lbs. (47 Nm).

4. Install the flywheel housing cover, and heat shield and connect the negative battery cable.

5. Check the system for proper operation.

1984–85 8–350 Diesel

1. Disconnect both batteries. Raise the vehicle and support it securely with jackstands.

2. Remove the flywheel cover.

3. Remove the starter heat shield upper bolt and side nut and then remove the shield.

4. Label the wires and then disconnect them, keeping attaching nuts in order. On the Olds 88 and 98 models, it may be necessary to work on the wiring from the front of the engine.

5. Support the starter from underneath. Remove the two mounting bolts that can be reached from underneath the starter, and remove it by pulling it out between the flywheel and exhaust crossover.

To install:

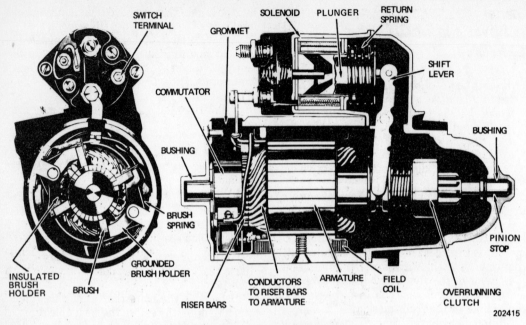

Cross section of typical starting motor

1. Support the starter and connect the wiring harness as previously marked.

2. Position the starter into the mounting area and install the shims (if used) and mounting bolts. Torque the mounting bolts to 35 ft. lbs. (47 Nm).

3. Install the flywheel cover and heat shield, if so equipped.

4. Connect the battery cables and start the engine to check for proper operation.

SHIMMING THE STARTER

Starter noise during cranking and after the engine fires is often a result of too much or too little distance between the starter pinion gear and the flywheel. A high pitched whine during cranking (before the engine fires) can be caused by the pinion and flywheel being too far apart. Likewise, a whine after the engine starts (as the key is released) is often a result of the pinion-

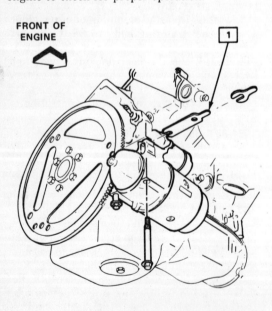

FRONT OF ENGINE

1 USE SHIMS AS REQUIRED

2 SHIELD

STARTER NOISE DIAGNOSTIC PROCEDURE

1. STARTER NOISE DURING CRANKING: REMOVE 1 – .015" DOUBLE SHIM OR ADD SINGLE .015" SHIM TO **OUTER** BOLT ONLY.

2. HIGH PITCHED WHINE AFTER ENGINE FIRES: ADD .015" DOUBLE SHIMS UNTIL NOISE DISAPPEARS.

SEE TEXT FOR COMPLETE PROCEDURE.

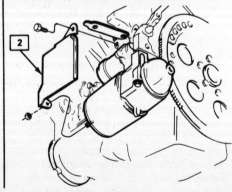

Starter motor mounting; V6 at left, diesel at right. Others similar

Meshing starter and flywheel teeth

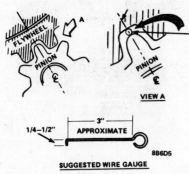

VIEW A

Flywheel-to-pinion clearance

flywheel relationship being too close. In both cases flywheel damage can occur. Shims are available in 0.015 in. (0.4mm) sizes to properly adjust the starter on its mount. You will also need a flywheel turning tool, available at most auto parts stores or from any auto tool store or salesperson.

If your vehicle's starter emits the above noises, follow the shimming procedure below:

1. Disconnect the negative battery cable.
2. Remove the flywheel inspection cover on the bottom of the bellhousing.
3. Using the flywheel turning tool, turn the flywheel and examine the flywheel teeth. If damage is evident, the flywheel should be replaced.
4. Insert a suitable prybar into the small hole in the bottom of the starter and move the starter pinion and clutch assembly so the pinion and flywheel teeth mesh. If necessary, rotate the flywheel so that a pinion tooth is directly in the center of the two flywheel teeth and on the centerline of the two gears, as shown in the accompanying illustration.
5. Check the pinion-to-flywheel clearance by using a 0.020 in. (0.5mm) wire gauge (a spark plug wire gauge may work here, or you can make your own). Make sure you center the pinion tooth between the flywheel teeth and the gauge, NOT in the corners, as you may get a false reading. If the clearance is under this minimum, shim the starter away from the flywheel by adding shim(s) one at a time to the starter mount. Check clearance after adding each shim.

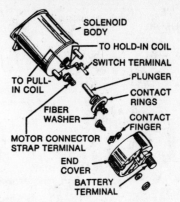

Removing the solenoid

6. If the clearance is a good deal over 0.020 in. (0.5mm), in the vicinity of 0.050 in. (1.27mm) plus, shim the starter toward the flywheel. Broken or severely mangled flywheel teeth are also a good indicator that the clearance here is too great. Shimming the starter toward the flywheel is done by adding shims to the outboard starter mounting pad only. Check the clearance after each shim is added. A shim of 0.015 in. (0.4mm) at this location will decrease the clearance about 0.010 in. (0.25mm).

SOLENOID REPLACEMENT

1. Disconnect the negative (–) battery cable.
2. Remove the starter motor from the vehicle as previously outlined.
3. Remove the screw and washer from the field strap terminal.
4. Remove the two solenoid-to-housing retaining screws and the motor terminal bolt.
5. Remove the solenoid by twisting the unit 90°.

To install:

1. install the solenoid and twist 90°. Make sure the return spring is on the plunger, and rotate the solenoid unit into place on the starter.
2. Install the retaining screws and torque to 100 inch lbs. (11 Nm).
3. Connect the field strap terminal, install the starter, connect the negative battery cable and start the engine to check for proper operation.

STARTER OVERHAUL

Drive Replacement

1. Disconnect the field coil straps from the solenoid.
2. Remove the through-bolts (usually 2), and separate the commutator end frame, field frame assembly, drive housing, and armature assembly from each other.

NOTE: *On diesel starters, remove the insulator from the end frame. The armature on the*

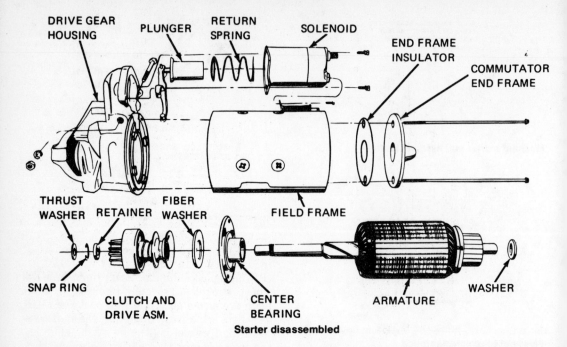

Starter disassembled

diesel starter remains in the drive end frame.

3. On diesel starters, remove the shift lever pivot bolt. On the diesel 25 MT starter only, remove the center bearing screws and remove the drive gear housing from the armature shaft. The shift lever and plunger assembly will now fall away from the starter clutch.

4. Slide the 2-piece thrust collar off the end of the armature shaft.

5. Slide a ⅝ in. deep socket, piece of pipe or an old pinion onto the shaft so that the end of the pipe, socket, or pinion butts up against the edge of the pinion retainer.

6. Place the lower end of the armature securely on a soft surface, such as a wooden block or thick piece of foam rubber. Tap the end of the socket, pipe or pinion, driving the retainer toward the armature end of the snapring.

7. Remove the snapring from the groove in the armature shaft with a pair of pliers. If the snapring is distorted, replace it with a new one during reassembly. Slide the retainer and starter drive from the shaft; on diesel starters, remove the fiber washer and the center bearing from the armature shaft. On gasoline engine starters, the shift lever and plunger may be disassembled at this time (if necessary) by removing the roll pin.

8. To reassemble, lubricate the drive end of the armature shaft with silicone lubricant. On diesel starters, install the center bearing with the bearing toward the armature winding, then install the fiber washer on the armature shaft.

9. Slide the starter drive onto the armature shaft with the pinion facing outward (away from the armature). Slide the retainer onto the

shaft with the cupped surface facing outward.

10. Again support the armature on a soft surface, with the pinion on the upper end. Center the snapring on the top of the shaft (use a new ring if the old one was misshapen or damaged). Gently place a block of wood on top of the snapring so as not to move it from a centered position. Tap the wooden block with a hammer in order to force the snapring around the shaft. Slide the ring down into the snapring groove.

11. Lay the armature down flat on your work surface. Slide the retainer close up onto the shaft and position it and the thrust collar next to the snapring. Using two pairs of pliers on opposite ends of the shaft, squeeze the thrust collar and the retainer together until the snapring is forced into the retainer.

12. Lube the drive housing bushing with a silicone lubricant.

13. Engage the shift lever yoke with the clutch. Position the front of the armature shaft

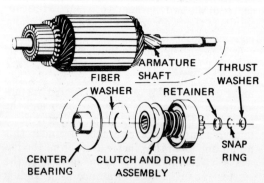

Starter drive assembly removed

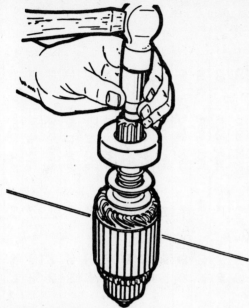

Use an old socket or piece of pipe to drive the retainer toward the snap-ring

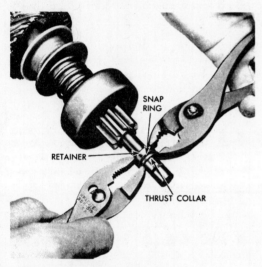

Forcing retainer over snap ring

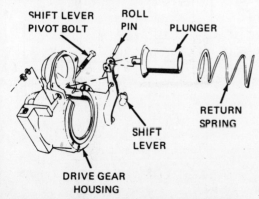

Removing shift lever and plunger from starter

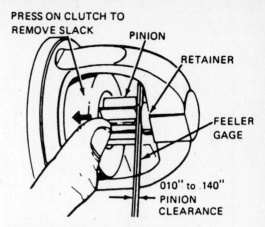

Checking starter pinion clearance

into the bushing, then slide the complete drive assembly into the drive gear housing.

NOTE: *On non-diesel starters the shift lever may be installed in the drive gear housing first.*

14. On the 25 MT diesel starter only, install the center bearing screws and the shift lever pivot bolt, and tighten securely.

15. Apply a sealing compound approved for this application onto the drive housing, to the solenoid flange where the field frame contacts it. Position the field frame around the armature shaft and against the drive housing. Work carefully and slowly to prevent damaging the starter brushes.

16. Lubricate the bushing in the commutator end frame with a silicone lubricant, place the leather washer onto the armature shaft, and then slide the commutator end frame over the shaft and into position against the field frame. On diesel starters, install the insulator and then the end frame onto the shaft. Line up the bolt holes, then install and tighten the through-bolts (make sure they pass through the bolt holes in the insulator).

17. Connect the field coil straps to the motor terminal of the solenoid.

NOTE: *If replacement of the starter drive fails to cure improper engagements of the starter pinion to the flywheel, there may be defective parts in the solenoid and/or shift lever. The best procedure is to take the assembly to a shop where a pinion clearance check can be made by energizing the solenoid on a test bench. If the pinion clearance is incorrect, disassemble the solenoid and shift lever, inspect, and replace the worn parts.*

Brush Replacement

1. Disassemble the starter by following steps 1 and 2 of the Drive Replacement procedure above.

Battery and Starter Specifications

Year	Engine No. Cyl Displacement (cu in.)	Engine VIN Code	Battery Ampere Hour Capacity②	Battery Volts	Battery Terminal Grounded	Lock Test Amps	Lock Test Volts	Lock Test Torque (ft. lbs.)	No-Load Test Amps	No-Load Test Volts	No-Load Test RPM	Brush String Tension (oz)①
1975	8-350	K	350	12	Neg			Not Recommended	45–80	9	3500–6000	35
	8-350	J	310	12	Neg			Not Recommended	55–80	9	3500–6000	35
	8-400	R③	430	12	Neg			Not Recommended	55–80	9	3500–6000	35
	8-400	S③	450	12	Neg			Not Recommended	55–80	9	3500–6000	35
	8-400	R④	430	12	Neg			Not Recommended	55–80	9	3500–6000	35
	8-400	S④	450	12	Neg			Not Recommended	55–80	9	3500–6000	35
	8-455	T③	450	12	Neg			Not Recommended	45–80	9	4000–6500	35
	8-455	T⑤	420	12	Neg			Not Recommended	45–80	9	4000–6500	35
	8-455	W④	420	12	Neg			Not Recommended	45–80	9	4000–6500	35
1976	8-350	R	350	12	Neg			Not Recommended	55–80	9	3500–6000	35
	8-350	J	350	12	Neg			Not Recommended	55–80	9	3500–6000	35
	3-350	P	350	12	Neg			Not Recommended	55–80	9	3500–6000	35
	8-400	R	450	12	Neg			Not Recommended	55–80	9	3500–6000	35
	8-400	S	430	12	Neg			Not Recommended	55–80	9	3500–6000	35
	8-403	K	420	12	Neg			Not Recommended	55–80	9	3500–6000	35
	8-455	T③	420	12	Neg			Not Recommended	45–80	9	4000–6500	35
	8-455	W④	420	12	Neg			Not Recommended	45–80	9	4000–6500	35
	8-455	Y⑤	420	12	Neg			Not Recommended	45–80	9	4000–6500	35
1977	6-231	C	275	12	Neg			Not Recommended	50–80	9	5500–10,000	35
	8-260	F	310	12	Neg			Not Recommended	55–80	9	7000–11,900	35
	8-301	Y	350	12	Neg			Not Recommended	55–80	9	3500–6000	35
	8-350	R③	350	12	Neg			Not Recommended	55–80	9	3500–6000	35
	8-350	L⑥	350	12	Neg			Not Recommended	60–95	9	7500–10,500	35

	8-350	P④	350	12	Neg	Not Recommended	65-95	9	7500-10,500	35
	8-350	J⑤	350	12	Neg	Not Recommended	55-80	9	3500-6000	35
	8-403	K	430	12	Neg	Not Recommended	55-80	9	3500-6000	35
1978	6-231	A,G,3	275	12	Neg	Not Recommended	60-85	9	6800-10,300	35
	8-260	F	310	12	Neg	Not Recommended	45-70	9	7000-11,900	35
	8-301	Y,W	310	12	Neg	Not Recommended	45-70	9	7000-11,900	35
	8-305	U	310	12	Neg	Not Recommended	60-85	9	6800-10,300	35
	8-350	R	310	12	Neg	Not Recommended	65-95	9	7500-10,500	35
	8-350	N	550	12	Neg	Not Recommended	40-140	9	8000-13,000	35
	8-350	L	310	12	Neg	Not Recommended	60-95	9	7500-10,500	35
	8-350	X	310	12	Neg	Not Recommended	60-85	9	6800-10,300	35
	8-400	Z	380	12	Neg	Not Recommended	65-95	9	7500-10,500	35
	8-403	K	430	12	Neg	Not Recommended	65-95	9	7500-10,500	35
1979	6-231	A,3	275	12	Neg	Not Recommended	60-85	9	6800-10,300	35
	8-260	F	310	12	Neg	Not Recommended	45-70	9	7000-11,900	35
	8-301	Y,W	350	12	Neg	Not Recommended	45-70	9	7000-11,900	35
	8-305	G	350	12	Neg	Not Recommended	60-85	9	6800-10,300	35
	8-350	R	350	12	Neg	Not Recommended	65-95	9	7500-10,500	35
	8-350	L	350	12	Neg	Not Recommended	65-95	9	7500-10,500	35
	8-350	X	350	12	Neg	Not Recommended	65-95	9	7500-10,500	35
	8-350	N	500	12	Neg	Not Recommended	40-140	9	8000-13,000	35
	8-400	Z	380	12	Neg	Not Recommended	65-95	9	7500-10,500	35
	8-403	K	430	12	Neg	Not Recommended	65-95	9	7500-10,500	35
1980	6-231	A,3	275	12	Neg	Not Recommended	60-85	9	6800-10,300	35
	6-252	4	350	12	Neg	Not Recommended	65-95	9	7500-10,500	35
	8-260	F	350	12	Neg	Not Recommended	45-70	9	7000-11,900	35
	8-265	S	350	12	Neg	Not Recommended	45-70	9	7000-11,900	35
	8-301	W	350	12	Neg	Not Recommended	45-70	9	7000-11,900	35

Battery and Starter Specifications (cont.)

Year	Engine No. Cyl Displacement (cu in.)	Engine VIN Code	Battery			Starter						Brush String Tension (oz) ①
			Volts	Ampere Hour Capacity	Terminal Grounded	Lock Test			No-Load Test			
						Amps	Volts	Torque (ft. lbs.)	Amps	Volts	RPM	
1980	8-307	Y	12	350	Neg	Not Recommended			45–70	9	7000–11,900	35
	8-350	R	12	350	Neg	Not Recommended			65–95	9	7500–10,500	35
	8-350	X	12	350	Neg	Not Recommended			65–95	9	7500–10,500	35
	8-350	N	12	550	Neg	Not Recommended			40–140	9	8000–13,000	35
1981	6-231	A	12	350	Neg	Not Recommended			60–85	9	6800–10,300	35
	6-252	4	12	350	Neg	Not Recommended			65–95	9	7500–10,500	35
	8-260	F	12	350	Neg	Not Recommended			45–70	9	7000–11,900	35
	8-265	S	12	370	Neg	Not Recommended			45–70	9	7000–11,900	35
	8-307	Y	12	350	Neg	Not Recommended			45–70	9	7000–11,900	35
	8-350	N	12	550	Neg	Not Recommended			100–230	9	8000–14,000	35
1982	6-231	A	12	350	Neg	Not Recommended			60–85	9	6800–10,300	35
	8-252	4	12	370	Neg	Not Recommended			65–95	9	7500–10,500	35
	8,260	8	12	350	Neg	Not Recommended			45–70	9	7000–11,900	35
	8-307	Y	12	350	Neg	Not Recommended			45–70	9	7000–11,900	35
	8-350	N	12	550	Neg	Not Recommended			160–220	9	4000–5500	35
1983	6-231	A	12	350	Neg	Not Recommended			60–85	9	6800–10,300	35
	6-252	4	12	370	Neg	Not Recommended			65–95	9	7500–10,500	35
	8-260	8	12	350	Neg	Not Recommended			45–70	9	7000–11,900	35
	8-305	H	12	350	Neg	Not Recommended			45–70	9	7000–11,900	35

Year	Engine									
'84–'85	8-307	Y	350	12	Neg	Not Recommended	45–70	9	7000–11,900	35
	8-350	N	550	12	Neg	Not Recommended	160–220	9	4000–5500	35
	6-231	A	315⑧	12	Neg	Not Recommended	70–110	10	6500–10,700	—
	6-252	4	390⑨	12	Neg	Not Recommended	70–110	10	6500–10,700	—
	8-305	H	500	12	Neg	Not Recommended	50–75	10	6000–11,900	—
	8-307	Y	390⑩	12	Neg	Not Recommended	50–75	10	6000–11,900	—
	8-350	N	405⑪	12	Neg	Not Recommended	160–240⑦	10	4400–6300	—
'86	6-231	A	500⑫	12	Neg	Not Recommended	70–110	10	6500–10,700	—
	8-307	Y	525⑫	12	Neg	Not Recommended	70–110	10	6500–10,700	—
'87	6-231	A	430	12	Neg	Not Recommended	60–90	10	6500–10,500	—
	8-307	Y	525	12	Neg	Not Recommended	50–75	10	6000–11,900	—
'88	8-307	Y	525	12	Neg	Not Recommended	50–75	10	6000–11,900	—
'89	8-307	Y	430	12	Neg	Not Recommended	50–75	10	6000–11,900	—
'90	8-307	Y	570⑫	12	Neg	Not Recommended	50–75	10	6000–11,900	—

NOTE: All 350 V8 diesels use 2 12 volt Batteries
① Minimum Tension
② Cold Cranking Power in amps @ 0°F
③ Olds
④ Pontiac
⑤ Buick
⑥ Chevrolet
⑦ Figures apply to 15MT. Some engines use the ALU/GR. Test figures are: 125–170 amps at 10 volts, 3200–4100 pinion rpm
⑧ Heavy Duty—500
  Olds 88—390
⑨ Heavy Duty—550
⑩ Heavy Duty—500
⑪ Heavy Duty—550
⑫ Heavy Duty—570
All diesels use two batteries

2. Replace the brushes one at a time to avoid having to mark the wiring. For each brush: remove the brush holding screw; remove the old brush and position the new brush in the same direction (large end toward center of field frame), position the wire connector on top of the brush, line up the holes, and reinstall the screw. Make sure the screw is snug enough to ensure good contact.

3. Reassemble starter according to Steps 8–17 above.

ENGINE MECHANICAL

Design

All Buick, Olds and Pontiac engines covered in this guide, whether V6 or V8, are watercooled powerplants with pushrod valve actuation. All engines use cast iron cylinder blocks and heads.

The gasoline V8s are all very similar in construction and share common design features such as chain-driven camshafts, hydraulic valve lifters and pressed-steel rocker arms. The Oldsmobile 307 cu. in. VIN Y engine uses roller valve lifters after 1985. The Buick engines, including V6s, differ in that they have their rockers mounted on shafts. Because of this similarity between the engines, many removal and installation procedures given here will simultaneously cover all three manufacturers' engines. Likewise, the 231 and 252 V6 engines are nearly identical to themselves and to the Buick V8s.

The 350 diesel is derived from the 350 cu. in. gasoline engine, but virtually all major engine parts were beefed up to withstand the higher compression ratio and combustion pressures. Fairly early in the production run the standard valve lifters were replaced with roller type hydraulic lifters because the particles generated in diesel combustion were causing camshaft and lifter wear problems. Diesel cylinder head design is radically different from gas engine design, especially in that the diesel incorporates a special steel insert that forms a precombustion chamber and must be properly fitted to ensure correct head gasket seal.

One especially important difference in the diesel relates to the high compression ratio. The area between the piston top surface and the lower surface of the cylinder head is very small and there is minimal clearance between the piston and valves. For this reason, any engine work related to the valves, lifters and intake manifold requires particular attention to special diesel service procedures. Failure to follow these procedures will often result in bent valves or valve gear.

The diesel fuel system is considerably more complex and precise than the typical gas engine carburetor or injection system. Particular attention must be paid to fuel cleanliness and maintenance of various fuel filters and water separators. Service on this system usually requires extensive specialized tooling and training. It should never be tampered with, as this can even result in personal injury. Make sure you are properly equipped and fully aware of proper service procedures before you begin work on it.

Engine Overhaul Tips

Most engine overhaul procedures are fairly standard. In addition to specific parts replacement procedures and complete specifications for your individual engine, this chapter also is a guide to accept rebuilding procedures. Examples of standard rebuilding practice are shown and should be used along with specific details concerning your particular engine.

Competent and accurate machine shop services will ensure maximum performance, reliability and engine life.

In most instances it is more profitable for the do-it-yourself mechanic to remove, clean and inspect the component, buy the necessary parts and deliver these to a shop for actual machine work.

On the other hand, much of the rebuilding work (crankshaft, block, bearings, piston rods, and other components) is well within the scope of the do-it-yourself mechanic.

TOOLS

The tools required for an engine overhaul or parts replacement will depend on the depth of your involvement. With a few exceptions, they will be the tools found in a mechanic's tool kit (see Chapter 1). More in-depth work will require any or all of the following:

- a dial indicator (reading in thousandths) mounted on a universal base
- micrometers and telescope gauges
- jaw and screw-type pullers
- scraper
- valve spring compressor
- ring groove cleaner
- piston ring expander and compressor
- ridge reamer
- cylinder hone or glaze breaker
- Plastigage®
- engine lift and stand

Use of most of these tools is illustrated in this chapter. Many can be rented for a one-time use from a local parts jobber or tool supply house specializing in automotive work.

Occasionally, the use of special tools is called

for. See the information on Special Tools and Safety Notice in the front of this book before substituting another tool.

INSPECTION TECHNIQUES

Procedures and specifications are given in this chapter for inspecting, cleaning and assessing the wear limits of most major components. Other procedures such as Magnaflux® and Zyglo® can be used to locate material flaws and stress cracks. Magnaflux® is a magnetic process applicable only to ferrous materials (not aluminum). The Zyglo® process coats the material with a fluorescent dye penetrant and can be used on any material. Checking for suspected surface cracks can be more readily made using spot check dye. The dye is sprayed onto the suspected area, wiped off and the area sprayed with a developer. Cracks will show up brightly.

OVERHAUL TIPS

Aluminum has become extremely popular for use in engines, due to its low weight. Observe the following precautions when handling aluminum parts:
- Never hot tank aluminum parts (the caustic hot tank solution will eat the aluminum.
- Remove all aluminum parts (identification tag, etc.) from engine parts prior to the tanking.
- Always coat threads lightly with engine oil or anti-seize compounds before installation, to prevent seizure.
- Never over-torque bolts or spark plugs especially in aluminum threads.

Stripped threads in any component can be repaired using any of several commercial repair kits (Heli-Coil®, Microdot®, Keenserts®, etc.).

When assembling the engine, any parts that will be frictional contact must be prelubed to provide lubrication at initial start-up. Any product specifically formulated for this purpose can be used, but engine oil is not recommended as a prelube.

When semi-permanent (locked, but removable) installation of bolts or nuts is desired, threads should be cleaned and coated with Loctite® or other similar, commercial non-hardening sealant.

REPAIRING DAMAGED THREADS

Several methods of repairing damaged threads are available. Heli-Coil® (shown here), Keenserts® and Microdot® are among the most widely used. All involve basically the same principle—drilling out stripped threads, tapping the hole and installing a prewound insert—making welding, plugging and oversize fasteners unnecessary.

Two types of thread repair inserts are usually supplied — a standard type for most Inch

Coarse, Inch Fine, Metric Course and Metric Fine thread sizes and a spark lug type to fit most spark plug port sizes. Consult the individual manufacturer's catalog to determine exact

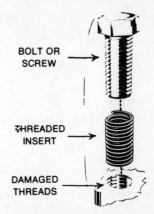

Damaged bolt holes can be repaired with thread repair inserts

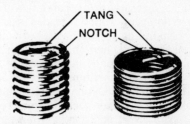

Standard thread repair insert (left) and spark plug thread insert (right)

Drill out the damaged threads with specified drill. Drill completely through the hole or to the bottom of a blind hole

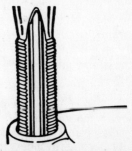

With the tap supplied, tap the hole to receive the thread insert. Keep the tap well oiled and back it out frequently to avoid clogging the threads

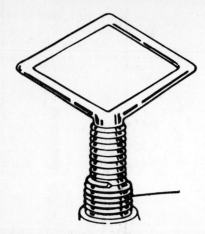

Screw the threaded insert onto the installation tool until the tang engages the slot. Screw the insert into the tapped hole until it is ¼–½ turn below the top surface, After installation break off the tang with a hammer and punch

applications. Typical thread repair kits will contain a selection of prewound threaded inserts, a tap (corresponding to the outside diameter threads of the insert) and an installation tool. Spark plug inserts usually differ because they require a tap equipped with pilot threads and a combined reamer/tap section. Most manufacturers also supply blister-packed thread repair inserts separately in addition to a master kit containing a variety of taps and inserts plus installation tools.

Before effecting a repair to a threaded hole, remove any snapped, broken or damaged bolts or studs. Penetrating oil can be used to free frozen threads; the offending item can be removed with locking pliers or with a screw or stud extractor. After the hole is clear, the thread can be repaired, as follows:

Checking Engine Compression

A noticeable lack of engine power, excessive oil consumption and/or poor fuel mileage measured over an extended period are all indicators of internal engine wear. Worn piston rings, scored or worn cylinder bores, blown head gaskets, sticking or burnt valves and worn valve seats are all possible culprits here. A check of each cylinder's compression will help you locate the problems.

As mentioned in the Tools and Equipment section of Chapter 1, a screw-in type compression gauge is more accurate that the type you simply hold against the spark plug hole, although it takes slightly longer to use. It's worth it to obtain a more accurate reading. Follow the procedures below for gasoline and diesel engined vehicles.

GASOLINE ENGINES

1. Warm up the engine to normal operating temperature. Turn the engine OFF.
2. Remove all spark plugs.
3. Disconnect the high tension lead from the ignition coil.
4. Fully open the throttle either by operating the carburetor throttle linkage by hand or by having an assistant floor the accelerator pedal.
5. Apply engine oil to the gauge fitting and screw the compression gauge into the no.1 spark plug hole until the fitting is snug.

NOTE: *Be careful not to crossthread the plug hole. On aluminum cylinder heads use extra care, as the threads in these heads are easily crossthreaded.*

6. Ask an assistant to depress the accelerator pedal fully on both carbureted and fuel injected vehicles. Then, while you read the compression gauge, ask the assistant to crank the engine two or three times in short bursts using the ignition switch.
7. Read the compression gauge at the end of each series of cranks, and record the highest of these readings. Repeat this procedure for each of the engine's cylinders. Compare the highest reading of each cylinder to the compression pressure specification in the Tune-Up Specifications chart in Chapter 2. The specs in this chart are maximum values.

A cylinder's compression pressure is usually acceptable if it is not less than 80% of maximum. The difference between each cylinder should be no more than 12–14 pounds.

8. If a cylinder is unusually low, pour a tablespoon of clean engine oil into the cylinder through the spark plug hole and repeat the compression test. If the compression comes up after adding the oil, it appears that the cylinder's piston rings or bore are damaged or worn. If the pressure remains low, the valves may not be seating properly (a valve job is needed), or the head gasket may be blown near that cylinder. If compression in any two adjacent cylin-

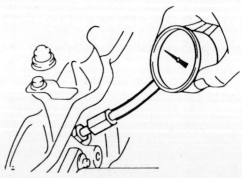

The screw-in type compression gauge is more accurate

Troubleshooting Basic Starting System Problems

Problem	Cause	Solution
Starter motor rotates engine slowly	• Battery charge low or battery defective	• Charge or replace battery
	• Defective circuit between battery and starter motor	• Clean and tighten, or replace cables
	• Low load current	• Bench-test starter motor. Inspect for worn brushes and weak brush springs.
	• High load current	• Bench-test starter motor. Check engine for friction, drag or coolant in cylinders. Check ring gear-to-pinion gear clearance.
Starter motor will not rotate engine	• Battery charge low or battery defective	• Charge or replace battery
	• Faulty solenoid	• Check solenoid ground. Repair or replace as necessary.
	• Damage drive pinion gear or ring gear	• Replace damaged gear(s)
	• Starter motor engagement weak	• Bench-test starter motor
	• Starter motor rotates slowly with high load current	• Inspect drive yoke pull-down and point gap, check for worn end bushings, check ring gear clearance
	• Engine seized	• Repair engine
Starter motor drive will not engage (solenoid known to be good)	• Defective contact point assembly	• Repair or replace contact point assembly
	• Inadequate contact point assembly ground	• Repair connection at ground screw
	• Defective hold-in coil	• Replace field winding assembly
Starter motor drive will not disengage	• Starter motor loose on flywheel housing	• Tighten mounting bolts
	• Worn drive end busing	• Replace bushing
	• Damaged ring gear teeth	• Replace ring gear or driveplate
	• Drive yoke return spring broken or missing	• Replace spring
Starter motor drive disengages prematurely	• Weak drive assembly thrust spring	• Replace drive mechanism
	• Hold-in coil defective	• Replace field winding assembly
Low load current	• Worn brushes	• Replace brushes
	• Weak brush springs	• Replace springs

ders is low, and if the addition of oil does not help the compression, there is leakage past the head gasket. Oil and coolant water in the combustion chamber can result from this problem. There may be evidence of water droplets on the engine dipstick when a head gasket has blown. Another sign of a blown head gasket is white smoke coming from the exhaust pipe when the engine is at normal operating temperature.

Diesel Engines

Checking cylinder compression on diesel engines is basically the same procedure as on gasoline engines except for the following:

1. A special compression gauge adaptor suitable for diesel engines (because these engines have much greater compression pressures) must be used.

2. Remove the injector tubes and remove the injectors from each cylinder.

NOTE: *Do not forget to remove the washer underneath each injector; otherwise, it may get lost when the engine is cranked.*

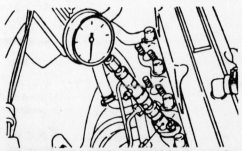

Diesel engines require a special compression gauge adaptor

Troubleshooting Engine Mechanical Problems

Problem	Cause	Solution
External oil leaks	• Fuel pump gasket broken or improperly seated	• Replace gasket
	• Cylinder head cover RTV sealant broken or improperly seated	• Replace sealant; inspect cylinder head cover sealant flange and cylinder head sealant surface for distortion and cracks
	• Oil filler cap leaking or missing	• Replace cap
	• Oil filter gasket broken or improperly seated	• Replace oil filter
	• Oil pan side gasket broken, improperly seated or opening in RTV sealant	• Replace gasket or repair opening in sealant; inspect oil pan gasket flange for distortion
	• Oil pan front oil seal broken or improperly seated	• Replace seal; inspect timing case cover and oil pan seal flange for distortion
	• Oil pan rear oil seal broken or improperly seated	• Replace seal; inspect oil pan rear oil seal flange; inspect rear main bearing cap for cracks, plugged oil return channels, or distortion in seal groove
	• Timing case cover oil seal broken or improperly seated	• Replace seal
	• Excess oil pressure because of restricted PCV valve	• Replace PCV valve
	• Oil pan drain plug loose or has stripped threads	• Repair as necessary and tighten
	• Rear oil gallery plug loose	• Use appropriate sealant on gallery plug and tighten
	• Rear camshaft plug loose or improperly seated	• Seat camshaft plug or replace and seal, as necessary
	• Distributor base gasket damaged	• Replace gasket
Excessive oil consumption	• Oil level too high	• Drain oil to specified level
	• Oil with wrong viscosity being used	• Replace with specified oil
	• PCV valve stuck closed	• Replace PCV valve
	• Valve stem oil deflectors (or seals) are damaged, missing, or incorrect type	• Replace valve stem oil deflectors
	• Valve stems or valve guides worn	• Measure stem-to-guide clearance and repair as necessary
	• Poorly fitted or missing valve cover baffles	• Replace valve cover
	• Piston rings broken or missing	• Replace broken or missing rings
	• Scuffed piston	• Replace piston
	• Incorrect piston ring gap	• Measure ring gap, repair as necessary
	• Piston rings sticking or excessively loose in grooves	• Measure ring side clearance, repair as necessary
	• Compression rings installed upside down	• Repair as necessary
	• Cylinder walls worn, scored, or glazed	• Repair as necessary
	• Piston ring gaps not properly staggered	• Repair as necessary
	• Excessive main or connecting rod bearing clearance	• Measure bearing clearance, repair as necessary
No oil pressure	• Low oil level	• Add oil to correct level
	• Oil pressure gauge, warning lamp or sending unit inaccurate	• Replace oil pressure gauge or warning lamp
	• Oil pump malfunction	• Replace oil pump
	• Oil pressure relief valve sticking	• Remove and inspect oil pressure relief valve assembly
	• Oil passages on pressure side of pump obstructed	• Inspect oil passages for obstruction

Troubleshooting Engine Mechanical Problems (cont.)

Problem	Cause	Solution
No oil pressure (cont.)	• Oil pickup screen or tube obstructed	• Inspect oil pickup for obstruction
	• Loose oil inlet tube	• Tighten or seal inlet tube
Low oil pressure	• Low oil level	• Add oil to correct level
	• Inaccurate gauge, warning lamp or sending unit	• Replace oil pressure gauge or warning lamp
	• Oil excessively thin because of dilution, poor quality, or improper grade	• Drain and refill crankcase with recommended oil
	• Excessive oil temperature	• Correct cause of overheating engine
	• Oil pressure relief spring weak or sticking	• Remove and inspect oil pressure relief valve assembly
	• Oil inlet tube and screen assembly has restriction or air leak	• Remove and inspect oil inlet tube and screen assembly. (Fill inlet tube with lacquer thinner to locate leaks.)
	• Excessive oil pump clearance	• Measure clearances
	• Excessive main, rod, or camshaft bearing clearance	• Measure bearing clearances, repair as necessary
High oil pressure	• Improper oil viscosity	• Drain and refill crankcase with correct viscosity oil
	• Oil pressure gauge or sending unit inaccurate	• Replace oil pressure gauge
	• Oil pressure relief valve sticking closed	• Remove and inspect oil pressure relief valve assembly
Main bearing noise	• Insufficient oil supply	• Inspect for low oil level and low oil pressure
	• Main bearing clearance excessive	• Measure main bearing clearance, repair as necessary
	• Bearing insert missing	• Replace missing insert
	• Crankshaft end play excessive	• Measure end play, repair as necessary
	• Improperly tightened main bearing cap bolts	• Tighten bolts with specified torque
	• Loose flywheel or drive plate	• Tighten flywheel or drive plate attaching bolts
	• Loose or damaged vibration damper	• Repair as necessary
Connecting rod bearing noise	• Insufficient oil supply	• Inspect for low oil level and low oil pressure
	• Carbon build-up on piston	• Remove carbon from piston crown
	• Bearing clearance excessive or bearing missing	• Measure clearance, repair as necessary
	• Crankshaft connecting rod journal out-of-round	• Measure journal dimensions, repair or replace as necessary
	• Misaligned connecting rod or cap	• Repair as necessary
	• Connecting rod bolts tightened improperly	• Tighten bolts with specified torque
Piston noise	• Piston-to-cylinder wall clearance excessive (scuffed piston)	• Measure clearance and examine piston
	• Cylinder walls excessively tapered or out-of-round	• Measure cylinder wall dimensions, rebore cylinder
	• Piston ring broken	• Replace all rings on piston
	• Loose or seized piston pin	• Measure piston-to-pin clearance, repair as necessary
	• Connecting rods misaligned	• Measure rod alignment, straighten or replace
	• Piston ring side clearance excessively loose or tight	• Measure ring side clearance, repair as necessary
	• Carbon build-up on piston is excessive	• Remove carbon from piston

Troubleshooting Engine Mechanical Problems (cont.)

Problem	Cause	Solution
Valve actuating component noise	• Insufficient oil supply	• Check for: (a) Low oil level (b) Low oil pressure (c) Plugged push rods (d) Wrong hydraulic tappets (e) Restricted oil gallery (f) Excessive tappet to bore clearance
	• Push rods worn or bent	• Replace worn or bent push rods
	• Rocker arms or pivots worn	• Replace worn rocker arms or pivots
	• Foreign objects or chips in hydraulic tappets	• Clean tappets
	• Excessive tappet leak-down	• Replace valve tappet
	• Tappet face worn	• Replace tappet; inspect corresponding cam lobe for wear
	• Broken or cocked valve springs	• Properly seat cocked springs; replace broken springs
	• Stem-to-guide clearance excessive	• Measure stem-to-guide clearance, repair as required
	• Valve bent	• Replace valve
	• Loose rocker arms	• Tighten bolts with specified torque
	• Valve seat runout excessive	• Regrind valve seat/valves
	• Missing valve lock	• Install valve lock
	• Push rod rubbing or contacting cylinder head	• Remove cylinder head and remove obstruction in head
	• Excessive engine oil (four-cylinder engine)	• Correct oil level

Troubleshooting the Cooling System

Problem	Cause	Solution
High temperature gauge indication—overheating	• Coolant level low	• Replenish coolant
	• Fan belt loose	• Adjust fan belt tension
	• Radiator hose(s) collapsed	• Replace hose(s)
	• Radiator airflow blocked	• Remove restriction (bug screen, fog lamps, etc.)
	• Faulty radiator cap	• Replace radiator cap
	• Ignition timing incorrect	• Adjust ignition timing
	• Idle speed low	• Adjust idle speed
	• Air trapped in cooling system	• Purge air
	• Heavy traffic driving	• Operate at fast idle in neutral intermittently to cool engine
	• Incorrect cooling system component(s) installed	• Install proper component(s)
	• Faulty thermostat	• Replace thermostat
	• Water pump shaft broken or impeller loose	• Replace water pump
	• Radiator tubes clogged	• Flush radiator
	• Cooling system clogged	• Flush system
	• Casting flash in cooling passages	• Repair or replace as necessary. Flash may be visible by removing cooling system components or removing core plugs.
	• Brakes dragging	• Repair brakes
	• Excessive engine friction	• Repair engine
	• Antifreeze concentration over 68%	• Lower antifreeze concentration percentage
	• Missing air seals	• Replace air seals
	• Faulty gauge or sending unit	• Repair or replace faulty component
	• Loss of coolant flow caused by leakage or foaming	• Repair or replace leaking component, replace coolant
	• Viscous fan drive failed	• Replace unit

Troubleshooting the Cooling System (cont.)

Problem	Cause	Solution
Low temperature indication—undercooling	• Thermostat stuck open • Faulty gauge or sending unit	• Replace thermostat • Repair or replace faulty component
Coolant loss—boilover	• Overfilled cooling system • Quick shutdown after hard (hot) run • Air in system resulting in occasional "burping" of coolant • Insufficient antifreeze allowing coolant boiling point to be too low • Antifreeze deteriorated because of age or contamination • Leaks due to loose hose clamps, loose nuts, bolts, drain plugs, faulty hoses, or defective radiator • Faulty head gasket • Cracked head, manifold, or block • Faulty radiator cap	• Reduce coolant level to proper specification • Allow engine to run at fast idle prior to shutdown • Purge system • Add antifreeze to raise boiling point • Replace coolant • Pressure test system to locate source of leak(s) then repair as necessary • Replace head gasket • Replace as necessary • Replace cap
Coolant entry into crankcase or cylinder(s)	• Faulty head gasket • Crack in head, manifold or block	• Replace head gasket • Replace as necessary
Coolant recovery system inoperative	• Coolant level low • Leak in system • Pressure cap not tight or seal missing, or leaking • Pressure cap defective • Overflow tube clogged or leaking • Recovery bottle vent restricted	• Replenish coolant to FULL mark • Pressure test to isolate leak and repair as necessary • Repair as necessary • Replace cap • Repair as necessary • Remove restriction
Noise	• Fan contacting shroud • Loose water pump impeller • Glazed fan belt • Loose fan belt • Rough surface on drive pulley • Water pump bearing worn • Belt alignment	• Reposition shroud and inspect engine mounts • Replace pump • Apply silicone or replace belt • Adjust fan belt tension • Replace pulley • Remove belt to isolate. Replace pump. • Check pulley alignment. Repair as necessary.
No coolant flow through heater core	• Restricted return inlet in water pump • Heater hose collapsed or restricted • Restricted heater core • Restricted outlet in thermostat housing • Intake manifold bypass hole in cylinder head restricted • Faulty heater control valve • Intake manifold coolant passage restricted	• Remove restriction • Remove restriction or replace hose • Remove restriction or replace core • Remove flash or restriction • Remove restriction • Replace valve • Remove restriction or replace intake manifold

NOTE: *Immediately after shutdown, the engine enters a condition known as heat soak. This is caused by the cooling system being inoperative while engine temperature is still high. If coolant temperature rises above boiling point, expansion and pressure may push some coolant out of the radiator overflow tube. If this does not occur frequently it is considered normal.*

Troubleshooting the Serpentine Drive Belt

Problem	Cause	Solution
Tension sheeting fabric failure (woven fabric on outside circumference of belt has cracked or separated from body of belt)	• Grooved or backside idler pulley diameters are less than minimum recommended	• Replace pulley(s) not conforming to specification
	• Tension sheeting contacting (rubbing) stationary object	• Correct rubbing condition
	• Excessive heat causing woven fabric to age	• Replace belt
	• Tension sheeting splice has fractured	• Replace belt
Noise (objectional squeal, squeak, or rumble is heard or felt while drive belt is in operation)	• Belt slippage	• Adjust belt
	• Bearing noise	• Locate and repair
	• Belt misalignment	• Align belt/pulley(s)
	• Belt-to-pulley mismatch	• Install correct belt
	• Driven component inducing vibration	• Locate defective driven component and repair
	• System resonant frequency inducing vibration	• Vary belt tension within specifications. Replace belt.
Rib chunking (one or more ribs has separated from belt body)	• Foreign objects imbedded in pulley grooves	• Remove foreign objects from pulley grooves
	• Installation damage	• Replace belt
	• Drive loads in excess of design specifications	• Adjust belt tension
	• Insufficient internal belt adhesion	• Replace belt
Rib or belt wear (belt ribs contact bottom of pulley grooves)	• Pulley(s) misaligned	• Align pulley(s)
	• Mismatch of belt and pulley groove widths	• Replace belt
	• Abrasive environment	• Replace belt
	• Rusted pulley(s)	• Clean rust from pulley(s)
	• Sharp or jagged pulley groove tips	• Replace pulley
	• Rubber deteriorated	• Replace belt
Longitudinal belt cracking (cracks between two ribs)	• Belt has mistracked from pulley groove	• Replace belt
	• Pulley groove tip has worn away rubber-to-tensile member	• Replace belt
Belt slips	• Belt slipping because of insufficient tension	• Adjust tension
	• Belt or pulley subjected to substance (belt dressing, oil, ethylene glycol) that has reduced friction	• Replace belt and clean pulleys
	• Driven component bearing failure	• Replace faulty component bearing
	• Belt glazed and hardened from heat and excessive slippage	• Replace belt
"Groove jumping" (belt does not maintain correct position on pulley, or turns over and/or runs off pulleys)	• Insufficient belt tension	• Adjust belt tension
	• Pulley(s) not within design tolerance	• Replace pulley(s)
	• Foreign object(s) in grooves	• Remove foreign objects from grooves
	• Excessive belt speed	• Avoid excessive engine acceleration
	• Pulley misalignment	• Align pulley(s)
	• Belt-to-pulley profile mismatched	• Install correct belt
	• Belt cordline is distorted	• Replace belt
Belt broken (Note: identify and correct problem before replacement belt is installed)	• Excessive tension	• Replace belt and adjust tension to specification
	• Tensile members damaged during belt installation	• Replace belt
	• Belt turnover	• Replace belt
	• Severe pulley misalignment	• Align pulley(s)
	• Bracket, pulley, or bearing failure	• Replace defective component and belt

Troubleshooting the Serpentine Drive Belt (cont.)

Problem	Cause	Solution
Cord edge failure (tensile member exposed at edges of belt or separated from belt body)	• Excessive tension • Drive pulley misalignment • Belt contacting stationary object • Pulley irregularities • Improper pulley construction • Insufficient adhesion between tensile member and rubber matrix	• Adjust belt tension • Align pulley • Correct as necessary • Replace pulley • Replace pulley • Replace belt and adjust tension to specifications
Sporadic rib cracking (multiple cracks in belt ribs at random intervals)	• Ribbed pulley(s) diameter less than minimum specification • Backside bend flat pulley(s) diameter less than minimum • Excessive heat condition causing rubber to harden • Excessive belt thickness • Belt overcured • Excessive tension	• Replace pulley(s) • Replace pulley(s) • Correct heat condition as necessary • Replace belt • Replace belt • Adjust belt tension

3. When fitting the compression gauge adaptor to the cylinder head, make sure the bleeder of the gauge (if equipped) is closed.

4. When reinstalling the injector assemblies, install new washers underneath each injector.

Engine

REMOVAL AND INSTALLATION

6-231 and 6-252

1. Scribe marks around the hood hinges and hinge bracket, so the hood can be installed easily. Remove the hood.

2. Disconnect both battery cables.

3. Drain the coolant into a suitable container; it can be reused if in fresh condition.

CAUTION: *When draining the coolant, keep in mind that cats and dogs are attracted by the ethylene glycol antifreeze, and are quite likely to drink any that is left in an uncovered container or in puddles on the ground. This will prove fatal in sufficient quantity. Always drain the coolant into a sealable container. Coolant should be reused unless it is contaminated or several years old.*

4. Remove the air cleaner.

5. Disconnect the radiator and heater hoses and position them out of the way.

6. On air conditioned vehicles, disconnect the A/C compressor ground wire from the mounting bracket. Remove the electrical connector from the compressor clutch, remove the compressor-to-mounting bracket attaching bolts and position the compressor out of the way. Do NOT disconnect the refrigerant hoses.

CAUTION: *If the compressor refrigerant lines do not have enough slack to position the compressor out of the way without discharging the refrigerant lines, the air conditioning system will have to be discharged by a trained air conditioning specialist. Under no circumstances should an untrained person attempt to disconnect the air conditioning refrigerant lines. These lines contain pressurized R-12 refrigerant, which can be extremely dangerous.*

7. Remove the fan blade, pulleys and belts.

8. Remove the fan shroud assembly.

9. Remove the power steering pump-to-mounting bracket bolts and position the pump out of the way.

10. Tag, remove and plug the fuel pump hoses.

11. Tag and disconnect the vacuum lines from the engine to parts not attached to the engine. Disconnect the engine wiring harness.

12. Disconnect and tag the throttle cable, downshift cable and/or throttle valve cable at the carburetor.

13. Disconnect the transmission oil cooler lines at the transmission. Disconnect the oil and coolant sending unit switch connections at the engine.

14. Disconnect the engine-to-body ground strap at the engine.

15. Raise and support the front end of the vehicle with jackstands. Disconnect the starter cables and the cable shield from the engine.

16. Disconnect the exhaust pipes from the exhaust manifolds and support the exhaust system.

17. Remove the flywheel cover pan. Remove the flywheel-to-torque converter bolts. Using a scribe or felt tip marker, matchmark the flywheel-to-torque converter relationship for later assembly.

18. Remove the transmission-to-engine attaching bolts from the transmission bell housing.

19. Remove the cruise control bracket, if so equipped.

Standard Torque Specifications and Fastener Markings

In the absence of specific torques, the following chart can be used as a guide to the maximum safe torque of a particular size/grade of fastener.

- There is no torque difference for fine or coarse threads.
- Torque values are based on clean, dry threads. Reduce the value by 10% if threads are oiled prior to assembly.
- The torque required for aluminum components or fasteners is considerably less.

U.S. Bolts

SAE Grade Number	1 or 2			5			6 or 7		
Number of lines always 2 less than the grade number.									
Bolt Size (Inches)—(Thread)	Maximum Torque			Maximum Torque			Maximum Torque		
	Ft./Lbs.	Kgm	Nm	Ft./Lbs.	Kgm	Nm	Ft./Lbs.	Kgm	Nm
¼—20	5	0.7	6.8	8	1.1	10.8	10	1.4	13.5
—28	6	0.8	8.1	10	1.4	13.6			
⁵⁄₁₆—18	11	1.5	14.9	17	2.3	23.0	19	2.6	25.8
—24	13	1.8	17.6	19	2.6	25.7			
³⁄₈—16	18	2.5	24.4	31	4.3	42.0	34	4.7	46.0
—24	20	2.75	27.1	35	4.8	47.5			
⁷⁄₁₆—14	28	3.8	37.0	49	6.8	66.4	55	7.6	74.5
—20	30	4.2	40.7	55	7.6	74.5			
½—13	39	5.4	52.8	75	10.4	101.7	85	11.75	115.2
—20	41	5.7	55.6	85	11.7	115.2			
⁹⁄₁₆—12	51	7.0	69.2	110	15.2	149.1	120	16.6	162.7
—18	55	7.6	74.5	120	16.6	162.7			
⅝—11	83	11.5	112.5	150	20.7	203.3	167	23.0	226.5
—18	95	13.1	128.8	170	23.5	230.5			
¾—10	105	14.5	142.3	270	37.3	366.0	280	38.7	379.6
—16	115	15.9	155.9	295	40.8	400.0			
⅞—9	160	22.1	216.9	395	54.6	535.5	440	60.9	596.5
—14	175	24.2	237.2	435	60.1	589.7			
1—8	236	32.5	318.6	590	81.6	799.9	660	91.3	894.8
—14	250	34.6	338.9	660	91.3	849.8			

Metric Bolts

Relative Strength Marking	4.6, 4.8			8.8		
Bolt Markings						
Bolt Size Thread Size x Pitch (mm)	Maximum Torque			Maximum Torque		
	Ft./Lbs.	Kgm	Nm	Ft./Lbs.	Kgm	Nm
6 x 1.0	2–3	.2–.4	3–4	3–6	.4–.8	5–8
8 x 1.25	6–8	.8–1	8–12	9–14	1.2–1.9	13–19
10 x 1.25	12–17	1.5–2.3	16–23	20–29	2.7–4.0	27–39
12 x 1.25	21–32	2.9–4.4	29–43	35–53	4.8–7.3	47–72
14 x 1.5	35–52	4.8–7.1	48–70	57–85	7.8–11.7	77–110
16 x 1.5	51–77	7.0–10.6	67–100	90–120	12.4–16.5	130–160
18 x 1.5	74–110	10.2–15.1	100–150	130–170	17.9–23.4	180–230
20 x 1.5	110–140	15.1–19.3	150–190	190–240	26.2–46.9	160–320
22 x 1.5	150–190	22.0–26.2	200–260	250–320	34.5–44.1	340–430
24 x 1.5	190–240	26.2–46.9	260–320	310–410	42.7–56.5	420–550

General Engine Specifications

BUICK

Year	Engine V.I.N. Code	Engine Type (No. of cyl-C.I.D.)	Engine Manufacturer	Carb Type	Horsepower @ rpm ①	Torque @ rpm (ft. lbs.) ①	Bore x Stroke (in.)	Compression Ratio	Oil Pressure (psi @ rpm)
1975	J	8-350	Buick	4 bbl	165 @ 3800	260 @ 2200	3.800 x 3.850	8.0:1	37 @ 2600
	T	8-455	Buick	4 bbl	205 @ 3800	345 @ 2000	4.312 x 3.900	7.9:1	40 @ 2400
1976	J	8-350	Buick	4 bbl	155 @ 3400	280 @ 1800	3.800 x 3.850	8.0:1	37 @ 2600
	Y	8-455	Buick	4 bbl	205 @ 3800	345 @ 2000	4.312 x 3.900	7.9:1	40 @ 2400
1977	C	6-231	Buick	2 bbl	105 @ 3200	185 @ 2000	3.800 x 3.400	8.0:1	37 @ 2600
	Y	8-301	Pont.	2 bbl	135 @ 4000	250 @ 1600	4.000 x 3.000	8.2:1	40 @ 2600
	J	8-350	Buick	4 bbl	155 @ 3400	275 @ 1800	4.057 x 3.385	8.0:1	37 @ 2600
	R	8-350	Olds.	4 bbl	170 @ 3800	275 @ 2400	4.057 x 3.385	8.0:1	40 @ 1500
	K	8-403	Olds.	4 bbl	185 @ 3600	315 @ 2400	4.351 x 3.385	7.9:1	40 @ 1500
1978	A	6-231	Buick	2 bbl	105 @ 3400	285 @ 2000	3.800 x 3.400	8.0:1	37 @ 2600
	G	6-231	Buick	2 bbl-Turbo	150 @ 3800	245 @ 2400	3.800 x 3.400	8.0:1	37 @ 2600
	3	6-231	Buick	4 bbl-Turbo	165 @ 4000	285 @ 2800	3.800 x 3.400	8.0:1	37 @ 2600
	Y	8-301	Pont.	2 bbl	140 @ 3600	235 @ 2000	4.000 x 3.000	8.2:1	37 @ 2600
	U	8-305	Chev.	4 bbl	160 @ 4000	285 @ 2400	3.736 x 3.480	8.5:1	35-40 @ 2400
	L	8-350	Chev.	4 bbl	170 @ 3800	275 @ 2000	4.000 x 3.480	8.5:1	35-40 @ 2400
	R	8-350	Olds.	4 bbl	170 @ 3600	265 @ 2000	4.057 x 3.385	8.0:1	40 @ 1500
	X	8-350	Buick	4 bbl	155 @ 3400	280 @ 1800	3.800 x 3.850	8.0:1	37 @ 2600
	K	8-403	Olds.	4 bbl	185 @ 3600	320 @ 2000	4.351 x 3.385	8.0:1	40 @ 1500
1979	A	6-231	Buick	2 bbl	115 @ 3800	190 @ 2000	3.800 x 3.400	8.0:1	37 @ 2600
	3	6-231	Buick	4 bbl-Turbo	165 @ 4000	285 @ 2800	3.800 x 3.400	8.0:1	37 @ 2600
	Y	8-301	Pont.	2 bbl	140 @ 3600	235 @ 2000	4.000 x 3.000	8.2:1	40 @ 2000
	G	8-305	Chev.	2 bbl	140 @ 3800	270 @ 2400	3.736 x 3.480	8.5:1	35-40 @ 2400
	R	8-350	Olds.	4 bbl	170 @ 3800	275 @ 2000	4.057 x 3.385	8.0:1	40 @ 1500

General Engine Specifications (cont.)

BUICK

Year	Engine V.I.N. Code	Engine Type (No. of cyl. C.I.D.)	Engine Manufacturer	Carb Type	Horsepower @ rpm ①	Torque @ rpm (ft. lbs.) ①	Bore x Stroke (in.)	Compression Ratio	Oil Pressure (psi @ rpm)
1979	X	8-350	Buick	4 bbl	155 @ 3400	280 @ 1800	3.800 x 3.850	8.0:1	37 @ 2400
	K	8-403	Pont.	4 bbl	185 @ 3600	320 @ 2000	4.351 x 3.385	8.0:1	40 @ 1500
1980	A	6-231	Buick	2 bbl	115 @ 3800	190 @ 2000	3.800 x 3.400	8.0:1	37 @ 2400
	3	6-231	Buick	4 bbl-Turbo	165 @ 4000	265 @ 2800	3.800 x 3.400	8.0:1	37 @ 2400
	4	6-252	Buick	4 bbl	125 @ 4000	205 @ 2000	3.965 x 3.400	8.0:1	37 @ 2400
	W	8-301	Pont.	4 bbl	150 @ 4000	240 @ 2000	4.000 x 3.000	8.2:1	40 @ 2600
	N	8-350	Olds.	Diesel	120 @ 3600	220 @ 2200	4.057 x 3.385	22.5:1	37 @ 1500
	R	8-350	Olds.	4 bbl	170 @ 3800	275 @ 2000	4.057 x 3.385	8.5:1	37 @ 1500
	X	8-350	Buick	4 bbl	155 @ 3400	280 @ 1800	3.800 x 3.850	8.0:1	37 @ 2400
1981	A	6-231	Buick	2 bbl	110 @ 3800	190 @ 1600	3.800 x 3.400	8.0:1	37 @ 2400
	4	6-252	Buick	4 bbl	125 @ 4000	205 @ 2000	3.965 x 3.400	8.0:1	37 @ 2400
	Y	8-307	Olds.	4 bbl	148 @ 3800	250 @ 2400	3.800 x 3.385	8.0:1	40 @ 1500
	N	8-350	Olds.	Diesel	125 @ 3600	225 @ 1600	4.057 x 3.385	22.5:1	40 @ 1500
1982–83	A	6-231	Buick	2 bbl	110 @ 3800	190 @ 1600	3.800 x 3.400	8.0:1	37 @ 2400
	4	6-252	Buick	4 bbl	125 @ 4000	205 @ 2000	3.965 x 3.400	8.0:1	37 @ 2400
	Y	8-307	Olds.	4 bbl	150 @ 3800	260 @ 2400	3.800 x 3.385	8.5:1	30–45 @ 1500
	N	8-350	Olds.	Diesel	105 @ 3200	200 @ 1600	4.057 x 3.385	21.6:1	30–45 @ 1500
'84–'85	A	6-231	Buick	2 bbl	110 @ 3800	190 @ 1600	3.800 x 3.400	8.0:1	37 @ 2400
	4	6-252	Buick	4 bbl	125 @ 4000	205 @ 2000	3.965 x 3.400	8.0:1	37 @ 2400
	Y	8-307	Olds.	4 bbl	140 @ 3600	240 @ 1600	3.800 x 3.385	8.5:1	30 @ 1500
	N	8-350	Olds.	Diesel	105 @ 3200	200 @ 1600	4.057 x 3.385	22.5:1	30–45 @ 1500
'86–'87	A	6-231	Buick	2 bbl	110 @ 3800	190 @ 1600	3.800 x 3.400	8.0:1	37 @ 2400
	Y	8-307	Olds.	4 bbl	140 @ 3200	255 @ 2000	3.800 x 3.385	8.5:1	30–45 @ 1500
	Y	8-307	Olds.	4 bbl	140 @ 3200	225 @ 2000	3.800 x 3.385	8.0:1	30 @ 1500

OLDSMOBILE

Year	Code	Engine	Make	Carb	HP @ RPM	Torque @ RPM	Bore x Stroke	Compression	Oil Pressure
1975	K	8-350	Olds.	4 bbl	160 @ 3800	275 @ 2400	4.057 x 3.385	8.5:1	30-45
	R	8-400	Olds.	2 bbl	180 @ 3600	290 @ 2200	4.121 x 3.750	8.5:1	30-45
	S	8-400	Olds.	4 bbl	185 @ 3600	300 @ 2200	4.121 x 3.750	8.5:1	30-45
	T	8-455	Olds.	4 bbl	190 @ 3400	350 @ 2000	4.126 x 4.250	8.5:1	30-45 @ 1500
1976	R	8-350	Olds.	4 bbl	170 @ 3800	275 @ 2400	4.057 x 3.385	8.5:1	30-45
	K	8-403	Olds.	4 bbl	185 @ 3600	320 @ 2200	4.351 x 3.385	8.0:1	40
	T	8-455	Olds.	4 bbl	190 @ 3400	350 @ 2000	4.126 x 4.250	8.5:1	30-45 @ 1500
1977	C	6-231	Buick	2 bbl	105 @ 3400	185 @ 2000	3.800 x 3.400	8.0:1	37
	F	8-260	Olds.	2 bbl	110 @ 3400	205 @ 1800	3.500 x 3.385	7.5:1	40
	L	8-350	Olds.	4 bbl	170 @ 3800	275 @ 2000	4.057 x 3.385	22.5:1	30-45
	R	8-350	Chev.	4 bbl	170 @ 3800	270 @ 2400	4.057 x 3.385	8.0:1	40
	K	8-403	Olds.	4 bbl	185 @ 3600	320 @ 2200	4.351 x 3.385	8.0:1	40
1973	A	6-231	Buick	2 bbl	105 @ 3400	185 @ 2000	3.800 x 3.400	8.0:1	37
	F	8-260	Olds.	2 bbl	110 @ 3400	205 @ 1800	3.500 x 3.385	7.5:1	40
	R	8-350	Olds.	4 bbl	170 @ 3800	275 @ 2000	4.057 x 3.385	8.0:1	40
	N	8-350	Olds.	Diesel	120 @ 3600	220 @ 1800	4.057 x 3.385	22.0:1	40
	K	8-403	Olds.	4 bbl	185 @ 3600	320 @ 2200	4.351 x 3.385	8.0:1	40
1979	A	6-231	Buick	2 bbl	115 @ 3800	190 @ 2000	3.800 x 3.400	8.0:1	37 @ 2000
	F	8-260	Olds.	2 bbl	105 @ 3600	205 @ 1800	3.500 x 3.385	7.5:1	40 @ 2000
	Y	8-301	Pont.	2 bbl	135 @ 3800	240 @ 1600	4.000 x 3.000	8.2:1	35 @ 2000
	N	8-350	Olds.	Diesel	125 @ 3600	225 @ 1600	4.057 x 3.385	22.5:1	40 @ 2000
	R	8-350	Olds.	4 bbl	170 @ 3800	275 @ 2000	4.057 x 3.385	8.0:1	40 @ 2000
	K	8-403	Olds.	4 bbl	175 @ 3600	310 @ 2000	4.351 x 3.385	7.8:1	40 @ 2000
1980	A	6-231	Buick	2 bbl	110 @ 3800	190 @ 1600	3.800 x 3.400	8.0:1	37 @ 2000
	S	8-265	Pont.	2 bbl	110 @ 3400	207 @ 1800	3.74 x 3.00	8.2:1	40 @ 2000
	Y	8-307	Olds.	4 bbl	148 @ 3800	250 @ 2400	3.800 x 3.385	7.9:1	40 @ 2000

General Engine Specifications (cont.)

Year	Engine V.I.N. Code	Engine Type (No. of cyl-C.I.D.)	Engine Manufacturer	Carb Type	Horsepower @ rpm ①	Torque @ rpm (ft. lbs.) ①	Bore x Stroke (in.)	Compression Ratio	Oil Pressure (psi @ rpm)
OLDSMOBILE									
1980	R	8-350	Olds.	4 bbl	170 @ 3800	275 @ 2000	4.057 x 3.385	8.0:1	40 @ 2000
	N	8-350	Olds.	Diesel	125 @ 3600	225 @ 1600	4.057 x 3.385	22.5:1	40 @ 2000
1981	A	6-231	Buick	2 bbl	110 @ 3800	190 @ 1600	3.800 x 3.400	8.0:1	37 @ 2000
	4	6-252	Buick	4 bbl	125 @ 4000	205 @ 2000	3.965 x 3.400	8.0:1	37 @ 2400
	F	8-260	Olds.	2 bbl	105 @ 3600	205 @ 1800	3.500 x 3.385	7.5:1	40 @ 1500
	Y	8-307	Olds.	4 bbl	148 @ 3800	250 @ 2400	3.800 x 3.385	8.0:1	40 @ 1500
	N	8-350	Olds.	Diesel	125 @ 3600	225 @ 1600	4.057 x 3.385	22.5:1	40 @ 1500
1982—83	A	6-231	Buick	2 bbl	110 @ 3800	190 @ 1600	3.800 x 3.400	8.0:1	37 @ 2000
	4	6-252	Buick	4 bbl	125 @ 4000	205 @ 2000	3.965 x 3.400	8.0:1	37 @ 2400
	F	8-260	Olds.	2 bbl	105 @ 3600	205 @ 1800	3.500 x 3.385	7.5:1	40 @ 1500
	Y	8-307	Olds.	4 bbl	148 @ 3800	250 @ 2400	3.800 x 3.385	8.0:1	40 @ 1500
	N	8-350	Olds.	Diesel	125 @ 3600	225 @ 1600	4.057 x 3.385	22.5:1	40 @ 1500
1984—85	A	6-231	Buick	2 bbl	110 @ 3800	190 @ 1600	3.800 x 3.400	8.0:1	37 @ 2400
	Y	8-307	Olds.	4 bbl	140 @ 3600	240 @ 1600	3.800 x 3.385	8.5:1	30 @ 1500
	N	8-350	Olds.	Diesel	105 @ 3200	200 @ 1600	4.06 x 3.39	22.5:1	30—45 @ 1500
1986—87	Y	8-307	Olds.	4 bbl	140 @ 3600	240 @ 1600	3.800 x 3.385	8.5:1	30 @ 1500
1988—90	Y	8-307	Olds.	4 bbl	140 @ 3600	225 @ 2000	3.800 x 3.385	8.0:1	30 @ 1500
PONTIAC									
1975	R	8-400	Pont.	2 bbl	170 @ 3600	315 @ 2000	4.12 x 3.75	8.0:1	55-60 @ 2600
	S	8-400	Pont.	4 bbl	185 @ 4000	320 @ 2400	4.12 x 3.75	8.0:1	55-60 @ 2600
	W	8-455	Pont.	4 bbl	200 @ 3600	355 @ 2400	4.15 x 4.21	8.0:1	55-60 @ 2600
1976	P	8-350	Pont.	4 bbl	175 @ 4000	280 @ 2000	3.876 x 3.750	7.6:1	55-60 @ 2600

Year	Code	Engine	Mfr	Carb	HP @ rpm	Torque @ rpm	Bore x Stroke	Compression	Oil Pressure
	R	8-400	Pont.	2 bbl	170 @ 4000	305 @ 2000	4.121 x 3.750	7.6:1	55–60 @ 2600
	S	8-400	Pont.	4 bbl	185 @ 3600	310 @ 1600	4.121 x 3.750	7.6:1	55–60 @ 2600
	K	8-403	Olds.	4 bbl	185 @ 3600	320 @ 2200	4.351 x 3.385	8.0:1	35–40 @ 2400
	W	8-455	Pont.	4 bbl	200 @ 3500	330 @ 2000	4.152 x 4.210	7.6:1	55–60 @ 2600
1977	R	8-350	Olds.	4 bbl	170 @ 3800	275 @ 2000	4.057 x 3.385	8.0:1	32–40
	P	8-350	Pont.	4 bbl	170 @ 4000	275 @ 1800	3.876 x 3.750	7.6:1	30–45 @ 2400
	K	8-403	Olds.	4 bbl	185 @ 3600	320 @ 2200	4.351 x 3.385	8.0:1	35–40 @ 2400
1978	A	6-231	Buick	2 bbl	105 @ 3200	185 @ 2000	3.800 x 3.400	8.0:1	37 @ 2600
	Y	8-301	Pont.	2 bbl	135 @ 4000	250 @ 1600	4.000 x 3.000	8.2:1	35–40 @ 2600
	W	8-301	Pont.	4 bbl	150 @ 4000	265 @ 1600	4.000 x 3.000	8.2:1	35–40 @ 2600
	X	8-350	Buick	4 bbl	290 @ 1600	165 @ 4000	3.800 x 3.850	8.0:1	37 ②
	R	8-350	Olds.	4 bbl	280 @ 1600	160 @ 4000	4.057 x 3.385	7.9:1	30–45 @ 1500
	L	8-350	Chev.	4 bbl	170 @ 3800	270 @ 2400	4.000 x 3.480	8.2:1	30–45 @ 2400
	Z	8-400	Pont.	4 bbl	180 @ 3600	325 @ 1600	4.120 x 3.750	7.7:1	35–40 @ 2600
	K	8-403	Olds.	4 bbl	180 @ 3400	315 @ 2200	4.351 x 3.385	7.9:1	30–45 @ 1500
1979	A	6-231	Buick	2 bbl	115 @ 3800	190 @ 2000	3.800 x 3.400	8.2:1	34
	Y	8-301	Pont.	2 bbl	140 @ 3600	235 @ 2000	4.000 x 3.000	8.1:1	35–40
	W	8-301	Pont.	4 bbl	150 @ 4000	240 @ 2000	4.000 x 3.000	8.1:1	35–40
	G	8-305	Chev.	2 bbl	140 @ 3800	270 @ 2400	3.736 x 3.480	8.5:1	40
	H	8-305	Chev.	4 bbl	160 @ 3800	235 @ 2400	3.736–3.480	8.5:1	40
	L	8-350	Chev.	4 bbl	160 @ 3800	260 @ 2400	4.000 x 3.480	8.5:1	40
	X	8-350	Buick	4 bbl	155 @ 3400	280 @ 1800	3.800 x 3.850	8.0:1	35
	R	8-350	Olds.	4 bbl	170 @ 3800	275 @ 2000	4.057 x 3.385	8.0:1	35
	Z	8-400	Pont.	4 bbl	180 @ 3600	325 @ 1600	4.120 x 3.750	7.7:1	35–40 @ 2600
	K	8-403	Olds.	4 bbl	185 @ 3600	320 @ 2200	4.351 x 3.385	8.0:1	40
1980	A	6-231	Buick	2 bbl	115 @ 3800	188 @ 2000	3.800 x 3.400	8.0:1	37
	S	8-265	Pont.	2 bbl	120 @ 3600	210 @ 1600	3.750 x 3.000	8.0:1	40 @ 2600

General Engine Specifications (cont.)

Year	Engine V.I.N. Code	Engine Type (No. of cyl- C.I.D.)	Engine Manufacturer	Carb Type	Horsepower @ rpm ①	Torque @ rpm (ft. lbs.) ①	Bore x Stroke (in.)	Compression Ratio	Oil Pressure (psi @ rpm)
				PONTIAC					
1980	W	8-301	Pont.	4 bbl	150 @ 4000	240 @ 2000	4.000 x 3.000	8.2:1	40 @ 2600
	R	8-350	Olds.	4 bbl	160 @ 3800	260 @ 2400	4.000 x 3.480	8.5:1	40
	N	8-350	Olds.	Diesel	125 @ 3600	225 @ 1600	4.057 x 3.385	22.5:1	40 @ 1500
1981	A	6-231	Buick	2 bbl	115 @ 3800	188 @ 2000	3.800 x 3.400	8.0:1	37
	S	8-265	Pont.	2 bbl	120 @ 3600	210 @ 1600	3.750 x 3.000	8.0:1	40 ②
	Y	8-307	Olds.	4 bbl	148 @ 3800	250 @ 2400	3.800 x 3.385	8.0:1	40 @ 1500
	N	8-350	Olds.	Diesel	105 @ 3200	205 @ 1600	4.057 x 3.385	22.5:1	40 @ 1500
'82	A	6-231	Buick	2 bbl	110 @ 3800	190 @ 1600	3.800 x 3.400	8.0:1	37
	4	6-252	Buick	4 bbl	125 @ 4000	205 @ 2000	3.965 x 3.400	8.0:1	37
	N	8-350	Olds.	Diesel	105 @ 3200	200 @ 1600	4.057 x 3.385	21.6:1	40
'83	A	6-231	Buick	2 bbl	110 @ 3800	190 @ 1600	3.800 x 3.400	8.0:1	37
	H	8-305	Chev.	4 bbl	150 @ 3800	240 @ 2400	3.735 x 3.480	8.6:1	45
	N	8-350	Olds.	Diesel	105 @ 3200	200 @ 1600	4.057 x 3.385	21.6:1	40 @ 1500
1984–85	A	6-231	Buick	2 bbl	110 @ 3800	190 @ 1600	3.800 x 3.400	8.0:1	37 @ 2400
	4	6-252	Buick	4 bbl	125 @ 4000	205 @ 2000	3.965 x 3.400	8.0:1	37 @ 2400
	H	8-305	Chev.	4 bbl	150 @ 4000	240 @ 2400	3.74 x 3.48	8.6:1	32–40 @ 2000
	Y	8-307	Olds.	4 bbl	140 @ 3600	240 @ 1600	3.800 x 3.385	8.5:1	30 @ 1500
	N	8-350	Olds.	Diesel	105 @ 3200	200 @ 1600	4.06 x 3.39	22.5:1	30–45 @ 1500
1981–87	A	6-231	Buick	2 bbl	110 @ 3800	190 @ 1600	3.800 x 3.400	8.0:1	37 @ 2400
	Y	8-307	Olds.	4 bbl	140 @ 3600	240 @ 1600	3.800 x 3.385	8.5:1	30 @ 1500
1988–89	Y	8-307	Olds.	4 bbl	140 @ 3600	225 @ 2000	3.800 x 3.385	8.0:1	30 @ 1500

C.I.D.—Cubic Inch Displacement
① Horsepower and torque are SAE net figures. They are measured at the rear of the transmission with all accessories installed and operating. Since the figures vary when a given engine is installed in different models, some are representative rather than exact.
② Above 2600 rpm

Valve Specifications

Year	Engine No. Cyl. Displacement (cu in.)	Seat Angle (deg)	Face Angle (deg)	Spring Text Pressure ▲ (lbs. @ in.)	Spring Installed Height (in.)	Stem to Guide Clearance (in.) Intake	Stem to Guide Clearance (in.) Exhaust	Stem Diameter (in.) Intake	Stem Diameter (in.) Exhaust
	BUICK								
1975–76	8-350 Buick	45	45	164 @ 1.34	14⁷/₆₄	.0015–.0035	.0015–.0032	.3407	.3409
	8-455 Buick	45	45	177 @ 1.45	15⁷/₆₄	.0015–.0035	.0015–.0032	.3725	.3727
1977	6-231 Buick	45	45	164 @ 1.34	14⁷/₆₄	.0015–.0035	.0015–.0035	.340	.340
	8-301 Pont.	46	45	170 @ 1.26	14⁷/₆₄	.0017–.0020	.0015–.0020	.340	.340
	8-350 Olds.	45 ②	44 ②	180 @ 1.34	14⁷/₆₄	.0010–.0027	.0015–.0032	.3425	.3420
	8-350 Buick	45	45	180 @ 1.34	14⁷/₆₄	.0015–.0032	.0015–.0032	.3730	.3727
	8-403 Olds.	45 ②	44 ②	180 @ 1.27	14⁷/₆₄	.0010–.0027	.0015–.0032	.3425	.3420
1978	6-231 Buick	45	45	168 @ 1.327	14⁷/₆₄	.0015–.0032	.0015–.0032	.3405–.3412	.3405–.3412
	8-301 Pont.	46	45	170 @ 1.260	14⁷/₆₄	.0017–.0020	.0017–.0020	.3400–.3405	.3400–.3405
	8-305 Chev.	46	45	200 @ 1.160	④	.0010–.0037	.0010–.0037	.3410–.3417	.3410–.3417
	8-350 Buick	45	45	③	14⁷/₆₄	.0015–.0035	.0015–.0032	.3720–.3730	.3723–.3730
	8-350 Chev.	46	45	200 @ 1.160	④	.0010–.0037	.0010–.0037	.3410–.3417	.3410–.3417
	8-350 Olds.	45 ②	44 ②	187 @ 1.270	14⁷/₆₄	.0010–.0027	.0015–.0032	.3425–.3432	.3420–.3427
	8-403 Olds.	45 ②	44 ②	187 @ 1.270	14⁷/₆₄	.0010–.0027	.0015–.0032	.3425–.3432	.3420–.3427
1979–'81	6-231 Buick	45	45	164 @ 1.34 ⑤	14⁷/₆₄	.0015–.0035	.0015–.0032	.3401–.3412	.3405–.3412
	6-252 Buick	45	45	164 @ 1.34 ⑤	14⁷/₆₄	.0015–.0035	.0015–.0032	.3401–.3412	.3405–.3412
	8-301 Pont.	46	45	170 @ 1.27	14⁷/₆₄	.0017–.0020	.0017–.0020	.3400	.3400
	8-305 Chev.	46	45	200 @ 1.25	12³/₃₂	.0010–.0020	.0010–.0047	.3414	.3414
	8-307 Olds.	⑦	⑧	③	14⁷/₆₄	.0010–.0027	.0015–.0032	.3428	.3424
	8-350 Buick	45	45	③	14⁷/₆₄	.0015–.0035	.0015–.0032	.3720–.3730	.3723–.3730
	8-350 Olds.	45 ②	44 ②	187 @ 1.27	14⁷/₆₄	.0010–.0027	.0015–.0032	.3425–.3432	.3420–.3427
	8-350 Olds. Diesel	45 ②⑨	44 ②⑨	151 @ 130 ⑥	14⁷/₆₄	.0010–.0027	.0015–.0032	.3425–.3432	.3420–.3427
	8-403 Olds.	45 ②	44 ②	187 @ 1.27	14⁷/₆₄	.0010–.0027	.0015–.0032	.3425–.3432	.3420–.3427

Valve Specifications (cont.)

Year	Engine No. Cyl. Displacement (cu in.)	Seat Angle (deg)	Face Angle (deg)	Spring Text Pressure▲ (lbs. @ in.)	Spring Installed Height (in.)	Stem to Guide Clearance (in.) Intake	Stem to Guide Clearance (in.) Exhaust	Stem Diameter (in.) Intake	Stem Diameter (in.) Exhaust
1982–83	6-231 Buick	45	45	164 @ 1.34 ⑤	1 47/64	.0015–.0035	.0015–.0032	.3401–.3412	.3405–.3412
	6-252 Buick	45	45	164 @ 1.34 ⑤	1 47/64	.0015–.0035	.0015–.0032	.3401–.3412	.3405–.3412
	8-307 Olds.	44 ②	45 ②	187 @ 1.27	1 47/64	.0010–.0027	.0015–.0032	.3425–.3432	.3400–.3427
	8-350 Diesel	45 ②	44 ②	210 @ 1.23	1 47/64	.0010–.0027	.0015–.0032	.3425–.3432	.3400–.3427
1984–85	6-231 Buick	46	45	56–69 @ 1.73	1 47/64	.0015–.0035	.0015–.0032	.3401–.3412	.3405–.3412
	6-252 Buick	46	45	56–69 @ 1.73	1 47/64	.0015–.0035	.0015–.0032	.3401–.3412	.3405–.3412
	8-307 Olds.	45 ②	44 ②	76–84 @ 1.67	1 43/64	.0010–.0027	.0015–.0032	.3425–.3432	.3420–.3427
	8-350 Diesel	45 ②	44 ②	85–95 @ 1.67	1 43/64	.0010–.0027	.0015–.0032	.3424–.3432	.3420–.3428
1986–87	6-231 Buick	45	45	88 @ 1.57	1 47/64	.0010–.0027	.0015–.0032	.3425–.3432	.3420–.3412
1988–90	8-307 Olds.	45 ②	44 ②	76–84 @ 1.670	1 43/64	.0010–.0027	.0015–.0032	.3425–.3432	.3420–.3427
	8-307 Olds.	45 ②	44 ②	76–84 @ 1.670	1 43/64	.0010–.0027	.0015–.0032	.3425–.3432	.3420–.3427
OLDSMOBILE									
1975	8-350 Olds.	⑪	⑫	187 @ 1.27	1 21/32	.0010–.0027	.0015–.0032	.3429	.3424
	8-400 Olds.	⑬	⑭	N.A.	1 21/32	.0016–.0033	.0021–.0038	.3419–.3412	.3414–.3407
	8-455 Olds.	⑪	⑫	187 @ 1.27	1 21/32	.0010–.0027	.0015–.0032	.3429	.3424
1976	8-350, 403	⑪	⑫	187 @ 1.27	1 21/32	.0010–.0027	.0015–.0032	.3429	.3424
	8-455	⑪	⑫	187 @ 1.27	1 21/32	.0010–.0027	.0015–.0032	.3429	.3424
1977	6-231 Buick	45	45	168 @ 1.327	1 46/64	.0015–.0032	.0015–.0032	.3409	.3409
	8-260 Olds.	⑪	⑫	187 @ 1.270	1 43/64	.0010–.0027	.0015–.0032	.3429	.3427
	8-350 Chev.	46	45	200 @ 1.250	1 45/64	.0010–.0037	.0010–.0037	.3414	.3414
	8-350 Olds.	⑪	⑫	187 @ 1.270	1 43/64	.0010–.0027	.0015–.0032	.3429	.3427
	8-403 Olds.	⑪	⑫	187 @ 1.270	1 43/64	.0010–.0027	.0015–.0032	.3429	.3427
1978	6-231 Buick	45	45	168 @ 1.327	1 47/64	.0015–.0032	.0015–.0032	.3405–.3412	.3405–.3412
	8-260 Olds.	⑪	⑫	187 @ 1.270	1 47/64	.0010–.0027	.0015–.0032	.3425–.3432	.3420–.3427

Year	Engine	Seat Angle (deg)	Face Angle (deg)	Spring Test Pressure (lbs. @ in.)	Spring Installed Height (in.)	Stem to Guide Clearance Intake (in.)	Stem to Guide Clearance Exhaust (in.)	Stem Diameter Intake (in.)	Stem Diameter Exhaust (in.)
	8-350 Olds.	⑪	⑫	187 @ 1.270	1 47/64	.0010–.0027	.0015–.0032	.3425–.3432	.3420–.3427
	8-350 Diesel	⑪	⑫	151 @ 1.300	1 47/64	.0010–.0027	.0015–.0032	.3425–.3432	.3420–.3427
	8-403 Olds.	⑪	⑫	187 @ 1.270	1 47/64	.0010–.0027	.0015–.0032	.3425–.3432	.3420–.3427
1979–'80	6-231 Buick	45	⑪	168 @ 1.340	1 47/64	.0015–.0035	.0015–.0032	.3402–.3412	.3405–.3412
	8-260 Olds.	⑪	⑫	187 @ 1.270	1 43/64	.0010–.0027	.0015–.0032	.3425–.3432	.3420–.3427
	8-265 Pont.	46	45	170 @ 1.290	1 43/64	.0010–.0027	.0010–.0027	.3425	.3425
	8-301 Pont.	46	45	170 @ 1.290	1 43/64	.0010–.0027	.0010–.0027	.3425	.3425
	8-307 Olds.	⑪	⑫	187 @ 1.270	1 43/64	.0010–.0027	.0015–.0032	.3429	.3424
	8-350 Olds.	⑪	⑫	187 @ 1.270	1 43/64	.0010–.0027	.0015–.0032	.3425–.3432	.3420–.3427
	8-350 Diesel	⑪	⑫	151 @ 1.300	1 47/64	.0010–.0027	.0015–.0032	.3425–.3432	.3420–.3427
	8-403 Olds.	⑪	⑫	187 @ 1.270	1 43/64	.0010–.0027	.0015–.0032	.3425–.3432	.3420–.3427
'81	6-231 Buick	45	45	182 @ 1.340	1 47/64	.0015–.0035	.0015–.0032	.3407	.3409
	6-252 Buick	45	45	182 @ 1.340	1 47/64	.0015–.0035	.0015–.0032	.3407	.3409
	8-260 Olds.	⑪	⑫	187 @ 1.270	1 43/64	.0010–.0027	.0015–.0032	.3429	.3424
	8-307 Olds.	⑪	⑫	187 @ 1.270	1 43/64	.0010–.0027	.0015–.0032	.3429	.3424
	8-350 Diesel	⑪	⑫	210 @ 1.22	1 43/64	.0010–.0027	.0015–.0032	.3429	.3424
'82	6-231 Buick	45	45	182 @ 1.340	1 47/64	.0015–.0035	.0015–.0032	.3407	.3409
	6-252 Buick	45	45	182 @ 1.340	1 47/64	.0015–.0035	.0015–.0032	.3407	.3409
	8-260 Olds.	⑪	⑫	187 @ 1.270	1 43/64	.0010–.0027	.0015–.0032	.3429	.3424
	8-307 Olds.	⑪	⑫	187 @ 1.270	1 43/64	.0010–.0027	.0015–.0032	.3429	.3429
	8-350 Diesel	⑪	②	210 @ 1.22	1 43/64	.0010–.0027	.0015–.0032	.3429	.3429
1983	6-231 Buick	45	45	182 @ 1.340	1 47/64	.0015–.0035	.0015–.0032	.3407	.3409
	6-252 Buick	45	45	182 @ 1.340	1 47/64	.0015–.0035	.0015–.0032	.3407	.3409
	8-260 Olds.	⑪	⑫	187 @ 1.270	1 43/64	.0010–.0027	.0015–.0032	.3429	.3424
	8-307 Olds.	⑪	⑫	187 @ 1.270	1 43/64	.0010–.0027	.0015–.0032	.3429	.3429
	8-350 Diesel	⑪	②	210 @ 1.22	1 43/64	.0010–.0027	.0015–.0032	.3429	.3429
1984–85	6-231 Buick	46	45	59–69 @ 1.73	1 47/64	.0015–.0035	.0015–.0032	.3401–.3412	.3405–.3412
	8-307 Olds.	45 ②	45 ②	76–84 @ 1.67	1 43/64	.0010–.0027	.0015–.0032	.3425–.3432	.3420–.3427
	8-350 Diesel	45 ②	45 ②	85–95 @ 1.67	1 49/64	.0010–.0027	.0015–.0032	.3424–.3432	.3420–.3428

Valve Specifications (cont.)

Year	Engine No. Cyl. Displacement (cu in.)	Seat Angle (deg)	Face Angle (deg)	Spring Text Pressure▲ (lbs. @ in.)	Spring Installed Height (in.)	Stem to Guide Clearance (in.)		Stem Diameter (in.)	
						Intake	Exhaust	Intake	Exhaust
					OLDSMOBILE				
1986–87	8-307 Olds.	45 ②	44 ②	76-84 @ 1.670	1 43/64	.0010-.0027	.0015-.0032	.3425-.3432	.3420-.3427
1988–90	8-307 Olds.	45 ②	44 ②	76-84 @ 1.670	1 43/64	.0010-.0027	.0015-.0032	.3425-.3432	.3420-.3427
					PONTIAC				
1975	8-400 2 bbl	45	44	139 @ 1.17	1 9/16	.0016-.0033	.0021-.0038	.3416	.3411
	8-400 4 bbl	45	44	143 @ 1.15	1 19/32	.0016-.0033	.0021-.0038	.3416	.3411
	8-455 4 bbl	45	44	143 @ 1.15	1 9/16	.0016-.0033	.0021-.0038	.3416	.3411
1976	8-350	30	29	131 @ 1.18 ⑧	1 19/32	.0016-.0033	.0021-.0038	.3416	.3411
	8-400 2 bbl	30	29	134 @ 1.16 ⑨	1 19/32	.0016-.0033	.0021-.0038	.3416	.3411
	8-400 4 bbl	30	29	135 @ 1.13 ⑩	1 9/16	.0016-.0033	.0021-.0038	.3416	.3411
	8-403 Olds.	⑪	⑫	187 @ 1.270	1 43/64	.0010-.0027	.0015-.0032	.3429	.3427
	8-455 Pont.	30	29	135 @ 1.16	1 9/16	.0016-.0033	.0021-.0038	.3416	.3411
1977	8-350 Olds.	45 ⑪	44 ⑫	180 @ 1.34	1 47/64	.0010-.0027	.0015-.0032	.3425	.3420
	8-350 Pont.	30	29	131 @ 1.19	1 19/32	.0016-.0033	.0021-.0038	.3416	.3411
	8-403 Olds.	45 ⑪	44 ⑫	180 @ 1.34	1 47/64	.0010-.0027	.0015-.0032	.3425	.3420
1978	6-231 Buick	45	45	182 @ 1.34	1 47/64	.0015-.0032	.0015-.0032	.3402-.3412	.3405-.3412
	8-301 Pont.	46	45	165 @ 1.29	1 2/3	.0010-.0027	.0010-.0027	.3425	.3425
	8-350 Buick	45	45	180 @ 1.34	1 47/64	.0015-.0032	.0015-.0035	.3720-.3730	.3723-.3730
	8-350 Olds.	45 ⑪	46 ⑫	190 @ 1.27	1 47/64	.0010-.0027	.0015-.0032	.3425-.3432	.3420-.3427
	8-350 Chev.	46	45	200 @ 1.16	④	.0010-.0037	.0010-.0037	.3410-.3417	.3410-.3417
	8-400 Pont.	30	29	135 @ 1.18	1 27/50	.0016-.0033	.0021-.0038	.3425	.3425
	8-403 Olds.	45 ⑪	46 ⑫	190 @ 1.27	1 47/64	.0010-.0027	.0015-.0032	.3425-.3432	.3420-.3427
1979–'80	6-231 Buick	45	45	182 @ 1.340	1 23/32	.0015-.0032	.0015-.0032	.3402-.3412	.3405-.3412
	8-265 Pont.	46	45	170 @ 1.290	1 43/64	.0010-.0027	.0010-.0027	.3425	.3425

Year	Engine	Seat Angle (deg)	Face Angle (deg)	Spring Test Pressure (lbs @ in)	Spring Installed Height (in)	Stem-to-Guide Clearance Intake (in)	Stem-to-Guide Clearance Exhaust (in)	Stem Diameter Intake (in)	Stem Diameter Exhaust (in)
	8-301 Pont.	46	45	170 @ 1.290	$1\frac{43}{64}$	.0010-.0027	.0010-.0027	.3425	.3425
	8-350 Olds.	45[2]	44[2]	187 @ 1.270	$1\frac{47}{64}$	.0010-.0027	.0015-.0032	.3425-.3432	.3420-.3427
	8-350 Buick	45	45	[3]	$1\frac{47}{64}$	.0015-.0035	.0015-.0032	.3720-.3730	.3723-.3730
	8-350 Diesel	45[2][9]	44[2][9]	151 @ 1.30 [6]	$1\frac{47}{64}$	.0010-.0027	.0015-.0032	.3425-.3432	.3420-.3427
	8-400 Pont.	30	29	135 @ 1.18	$1\frac{27}{50}$	.0016-.0033	.0021-.0038	.3425	.3425
	8-403 Olds.	45[2]	44[2]	187 @ 1.27	$1\frac{47}{64}$	.0010-.0027	.0015-.0032	.3425-.3432	.3420-.3427
'81	6-231 Buick	45	45	182 @ 1.340[15]	$1\frac{47}{64}$	.0015-.0035	.0015-.0032	.3401-.3412	.3405-.3412
	8-265 Pont.	46	45	175 @ 1.290	$1\frac{43}{64}$	.0010-.0027	.0010-.0027	.3418-.3425	.3418-.3425
	8-307 Olds.	[11]	[9]	187 @ 1.270	$1\frac{43}{64}$	.0010-.0027	.0015-.0032	.3429	.3424
	8-350 Olds. Diesel	45[2][9]	44[2][9]	210 @ 1.300	$1\frac{43}{64}$	.0010-.0027	.0015-.0032	.3429	.3424
'82	6-231 Buick	45	45	182 @ 1.340	$1\frac{23}{32}$	.0015-.0032	.0015-.0032	.3402-.3412	.3405-.3412
	6-252 Buick	45	45	182 @ 1.340	$1\frac{47}{64}$	.0015-.0032	.0015-.0032	.3407	.3407
	8-350 Diesel	45[2][9]	44[2][9]	210 @ 1.300	$1\frac{43}{64}$	.0010-.0027	.0015-.0032	.3429	.3424
'83	6-231 Buick	45	45	182 @ 1.340	1.72	.0015-.0032	.0015-.0032	.3402-.3412	.3405-.3412
	8-305 Chev.	46	45	200 @ 1.25	1.70	.0010-.0027	.0010-.0027	.3414	.3414
	8-350 Diesel	45[2][9]	44[2][9]	210 @ 1.22	$1\frac{43}{64}$	.0010-.0027	.0015-.0032	.3429	.3429
1984-85	6-231 Buick	46	45	56-69 @ 1.73	$1\frac{47}{64}$	.0015-.0035	.0015-.0032	.3401-.3412	.3405-.3412
	8-305 Chev.	46	45	76-84 @ 1.70	$1\frac{45}{64}$	.0010-.0027	.0010-.0027	—	—
	8-350 Diesel	45[2]	44[2]	85-95 @ 1.67	$1\frac{43}{64}$	.0010-.0027	.0015-.0032	.3424-.3432	.3420-.3428
1986	6-231 Buick	46	45	76-84 @ 1.70	$1\frac{46}{64}$	.0010-.0027	.0010-.0027	.3462-.3412	.3405-.3412
	8-307 Olds.	46[16]	45[16]	76-84 @ 1.670	$1\frac{43}{64}$	.0010-.0027	.0015-.0032	.3425-.3432	.3420-.3426
1987	6-231 Buick	46	45	62-72 @ 1.727	$1\frac{46}{64}$	.0015-.0035	.0010-.0027	.3412-.3401	.3412-.3412
	8-307 Olds.	45[2]	44[2]	76-84 @ 1.670	$1\frac{43}{64}$	.0010-.0027	.0015-.0032	.3425-.3432	.3420-.3426
1988-89	8-307 Olds.	45[2]	44[2]	76-84 @ 1.670	$1\frac{43}{64}$	.0010-.0027	.0015-.0032	.3425-.3432	.3420-.3426

▲ Spring test pressures with valve open

N.A. Not Available

[1] Exhaust—175 @ 1.34
[2] Exhaust valve seat angle—31, exhaust valve face angle—30
[3] Intake: 180 @ 1.340 Exhaust: 177 @ 1.450
[4] Intake: $1\frac{23}{32}$ Exhaust: $1\frac{19}{32}$
[5] Exhaust: 182 @ 1.34
[6] 1981 210 @ 1.23
[7] Intake—45°, exhaust—59°
[8] Intake—56°, exhaust—60°
[9] 1981 Seat: Intake—45°, exhaust—59° Face: Intake—46°, exhaust—60°
[10] Exhaust: 140 @ 1.12
[11] Intake—45°, exhaust 31°
[12] Intake—44°, exhaust 30°
[13] Intake—30°, exhaust 45°
[14] Intake—29°, exhaust 44°
[15] Intake: 164 @ 1.34
[16] Exhaust—59°, 60°
[17] Exhaust—31°, 30°

Piston and Ring Specifications

Year	Engine	Piston-Bore Clearance	Ring Side Clearance			Ring Gap		
			Top Compression	Bottom Compression	Oil Control	Top Compression	Bottom Compression	Oil Control
			BUICK					
1975–76	8-350	.0008–.0014	.003–.005	.003–.005	.0035 Max.	.013–.023	.015–.035	.015–.035
	8-455	.0010–.0016	.003–.005	.003–.005	.0035 Max.	.013–.023	.013–.023	.015–.035
1977	6-231	.0008–.0020	.003–.005	.003–.005	.0035 Max.	.013–.023	.015–.035	.015–.035
	8-301	.0025–.0033	.0015–.0035	.0015–.0035	.0015–.0035	.010–.020	.010–.020	.035
	8-350 Olds.	.0010–.0020	.0020–.0040	.0020–.0040	.0015–.0035	.010–.023	.010–.023	.015–.055
	8-350 Buick	.0008–.0014	.003–.005	.003–.005	.0035 Max.	.013–.023	.013–.023	.015–.055
	8-403	.0010–.0020	.002–.004	.002–.004	.0015–.0035	.010–.023	.010–.023	.015–.055
1978	6-231	.0008–.0020 [1]	.003–.005	.003–.005	.0035	.010–.020	.010–.020	.015–.035
	8-301	.0025–.0033	.0015–.0035	.0015–.0035	.0015–.0035	.010–.020	.010–.020	.035
	8-305	.0027 Max.	.0012–.0042	.0012–.0042	.0020–.0080	.010–.030	.010–.035	.015–.065
	8-350 Olds.	.0010–.0020	.0020–.0040	.0020–.0040	.0015–.0035	.010–.023	.010–.023	.015–.055
	8-350 Chev.	.0027 Max.	.0012–.0042	.0012–.0042	.0020–.0080	.010–.030	.010–.035	.015–.056
	8-350 Buick	.0008–.0020 [1]	.003–.005	.003–.005	.0035	.010–.020	.010–.020	.015–.035
	8-403	.0010–.0020	.0020–.0040	.0020–.0040	.0015–.0035	.010–.023	.010–.023	.015–.035
1979–80	6-231	.0008–.0020 [1]	.003–.005	.003–.005	.0035	.013–.023	.013–.023	.015–.035
	6-252	.0008–.0020 [1]	.003–.005	.003–.005	.0035	.013–.023	.013–.023	.015–.035
	8-301	.0025–.0023	.0015–.0035	.0015–.0035	.0015–.0035	.010–.020	.010–.020	.035 Max.
	8-305	.0027 Max.	.0012–.0032	.0012–.0032	.0020–.0080	.010–.030	.010–.035	.015–.065
	8-350 Olds.	.0010–.0027	.0020–.0040	.0020–.0040	.001–.005	.010–.023 [2]	.010–.023 [2]	.015–.055
	8-350 Buick	.0008–.0020 [1]	.0030–.0050	.0030–.0050	.0035	.010–.020 [3]	.010–.020 [3]	.015–.055
	8-350 Diesel	.005–.006	.004–.006	.0018–.0038	.001–.005	.015–.025	.015–.025	.015–.055
	8-403	.0010–.0020	.0020–.0040	.0020–.0040	.001–.005	.010–.023 [2]	.010–.023 [2]	.015–.055
1981–83	6-231	.0008–.0020 [1]	.003–.005	.003–.005	.0035	.013–.023	.013–.023	.015–.035

Year	Engine	Piston Clearance	Ring Gap — Top Comp.	Ring Gap — Bottom Comp.	Ring Gap — Oil Control	Ring Side Clearance — Top Comp.	Ring Side Clearance — Bottom Comp.	Ring Side Clearance — Oil Control
	6-252	.0008–.0020[1]	.013–.023	.013–.023	.015–.035	.003–.005	.003–.005	.0035
	8-307	.0075–.00175	.019–.019[4]	.009–.019[4]	.015–.055[5]	.0020–.0040	.0020–.0040	.0010–.0050
	8-350 Diesel	.005–.006	.015–.025	.015–.025	.015–.055	.004–.006	.004–.006	.001–.005
1984–85	6-231	.0008–.0020[6]	.013–.023	.013–.023	.015–.035	.003–.005	.003–.005	.0035
	6-252	.0008–.0020[6]	.013–.023	.013–.023	.015–.035	.003–.005	.003–.005	.0035
	8-307	.00075–.00175[6]	.009–.020	.009–.019	.01–.025	.002–.004	.002–.004	.001–.005
	8-350 Diesel	.0035–.0045[6]	.019–.027	.013–.021	.015–.035	.005–.007	.003–.005	.001–.005
1986–87	6-231	.0013–.0035	.010–.020	.010–.020	.015–.035	.003–.005	.003–.005	.0035
	8-307	.00075–.00175	.009–.019	.009–.019	.015–.055	.0018–.0038	.0018–.0038	.001–.005
1988–90	8-307	.00075–.00175	.009–.019	.009–.019	.015–.055	.0018–.0038	.0018–.0038	.001–.005

OLDSMOBILE

Year	Engine	Piston Clearance	Ring Gap — Top Comp.	Ring Gap — Bottom Comp.	Ring Gap — Oil Control	Ring Side Clearance — Top Comp.	Ring Side Clearance — Bottom Comp.	Ring Side Clearance — Oil Control
1975	8-350	.0010–.0020	.010–.023	.010–.023	.015–.055	.0020–.0040	.0020–.0040	.001–.005
	8-455	.0010–.0020	.010–.023	.010–.023	.015–.055	.0020–.0040	.0020–.0040	.002–.008
1976	8-350	.0010–.0020	.010–.023	.010–.023	.015–.055	.0020–.0040	.0020–.0040	.001–.005
	8-403	.0010–.0020	.010–.023	.010–.023	.015–.055	.0020–.0040	.0020–.0040	.001–.005
	8-455	.0010–.0020	.010–.023	.010–.023	.015–.055	.0020–.0040	.0020–.0040	.002–.008
1977	8-231	.0013–.0035[6]	.013–.023	.015–.035	.015–.035	.0030–.0050	.0030–.0050	.0035
	8-260	.0010–.0020	.010–.023	.010–.023	.015–.055	.0020–.0040	.0020–.0040	.005–.011
	8-350 Olds.	.0010–.0020	.010–.023	.010–.023	.015–.055	.0020–.0040	.0020–.0040	.001–.005
	8-350 Chev.	.0027 Max.	.010–.030	.010–.035	.015–.065	.0012–.0032	.0012–.0032	.001–.005
	8-403	.0010–.0020	.010–.023	.010–.035	.015–.055	.0020–.0040	.0020–.0040	.001–.005
1978–80	6-231	.0013–.0035[6]	.010–.020[7]	.010–.020	.015–.035	.0030–.0050	.0030–.0050	.0035
	8-260	.0008–.0018[6][8]	.010–.020[12]	.010–.020[12]	.015–.055[9]	.0020–.0040	.0020–.0040	.005–.011
	8-265	.0017–.0041[6]	.010–.022	.010–.028	.010–.055	.0015–.0035	.0015–.0035	.0015–.0035
	8-301	.0025–.0033	.010–.020	.010–.020	.0035	.0015–.0035	.0015–.0035	.0015–.0035
	8-307	.0005–.0015	.009–.019	.009–.019	.015–.055	.0020–.0040	.0020–.0040	.001–.005
	8-350 Olds.	.0008–.0018[8]	.013–.023[10][2]	.013–.023[10][2]	.015–.055	.0020–.0040	.0020–.0040	.001–.005
	8-350 Diesel	.005–.006[6]	.015–.025	.015–.025	.015–.055	.005–.007	.0018–.0038	.0010–.0050

Piston and Ring Specifications (cont.)

Year	Engine	Piston-Bore Clearance	Ring Side Clearance			Ring Gap		
			Top Compression	Bottom Compression	Oil Control	Top Compression	Bottom Compression	Oil Control
OLDSMOBILE								
1978–80	8-403	.0005–.0015 ⑪	.0020–.0040	.0020–.0040	.001–.005	.010–.020 ⑫	.010–.020 ⑫	.015–.055
1981–83	6-231	.0016–.0038 ⑥	.0030–.0050	.0030–.0050	.0035	.013–.023	.013–.023	.015–.055
	6-252	.0016–.0038 ⑥	.0030–.0050	.0030–.0050	.0035	.013–.023	.013–.023	.015–.055
	8-260	.0008–.0018 ⑥	.0020–.0040	.0020–.0040	.005–.011	.010–.020 ⑫	.010–.020 ⑫	.015–.055 ⑨
	8-307	.0008–.0018	.0020–.0040	.0020–.0040	.001–.005	.009–.019	.009–.019	.015–.055
	8-350 Diesel	.005–.006 ⑥	.005–.007	.0018–.0038	.0010–.0050	.015–.025	.015–.025	.015–.055
1984–85	6-231	.008–.020	.003–.005	.003–.005	.0035	.013–.023	.013–.023	.015–.035
	8-307	.00075–.00175	.002–.004	.002–.004	.001–.005	.009–.019 ④	.009–.019 ④	.015–.055 ⑤
	8-350	.0035–.0045 ①	.005–.007	.003–.005	.001–.005	.019–.027	.013–.021	.010–.022
1986–87	8-307	.00075–.00175	.0018–.0038	.0018–.0038	.001–.005	.009–.019	.009–.019	.015–.055
1988–90	8-307	.00075–.00175	.0018–.0038	.0018–.0038	.001–.005	.009–.019	.009–.019	.015–.055
PONTIAC								
1975	8-400	.0029–.0037 ①	.0015–.005	.0015–.005	.0015–.005	.010–.030	.010–.030	.015–.055
	8-455	.0021–.0029	.0020–.0040	.0020–.0040	.0021–.0031	.010–.023	.010–.023	.015–.055
1976	8-350 Pont.	.0029–.0037	.0015–.0050	.0015–.0050	.0015–.0050	.010–.020	.010–.020	.015–.035
	8-400	.0029–.0037	.0015–.0035	.0015–.0035	.0015–.0050	.010–.020	.010–.020	.015–.055
	8-403	.0008–.0018	.0020–.0040	.0020–.0040	.001–.005	.010–.023	.010–.023	.015–.055
	8-455	.0021–.0029	.0015–.0050	.0015–.0050	.0015–.0050	.010–.030	.010–.030	.015–.055
1977	8-350 Pont.	.0025–.0033 ⑭	.0015–.0050	.0015–.005	.0015–.0050	.010–.020	.010–.020	.015–.035
	8-360 Olds.	.0008–.0018 ⑮	.0020–.0040	.0020–.0040	.001–.005	.010–.020	.010–.020	.015–.055
	8-403	.0008–.0018 ①	.0020–.0040	.0020–.0040	.001–.005	.010–.020	.010–.020	.015–.055
1978–80	6-231	.0008–.0020 ①	.0030–.0050	.0030–.0050	.0035 Max.	.013–.023	.013–.023	.015–.035
	8-265	.0017–.0041 ⑥	.0015–.0035	.0015–.0035	.0015–.0035	.010–.022	.010–.028	.010–.055

Year	Engine							
	8-301	.0025–.0033⑭	.0015–.0035	.0015–.0035	.0015–.0035	.010–.020	.010–.020	.0035
	8-350 Olds.	.0008–.0018⑮	.020–.0040	.020–.0040	.001–.005	.013–.023⑩②	.013–.023⑩②	.015–.055
	8-350 Chev.	.0007–.0017⑭	.0012–.0032	.0010–.0032⑯	.0020–.0070⑰	.010–.030	.010–.035	.015–.055
	8-350 Buick	.0013–.0035⑥	.0030–.0050	.0030–.0050	.0035 Max.	.010–.020	.010–.020	.015–.055
	8-350 Diesel	.005–.006⑥	.005–.007	.018–.0038	.0010–.0050	.015–.025	.015–.025	.015–.055
	8-400	.0025–.0033⑭	.0015–.0035	.0015–.0035	.0015–.0035	.009–.019	.005–.015	.015–.035
	8-403	.0008–.0018⑮	.0020–.0040	.0020–.0040	.001–.005	.010–.020	.010–.020	.015–.055
1981–83	6-231	.0016–.0038⑥	.0030–.0050	.0030–.0050	.0035 Max.	.013–.023	.013–.023	.015–.035
	6-252	.0016–.0038⑥	.0030–.0050	.0030–.0050	.0035 Max.	.010–.020	.010–.020	.015–.055
	8-265	.0017–.0041⑥	.0015–.0035	.0015–.0035	.0015–.0035	.010–.022	.010–.028	.010–.050
	8-305	.0012 Max.	.0012–.0032	.0012–.0032	.002–.007	.010–.020	.010–.025	.015–.055
	8-307	.0006–.0018	.0020–.0040	.0020–.0040	.001–.005	.009–.019	.009–.019	.015–.055
	8-350 Diesel	.005–.006	.005–.007	.005–.007	.001–.005	.015–.025	.015–.025	.015–.055
1984–85	6-231	.001–.002①	.003–.005	.003–.005	.0035	.01–.02	.01–.02	.015–.035
	8-305	.00075–.00175①	.012–.0032	.012–.0032	.002–.007	.01–.02	.01–.02	.01–.055
	8-350 Diesel	.0035–.0045①	.005–.007	.003–.005	.001–.005	.019–.027	.013–.021	.015–.055
1986–87	6-231	.0013–.0035	.003–.005	.003–.005	.0035	.010–.020	.010–.020	.015–.055
	8-307	.00075–.00175	.0018–.0038	.0018–.0038	.001–.005	.009–.019	.009–.019	.015–.055
1988–89	8-307	.0075–.00175	.0018–.0038	.0018–.0038	.001–.005	.009–.019	.009–.019	.015–.055

① Measured at skirt top
② w/Sealed Power rings—.010–.020 in.
③ 1980—.013–.023 in.
④ w/TRW rings .010–.020 in.
⑤ w/TRW rings .010–.025
⑥ Measured at bottom of skirt
⑦ 1980—.013–.023 in. in both rings
⑧ 1978—.0010–.0020 in.
⑨ 1979–81 260 w/Muskegon rings—.010–.035 in.
⑩ 1978—.010–.023 in.
⑪ 1978—.0010–.0022 in.
⑫ w/Sealed Power rings—.009–.019 in.
⑭ Measured 1.1 in. from the top of piston
⑮ Measured ¾ in. below piston pin centerline
⑯ 1978 .0012–.0027 in.
⑰ 1978 .0050 Max.

Crankshaft and Connecting Rod Specifications

BUICK

Year	Engine Displacement (cu In.)	Crankshaft					Connecting Rod	
		Main Brg. Journal Dia	Main Brg. Oil Clearance	Shaft End-Play	Thrust on No.	Journal Diameter	Oil Clearance	Side Clearance
1975–78	8-350	2.9995	.0004–.0015	.002–.006	3	1.9995	.0005–.0026	.006–.026
	8-455	3.2500	.0007–.0018	.003–.009	3	2.2491	.0005–.0026	.005–.025
1977	231 Buick	2.4995	.0004–.0015	.004–.008	2	2.000	.0005–.0026	.006–.027
	3.01 Pont.	3.0000	.0004–.0020	.003–.009	4	2.000	.0005–.0025	.006–.027
	8-350 Buick	2.9995	.0004–.0015	.002–.006	3	1.9995	.0005–.0026	.006–.026
	350 Olds.	2.4990	.0005–.0021 ①	.004–.014	3	2.1243	.0004–.0015	.006–.027
	403 Olds.	2.4990	.0005–.0021 ①	.004–.014	3	2.1243	.0005–.0026	.006–.020
1978	6-231 Buick	2.4995	.0003–.0017	.004–.008	2	2.2487–2.2495	.0005–.0026	.006–.027
	8-301 Pont.	3.0000	.0004–.0020	.006–.022	4	2.2500	.0005–.0025	.006–.022
	8-305 Chev.	③	.0010–.0035 ⑤	.002–.006	5	2.0990–2.1000	.0010–.0035	.008–.014
	8-350 Buick	3.0000	.0004–.0015	.003–.009	3	1.9910–2.0000	.0005–.0026	.006–.027
	8-350 Chev.	③	.0010–.0035 ⑤	.002–.006	5	2.0990–2.1000	.0010–.0035	.008–.014
	8-350 Olds.	2.4985–2.4995 ②	.0005–.0021 ①	.0035–.0135	3	2.1238–2.1248	.0004–.0033	.006–.020
	8-403 Olds.	2.4985–2.4995 ②	.0005–.0021 ①	.0035–.0135	3	2.1238–2.1248	.0004–.0033	.006–.020
1979–81	6-231 Buick	2.4995	.0003–.0018	.003–.009	2	2.2487–2.2498	.0005–.0026	.006–.023
	6-252 Buick	2.4995	.0003–.0018	.003–.009	2	2.2487–2.2495	.0005–.0026	.006–.023
	8-301 Pont.	3.000	.0004–.0020	.006–.022	4	2.250	.0005–.0025	.006–.022
	8-305 Chev.	③	④	.002–.006	5	2.099–2.100	.0035 max	.006–.014
	8-307 Olds.	2.49793–2.4998 ⑥	.0005–.0021 ①	.0035–.0135	3	2.1238–2.1248	.0004–.0033	.006–.020
	8-350 Buick	3.000	.0004–.0015	.003–.009	3	1.991–2.000	.0005–.0026	.006–.023
	8-350 Olds.	2.4985–2.4995 ②	.0005–.0021 ①	.0035–.0135	3	2.1238–2.1248	.0004–.0033	.006–.020
	8-350 Olds. Diesel	2.9993–3.003	.0005–.0021 ①	.0035–.0135	3	2.2495–2.2500	.0005–.0026	.006–.020
	8-403 Olds.	2.4985–2.4995	.0005–.0021 ①	.0035–.0135	3	2.1238–2.1248	.0005–.0033	.006–.020

Year	Engine						
1982–83	6-231 Buick	2.4995	.0003–.0018	.003–.009	2	2.2487–2.2495	.0005–.0026	.006–.023
	6-252 Buick	2.4995	.0003–.0018	.003–.009	2	2.2487–2.2495	.0005–.0026	.006–.023
	8-307 Olds.	2.4973–2.4998 ⑥	.0005–.0021 ①	.0035–.0135	3	2.1238–2.1248	.0004–.0033	.006–.020
	8-350 Olds. Diesel	2.9993–3.003	.0005–.0021 ①	.0035–.0135	3	2.2495–2.2500	.0005–.0026	.006–.020
1984–85	6-231 Buick	2.4995	.0003–.0018	.003–.009	2	2.2487–2.2495	.0005–.0026	.005–.026
	6-252 Buick	2.4995	.0003–.0018	.003–.009	2	2.2487–2.2495	.0005–.0026	.005–.026
	8-307 Olds.	2.4990–2.4995 ⑫	.0015–.0021 ⑧	.0035–.0135	3	2.1238–2.1248	.0004–.0033	.006–.020
	8-350 Olds. Diesel	2.9993–3.0003	.0021–.005 ⑨	.0035–.0135	3	2.1238–2.1248	.0005–.0025	.006–.020
1986–87	6-231 Buick	2.4995	.0003–.0018	.003–.009	2	2.2487–2.2495	.0005–.0026	.004–.015
	8-307 Olds.	2.4985–2.4995 ⑬	.0005–.0021 ⑧	.0035–.0135	3	2.1238–2.1248	.0004–.0033	.006–.020
1988–90	8-307 Olds.	2.4985–2.4995 ⑬	.0005–.0021 ⑧	.0035–.0135	3	2.1238–2.1248	.0004–.0033	.006–.020

OLDSMOBILE

Year	Engine						
1975	8-350 Olds.	2.4990 ⑦	.0005–.0021 ⑧	.004–.008	3	2.1238–2.1248	.0004–.0033	.006–.020
	8-400 Olds.	3.000	.0002–.0017	.0035–.0085	4	2.250	.0005–.0026	.012–.017
	8-455 Olds.	2.9998	.0005–.0021 ⑨	.004–.008	3	2.4988–2.4998	.0004–.0033	.006–.020
1976	8-350 Olds.	2.4990 ⑦	.0005–.0021 ⑧	.004–.008	3	2.1238–2.1248	.0004–.0033	.006–.020
	8-403 Olds.	2.4990 ⑦	.0005–.0021 ⑨	.004–.008	3	2.1238–2.1248	.0004–.0033	.006–.020
	8-455 Olds.	2.9998	.0005–.0021 ⑦	.004–.008	3	2.4988–2.4998	.0004–.0033	.006–.020
1977	6-231 Buick	2.4995	.0004–.0015	.004–.008	2	1.9960	.0005	.006–.027
	8-260 Olds.	2.4990 ⑦	.0005–.0021	.004–.014	3	2.21243	.0004–.0033	.006–.020
	8-350 Chev.	⑥	.0035 max ⑤	.002–.006	3	2.1995	.0035 max	.008–.014
	8-350 Olds.	2.4990 ⑦	.0005–.0021	.004–.014	3	2.21243	.0004–.0033	.006–.020
1978	6-231 Buick	2.4995	.0003–.0017	.004–.008	2	2.2487–2.2495	.0005–.0026	.006–.027
	8-260 Olds.	2.4985–2.4995 ②	.0005–.0021 ⑧	.0035–.0135	3	2.1238–2.1248	.0004–.0033	.006–.020
	8-350 Olds.	2.4985–2.4995 ②	.0005–.0021 ⑧	.0035–.0135	3	2.1238–2.1248	.0004–.0033	.006–.020
	8-350 Diesel	2.9993–3.0003	.0005–.0021 ⑧	.0035–.0135	3	2.1238–2.1248	.0005–.0026	.006–.020
	8-403 Olds.	2.4985–2.4995 ②	.0005–.0021 ⑧	.0035–.0135	3	2.1238–2.1248	.0004–.0033	.006–.020
1979–80	6-231 Buick	2.4995	.0003–.0018	.004–.008	2	2.2487–2.2495	.0005–.0026	.006–.027

Crankshaft and Connecting Rod Specifications (cont.)

Year	Engine Displacement (cu in.)	Crankshaft				Connecting Rod		
		Main Brg. Journal Dia	Main Brg. Oil Clearance	Shaft End-Play	Thrust on No.	Journal Diameter	Oil Clearance	Side Clearance
OLDSMOBILE								
1979–80	8-260 Olds.	2.4985–2.4995 ②	.0005–.0021 ⑧	.0035–.0135	3	2.1238–2.1248	.0004–.0033	.006–.020
	8-265 Pont.	3.000	.0004–.0020	.006–.022	4	2.000	.0005–.0025	.006–.022
	8-301 Pont.	3.000	.0002–.0020	.003–.009	4	2.250 ⑪	.0005–.0025	.006–.022
	8-305 Chev.	③	⑩	.002–.006	3	2.0986–2.0998	.003 max	.006–.014
	8-307 Olds.	2.4985–2.4995 ②	.0005–.0021 ⑧	.0035–.0135	3	2.1238–2.1248	.0004–.0033	.006–.020
	8-350 Olds.	2.4985–2.4995 ②	.0005–.0021 ⑧	.0035–.0135	3	2.1238–2.1248	.0004–.0033	.006–.020
	8-350 Diesel	2.9993–3.0003	.0005–.0021 ⑧	.0035–.0135	3	2.1238–2.1248	.0005–.0026	.006–.020
	8-403 Olds.	2.4985–2.4995 ②	.0005–.0021 ⑧	.0035–.0135	3	2.1238–2.1248	.0004–.0033	.006–.020
1981–83	6-231 Buick	2.4995	.0003–.0018	.011–.003	2	2.2487–2.2495	.0005–.0026	.006–.023
	6-252 Buick	2.4955	.0003–.0018	.011–.003	2	2.2487–2.2495	.0005–.0026	.006–.023
	8-260 Olds.	2.5000	.0005–.0021 ⑧	.0035–.0135	3	2.1238–2.1248	.0004–.0033	.006–.020
	8-307 Olds.	2.4990–2.4995	.0005–.0021 ⑧	.0035–.0135	3	2.1238–2.1248	.0004–.0033	.006–.020
	8-350 Diesel	2.9993–3.0003	.0005–.0021 ⑧	.0035–.0135	3	2.24995–2.500	.0005–.0026	.006–.020
1984–85	6-231	2.4995	.0003–.0018	.003–.009	2	2.2487–2.2495	.0005–.0026	.005–.026
	8-307	2.4990–2.4995 ⑫	.0015–.0021 ⑧	.0035–.0135	3	2.1238–2.1248	.0004–.0033	.006–.020
	8-350 Diesel	2.9993–3.0003	.0009–.0021 ⑨	.0035–.0135	3	2.1238–2.1248	.0005–.0025	.006–.020
1986–87	8-307	2.4985–2.4995 ⑬	.0005–.0021 ⑧	.0035–.0135	3	2.1238–2.1248	.0004–.0033	.006–.020
1988–90	8-307 Olds.	2.4985–2.4995 ⑬	.0005–.0021 ⑧	.0035–.0135	3	2.1238–2.1248	.0004–.0033	.006–.020
PONTIAC								
1975	8-400	3.000	.0002–.0017	.0030–.0090	4	2.250	.0005–.0025	.012–.017
	8-455	3.250	.0005–.0021	.0030–.0090	4	2.250	.0010–.0031	.012–.017
1976	8-350 Pont.	3.000	.0002–.0017	.0030–.0090	4	2.250	.0005–.0025	.012–.017
	8-400	3.000	.0002–.0017	.0030–.0090	4	2.250	.0005–.0025	.012–.017

Year	Engine							
1977	8-403	2.4990 ⑦	.0005-.0021 ⑧	.004-.008	3	2.1238-2.1248	.0004-.0033	.006-.020
	8-455	3.250	.0005-.0021	.0030-.0090	4	2.250	.0005-.0025	.012-.017
	8-350 Pont.	3.000	.0002-.0017	.0035-.0085	4	2.250	.0005-.0026	.002-.017
	8-350 Olds.	2.500	.0005-.0021 ⑧	.0035-.0085	3	2.124	.0005-.0026	.006-.020
	8-403	2.500	.0005-.0021 ⑧	.0035-.0085	3	2.124	.0005-.0026	.006-.020
1978-80	6-231	2.4995-2.5000	.0003-.0017	.003-.009	2	2.2487-2.2495	.0005-.0026	.006-.020
	8-265	3.00	.0002-.0018	.003-.009	4	2.000	.0005-.0025	.006-.022
	8-301	3.0000	.0004-.0020	.003-.009	4	2.2500	.0005-.0025	.006-.022
	8-350 Olds.	2.4985-2.4995 ⑬	.0005-.0021 ⑧	.0035-.0135	3	2.1238-2.1248	.0004-.0033	.006-.020
	8-350 Chev.	③	⑭	.002-.007	5	2.0990-2.1000	.0013-.0035	.006-.016
	8-350 Buick	3.0000-3.0005	.0004-.0015	.003-.009	3	1.9910-2.0000	.0005-.0026	.006-.027 ⑮
1981	8-350 Diesel	2.9993-3.0003	.0005-.0021 ⑧	.0035-.0135	3	2.1238-2.1248	.0005-.0026	.006-.020
	8-400	3.0000	.0002-.0020	.003-.009	4	2.2500	.0005-.0025	.006-.022
	8-403	2.4985-2.4995	.005-.0021 ⑧	.0035-.0135	5	2.1238-2.1248	.0009-.0026	.006-.020
	6-231	2.4995-2.5000	.0003-.0018	.003-.009	2	2.2487-2.2495	.0005-.0026	.006-.023
	8-265	3.0000	.0002-.0018	.0035-.0085	4	2.0000	.0005-.0026	.006-.022
	8-307	2.4985-2.4995 ⑬	.0005-.0021 ⑧	.0035-.0135	3	2.1238-2.1248	.0004-.0033	.006-.020
	8-350 Diesel	2.9993-3.0003	.0005-.0021 ⑧	.0035-.0135	3	2.1238-2.1248	.0005-.0026	.006-.020
1982	6-231	3.4955	.0003-.0018	.003-.011	2	2.2491	.0005-.0026	.006-.023
	6-252	2.4955	.0003-.0018	.003-.009	2	2.2487-2.2495	.0005-.0026	.006-.023
	8-350	3.000	.0005-.0021 ⑧	.0035-.0135	3	2.1243	.0005-.0026	.006-.020
1983-84	6-231	3.4955	.0003-.0018	.003-.011	2	2.2491	.0005-.0026	.006-.020
	8-305 Chev.	③	⑯	.002-.00	5	2.0995	.0013-.0035	.006-.016
	8-350 Diesel	2.9998	.0005-.0021	.0035-.0135	3	2.1243	.0005-.0026	.006-.020
1985	6-231	3.4995	.0003-.0018	.003-.011	2	2.1243	.0005-.0026	.006-.020
	8-305 Chev.	③	⑯	.002-.006	5	2.0995	.0013-.0035	.006-.016
	8-350 Diesel	2.9998	.0005-.0021	.0035-.0135	3	2.1243	.0005-.0026	.006-.020

Crankshaft and Connecting Rod Specifications (cont.)

| Year | Engine Displacement (cu in.) | Crankshaft | | | | | Connecting Rod | | |
		Main Brg. Journal Dia	Main Brg. Oil Clearance	Shaft End-Play	Thrust on No.	Journal Diameter	Oil Clearance	Side Clearance
PONTIAC								
1986–87	6-231 Buick	2.4988–2.4998	.0003–.0018	.003–.011	2	2.2487–2.2495	.0005–.0026	.004–.015
	8-307 Olds.	2.4985–2.4995 ⑬	.0005–.0021 ⑧	.0035–.0135	3	2.1238–2.1248	.0004–.0033	.006–.020
1988–89	8-307 Olds.	2.4985–2.4995 ⑬	.0005–.0021 ⑧	.0035–.0135	3	2.1238–2.1248	.0004–.0033	.006–.020

Note: Side clearance is total for 2 rods
① Number five main bearing clearance—.0015–.0031
② —1: 2.4988–2.4998
③ #1: 2.4484–2.4493 2,3,4: 2.4481–2.4490 #5: 2.4479–2.4488
④ 1979 #1: .0020, all others .0035. 1980: #1: .0015, #2,3,4: .0025, #5: .0035
⑤ #1: .0020 max.
⑥ 2.4990–2.4995 (#2,3,4,5)
⑦ #1: 2.4993 in.
⑧ #5: .0015–.0031 in.
⑨ #5: .0020–.0034 in.
⑩ Front—.001–.0015
Intermediate—.001–.0025
Rear—.0025–.0035
⑪ Diameter may also be 2.240
⑫ #1: 2.4973–2.4998
⑬ #1: 2.4988–2.4998
⑭ #1: .001–.0015 #2,3,4: .001–.0025 #5: .0025–.0035
⑮ 1979 and later: .006–.023
⑯ #1: .0008–.0020
#2: .0011–.0023
#3: .0017–.0033

Torque Specifications
(All readings in ft. lbs.)

Year	Engine	Cylinder Head Bolts	Rod Bearing Bolts	Main Bearing Bolts	Crankshaft Damper or Pulley Bolt	Flywheel to Crankshaft Bolts	Manifold	
							Intake	Exhaust
			BUICK					
1975–76	8-350 Buick	80	40	115	140	60	45	28
	8-455 Buick	100	45	115	200	60	45	28
1977	231 Buick	85	42	80 ③	310	60	40	25
	301 Pont.	90	35	60 ①	160	95	40	35
	8-350 Buick	80	40	115	175	60	45	25
	350, 403 Olds.	130 ⑤	42	80 ③	200–310	60	40 ⑤	25
1978–82	6-231 Buick	80	40	100	225 ②	60	45	25
	6-252 Buick	80	40	100	225 ②	60	45	25
	8-301 Pont.	90	35	60 ①	160	95	40	35
	8-305 Chev.	65	45	70	60	60	30	20
	8-350 Buick	80	40	100	225 ②	60	45	25
	8-350 Chev.	65	45	70	60	60	30	20
	8-307, 350, 403 Olds.	130 ⑤	42	80 ③	255 ②	60	40 ⑤	25
	8-350 Olds. Diesel	130 ⑤	42	120	200–310 ②	60	40 ⑤	25
1983–85	6-231 Buick	80	40	100	225	60	45	25
	6-252 Buick	80	40	100	225	60	45	25
	8-307 Olds.	125	42	80 ③	200–310	60	45	25
	8-350 Diesel	130	42	120	200–310	60	45	25
1986–87	6-231 Buick	25 ⑨	40	135	135	60	45	20
	8-307 Olds.	125	42	④	200–310	60	40 ⑤	25
1988–90	8-307 Olds.	40 ⑤ ⑩	18 ⑪	④	200–310	60	40 ⑤	25
			OLDSMOBILE					
1975	8-350 Olds.	85	42	120 ④	200–310	60	40	25
	8-400 Olds.	95	43	100 ③	160	95	40	30
	8-455 Olds.	85 ⑤	42	120	200–310	60	40	25
1976	8-350, 403, 455	85 ⑤	42	120 ④	200–310	60	40	25
1977	6-231 Buick	80	40	115	175	60	45	25
	8-260 Olds.	85	42	④	200–310	60	40	25
	8-350 Chev.	65	45	70	60	60	30	20
	8-350 Olds. Diesel	130 ⑤	42	120	200–300	60	40 ⑤	25
	8-350, 403 Olds.	130 ⑤	42	④	200–310	60	40 ⑤	25
1978–81	6-231 Buick	80	40	100	225	60	45	25
	6-252 Buick	80	40	100	225	60	45	25
	8-260 Olds.	85 ⑤	42	④	200–310	60	40 ⑤	25
	8-301 Pont.	95	35	⑧	160	95	40	25
	8-307 Olds.	130 ⑤	42	④	200–310	60	40 ⑤	25
	8-350 Olds.	130 ⑤	42	④	200–310	60	40 ⑤	25
	8-350 Diesel	130 ⑤	42	120	200–310	60	40 ⑤	25

Torque Specifications (cont.)
(All readings in ft. lbs.)

Year	Engine	Cylinder Head Bolts	Rod Bearing Bolts	Main Bearing Bolts	Crankshaft Damper or Pulley Bolt	Flywheel to Crankshaft Bolts	Manifold Intake	Manifold Exhaust
				OLDSMOBILE				
1978–81	8-403 Olds.	130 ⑤	42	④	200–310	60	40 ⑤	25
1982	6-231 Buick	80	40	100	225	60	45	25
	6-252 Buick	80	40	100	225	60 ⑥	45	25
	8-260 Olds.	85 ⑤	42	④	200–310	60	40 ⑤	25
	8-307 Olds.	130 ⑤	42	④	200–310	60	40 ⑤	25
	8-350 Diesel	130 ⑤	42	120	200–310	60	40 ⑤	25
1983–85	6-231 Buick	80	40	100	225	60	45	25
	8-307 Olds.	130 ⑤	42	④	200–310	60	40 ⑤	25
	8-350 Diesel	130 ⑤	42	120	200–310	60	40 ⑤	25
1986–87	8-307 Olds.	125 ⑤	42	④	200–310	60	40 ⑤	25
1988–90	8-307 Olds.	40 ⑤⑩	18 ⑪	④	200–310	60	40 ⑤	25
				PONTIAC				
1975	8-400 Pont.	95	43	100 ③	160	95	40	30
	8-455 Pont.	95	43 ⑦	100 ③	160	95	40	30
1976	8-350 Pont.	95	43	100 ③	160	95	40	30
	8-400 Pont.	95	43	100 ③	160	95	40	30
	8-403 Olds.	130	42	80 ③	200 Min.	60	40	25
	8-455 Pont.	95	43 ⑦	100 ③	160	95	40	30
1977	8-350 Pont.	100	40	100 ③	160	95	35	40
	8-350 Olds.	130	42	80 ③	200 Min.	60	40	25
	8-403 Olds.	130	42	80 ③	200 Min.	60	40	25
1978–79	6-231 Buick	80	40	100	225	60	45	25
	8-301 Pont.	95	30	70 ⑧	160	95	35	40
	8-350 Chev.	65	45	70	60	60	30	20
	8-350 Buick	80	40	100	225	60	45	25
	8-350 Olds.	130	42	80 ③	220	60	40	25
	8-400 Pont.	95	40	100 ③	160	95	35	40
	8-403 Olds.	130	42	80 ③	220	60	40	25
1980–81	6-231 Buick	80	40	100	225	60	45	25
	8-265, 301 Pont.	95	30	⑧	160	95	35	40
	8-307 Olds.	130 ⑤	45	70 ③	200–310	60	40 ⑤	25
	8-350 Olds.	130 ⑤	45	70	200–310	60	40 ⑤	25
	8-350 Diesel	130 ⑤	42	④	200–310	60	40 ⑤	25
1982–83	6-231 Buick	80	40	100	225	60	40	25
	6-252 Buick	80	40	100	225	60	40	25
	8-305 Chev.	65	45	70	60	60	30	20
	8-350 Diesel	130 ⑤	42	④	200–310	60	40 ⑤	25
1983–84	6-231 Buick	80	40	100	225	60	45	25

Torque Specifications (cont.)

(All readings in ft. lbs.)

Year	Engine	Cylinder Head Bolts	Rod Bearing Bolts	Main Bearing Bolts	Crankshaft Damper or Pulley Bolt	Flywheel to Crankshaft Bolts	Manifold	
							Intake	Exhaust
				PONTIAC				
1983–84	8-305 Chev.	65	45	70	60	60	30	20
	8-350 Diesel	130 ⑤	42	120	200–310	60	40 ③	25
1985	6-231 Buick	80	40	100	225	60	45	25
	8-305 Chev.	65	45	70	60	60	30	20
	8-350 Diesel	130 ③	42	120	200–310	60	40 ③	25
1986–87	6-231	25 ⑨	45	100	200	60	45	20
	8-307	125 ⑤	42	80 ④	200–310	60	40	25
1988–89	8-307	40 ⑤ ⑩	18 ⑪	④	200–310	60	40 ⑤	25

① Rear main—100 ft. lbs.
② Fan pulley to balancer—20 ft. lbs.
③ Rear main—120 ft. lbs.
④ 80 ft. lbs. on No. 1—4, 120 ft. lbs. on No. 5
⑤ Dip bolt in oil before torquing
⑥ '83—48 ft. lbs.
⑦ 63 ft. lbs. on 455 S.D. engines
⑧ ⁷⁄₁₆ in. bolt—70; ½ in. bolt—100; rear main—100
⑨ See text for the complete procedure, as bolts are final-torqued using angle torquing

Camshaft Specifications

All measurements given in inches.

Year	VIN	No. Cylinder Displacement cu. in. (liter)	Journal Diameter					Lobe Lift		Bearing Clearance	Camshaft End Play
			1	2	3	4	5	In.	Ex.		
1982	A	6-231 (3.8)	1.785	1.785	1.785	1.785	—	NA	NA	.0005–.0035 ①	NA
	4	6-252 (4.1)	1.785	1.785	1.785	1.785	—	NA	NA	.0005–.0035 ①	NA
	8	8-260 (4.3)	2.0361	2.0161	1.9961	1.9761	1.9561	3.96	4.00	.0039	.011–.077
	V	6-260 (4.3)	—	2.205	2.18501	2.165	—	NA	NA	.0040	.0008–.0228
	Y	8.307 (5.0)	2.0365	2.0166	1.9965	1.9765	1.9565	4.00	4.00	.0020–.0058	.011–.077
	N	8-350 (5.7)	2.0361	2.0161	1.9961	1.9761	1.9561	NA	NA	.0039	.011–.077
1983	A	6-231 (3.8)	1.785	1.785	1.785	1.785	—	NA	NA	.0005–.0035 ①	NA
	4	6-252 (4.1)	1.785	1.785	1.785	1.785	—	NA	NA	.0005–.0035 ①	NA
	V	6-260 (4.3)	—	2.205	2.18501	2.165	—	NA	NA	.0040	.0008–.0228
	H	8-305 (5.0)	1.8682–1.8692	1.8682–1.8692	1.8682–1.8692	1.8682–1.8692	1.8682–1.8692	.234	.257	NA	.004–.012

Camshaft Specifications (cont.)
All measurements given in inches.

Year	VIN	No. Cylinder Displacement cu. in. (liter)	Journal Diameter					Lobe Lift		Bearing Clearance	Camshaft End Play
			1	2	3	4	5	In.	Ex.		
1983	Y	8-307 (5.0)	2.0365	2.0166	1.9965	1.9765	1.9565	4.00	4.00	.0020–.0058	.011–.077
	N	8-350 (5.7)	2.0361	2.0161	1.9961	1.9761	1.9561	NA	NA	.0039	.011–.077
1984	A	6-231 (3.8)	1.785	1.785	1.785	1.785	—	NA	NA	.0005–.0035 ①	NA
	4	6-252 (4.1)	1.785	1.785	1.785	1.785	—	NA	NA	.0005–.0035 ①	NA
	V	6-260 (4.3)	—	2.205	2.18501	2.165	—	NA	NA	.0040	.0008–.0228
	H	8-305 (5.0)	1.8682–1.8692	1.8682–1.8692	1.8682–1.8692	1.8682–1.8692	1.8682–1.8692	.234	.257	NA	.004–.012
	Y	8-307 (5.0)	2.0361	2.0161	1.9961	1.9761	1.9561	4.00	4.00	.0020–.0058	.011–.077
	N	8-350 (5.7)	2.0361	2.0161	1.9961	1.9761	1.9561	NA	NA	.0039	.011–.077
1985	A	6-231 (3.8)	1.785	1.785	1.785	1.785	—	NA	NA	.0005–.0035 ①	NA
	Z	6-262 (4.3)	1.8682–1.8692	1.8682–1.8692	1.8682–1.8692	1.8682–1.8692	1.8682–1.8692	.234	.257	NA	.004–.012
	H	8-305 (5.0)	1.8682–1.8692	1.8682–1.8692	1.8682–1.8692	1.8682–1.8692	1.8682–1.8692	.234	.257	NA	.004–.012
	Y	8-307 (5.7)	2.0365	2.0166	1.9965	1.9765	1.9565	.247	.251	.0020–.0058	.006–.022
	9	8-307 (5.0)	2.0361	2.0161	1.9961	1.9761	1.9561	.275	.275	.0039	.006–.022
	N	8-350 (5.7)	2.0361	1.0161	1.9961	1.9761	1.9561	NA	NA	.0039	.011–.077
1986	A	6-231 (3.8)	1.785	1.785	1.785	1.785	—	NA	NA	.0005–.0035	NA
	Z	6-262 (4.3)	1.8682–1.8692	1.8682–1.8692	1.8682–1.8692	1.8682–1.8692	1.8682–1.8692	.234	.257	NA	.004–.012
	H	8-305 (5.0)	1.8682–1.8692	1.8682–1.8692	1.8682–1.8692	1.8682–1.8692	1.8682–1.8692	.234	.257	NA	.004–.012
	Y	8-307 (5.0)	2.0365	2.0166	1.9965	1.9765	1.9565	.247	.251	.0020–.0058	.006–.022
	9	8-307 (5.0)	2.0359	2.0360	1.9959	1.9759	1.9559	.272	.274	.0038–	.006–.022
1987	A	6-231 (3.8)	1.785	1.785	1.785	1.785	—	NA	NA	.0005–.0035 ①	NA
	H	8-305 (5.0)	1.8682–1.8692	1.8682–1.8692	1.8682–1.8692	1.8682–1.8692	1.8682–1.8692	.234	.257	NA	.004–.012
	Y	8-307 (5.0)	2.0365	2.0166	1.9965	1.9765	1.9565	.247	.251	.0020–.0058	.006–.022

Camshaft Specifications (cont.)

All measurements given in inches.

Year	VIN	No. Cylinder Displacement cu. in. (liter)	Journal Diameter					Lobe Lift		Bearing Clearance	Camshaft End Play
			1	2	3	4	5	In.	Ex.		
	9	8-307 (5.0)	2.0359	2.0360	1.9959	1.9759	1.9559	.272	.274	.0038	.006–.022
1988–90	Y	8-307 (5.0)	2.0365	2.0166	1.9965	1.9765	1.9565	.247	.251	.0020–.0058	.006–.022

NA—Not available at time of publication
① No. 1—.0005–.0025

20. Remove the motor mount bolts.
21. Lower the vehicle and support the transmission with a floor jack.
22. Check to make sure that all wiring and hoses have been disconnected. Attach a lifting device to the engine and raise the engine just enough so that the engine mount through-bolts can be removed.
23. Raise the engine and transmission alter-nately until the engine can be disengaged and removed.

To install:
1. It may be necessary to alternately raise and lower the transmission to fit the motor mount through-bolts into position. Torque the through-bolt nuts to 35 ft. lbs. (48 Nm). Torque the automatic transmission-to-engine bolts to 35 ft. lbs. (48 Nm).

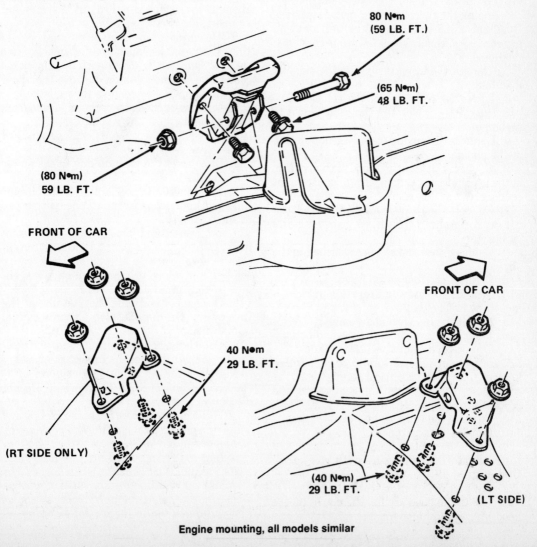

Engine mounting, all models similar

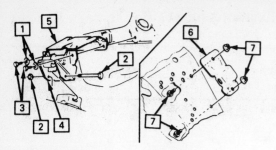

1. Flat washer (4)
2. 55 ft. lbs. (73 Nm)
3. 75 ft. lbs. (100 Nm)
4. Mount assembly
5. Shield
6. Bracket
7. 35 ft. lbs. (48 Nm)

Engine mounts—late model V8 (VIN Y)

2. Raise the vehicle and support the transmission with a floor jack.

3. Install the motor mount bolts and torque to 55 ft. lbs. (75 Nm).

4. Install the cruise control bracket, if so equipped.

5. Install the transmission-to-engine attaching bolts to the transmission bell housing.

6. Install the flywheel cover pan. Install the flywheel-to-torque converter bolts at the matchmark of the flywheel-to-torque converter relationship.

7. Connect the exhaust pipes to the exhaust manifolds.

8. Lower the front end of the vehicle. Connect the starter cables and the cable shield to the engine.

9. Connect the engine-to-body ground strap at the engine.

10. Connect the transmission oil cooler lines at the transmission. Connect the oil and coolant sending unit switch connections at the engine.

11. Connect the throttle cable, downshift cable and/or throttle valve cable at the carburetor.

12. Connect the vacuum lines attached to the engine. Connect the engine wiring harness.

13. Connect the fuel pump hoses.

14. Install the power steering pump-to-mounting bracket bolts.

15. Install the fan shroud assembly.

16. Install the fan blade, pulleys and belts.

17. On air conditioned vehicles, connect the A/C compressor ground wire to the mounting bracket. Install the electrical connector to the compressor clutch, install the compressor and bracket attaching bolts.

18. Connect the radiator and heater hoses.

19. Install the air cleaner.

20. Refill the coolant into the radiator and reservoir. **Refill the engine with the specified engine oil.**

22. Connect both battery cables.

23. Install the hood around the marks on the hood hinges and hinge bracket.

24. Start the engine and check for vacuum, coolant, oil, fuel and refrigerant leaks. Adjust timing and idle speed to specification found in Chapter 2.

V8 Including Diesel

1. Drain the cooling system.
CAUTION: *When draining the coolant, keep in mind that cats and dogs are attracted by the ethylene glycol antifreeze, and are quite likely to drink any that is left in an uncovered container or in puddles on the ground. This will prove fatal in sufficient quantity. Always drain the coolant into a sealable container. Coolant should be reused unless it is contaminated or several years old.*

2. Scribe the hinge outline on the underside of the hood. Remove the hood attaching bolts and remove the hood.

3. Disconnect the battery cables.

4. Remove the radiator and heater hoses and remove the air cleaner.

5. Remove the V-belts to avoid damaging them as the engine is pulled out of the engine compartment.

6. Disconnect the transmission oil cooler lines. Remove the fan shroud, fan belts, and pulleys. On diesels, disconnect the engine oil cooler lines at the radiator. Remove the upper radiator support and remove the radiator.

7. Disconnect the battery ground cable from the engine. Remove the radiator.

8. Disconnect the exhaust pipe or pipes or crossover at the exhaust manifolds.

9. Disconnect the vacuum line to the power brake unit.

10. Disconnect the accelerator to carburetor linkage. On diesels, disconnect the hairpin clip at the bellcrank.

11. Disconnect and label all the engine component wiring that would interfere with the engine removal, such as alternator wires, gauge sending unit wires, primary ignition wires, engine-to-body ground strap, etc.

12. Disconnect and plug the fuel line at the fuel pump. On diesels, also disconnect fuel pump wiring.

13. Detach the power steering pump and position to the left. Do not disconnect the hoses.

14. Detach the air conditioner compressor at the bracket and position to the right. Do not disconnect the hoses.
CAUTION: *If the compressor refrigerant lines do not have enough slack to position the compressor out of the way without disconnecting the refrigerant lines, the air conditioning system will have to be discharged by a trained air conditioning specialist. Under no conditions should an untrained person attempt to disconnect the air conditioning re-*

frigerant lines. These lines contain pressurized R-12 gas which can be extremely dangerous.

15. Disconnect the starter cable and remove the cable shield.

16. On 1987 vehicles, disconnect the AIR pipe-to-catalytic converter, if there is one.

17. Remove the flywheel cover pan. Remove the flywheel-to-torque converter bolts. Matchmark the flywheel and torque converter for reassembly.

18. Separate the engine from the transmission at the bell housing. On 1987 models, remove 5 of the bolts and leave the lower/left bolt in place.

19. Remove the cruise control bracket, if so equipped.

20. Support the transmission with a floor jack.

21. Attach a lifting device to the engine and raise the engine slightly so the engine mount through-bolts can be removed.

22. Check to make sure all of the wiring and hoses have been disconnected. Raise the engine enough to clear the motor mounts.

23. Raise the engine and transmission alternately until the engine can be disengaged and removed. Once both are raised slightly, remove the remaining transmission-to-engine bolt on the 1987 models.

24. Install by reversing the procedure. When installing an engine, the front mounting pad to frame bolts should be the last mounting bolts to be tightened. Note that there are dowel pins in the block that have matching holes in the bellhousing. These pins must be in almost perfect alignment before the engine will go together with the transmission. Torque the through-bolt nuts to 35 ft. lbs. (48 Nm). Torque the automatic transmission-to-engine bolts to 35 ft. lbs. (48 Nm). When tightening the three converter-to-drive plate bolts, first tighten all three finger tight, and then torque to 46 ft. lbs. (63 Nm), all three. Make sure to retighten and torque the first bolt tightened.

To install:

1. When installing an engine, the front mounting pad to frame bolts should be the last mounting bolts to be tightened.

NOTE: *There are dowel pins in the block that have matching holes in the bellhousing. These pins must be in almost perfect alignment before the engine will go together with the transmission.*

2. Torque the through-bolt nuts to 35 ft.lbs. (48 Nm). Torque the automatic transmission-to-engine bolts to 35 ft.lbs. (48 Nm). When tightening the three converter-to-drive plate bolts, first tighten all three finger tight, and then torque (46 ft.lbs. 63 Nm), all three. Make

sure to retighten and torque the first bolt tightened.

3. Lower the engine and transmission alternately until the engine can be engaged. Once both are lowered slightly, install the remaining transmission-to-engine bolts.

4. Check to make sure all of the wiring and hoses have not gotten pinched between the engine and transmission. Lower the engine enough to engage the motor mounts.

5. Using the lifting device, raise the engine slightly so the engine mount through-bolts can be installed.

6. Support the transmission with a floor jack.

7. Install the cruise control bracket, if so equipped.

8. Install and tighten the flywheel-to-torque converter bolts to 50 ft. lbs. (68 Nm). Install the flywheel cover. Matchmark the flywheel and torque converter.

9. On 1987–90 vehicles, connect the AIR pipe-to-catalytic converter, if there is one.

10. Connect the starter cable and install the cable shield.

11. Reposition the air conditioner compressor to the bracket.

12. Connect the power steering pump. Do not disconnect the hoses.

13. Connect the fuel line at the fuel pump. On diesels, also connect the fuel pump wiring.

14. Connect all the engine component wiring that would interfere with the engine installation, such as alternator wires, gauge sending unit wires, primary ignition wires, engine-to-body ground strap, etc.

15. Connect the accelerator to carburetor linkage. On diesels, connect the hairpin clip at the bellcrank.

16. Connect the vacuum line to the power brake unit.

17. Connect the exhaust pipe or pipes or crossover at the exhaust manifolds.

18. Connect the battery ground cable to the engine. Install the radiator.

19. Connect the transmission oil cooler lines. Install the fan shroud, fan belts, and pulleys. On diesels, connect the engine oil cooler lines at the radiator. Install the upper radiator support.

20. Install the V-belts.

21. Install the radiator, heater hoses and install the air cleaner.

22. Connect the battery cables.

23. Install the hood and attaching bolts at the scribes on the hinge outline on the underside of the hood.

24. Refill the cooling system. **Refill the engine with the specified engine oil**.

25. Start the engine and check for vacuum, coolant, oil, fuel and refrigerant leaks. Adjust

timing and idle speed to specification found in Chapter 2.

Valve Cover

REMOVAL AND INSTALLATION

1. Remove air cleaner and negative battery cable.

2. Disconnect, LABEL and reposition as necessary any vacuum or PCV hoses that obstruct the valve covers.

3. Disconnect and label electrical wire(s) (spark plug, etc.) from the valve cover clips.

4. Unbolt and remove the valve covers.

NOTE: *Do not pry the covers off if they seem stuck. Instead, use a seal breaker tool J-34144 or gently tap around each cover with a rubber mallet until the old gasket or sealer breaks loose.*

To install:

5. Use a new valve cover gasket and/or RTV (or any equivalent) sealer. If using sealer, follow directions on the tube. Install valve cover and tighten cover bolts to 36 inch lbs. (4 Nm).

6. Install all wires and hoses in the same location as removed.

7. Connect and reposition all vacuum and

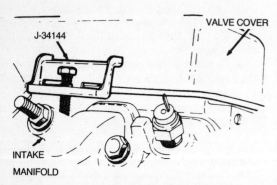

Removing the valve cover with a seal breaker

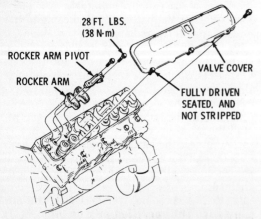

Valve cover and rocker arm removal, all engines except Buick V6 and V8. Rocker arms are marked "L" (left) and "R" (right)

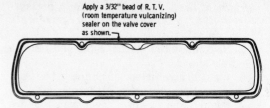

Apply sealer to the valve cover before assembling

PCV hoses, and reconnect electrical and/or spark plug wires at the cover clips. Install the air cleaner.

Rocker Arms

REMOVAL AND INSTALLATION

V6, 8-350 (VIN X) and 8-455 (VIN T)

1. Disconnect the negative battery cable and remove the valve covers as previously outlined.

2. Remove the rocker arm shaft assembly bolts.

3. Remove the rocker arm shaft assembly and place it on a clean surface.

4. To remove the rocker arms from the shaft, you must first remove the nylon arm retainers. These can be removed with locking jaw pliers, by prying them out, or by breaking them by hitting them below the head with a chisel.

5. Remove the rocker arms from the shaft. Make sure you keep them in order. Also note that the external rib on each arm points away from the rocker arm shaft bolt located between each pair of rocker arms.

6. If you are installing new rocker arms, note that the replacement rocker arms are marked **R** and **L** for right and left side installation. Do not interchange them.

To install:

1. Install the rocker arms on the shaft and lubricate them with oil.

NOTE: *Install the rocker arms for each cylinder only when the lifters are off the cam lobe and both valves are closed.*

2. Center each arm on the ¼ in. (6.3mm)

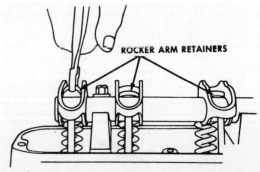

Removing nylon retainers—Buick V6 and V8 rocker shafts

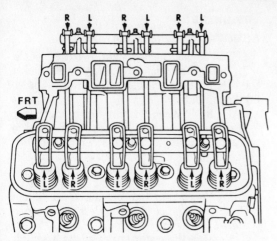

Rocker arm positioning—Buick engines

hole in the shaft. Install new nylon rocker arm retainers in the holes using a ½ in. (12.7mm) drift.

3. Locate the pushrods in the rocker arm cups and insert the shaft bolts. Tighten the bolts a little at a time to 30 ft. lbs. (34 Nm).

4. Install the valve covers using sealer or new gaskets as previously outlined in this chapter.

5. Start the engine and check for oil leaks.

All Other V8s except Diesel

1. Disconnect the negative (–) battery cable.

2. Remove the valve cover.

3. Remove the rocker arm flanged bolts, and remove the rocker pivots.

4. Remove the rocker arms.

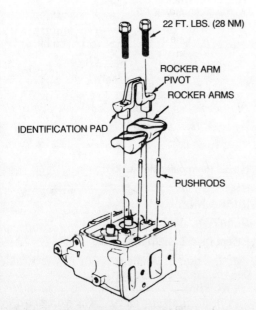

22 FT. LBS. (28 NM)

ROCKER ARM PIVOT

ROCKER ARMS

IDENTIFICATION PAD

PUSHRODS

Rocker arm assembly—Oldsmobile V8

NOTE: *Remove each set of rocker arms (one set per cylinder) as a unit.*

To install:

1. Position a set of rocker arms (for one cylinder) in the proper location.

NOTE: *Install the rocker arms for each cylinder only when the lifters are off the cam lobe and both valves are closed.*

2. Coat the replacement rocker arm and pivot with SAE 90 gear oil and install the pivots.

3. Install the flanged bolts and tighten alternately. Torque the bolts as follows:

- Early Buick and Pontiac V8 to 25 ft. lbs. (34 Nm)
- Early Oldmobile V8 28 ft. lbs. (35 Nm)
- Late model Buick, Olds, Pontiac 307 V8 22 ft. lbs. (28 Nm)

4. Install the valve cover, connect the negative battery cable, start the engine and check for oil leaks.

Diesel

NOTE: *When the diesel engine rocker arms are removed or loosened, the lifters must be bled down to prevent oil pressure buildup inside each lifter, which could cause it to raise up higher than normal and bring the valves within striking distance of the pistons.*

1. Disconnect the negative (–) battery cable.

2. Remove the valve cover.

3. Remove the rocker arm pivot bolts, the bridged pivot and rocker arms.

4. Remove each rocker set as a unit.

To install:

1. Lubricate the pivot wear points and position each set of rocker arms in its proper location. Do not tighten the pivot bolts for fear of bending the valves when the engine is turned.

2. On 1980 and earlier models: The lifters can be bled down for six cylinders at once with the crankshaft in either of the following two positions:

   a. For cylinders numbered 3, 5, 7, 2, 4 and 8, turn the crankshaft so the saw slot on the harmonic balancer is at 0° on the timing indicator.

   b. For cylinders 1, 3, 7, 2, 4 and 6, turn the crankshaft so the saw slot on the harmonic balancer is at 4 o'clock.

3. On these models only, tighten the rocker arm bolts on the numbered cylinders for the position the engine is in only. Torque to 28 ft. lbs. (35 Nm). It will take 45 minutes to completely bleed down the lifters. If additional lifters must be bled, wait till the 45 minutes has passed, and then turn the engine to the other position. Then tighten the remaining rocker arm pivot bolts and torque them to 28 ft. lbs. (35 Nm). Make sure you again wait 45 minutes before turning the crankshaft.

On 1981 and later models: Before installing any rockers, turn the crankshaft so No. 1 cylinder is at 32° before Top Dead Center on the compression stroke. 32° BTC is 50mm or 2 in. counterclockwise from the 0° pointer. If only the right valve cover was removed for the work you did so that No. 1 cylinder's valves have not been disturbed you can determine that you're on the compression stroke for No. 1 by removing the glow plug for that cylinder and feeling for expulsion of air through that hole as you turn the engine (in the direction of normal rotation) up to the required position. If you have disturbed the rockers for No. 1, the left side valve cover will be off and you can rotate the crankshaft until the No. 5 cylinder intake valve pushrod ball is 7mm or 0.28 in. above the No. 5 cylinder exhaust pushrod ball. If this cover is off even if you did not disturb No. 1 cylinder, you may wish to use the pushrod measurement method to save time.

Once the engine is in proper position, install the No. 5 cylinder rockers and rocker nuts, but DO NOT TIGHTEN THEM FULLY. Instead, turn them down by hand cautiously, alternating between intake and exhaust valves and turning both nuts an equal amount just until the intake valve nut begins to be harder to turn, indicating that the intake valve has just begun to crack open. Proceed cautiously so you don't turn too far. You'll see the valve begin to be depressed by the rocker, too.

4. At this point, torque all the remaining rocker nuts except those for cylinder No. 3. For cylinders No. 3 and 5, you'll have to turn the rocker bolts down very cautiously. On these cylinders, the cams are in such a position that installing the rocker nuts fully would open the valves all the way and then bend the pushrods. So, you'll have to feel very carefully for increased resistance as the valve reaches fully open position. Continue to turn the rocker nuts down on these three valves, always proceeding cautiously and stopping just as increased resistance is felt. Alternate, giving some time between tightening operations for the lifters to bleed down somewhat, until you can torque the nuts smoothly (without a sudden increase in resistance) to the required 28 ft. lbs. (35 Nm). Now, wait a full 45 minutes before the crankshaft is turned for any reason to permit all the lifters to bleed down fully.

5. Assemble the remaining components in reverse of disassembly. The rocker covers do not use gaskets, but are sealed with a bead of RTV (Room Temperature Vulcanizing) silicone sealer.

6. Connect the negative battery cable, start the engine and check for oil leaks.

Thermostat
REMOVAL AND INSTALLATION

1. Disconnect the negative (−) battery cable.
2. Drain the radiator until the level is below the thermostat level (below the level of the intake manifold).

CAUTION: *When draining the coolant, keep in mind that cats and dogs are attracted by the ethylene glycol antifreeze, and are quite likely to drink any that is left in an uncovered container or in puddles on the ground. This will prove fatal in sufficient quantity. Always drain the coolant into a sealable container. Coolant should be reused unless it is contaminated or several years old.*

3. Remove the water outlet elbow assembly from the engine. Remove the thermostat from inside the elbow.

4. Install new thermostat in the reverse order of removal, making sure the spring side is inserted into the elbow. Clean the gasket surfaces on the water outlet elbow and the intake manifold. Use a new gasket and RTV sealer when installing the elbow to the manifold. Refill the radiator to approximately 2½ inches below the filler neck or, if there is a coolant recovery system, fill it up all the way.

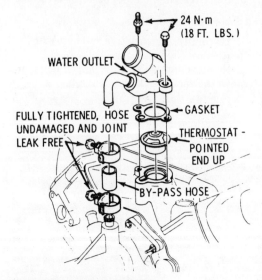

Typical thermostat installation

Intake Manifold
REMOVAL AND INSTALLATION
Except Diesel, 6–231 and 6–252

1. Disconnect the negative (−) battery cable and drain the cooling system.

CAUTION: *When draining the coolant, keep in mind that cats and dogs are attracted by*

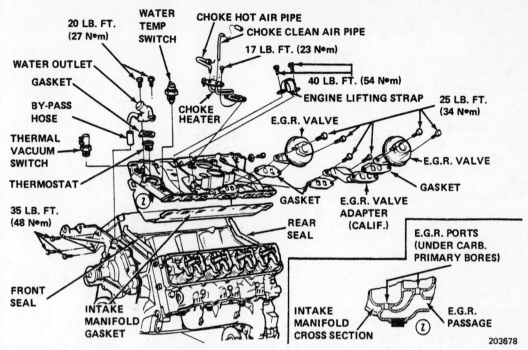

Typical gasoline V6 and V8 intake manifold installation

the ethylene glycol antifreeze, and are quite likely to drink any that is left in an uncovered container or in puddles on the ground. This will prove fatal in sufficient quantity. Always drain the coolant into a sealable container. Coolant should be reused unless it is contaminated or several years old.

2. Remove the air cleaner assembly.

3. Remove the thermostat housing and the bypass hose. It is not necessary to disconnect the top radiator hose at the thermostat housing.

4. Disconnect the heater hose at the rear of the manifold.

5. Disconnect all electrical connections and vacuum lines from the manifold. Remove the EGR valve if necessary.

6. On vehicles equipped with power brakes remove the vacuum line from the vacuum booster to the manifold.

7. Mark rotor and distributor housing-to-block locations. Remove the distributor (if necessary).

8. Remove the fuel line to the carburetor.

9. Remove the carburetor linkage.

10. Remove the carburetor. Refer to Chapter 5 for assistance.

11. Remove the intake manifold bolts. Remove the manifold and the gaskets. Remember to reinstall the O-ring seal between the intake

manifold and timing chain cover during assembly, if so equipped.

To install:

1. Clean all gasket mating surfaces with a gasket scraper and solvent.

NOTE: *Use care not to damage aluminum engine parts during gasket removal.*

Use plastic gasket retainers to prevent the manifold gasket from slipping out of place, if so equipped.

2. Install the intake manifold gaskets. Remember to reinstall the O-ring seal between the intake manifold and timing chain cover during assembly, if so equipped. With an assistant, carefully position the manifold onto the engine.

WARNING: *Do NOT slid the manifold into position if the bolts will not line up. This may cause the gasket to become dislodged. With an assistant, remove the manifold, reposition the gasket and try again until the manifold bolts will thread.*

3. Torque the intake manifold in the proper tightening sequence and to the proper torque. Refer to the "Torquing Sequence" illustrations in this section and to the Torque Specifications chart in the beginning of this chapter.

4. Install the carburetor. Refer to Chapter 5 for assistance.

5. Install the carburetor linkage.

6. Install the fuel line to the carburetor.

7. Install the distributor at the housing-to-block and rotor locations. Install the distributor (if removed).

8. On vehicles equipped with power brakes install the vacuum line from the vacuum booster to the manifold.

9. Connect all electrical connections and vacuum lines to the manifold. Install the EGR valve if necessary.

10. Connect the heater hose at the rear of the manifold.

11. Install the thermostat housing and the bypass hose.

12. Install the air cleaner assembly.

13. Connect the negative (−) battery cable and refill the cooling system.

14. Start the engine and check for oil, vacuum, coolant and fuel leaks.

6–231 and 6–252

1. Disconnect the battery, remove the air cleaner and drain the radiator.

CAUTION: *When draining the coolant, keep in mind that cats and dogs are attracted by the ethylene glycol antifreeze, and are quite likely to drink any that is left in an uncovered container or in puddles on the ground. This will prove fatal in sufficient quantity. Always drain the coolant into a sealable container. Coolant should be reused unless it is contaminated or several years old.*

2. Disconnect the following:

   a. The upper radiator hose and coolant bypass hose at the manifold. If the dipstick tube connects to the alternator adjusting brace, remove it, also, at this time.

   b. The alternator upper bracket, on 1986–87 models.

   c. Accelerator downshift and/or throttle valve cable(s) and bracket at the manifold.

   d. Booster vacuum pipe at the manifold.

   e. The EFE valve vacuum line at the manifold, if so equipped.

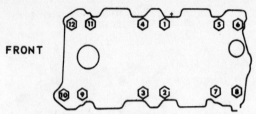

FRONT

Chevrolet-built 305 and 350 V8 intake manifold bolt torquing sequence

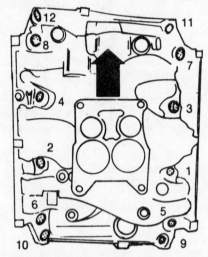

Intake manifold bolt torquing sequence, Buick-built 350 and 455 V8. Arrow points to front

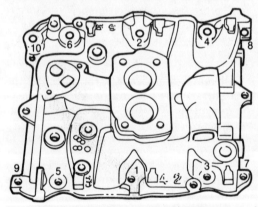

231 and 252 V6 intake manifold bolt sequence

f. Carburetor fuel line and choke pipes. If the engine has throttle body injection, unclip and disconnect the fuel lines at the TBI unit.

g. Automatic transmission vacuum modulator line.

h. Idle stop solenoid wire or idle Speed Control wiring.

i. Distributor primary wires and the temperature sending unit wires.

j. Any remaining vacuum hoses. On 1983 Olds, remove the A/C top bracket, if so equipped. On 1986–90 models, remove the

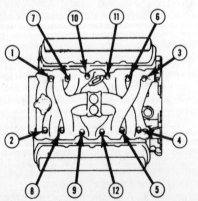

V8 intake manifold bolt torquing sequence, Olds-built gasoline and diesel engines

air conditioner compressor brace and disconnect the bracket at the manifold.

3. Remove the distributor cap and rotor for access to the left side manifold head bolt that is a Torx® type bolt on engines built before 1986. On 1986–87 models, remove the distributor and, if there is a separate coil, the coil as well.

4. Remove the plug wires and accelerator linkage springs.

5. Remove the manifold bolts. The Torx® bolt may be removed with a No. 45 Torx® socket. Remove the manifold.

To install:

1. Clean all gasket surfaces with a gasket scraper and solvent.

2. Place a new gasket and rubber seals in position at the front and rear rail of the block. Make sure the pointed end of the seal fits snugly against both the block and head. Coat both ends of these seals with RTV (Room Temperature Vulcanizing) sealant.

3. With an assistant, carefully position the manifold over the seals and gasket so that the seals and gasket remain in proper position.

WARNING: *Do NOT slid the manifold into position if the bolts will not line up. This may cause the gasket to become dislodged. With an assistant, remove the manifold, reposition the gasket and try again until the manifold bolts will thread.*

4. Start the manifold bolts.

5. Tighten the No. 1 and No. 2 bolts first until snug. Refer to the "Tightening sequence" illustration and Torque Specifications chart in this chapter. Then, continue with the rest of the bolts in sequence until all are just snug. Finally, torque in sequence to 45 ft. lbs. (61 Nm).

6. Install the plug wires and accelerator linkage springs.

7. Install the distributor, cap and rotor, if removed. Adjust the timing after all components have been installed.

8. Install any remaining vacuum hoses. On 1983 Olds, install the A/C top bracket, if so equipped. On 1986–87 models, install the air conditioner compressor brace and connect the bracket at the manifold.

9. Install the distributor primary wires and the temperature sending unit wires.

10. Connect the idle stop solenoid wire or idle Speed Control wiring.

11. Connect the automatic transmission vacuum modulator line.

12. Connect the carburetor fuel line and choke pipes. If the engine has throttle body injection, connect the fuel lines at the TBI unit.

13. Connect the EFE valve vacuum line at the manifold, if so equipped.

14. Connect the booster vacuum pipe at the manifold.

15. Install the accelerator downshift and/or throttle valve cable(s) and bracket at the manifold.

16. Install the alternator upper bracket, on 1986–87 models.

17. Install the upper radiator hose and coolant bypass hose at the manifold. If the dipstick tube connects to the alternator adjusting brace, install it, also, at this time.

18. Connect the battery, install the air cleaner and refill the radiator with engine coolant.

19. Start the engine and check for leaks. Adjust the timing at this time.

6–262 Diesel
8–350 Diesel

1. Remove the air cleaner.

2. Drain the radiator. Loosen the upper bypass hose clamp, remove the thermostat housing bolts, and remove the housing and the thermostat from the intake manifold.

CAUTION: *When draining the coolant, keep in mind that cats and dogs are attracted by the ethylene glycol antifreeze, and are quite likely to drink any that is left in an uncovered container or in puddles on the ground. This will prove fatal in sufficient quantity. Always drain the coolant into a sealable container. Coolant should be reused unless it is contaminated or several years old.*

3. Remove the breather pipes from the rocker covers and the air crossover. Remove the air crossover.

4. Disconnect the throttle rod and the return spring. If equipped with cruise control, remove the servo.

5. Remove the hairpin clip at the bellcrank and disconnect the cables. Remove the throttle cable from the bracket on the manifold; position the cable away from the engine. Disconnect and label any wiring as necessary.

6. Remove the alternator bracket if necessary. If equipped with air conditioning, remove the compressor mounting bolts and move the

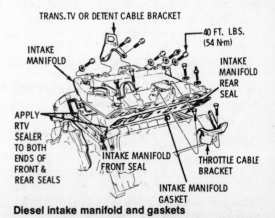

Diesel intake manifold and gaskets

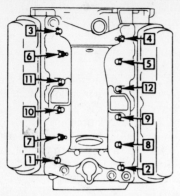

350 5.7L Diesel intake manifold torque sequence

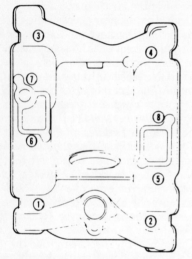

262 4.3L Diesel intake manifold torque sequence

262 4.3L Diesel intake manifold

compressor aside, without disconnecting any of the hoses. Remove the compressor mounting bracket from the intake manifold.

7. Disconnect the fuel line from the pump and the fuel filter. Remove the fuel filter and bracket.

8. Remove the fuel injection pump and lines See Chapter 5, Fuel System, for procedures.

9. Disconnect and remove the vacuum pump or oil pump drive assembly from the rear of the engine.

10. Remove the intake manifold drain tube.

11. Remove the intake manifold bolts and remove the manifold. Remove the adapter seal. Remove the injection pump adapter.

To install:

1. Clean the mating surfaces of the cylinder heads and the intake manifold using a gasket scraper and solvent.

2. Coat both sides of the gasket surface that seal the intake manifold to the cylinder heads with G.M. sealer #1050026 or the equivalent.

WARNING: *Do NOT slide the manifold into*

position if the bolts will not line up. This may cause the gasket to become dislodged. With an assistant, remove the manifold, reposition the gasket and try again until the manifold bolts will thread.

3. With an assistant, position the intake manifold gaskets on the cylinder heads. Install the end seals, making sure that the ends are positioned under the cylinder heads.

4. Carefully lower the intake manifold into place on the engine.

5. Clean the intake manifold bolts thoroughly, then dip them in clean engine oil. Install the bolts and torque to 15 ft. lbs. (20 Nm) in the sequence shown. Next, torque all the bolts to 30

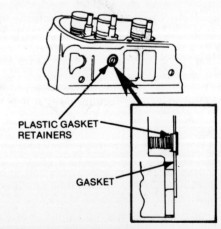

Plastic manifold gasket retainers

ft. lbs. (41 Nm), in sequence, and finally tighten to 40 ft. lbs. (54 Nm) in sequence.

6. Install the intake manifold drain tube and clamp.

7. Install injection pump adapter. See Chapter 5. Make sure not to run the engine without the vacuum pump in place as this drives the oil pump.

8. Install the fuel injection pump and lines. See Chapter 5, Fuel System, for procedures.

9. Connect the fuel line to the pump and the fuel filter. Install the fuel filter and bracket.

10. Install the alternator bracket if removed. If equipped with air conditioning, install the compressor bracket and compressor. Install the compressor mounting bracket bolts to the intake manifold.

11. Install the hairpin clip to the bellcrank and connect the cables. Install the throttle cable to the bracket on the manifold.

12. Connect any wiring as necessary.

13. Connect the throttle rod and the return spring. If equipped with cruise control, install the servo.

14. Install the air crossover and connect the breather pipes to the rocker covers and the air crossover.

15. Install the thermostat, gasket and housing bolts to the intake manifold.

16. Refill the radiator with engine coolant.

17. Connect the negative battery cable and install the air cleaner.

18. Start the engine and check for leaks and proper engine operation.

Exhaust Manifold

REMOVAL AND INSTALLATION

Tab locks are used on the front and rear pairs of bolts on each exhaust manifold. When removing the bolts, straighten the tabs from beneath the vehicle using a suitable tool. When installing the tab locks, bend the tabs against the flats on the sides of the bolt, not over the top of the bolt.

1. Disconnect the negative (–) battery cable.

2. Remove the air cleaner. Number and then disconnect the spark plug wires.

3. Remove the hot air shroud (if so equipped). If the vehicle has Early Fuel Evaporation, disconnect the vacuum hose, if it is in the way.

4. Loosen the alternator and remove its lower bracket. Disconnect the pipe for the Air Injection Reactor system.

5. Raise the vehicle and support it with jackstands.

6. Disconnect the crossover pipe from both manifolds.

7. On models with air conditioning, especial-

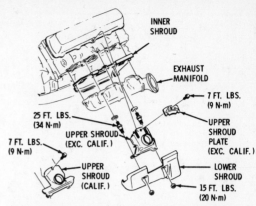

Typical exhaust manifold and hot air shrouds

ly on V8 engines when removing the left side manifold, it may be necessary to remove the compressor and tie it out of the way. On V8s, to remove the left manifold, loosen the compressor mounting bracket at the front of the head, remove the rear bracket, and then hang the compressor so you don't put strain on the refrigerant lines.

CAUTION: *Do not disconnect the compressor lines! You could be injured by frostbite as the refrigerant escapes!*

8. Remove the manifold bolts and remove the manifold(s). Some models have lock tabs on the front and rear manifold bolts which must be removed before removing the bolts. These tabs can be bent with a drift pin.

To install:

1. Install the manifold and bolts. Some models have lock tabs on the front and rear manifold bolts which must be bent over the flats of the bolts to prevent loosening. These tabs can be bent with a drift pin. Torque the bolts to specifications found in the Torque specifications chart in the beginning of this chapter.

2. On models with air conditioning, especially on V8 engines when installing the left side manifold, reinstall the compressor, tighten the belt and mounting bolts. Do NOT put strain on the refrigerant lines.

3. Raise the vehicle and support it with jackstands.

4. Connect the crossover pipe to both manifolds. Lower the vehicle.

5. Tighten the alternator and install its lower bracket. Connect the pipe for the Air Injection Reactor system.

6. Install the hot air shroud (if so equipped). If the vehicle has Early Fuel Evaporation, connect the vacuum hose, if it was disconnected.

7. Install the air cleaner. Connect the spark plug wires.

8. Connect the negative (–) battery cable, start the engine and check for exhaust leaks.

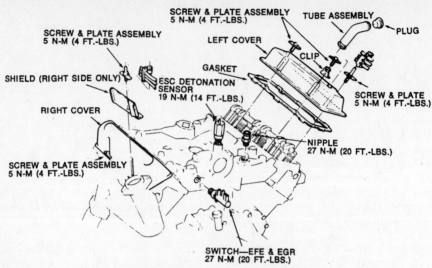

ECS detonation sensor, turbo V6

Turbocharger

COMPONENT PART REMOVAL AND INSTALLATION

6–231

CAUTION: *If the turbocharger unit has to be removed, first clean around the unit thoroughly with a non-caustic solution. When removing the turbocharger, take great care to avoid bending, nicking or in ANY WAY damaging the compressor or turbine blades. Any damage to the blades will result in imbalance, failure of the center housing bearing, damage to the unit and possible personal injury or damage to the other engine parts.*

ESC DETONATION SENSOR

1. Disconnect the negative (–) battery cable.
2. Squeeze the side of the connector and carefully pull it straight up.
3. Using a deep socket, unscrew the sensor.
4. To install, reverse the removal procedure. Torque the sensor to 14 ft. lbs. (19 Nm). Do not overtorque the sensor or apply a side load when installing. Connect the negative battery cable and check operation.

WASTEGATE ACTUATOR ASSEMBLY

1. Disconnect the negative (–) battery cable and two hoses from the actuator.
2. Remove the wastegate linkage-to-actuator rod clip.

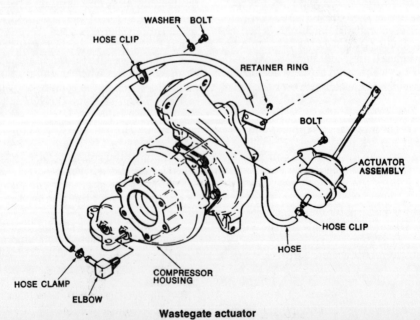

Wastegate actuator

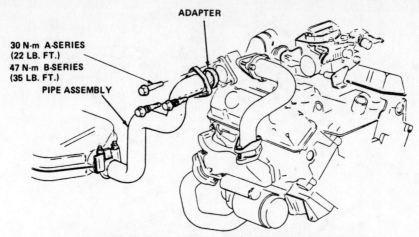

231 V6 turbocharger outlet-to-exhaust pipe connection

3. Remove the two bolts attaching the actuator to the compressor housing.

4. Installation is the reverse of removal. Torque the bolts to 100 inch lbs. (11 Nm). Connect the negative battery cable and check for proper operation.

TURBOCHARGER UNIT AND ACTUATOR ASSEMBLY

1. Disconnect the negative (–) battery cable and remove the air cleaner.

2. Disconnect the exhaust inlet and outlet pipes from the turbocharger.

3. Disconnect the oil feed pipe from the center housing.

4. Remove the nut attaching the air intake elbow to the carburetor and remove the elbow and flex tube from the carburetor.

5. Disconnect and tag the accelerator, cruise control and detent linkages from the carburetor. Disconnect the plenum linkage bracket.

6. Remove the two bolts attaching the plenum to the side bracket.

7. Disconnect and tag the fuel line and all vacuum lines from the carburetor.

8. Drain the cooling system and save the coolant if it is in good condition.

CAUTION: *When draining the coolant, keep in mind that cats and dogs are attracted by the ethylene glycol antifreeze, and are quite likely to drink any that is left in an uncovered container or in puddles on the ground. This will prove fatal in sufficient quantity. Always drain the coolant into a sealable container. Coolant should be reused unless it is contaminated or several years old.*

9. Disconnect the coolant lines from the front and rear of the plenum.

10. Disconnect and tag the power brake vacuum line from the plenum.

11. Remove the two bolts attaching the tur-

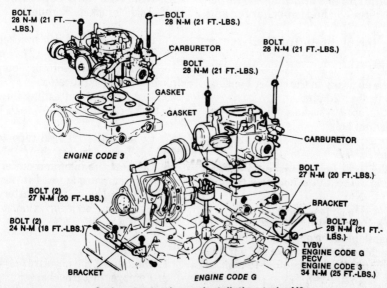

Carburetor-to-plenum installation, turbo V6

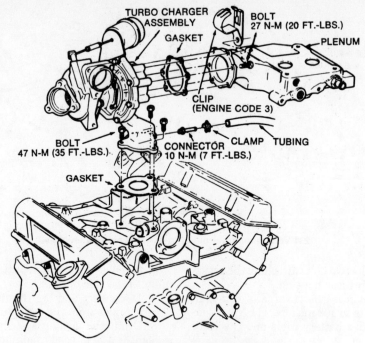

Turbocharger and plenum assembly

bine housing to the intake manifold bracket.

12. Remove the two bolts attaching the EGR valve manifold to the plenum. Loosen the two bolts attaching the EGR valve to the intake manifold.

13. Remove the AIR bypass hose from the check valve.

14. Remove the three bolts attaching the compressor housing to the intake manifold.

15. Remove the turbocharger, actuator, carburetor and plenum from the engine.

16. Remove the six bolts attaching the carburetor and plenum to the turbocharger and actuator.

17. Remove the oil drain from the center housing.

To install:

1. Install the oil drain on the center housing. Torque to 15 ft. lbs. (20 Nm).

2. Install the six turbocharger/actuator-to-carburetor/plenum bolts.

3. Place the assembly on the engine and connect all vacuum hoses.

4. Install the three bolts attaching the compressor housing to the intake manifold. Torque to 35 ft. lbs. (48 Nm).

5. Install the AIR bypass hose.

6. Loosely install the two bolts attaching the EGR valve manifold to the plenum. Tighten the two bolts attaching the EGR valve to 15 ft. lbs. (20 Nm). Tighten the EGR manifold-to-plenum bolts to 15 ft. lbs. (20 Nm).

7. Install the two bolts attaching the turbine

housing to the intake manifold bracket. Torque to 20 ft. lbs. (27 Nm).

8. Connect the power brake vacuum line at the plenum. Torque to 10 ft. lbs. (14 Nm).

9. Connect the plenum front bracket and install one bolt attaching the bracket to the manifold. Torque to 20 ft. lbs. (27 Nm).

10. Connect the coolant hoses to the plenum.

11. Refill the cooling system.

12. Connect the carburetor fuel line and remaining vacuum hoses.

13. Install the two bolts attaching the plenum to the side bracket. Torque to 20 ft. lbs. (27 Nm).

14. Connect the linkage bracket to the plenum. Torque to 20 ft. lbs. (27 Nm).

15. Connect the accelerator, detent and cruise linkages to the carburetor.

16. Install the nut attaching the air intake elbow to the carburetor. Torque to 15 ft. lbs. (20 Nm).

17. Connect the oil feed pipe to the center housing. Torque to 7 ft. lbs. (10 Nm).

18. Connect the inlet and outlet pipes to the turbocharger. Torque to 14 ft. lbs. (19 Nm).

19. Connect the negative battery cable, start the engine and check for exhaust, coolant and vacuum leaks.

PLENUM

1. Disconnect the negative (–) battery cable.

2. Remove the turbocharger and actuator assembly as previously described.

3. Remove the four bolts attaching the carburetor to the plenum.

4. Installation is the reverse of removal. Torque the bolts to 20 ft. lbs. (27 Nm).

5. Connect the negative battery cable and start the engine to check for normal operation.

Air Conditioning Compressor

REMOVAL AND INSTALLATION

1. Disconnect the negative (−) battery cable.

2. Discharge the A/C system as follows. Also refer to Chapter 1 for assistance:

CAUTION: *Always wear safety goggles when working on a system to protect the eyes. If refrigerant contacts the eye, it is advisable in all cases to see a physician as soon as possible.*

a. Remove the caps from the high and low pressure charging valves in the high and low pressure lines.

b. Turn both manifold gauge set hand valves to the fully closed (clockwise) position.

c. Connect a gauge set (engine not running). The LOW side gauge hose to the suction line near the accumulator and the HIGH side gauge hose to the liquid line or muffler. The muffler is a round shaped can about three times larger than the liquid line.

d. Place the end of the center hose away from you and the vehicle and into a suitable container.

e. Open the low pressure gauge valve slightly and allow the system pressure to bleed off.

f. When the system is just about empty, open the high pressure valve very slowly to avoid losing an excessive amount of refrigerant oil. Allow any remaining refrigerant to escape.

3. Note routing and remove the compressor drive belt from the pulleys.

4. Disconnect the electrical connectors at the compressor.

5. Remove the screw and O-ring from the refrigerant line connector block at the rear of the compressor. **Important**, seal both open ports in the connector block with tape to prevent dirt and moisture from contaminating the system.

6. Remove the compressor mounting bolts, nuts and spacers.

7. Remove compressor from the brackets. The bracket bolts may have to be loosened to permit removal.

To install:

1. If no refrigerant oil has been lost due to

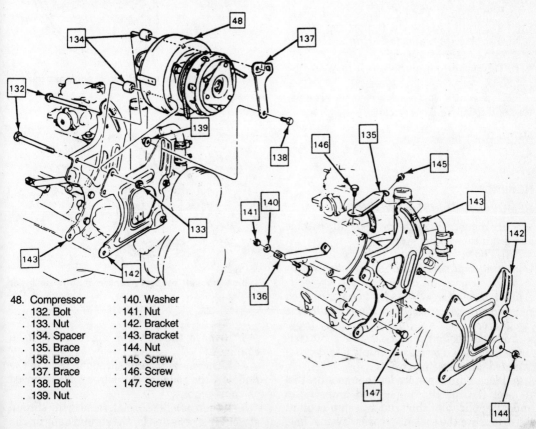

48. Compressor	140. Washer
. 132. Bolt	. 141. Nut
. 133. Nut	. 142. Bracket
. 134. Spacer	. 143. Bracket
. 135. Brace	. 144. Nut
. 136. Brace	. 145. Screw
. 137. Brace	. 146. Screw
. 138. Bolt	. 147. Screw
. 139. Nut	

A/C compressor removal

leakage, empty the oil out of old compressor into a measuring cylinder. Record this amount then empty the oil out of the new compressor. If the amount from the old is less than 1 fluid oz. (30ml), add 2 fluid oz. (60ml) to the new compressor. If the amount from the old is more than 1 fluid oz. (30ml), add the same amount to the new compressor.

NOTE: *Replacement compressors may or may not have refrigerant oil from the factory. Always drain the new compressor to make sure that the system will not be over or under filled with oil after installation, causing low cooling capacity.*

Only use 525 viscosity refrigerant oil in any GM air conditioning system unless instructed otherwise. Severe A/C system damage may occur if lubrication substitutes are used.

2. If the system has been flushed, **the TO-TAL system oil capacity is 6 fluid oz. (180ml)**.

3. Install the compressor, bolts, spacers and nuts. Do not tighten until the drive belt has been adjusted.

4. Adjust the drive belt to the specification in Chapter 1.

5. Torque the long mounting bolts to 61 ft. lbs. (83 Nm) and the short bolts to 37 ft. lbs. (50 Nm).

6. Unplug, coat O-ring with oil and install the refrigerant lines to the compressor.

NOTE: *Always use new O-ring seals when installing the refrigerant lines.*

7. Torque the retaining screw to 25 ft. lbs. (34 Nm).

8. Connect the compressor electrical connectors and negative battery cable.

9. Evacuate and recharge the system. Refer to Chapter 1 for assistance.

Radiator

REMOVAL AND INSTALLATION

1. Disconnect the negative (−) battery cable and drain the cooling system.

CAUTION: *When draining the coolant, keep in mind that cats and dogs are attracted by the ethylene glycol antifreeze, and are quite likely to drink any that is left in an uncovered container or in puddles on the ground. This will prove fatal in sufficient quantity. Always drain the coolant into a sealable container. Coolant should be reused unless it is contaminated or several years old.*

2. Place a drain pan under the radiator. Disconnect the radiator upper and lower hoses and, if applicable, the transmission coolant lines. Remove the coolant recovery system line, if so equipped.

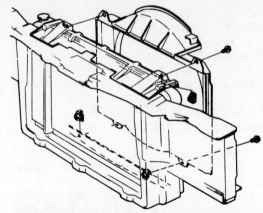

Radiator fan shroud mounting, diesel sedans and wagons. Gasoline-engined cars similar

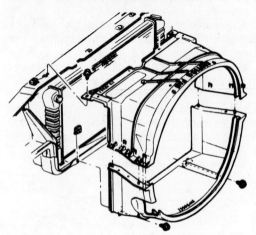

Radiator fan shroud mounting, V6 equipped cars

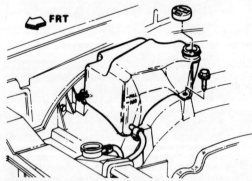

Typical coolant recovery tank mounting on inner fender

3. Remove the radiator upper panel if so equipped.

4. If there is a radiator shroud in front of the radiator, the radiator and shroud are removed as an assembly.

5. If there is a fan shroud, remove the shroud attaching screws and let the shroud hang on the fan.

6. Remove the radiator attaching bolts and remove the radiator.

To install:

1. Install the radiator and attaching bolts. Torque the bolts to 15 ft. lbs. (20 Nm).

2. If there is a fan shroud, install the shroud and attaching screws.

3. Install the radiator upper panel if so equipped.

4. Connect the radiator upper and lower hoses and, if applicable, the transmission coolant lines. Connect the coolant recovery system line, if so equipped.

5. Connect the negative (−) battery cable and refill the cooling system with the specified amount of engine coolant. Start the engine and check for coolant and transmission fluid leaks.

Air Conditioning Condenser

REMOVAL AND INSTALLATION

1. Disconnect the negative (−) battery cable. CAUTION: *Always wear safety goggles when working on a system to protect the eyes. If refrigerant contacts the eye, it is advisable in all cases to see a physician as soon as possible.*

2. Discharge the A/C system as outlined in the "Compressor" section in this chapter or the "A/C" section in Chapter 1.

3. Remove the radiator as previously outlined.

4. Disconnect the refrigerant lines from the condenser and plug all open line connections. **Important**, seal both open ports in the condenser lines with tape to prevent dirt and moisture from contaminating the system.

5. Remove the retaining screws and insulators.

6. Carefully lift up on the condenser to remove it from the insulators at the bottom channel of the radiator support.

7. Inspect the condenser for leaks, damaged fins, faulty connections and other damage.

To install:

1. Add 1 fluid oz. (30 ml) of 525 viscosity refrigerant oil into the condenser fittings.

2. Fit the lower end of the condenser into the insulators at the bottom of the support channel.

3. Install the upper insulators and retainers. Torque the retaining screws to 42 inch lbs. (5 Nm).

4. Install new O-ring seals and reconnect the condenser refrigerant lines. Torque steel fittings to 32 ft. lbs. (44 Nm). Torque aluminum or copper fittings to 17 ft. lbs. (23 Nm). **Always use a backup and flare nut wrench to tighten any refrigerant lines.**

5. Install the radiator as outlined in this chapter.

6. Connect the negative battery cable.

7. Evacuate and recharge the A/C system. Refer to the "A/C" section in Chapter 1 for assistance.

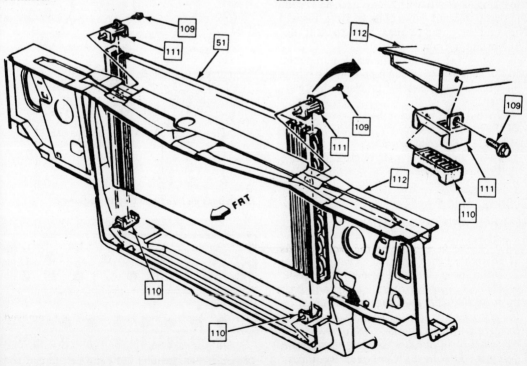

A/C condenser removal

Water Pump

REMOVAL AND INSTALLATION

1. Disconnect the negative (–) battery cable.
2. Drain the radiator.

CAUTION: *When draining the coolant, keep in mind that cats and dogs are attracted by the ethylene glycol antifreeze, and are quite likely to drink any that is left in an uncovered container or in puddles on the ground. This will prove fatal in sufficient quantity. Always drain the coolant into a sealable container. Coolant should be reused unless it is contaminated or several years old.*

3. Loosen the alternator and other accessories at their adjusting points, and remove the fan belts from the fan pulley.
4. Remove the fan and pulley.
5. Remove any accessory brackets that might interfere with water pump removal.
6. Disconnect the hose from the water pump inlet and the heater hose from the nipple on the pump. Remove the bolts, pump assembly and old gasket from the timing chain cover.
7. Check the pump shaft bearings for end play or roughness in operation. Water pump bearings usually emit a squealing sound with the engine running when the bearings need to be replaced. Replace the pump if the bearings are not in good shape or have been leaking.

To install:
1. Make sure the gasket surfaces on the pump and timing chain cover are clean. Install the pump assembly with a new gasket. Torque the pump-to-front cover bolts to 10 ft. lbs. (14 Nm) and the pump-to-block bolts to 22 ft. lbs. (30 Nm), uniformly.
2. Connect the hose to the water pump inlet and the heater hose to the nipple on the pump.
3. Install any accessory brackets that were removed.
4. Install the fan and pulley.
5. Tighten the alternator and other accessories at their adjusting points.
6. Refill the radiator with engine coolant.
7. Connect the negative (–) battery cable.

Cylinder Head

REMOVAL AND INSTALLATION

Gasoline Engines

1. Disconnect the negative (–) battery cable.
2. Drain the coolant and save it if still fresh.

CAUTION: *When draining the coolant, keep in mind that cats and dogs are attracted by the ethylene glycol antifreeze, and are quite likely to drink any that is left in an uncovered container or in puddles on the ground. This will prove fatal in sufficient quantity. Always drain the coolant into a sealable container.*

Coolant should be reused unless it is contaminated or several years old.

3. Remove the air cleaner.
4. Remove the air conditioning compressor,

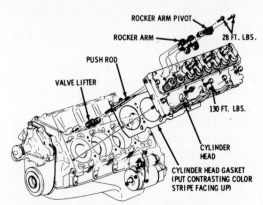

Cylinder head removal, all engines similar

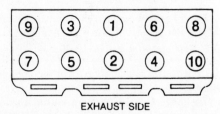

Buick-built 350 and 455 V8 cylinder head bolt torque sequence

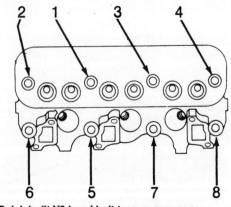

Buick-built V6 head bolt torque sequence

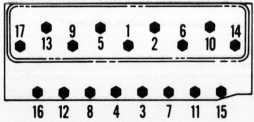

Chevrolet-built 305 and 350 head bolt torque sequence

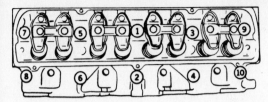

Cylinder head torque sequence—Oldsmobile 260, 307, 350, 403 and 455 V8 engines

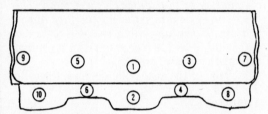

Pontiac-built 265, 301, 350, 400 and 455 head bolt torque sequence

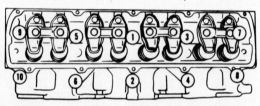

Olds-built 350 diesel cylinder head torque sequence

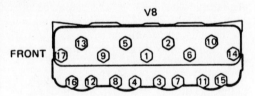

Torque sequences for the 307 V8 built in 1985–87

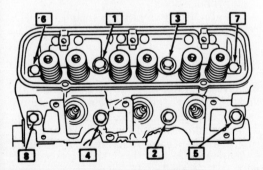

Torque sequence for the 231 V6 1985–87

but do not disconnect any A/C lines. Secure the compressor to one side.

5. Disconnect the AIR hose at the check valve. Remove the turbocharger assembly, if so equipped.

6. Remove the intake manifold.

7. When removing the right cylinder head,

loosen the alternator belt, disconnect the wiring and remove the alternator.

8. When removing the left cylinder head, remove the dipstick, power steering pump and air pump if so equipped.

9. Label the spark plug wires and disconnect them.

10. Disconnect the exhaust manifold from the head being removed.

11. Remove the valve cover. Scribe the rocker arms with an identifying mark for reassembly; it is important that the rocker assembly is reinstalled in the same position as it was removed. Remove the rocker arm bolts, rocker arms and pivots.

12. Take a piece of heavy cardboard and cut 16 or 12 holes (depending on whether the engine is a V6 or a V8 or 8 or 6 holes if you are only removing one head) in it the same diameter as the pushrod stems. Number the holes in relation to the pushrods being removed. This cardboard holder will keep the pushrods in order (and hopefully out of harm's way) while they are out of the engine. Remove the pushrods.

NOTE: *Pushrods MUST be returned to their original locations.*

13. On models equipped with power brakes, it is necessary to disconnect the brake booster and turn it sideways to remove the No. 7 pushrod.

14. Remove the cylinder head bolts, and remove the cylinder head and gasket. If the head seems stuck to the block, gently tap around the edge of the head with a rubber mallet until the joint breaks.

To install:

1. NEW head gasket(s) should always be used. Match the old gasket with the new one to make sure they are exactly the same. Gaskets on the 260 V8 must be installed with the stripe facing up: 307 V8 gaskets do not have a stripe. If the gasket has a bead, install it so the bead is upward. If there are dowel pins, locate the holes in the gasket over them. On the 285 and 301 engines, coat all rocker stud lower threads, the cylinder head bolt threads, and the underside of the bolt head with thread sealer. On 1986–87 3.8L V6 engines, coat the bolt threads with a heavy body thread sealer. On all engines, the head bolts should be dipped in clean oil before installing. Except on 1986–87 V6, tighten all head bolts in sequence and in small stages to the specified torque (see Torque Specifications chart in this chapter). On the 1986–87 V6, see the next step.

2. **On the 1986–87 V6:**

a. First follow the sequence, torquing the bolts to 25 ft. lbs. (34 Nm).

b. Watching the torque reading, turn the bolts, in the same sequence, 90° tighter. If the torque reading reaches 60 ft. lbs. (81 Nm), stop turning that bolt and proceed to the next one.

c. Repeat the step above, turning the bolts another 90° in sequence, but, again, stopping if a bolt reaches 60 ft. lbs. (81 Nm).

NOTE: *When installing the intake manifold remember to use new gaskets and new O-ring seals, if the manifold has them.*

Pushrods MUST be returned to their original locations.

3. Install the pushrods into their original location as removed.

4. Install the rocker arm assemblies into their original location. It is important that the rocker assembly is reinstalled in the same position as it was removed. Torque the bolts to specifications. Also, refer to the "Rocker Arm" section in this chapter.

5. Install the valve cover with a new gasket.

6. Connect the exhaust manifold to the head that was removed.

7. Reconnect the spark plug wires.

8. When installing the left cylinder head, install the dipstick, power steering pump and air pump if so equipped.

9. When installing the right cylinder head, install the alternator, connect the wiring and tighten the belt.

10. Install the intake manifold using a new gasket.

11. Connect the AIR hose at the check valve. Install the turbocharger assembly, if so equipped.

12. Install the air conditioning compressor if so equipped.

13. Install the air cleaner.

14. Refill the radiator with coolant.

15. Connect the negative (−) battery cable.

Diesel Engines

1. Disconnect the negative (−) battery cable. Remove the intake manifold, using the procedure outlined in the "Intake Manifold" section in this chapter.

2. Remove the rocker arm cover(s), after removing any accessory brackets which interfere with cover removal.

3. Disconnect and label the glow plug wiring.

4. If the right cylinder head is being removed, remove the ground strap from the head.

5. Remove the rocker arm bolts, the bridged pivots, the rocker arms, and the pushrods, keeping all the parts in order so that they can be returned to their original positions. It is a good practice to number or mark the parts to avoid interchanging them.

6. Remove the fuel return lines from the nozzles.

7. Remove the exhaust manifold(s), using the procedure outlined above.

8. Remove the engine block drain plug on the side of the engine from which the cylinder head is being removed.

CAUTION: *When draining the coolant, keep in mind that cats and dogs are attracted by the ethylene glycol antifreeze, and are quite likely to drink any that is left in an uncovered container or in puddles on the ground. This will prove fatal in sufficient quantity. Always drain the coolant into a sealable container. Coolant should be reused unless it is contaminated or several years old.*

9. Remove the head bolts. Remove the cylinder head.

To install:

1. Clean the mating surfaces thoroughly with a gasket scraper and solvent. Install new head gaskets on the engine block. Make sure the new gasket matches the old gasket exactly. Do NOT coat the gaskets with any sealer. The gaskets have a special coating that eliminates the need for sealer. The use of sealer will interfere with this coating and cause leaks.

2. Install the cylinder head onto the block.

3. Clean the head bolts thoroughly. Dip the bolts in clean engine oil and install into the cylinder block until the heads of the bolts lightly contact the cylinder head.

4. Torque the bolts, in the sequence illustrated, to 100 ft. lbs. (136 Nm). When all bolts have been tightened to this figure, begin the torquing sequence again, and torque all bolts to 130 ft. lbs. (176 Nm).

5. Install the engine block drain plugs, the exhaust manifolds, the fuel return lines, the glow plug wiring, and the ground strap for the right cylinder head.

6. **Valve lifter draining:** Install the valve train assembly. You'll have to remove, disassemble, and drain oil from all eight lifters associated with the removal of one cylinder head or, if both heads have been removed, all 16 lifters. Remove the valve lifter guide retaining bolts, and then remove the lifter guide. Then, remove each lifter from its bore, keeping it in order for replacement in the same bore. This is especially important since some lifters are 0.010 in. (0.254mm) oversize (these bores are marked with an oval).

To disassemble each lifter, remove the retainer ring with a small prybar. Then, remove the pushrod seat and oil metering valve. Remove the plunger and plunger spring (the plunger, valve disc, spring, and check retainer may remain fully assembled). Now, turn the lifter upside down and drain the oil from the lifter body completely.

Don't wipe any of the parts dry, however, as

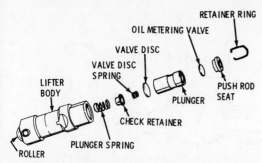

Disassembly of gasoline and diesel V8 engines with roller valve lifters

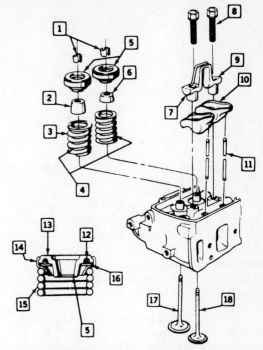

1. Valve keys	10. Rocker arms
2. Intake valve seal	11. Pushrods
3. Spring	12. Coil spring
4. Dampener Spring	13. Body
5. Valve rotator	14. Collar
6. Exhaust valve seal	15. Valve spring
7. Identification pad	16. Flat washer
8. 22 ft. lbs. (28 Nm)	17. Intake valve
9. Rocker arm pivot	18. Exhaust valve

Valve train exploded view—all engines similar except Buick with rocker shafts

there must be some lubrication at startup. Then, reassemble each lifter by first installing the plunger spring over the check retainer. Hold the plunger upside down so that the spring will not cock and insert it into the lifter bore. Then, install the oil metering valve and pushrod seat into the bore and install the retaining ring.

Install the lifters (in original bores) and the lifter guide and retaining bolts. Install the pushrods in their original positions with the wing at the top. Install the rockers and pivots and bolts, torquing the bolts alternately to 28 ft. lbs. (37 Nm).

7. Install the intake manifold. Refer to the procedure in the "Intake Manifold" section in this chapter.

8. Install the valve covers. These are sealed with RTV (Room Temperature Vulcanizing) silicone sealer instead of a gasket. Use GM #1052434 or an equivalent. Install the cover to the head within 10 minutes, while the sealer is still wet.

Valves and Springs

REMOVAL AND INSTALLATION

1. Remove the head(s), and place on a clean work surface.

2. Using a suitable spring compressor (for pushrod-type overhead valve engines), compress the valve spring and remove the valve spring cap keys. Release the spring compressor and remove the valve spring and cap (and valve rotator on some engines). If the keys will not release, tap on the valve cap with a brass hammer with the compressor removed.

NOTE: *Use care in removing the keys; they are easily lost.*

3. Remove the valve seals from the intake valve guides. Throw these old seals away, as you'll be installing new seals during reassembly.

4. Slide the valves out of the head from the combustion chamber side.

5. Make a holder for the valves out of a piece

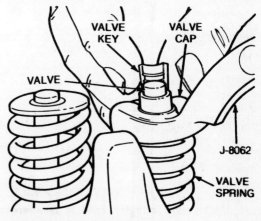

Installing valve retaining keys

of wood or cardboard, as outlined for the pushrods in Cylinder Head Removal. Make sure you number each hole in the cardboard to keep the valves in proper order. Slide the valves out of the head from the combustion chamber side; they MUST be installed as they were removed.

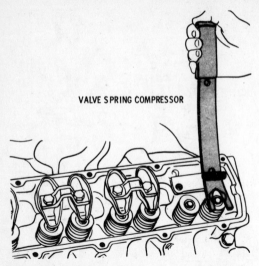

VALVE SPRING COMPRESSOR

Removing the valve springs

INSPECTION

Inspect the valve faces and seats (in the head) for pits, burned spots and other evidence of poor seating. If a valve face is in such bad shape that the head of the valve must be ground in order to true up the face, discard the valve because the sharp edge will run too hot. Check the "Valve Specification" chart in this chapter for

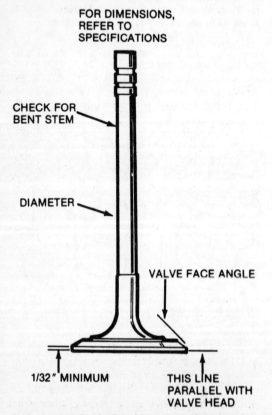

FOR DIMENSIONS, REFER TO SPECIFICATIONS

CHECK FOR BENT STEM

DIAMETER

VALVE FACE ANGLE

1/32″ MINIMUM

THIS LINE PARALLEL WITH VALVE HEAD

Critical valve dimensions

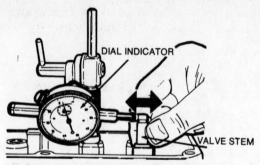

DIAL INDICATOR

VALVE STEM

Checking the valve stem-to-guide clearance

the correct angle for the valve faces. We recommend the refacing be done at a reputable machine shop.

Check the valve stem for scoring and burned spots. If not noticeably scored or damaged, clean the valve stem with solvent to remove all gum and varnish. Clean the valve guides using solvent and an expanding wire-type valve guide cleaner. If you have access to a dial indicator for measuring valve stem-to-guide clearance, mount it so that the stem of the indicator is at 90° to the valve stem, and as close to the valve guide as possible. Move the valve off its seat, and measure the valve guide-to-stem clearance by rocking the stem back and forth to actuate the dial indicator. Measure the valve stems using a micrometer, and compare to specifications to determine whether stem or guide wear is responsible for the excess clearance. If a dial indicator and micrometer are not available to you, take your cylinder head and valves to a reputable machine shop for inspection.

Some of the engines covered in this guide are equipped with valve rotators, which double as valve spring caps. In normal operation the rotators put a certain degree of wear on the tip of the valve stem; this wear appears as concentric rings on the stem tip. However, if the rotator is not working properly, the wear may appear as straight notches or **X** patterns across the valve stem tip. Whenever the valves are removed from the cylinder head, the tips should be inspected for improper pattern, which could indi-

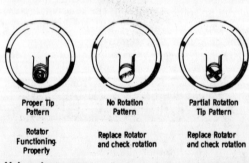

Proper Tip Pattern	No Rotation Pattern	Partial Rotation Tip Pattern
Rotator Functioning Properly	Replace Rotator and check rotation	Replace Rotator and check rotation

Valve stem wear

cate valve rotator problems. Valve stem tips will have to be ground flat if rotator patterns are severe.

Valve Guides

The V6 and V8 engines covered in this guide use integral valve guides; that is, they are a part of the cylinder head and cannot be replaced. The guides can, however, be reamed oversize if they are found to be worn past an acceptable limit. Occasionally, a valve guide bore will be oversize as manufactured. These are marked on the inboard side of the cylinder heads on the machined surface just above the intake manifold.

If the guides must be reamed (this service is available at most machine shops), then valves with oversize stems must be fitted. Valves are usually available in 0.001 in. (0.025mm), 0.003 in. (0.076mm) and 0.005 in. (0.127mm) stem oversizes. Valve guides which are not excessively worn or distorted may, in some cases, be knurled rather than reamed. Knurling is a process in which the metal on the valve guide bore is displaced and raised, thereby reducing clearance. Knurling also provides excellent oil control. The option of knurling rather than reaming valve guides should be discussed with a reputable machinist or engine specialist.

CYLINDER HEAD CLEANING AND INSPECTION

NOTE: *Any diesel cylinder head work should be handled by a reputable machine shop familiar with diesel engines. Disassembly, valve lapping, and assembly can be completed by following the gasoline engine procedures.*

Gasoline Engines

Once the complete valve train has been removed from the cylinder head(s), the head itself can be inspected, cleaned and machined (if necessary). Set the head(s) on a clean work space, so the combustion chambers are facing up. Begin cleaning the chambers and ports with a hardwood chisel or other non-metallic tool (to avoid nicking or gouging the chamber, ports, and especially the valve seats). Chip away the

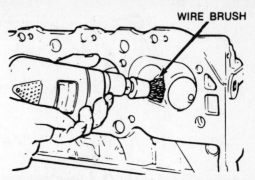

Use a wire brush and electric drill to remove carbon from the combustion chambers and exhaust ports

major carbon deposits, then remove the remainder of carbon with a wire brush fitted to an electric drill.

NOTE: *Be sure that the carbon is actually removed, rather than just burnished.*

After decarbonizing is completed, take the head(s) to a machine shop and have the head hot tanked (cast iron only). In this process, the head is lowered into a hot chemical bath that very effectively cleans all grease, corrosion, and scale from all internal and external head surfaces. Also have the machinist check the valve seats and re-cut them if necessary. When you bring the clean head(s) home, place them on a clean surface. Completely clean the entire valve train with solvent.

CHECKING FOR HEAD WARPAGE

Lay the head down with the combustion chambers facing up. Place a straightedge across the gasket surface of the head, both diagonally and straight across the center. Using a flat feeler gauge, determine the clearance at the center of the straightedge. If warpage exceeds 0.003 in. (0.076mm) in a 6 in. (152mm) span, or 0.006 in. (0.152mm) over the total length, the cylinder head must be resurfaced (which is similar to planing a piece of wood). Resurfacing can be performed at most machine shops.

NOTE: *When resurfacing the cylinder head(s) of V6 or V8 engines, the intake mani-*

1 & 3 CHECK DIAGONALLY
2 CHECK ACROSS CENTER

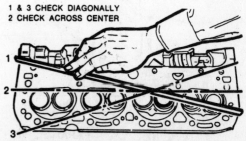

Check the cylinder head mating surface for warpage with a precision straight edge

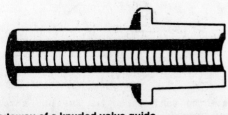

Cutaway of a knurled valve guide

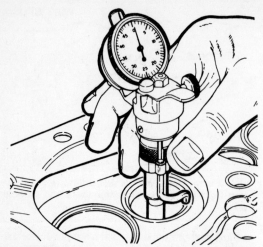

Have the valve seat concentricity checked at a machine shop

Home-made valve lapping tool

fold mounting position is altered, and must be corrected by machining a proportionate amount from the intake manifold flange.

LAPPING THE VALVES

When valve faces and seats have been refaced and recut, or if they are determined to be in good condition, the valves must be lapped in to ensure efficient sealing when the valve closes against the seat. Do not lap new valves, however, as a protective coating will be destroyed.

1. Invert the cylinder head so that the combustion chambers are facing up.

2. Lightly lubricate the valve stems with clean oil, and coat the valve seats with valve grinding compound. Install the valves in the head as numbered.

3. Attach the suction cup of a valve lapping tool to a valve head. You'll probably have to moisten the cup to securely attach the tool to the valve.

4. Rotate the tool between the palms, changing position and lifting the tool often to prevent

grooving. Lap the valve until a smooth, polished seat is evident (you may have to add a bit more compound after some lapping is done).

5. Remove the valve and tool, and remove ALL traces of grinding compound with solvent-soaked rag, or rinse the head with solvent.

NOTE: *Valve lapping can also be done by fastening a suction cup to a piece of drill rod in a hand eggbeater type drill. Proceed as above, using the drill as a lapping tool. Due to the higher speeds involved when using the hand drill, care must be exercised to avoid grooving the seat. Lift the tool and change direction of rotation often.*

Valve Springs

HEIGHT AND PRESSURE CHECK

1. Place the valve spring on a flat, clean surface next to a square.

2. Measure the height of the spring, and rotate it against the edge of the square to measure distortion (out-of-roundness). If spring height varies between springs by more than $\frac{1}{16}$ in. (1.6mm) or if the distortion exceeds $\frac{1}{16}$ in. (1.6mm), replace the spring.

A valve spring tester is needed to test spring

Lapping the valves by hand

Have the valve spring test pressure checked professionally

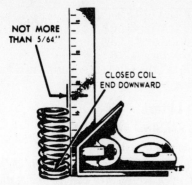

Check the valve spring free length and squareness

test pressure, so the valve springs must usually be taken to a professional machine shop for this test. Spring pressure at the installed and compressed heights is checked, and a tolerance of plus or minus 5 lbs. (plus or minus 1 lb. on the 231 V6 is permissible on the springs covered in this guide.

VALVE INSTALLATION

New valve seals must be installed when the valve train is put back together. Umbrella seals slip over the valve stem and guide boss, while others require that the boss be machined. In some applications Teflon guide seals are available. Check with a machinist and/or automotive parts store for a suggestion on the proper seals to use.

NOTE: *Remember that when installing valve seals, a small amount of oil must be able to pass the seal to lubricate the valve guides; otherwise, excessive wear will result.*

To Install the Valves and Rocker Assembly:

1. Lubricate the valve stems with clean engine oil.

2. Install the valves in the cylinder head, one at a time, as numbered.

3. Lubricate and position the seals and valve springs, again one valve at a time.

4. Install the spring retainers, and compress the springs.

5. With the valve key groove exposed above the compressed valve spring, wipe some wheel bearing grease around the groove. This will retain the keys as you release the spring compressor.

6. Using needlenose pliers (or your fingers), place the keys in the key grooves. The grease should hold the keys in place. Slowly release the spring compressor; the valve cap or rotator will raise up as the compressor is released, retaining the keys.

7. Install the rocker assembly, and install the cylinder head(s).

VALVE ADJUSTMENT

All engines covered by this guide use hydraulic valve lifters which require no periodic maintenance or adjustment. However, in the event the cylinder head or heads is removed or valve gear must be worked on, **Chevrolet** engines require adjustment of the valve lash. Olds and Buick engines do not require or permit adjustment; instead, the bolts which retain the rocker pivots are torqued. However, in the case of the Olds V8 Diesel, a special procedure must be followed to ensure the lifters are drained of oil prior to engine reassembly.

See the procedure below for the adjustment of Chevrolet valves only. See the procedure for cylinder head removal of the Olds Diesel for the procedure to be followed in draining oil from the valve lifters.

Chevrolet Built V8 and V6

1. Remove the valve covers and crank the engine until the mark on the damper aligns with

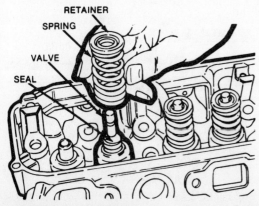

Installing valve stem seals

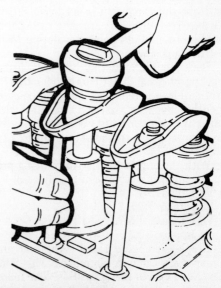

Typical valve adjustment

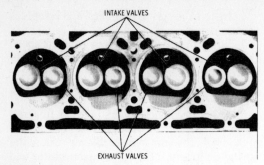

Olds-built V8 valve location

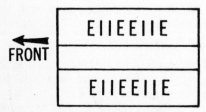

FRONT ←

Valve location, Chevrolet-built 305, 350 V8

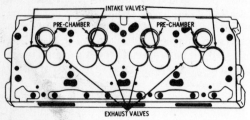

Diesel V8 valve location

the TDC or 0° mark on the timing tab and the engine is in the No. 1 firing position. This can be determined by placing the fingers on the No. 1 cylinder valves as the marks align. If the valves do not move, it is in the No. 1 firing position. If the valves move, it is in the No. 6 firing position (No. 4 on V6) and the crankshaft should be rotated one more revolution to the No. 1 firing position.

2. Back out the adjusting nut until lash is felt at the pushrod, then turn the adjusting nut in until all lash is removed. This can be determined by checking pushrod end play while turning the adjusting nut. When all play has been removed, turn the adjusting nut in 1 full turn.

3. With the engine in the No. 1 firing position, the following valves can be adjusted:
- V8 Exhaust: 1,3,4,8
- V8 Intake: 1,2,5,7
- V6 Exhaust: 1,5,7
- V6 Intake: 1,2,3

4. Crank the engine 1 full revolution until the marks are again in alignment. This is the No. 6 (No. 4 on V6) firing position. The following valves can now be adjusted:

- V8 Exhaust: 2,5,6,7
- V8 Intake: 3,4,6,8
- V6 Exhaust: 2,3,4
- V6 Intake: 4,5,6

5. Install the valve covers using new gaskets or sealer as required.

Valve Lifters

REMOVAL AND INSTALLATION

Gasoline and Diesel

NOTE: *Valve lifters and pushrods should be kept in order so they can be reinstalled in their original position. Some engines will have both standard size and oversize 0.010 in. (0.254mm) valve lifters as original equipment. The oversize lifters are etched with an O on their sides; the cylinder block will also be marked with an O if the oversize lifter is used.*

1. Remove the intake manifold and gasket.

2. Remove the valve covers, rocker arm assemblies and pushrods.

3. If the lifters are coated with varnish, apply carburetor cleaning solvent to the lifter body. The solvent should dissolve the varnish in about 10 minutes.

4. Remove the lifters. On engines equipped with roller lifters, remove the lifter retainer guide bolts, and remove the guides. A special tool for removing lifters is available, and is helpful for this procedure.

5. New lifters must be primed before installation, as dry lifters will seize when the engine is started. Submerge the lifters in clean engine oil and work the lifter plunger up and down. On Olds diesels, the lifters must be internally and externally lubricated before assembly, but they must be virtually empty of oil. New lifters

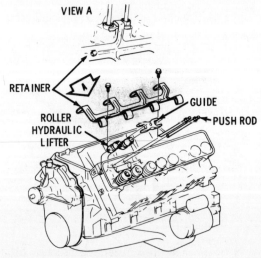

Roller valve lifter guide and retainer

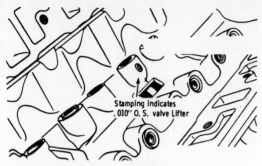

Oversize valve lifter identification

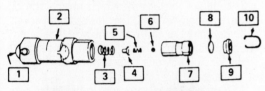

1. Roller
2. Lifter body
3. Plunger spring
4. Check ball retainer
5. Check ball spring
6. Check ball
7. Plunger
8. Oil metering valve
9. Pushrod seat
10. Retainer ring

Roller valve lifter exploded view—flat lifter similar

should be disassembled and thoroughly lubricated on all wear surfaces, but accumulated oil should be drained out prior to reassembly. Reuseable lifters should be disassembled and drained of oil but left damp with oil. Do not attempt to wipe them dry! If they have been cleaned, use the procedure for new lifters. See the procedure for cylinder head removal for lifter disassembly procedures.

6. Install the lifters and pushrods into the cylinder block in their original order. On roller lifter engines, install the lifter retainer guide.

7. Install the intake manifold gaskets and manifold.

8. Position the rocker arms, pivots and bolts on the cylinder head.

9. Install the valve covers, connect the spark plug wires and install the air cleaner.

Oil Pan

REMOVAL AND INSTALLATION

Gasoline Engines

NOTE: *Pan removal may be easier if the engine is turned to No. 1 cylinder firing position. This positions the crankshaft in the path of least resistance for pan removal.*

1. Disconnect the negative battery terminal.

2. Remove the fan shroud-to-radiator tie bar screws.

3. Remove the air cleaner and disconnect the throttle linkage.

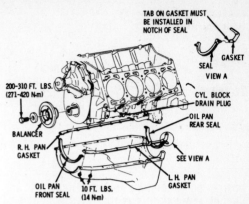

Oil pan installation; gaskets and seals may differ among engines

4. Raise the vehicle and support it on jackstands.

5. Drain the oil.

6. Remove the lower flywheel housing, remove the shift linkage attaching bolt and swing it out of the way, and disconnect the exhaust crossover pipe at the engine.

7. Remove the front engine mounting bolts.

8. Raise the engine by placing a jack under the crankshaft pulley mounting.

CAUTION: *On air conditioned vehicles, place a support under the right side of the transmission before raising the engine. If you don't do this, the engine and transmission will cock to the right due to the weight of the air conditioning equipment.*

9. Remove the oil pan bolts and remove the pan.

To install:

1. Use gasket sealer and new gaskets (if gaskets are used). Torque the pan bolts to 14 ft. lbs. (18 Nm).

2. Lower the engine with a jack under the crankshaft pulley mounting.

3. Install the front engine mounting bolts.

4. Install the lower flywheel housing, shift linkage attaching bolt, and connect the exhaust crossover pipe at the engine.

5. Refill the engine with oil.

6. Lower the vehicle.

7. Install the air cleaner and connect the throttle linkage.

8. Install the fan shroud-to-radiator tie bar screws.

9. Connect the negative battery terminal.

Diesel Engines

1. Remove the vacuum pump and drive (with A/C or the oil pump drive (without A/C).

2. Disconnect the batteries and remove the dipstick.

3. Remove the upper radiator support and fan shroud.

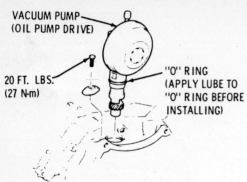

VACUUM PUMP
(OIL PUMP DRIVE)

20 FT. LBS.
(27 N·m)

"O" RING
(APPLY LUBE TO
"O" RING BEFORE
INSTALLING)

NOTICE: DO NOT OPERATE ENGINE WITHOUT
VACUUM PUMP AS THIS IS THE DRIVE
FOR THE ENGINE OIL PUMP AND ENGINE
DAMAGE WOULD OCCUR.

Diesel engine vacuum/oil pump drive

4. Raise and support the vehicle. Drain the oil.

5. Remove the flywheel cover.

6. Disconnect the exhaust and crossover pipes.

7. Remove the oil cooler lines at the filter base.

8. Remove the starter assembly. Support the engine with a jack.

9. Remove the engine mounts from the block.

10. Raise the front of the engine and remove the oil pan.

To install:

1. Install the oil pan, torque the retaining bolts 12 ft. lbs. (16 Nm).

2. Install the engine mounts to the block.

3. Install the starter assembly.

4. Install the oil cooler lines at the filter base.

5. Connect the exhaust and crossover pipes.

6. Install the flywheel cover.

7. Lower the vehicle.

8. Refill the engine with the proper amount of high quality engine oil suitable for diesel engines.

9. Install the upper radiator support and fan shroud.

10. Connect the batteries and install the dipstick.

11. Install the vacuum pump and drive.

12. Start the engine and check for oil leaks.

Oil Pump

REMOVAL AND INSTALLATION

Gasoline (except V6) and Diesel

The oil pump is mounted to the bottom of the block and is accessible only by removing the oil pan.

On V8 engines, including diesel, remove the oil pan, then unbolt and remove the oil pump

and screen as an assembly. Torque the pump bolts to 35 ft. lbs. (47 Nm).

OVERHAUL

V6

The oil pump is located in the timing chain cover and is connected by a drilled passage to the oil screen housing and pipe assembly in the oil pan. All oil is discharged from the pump to the oil pump cover assembly, on which the oil filter is mounted.

1. To remove the oil pump cover and gears, first remove the oil filter.

2. Remove the screws which attach the oil pump cover assembly to the timing chain cover.

3. Remove the cover assembly and slide out the oil pump gears. Clean the gears and inspect them for any obvious defects such as chipping or scoring.

4. Remove the oil pressure relief valve cap, spring and valve. Clean them and inspect them for wear or scoring. Check the relief valve spring to see that it is not worn on its side or collapsed, Replace the spring if it seems questionable.

5. Check the relief valve for a correct fit in its bore. It should be an easy slip fit and no more. If any perceptible shake can be felt, the valve and/or the cover should be replaced.

6. Install the oil pump gears (if removed) and

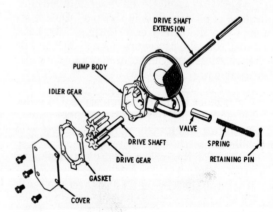

DRIVE SHAFT
EXTENSION

PUMP BODY

IDLER GEAR

DRIVE SHAFT

DRIVE GEAR

VALVE

SPRING

RETAINING PIN

GASKET

COVER

Oil pump exploded view

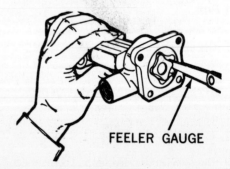

FEELER GAUGE

Measuring oil pump side clearance, typical

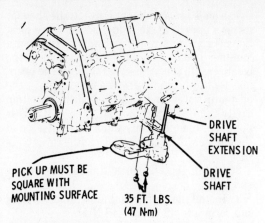

PICK UP MUST BE
SQUARE WITH
MOUNTING SURFACE

DRIVE
SHAFT
EXTENSION

DRIVE
SHAFT

35 FT. LBS.
(47 N·m)

Oil pump installation

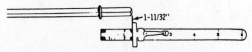

←—1-11/32"

Oil pump driveshaft retainer measurement

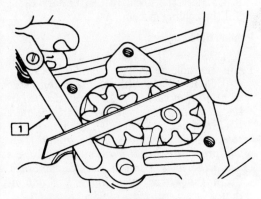

Checking oil pump end clearance

the shaft in the oil pump body section of the timing chain cover to check the gear end clearance and gear side clearance. Check gear end clearance by placing a straight edge over the gears and measure the clearance between the straight edge and the gasket surface. Clearance should be 0.002–0.006 in. (0.050–0.152mm). Check gear side clearance by inserting the feeler gauge between the gear teeth and the side wall of the pump body. Clearance should be 0.002–0.005 in. (0.050–0.127mm).

7. Check the pump cover flatness by placing a straight edge across the cover face, with a feeler gauge between the straight edge and the cover. If clearance is 0.001 in. (0.025mm) or more, replace the cover.

To install:

1. Lubricate the pressure relief valve and spring and place them in the cover. Install the cap and the gasket. Torque the cap to 35 ft. lbs. (48 Nm).

2. Pack the oil pump gear cavity full of petroleum jelly. Do not use gear lube. Reinstall the oil pump gears so that the petroleum jelly is forced into every cavity of the gear pocket, and between the gear teeth. There must be no air spaces. This step is very important.

CAUTION: *Unless the pump is primed this way, it won't produce any oil pressure when the engine is started.*

3. Install the cover assembly using a new gasket and sealer. Tighten the screws to 10 ft. lbs. (14 Nm).

4. Install the oil filter.

V8 Including Diesel

1. Remove the oil pump driveshaft extension.

2. Remove the cotter pin, spring and the pressure regulator valve.

CAUTION: *Place your thumb over the pressure regulator bore before removing the cotter pin, as the spring is under pressure.*

3. Remove the oil pump cover attaching screws and remove the oil pump cover and gasket. Clean the pump in solvent or kerosene, and wash out the pick-up screen.

4. Remove the drive gear and idler gear from the pump body.

5. Check the gears for scoring and other damage. Install the gears if in good condition, or replace them if damaged. Check gear end clearance by placing a straight edge over the gears and measure the clearance between the straight edge and the gasket surface with a feeler gauge. End clearance for the diesel is 0.0005–0.0075 in. (0.0127–0.1905mm); 350 (R) and 403 (K) is 0.0015–0.0085 in. 0.0381–0.2159mm); and other V8s is 0.002–0.0065 in. (0.0508–0.1651mm). If end clearance is excessive, check for scores in the cover that would bring the total clearance over the specs.

6. Check gear side clearance by inserting the feeler gauge between the gear teeth and the side wall of the pump body. Clearance should be 0.002–0.005 in. (0.0508–0.1270mm).

To install:

1. Pack the inside of the pump completely with petroleum jelly. DO NOT Use engine oil. The pump MUST be primed this way or it won't produce any oil pressure when the engine is started.

2. Install the cover screws and tighten alternately and evenly to 8 ft. lbs. (11 Nm).

3. Position the pressure regulator valve into the pump cover, closed end first, then install the spring and retaining pin.

NOTE: *When assembling the driveshaft extension to the driveshaft, the end of the extension nearest the washers must be inserted into the driveshaft.*

4. Insert the driveshaft extension through the opening in the main bearing cap and block until the shaft mates into the distributor drive gear.

5. Install the pump onto the rear main bearing cap and install the attaching bolts. Torque the bolts to 35 ft. lbs. (48 Nm).

6. Install the oil pan.

7. Start the engine and check for oil leaks.

Timing Chain Cover and Front Oil Seal

REMOVAL AND INSTALLATION

Buick Built Engines

1. Disconnect the negative (−) battery cable. Drain the cooling system.

CAUTION: *When draining the coolant, keep in mind that cats and dogs are attracted by the ethylene glycol antifreeze, and are quite likely to drink any that is left in an uncovered container or in puddles on the ground. This will prove fatal in sufficient quantity. Always drain the coolant into a sealable container. Coolant should be reused unless it is contaminated or several years old.*

2. Remove the radiator, fan, pulley and belt.

3. Remove the fuel pump and alternator, if necessary to remove cover.

4. Remove the distributor. If the timing chain and sprockets will not be disturbed, note the position of the distributor for installation in the same position.

5. Remove the thermostat bypass hose.

6. Remove the harmonic balancer.

7. Remove the timing chain-to-crankcase bolts.

8. Remove the oil pan-to-timing chain cover bolts and remove the timing chain cover.

9. Using a punch, drive out the old seal and the shedder toward the rear of the seal.

To install:

1. Coil the new packing around the opening so the ends are at the top. Drive in the shedder using a punch. Stake it in place at three locations. Properly size the packing by rotating a hammer handle around the packing until the balancer hub can be inserted through the opening. Before beginning reassembly, remove the oil pump cover and pack the entire oil pump cavity tightly with petroleum grease. If this is not done, the oil pump cannot prime itself and the engine will be damaged. Coat the cover bolts with sealer.

2. Install the oil pan-to-timing chain cover and bolts.

3. Install the timing chain-to-crankcase bolts and torque to 35 ft. lbs. (48 Nm).

4. Install the harmonic balancer using balancer installer tool.

5. Install the thermostat bypass hose.

6. Install the distributor to the same position as removed.

7. Install the fuel pump and alternator.

8. Install the radiator, fan, pulley and belt.

9. Connect the negative (−) battery cable. Refill the cooling system.

Pontiac Built Engines

1. Disconnect the negative (−) battery cable. Drain the radiator and the cylinder block.

CAUTION: *When draining the coolant, keep in mind that cats and dogs are attracted by the ethylene glycol antifreeze, and are quite likely to drink any that is left in an uncovered container or in puddles on the ground. This will prove fatal in sufficient quantity. Always drain the coolant into a sealable container. Coolant should be reused unless it is contaminated or several years old.*

2. Loosen the alternator adjusting bolts.

3. Remove the fan, fan pulley, accessory drive belts, and water pump.

4. Disconnect the radiator hoses.

5. Remove the fuel pump.

6. Remove the harmonic balancer bolt and washer.

7. Remove harmonic balancer.

NOTE: *Do not pry on rubber mounted balancers. If only the seal is to be replaced, proceed to Step 2.*

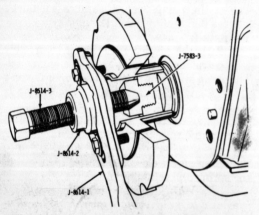

J-7583-3
J-8514-3
J-8514-2
J-8514-1

Removing the harmonic balancer using a puller—caution, use this type only

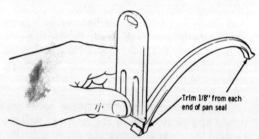

Trim 1/8" from each end of pan seal

Trimming pan seal with razor blade

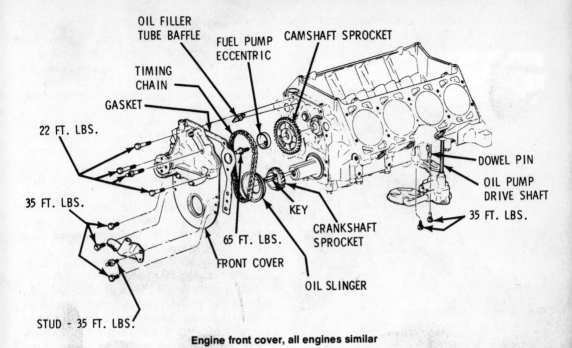

Engine front cover, all engines similar

8. Remove the front four oil pan to timing cover bolts.

9. Remove the timing cover bolts and nuts and cover to intake manifold bolt.

10. Pull the cover forward and remove.

11. Remove the O-ring from the recess in the intake manifold.

To install:

1. Clean all the gasket surfaces.

2. To replace the seal, pry it out of the cover using a prybar. Install the new seal with the lip inward.

NOTE: *The seal can be replaced with the cover installed.*

3. Making sure all gaskets are replaced. Torque the four oil pan bolts to 12 ft. lbs. (16 Nm), and the fan pulley bolts to 20 ft. lbs. (27 Nm).

4. Install harmonic balancer and torque the bolt to specifications.

5. Install the fuel pump.

6. Connect the radiator hoses.

7. Install the water pump, fan, pulley, accessory drive belts.

8. Tighten the alternator adjusting bolts.

9. Connect the negative (−) battery cable. Refill the radiator and the cylinder block.

Oldsmobile Built Gasoline Engines

1. Disconnect the negative (−) battery cable. Drain the coolant. Disconnect the radiator hose and the bypass hose. Remove the fan, belts and pulley.

CAUTION: *When draining the coolant, keep in mind that cats and dogs are attracted by*

the ethylene glycol antifreeze, and are quite likely to drink any that is left in an uncovered container or in puddles on the ground. This will prove fatal in sufficient quantity. Always drain the coolant into a sealable container. Coolant should be reused unless it is contaminated or several years old.

2. Remove the vibration damper and crankshaft pulley.

3. On 1975–76 models only (which have no dowel pins), remove the oil pan.

4. Remove the front cover attaching bolts and remove the cover, timing indicator and water pump from the front of the engine. This requires removing all the bolts (four) that hold the cover on at the bottom, and four larger water pump mounting bolts that go right through the cover into the block. The two top center wa-

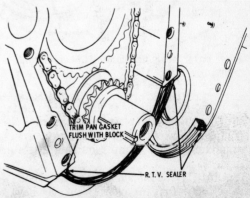

Sealer application, Chevrolet and Olds-built engines

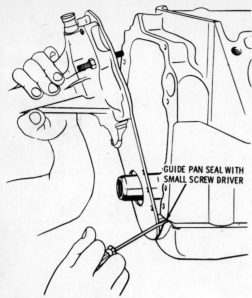

Guiding front cover into place

Chamfer on dowel pin, Olds-built engines

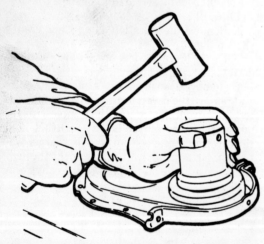

Front cover seal installation, Chevrolet-built engines

ter pump mounting bolts and the two bottom such bolts remain in place and retain the water pump and gasket to the front of the cover. The other four water pump mounting bolts are removed.

On 1977 and later models, remove the two dowel pins from the block. You may have to grind a flat on each pin to get a good grip.

5. On 1977 and later models, grind a chamfer on the end of each dowel pin as illustrated. When installing the dowel pins, they must be inserted chamfered end first. Trim about ⅛ in. (3.1mm) from each end of the new front pan seal and trim any excess material from the front edge of the oil pan gasket. Be sure all mating surfaces are clean.

6. On 1975–76 models apply a sealer around water holes on the new cover gasket before applying it to the block.

6a. On 1977 and later models:

a. Clean all seal mating surfaces with solvent.

b. When installing the new front cover gasket, first apply sealer to the water pump bolt hole areas of the seal and then position the gasket to the block.

c. Apply RTV sealer to the junction of block, pan, and front cover.

d. In positioning the front cover onto the block and gasket, press it downward to compress the seal. Then, rotate the cover left and right while you guide the pan seal into the cavity with a small prybar, as shown. Now, apply oil to the threads and install two of the bolts finger tight to hold the cover in place. Install the two dowel pins, chamfered end first.

7. **To install:** note these points:

a. When installing cover bolts, first coat them with engine oil. Tighten evenly, torquing the four lower bolts to 35 ft. lbs. (48 Nm) and the four bolts passing through the water pump to 22 ft. lbs. (30 Nm).

b. Apply a high quality lubricant (an example is GM 1050169) to the sealing surface of the balancer.

c. When installing the balancer bolt, torque to 200–310 ft. lbs. (270–420 Nm). Crankshaft pulley attaching bolts are torqued to 10 ft. lbs. (14 Nm); fan pulley attaching bolts are torqued to 20 ft. lbs. (27 Nm).

Chevrolet Built Engines

1. Disconnect the negative (–) battery cable. Drain the cooling system.

CAUTION: *When draining the coolant, keep in mind that cats and dogs are attracted by the ethylene glycol antifreeze, and are quite likely to drink any that is left in an uncovered container or in puddles on the ground. This will prove fatal in sufficient quantity. Always drain the coolant into a sealable container. Coolant should be reused unless it is contaminated or several years old.*

2. Remove the crankshaft pulley with a puller. Remove the water pump. Remove the screws holding the timing case cover to the block and remove the cover and gaskets.

3. Use a suitable tool to pry the old seal out of the front face of the cover.

To install:

1. Install the new seal so that open end is toward the inside of the cover.

NOTE: *Coat the lip of the new seal with oil prior to installation.*

2. Check that the timing chain oil slinger is in place against the crankshaft sprocket.

3. Apply a ⅛ in. (3.1mm) bead of RTV sealer to the joint formed by the oil pan and cylinder block.

4. Coat the cover gasket with sealer and position it on the block. Coat the bottom of the crankshaft seal with engine oil and carefully position the cover over the crankshaft and onto the locating dowels. Make sure you don't force the cover over the dowels, or it will be distorted. Now, loosely install the cover-to-block upper attaching screws.

5. Tighten the screws alternately in several stages, while you hold the cover downward and in position so that the dowels do not bind in the cover holes. Install the remaining screws and tighten alternately and in several stages to 6–8 ft. lbs. (8–11 Nm).

6. Install the vibration damper and water pump. Torque the vibration damper bolt to 200–310 ft. lbs. (270–420 Nm).

7. Connect the negative battery cable, refill the engine with coolant, start the engine and check for leaks.

Diesel Engine

1. Disconnect the negative (−) battery cable. Drain the cooling system and disconnect the radiator hoses.

CAUTION: *When draining the coolant, keep in mind that cats and dogs are attracted by the ethylene glycol antifreeze, and are quite likely to drink any that is left in an uncovered container or in puddles on the ground. This will prove fatal in sufficient quantity. Always drain the coolant into a sealable container. Coolant should be reused unless it is contaminated or several years old.*

2. Remove all belts, fan and pulley, crankshaft pulley and balancer, using a balancer puller.

CAUTION: *The use of any other type of puller, such as a universal claw type which pulls on the outside of the hub, can destroy the balancer. The outside ring of the balancer is bonded in rubber to the hub. Pulling on the outside will break the bond. The timing mark is on the outside ring. If it is suspected that the bond is broken, check that the center of the keyway is 16° from the center of the timing slot. In addition, there are chiseled aligning marks between the weight and the hub.*

3. Unbolt and remove the cover, timing indicator and water pump.

4. Remove the two dowel pins from the block. It may be necessary to grind a flat on each pin to get a grip on it.

To install:

1. Grind a chamfer on one end of each dowel pin.

2. Cut the excess material from the front end of the oil pan gasket on each side of the block.

3. Clean the block, oil pan and front cover mating surfaces with solvent and a gasket scraper.

4. Trim about ⅛ in. (3.1mm) off each end of a new front pan seal.

5. Install a new front cover gasket on the block and a new seal in the front cover.

6. Apply sealer to the gasket around the coolant holes.

7. Apply sealer to the block at the junction of the pan and front cover.

8. Place the cover on the block and press down to compress the seal. Rotate the cover left and right and guide the pan seal into the cavity using a small prybar. Oil the bolt threads and install two bolts to hold the cover in place. Install both dowel pins (chamfered end first), then install the remaining front cover bolts.

9. Apply a lubricant, compatible with rubber, on the balancer seal surface.

10. Install the balancer and bolt. Torque the bolt to 200–310 ft. lbs. (270–420 Nm).

11. Install the belts, connect the negative battery cable, refill the engine with coolant, start the engine and check for leaks.

Timing Chain
REMOVAL AND INSTALLATION
Buick Built V6 and V8

1. Disconnect the negative (−) battery cable. Remove the front cover as previously outlined.

2. Align the timing marks on the sprockets.

3. Remove the camshaft sprocket bolt without changing the position of the sprocket. On the V6 and 455, remove the oil pan.

4. Remove the front crankshaft oil slinger.

5. On the 350, remove the crankshaft distributor drive gear retaining bolt and washer. Remove the drive gear and the fuel pump eccentric. On the V6 and the 455, remove the camshaft sprocket bolts.

6. Using two large prybars, carefully pry the camshaft sprocket and the crankshaft sprocket forward until they are free. Remove the sprockets and the chain.

7. Remove the crankshaft sprocket using a jaw puller or equivalent tool.

To install:

1. Make sure, with sprockets temporarily in-

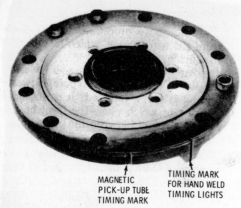

MAGNETIC
PICK-UP TUBE
TIMING MARK

TIMING MARK
FOR HAND WELD
TIMING LIGHTS

Harmonic balancer timing marks, V6

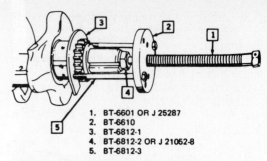

1. BT-6601 OR J 25287
2. BT-6610
3. BT-6812-1
4. BT-6812-2 OR J 21052-8
5. BT-6812-3

Removing crankshaft timing sprocket

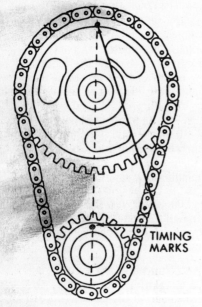

TIMING
MARKS

Pontiac V8 valve timing marks. Olds 400 V8 similar

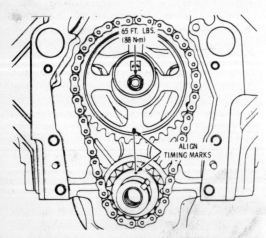

65 FT. LBS.
(88 N·m)

ALIGN
TIMING MARKS

Timing chain and sprocket alignment—all V6 and V8 engines except Pontiac V8 and Olds 400

stalled, that No. 1 piston is at top dead center and the camshaft sprocket O-mark is straight down and on the centerline of both shafts. Refer to the "Timing Chain Alignment" illustrations in this section.

2. Remove the camshaft sprocket and assemble the timing chain on both sprockets. Then slide the sprockets-and-chain assembly on the shafts with the O-marks in their closest together position and on a centerline with the sprocket hubs.

3. Assemble the slinger on the crankshaft with I.D. against the sprocket, (concave side toward the front of engine). Install the oil pan, if removed.

4. On the 350, slide the fuel pump eccentric on the camshaft and the Woodruff key with the oil groove forward. On the six cylinder and the 455, install the camshaft sprocket bolts.

5. Install the distributor drive gear.

6. Install the drive gear and eccentric bolt and retaining washer Torque to 40–55 ft. lbs. (54–75 Nm). Turn the crankshaft over twice to see if the timing marks align. If they do not align, the chain is not in the right position and will have to be realigned.

7. Install the timing case cover. Install a new seal by lightly tapping it in place. The lip of the seal faces inward. Pay particular attention to the following points.

a. Remove the oil pump cover and pack the space around the oil pump gears completely full of petroleum jelly. There must be no air space left inside the pump. Reinstall the pump cover using a new gasket.

b. The gasket surface of the block and timing chain cover must be clean and smooth. Use a new gasket correctly positioned.

c. Install the chain cover being certain the dowel pins engage the dowel pin holes before starting the attaching bolts.

d. Lube the bolt threads before installation and install them.

e. If the vehicle has power steering the front pump bracket should be installed at this time.

f. Lube the O.D. of the harmonic balancer

hub before installation to prevent damage to the seal when starting the engine.

NOTE: *The V6 engine has two timing marks on the harmonic balancer. A 1 in. (25.4mm) long, thin scribe mark is used for strobe light timing. Another mark, 4 in. (102mm) back, has a wider slot and is about ½ in. (12.7mm) long. This mark is used for magnetic pick-up timing.*

Pontiac Built Engines

1. Disconnect the negative (–) battery cable. Remove the timing chain cover as previously outlined in this chapter.

2. Remove the camshaft bolt, fuel pump eccentric and bushing.

3. Align the timing marks to simplify proper positioning of the sprockets during reassembly.

4. Slide the timing chain and camshaft gear off at the same time.

NOTE: *If you intend to remove the gear on the crankshaft you will need a puller to do so.*

To install:

1. Install the new timing chain and or sprockets, making sure the marks on both sprockets are exactly on a straight line passing through the shaft centers. The camshaft should extend through the sprocket so that the hole in the fuel pump eccentric will locate on the shaft.

6. Install the fuel pump eccentric and bushing. Install the retainer bolt and tighten it to 40 ft. lbs. (54 Nm).

7. Reinstall the timing gear cover, water pump, and harmonic balancer. Remember to install a new O-ring in the water passage. Connect the negative batter cable and check for proper operation.

NOTE: *When rassembling the timing case cover, extra care should be taken to make sure that the oil seal between the bottom of the timing case cover and the front of the oil pan is still good. Gasket cement should be used at the joint to prevent oil leaks.*

Oldsmobile Built Engines

1. Disconnect the negative (–) battery cable.

2. Remove the timing case cover and take off the camshaft gear.

NOTE: *The fuel pump operating cam is bolted to the front of the camshaft sprocket and the sprocket is located on the camshaft by means of a dowel.*

3. Remove the oil slinger, timing chain, and the camshaft sprocket. If the crankshaft sprocket is to be replaced, remove it also at this time. Remove the crankshaft key before using the puller. If the key can not be removed, align the puller so it does not overlap the end of the key, as the keyway is only machined part of the way into the crankshaft gear.

To install:

1. Reinstall the crankshaft sprocket being careful to start it with the keyway in perfect alignment since it is rather difficult to correct for misalignment after the gear has been started on the shaft. Turn the timing mark on the crankshaft gear until it points directly toward the center of the camshaft. Mount the timing chain over the camshaft gear and start the camshaft gear up on to its shaft with the timing marks as close as possible to each other and in line between the shaft centers. Rotate the camshaft to align the shaft with the new gear.

2. Install the fuel pump eccentric with the flat side toward the rear.

3. Drive the key in with a hammer until it bottoms.

4. Install the oil slinger.

5. Install the timing cover, vibration damper, belts, fan, connect the negative battery cable. Start the engine and check for normal operation.

NOTE: *Any time the timing chain and gears are replaced on the diesel engine it will be necessary to retime the engine. Refer to the paragraph on Diesel Engine Injection Timing in Chapter 5.*

Chevrolet Built Engines

To replace the chain, remove the radiator, water pump, the harmonic balancer and the crankcase front cover. This will allow access to the timing chain. Crank the engine until the timing marks on both sprockets are nearest each other and in line between the shaft centers. Then take out the three bolts that hold the camshaft gear to the camshaft. This gear is a light press fit on the camshaft and will come off easily. It is located by a dowel.

The chain comes off with the camshaft gear.

A gear puller will be required to remove the crankshaft gear.

Without disturbing the position of the engine, mount the new crankshaft gear on the shaft, and mount the chain over the camshaft gear. Arrange the camshaft gear in such a way that the timing marks will line up between the shaft centers and the camshaft locating dowel will enter the dowel hole in the cam sprocket.

Place the cam sprocket, with its chain mounted over it, in position on the front of the vehicle and pull up with the three bolts that hold it to the camshaft.

After the gears are in place, turn the engine two full revolutions to make certain that the timing marks are in correct alignment between the shaft centers.

End play of the camshaft is zero.

Camshaft

REMOVAL AND INSTALLATION

V6

1. Disconnect the negative (−) battery cable. Drain and remove the radiator. Remove the air conditioning condenser. If disconnected, immediately cap condenser openings. Remove the A/C condenser.

CAUTION: *When draining the coolant, keep in mind that cats and dogs are attracted by the ethylene glycol antifreeze, and are quite likely to drink any that is left in an uncovered container or in puddles on the ground. This will prove fatal in sufficient quantity. Always drain the coolant into a sealable container. Coolant should be reused unless it is contaminated or several years old.*

2. Remove valve covers.
3. Remove rocker arm and shaft assemblies, pushrods and valve lifters. Mark parts as necessary and keep pushrods in order for later assembly.
4. Remove timing chain cover, timing chain and sprocket.
5. Install long bolts into the camshaft sprocket bolt holes to help support the camshaft. Carefully slide camshaft forward, out of the bearing bores, working slowly to avoid marring the bearing surfaces. Remove camshaft.

To install:

1. Liberally coat the entire cam with assembly lube or equivalent. Slowly slide the camshaft into the engine block, exercising extreme care not to damage the cam bearings.
2. Install the timing chain and sprockets and timing chain cover.
3. Install the rocker arm and shaft assem-

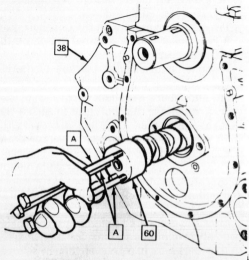

Removing camshaft from the engine—be careful not to damage bearings

blies, pushrods and valve lifters into their original locations as removed.

4. Install valve covers.
5. Install the air conditioning condenser. Evacuate and recharge the A/C system as outlined in Chapter 1.
6. Connect the negative (−) battery cable. Refill the radiator.
7. Start the engine and check for proper operation and leaks.

Gasoline V8

1. Disconnect the negative (−) battery cable.
2. Drain and remove the radiator.

CAUTION: *When draining the coolant, keep in mind that cats and dogs are attracted by the ethylene glycol antifreeze, and are quite likely to drink any that is left in an uncovered container or in puddles on the ground. This will prove fatal in sufficient quantity. Always drain the coolant into a sealable container. Coolant should be reused unless it is contaminated or several years old.*

3. Disconnect the fuel line at the fuel pump. Remove the pump on 1978 and later models.
4. Disconnect the throttle cable and the air cleaner.
5. Remove the alternator belt, loosen the alternator bolts, and move the alternator to one side.
6. Remove the power steering pump from its brackets and move it out of the way.
7. Remove the air conditioning compressor from its brackets and move the compressor out of the way without disconnecting the lines.
8. Disconnect the hoses from the water pump.
9. Disconnect the electrical and vacuum connections.
10. Mark the distributor as to location in the block. Remove the distributor.

On 1977 and later model Olds engines, remove the crankshaft pulley and the hub attaching bolt. Remove the crankshaft hub. Proceed to Step 19.
11. Raise the vehicle and drain the oil pan.
12. Remove the exhaust crossover pipe and starter motor.
13. Disconnect the exhaust pipe at the manifold.
14. Remove the harmonic balancer and pulley.
15. Support the engine and remove the front motor mounts.
16. Remove the flywheel inspection cover.
17. Remove the engine oil pan.
18. Support the engine by placing wooden blocks between the exhaust manifolds and the front crossmember.
19. Remove the engine front cover.

20. Remove the valve covers.

21. Remove the intake manifold, oil filler pipe, and temperature sending switch.

22. Mark the lifters, pushrods, and rocker arms as to location so that they may be installed in the same position. Remove these parts.

23. If the vehicle is equipped with air conditioning, discharge the A/C system and remove the condenser. See CAUTION above.

24. Remove the fuel pump eccentric, camshaft gear, oil slinger, and timing chain. Remove the camshaft thrust plate (on front of camshaft) if equipped.

25. Carefully remove the camshaft from the engine.

26. Inspect the shaft for signs of excessive wear or damage.

To install:

1. Liberally coat camshaft and bearings with engine assembly lubricant and insert the cam into the engine. Be careful not to damage the cam bearings.

2. Align the timing marks on the camshaft and crankshaft gears. See Timing Chain Replacement and Valve Timing for details.

3. Install the distributor using the locating marks made during removal. If any problems are encountered, see Distributor Installation.

4. Pay attention to the following points:

   a. Install the timing indicator before installing the power steering pump bracket.

   b. Install the flywheel inspection cover after installing the starter.

   c. Replace the engine oil and radiator coolant.

Diesel Engine

NOTE: *If equipped with air conditioning, the system must be discharged before the camshaft can be removed. The condenser must also be removed from the vehicle.*

Removal of the camshaft also requires re-

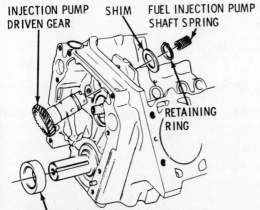

INJECTION PUMP DRIVEN GEAR   SHIM   FUEL INJECTION PUMP SHAFT SPRING

RETAINING RING

FUEL PUMP ECCENTRIC

Diesel injection pump drive

moval of the injection pump drive and driven gears, removal of the intake manifold, disassembly of the valve lifters, and re-timing of the injection pump.

1. Disconnect the negative battery cables. Drain the coolant. Remove the radiator.

CAUTION: *When draining the coolant, keep in mind that cats and dogs are attracted by the ethylene glycol antifreeze, and are quite likely to drink any that is left in an uncovered container or in puddles on the ground. This will prove fatal in sufficient quantity. Always drain the coolant into a sealable container. Coolant should be reused unless it is contaminated or several years old.*

2. Remove the intake manifold and gasket and the front and rear intake manifold seals. Refer to the "Intake Manifold" removal and installation procedure in this chapter.

3. Remove the balancer pulley and the balancer. See Caution under diesel engine front cover removal and installation, above. Remove the engine front cover using the appropriate procedure.

4. Remove the valve covers. Remove the rocker arms, pushrods and valve lifters. Be sure to keep the parts in order so that they may be returned to their original positions.

5. Remove the camshaft sprocket retaining bolt, and remove the timing chain and sprockets, using the procedure outlined earlier.

6. Position the camshaft dowel pin at the 3 o'clock position on the V8.

7. On V8s, push the camshaft rearward and hold it there, being careful not to dislodge the oil gallery plug at the rear of the engine. Remove the fuel injection pump drive gear by sliding it from the camshaft while rocking the pump driven gear.

8. To remove the fuel injection pump driven gear, remove the pump adapter, the snapring, and remove the selective washer. Remove the driven gear and spring.

NOTE: *Thread long bolts into the camshaft-to-sprocket bolt holes. The bolts are used to support the camshaft during removal.*

9. Remove the camshaft by sliding it out the front of the engine. Be extremely careful not to allow the cam lobes to contact any of the bearings, or the journals to dislodge the bearings during camshaft removal. Do not force the camshaft, or bearing damage will result.

To install:

1. If either the injection pump drive or driven gears are to be replaced, replace both gears.

2. Coat the camshaft and the cam bearings with a high quality assembly lube, GM lubricant #1052365 or the equivalent.

3. Carefully slide the camshaft into position in the engine.

4. Fit the crankshaft and camshaft sprockets, aligning the timing marks as shown in the timing chain removal and installation procedure, above. Remove the sprockets without disturbing the timing.

5. Install the injection pump driven gar, spring, shim, and snapring. Check the gear end play. If the end play is not within 0.002–0.006 in. (0.0508–0.1524mm) on V8s through 1979, and 0.002–0.015 in. (0.0508–0.3810mm) on 1980 and later, replace the shim to obtain the specified clearance. Shims are available in 0.003 in. (0.0762mm) increments, from 0.080–0.115 in. (0.2032–2.9210mm).

6. Position the camshaft dowel pin at the 3 o'clock position. Align the zero marks on the pump drive gear and pump driven gear. Hold the camshaft in the rearward position and slide the pump drive gear onto the camshaft. Install the camshaft bearing retainer.

7. Install the timing chain and sprockets, making sure the timing marks are aligned.

8. Install the lifters, pushrods and rocker arms. See the procedure for cylinder head removal for diesel engines for lifter disassembly and draining procedures. If the lifters are not disassembled and drained, valves could be bent or pushrods damaged at start-up.

9. Install the injection pump adapter and injection pump. See the appropriate sections under Fuel System above for procedures.

10. Install the valve covers after the rocker arms have been adjusted. Be sure to install all valve parts into their original positions.

11. Install the front cover, balancer and pulley. Torque the balancer bolt to 200–310 ft. lbs. (270–420 Nm). See Caution under diesel engine front cover removal and installation, above.

13. Install the intake manifold and gaskets. Refer to the "Intake Manifold" removal and installation procedure in this chapter.

14. Connect the negative battery cables. Install the radiator and refill the engine coolant.

CAMSHAFT INSPECTION

Completely clean the camshaft with solvent, paying special attention to cleaning the oil holes. Visually inspect the cam lobes and bearing journals for excessive wear. If a lobe is questionable, have the cam checked at a reputable machine ship; if a journal or lobe is worn, the camshaft must be reground or replaced. Also have the camshaft checked for straightness on a dial indicator.

NOTE: *If a cam journal is worn, there is a good chance that the bearings are worn.*

CAMSHAFT BEARINGS
REMOVAL AND INSTALLATION

If excessive camshaft wear is found, or if the engine is being completely rebuilt, the camshaft bearings should be replaced.

NOTE: *The front and rear bearings should be removed last, and installed first. Those bearings act as guides for the other bearings and pilot.*

1. Drive the camshaft rear plug from the block.

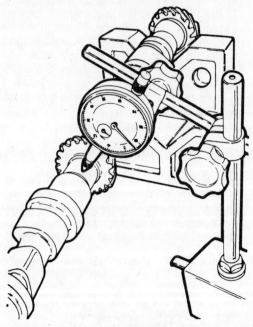

Checking camshaft for straightness

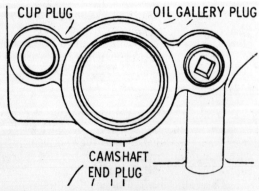

Camshaft and oil gallery plugs at rear of block

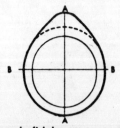

Camshaft lobe measurement

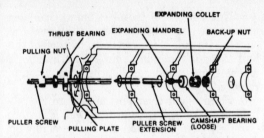

Camshaft bearing removal and installation tool

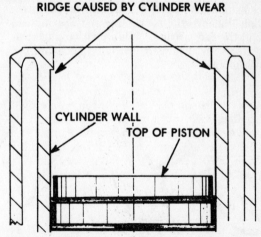

RIDGE CAUSED BY CYLINDER WEAR

CYLINDER WALL

TOP OF PISTON

Ridge formed by piston rings at the top of their travel

2. Assemble the removal puller with its shoulder on the bearing to be removed. Gradually tighten the puller nut until the bearing is removed.

3. Remove the remaining bearings, leaving the front and rear for last. To remove these, reverse the position of the puller, so as to pull the bearings toward the center of the block. Leave the tool in this position, pilot the new front and rear bearings on the installer, and pull them into position.

4. Return the puller to its original position and pull the remaining bearings into position.

NOTE: *Ensure that the oil holes align when installing the bearings. This is very important!*

5. Replace the camshaft rear plug, and stake it into position.

6. Coat the bearings and camshaft with high quality assembly lube before installing the camshaft. Use long bolts threaded into the camshaft-to-sprocket bolt holes to ease installation and help prevent bearing damage.

Pistons And Connecting Rods
REMOVAL AND INSTALLATION

Before removing the pistons, the top of the cylinder bore must be examined for a ridge. A ridge at the top of the bore is the result of normal cylinder wear, caused by the piston rings only traveling so far up the bore in the course of the piston stroke. The ridge can be felt by hand; it must be removed before the pistons are removed.

A ridge reamer is necessary for this operation. Place the piston at the bottom of its stroke, and cover it with a rag. Cut the ridge away with the ridge reamer, using extreme care to avoid cutting too deeply. Remove the rag, and remove the cuttings that remain on the piston with a magnet and a rag soaked in clean oil. Make sure the piston top and cylinder bore are absolutely clean before removing the piston.

1. Remove intake manifold and cylinder head or heads.

2. Remove oil pan.

3. Remove oil pump assembly if necessary.

4. Matchmark the connecting rod cap to the connecting rod with a scribe; each cap must be

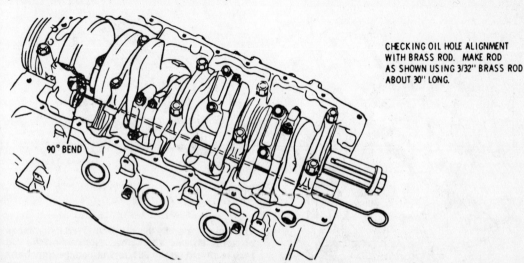

CHECKING OIL HOLE ALIGNMENT WITH BRASS ROD. MAKE ROD AS SHOWN USING 3/32" BRASS ROD ABOUT 30" LONG.

90° BEND

Checking camshaft bearing oil hole alignment

reinstalled on its proper rod in the proper direction. Remove the connecting rod bearing cap and the rod bearing. Number the top of each piston with silver paint or a felt tip pen for later assembly.

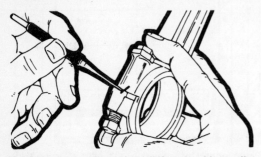

Match the connecting rods to their caps with a scribe mark

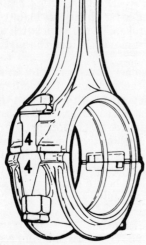

Match the connecting rods to their cylinders with a number stamp

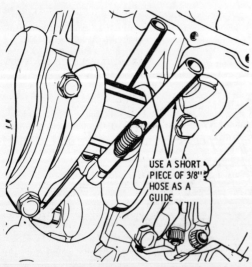

Connecting rod bolt guide

5. Cut lengths of ⅜ in. (9.5mm) diameter hose to use as rod bolt guides. Install the hose over the threads of the rod bolts, to prevent the bolt threads from damaging the crankshaft journals and cylinder walls when the piston is removed.

6. Squirt some clean engine oil onto the cylinder wall from above, until the wall is coated. Carefully push the piston and rod assembly up and out of the cylinder by tapping on the bottom of the connecting rod with a wooden hammer handle.

7. Place the rod bearing and cap back on the connecting rod, and install the nuts temporarily. Using a number stamp or punch, stamp the cylinder number on the side of the connecting rod and cap; this will help keep the proper piston and rod assembly on the proper cylinder.

NOTE: *On V6 engines, starting at the front the cylinders are numbered 2–4–6 on the*

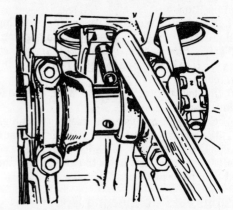

Push the piston and rod out with a hammer handle

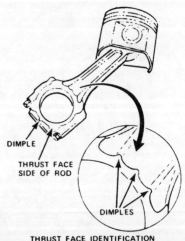

THRUST FACE IDENTIFICATION

The dimples identify the connecting rod thrust faces on some Pontiac V8 engines. Notches on the rod face rearward on the 301, forward on the right bank and rearward on the left bank on the 350 and 400 V8s.

right bank and 1–3–5 on the left. On all V8s, starting at the front the right bank cylinders are 2–4–6–8 and the left bank 1–3–5–7.

8. Remove remaining pistons in a similar manner.

On all engines, the notch on the piston will face the front of the engine for assembly. The chamfered corners of the bearing caps should face toward the front of the engine for the right bank and to the rear of the engine on the left bank. On some Pontiac built engines, the rods

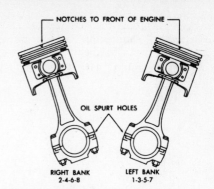

Pontiac V8 piston and rod assembly

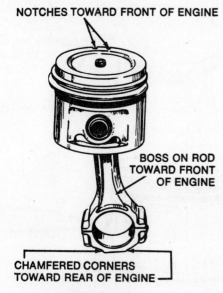

Right bank piston and rod assembly, 231 and 252 V6s

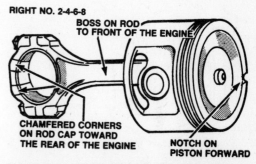

Buick V8 piston and rod assembly, right bank

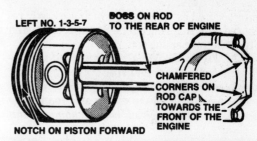

Buick V8 piston and connecting rod assembly, left bank

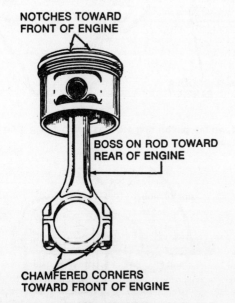

Left bank piston and rod assembly, V6s

have three dimples on one side of the rod and a single dimple on the rod cap. The dimples must face to the rear on the right bank and forward on the left. Where there are numbers on the pistons and rods, the numbers must be on the same side when the two are assembled.

On various engines, the piston compression rings are marked with a dimple, a letter **T**, a letter **O**, **GM** or the word **TOP** to identify the side of the ring which must face toward the top of the piston.

Piston Ring and Wrist Pin
REMOVAL

Most of the engines covered in this guide utilize pistons with pressed-in wrist pins; these must be removed by a special press designed for this purpose. Other pistons have their wrist

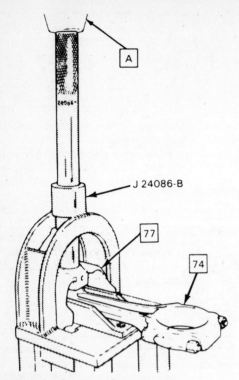

Removing piston pin—pressed-in type

pins secured by snaprings, which are easily removed with snapring pliers. Separate the piston from the connecting rod.

CAUTION: *Do NOT try to press out the piston wrist pin without using the specified tools (unless retained by snaprings). Severe damage may occur to the piston and connecting rod, causing internal engine damage and failure.*

A piston ring expander is necessary for removing piston rings without damaging them; any other method (screwdriver blades, pliers, etc.) usually results in the rings being bent, scratched or distorted, or the piston itself being damaged. When the rings are removed, clean the ring grooves using an appropriate ring

groove cleaning tool, using care not to cut too deeply. Thoroughly clean all carbon and varnish from the piston with a non-caustic solvent.

CAUTION: *Do not use a wire brush or caustic solvent (acids, etc.) on pistons.*

Inspect the pistons for scuffing, scoring, cracks, pitting, or excessive ring groove wear. If these are evident, the piston must be replaced.

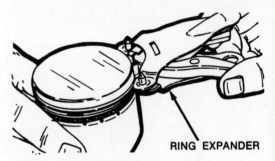

RING EXPANDER

Remove the piston rings

Install the piston lock-rings, if used

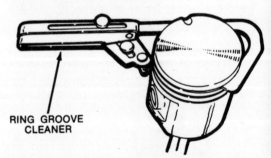

RING GROOVE CLEANER

Clean the piston ring grooves using a ring groove cleaner

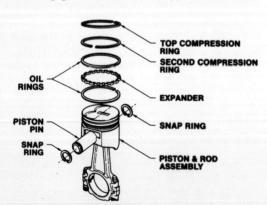

Piston rings and wrist pin

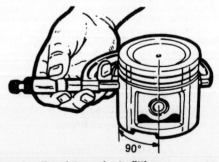

Measuring the piston prior to fitting

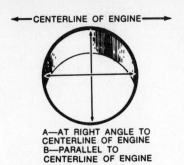

A—AT RIGHT ANGLE TO
CENTERLINE OF ENGINE
B—PARALLEL TO
CENTERLINE OF ENGINE

Cylinder bore measuring points

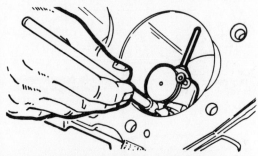

Measuring cylinder bore with a dial gauge

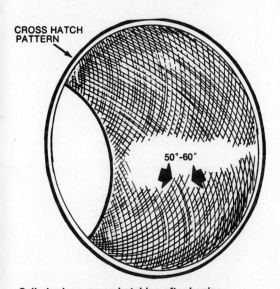

CROSS HATCH
PATTERN

50°-60°

Cylinder bore cross-hatching after honing

The piston should also be checked in relation to the cylinder diameter. Using a telescoping gauge and micrometer, or a dial gauge, measure the cylinder bore diameter perpendicular (90%) to the piston pin, 2½ in. (63.5mm) below the cylinder block deck (surface where the block mates with the heads). Then, with the micrometer, measure the piston perpendicular to its wrist pin on the skirt. The difference between the two measurements is the piston clearance. If the clearance is within specifications or slightly below (after the cylinders have been

bored or honed), finish honing is all that is necessary. If the clearance is excessive, try to obtain a slightly larger piston to bring clearance to within specifications. If this is not possible, obtain the first oversize piston and bore the cylinder to size. Generally, if the cylinder bore is tapered 0.005 in. (0.127mm) or more or is out-of-round 0.003 in. (0.0762mm) or more, it is advisable to rebore for the smallest possible oversize piston and rings.

After measuring, mark pistons with a felt-tip for reference and for assembly.

NOTE: *Cylinder honing and/or boring should be performed by a reputable, professional machine shop with the proper equipment. In some cases, clean-up honing can be done with the cylinder block in the vehicle, but most excessive honing and all cylinder boring must be done with the block stripped and removed from the vehicle.*

PISTON RING END GAP

Piston ring end gap should be checked while the rings are removed from the pistons. Incorrect end gap indicates that the wrong size rings are being used; ring breakage could occur.

Compress the piston rings to be used in a cylinder, one at a time, into that cylinder. Squirt clean oil into the cylinder, so that the rings and the top 2 in. (51mm) of cylinder wall are coated. Using an inverted piston, press the rings approximately 1 in. (25mm) below the deck of the block (on diesels, measure ring gap clearance with the ring positioned at the bottom of ring travel in the bore). Measure the ring end gap with a feeler gauge, and compare to the Ring Gap chart in this chapter. Carefully pull the ring out of the cylinder and file the ends squarely with a fine file to obtain the proper clearance.

PISTON RING SIDE CLEARANCE CHECK AND INSTALLATION

Check the pistons to see that the ring grooves and oil return holes have been properly cleaned.

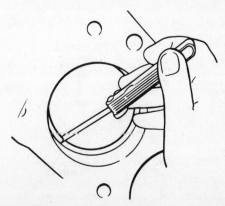

Checking piston ring end gap with a feeler gauge

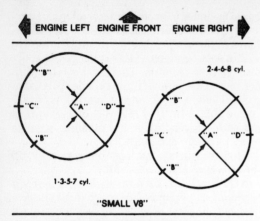

← ENGINE LEFT ENGINE FRONT ENGINE RIGHT →

2-4-6-8 cyl.

1-3-5-7 cyl.

"SMALL V8"

"A" OIL RING SPACER GAP
(Tang in Hole or Slot within Arc)

"B" OIL RING RAIL GAPS

"C" 2ND COMPRESSION RING CAP

"D" TOP COMPRESSION RING GAP

Ring gap location—Chevrolet, Olds, Pontiac V8

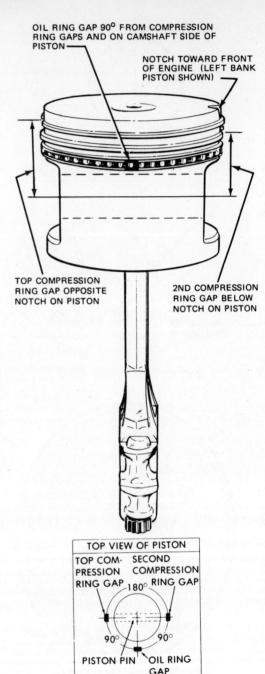

OIL RING GAP 90° FROM COMPRESSION RING GAPS AND ON CAMSHAFT SIDE OF PISTON

NOTCH TOWARD FRONT OF ENGINE (LEFT BANK PISTON SHOWN)

TOP COMPRESSION RING GAP OPPOSITE NOTCH ON PISTON

2ND COMPRESSION RING GAP BELOW NOTCH ON PISTON

TOP VIEW OF PISTON

TOP COM- SECOND
PRESSION COMPRESSION
RING GAP 180° RING GAP

90° 90°

PISTON PIN OIL RING GAP

CAMSHAFT

Piston ring gap location—Buick-built V6, V8

Slide a piston ring into its groove, and check the side clearance with a feeler gauge. On gasoline engines, make sure you insert the gauge between the ring and its lower land (lower edge of the groove), because any wear that occurs forms a step at the inner portion of the lower land. On diesels, insert the gauge between the ring and the upper land. If the piston grooves have worn to the extent that relatively high steps exist on the lower land, the piston should be replaced, because these will interfere with the operation of the new rings and ring clearances will be excessive. Piston rings are not furnished in oversize widths to compensate for ring groove wear.

Install the rings on the piston, lowest ring first, using a piston ring expander. There is a high risk of breaking or distorting the rings, or scratching the piston, if the rings are installed by hand or other means.

Position the rings on the piston as illustrated; spacing of the various piston ring gaps is crucial to proper oil retention and even cylinder

wear. When installing new rings, refer to the installation diagram furnished with the new parts.

Connecting Rod Bearings

Connecting rod bearings for the engines covered in this guide consist of two halves or shells which are interchangeable in the rod and cap.

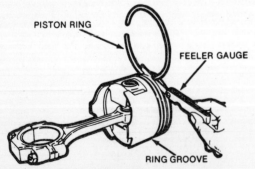

PISTON RING

FEELER GAUGE

RING GROOVE

Checking ring side clearance

When the shells are placed in position, the ends extend slightly beyond the rod and cap surfaces so that when the rod bolts are torqued the shells will be clamped tightly in place to insure positive seating and to prevent turning. A tang holds the shells in place.

NOTE: *The ends of the bearing shells must never be filed flush with the mating surface of the rod and cap.*

If a rod bearing becomes noisy or is worn so that its clearance on the crank journal is sloppy, a new bearing of the correct undersize must be selected and installed since there is no provision for adjustment.

CAUTION: *Under no circumstances should the rod end or cap be filed to adjust the bearing clearance, nor should shims of any kind be used.*

Inspect the rod bearings while the rod assemblies are out of the engine. If the shells are scored or show flaking, they should be replaced. If they are in good shape check for proper clearance on the crank journal (see below). Any scoring or ridges on the crank journal means the crankshaft must be replaced, or reground and fitted with undersized bearings.

NOTE: *If turbo V6 crank journals are scored or ridged the crankshaft must be replaced, as regrinding will reduce the durability and strength of the crankshaft.*

CHECKING BEARING CLEARANCE AND REPLACING BEARINGS

NOTE: *Make sure connecting rods and their caps are kept together, and that the caps are installed in the proper direction. On some engines like the Buick built 350 V8, the caps can only be installed one way.*

Replacement bearings are available in standard size, and in undersizes for reground crankshafts. Connecting rod-to-crankshaft bearing clearance is checked using Plastigage®

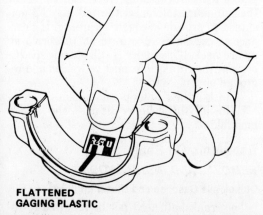

FLATTENED GAGING PLASTIC

Checking rod bearing clearance with Plastigage® or equivalent

at either the top or bottom of each crank journal. The Plastigage® has a range of 0.001–0.003 in. (0.0254–0.0762mm).

1. Remove the rod cap with the bearing shell. Completely clean the bearing shell and the crank journal, and blow any oil from the oil hole in the crankshaft; Plastigage® is soluble in oil.

2. Place a piece of Plastigage® lengthwise along the bottom center of the lower bearing shell, then install the cap with shell and torque the bolt or nuts to specification. DO NOT turn the crankshaft with Plastigage® in the bearing.

3. Remove the bearing cap with the shell. The flattened Plastigage® will be found sticking to either the bearing shell or crank journal. Do not remove it yet.

4. Use the scale printed on the Plastigage® envelope to measure the flattened material at its widest point. The number within the scale which most closely corresponds to the width of the Plastigage® indicates bearing clearance in thousandths of an inch.

5. Check the specifications chart in this chapter for the desired clearance. It is advisable to install a new bearing if clearance exceeds 0.003 in. (0.0762mm); however, if the bearing is in good condition and is not being checked because of bearing noise, bearing replacement is not necessary.

6. If you are installing new bearings, try a standard size, then each undersize in order until one is found that is within the specified limits when checked for clearance with Plastigage®. Each undersize shell has its size stamped on it.

7. When the proper size shell is found, clean off the Plastigage®, oil the bearing thoroughly, reinstall the cap with its shell and torque the rod bolt nuts to specification.

NOTE: *With the proper bearing selected and the nuts torqued, it should be possible to move the connecting rod back and forth freely on the crank journal as allowed by the specified connecting rod and clearance. If the rod cannot be moved, either the rod bearing is too far undersize or the rod is misaligned.*

PISTON AND CONNECTING ROD ASSEMBLY AND INSTALLATION

Install the connecting rod to the piston, making sure piston installation notches and any marks on the rod are in proper relation to one another. Lubricate the wrist pin with clean engine oil, and install the pin into the rod and piston assembly, either by hand or by using a wrist pin press as required. Install snaprings if equipped, and rotate them in their grooves to make sure they are seated. To install the piston and connecting rod assembly:

1. Make sure connecting rod big end bear-

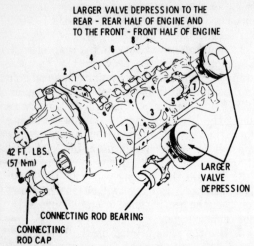

LARGER VALVE DEPRESSION TO THE
REAR - REAR HALF OF ENGINE AND
TO THE FRONT - FRONT HALF OF ENGINE

42 FT. LBS.
(57 N·m)

LARGER
VALVE
DEPRESSION

CONNECTING ROD BEARING

CONNECTING
ROD CAP

Piston locations in block, diesels up to 1981. On '82 and later models, pistons are notched, and the notch faces front.

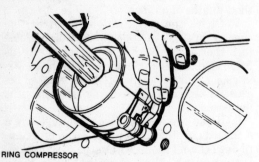

RING COMPRESSOR

Using a wooden hammer handle, tap the piston down through the ring compressor and into the cylinder

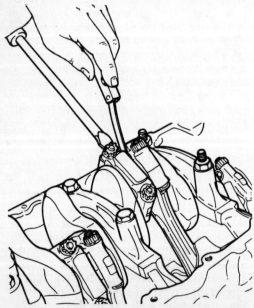

Checking connecting rod side clearance with a feeler gauge. Use a small pry bar to carefully spread the connecting rods

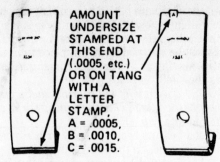

AMOUNT UNDERSIZE STAMPED AT THIS END (.0005, etc.) OR ON TANG WITH A LETTER STAMP, A = .0005, B = .0010, C = .0015.

Bearing insert markings

ings (including end cap) are of the correct size and properly installed.

2. Fit rubber hoses over the connecting rod bolts to protect the crankshaft journals, as in the Piston Removal procedure. Coat the rod bearings with high quality assembly lube (not engine oil).

3. Using the proper ring compressor, insert the piston assembly into the cylinder so that the notch in the top of the piston faces the front of the engine (this assumes that the dimple(s) or other markings on the connecting rods are in correct relation to the piston notch(es).

4. From beneath the engine, coat each crank journal with assembly lube. Pull the connecting rod, with the bearing shell in place, into position against the crank journal.

5. Remove the rubber hoses. Install the bearing cap and cap nuts and torque to specification.

NOTE: *When more than one rod and piston assembly is being installed, the connecting rod cap attaching nuts should only be tightened enough to keep each rod in position until all have been installed. This will ease the installation of the remaining piston assemblies.*

6. Check the clearance between the sides of the connecting rods and the crankshaft using a feeler gauge. Spread the rods slightly with a prybar to insert the gauge. If clearance is below the minimum tolerance, the rod may be machined to provide adequate clearance. If clearance is excessive, substitute an unworn rod, and recheck. If clearance is still outside specifications, the crankshaft must be welded and reground or replaced.

7. Install the oil pump and oil pan.

8. Install the cylinder head(s) and intake manifold.

Rear Main Oil Seal

REMOVAL AND INSTALLATION

Oldsmobile Gasoline and Diesel Engines

The crankshaft need not be removed to replace the rear main bearing upper oil seal. The lower seal is installed in the bearing cap.

1. Drain the crankcase oil and remove the oil pan and rear main bearing cap.

2. Using a special main seal tool or a tool that can be made from a dowel (see illustration), drive the upper seal into its groove on each side until it is tightly packed. This is usually ¼–¾ in. (6–19mm).

3. Measure the amount the seal was driven up on one side; add $\frac{1}{16}$ in. (1.6mm) and cut another length from the old seal. Use the main bearing cap as a holding fixture when cutting the seal as illustrated. Carefully trim the protruding seal.

4. Work these two pieces of seal up into the

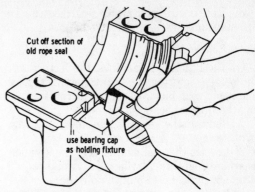
Cutting off the lower seal ends.

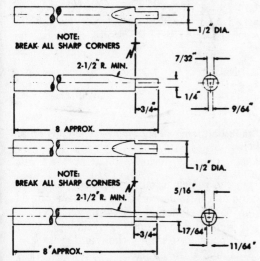
Make a rear main bearing seal tool from a wooden dowel. The upper tool dimensions are for engines up to 400 cu. in.; the bottom is for 455s.

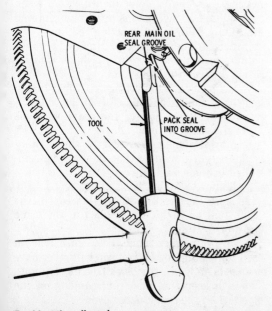
Packing the oil seal.

NEOPRENE COMPOSITION SEAL

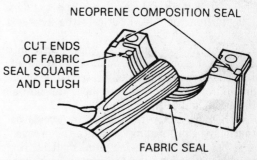
Installing lower main bearing oil seal—fabric type

cylinder block on each side with two nailsets or small prybars. Using the packing tool again, pack these pieces into the block, then trim the flush with a razor blade or hobby knife as shown. Do not scratch the bearing surface with the razor.

5. Install a new seal in the rear main bearing cap. Run a $\frac{1}{16}$ in. (1.6mm) bead of sealer onto the outer mating surface of the bearing cap. Assemble the cap to the block and torque to specifications.

Pontiac Built Engines

1. Remove the oil pan, baffle, and oil pump.

2. Remove the rear main bearing cap.

3. Obtain an oil seal tool, or construct one from a dowel as illustrated. Insert the tool against one end of the oil seal in the block and drive the seal gently into the groove about ¾ in. (19mm). Repeat on the other end of the seal.

4. Using the bearing cap as a holder, form a new upper bearing seal in the cap. Cut four ⅜ in. (9.5mm) long pieces from this seal.

5. Work two of the pieces into each of the gaps which have been made at the end of the seal in the cylinder block. Do not cut off any material to make the pieces fit.

6. Press a new seal into the bearing cap.

7. Apply a $\frac{1}{16}$ in. (1.6mm) bead of sealer across the outer mating surface of the bearing cap.

8. Reassemble the cap and torque to specifications.

Buick Built V6 and V8

On the Buick built engines, the factory recommends removing the crankshaft to replace the upper seal, but the seal can be replaced using the method below.

1. Remove the oil pan and the rear main bearing cap.

2. Loosen the rest of the crankshaft main bearings slightly and allow the crankshaft to drop about $\frac{1}{16}$ in. (1.6mm), no more.

3. Remove the old upper half of the oil seal.

4. Wrap some soft copper wire around the end of the new seal and leave about 12 in. (305mm) on the end. Lubricate the new seal generously with clean oil.

5. Slip the free end of the copper wire into the oil seal groove and around the crankshaft. Pull the wire until the seal protrudes an equal amount on each side. Rotate the crankshaft as the seal is pulled into place.

6. Remove the wire. Push any excess seal that may be protruding back into the groove.

7. Before tightening the crankshaft bearing caps, visually check the bearings to make sure they are in place. Torque the bearing cap bolts to specification. Make sure there is no oil on the mating surfaces.

8. To replace the seal in the main bearing cap, remove the old seal and place a new seal in the groove with both ends projecting above the mating surface of the cap.

9. Force the seal into the cap groove by rubbing down on it with a hammer handle or other smooth round tool, until the seal projects above the groove not more than $\frac{1}{16}$ in. (1.6mm). Using a razor blade, cut the ends off flush with the surface of the cap.

10. On the V6s and Buick built 350 V8, place new neoprene seals in the grooves in the sides of the bearing caps after soaking the seals in kerosene for two minutes.

NOTE: *The neoprene seals will swell up once exposed to the oil and heat. It is normal for the seals to leak for a short time, until they become properly seated. The seals must NOT be cut to fit.*

11. Reverse the above procedure for installation. Use a small bead of sealer on the outer edge of the bearing cap mating surface.

12. Install the oil pan. Run the engine at low rpm for the first few minutes of operation.

Crankshaft and Main Bearings
CRANKSHAFT REMOVAL

1. Disconnect the negative (−) battery cable. Drain the engine oil and remove the engine

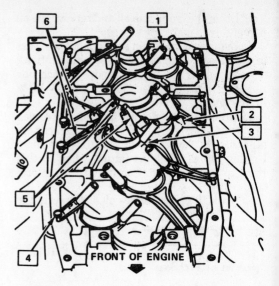

1. Rubber	5. Note overlap of
2. #4 Rod	adjacent rods
3. #3 Rod	6. Rubber
4. Oil pan bolt	bands

Crankshaft removal showing hose lengths on rod bolts

from the vehicle. Mount the engine on a work stand in a suitable working area. Invert the engine, so the oil pan is facing up.

2. Remove the engine front (timing) cover.

3. Remove the timing chain and gears.

4. Remove the oil pan.

5. Remove the oil pump.

6. Stamp the cylinder number on the machined surfaces of the bolt bosses of the connecting rods and caps for identification when reinstalling. If the pistons are to be removed eventually from the connecting rod, mark the cylinder number on the pistons with silver paint or felt-tip pen for proper cylinder identification and cap-to-rod location.

7. Remove the connecting rod caps. Install lengths of rubber hose on each of the connecting rod bolts, to protect the crank journals when the crank is removed.

8. Mark the main bearing caps with a number punch or punch so that they can be reinstalled in their original positions.

9. Remove all main bearing caps.

10. Note the position of the keyway in the crankshaft so it can be installed in the same position.

11. Install rubber bands between a bolt on each connecting rod and oil pan bolts that have been reinstalled in the block (see illustration). This will keep the rods from banging on the block when the crank is removed.

12. Carefully lift the crankshaft out of the

block. The rods will pivot to the center of the engine when the crank is removed.

MAIN BEARING INSPECTION AND REPLACEMENT

Like connecting rod bearings, the crankshaft main bearings are shell type inserts that do not utilize shims and cannot be adjusted. The bearings are available in various standard and undersizes; if main bearing clearance is found to be too sloppy, a new bearing (both upper and lower halves) is required.

NOTE: *Factory undersized crankshafts are marked, sometimes with a 9 and/or a large spot of light green paint; the bearing caps also will have the paint on each side of the undersized journal.*

Generally, the lower half of the bearing shell (except No. 1 bearing) shows greater wear and fatigue. If the lower half only shows the effects of normal wear (no heavy scoring or discoloration), it can usually be assumed that the upper half is also in good shape; conversely, if the lower half is heavily worn or damaged, both halves should be replaced. Never replace one bearing half without replacing the other.

CHECKING CLEARANCE

Main bearing clearance can be checked with the crankshaft in the vehicle and with the engine out of the vehicle. If the engine block is still in the vehicle, the crankshaft should be supported both front and rear (by the damper and to remove clearance from the upper bearing. Total clearance can then be measured between the lower bearing and journal. If the block has been removed from the vehicle, and is inverted, the crank will rest on the upper bearings and the total clearance can be measured between the lower bearing and journal. Clearance is checked in the same manner as the connecting rod bearings, with Plastigage®.

NOTE: *Crankshaft bearing caps and bearing shells should NEVER be filed flush with the cap-to-block mating surface to adjust for wear in the old bearings. Always install new bearings. The low cost of new bearings outways the aggravation of having to do the job twice because of failed bearings.*

1. If the crankshaft has been removed, install it (block removed from vehicle). If the block is still in the vehicle, remove the oil pan and oil pump. Starting with the rear bearing cap, remove the cap and wipe all oil from the crank journal and bearing cap.

2. In order to check bearing clearance, the crankshaft *must* rest against the upper bearings. If the engine is out of the vehicle, turning the block upside down will take care of this requirement. If the engine is in the vehicle, the crankshaft must be supported at either end so that it rests against the upper bearings and all clearance is present at the lower bearing.

3. Place a strip of Plastigage® the full width of the bearing, (parallel to the crankshaft), on the journal.

CAUTION: *Do not rotate the crankshaft while the gauging material is between the bearing and the journal.*

4. Install the bearing cap and evenly torque the cap bolts to specification.

5. Remove the bearing cap. The flattened Plastigage® will be sticking to either the bearing shell or the crank journal.

6. Use the graduated scale on the Plastigage® envelope to measure the material at its widest point.

NOTE: *If the flattened Plastigage® tapers toward the middle or ends, there is a difference in clearance indicating the bearing or journal has a taper, low spot or other irregularity. If this is indicated, measure the crank journal with a micrometer.*

7. If bearing clearance is within specifications, the bearing insert is in good shape. Replace the insert if the clearance is not within specifications. Always replace both upper and lower inserts as a unit.

8. Standard, 0.001 in. (0.0254mm) or 0.002 in. (0.0508mm) undersize bearings should produce the proper clearance. If these sizes still produce too sloppy a fit, the crankshaft must be reground for use with the next undersize bearing. Recheck all clearances after installing new bearings.

9. Replace the rest of the bearings in the same manner. After all bearings have been checked, rotate the crankshaft to make sure there is no excessive drag. When checking the No. 1 main bearing, loosen the accessory drive belts (engine in vehicle) to prevent a tapered reading with the Plastigage®.

MAIN BEARING REPLACEMENT

Engine Out of vehicle

1. Remove and inspect the crankshaft.

2. Remove the main bearings from the bearing saddles in the cylinder block and main bearing caps.

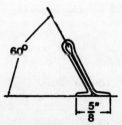

Home-made bearing roll-out pin

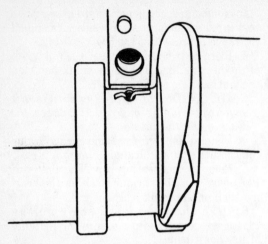

Roll-out pin installed for removing the upper half of the main bearing

3. Coat the bearing surfaces of the new, correct size main bearings with high quality assembly lube and install them in the bearing saddles in the block and in the main bearing caps. Make sure the tabs in the bearing insert align with the notch in the block and bearing cap.

4. Install the crankshaft. See Crankshaft Installation.

Engine in vehicle

1. With the oil pan, oil pump and spark plugs removed, remove the cap from the main bearing needing replacement and remove the bearing from the cap.

2. Make a bearing roll-out pin, using a bent cotter pin as shown in the illustration. Install the end of the pin in the oil hole in the crankshaft journal.

3. Rotate the crankshaft clockwise as viewed from the front of the engine. This will roll the upper bearing out of the block.

NOTE: *Turn the crankshaft in the opposite direction of the bearing insert tab. The bearing insert will only turn on way.*

4. Lube the new upper bearing with clean engine oil and insert the plain (unnotched) end between the crankshaft and the indented or notched side of the block. Roll the bearing into place, making sure that the oil holes are aligned. Remove the roll pin from the oil hole.

5. Lube the new lower bearing and install the main bearing cap. Install the main bearing cap, making sure it is positioned in proper direction with the matchmarks in alignment.

6. Torque the main bearing cap bolts to specification.

NOTE: *See Crankshaft Installation for thrust bearing alignment.*

CRANKSHAFT END PLAY AND INSTALLATION

When main bearing clearance has been checked, bearings examined and/or replaced, the crankshaft can be installed. Thoroughly clean the upper and lower bearing surfaces, and lube them with clean engine oil. Install the crankshaft and main bearing caps.

Dip all main bearing cap bolts in clean oil, and torque all main bearing caps, excluding the thrust bearing cap, to specifications (see the Crankshaft and Connecting Rod chart in this chapter to determine which bearing is the thrust bearing). Tighten the thrust bearing bolts finger tight. To align the thrust bearing, pry the crankshaft the extent of its axial travel several times, holding the last movement toward the front of the engine. Add thrust washers if required for proper alignment. Torque the thrust bearing cap to specifications.

To check crankshaft end play, pry the crankshaft to the extreme rear of its axial travel, then to the extreme front of its travel. Using a feeler gauge, measure the end play at the front of the rear main bearing. End play may also be measured at the thrust bearing. Install a new rear main bearing oil seal in the cylinder block and main bearing cap. Continue to reassemble the engine.

On the 1986 and 1987 231 and 307 cu. in. engines, it is necessary to line up the rear main bearing and crankshaft thrust surfaces. Torque all main caps to specification except the one at the rear. Torque the rear main cap to 10–12 ft.

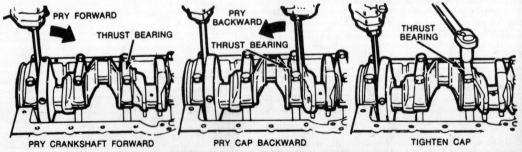

Aligning the crankshaft thrust bearing

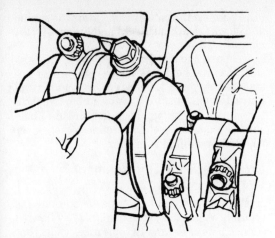

Checking crankshaft end-play

lbs. (14–16 Nm). Using a lead hammer, tap the end of the crankshaft first backward and then forward. Now, retorque all caps to specification.

Flywheel and Ring Gear
REMOVAL AND INSTALLATION

The ring gear is an integral part of the flywheel and is not replaceable.

1. Remove the transmission. Refer to the "Automatic Transmission" section in Chapter 7.

2. Remove the six bolts attaching the flywheel to the crankshaft flange. Remove the flywheel.

3. Inspect the flywheel for cracks, and inspect the ring gear for burrs or worn teeth. Replace the flywheel if any damage is apparent. Remove burrs with a mill file.

4. Install the flywheel. The flywheel will only attach to the crankshaft in one position, as the bolt holes are unevenly spaced. Install the bolts and torque to specification.

EXHAUST SYSTEM

Safety Precautions

For a number of reasons, exhaust system work can be the most dangerous type of work you can do on your vehicle. Always observe the following precautions:

• Support the vehicle extra securely. Not only will you often be working directly under it, but you'll frequently be using a lot of force, say, heavy hammer blows, to dislodge rusted parts. This can cause a vehicle that's improperly supported to shift and possibly fall.

• Wear goggles. Exhaust system parts are always rusty. Metal chips can be dislodged, even when you're only turning rusted bolts. At-

tempting to pry pipes apart with a chisel makes the chips fly even more frequently.

• If you're using a cutting torch, keep it a great distance from either the fuel tank or lines. Stop what you're doing and feel the temperature of the fuel bearing pipes on the tank frequently. Even slight heat can expand and/or vaporize fuel, resulting in accumulated vapor, or even a liquid leak, near your torch.

• Watch where your hammer blows fall and make sure you hit squarely. You could easily tap a brake or fuel line when you hit an exhaust system part with a glancing blow. Inspect all lines and hoses in the area where you have been working.

Special Tools

A number of special exhaust system tools can be rented from auto supply houses or local stores that rent special equipment. A common one is a tail pipe expander, designed to enable you to join pipes of identical diameter.

It may also be quite helpful to use solvents designed to loosen rusted bolts or flanges. Soaking rusted parts the night before you do the job can speed the work of freeing rusted parts considerably. Remember that these solvents are are often flammable. Apply only to parts after they are cool!

Exhaust Manifold
REMOVAL AND INSTALLATION

Exhaust manifolds rarely rust through, but they may crack due to road damage or thermal shock.

Remove parts that are in the way. These may include the hot air shroud, or various accessory brackets on the engine. You may have to disconnect the steering shaft on certain vehicles. Disconnect the oxygen sensor, if it's on the manifold.

1. Place safety glasses over your eyes. Disconnect the negative (–) battery cable. Remove the air cleaner.

2. The first step is to disconnect the exhaust pipe or crossover pipe by removing the nuts from the manifold studs.

3. Then slide the collar or pull the flanged portion of the exhaust pipe or crossover away. In some cases, you may have to loosen the crossover pipe on the other side in order to gain clearance for easy manifold removal. Make sure you remove and replace seals.

4. If the Early Fuel Evaporation valve is involved remove it and install it later with all new seals.

To install:

NOTE: *Be careful to ensure that seals are in-*

224
234

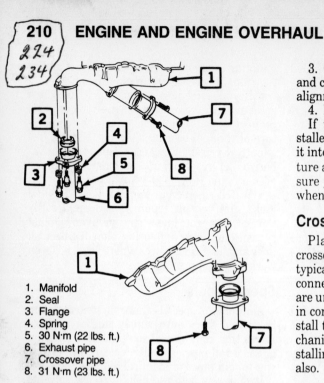

1. Manifold
2. Seal
3. Flange
4. Spring
5. 30 N·m (22 lbs. ft.)
6. Exhaust pipe
7. Crossover pipe
8. 31 N·m (23 lbs. ft.)

Disconnecting crossover and exhaust pipes—5.7 l Diesel

stalled facing in the proper direction so all exhaust ports are fully open and all bolt or stud holes or slots are in proper position. Install nuts loosely and then tighten in several stages, going around the manifold, until you reach the specified torque.

1. Reinstall the manifold, heat shields, gaskets and other hardware. Torque the manifold-to-block bolts to specifications in the Torque Specifications chart in the beginning of this chapter.

2. Install a new manifold-to-pipe gasket and torque the bolts to 23 ft. lbs. (31 Nm).

3. Connect the battery cable, start the engine and check for exhaust leaks and proper system alignment.

4. Install the air cleaner.

If the manifold has an oxygen sensor installed in it, you'll have to remove it and install it into the new manifold, using a high temperature anti-seize compound on the threads. Make sure you don't forget to reconnect the sensor when the manifold is in place.

Crossover Pipe Replacement

Place safety glasses over your eyes. The crossover pipe (used on V-type engines only) is typically connected to the manifolds by flanged connections or collars. In some cases, bolts that are unthreaded for part of their length are used in conjunction with springs. Make sure you install the springs and that they are in good mechanical condition (no broken coils) when installing the new pipe. Replace ring type seals, also.

Headpipe Replacement

Place safety glasses over your eyes. The headpipe is typically attached to the rear of one exhaust manifold with a flange or collar type connector and flagged to the front of the catalytic converter. Remove nuts and bolts and if springs are used to maintain the seal. The pipe may then be separated from the rest of the system at both flanges.

Replace ring seals; inspect springs and replace them if any coils are broken.

Catalytic Converter

CAUTION: *The catalytic converter maintains a high temperature for an extended time*

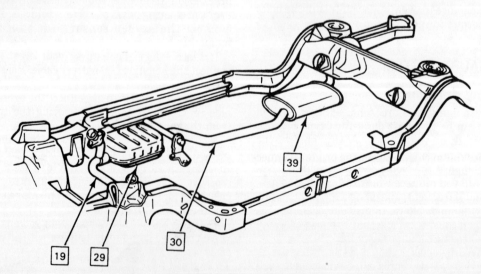

Typical "B" body exhaust system

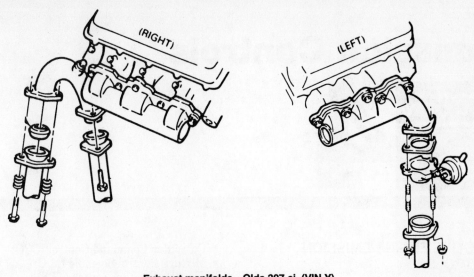

Exhaust manifolds—Olds 307 ci. (VIN Y)

after the engine is turned off. Allow the vehicle to cool for at least two hours before servicing the exhaust system or personal injury may occur.

Place safety glasses over your eyes. Remove bolts at the flange at the rear end. Then, loosen nuts and remove U-clamp to remove the catalyst. Slide the catalyst out of the outlet pipe. Replace all ring seals. In some cases, you'll have to disconnect an air line coming from the engine compartment before catalyst removal. In some cases, a hanger supports the converter via one of the flange bolts. Make sure the hanger gets properly reconnected. Also, be careful to retain all parts used to heat shield the converter and reinstall them.

Make sure the converter is replaced for proper direction of flow and air supply connections.

Mufflers and Tailpipes

Place safety glasses over your eyes. These units are typically connected by flanges at the rear of the converter and at either end of mufflers either by an original weld or by U-clamps working over a pipe connection in which one side of the connection is slightly larger than the other. You may have to cut the original connection and use the pipe expander to allow the original equipment exhaust pipe to be fitted over the new muffler. In this case, you'll have to purchase new U-clamps to fasten the joints. GM recommends that whenever you replace a muffler, all parts to the rear of the muffler in the exhaust system must be replaced. Also, all slip joints rearward of the converter should be coated with sealer before they are assembled.

Place safety glasses over your eyes. Be careful to connect all U-clamps or other hanger arrangements so the exhaust system will not flex. Assemble all parts loosely and rotate parts inside one another or clamps on the pipes to ensure proper routing of all exhaust system parts to avoid excessive heating of the floorpan, fuel lines and tank, etc. Also, make sure there is clearance to prevent the system from rattling against spring shackles, the differential, etc. You may be able to bend long pipes slightly by hand to help get enough clearance, if necessary.

While disassembling the system, keep your eye open for any leaks or for excessively close clearance to any brake system parts. Inspect the brake system for any sort of heat damage and repair as necessary.

1. Hanger
2. 20 N·m (15 lbs. ft.)
3. 52 N·m (38 lbs. ft.)
4. Converter
5. Clamp
6. 35 N·m (26 lbs. ft.)
7. Outlet pipe
8. Intermediate pipe

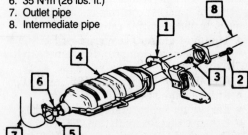

Disconnecting the catalytic converter—late model Oldsmobile

Emission Controls

GASOLINE ENGINE EMISSION CONTROLS

In its normal operation, the internal combustion engine releases several compounds into the atmosphere. Since most of these compounds are harmful to our health if inhaled or ingested for long periods in sufficient quantity, the Federal Government has placed a limit on the quantities of the three main groups of compounds: unburned hydrocarbons (HC); carbon monoxide (CO); and oxides of nitrogen (NOx).

The emissions systems covered in this chapter are designed to regulate the output of these noxious fumes by your vehicle's engine and fuel system. Three areas of the automobile are covered, each with its own anti-pollution system or systems; the engine crankcase, which emits unburned hydrocarbons in the form of oil and fuel vapors; the fuel storage system (fuel tank and carburetor), which also emits unburned hydrocarbons in the form of evaporated gasoline; and the engine exhaust. Exhaust emissions comprise the greatest quantity of auto emissions, in the forms of unburned hydrocarbons, carbon monoxide, and oxides of nitrogen. Because of this, there are more pollution devices on your vehicle dealing with exhaust emissions than there are dealing with the other two emission types.

Exhaust emission controls comprise the largest body of emission controls installed on your vehicle. Included in this category are:

- Thermostatic Air Cleaner (THERMAC)
- Air Injection Reactor System (A.I.R., 1975–80)
- Air Management System (1981 and later)
- Anti-Dieseling Solenoid
- Early Fuel Evaporation system (EFE)
- Exhaust Gas Recirculation
- Controlled Combustion System (CCS)
- Computer Controlled Catalytic Converter system (C-4)
- Computer Command Control (CCC)
- Mixture Control Solenoid (M/C)
- Throttle Position Sensor (TPS)
- Idle Speed Control (ISC)
- Electronic Spark Timing (EST)
- Electronic Spark Control (ESC)
- Transmission Converter Clutch (TCC)
- Catalytic Converter and the Oxygen Sensor system

A brief description of each system and any applicable service procedures follows.

Positive Crankcase Ventilation

OPERATION

All Buick, Olds, Chevrolet and Pontiac engines covered in this guide are equipped with a positive crankcase ventilation (PCV) system to control crankcase blow-by vapors. The system functions as follows:

When the engine is running, a small portion of the gases which are formed in the combustion chamber leak by the piston rings and enter the crankcase. Since these gases are under pressure, they tend to escape from the crankcase and enter the atmosphere. If these gases are allowed to remain in the crankcase for any period of time, they contaminate the engine oil and cause sludge to build up in the crankcase. If the gases are allowed to escape into the atmosphere, they pollute the air with unburned hydrocarbons. The job of the crankcase emission control equipment is to recycle these gases back into the engine combustion chamber where they are reburned.

The crankcase (blow-by) gases are recycled in the following way: as the engine is running, clean, filtered air is drawn through the air filter and into the crankcase. As the air passes through the crankcase, it picks up the combustion gases and carries them out of the crankcase, through the oil separator, through the PCV valve, and into the induction system. As they enter the intake manifold, they are drawn into the combustion chamber where they are reburned.

The most critical component in the system is the PCV valve. Located in the valve cover or intake manifold, this valve controls the amount of gases which are recycled into the combustion chamber. At low engine speeds, the valve is partially closed, limiting the flow of the gases into the intake manifold. As engine speed increases, the valve opens to admit greater quantities of the gases into the intake manifold. As engine speed increases, the valve opens to admit greater quantities of the gases into the intake manifold. If the valve should become blocked or plugged, the gases will be prevented from escaping from the crankcase by the normal route. Since these gases are under pressure, they will find their own way out of the crankcase. This alternate route is usually a weak oil seal or gasket in the engine. As the gas escapes by the gasket, it also creates an oil leak. Besides causing oil leaks, a clogged PCV valve also allows these gases to remain in the crankcase for an extended period of time, promoting the formation of sludge in the engine. *See Chapter 1 for PCV valve replacement intervals.*

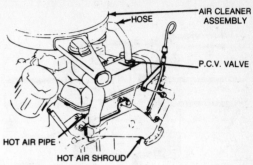

V6 PCV valve

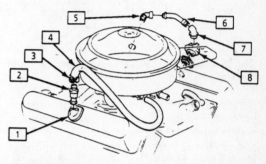

V8 PCV system

PCV VALVE SERVICE

Slow, unstable idling, frequent stalling, oil leaks and oil in the air cleaner are all signs that the PCV valve may be clogged or faulty. Follow the PCV valve testing procedure in Chapter 1 and replace the valve if necessary. Check the valve at every tune-up.

1. Remove the valve by gently pulling it out of the valve cover or manifold.

2. Then open the clamp on the hose end with a pair of pliers. Hold the clamp open while sliding it 1–2 in. (25–51mm) down the hose (away from the valve), and then remove the valve.

3. If the end of the hose is hard or cracked where it holds the valve, it may be feasible to cut the end off if there is plenty of extra hose. Otherwise, replace the hose. Replace the grommet in the valve cover if it is cracked or hard, and replace the clamp if it is broken or weak.

4. In replacing the valve, make sure it is fully inserted in the hose, that the clamp is moved over the ridge on the valve so that the valve will not slip out of the hose, and that the valve is fully inserted into the grommet in the valve cover.

PCV FILTER REMOVAL AND INSTALLATION

1. Slide the rubber coupling that joins the tube coming from the valve cover to the filter off the filter nipple. Then, remove the top of the air cleaner. Slide the spring clamp off the filter,

and remove the filter. See illustration in Chapter 1.

2. Inspect the rubber grommet in the valve cover and the rubber coupling for brittleness and cracking. Replace parts as necessary.

3. Insert the new PCV filter through the hole in the air cleaner with the open portion of the filter upward (See illustration in Chapter 1). Make sure that the square portion of filter behind the nipple fits into the (square) hole in the air cleaner.

4. Install a new spring clamp onto the nipple. Make sure the clamp goes under the ridge on the filter nipple all the way around. Then, reconnect the rubber coupling and install the air cleaner cover.

Evaporative Emission Control System

OPERATION

This system reduces the amount of escaping gasoline vapors. Float bowl emissions are controlled by internal carburetor modifications. Redesigned bowl vents, reduced bowl capacity, heat shields, and improved intake manifold-to-carburetor insulation reduce vapor loss into the atmosphere. The venting of fuel tank vapors into the air has been stopped by means of the carbon canister storage method. This method transfers fuel vapors to an activated carbon

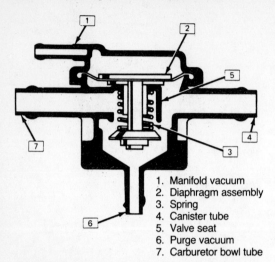

1. Manifold vacuum
2. Diaphragm assembly
3. Spring
4. Canister tube
5. Valve seat
6. Purge vacuum
7. Carburetor bowl tube

The Canister Control Valve used on 1984 cars with V-6 engines

storage device which absorbs and stores the vapor that is emitted from the engine's induction system while the engine is not running. When the engine is running, the stored vapor is purged from the carbon storage device by the intake air flow and then consumed in the normal combustion process. As the manifold vacuum reaches a certain point, it opens a purge control valve atop the charcoal storage canister. This allows air to be drawn into the canister, thus forcing the existing fuel vapors back into the engine to be burned normally.

On 1981 and later V6s, the purge function is electronically controlled by a purge solenoid in the line which is itself controlled by the Electronic Control Module (ECM). When the system is in the Open Loop mode, the solenoid valve is energized, blocking all vacuum to the purge valve. When the system is in the Closed Loop mode, the solenoid is de-energized, thus allowing existing vacuum to operate the purge valve. This releases the trapped fuel vapor and it is forced into the induction system.

Some canister systems (those without a vapor vent valve) starting in 1981 have a Canister Control Valve (C.C.V.). This is mounted near the carburetor and has four hoses connected to it. When the engine is off, manifold vacuum is non-existent at the C.C.V. and a spring loaded valve in the C.C.V. interconnects the carburetor vent hose to the canister via a Thermostatic Vacuum Valve which opens at 170°F (77°C). Vapors generated in the carburetor float bowl thus pass into the canister. When the engine is restarted, this valve closes as manifold vacuum is applied to it. When the TVS is open, the canister is purged as fuel vapors are drawn out of the canister and into the carburetor throttle body.

Most carbon canisters used are of the Open design, which means that the incoming air is drawn directly from the air cleaner.

SERVICE

The only service required for the evaporative emissions system is the periodic replacement of the charcoal canister filter. This procedure is covered in Chapter 1. Closed canisters do not require that this operation be performed. If the fuel tank cap on your vehicle ever requires replacement, make sure that it is of the same type as the original.

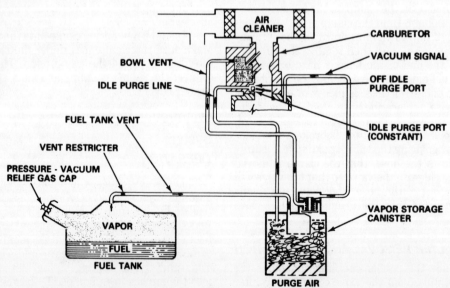

Open canister evaporative emission control system (EECS). This system is more common than the closed system.

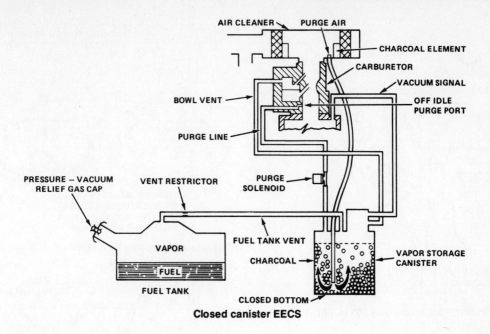

AIR CLEANER   PURGE AIR

CHARCOAL ELEMENT

CARBURETOR

VACUUM SIGNAL

BOWL VENT

OFF IDLE
PURGE PORT

PURGE LINE

PRESSURE – VACUUM
RELIEF GAS CAP   VENT RESTRICTOR   PURGE
SOLENOID

VAPOR

FUEL

FUEL TANK

FUEL TANK VENT

CHARCOAL

VAPOR STORAGE
CANISTER

CLOSED BOTTOM

Closed canister EECS

Exhaust Gas Recirculation (EGR)
OPERATION

All engines covered in this guide are equipped with exhaust gas recirculation (EGR). This system consists of a metering valve, a vacuum line to the carburetor, and cast-in exhaust gas passages in the intake manifold. The EGR valve is controlled by carburetor vacuum, and accordingly opens and closes to admit exhaust gases into the fuel/air mixture. The exhaust gases lower the combustion temperature, and reduce the amount of oxides of nitrogen (NOx) produced. The valve is closed at idle between the two extreme throttle positions.

In most installations, vacuum to the EGR valve is controlled by a thermal vacuum switch (TVS); the switch, which is installed into the engine block, shuts off vacuum to the EGR valve until the engine is hot. This prevents the stalling and rough idle which would result if EGR occurred when the engine was cold.

As the vehicle accelerates, the carburetor throttle plate uncovers the vacuum port for the EGR valve. At 3–5 in. Hg, the EGR valve opens and then some of the exhaust gases are allowed to flow into the air/fuel mixture to lower the combustion temperature. At full throttle the valve closes again.

Some California engines are equipped with a dual diaphragm EGR valve. This valve further limits the exhaust gas opening (compared to the single diaphragm EGR valve) during high intake manifold vacuum periods, such as high speed cruising, and provides more exhaust gas recirculation during acceleration when mani-

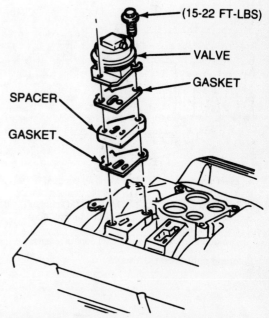

(15-22 FT-LBS)

VALVE

GASKET

SPACER

GASKET

Typical EGR valve location, gasoline engines

fold vacuum is low. In addition to the hose running to the thermal vacuum switch, a second hose is connected directly to the intake manifold.

For 1977, all California models and vehicles delivered in areas above 4000 feet are equipped with back pressure EGR valves. This valve is also used on all 1978–81 models. The EGR valve receives exhaust back pressure through its hollow shaft. This exerts a force on the bottom of the control valve diaphragm, opposed by

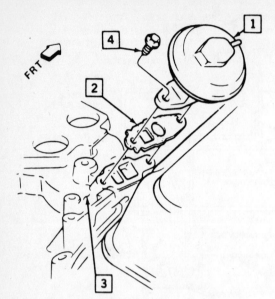

EGR valve—late model Olds 307 ci. (VIN Y)

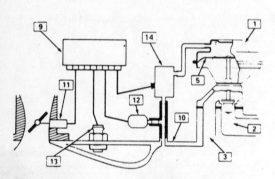

1. EGR valve
2. Exhaust gas
3. Intake air
5. Diaphragm
9. Electronic control module
10. Manifold vacuum
11. Throttle position sensor
12. MAP or VAC sensor
13. Coolant temperature sensor
14. EGR control solenoid

Solenoid controlled EGR valve

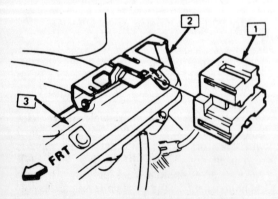

EGR solenoid—Olds 307 ci. (VIN Y)

NOTE. IDENTIFY POSITIVE PRESSURE MODULATED EGR VALVE BY DIAPHRAGM PLATE DESIGN

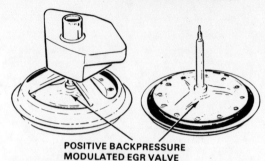

POSITIVE BACKPRESSURE MODULATED EGR VALVE HAS LOW REINFORCEMENT ON DIAPHRAGM PLATE

Positive backpressure EGR valve

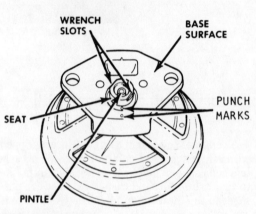

EGR valve cleaning

a light spring. Under low exhaust pressure (low engine load and partial throttle), the EGR signal is reduced by an air bleed. Under conditions of high exhaust pressure (high engine load and large throttle opening), the air bleed is closed and the EGR valve responds to an unmodified vacuum signal. At wide open throttle, the EGR flow is reduced in proportion to the amount of vacuum signal available.

1979 and later models have a ported signal vacuum EGR valve. The valve opening is controlled by the amount of vacuum obtained from a ported vacuum source on the carburetor and the amount of backpressure in the exhaust system.

Some late model vehicles with V6 and V8 engines use EGR Vacuum Control. This system uses a solenoid controlled by the Electronic Control Module to control vacuum going to the EGR valve. The ECM evaluates a number of engine parameters to determine EGR requirements, and then opens and closes the solenoid many times a second to produce the required vacuum. The length of each open cycle is increased to transmit increased vacuum.

EGR VALVE REMOVAL AND INSTALLATION

1. Detach the vacuum lines from the EGR valve.

2. Unfasten the two bolts or bolt and clamp which attach the valve to the manifold. Withdraw the valve.

To install:

3. Clean the valve and intake manifold as outlined in the Valve Cleaning section.

4. Always use a new gasket between the valve and the manifold. Torque the retaining bolts or nuts to 15 ft. lbs. (20 Nm). On dual diaphragm valves, attach the carburetor vacuum line to the tube at the top of the valve, and the manifold vacuum line to the tube at the center of the valve.

EGR VALVE CLEANING

Valves That Protrude from Mounting Face

WARNING: *Do NOT wash the valve assembly in solvents or degreasers; permanent damage to the valve diaphragm may result.*

1. Remove the vacuum hose from the EGR valve assembly. Remove the two attaching bolts, remove the EGR valve from the intake manifold and discard the gasket.

2. Holding the valve assembly in hand, tap the valve lightly with a small plastic hammer to remove exhaust deposits from the valve seat. Shake out any loose particles. DO NOT Put the valve in a vise.

3. Carefully remove any exhaust deposits from the mounting surface of the valve with a wire wheel or putty knife. Do not damage the mounting surface.

4. Depress the valve diaphragm and inspect the valve seating area through the valve outlet for cleanliness. If the valve and/or seat are not completely clean, repeat step 2.

5. Look for exhaust deposits in the valve outlet, and remove any deposits with a suitable cleaning tool.

6. Clean the mounting surfaces of the intake manifold and valve assembly.

7. Scrap any deposits from the intake manifold. With the valve removed, start the engine for two seconds to blow out the loose carbon deposits.

8. Using a new gasket, install the valve assembly to the intake manifold. Torque the bolts to 15 ft. lbs. (20 Nm). Connect the vacuum hose.

Shielded Valves or Valves That Do Not Protrude

1. Clean the base of the valve with a wire brush or wheel to remove exhaust deposits from the mounting surface.

2. Clean the valve seat and valve in an abrasive-type spark plug cleaning machine or sand-blaster. Most machine shops provide this service. Make sure the valve portion is cleaned (blasted) for about 30 seconds, and that the valve is also cleaned with the diaphragm spring fully compressed (valve unseated). The cleaning should be repeated until all deposits are removed.

3. The valve must be blown out with compressed air thoroughly to ensure all abrasive material is removed from the valve.

4. Clean the mounting surface of the intake manifold and valve assembly.

5. With the valve removed, start the engine for two second to blow out the loose carbon deposits.

6. Using a new gasket, install the valve assembly to the intake manifold. Torque the bolts to 15 ft. lbs. (20 Nm). Connect the vacuum hose.

TVS (Thermal Vacuum Switch)

REMOVAL AND INSTALLATION

1. Disconnect the negative (–) battery cable. Drain the radiator.

CAUTION: *When draining the coolant, keep in mind that cats and dogs are attracted by the ethylene glycol antifreeze, and are quite likely to drink any that is left in an uncovered container or in puddles on the ground. This will prove fatal in sufficient quantity. Always drain the coolant into a sealable container. Coolant should be reused unless it is contaminated or several years old.*

2. Disconnect the vacuum lines from the switch noting their locations. Remove the switch.

To install:

3. Apply sealer to the threaded portion of the new switch, and install it, torquing to 15 ft. lbs. (20 Nm).

4. Rotate the head of the switch to a position that will permit easy hookup of vacuum hoses. Then connect the vacuum hoses to the proper connectors and battery cable.

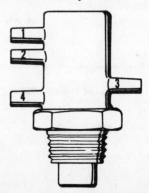

Thermostatic vacuum switch (TVS); nipple 1 is to distributor; 2 to TCS solenoid; 4 to intake manifold

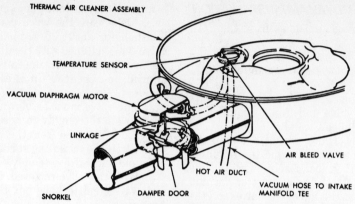

THERMAC AIR CLEANER ASSEMBLY
TEMPERATURE SENSOR
VACUUM DIAPHRAGM MOTOR
LINKAGE
AIR BLEED VALVE
HOT AIR DUCT
SNORKEL
DAMPER DOOR
VACUUM HOSE TO INTAKE MANIFOLD TEE

Typical THERMAC air cleaner

Thermostatic Air Cleaner (THERMAC)

OPERATION

All engines covered in this guide utilize the THERMAC system (in 1978 it was called TAC, but was the same). This system is designed to warm the air entering the carburetor when underhood temperatures are low, and to maintain a controlled air temperature into the carburetor at all times. By allowing preheated air to enter the carburetor, the amount of time the choke is on is reduced, resulting in better fuel economy and lower emissions. Engine warm-up time is also reduced.

The Thermac system is composed of the air cleaner body, a filter, sensor unit, vacuum diaphragm, damper door, and associated hoses and connections. Heat radiating from the exhaust manifold is trapped by a heat stove and is ducted to the air cleaner to supply heated air to the carburetor. A movable door in the air cleaner case snorkel allows air to be drawn in from the heat stove (cold operation) or from

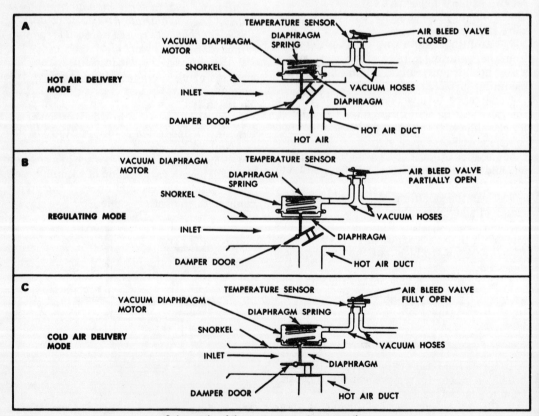

A   HOT AIR DELIVERY MODE
TEMPERATURE SENSOR
VACUUM DIAPHRAGM MOTOR
DIAPHRAGM SPRING
AIR BLEED VALVE CLOSED
SNORKEL
VACUUM HOSES
INLET
DIAPHRAGM
DAMPER DOOR
HOT AIR
HOT AIR DUCT

B   REGULATING MODE
VACUUM DIAPHRAGM MOTOR
TEMPERATURE SENSOR
DIAPHRAGM SPRING
AIR BLEED VALVE PARTIALLY OPEN
SNORKEL
VACUUM HOSES
INLET
DIAPHRAGM
DAMPER DOOR
HOT AIR DUCT

C   COLD AIR DELIVERY MODE
TEMPERATURE SENSOR
VACUUM DIAPHRAGM MOTOR
DIAPHRAGM SPRING
AIR BLEED VALVE FULLY OPEN
SNORKEL
VACUUM HOSES
INLET
DIAPHRAGM
DAMPER DOOR
HOT AIR DUCT

Schematic of the vacuum motor operation

underhood air (warm operation). The door position is controlled by the vacuum motor, which receives intake manifold vacuum as modulated by the temperature sensor.

SYSTEM CHECKS

1. Check the vacuum hoses for leaks, kinks, breaks, or improper connections and correct any defects.

2. With the engine off, check the position of the damper door within the snorkel. A mirror can be used to make this job easier. The damper door should be open to admit outside air.

3. Apply at least 7 in. Hg of vacuum to the damper diaphragm unit. The door should close. If it does not, check the diaphragm linkage for binding and correct hookup.

4. With vacuum still applied and the door closed, clamp the tube to trap the vacuum. If the door does not remain closed, there is a leak in the diaphragm assembly.

5. If the diaphragm is holding vacuum and the system has source vacuum, the last choose is the air bleed valve located in the air cleaner assembly.

6. The air bleed may be holding the damper door closed even after the vehicle has warmed up. Or the valve may not close the door at all. In any case, if the damper diaphragm and vacuum source are OK, replace the air bleed valve.

Air Injection Reactor System (A.I.R.)
OPERATION

The AIR system injects compressed air into the exhaust system, near enough to the exhaust valves to continue the burning of the normally unburned segment of the exhaust gases. To do this it employs an air injection pump and a system of hoses, valves, tubes, etc., necessary to carry the compressed air from the pump to the exhaust manifolds. Carburetors and distributors for AIR engines have specific modifications to adapt them to the air injection system; those components should not be interchanged with those intended for use on engines that do not have the system.

A diverter valve is used to prevent backfiring. The valve senses sudden increases in manifold vacuum and ceases the injection of air during fuel rich periods. During coasting, this valve diverts the entire air flow through the pump muffler and during high engine speeds, expels it through a relief valve. Check valves in the system prevent exhaust gases from entering the pump.

NOTE: *The AIR system on the V6 engines is slightly different, but its purpose remains the same.*

SERVICE

The AIR system's effectiveness depends on correct engine idle speed, ignition timing, and dwell. These settings should be strictly adhered to and checked frequently. All hoses and fittings should be inspected for condition and tightness of connections. Check the drive belt for wear and tension every 12 months or 12,000 miles.

REMOVAL AND INSTALLATION
Air Pump

CAUTION: *Do not pry on the pump housing or clamp the pump in a vise; the housing is*

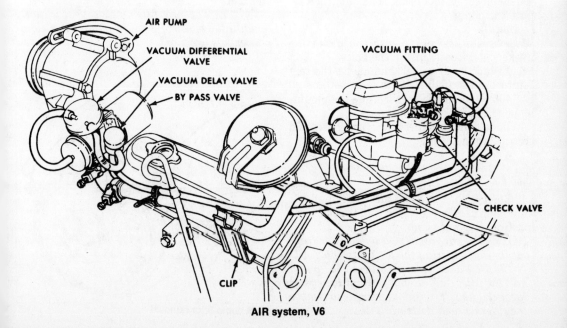

AIR PUMP

VACUUM DIFFERENTIAL VALVE

VACUUM DELAY VALVE

BY PASS VALVE

VACUUM FITTING

CHECK VALVE

CLIP

AIR system, V6

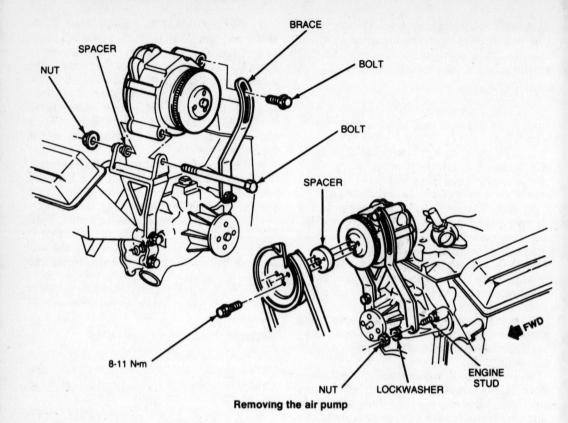

Removing the air pump

soft aluminum and may become distorted.

1. Disconnect the negative (−) battery cable and the air hoses at the pump.

2. Hold the pump pulley from turning and loosen the pulley bolts.

3. Loosen the pump mounting bolt and adjustment bracket bolt. Remove the drive belt.

4. Remove the mounting bolts, and then remove the pump.

To install:

5. Position the pump into the mounting brackets and loosely install the bolts.

6. Install the drive belt and adjust the tension to 146 lbs. (650 N) for a new belt and 90 lbs. (400 N) for an old belt. Torque the mounting bolts to 25 ft. lbs. (34 Nm).

7. Install and reconnect the pump hoses and electrical connections.

Pump Filter

1. Remove the drive belt and pump pulley.

2. Using needlenose pliers, pull the fan/filter unit from the pump hub.

NOTE: *Use care to prevent any dirt or fragments from entering the air intake hole. DO NOT insert a screwdriver between the pump and the filter, and do not attempt to remove the metal hub. It is seldom possible to remove the filter without destroying it.*

3. To install a new filter, draw it on with the pulley and pulley bolts. Do not hammer or press the filter onto the pump.

4. Draw the filter down evenly by torquing the bolts alternately. Make sure the outer edge of the filter slips into the housing. A slight amount of interference with the housing bore is normal.

NOTE: *The new filter may squeal initially until the sealing lip on the pump outer diameter has worn in.*

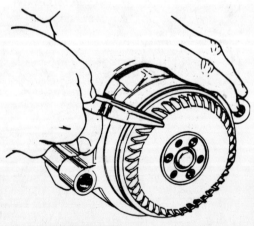

AIR pump filter removal

Diverter (Anti-afterburn) Valve

1. Detach the vacuum sensing line and electrical connections from the valve.

2. Remove the other hose(s) from the valve.

3. Unfasten the diverter valve from the elbow or the pump body.

To install:

4. Always use a new gasket. Tighten the valve securing bolts to 85 inch lbs. (10 Nm).

Air Management System

OPERATION

The Air Management System is used on 1981 and later vehicles to provide additional oxygen to continue the combustion process after the exhaust gases leave the combustion chamber; it works in much the same way as the AIR system described earlier in this chapter. Air is injected into either the exhaust port(s), the exhaust manifold(s) or the catalytic converter by an engine driven air pump. The system is in operation at all times and will bypass air only momentarily during deceleration and at high speeds. The bypass function is performed by the Air Management Valve, while the check valve protects the air pump by preventing any backflow of exhaust gases.

The AIR system helps to reduce HC and CO contents in the exhaust gases by injecting air into the exhaust ports during cold engine operation. This air injection also helps the catalytic converter to reach the proper temperature quicker during warm-up. When the engine is warm (closed loop), the AIR system injects air into the beds of a three-way converter to lower the HC and CO content in the exhaust.

The Air Management System utilizes the following components:

1. An engine driven air pump

2. Air management valves (Air Control and Air Switching)

3. Air flow and control hoses

4. Check valves

5. A dual-bed, three-way catalytic converter

The belt driven, vane type air pump is located at the front of the engine and supplies clean air to the system for purposes already stated. When the engine is cold, the Electronic Control Module (ECM) energizes an air control solenoid. This allows air to blow to the air switching valve. The air switching valve is then energized to direct air into the exhaust ports.

When the engine is warm, the ECM de-energizes the air switching valve, thus directing the air between the beds of the catalytic converter. This then provides additional oxygen for the oxidizing catalyst in the second bed to decrease HC and CO levels, while at the same time keeping oxygen levels low in the first bed, enabling the reducing catalyst to effectively decrease the levels of NOx.

If the air control valve detects a rapid increase in manifold vacuum (deceleration), certain operating modes (wide open throttle, etc.) or if the ECM self-diagnostic system detects any problems in the system, air is diverted to the air cleaner or directly into the atmosphere.

The primary purpose of the ECM's divert mode is to prevent backfiring. Throttle closure at the beginning of deceleration will temporarily create air/fuel mixtures which are too rich to burn completely. These mixtures will become burnable when they reach the exhaust if they are combined with injection air. The next firing of the engine will ignite the mixture causing an exhaust backfire. Momentary diverting of the injection air from the exhaust prevents this.

The Air Management System check valves and hoses should be checked periodically for any leaks, cracks or deterioration.

REMOVAL AND INSTALLATION

Air Pump

1. Disconnect the negative (–) battery cable. Remove the valves and/or adapter at the air pump.

2. Loosen the air pump adjustment bolt and remove the drive belt.

3. Unscrew the three mounting bolts and then remove the pump pulley.

4. Unscrew the pump mounting bolts and then remove the pump.

To install:

1. Be sure to adjust the drive belt tension after installing the pump.

2. Install the three mounting bolts and adjust the belt to 146 lbs. (650 N) for a new belt and 90 lbs. (300 N) for an old belt.

3. Torque the air pump adjustment bolt to 25 ft. lbs. (34 Nm).

4. Connect the negative (–) battery cable. Install the valves and/or adapter at the air pump.

Check Valve

1. Disconnect the negative (–) battery cable. Release the clamp and disconnect the air hoses from the valve.

NOTE: *The valve may be seized to the injection pipe due to rust. Soak the fitting with penetrating oil for an hour or two before attempting removal. Always use a backup wrench when attempting to remove the valve.*

2. Unscrew the check valve from the air injection pipe.

3. Install the valve and torque to 30 ft. lbs. (41 Nm). Connect all disconnected hoses and negative battery cable.

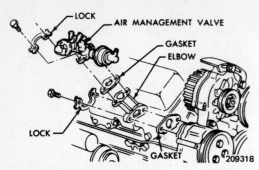

Air management valve—typical

Anti-dieseling solenoid

Air Management Valve

1. Disconnect the negative battery cable.
2. Remove the air cleaner.
3. Tag and disconnect the vacuum hose from the valve.
4. Tag and disconnect the air outlet hoses from the valve
5. Bend back the lock tabs and then remove the bolts holding the elbow to the valve.
6. Tag and disconnect any electrical connections at the valve and then remove the valve from the elbow.

To install:

1. Install the valve and connect any electrical connections at the valve.
2. Torque the valve bolts to 10 ft. lbs. (14 Nm) and bend back the lock tabs.
3. Connect the air outlet hoses to the valve
4. Connect the vacuum hose to the valve.
5. Install the air cleaner.
6. Connect the negative battery cable.

Anti-Dieseling Solenoid

Some 1975 models have idle solenoids. Due to the leaner carburetor settings required for emission control, the engine may have a tendency to diesel or run-on after the ignition is turned off. The carburetor solenoid energized when the ignition is on, maintains the normal idle speed. When the ignition is turned off, the solenoid is de-energized and permits the throttle valves to fully close, thus preventing run-on. For adjustment of carburetors with idle solenoids see the section on carburetor adjustments later in this chapter.

Early Fuel Evaporation (EFE) System
OPERATION

Two types of EFE have been used on the engines covered in this guide. Both provide quick heat to the induction system. This helps evaporate fuel (allowing the choke to close faster and

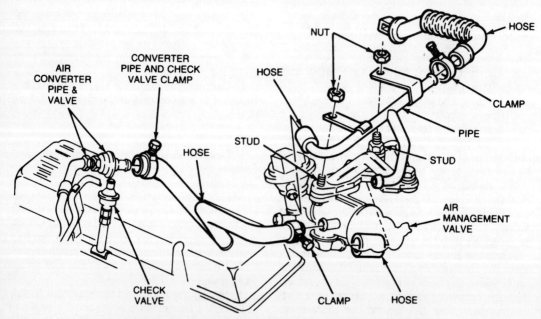

Check valve and hoses—1981 and later air management system

thus reducing emissions) when the engine is cold. It also aids cold driveability. The Vacuum Servo EFE system uses a valve between the exhaust manifold and exhaust pipe, operated by vacuum and controlled by either a thermal vacuum valve or electric solenoid. The valve causes hot exhaust gas to enter the intake manifold heat riser passages, heating the incoming fuel mixture. The Heated type EFE uses a ceramic heater plate located under the carburetor, controlled through the ECM. The vacuum type EFE should be checked for proper operation at every tune-up.

NOTE: *On 1981 and later V6 engines, the EFE system is controlled by the ECM.*

To check the valve:

1. Locate the EFE valve on the exhaust manifold and not the position of the actuator arm. On some vehicles, the valve and arm are covered by a two-piece cover which must be removed for access. Make sure the engine is overnight cold.

2. Watch the actuator arm when the engine is started. The valve should close when the engine is started cold; the actuator link will be pulled into the diaphragm housing.

3. If the valve does not close, stop the engine. Remove the hose from the EFE valve and apply 10 in. Hg of vacuum by hand pump. The valve should close and stay closed for at least 20 seconds (you will hear it close). If the valve opens in less than 20 seconds, replace it. The valve could also be seized if it does not close; lubricate it with spray type manifold heat valve lube. If

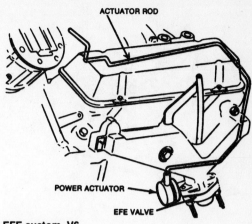

EFE system, V6

the valve does not close when vacuum is applied and when it is lubricated, replace the valve.

4. If the valve closes, the problem is not with the valve. Check for loose, cracked, pinched or plugged hoses, and replace as necessary. Test the EFE solenoid (located on the valve cover bracket); if it is working, the solenoid plunger will emit a noise when the current is applied.

5. Warm up the engine to operating temperature.

6. Watch the EFE valve to see if it has opened. It should now be open. If the valve is still closed, replace the solenoid if faulty, and/or check the engine thermostat; the engine coolant may not be reaching normal operating temperature.

EFE VALVE
REMOVAL AND INSTALLATION

NOTE: *If the vehicle is equipped with an oxygen sensor, it is located near the EFE valve. Use care when removing the EFE valve as not to damage the oxygen sensor.*

1. Disconnect the negative (−) battery cable and vacuum hose at the EFE valve.

2. Remove the exhaust pipe-to-manifold nuts, and the washers and tension springs if used.

3. Lower the exhaust cross-over pipe. On some models, complete removal of the pipe is not necessary.

4. Remove the EFE valve.

To install: Always install new seals and gaskets. Torque the exhaust nuts to 22 ft. lbs. (30 Nm). Connect the negative battery cable and vacuum hose to the valve.

EFE SOLENOID
REMOVAL AND INSTALLATION

1. Disconnect the battery ground.

2. Remove the air cleaner assembly if necessary.

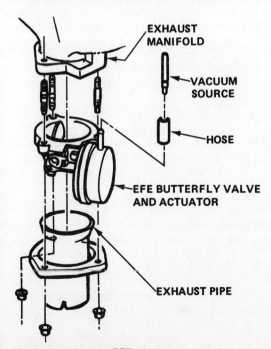

Vacuum-servo type EFE system

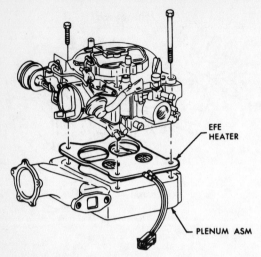

Electrically-heated type EFE

3. Disconnect and tag all electrical and vacuum hoses as required.

4. Remove the screw securing the solenoid to the valve cover bracket and remove the solenoid.

5. Installation is reverse of removal.

ELECTRIC TYPE EFE REPLACEMENT

Turbo

1. Remove the air cleaner.

2. Disconnect all vacuum, electrical and fuel connections from the carburetor.

3. Disconnect the EFE heater electrical connector.

4. Remove the carburetor.

5. Remove the EFE heater insulator (plate) assembly.

6. Installation is the reverse of removal.

THERMAL VACUUM SWITCH (TVS) REMOVAL AND INSTALLATION

1. Disconnect the negative (–) battery cable.

2. Remove the air cleaner.

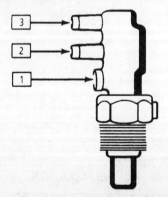

Thermal vacuum switch (TVS) located in the intake manifold—activates the EFE valve during cold operation

3. Partially drain the engine coolant.

4. Remove the hoses from the TVS assembly located in the engine coolant outlet housing or at the rear of the intake manifold. Remove the switch from the engine.

To install:

1. Refer to the number stamped on the base of the TVS for calibration temperature.

2. Apply a soft setting pipe sealant to the switch threads.

3. Install the switch and torque to 120 inch lbs. (14 Nm). Reconnect the vacuum hoses and negative battery cable.

4. Install the air cleaner assembly.

Controlled Combustion System
OPERATION

The CCS system relies upon leaner air/fuel mixtures and altered ignition timing to improve combustion efficiency. A special air cleaner with a thermostatically controlled opening is used on most CCS equipped models to ensure that air entering the carburetor is kept at 100°F (38°C). This allows leaner carburetor settings and improves engine warm-up. A 15°F higher temperature thermostat is employed on CCS vehicles to further improve emission control.

SERVICE

Since the only extra component added with a CCS system is the thermostatically controlled air cleaner, there is no additional maintenance required; however, tune-up adjustments such as idle speed, ignition timing, and dwell become much more critical. Care must be taken to ensure that these settings are correct, both for trouble free operation and a low emission level.

Computer Controlled Catalytic Converter System (C–4)
OPERATION

The C–4 System, installed on certain 1979 and all 1980 vehicles sold in California, is an electronically controlled exhaust emissions system. The purpose of the system is to maintain the ideal air/fuel ratio at which the catalytic converter is most effective.

Major components of the system include an Electronic Control Module (ECM), an oxygen sensor, an electronically controlled carburetor, and a three-way oxidation reduction catalytic converter. The system also includes a maintenance reminder flag connected to the odometer which becomes visible in the instrument cluster at regular intervals, signaling the need for oxygen sensor replacement.

The oxygen sensor, installed in the exhaust manifold generates a voltage which varies with

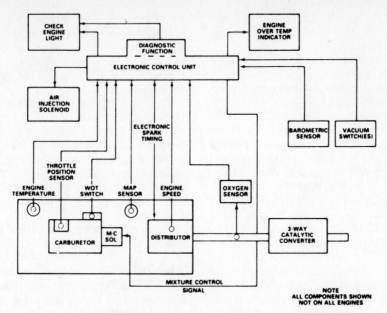

Computer Controlled Catalytic Converter (C-4) system schematic

exhaust gas oxygen content. Lean mixtures (more oxygen) reduce voltage; rich mixtures (less oxygen) increase voltage. Voltage output is sent to the ECM.

An engine temperature sensor installed in the engine coolant outlet monitors engine coolant temperatures. Vacuum control switches and throttle position sensors also monitor engine conditions and supply signals to the ECM.

The Electronic Control Module receives input signals from all sensors. It processes these signals and generates a control signal sent to the carburetor. The control signal cycles between on (lean command) and off (rich command). The amount of on and off time is a function of the input voltage sent to the ECM by the oxygen sensor.

Rochester Dualjet (2-barrel) E2ME and E4ME carburetors are used with the C-4 System. Basically, an electrically operated mixture control solenoid is installed in the carburetor float bowl. The solenoid controls the air/fuel mixture metered in the idle and main metering systems. Air metering to the idle system is controlled by an idle air bleed valve. It follows the movement of the mixture solenoid to control the amount of air bled into the idle system, enriching or leaning out the mixture as appropriate. Air/fuel mixture enrichment occurs when the fuel valve is open and the air bleed valve is closed. All cycling of this system, which occurs ten times per second, is controlled by the ECM. A throttle position sensor informs the ECM of open or closed throttle operation. A number of different switches are used, varying with application. When the ECM receives a signal from

the throttle sensor, indicating a change of position, it immediately searches its memory for the last set of operating conditions that resulted in an ideal air/fuel ratio, and shifts to that set of conditions. The memory is continually updated during normal operation.

A *Check Engine Light* is included in the C-4 System installation. When a fault develops, the light comes on, and a trouble code is set into the ECM memory. However, if the fault is intermittent, the light will go out, but the trouble code will remain in the ECM memory as long as the engine is running. The trouble codes are used as a diagnostic aid, and are pre-programmed.

Unless the required tools are available, troubleshooting the C-4 System should be confined to mechanical checks of electrical connectors, vacuum hoses and the like. All diagnosis and repair should be performed by a qualified mechanic with the proper diagnostic equipment.

Computer Command Control System
OPERATION

The Computer Command Control System, installed on all 1981 and later vehicles, is basically a modified version of the C-4 system. Its main advantage over its predecessor is that it can monitor and control a larger number of interrelated emission control systems.

This new system can monitor up to 15 engine/vehicle operating conditions and then use this information to control as many as 9 engine related systems. The system is thereby making constant adjustments to maintain good vehicle performance under all normal driving conditions while at the same time allowing the catalytic converter to effectively control the emissions of NOx, HC and CO.

In addition, the system has a built in diagnostic system that recognizes and identifies possible operational problems and alerts the driver through a Check Engine light in the instrument panel. The light will remain ON until the problem is corrected. The system also has built in back-up systems that in most cases of an operational problem, will allow for the continued operation of the vehicle in a near normal manner until the repairs can be made.

The CCC system has some components in common with the C-4 system, although they are not interchangeable. These components include the Electronic Control Module (ECM), which, as previously stated, controls many more functions than does its predecessor, an oxygen sensor system, an electronically controlled variable mixture carburetor, a 3-way catalytic converter, throttle position and coolant sensors, a Barometric Pressure Sensor (BARO), a Manifold Absolute Pressure Sensor (MAP) and a Check Engine light in the instrument panel.

Components unique to the CCC system include the Air Injection Reaction (AIR) management system, a charcoal canister purge solenoid, EGR valve controls, a vehicle speed sensor (in the instrument panel), a transmission converter clutch solenoid (only on models with automatic transmission), idle speed control and Electronic Spark Timing (EST).

The ECM, in addition to monitoring sensors and sending out a control signal to the carburetor, also controls the following components or sub-systems: charcoal canister purge control, the AIR system, idle speed, automatic transmission converter lock-up, distributor ignition timing, the EGR valve, and the air conditioner converter clutch.

The EGR valve control solenoid is activated by the ECM in a fashion similar to that of the charcoal canister purge solenoid described earlier in this chapter. When the engine is cold, the ECM energizes the solenoid, which blocks the vacuum signal to the EGR valve. When the engine is warm, the ECM de-energizes the solenoid and the vacuum signal is allowed to reach and then activate the EGR valve.

The Transmission Converter Clutch (TCC) lock is controlled by the ECM through an electrical solenoid in the automatic transmission. When the vehicle speed sensor in the dash signals the ECM that the vehicle has attained the predetermined speed, the ECM energizes the solenoid which then allows the torque converter to mechanically couple the engine to the transmission. When the brake pedal is pushed, or during deceleration or passing, etc., the ECM returns the transmission to fluid drive.

The idle speed control adjusts the idle speed to all particular engine load conditions and will lower the idle under no-load or low-load conditions in order to conserve fuel.

NOTE: *Not all engines use all systems. Control applications may differ.*

BASIC TROUBLESHOOTING

NOTE: *The following explains how to activate the Trouble Code signal light in the in-*

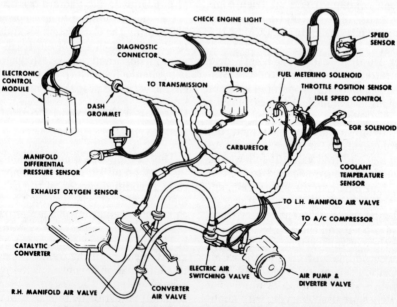

Computer Command Control (CCC) system schematic

strument cluster. This is not a full fledged C-4 or CCC system troubleshooting and isolation procedure.

Before suspecting the C-4 or CCC system, or any of its components as being faulty, check the ignition system (distributor, timing, spark plugs and wires). Check the engine compression, the air cleaner and any of the emission control components that are not controlled by the ECM. Also check the intake manifold for any leaks. Check the carburetor mounting bolts for tightness. Inspect all vacuum hoses for correct routing, pinching by a harness tie or any object in the engine compartment, cuts, cracks, or loose connections. Make sure to follow them

under the air cleaner, generator, or other object to make sure they are in good condition and not pinched along their entire length. Inspect all wiring in a similar manner, checking for chafing of the insulation, burned spots, pinching (which could ground a wire), contact with any sharp edge, or routing too near any hot portion of the engine. Also check that all connections are clean and tight. This visual inspection is extremely important as many operating problems can be cleared up only by repair of bad wiring or vacuum hoses.

The following symptoms could indicate a possible problem area with the C-4 or CCC systems:

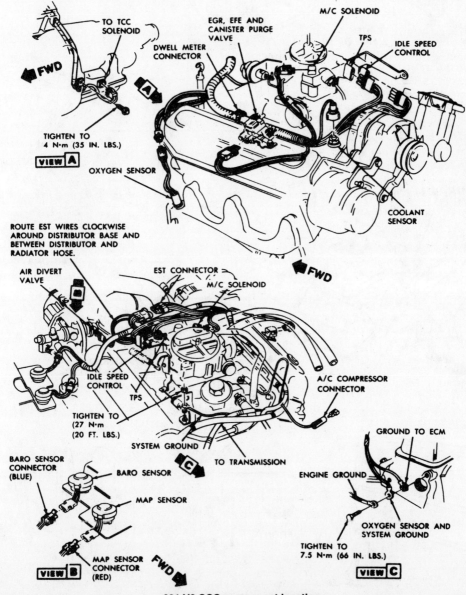

231 V6 CCC component location

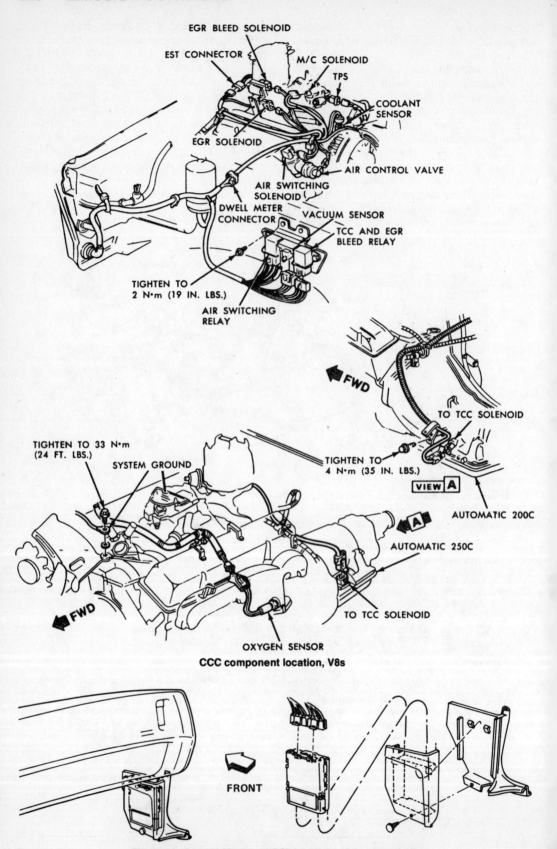

EGR BLEED SOLENOID

EST CONNECTOR

M/C SOLENOID

TPS

COOLANT SENSOR

EGR SOLENOID

AIR CONTROL VALVE

AIR SWITCHING SOLENOID

DWELL METER CONNECTOR

VACUUM SENSOR

TCC AND EGR BLEED RELAY

TIGHTEN TO 2 N·m (19 IN. LBS.)

AIR SWITCHING RELAY

FWD

TO TCC SOLENOID

TIGHTEN TO 33 N·m (24 FT. LBS.)

SYSTEM GROUND

TIGHTEN TO 4 N·m (35 IN. LBS.)

VIEW A

AUTOMATIC 200C

A

AUTOMATIC 250C

FWD

TO TCC SOLENOID

OXYGEN SENSOR

CCC component location, V8s

FRONT

Electronic Control Module (ECM) location, all models similar

1. Detonation;
2. Stalling or rough idling when the engine is cold;
3. Stalling or rough idling when the engine is hot;
4. Missing;
5. Hesitation;
6. Surging;
7. Poor gasoline mileage;
8. Sluggish or spongy performance;
9. Hard starting when engine is cold;
10. Hard starting when the engine is hot;
11. Objectionable exhaust odors;
12. Engine cuts out;
13. Improper idle speed (CCC only).

As a bulb and system check, the Check Engine light will come on when the ignition switch is turned to the ON position but the engine is not started.

The Check Engine light will also produce the trouble code/codes by a series of flashes which translate as follows: When the diagnostic test

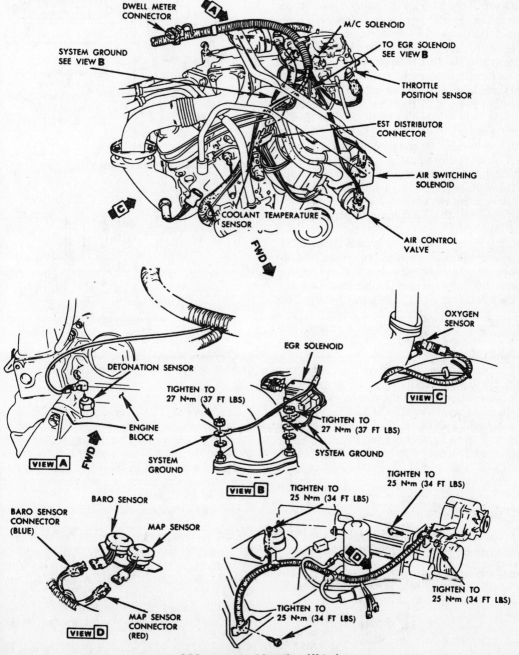

CCC component location, V6 turbo

lead (C-4) or terminal (CCC) under the instrument panel is grounded, with the ignition in the ON position and the engine not running, the Check Engine light will flash once, pause, and then flash twice in rapid succession. This is a Code 12, which indicates that the diagnostic system is working. After a long pause, the Code 12 will repeat itself two more times. This whole cycle will then repeat itself until the engine is started or the ignition switch is turned OFF.

When the engine is started, the Check Engine light will remain on for a few seconds and then turn off. If the Check Engine light remains on, the self-diagnostic system has detected a problem. If the test lead (C-4) or test terminal (CCC) is then grounded, the trouble code will flash (3) three times. If more than one problem is found to be in existence, each trouble code will flash (3) three times and then change to the next one. Trouble codes will flash in numerical order (lowest code number to highest). The trouble code series will repeat themselves for as long as the test leads or terminal remains grounded.

A trouble code indicates a problem with a given circuit. For example, trouble code 14 indicates a problem in the cooling sensor circuit. This includes the coolant sensor, its electrical harness and the Electronic Control Module (ECM).

Since the self-diagnostic system cannot diagnose every possible fault in the system, the absence of a trouble code does not necessarily mean that the system is trouble free. To determine whether or not a problem with the system exists that does not activate a trouble code, a system performance check must be made. This job should be left to a qualified service technician.

In the case of an intermittent fault in the system, the Check Engine light will go out when the fault goes away, but the trouble code will remain in the memory of the ECM. Therefore, if a trouble code can be obtained even though the Check Engine light is not on, it must still be evaluated. It must be determined if the fault is

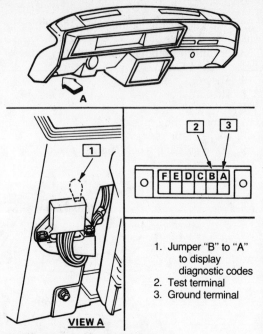

1. Jumper "B" to "A" to display diagnostic codes
2. Test terminal
3. Ground terminal

VIEW A

Under dash test terminal location

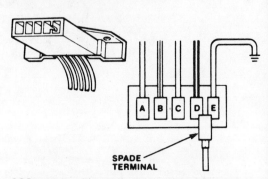

CCC system diagnostic test terminal located underneath the left side of the instrument panel

intermittent or if the engine must be operating under certain conditions (acceleration, deceleration, etc.) before the Check Engine light will come on. In some cases, certain trouble codes will not be recorded in the ECM until the engine has been operated at part throttle for at least 5 to 18 minutes.

On the C-4 system, the ECM erases all trouble codes every time that the ignition is turned off. In the case of intermittent faults, a long term memory is desirable. This can be produced by connecting the orange connector/lead from terminal **S** of the ECM directly to the battery (or to a 'hot' fuse panel terminal). This terminal must always be disconnected immediately after diagnosis as it puts an undue strain on the battery.

On the CCC system, a trouble code will be stored until the terminal 'R' at the ECM has

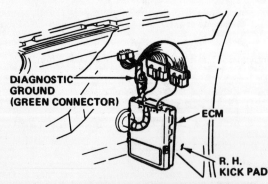

DIAGNOSTIC GROUND (GREEN CONNECTOR)

ECM

R. H. KICK PAD

C-4 system diagnostic test lead location, above ECM

Trouble Code Identification Chart

NOTE: Always ground the test lead/terminal AFTER the engine is running

Trouble Code	Applicable System	Possible Problem Area
12	C-4, CCC	No reference pulses to the ECM. This is not stored in the memory and will only flash when the fault is present (not to be confused with the Code 12 discussed earlier).
13	C-4, CCC	Oxygen sensor circuit. The engine must run for at least 5 min. (18 min. on the C-4 equipped 231 V6) at part throttle before this code will show.
13 & 14 (at same time)	C-4	See code 43.
13 & 43 (at same time)	C-4	See code 43.
14	C-4, CCC	Shorted coolant sensor circuit. The engine must run 2–5 min. before this code will show.
15	C-4, CCC	Open coolant sensor circuit. The engine must run for at least 5 min. (18 min. on the C-4 equipped 231 V6) before this code will show.
21	C-4	Shorted wide open throttle switch and/or open closed-throttle switch circuit (when used).
	C-4, CCC	Throttle position sensor circuit. The engine must run for at least 10 sec. (25 sec.—CCC) below 800 rpm before this code will show.
21 & 22 (at same time)	C-4	Grounded wide open throttle switch circuit (231 V6).
22	C-4	Grounded closed throttle or wide open throttle switch circuit (231 V6).
23	C-4, CCC	Open or grounded carburetor mixture control (M/C) solenoid circuit.
24	CCC	Vehicle speed sensor circuit. The engine must run for at least 5 min, at normal speed before this code will show.
32	C-4, CCC	Barometric pressure sensor (BARO) circuit output is low.
32 & 55 (at same time)	C-4	Grounded +8V terminal or V(REF) terminal for BARO sensor, or a faulty ECM.
34	C-4	Manifold absolute pressure sensor (MAP) output is high. The engine must run for at least 10 sec. below 800 rpm before this code will show.
	CCC	Manifold absolute pressure sensor (MAP) circuit or vacuum sensor circuit. The engine must run for at least 5 min. below 800 rpm before this code will show.
35	CCC	Idle speed control circuit shorted. The engine must run for at least 2 sec. above ½ throttle before this code will show.
42	CCC	Electronic spark timing (EST) bypass circuit grounded.
43	C-4	Throttle position sensor adjustment. The engine must run for at least 10 sec. before this code will show.
44	C-4, CCC	Lean oxygen sensor indication. The engine must run for at least 5 min. in closed loop (oxygen sensor adjusting carburetor mixture) at part throttle under load (drive car) before this code will show.
44 & 55 (at same time)	C-4, CCC	Faulty oxygen sensor circuit.
45	C-4, CCC	Rich oxygen sensor indication. The engine must run for at least 5 min. before this code will show (see 44 for conditions).
51	C-4, CCC	Faulty calibration unit (PROM) or improper PROM installation in the ECM. It will take at least 30 sec. before this code will show.
52 & 53	C-4	"Check Engine" light off: intermittant ECM problem. "Check Engine" light on: faulty ECM—replace.
52	C-4, CCC	Faulty ECM.
53	CCC	Faulty ECM.

Trouble Code Identification Chart (cont.)

NOTE: Always ground the test lead/terminal AFTER the engine is running

Trouble Code	Applicable System	Possible Problem Area
54	C-4, CCC	Faulty mixture control solenoid circuit and/or faulty ECM.
55	C-4	Faulty throttle position sensor or ECM (all but 231 V6). Faulty oxygen sensor, open MAP sensor or faulty ECM (231 V6 only).
	CCC	Grounded +8V supply (terminal 19 on ECM connector), grounded 5V reference (terminal 21 on ECM connector), faulty oxygen sensor circuit or faulty ECM.

NOTE: *Not all codes will apply to every model.*

been disconnected from the battery for at least 10 seconds.

ACTIVATING THE TROUBLE CODE

On the C-4 system, activate the trouble code by grounding the trouble code test lead. Use the illustrations to help you locate the test lead under the instrument panel (usually a white and black wire with a green connector). Run a jumper wire from the lead to a suitable ground.

On the CCC system, locate the test terminal under the instrument panel (see illustration). Use a jumper wire and ground only the lead. Jumper **B** to **A** on all models where letters run from **F** to **A** going from right to left.

NOTE: *Ground the test lead/terminal according to the instructions given previously in the Basic Troubleshooting section.*

Mixture Control Solenoid (M/C)

OPERATION

The fuel flow through the carburetor idle main metering circuits is controlled by a mixture control (M/C) solenoid located in the carburetor. The M/C solenoid changes the air/fuel mixture to the engine by controlling the fuel flow through the carburetor. The ECM controls the solenoid by providing a ground. When the solenoid is energized, the fuel flow through the carburetor is reduced, providing a leaner mixture. When the ECM removes the ground, the solenoid is de-energized, increasing the fuel flow and providing a richer mixture. The M/C solenoid is energized and de-energized at a rate of 10 times per second.

Throttle Position Sensor (TPS)
1980 and Later

OPERATION

The throttle position sensor is mounted in the carburetor body and is used to supply throttle position information in the ECM. The ECM memory stores an average of operating conditions with the ideal air/fuel ratios for each of those conditions. When the ECM receives a signal that indicates throttle position change, it immediately shifts to the last remembered set of operating conditions that resulted in an ideal air/fuel ratio control. The memory is continually being updated during normal operations.

Idle Speed Control (ISC)

OPERATION

V6 (Except Turbo)

The idle speed control does just what its name implies; it controls the idle. The ISC is used to maintain low engine speeds while at the same time preventing stalling due to engine load changes. The system consists of a motor

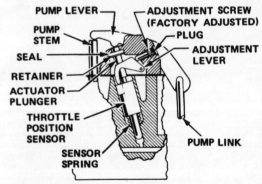

Throttle position sensor, mounted on carburetor body

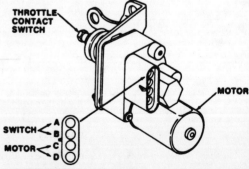

The Idle Speed Control (ISC) motor is attached to the carburetor

assembly mounted on the carburetor which moves the throttle lever so as to open or close the throttle blades.

The whole operation is controlled by the ECM. The ECM monitors engine load to determine the proper idle speed. To prevent stalling, it monitors the air conditioning compressor switch, the transmission, the park/neutral switch and the ISC throttle switch. The ECM processes all this information and then uses it to control the ISC motor which in turn will vary the idle speed as necessary.

Instructions for adjusting the ISC are contained in Chapter 2.

Electronic Spark Timing (EST)
OPERATION

All 1980 models with the 231 V6 engine and all 1981 and later models use EST. The EST distributor, as described in an earlier chapter, contains no vacuum or centrifugal advance mechanism and uses a seven terminal HEI module. It has four wires going to a four terminal connector in addition to the connectors normally found on HEI distributors. A reference pulse, indicating engine rpm is sent to the ECM. The ECM determines the proper spark advance for the engine operating conditions and then sends an "EST" pulse back to the distributor.

Under most normal operating conditions, the ECM will control the spark advance. However, under certain operating conditions such as cranking or when setting base timing, the distributor is capable of operating without ECM control. This condition is called BYPASS and is determined by the BYPASS lead which runs from the ECM to the distributor. When the BYPASS lead is at the proper voltage (5), the ECM will control the spark. If the lead is grounded or

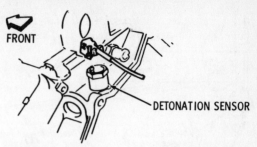

V6 turbo detonation sensor, mounted on intake manifold

open circuited, the HEI module itself will control the spark. Disconnecting the 4-terminal EST connector will also cause the engine to operate in the BYPASS mode.

Electronic Spark Control (ESC)
OPERATION
231 V6 TURBO, 252 V6 and Later Olds 307

The Electronic Spark Control (ESC) system is a closed loop system that controls engine detonation by adjusting the spark timing. There are two basic components in this system, the module and the detonation sensor.

The module processes the sensor signal and remodifies the EST signal to the distributor to adjust the spark timing. The process is continuous so that the presence of detonation is monitored and controlled. The module is not capable of memory storage.

The sensor is a magnetorestrictive device (meaning that is magnetically controls the flow of electricity), mounted in the engine block that detects the presence, or absence, and intensity of detonation according to the vibration characteristics of the engine. The output is an electrical signal which is sent to the controller.

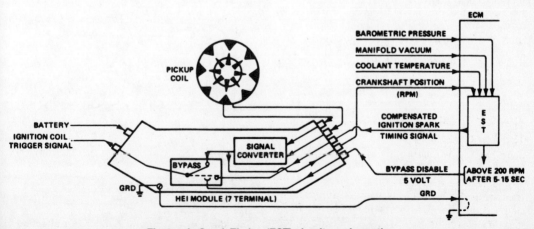

Electronic Spark Timing (EST) circuitry schematic

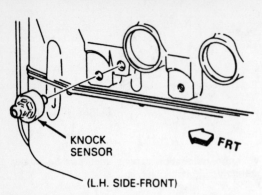

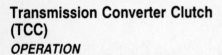

ESC knock sensor located on the engine block left side—Olds 307 ci. (VIN Y)

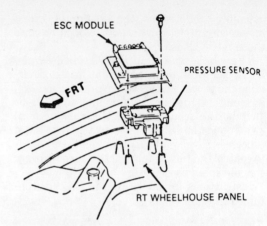

ESC module located on the right wheelhouse panel—Olds 307 ci. (VIN Y)

Transmission Converter Clutch (TCC)

OPERATION

All 1981 and later models with an automatic transmission use TCC. The ECM controls the converter by means of a solenoid mounted in the transmission. When the vehicle speed reaches a certain level, the ECM energizes the solenoid and allows the torque converter to mechanically couple the transmission to the engine. When the operating conditions indicate that the transmission should operate as a normal fluid coupled transmission, the ECM will de-energize the solenoid. Depressing the brake will also return the transmission to normal automatic operation.

The TCC may lock up early and give a feeling of engine lugging or vibration if you install over-size tires on your vehicle. This is because the clutch engages at a certain vehicle speed, not at a certain engine rpm. You can usually install tires one size larger than the original equipment tires, but if they are two sizes or more larger than original equipment, you may experience this form of engine roughness.

Catalytic Converter

OPERATION

The catalytic converter is a muffler-like container built into the exhaust system to aid in the reduction of exhaust emissions. The catalyst element consists of individual pellets or a honeycomb monolithic substrate coated with a metal such as platinum, palladium, rhodium or

39. Electrical connector
53. Solenoid assembly
75. Presssure switch
79. Solenoid wire clip
82. Filter retainer clip
84. Oil pipe retainer
89. Temperature switch

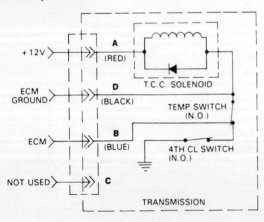

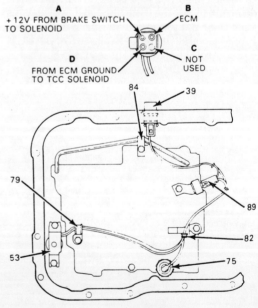

Torque converter clutch (TCC) solenoid (53)—Turbo Hydra-Matic 200-4R

a combination. When the exhaust gases come into contact with the catalyst, a chemical reaction occurs which will reduce the pollutants into harmless substances like water and carbon dioxide.

There are essentially two types of catalytic converters: an oxidizing type is used on all 1975–80 models with the exception of those 1980 models built for California. It requires the addition of oxygen to spur the catalyst into reducing the engine's HC and CO emissions into H_2O and CO_2. Because of this need for oxygen, the AIR system is used with all these models.

The oxidizing catalytic converter, while effectively reducing HC and CO emissions, does nothing in the way of reducing NOx emissions. Thus, the three-way catalytic converter was developed to reduce the NOx emissions.

The three-way converter, unlike the oxidizing type, is capable of reducing HC, CO and

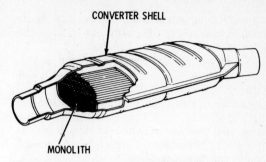

Single bed monolith catalytic converter

NOx, emissions, all at the same time. In theory, it seems impossible to reduce all three pollutants in one system since the reduction of HC and CO requires the addition of oxygen, while the reduction of NOx calls for the removal of oxygen. In actuality, the three-way system really can reduce all three pollutants, but only if the amount of oxygen in the exhaust system is precisely controlled. Due to this precise oxygen control requirement, the three-way converter system is used only in vehicles equipped with an oxygen sensor system (1980 Calif. vehicles and all 1981 and later models).

There are no service procedures required for the catalytic converter, although the converter body should be inspected occasionally for damage. Some models with the V6 engine require a catalyst change at 30,000 mile intervals (consult your Owner's Manual).

PRECAUTIONS

1. Use only unleaded fuel.
2. Avoid prolonged idling; the engine should run no longer than 20 min. at curb idle and no longer than 10 min. at fast idle.
3. Do not disconnect any of the spark plug leads while the engine is running.
4. Make engine compression checks as quickly as possible.

CATALYST TESTING

At the present time there is no known way to reliably test catalytic converter operation in the field. The only reliable test is a 12 hour and 40 min. soak test (CVS) which must be done in a laboratory.

A infrared HC/CO tester is not sensitive enough to measure the higher tailpipe emissions from a failing converter. Thus, a bad converter may allow enough emissions to escape so that the vehicle is no longer in compliance with Federal or state standards, but will still not cause the needle on a tester to move off zero.

The chemical reactions which occur inside a catalytic converter generate a great deal of heat. Most converter problems can be traced to fuel or ignition system problems which cause

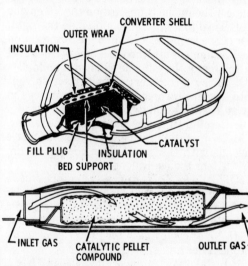

Bead type catalytic converter

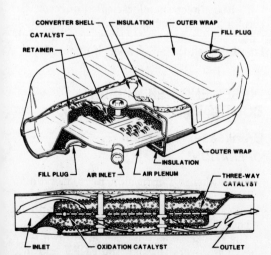

Dual bed type catalytic converter

unusually high emissions. As a result of the increased intensity of the chemical reactions, the converter literally burns itself up.

A completely failed converter might cause a tester to show a high reading. As a result, it is possible to detect a faulty converter.

As long as you avoid severe overheating and the use of leaded fuels it is reasonably safe to assume that the converter is working properly. If you are in doubt, take the vehicle to a diagnostic center that has a tester.

Oxygen Sensor

OPERATION

An oxygen sensor is used on all 1980 models built for California and on all 1981 and later models for all 50 states. The sensor protrudes into the exhaust stream and monitors the oxygen content of the exhaust gases. The difference between the oxygen content of the exhaust gases and that of the outside air generates a voltage signal to the ECM. The ECM monitors this voltage and, depending upon the value of the signal received, issues a command to adjust for a rich or a lean condition.

No attempt should ever be made to measure the voltage output of the sensor. The current drain of any conventional voltmeter would be such that it would permanently damage the sensor. No jumpers, test leads or any other electrical connections should ever be made to the sensor. Use these tools ONLY on the ECM side of the wiring harness connector AFTER disconnecting it from the sensor.

REMOVAL AND INSTALLATION

The oxygen sensor must be replaced every 30,000 miles (48,000 km.). The sensor may be difficult to remove when the engine temperature is below 120°F (48°C). Excessive removal force may damage the threads in the exhaust manifold or pipe; follow the removal procedure carefully.

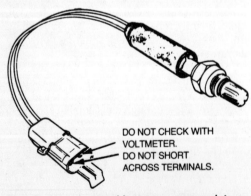

DO NOT CHECK WITH VOLTMETER.
DO NOT SHORT ACROSS TERMINALS.

Oxygen sensor assembly; sensor screws into exhaust manifold

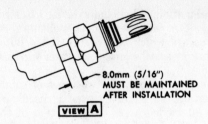

8.0mm (5/16")
MUST BE MAINTAINED
AFTER INSTALLATION

VIEW **A**

Oxygen sensor mounting

1. Locate the oxygen sensor. On the V8 engines, it is on the front of the left side exhaust manifold, just above the point where it connects to the exhaust pipe. On the V6 engines, it is on the inside of the exhaust pipe where it bends toward the back of the vehicle.

NOTE: *On the V6 engine you may find it necessary to raise the front of the vehicle and remove the oxygen sensor from underneath.*

2. Trace the wires leading from the oxygen sensor back to the first connector and then disconnect them (the connector on the V6 engine is attached to a bracket mounted on the right, rear of the engine block, while the connector on the V8 engine is attached to a bracket mounted on the top of the left side exhaust manifold.

3. Spray a commercial heat riser solvent onto the sensor threads and allow it to soak in for at least five minutes.

4. Carefully unscrew and remove the sensor.

5. To install, first coat the new sensor's threads with G.M. anti-seize compound no. 5613695 or the equivalent.

NOTE: *The G.M. anti-seize compound is NOT a conventional anti-seize paste. The use of a regular paste may electrically insulate the sensor, rendering it useless. The threads MUST be coated with the proper electrically conductive anti-seize compound.*

6. Installation torque is 30 ft. lbs. (42 Nm.). *Do not overtighten!*

7. Reconnect the electrical connector. Be careful not to damage the electrical pigtail. Check the sensor boot for proper fit and installation. Install the air cleaner, if removed.

DIESEL ENGINE EMISSION CONTROLS

Crankcase Ventilation

OPERATION

A Crankcase Depression Regulator Valve (CDRV) is used to regulate (meter) the flow of crankcase gases back into the engine to be burned. The CDRV is designed to limit vacuum in the crankcase as the gases are drawn from the valve covers through the CDRV and into the intake manifold (air crossover).

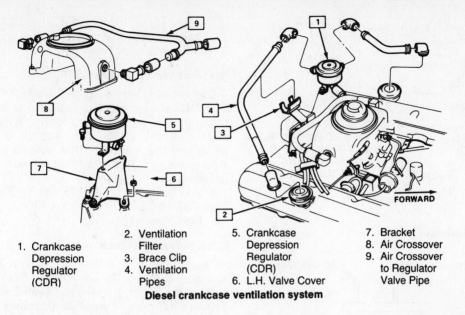

1. Crankcase
   Depression
   Regulator
   (CDR)

2. Ventilation
   Filter
3. Brace Clip
4. Ventilation
   Pipes

5. Crankcase
   Depression
   Regulator
   (CDR)
6. L.H. Valve Cover

7. Bracket
8. Air Crossover
9. Air Crossover
   to Regulator
   Valve Pipe

Diesel crankcase ventilation system

Fresh air enters the engine through the combination filter, check valve and oil fill cap. The fresh air mixes with blow-by gases and enters both valve covers. The gases pass through a filter installed on the valve covers and are drawn into connecting tubing.

Intake manifold vacuum acts against a spring loaded diaphragm to control the flow of crankcase gases. Higher intake vacuum levels pull the diaphragm closer to the top of the outlet tube. This reduces the amount of gases being drawn from the crankcase and decreases the vacuum level in the crankcase. As the intake vacuum decreases, the spring pushes the dia-phragm away from the top of the outlet tube allowing more gases to flow to the intake manifold.

NOTE: *Do not allow any solvent to come in contact with the diaphragm of the Crankcase Depression Regulator Valve because the diaphragm will fail.*

Exhaust Gas Recirculation (EGR)
OPERATION

To lower the formation of nitrogen oxides (NOx) in the exhaust, it is necessary to reduce combustion temperatures. This is done in the diesel, as in the gasoline engine, by introducing exhaust gases into the cylinders through the EGR valve.

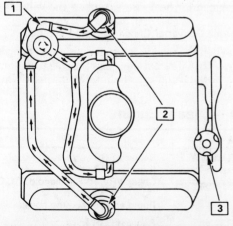

**CRANKCASE VENTILATION SYSTEM SCHEMATIC
V-TYPE DIESEL ENGINE
WITH DEPRESSION REGULATOR VALVE**

1. Crankcase
   Depression
   Regulator
2. Ventilation
   Filter
3. Breather Cap

Diesel crankcase ventilation flow

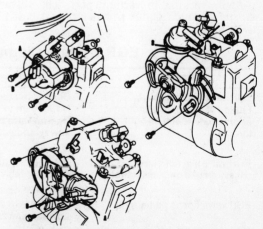

Diesel vacuum regulator valve, mounted to injection pump

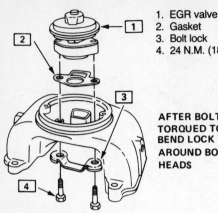

1. EGR valve
2. Gasket
3. Bolt lock
4. 24 N.M. (18 ft. lbs.)

AFTER BOLTS ARE
TORQUED TO SPECS
BEND LOCK TABS
AROUND BOLT
HEADS

210837

Diesel EGR valve location

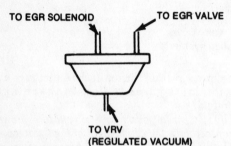

TO EGR SOLENOID

TO EGR VALVE

TO VRV
(REGULATED VACUUM)

Diesel EGR vacuum reducer—except California

FUNCTIONAL TESTS OF COMPONENTS

Vacuum Regulator Valve (VRV)

The Vacuum Regulator Valve is attached to the side of the injection pump and regulates vacuum in proportion to throttle angle. Vacuum from the vacuum pump is supplied to port A and vacuum at port B is reduced as the throttle is opened. At closed throttle, the vacuum is 15 in. Hg; at half throttle, 6 in. Hg; at wide open throttle there is zero vacuum.

Exhaust Gas Recirculation (EGR) Valve

Apply vacuum to vacuum port. The valve should be fully open at 10.5 in. Hg and closed below 6 in. Hg on 1984 and earlier models. On 1985 models, the valve should be wide open at 21 in. Hg and closed below 6 in. Hg.

Response Vacuum Reducer (RVR)

Connect a vacuum gauge to the port marked **To EGR valve or T.C.C. solenoid.** Connect a hand operated vacuum pump to the VRV port. Draw a 50.66 kPa (15 in. Hg) vacuum on the pump and the reading on the vacuum gauge should be lower than the vacuum pump reading as follows:
- Models up to 1983: 0.75 in. Hg Except High Altitude; 2.5 in. Hg High Altitude
- 1984 Models: 2 in. Hg

Quick Vacuum Response Valve

This valve is used on 1985 models only. Tee a vacuum gauge into the line running from this valve to the EPR valve, which is located on the bottom of the exhaust manifold. Disconnect the hose that runs from the inlet port **S** and connect a hand vacuum pump to the open end of the hose. Draw a vacuum of 22 in. Hg at the pump. The gauge located on the outlet side should read 20.7 in. Hg within less than two seconds. Reduce the vacuum coming from the pump to 0.9 in. Hg. The vacuum gauge should read 0.9 in. Hg within half a second.

Exhaust Pressure Regulator Valves

Disconnect the vacuum hose leading to each valve and apply vacuum with a vacuum pump. Vacuum should hold steady when you stop pumping. The valve should be open through 7 in. Hg vacuum and be fully closed by 12 in. Hg. If the valve cannot be freed up with a solvent designed for heat risers, replace the valve.

Torque Converter Clutch Operated Solenoid

When the torque converter clutch is engaged, an electrical signal energizes the solenoid allowing ports 1 and 2 to be interconnected. When

EGR System Diagnosis—Diesel Engine

Condition	Possible Causes	Correction
EGR valve will not open. Engine stalls on deceleration Engine runs rough on light throttle	Binding or stuck EGR valve. No vacuum to EGR valve. Control valve blocked or air flow restricted.	Replace EGR valve. Replace EGR valve. Check VRV, RVR, solenoid, T.C.C. Operation, Vacuum Pump and connecting hoses.
EGR valve will not close. (Heavy smoke on acceleration).	Binding or stuck EGR valve. Constant high vacuum to EGR valve.	Replace EGR valve. Check VRV, RVR, solenoid, and connecting hoses.
EGR valve opens partially.	Binding EGR valve. Low vacuum at EGR valve.	Replace EGR valve. Check VRV, RVR, solenoid, vacuum pump, and connecting hoses.

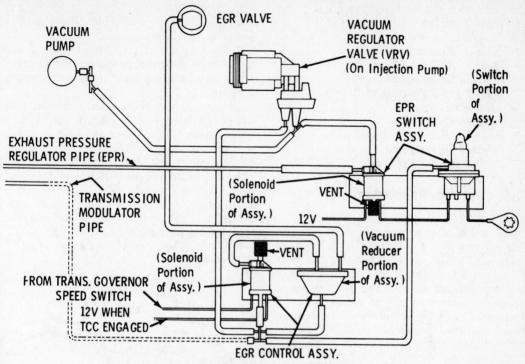

Diesel EGR system, 49-states, up to 1983

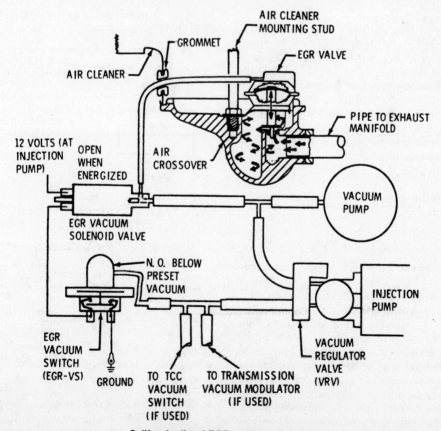

California diesel EGR system, up to 1983

the solenoid is not energized, port 1 is closed and ports 2 and 3 are interconnected.

- Models up to 1983:
  Solenoid Energized
  Ports 1 and 3 are connected
  Solenoid De-energized
  Ports 2 and 3 are connected
- 1984 Models:
  Solenoid Energized
  Ports 1 and 2 are connected
  Solenoid De-energized
  Ports 2 and 3 are connected

Quick Vacuum Response Valve (1984 only)

Connect a vacuum gauge into the vacuum line running from the GVR valve to the EGR valve with a Tee. Then, disconnect the hose from the inlet (**S**) port of the QVR and connect a hand operated vacuum pump which has a gauge that shows its output. Quickly draw a vacuum of 22 in. Hg as you watch the vacuum gauge connected to the outlet port. Outlet vacuum should reach 20.7 in. Hg within 1.7 seconds.

Engine Temperature Sensor (ETS) (Models to 1983)

OPERATION

The engine temperature sensor has two terminals. Twelve volts are applied to one terminal and the wire from the other terminal leads to the fast idle solenoid and Housing Pressure Cold Advance solenoid that is part of the injection pump.

The switch contacts are closed below 125°F (52°C). At the calibration point, the contacts are open, which turns off the solenoids.

Above calibration
- Open circuit.

Below calibration
- Closed circuit.

EGR-TVS (1984–85 Models)

1. Drain coolant from the engine until the level is below the EGR-TVS. Then, remove the valve from the engine by disconnecting all vacuum lines and electrical leads and unscrewing it with a wrench on the flats.

CAUTION: *When draining the coolant, keep in mind that cats and dogs are attracted by the ethylene glycol antifreeze, and are quite likely to drink any that is left in an uncovered container or in puddles on the ground. This will prove fatal in sufficient quantity. Always drain the coolant into a sealable container. Coolant should be reused unless it is contaminated or several years old.*

2. Inspect the valve for any visible defects and replace it if any are visible. Allow the valve to cool to room temperature.

3. Connect a vacuum gauge to port 2 and hand operated vacuum pump to port 4. Connect a self-powered test lamp across the switch terminals.

5. Immerse just the bottom (threaded portion) of the valve in a pan of cool water. Put a thermometer in the water and then heat the water slowly as you pull vacuum and watch the vacuum gauge and also watch the test lamp. The two functions of the switch should respond as specified below:

Vacuum: Port 2 and 3 should become connected and Port 1 should become blocked as the temperature passes 100°F ± 3.6° (38°C).

Electrical: The contacts should open at 107°F ± 3.6° (42°C).

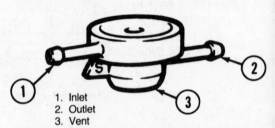

1. Inlet
2. Outlet
3. Vent

The Quick Vacuum Response valve used to V-8 diesel EGR systems

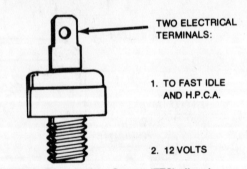

TWO ELECTRICAL TERMINALS:

1. TO FAST IDLE AND H.P.C.A.

2. 12 VOLTS

Engine Temperature Sensor (ETS), diesel

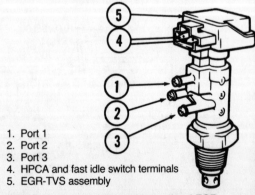

1. Port 1
2. Port 2
3. Port 3
4. HPCA and fast idle switch terminals
5. EGR-TVS assembly

EGR-TVS used on 1984 and later diesel EGR

6. Now remove the water from heat, watch the temperature, and check for an appropriate response as the temperature falls:

Vacuum: Port 2 and 1 should be connected and port 3 blocked as the temperature falls below 89°F ± 3.6° (32°C).

Electrical: The contacts should close at 89°F ± 3.6° (32°C).

6. If any of the tests are failed, the valve must be replaced. Coat the threads of the old or replacement valve with sealer and install it. Make all vacuum and electrical connections, replace water/antifreeze mix, operate the engine until hot and check for leaks.

Service Reminder Light
RESETTING
"Service Engine Soon" or "Check Engine" Light

The later model vehicles are equipped with a **"Service Engine Soon" or "Check Engine"** light. This light is on the instrument panel below the fuel gauge. The light will come ON during engine starting to let you know the bulb is working. Have the system serviced by your dealer if the light does not come on during starting, intermittently or continuously while driving. These conditions may indicate that the Computer Command Control system needs servicing. In most cases, the vehicle will not have to be towed, but get to your General Motors dealer as soon as possible.

For more information about the service reminder light, refer to the "Computer Command Control" basic troubleshooting section in this chapter.

VACUUM DIAGRAMS

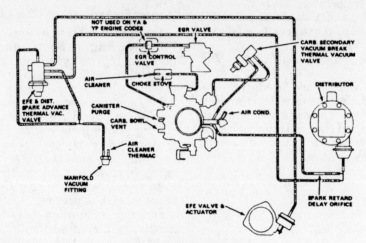

1975–76 Pontiac 350 2bbl

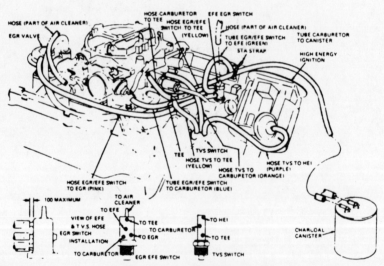

1975–77 Buick 350 4bbl with A/C

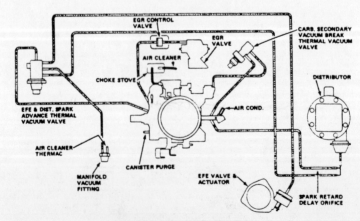

1975–76 Pontiac 350, 400 4bbl

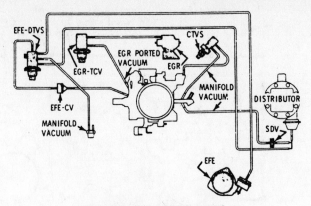

1975 Olds 400 4bbl (49 states)

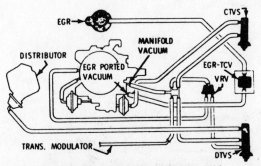

1975–76 Olds 350, 455 4bbl (49 states)

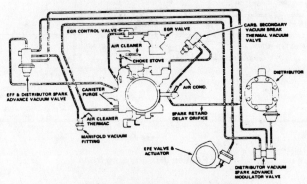

1975–76 Pontiac 455 (49 states)

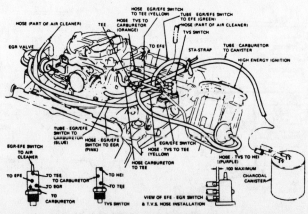

1975–77 Buick 455

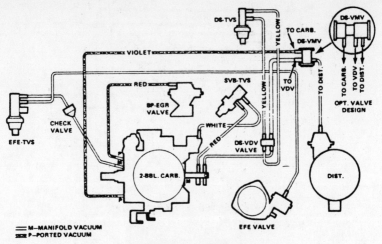

1977 Pontiac 301 with A/C

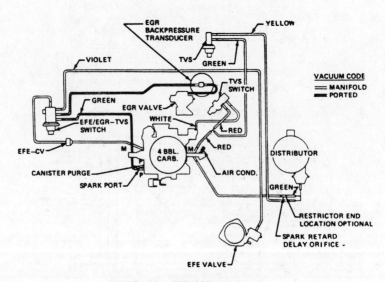

1977 Pontiac 350, 400 auto trans

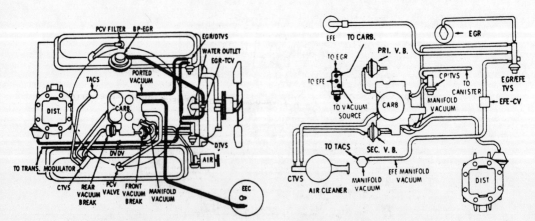

1977 Olds 350, 403 (49 states)   1978 Olds 231 (49 states)

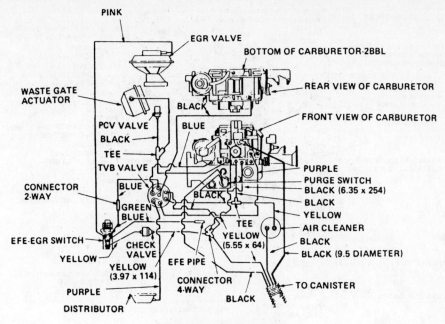

PINK

EGR VALVE

BOTTOM OF CARBURETOR-2BBL

REAR VIEW OF CARBURETOR

WASTE GATE
ACTUATOR

BLACK

FRONT VIEW OF CARBURETOR

PCV VALVE

BLUE

BLACK

TEE

TVB VALVE

PURPLE

PURGE SWITCH

CONNECTOR
2-WAY

BLUE

BLACK (6.35 x 254)

BLACK

GREEN
BLUE

BLACK

YELLOW

EFE-EGR SWITCH

TEE

AIR CLEANER

CHECK
VALVE

YELLOW
(5.55 x 64)

BLACK

YELLOW

BLACK (9.5 DIAMETER)

YELLOW
(3.97 x 114)

EFE PIPE

CONNECTOR
4-WAY

TO CANISTER

PURPLE

BLACK

DISTRIBUTOR

1978 Buick 231 2 bbl Turbo

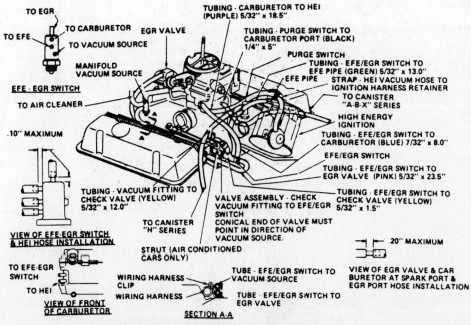

TO EGR

TUBING - CARBURETOR TO HEI
(PURPLE) 5/32" x 18.5"

TO CARBURETOR

EGR VALVE

TUBING - PURGE SWITCH TO
CARBURETOR PORT (BLACK)
1/4" x 5"

TO EFE

TO VACUUM SOURCE

PURGE SWITCH

MANIFOLD
VACUUM SOURCE

TUBING - EFE/EGR SWITCH TO
EFE PIPE (GREEN) 5/32" x 13.0"

EFE PIPE

STRAP - HEI VACUUM HOSE TO
IGNITION HARNESS RETAINER

EFE - EGR SWITCH

TO CANISTER
"A-B-X" SERIES

TO AIR CLEANER

HIGH ENERGY
IGNITION

.10" MAXIMUM

TUBING - EFE/EGR SWITCH TO
CARBURETOR (BLUE) 7/32" x 8.0"

EFE/EGR SWITCH

TUBING - EFE/EGR SWITCH TO
EGR VALVE (PINK) 5/32" x 23.5"

TUBING - VACUUM FITTING TO
CHECK VALVE (YELLOW)
5/32" x 12.0"

VALVE ASSEMBLY - CHECK
VACUUM FITTING TO EFE/EGR
SWITCH

TUBING - EFE/EGR SWITCH TO
CHECK VALVE (YELLOW)
5/32" x 1.5"

TO CANISTER
"H" SERIES

CONICAL END OF VALVE MUST
POINT IN DIRECTION OF
VACUUM SOURCE.

.20" MAXIMUM

**VIEW OF EFE-EGR SWITCH
& HEI HOSE INSTALLATION**

STRUT (AIR CONDITIONED
CARS ONLY)

**VIEW OF EGR VALVE & CAR
BURETOR AT SPARK PORT &
EGR PORT HOSE INSTALLATION**

TO EFE-EGR
SWITCH

TO HEI

WIRING HARNESS
CLIP

WIRING HARNESS

TUBE - EFE/EGR SWITCH TO
VACUUM SOURCE

TUBE - EFE/EGR SWITCH TO
EGR VALVE

**VIEW OF FRONT
OF CARBURETOR**

SECTION A-A

1978 Buick 196, 231 V6 2 bbl (49 state, auto trans)

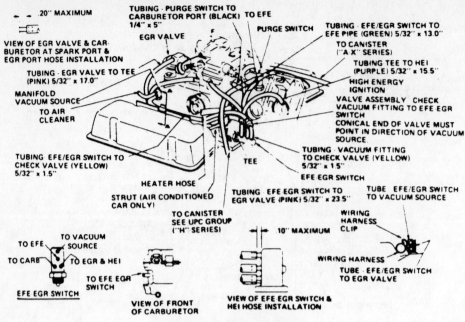

.20" MAXIMUM

VIEW OF EGR VALVE & CAR-
BURETOR AT SPARK PORT &
EGR PORT HOSE INSTALLATION

TUBING - EGR VALVE TO TEE
(PINK) 5/32" x 17.0"

MANIFOLD
VACUUM SOURCE
TO AIR
CLEANER

TUBING EFE/EGR SWITCH TO
CHECK VALVE (YELLOW)
5/32" x 1.5"

HEATER HOSE

STRUT (AIR CONDITIONED
CAR ONLY)

TO CANISTER
SEE UPC GROUP
("H" SERIES)

TUBING · PURGE SWITCH TO
CARBURETOR PORT (BLACK)
1/4" x 5"   TO EFE

EGR VALVE   PURGE SWITCH

TUBING - EFE/EGR SWITCH TO
EFE PIPE (GREEN) 5/32" x 13.0"

TO CANISTER
("A X" SERIES)

TUBING TEE TO HEI
(PURPLE) 5/32" x 15.5"

HIGH ENERGY
IGNITION

VALVE ASSEMBLY CHECK
VACUUM FITTING TO EFE EGR
SWITCH

CONICAL END OF VALVE MUST
POINT IN DIRECTION OF VACUUM
SOURCE

TUBING · VACUUM FITTING
TO CHECK VALVE (YELLOW)
5/32" x 1.5"

EFE-EGR SWITCH

TEE

TUBING · EFE EGR SWITCH TO
EGR VALVE (PINK) 5/32" x 23.5"

TUBE EFE/EGR SWITCH
TO VACUUM SOURCE

WIRING
HARNESS
CLIP

WIRING HARNESS

TUBE · EFE/EGR SWITCH
TO EGR VALVE

TO EFE   TO VACUUM
SOURCE

TO CARB   TO EGR & HEI

TO EFE EGR
SWITCH

EFE EGR SWITCH

VIEW OF FRONT
OF CARBURETOR

.10" MAXIMUM

VIEW OF EFE-EGR SWITCH &
HEI HOSE INSTALLATION

1978 Buick 231 2bbl (49 states)

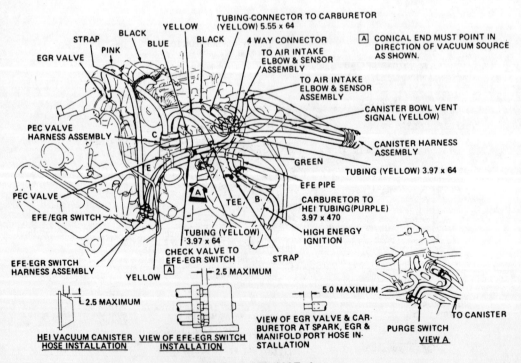

STRAP   BLACK   YELLOW

PINK   BLUE   BLACK

EGR VALVE

TUBING-CONNECTOR TO CARBURETOR
(YELLOW) 5.55 x 64

4 WAY CONNECTOR
TO AIR INTAKE
ELBOW & SENSOR
ASSEMBLY

TO AIR INTAKE
ELBOW & SENSOR
ASSEMBLY

A CONICAL END MUST POINT IN
DIRECTION OF VACUUM SOURCE
AS SHOWN.

PEC VALVE
HARNESS ASSEMBLY

CANISTER BOWL VENT
SIGNAL (YELLOW)

CANISTER HARNESS
ASSEMBLY

TUBING (YELLOW) 3.97 x 64

PEC VALVE

EFE/EGR SWITCH

EFE-EGR SWITCH
HARNESS ASSEMBLY

YELLOW

TUBING (YELLOW)
3.97 x 64

CHECK VALVE TO
EFE-EGR SWITCH

A

C

E

A   TEE   B

GREEN

EFE PIPE

CARBURETOR TO
HEI TUBING(PURPLE)
3.97 x 470

HIGH ENERGY
IGNITION

STRAP

2.5 MAXIMUM

2.5 MAXIMUM

HEI VACUUM CANISTER
HOSE INSTALLATION

VIEW OF EFE-EGR SWITCH
INSTALLATION

5.0 MAXIMUM

VIEW OF EGR VALVE & CAR-
BURETOR AT SPARK, EGR &
MANIFOLD PORT HOSE IN-
STALLATION

PURGE SWITCH

TO CANISTER

VIEW A

1978 Buick 231 4bbl Turbo

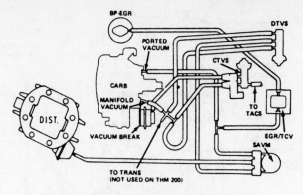

1978 Olds 260 (49 states)

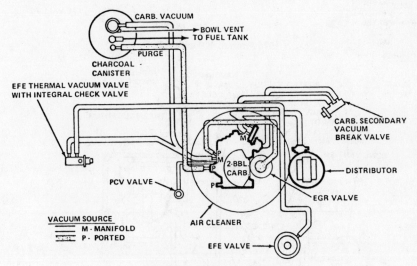

1978 Pontiac 301 auto trans

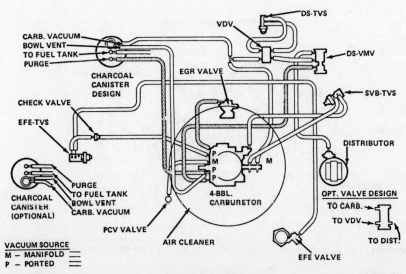

1978 Pontiac 301 4bbl

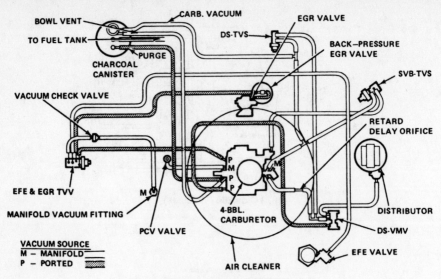

1978 Pontiac 400 with A/C

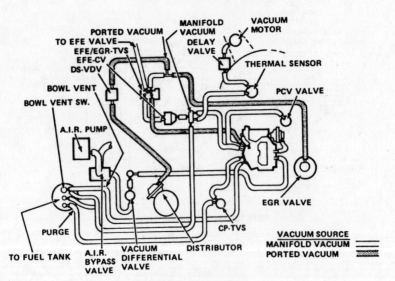

1979 Pontiac 231 V6

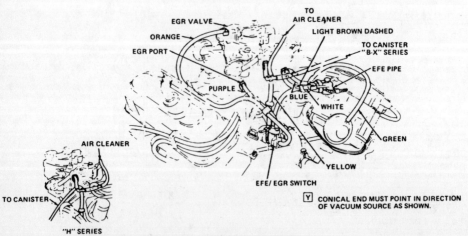

1979 Buick 231 2 bbl

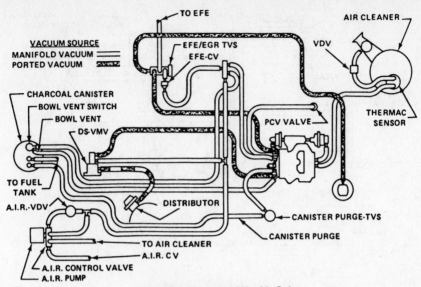

VACUUM SOURCE
MANIFOLD VACUUM
PORTED VACUUM

1979–80 Pontiac 231 V6 with C-4

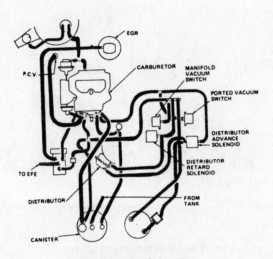

1979–80 Buick C-4 system

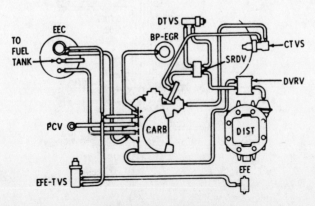

1979 Olds 301 (49 states)

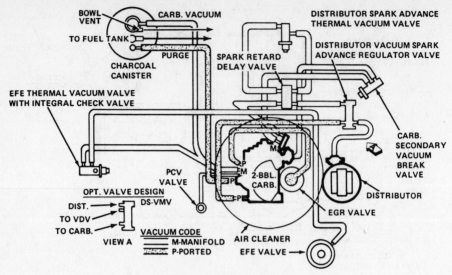

1979 Pontiac 301 2bbl

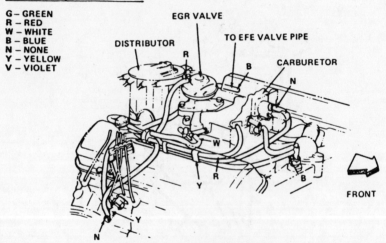

1979 Buick 307 2bbl (49 states)

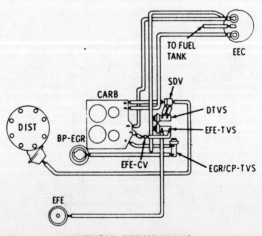

1979 Olds 307 (49 states)

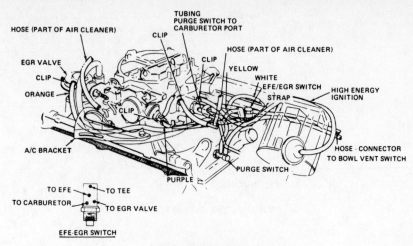

1979 Buick 350 4bbl

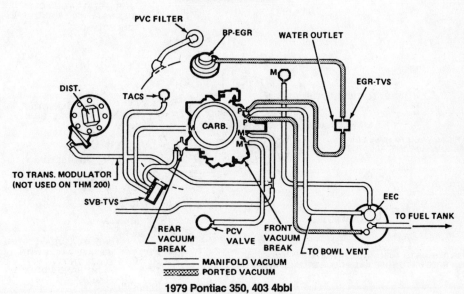

MANIFOLD VACUUM
PORTED VACUUM

1979 Pontiac 350, 403 4bbl

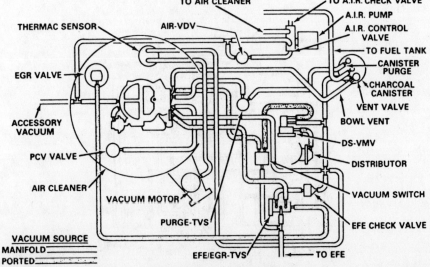

VACUUM SOURCE
MANIFOLD
PORTED

1979–80 Pontiac 350 4bbl

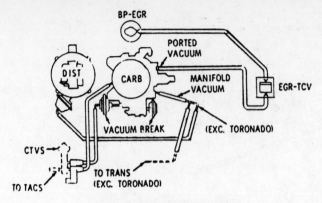

1979 Olds 350, 403 (49 states)

IF LUBRICANT IS REQUIRED
FOR INSTALLATION OF HOSES,
USE WATER ONLY AND APPLY
ONLY TO HOSE.

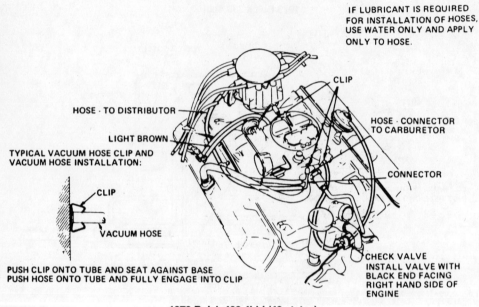

1979 Buick 403 4bbl (49 states)

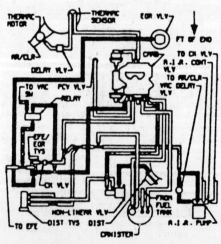

1980–84 231 V6 EGR, EFE

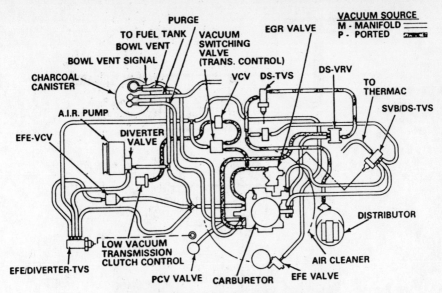

1980 Pontiac 301 with lock-up torque converter

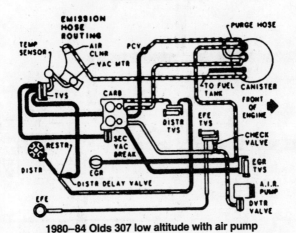

1980—84 Olds 307 low altitude with air pump

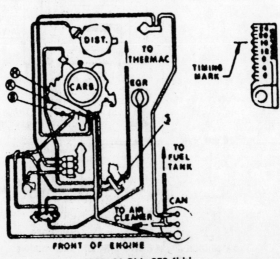

1980—81 Olds 350 4bbl

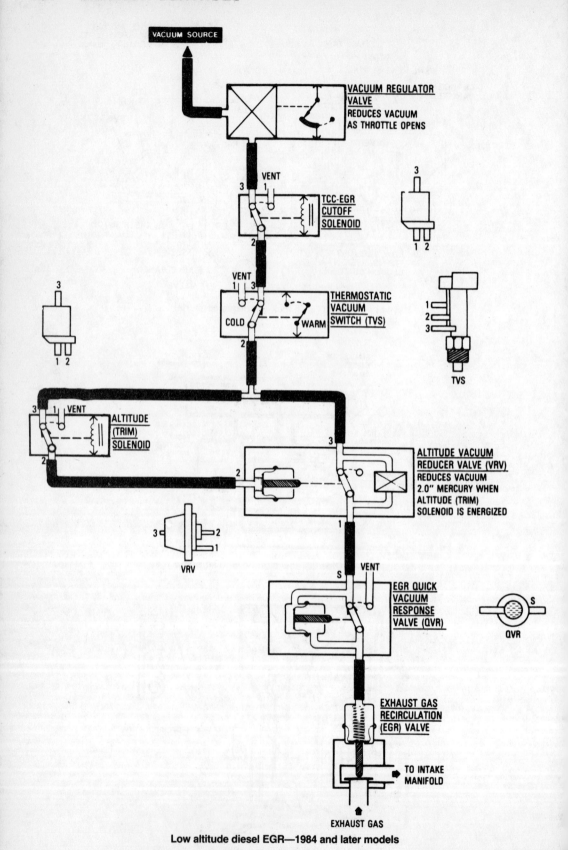

VACUUM SOURCE

VACUUM REGULATOR
VALVE
REDUCES VACUUM
AS THROTTLE OPENS

VENT

TCC-EGR
CUTOFF
SOLENOID

VENT

THERMOSTATIC
VACUUM
SWITCH (TVS)

COLD   WARM

TVS

ALTITUDE
(TRIM)
SOLENOID

VENT

ALTITUDE VACUUM
REDUCER VALVE (VRV)
REDUCES VACUUM
2.0" MERCURY WHEN
ALTITUDE (TRIM)
SOLENOID IS ENERGIZED

VRV

VENT

EGR QUICK
VACUUM
RESPONSE
VALVE (QVR)

QVR

EXHAUST GAS
RECIRCULATION
(EGR) VALVE

TO INTAKE
MANIFOLD

EXHAUST GAS

Low altitude diesel EGR—1984 and later models

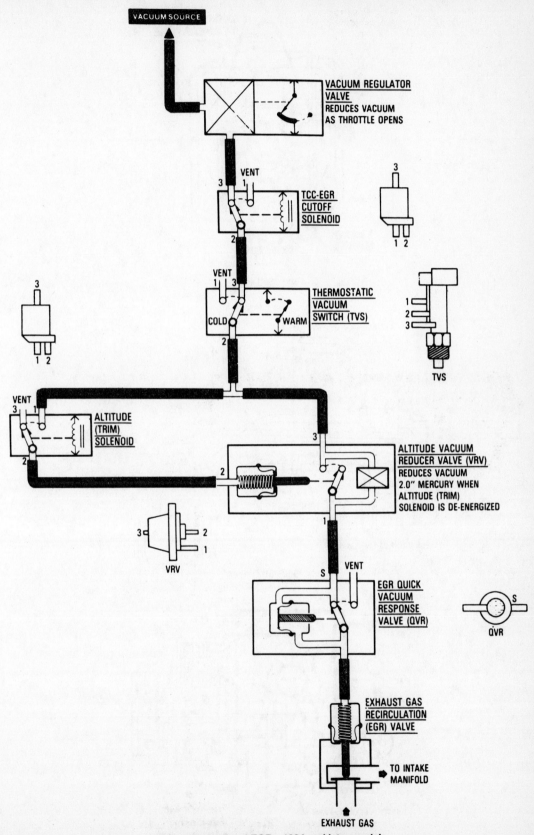

VACUUM SOURCE

VACUUM REGULATOR
VALVE
REDUCES VACUUM
AS THROTTLE OPENS

VENT

3
1

TCC-EGR
CUTOFF
SOLENOID

3

1 2

VENT
1   3

THERMOSTATIC
VACUUM
SWITCH (TVS)

COLD   WARM

2

3

1
2

1
2
3

TVS

VENT
3   1

ALTITUDE
(TRIM)
SOLENOID

2

3

ALTITUDE VACUUM
REDUCER VALVE (VRV)
REDUCES VACUUM
2.0" MERCURY WHEN
ALTITUDE (TRIM)
SOLENOID IS DE-ENERGIZED

2

3   2

1

VRV

1

S   VENT

EGR QUICK
VACUUM
RESPONSE
VALVE (QVR)

S

QVR

EXHAUST GAS
RECIRCULATION
(EGR) VALVE

TO INTAKE
MANIFOLD

EXHAUST GAS

High altitude diesel EGR—1984 and later models

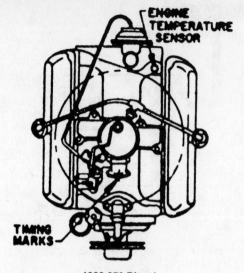

1980 350 Diesel

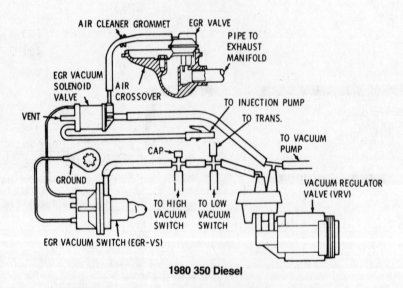

1980 350 Diesel

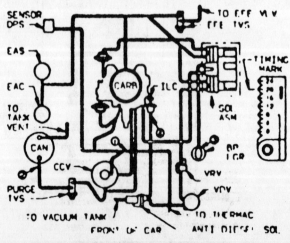

1981–84 Olds 307 VIN Y (CCC)

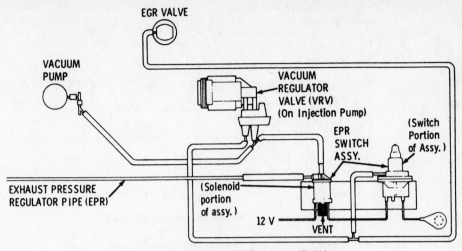

1981–83 350 Diesel EGR system (Calif.)

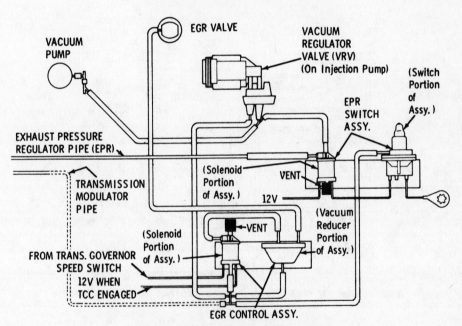

1981–83 350 Diesel EGR system (exc Calif.)

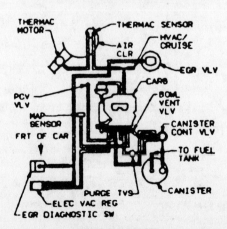

1985 Buick 231 V6

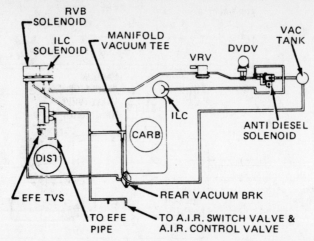

1985–87 Olds 307 VIN Y, idle load compensator and rear vacuum break

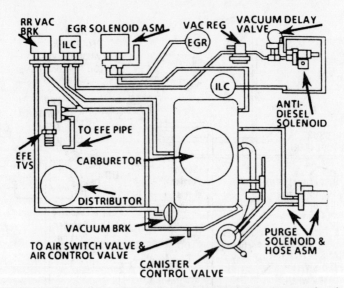

1988–89 Olds 307 VIN Y, idle load compensator and rear vacuum break

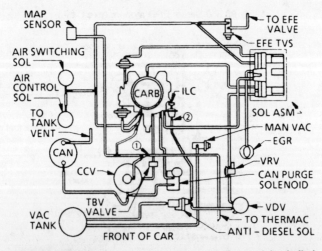

1987–90 Olds 307 VIN Y 4bbl, auto/trans (earlier models similar)

Fuel System

5

GASOLINE FUEL SYSTEM

Fuel Pump

OPERATION

Fuel pumps used on all engines are of the single-action mechanical type. The fuel pump rocker arm is held in constant engagement with the eccentric on the camshaft by the rocker arm spring. As the end of the rocker arm which is in contact with the eccentric moves upward, the fuel link pulls the fuel diaphragm downward. The action of the diaphragm enlarges the fuel chamber, drawing fuel from the tank. Fuel flows to the carburetor only when the pressure in the outlet line is less than the pressure maintained by the diaphragm spring.

The fuel pumps on all engines are not serviceable and must be replaced if defective.

REMOVAL AND INSTALLATION

NOTE: *To remove the fuel pump on some engines, the alternator and/or the A/C compressor may have to be moved out of the way. Do NOT disconnect the A/C hoses from the compressor.*

Troubleshooting Basic Fuel System Problems

Problem	Cause	Solution
Engine cranks, but won't start (or is hard to start) when cold	• Empty fuel tank • Incorrect starting procedure • Defective fuel pump • No fuel in carburetor • Clogged fuel filter • Engine flooded • Defective choke	• Check for fuel in tank • Follow correct procedure • Check pump output • Check for fuel in the carburetor • Replace fuel filter • Wait 15 minutes; try again • Check choke plate
Engine cranks, but is hard to start (or does not start) when hot— (presence of fuel is assumed)	• Defective choke	• Check choke plate
Rough idle or engine runs rough	• Dirt or moisture in fuel • Clogged air filter • Faulty fuel pump	• Replace fuel filter • Replace air filter • Check fuel pump output
Engine stalls or hesitates on acceleration	• Dirt or moisture in the fuel • Dirty carburetor • Defective fuel pump • Incorrect float level, defective accelerator pump	• Replace fuel filter • Clean the carburetor • Check fuel pump output • Check carburetor
Poor gas mileage	• Clogged air filter • Dirty carburetor • Defective choke, faulty carburetor adjustment	• Replace air filter • Clean carburetor • Check carburetor
Engine is flooded (won't start accompanied by smell of raw fuel)	• Improperly adjusted choke or carburetor	• Wait 15 minutes and try again, without pumping gas pedal • If it won't start, check carburetor

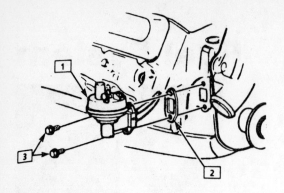

Mechanical fuel pump—gasoline engines

1. Disconnect the negative (−) battery cable.

2. Locate the fuel pump on the side of the cylinder block, open the fuel filler cap and disconnect the fuel lines. Be careful of the fuel leakage.

3. Remove the two pump mounting bolts.

NOTE: *On 305 and 350 Chevrolet built engines: if the pushrod is to be removed, take out the two adaptor bolts and lockwashers and remove the adaptor and gasket. For installation use heavy grease to hold the pushrod in place. Coat the pipe plug threads or adaptor gasket with sealer if pushrod was removed.*

4. Remove the pump and the gasket.

5. Use a new gasket when installing the pump. Torque the mounting bolts to 22 ft. lbs. (30 Nm).

6. Install the fuel lines, connect the negative battery cable, tighten the filler cap, start the engine and check for leaks.

TESTING

The fuel line from the tank to the pump is the suction side of the system and the line from the pump to the carburetor is the pressure side of the system. A leak on the pressure side, therefore, would be made apparent by dripping fuel, but a leak on the suction side would not be apparent except for the reduction of the volume of fuel on the pressure side.

1. Tighten any loose line connections and look for bends or kinks.

2. Disconnect the fuel pipe at the carburetor. Disconnect the distributor-to-coil primary wire so that the engine can be cranked without firing. Place a container at the end of the pipe and crank the engine a few revolutions. If little or no gasoline flows from the open end of the pipe, the fuel pipe is clogged or the pump is defective.

3. If fuel flows from the pump in good volume from the pipe at the carburetor, check fuel pressure to be certain that the pump is operating within specified limits as follows:

a. Attach a fuel pump pressure test gauge to the disconnected end of the pipe;

b. Run the engine at approximately 450 to 1000 rpm on the gasoline still remaining in the carburetor bowl. Note the reading on the pressure gauge.

c. If the pump is operating properly the pressure will be within the specifications listed in the Tune-Up Specifications chart found in Chapter 2. The pressure will remain constant between speeds of 450 to 1000 rpm. If the pressure is too low or too high at different speeds, the pump should be replaced.

NOTE: *There are no adjustments that can be made on these fuel pumps.*

Carburetor

ADJUSTMENTS

Float Level Adjustment

2-BBL CARBURETOR (MODEL 2GC-2GE)

1. Remove the air horn assembly from the carburetor.

2. Hold the air horn assembly upside down and measure the distance from the air horn gasket to the lip at the toe of the float. See the chart for the proper measurement.

3. Bend the float arm to adjust the float level to the proper specifications.

2-BBL CARBURETOR (MODEL 2MC)

1. Remove the air horn assembly from the carburetor. Remove the gasket.

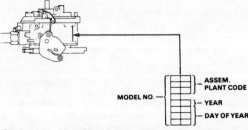

Carburetor identification location; all models similar

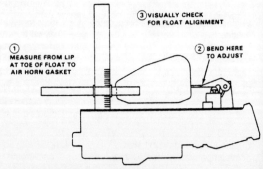

Model 2GC, GE, GV float adjustment

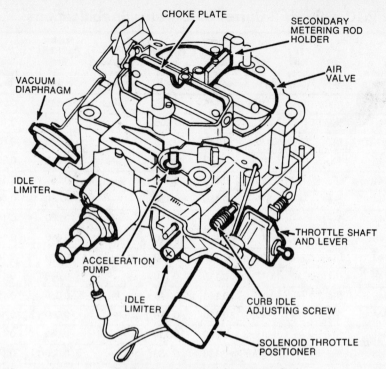

Rochester 4-barrel carburetor, typical

2. Measure the distance from the air horn gasket surface to the top of the float at the toe ($^1/_{16}$ in. (1.6mm) back from the toe on 1975 models; $^3/_{16}$ in. (4.7mm) back on 1976 and later models).

3. After making sure the retaining pin is in place, bend the float arm to adjust the float level.

2-bbl Carburetor (E2MC, E2ME)
4-bbl Carburetor (E4MC, E4ME)

1. Remove the air horn.

2. Hold the float retainer in place and lightly push down on the float against the needle.

3. Measure the gap between the casting surface and the top of the float at a point $^3/_{16}$ in. (4.7mm) back from the float toe.

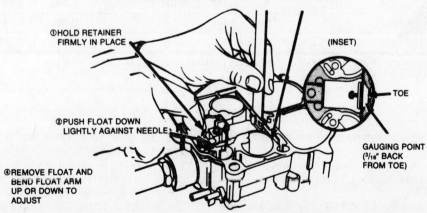

③GAUGE FROM TOP OF CASTING TO TOP OF FLOAT—GAUGING POINT ³/₁₆" BACK FROM END OF FLOAT AT TOE (SEE INSET)

①HOLD RETAINER FIRMLY IN PLACE

(INSET)

②PUSH FLOAT DOWN LIGHTLY AGAINST NEEDLE

TOE

GAUGING POINT (³/₁₆" BACK FROM TOE)

④REMOVE FLOAT AND BEND FLOAT ARM UP OR DOWN TO ADJUST

⑤VISUALLY CHECK FLOAT ALIGNMENT AFTER ADJUSTING

2MC float level adjustment; models M2ME, E2ME similar

2GC, GE, GV 2-Barrel Carburetor Specifications

Year	Carburetor Identification ①	Float Level (in.)	Air Valve Spring (turn)	Pump Rod (in.)	Primary Vacuum Break (in. or deg.)	Secondary Vacuum Break (in.)	Secondary Opening (in.)	Fast Idle Cam (Choke Rod) (in. or deg.)	Choke Unloader (in.)	Fast Idle Speed (rpm)
1975	7045160	9/16	17/32	1 11/32	0.145	0.265	1 Rich	0.085	0.180	Preset
	7045161	9/16	17/32	1 11/32	0.145	0.265	1 Rich	0.085	0.180	Preset
1976	Pontiac 400	9/16	19/32	1 11/32	0.165	0.285	1 Rich	0.085	0.180	—
1977	17057140	15/32	—	1 9/16	0.140	0.100	—	0.080	0.325	②
	17057141	7/16	—	1 1/2	0.110	0.110	—	0.080	0.140	②
	17057144	7/16	—	1 17/32	0.130	0.130	—	0.080	0.140	②
	17057145	7/16	—	1 1/2	0.110	0.110	—	0.080	0.140	②
	17057146	7/16	—	1 17/32	0.110	0.110	—	0.080	0.140	②
	17057147	7/16	—	1 1/2	0.110	0.110	—	0.080	0.140	②
	17057148	7/16	—	1 17/32	0.110	0.110	—	0.080	0.140	②
	17057445	7/16	—	1 1/2	0.140	0.140	—	0.080	0.140	②
	17057446	7/16	—	1 1/2	0.130	0.130	—	0.080	0.140	②
	17057447	7/16	—	1 1/2	0.130	0.130	—	0.080	0.140	②
	17057448	7/16	—	1 1/2	0.130	0.130	—	0.080	0.140	②
	17057112	19/32	—	1 21/32	—	0.130	—	0.260	0.325	②
	17057113	19/32	—	1 21/32	—	0.130	—	0.260	0.325	②
	17057114	19/32	—	1 21/32	—	0.130	—	0.260	0.325	②
1978	17058145	7/16	—	1 19/32	0.110	0.060	—	0.080	0.160	②
	17058182	7/16	—	1 19/32	0.110	0.080	—	0.080	0.140	②
	17058183	7/16	—	1 19/32	0.110	0.080	—	0.080	0.140	②
	17058185	7/16	—	1 19/32	0.110	0.050	—	0.080	0.140	②
	17058187	7/16	—	1 19/32	0.110	0.080	—	0.080	0.140	②
	17058189	7/16	—	1 19/32	0.110	0.080	—	0.080	0.140	②
	17058147	7/16	—	1 19/32	0.140	0.100	—	0.080	0.140	②
	17058444	7/16	—	1 19/32	0.140	0.100	—	0.080	0.140	②
	17058448	7/16	—	1 19/32	0.140	0.100	—	0.080	0.140	②
	17058440	7/16	—	1 19/32	0.140	0.100	—	0.080	0.140	②
	17058446	7/16	—	1 5/8	0.140	0.140	—	0.080	0.140	②

① Carburetor identification number is stamped on the float bowl next to the fuel inlet nut
② See underhood decal

4. To adjust, remove the float and bend the float arm.

5. On CCC carburetors, if the float level varies more than 1/16 in. (1.6mm) either way, adjust as follows:

a. Level too high. Hold the float retainer firmly in place and push down on the center of the float body until the correct gap is attained.

b. Level too low: Lift out the metering rods. Remove the solenoid connector screw. Turn the lean mixture solenoid screw clockwise counting the number of turns until the screw is lightly seated. Then, remove the screw. Lift the solenoid and connector from the float bowl. Remove the float and bend the arm to adjust. Instal the float and check the adjustment. Install the mixture screw to the exact number of turns noted earlier. Install all other parts.

2MC, M2MC, M2ME, E2MC, E2ME 2-Barrel Carburetor Specifications

Year	Carburetor Identification ①	Float Level (in.)	Fast Idle Cam (Choke Rod) (deg./in.)	Choke Unloader (deg./in.)	Vacuum Break Lean or Front (deg./in.)	Vacuum Break Rich or Rear (deg./in.)	Pump Rod (in.)	Choke Coil Lever (in.)	Automatic Choke (notches)
1977	17057150	$1/8$	.085	0.190	0.160	0.090	$11/32$ ③	0.120	2 Rich
	17057152	$1/8$	.085	0.190	0.160	0.090	$11/32$ ③	0.120	2 Rich
	17057156	$1/8$	.085	0.190	0.160	0.090	$11/32$ ③	0.120	1 Rich
	17057158	$1/8$	.085	0.190	0.160	0.090	$11/32$ ③	0.120	1 Rich
	17057172	$11/32$	.075	0.240	0.135	0.240	$3/8$ ③	0.120	2 Rich
1978	17058150	$3/8$	0.065	0.203	0.203	0.133	$1/4$ ②	0.120	2 Rich
	17058151	$3/8$	0.065	0.203	0.229	0.133	$11/32$ ③	0.120	2 Rich
	17058152	$3/8$	0.065	0.203	0.203	0.133	$1/4$ ②	0.120	2 Rich
	17058154	$3/8$	0.065	0.203	0.146	0.245	$11/32$ ③	0.120	2 Rich
	17058155	$3/8$	0.065	0.203	0.146	0.245	$11/32$ ③	0.120	2 Rich
	17058156	$3/8$	0.065	0.230	0.229	0.133	$11/32$ ③	0.120	2 Rich
	17058158	$3/8$	0.065	0.203	0.229	0.133	$11/32$ ③	0.120	2 Rich
	17058450	$3/8$	0.065	0.203	0.146	0.289	$11/32$ ③	0.120	2 Rich
1979	17059160	$11/32$	0.110	0.195	0.129	0.187	$1/4$ ②	0.120	2 Rich
	17059150	$3/8$	0.071	0.220	0.195	0.129	$1/4$ ②	0.120	2 Rich
	17059151	$3/8$	0.071	0.220	0.243	0.142	$11/32$ ③	0.120	2 Rich
	17059152	$3/8$	0.071	0.220	0.195	0.129	$1/4$ ②	0.120	2 Rich
	17059180	$11/32$	0.039	0.243	0.103	0.090	$1/4$ ②	0.120	2 Rich
	17059190	$11/32$	0.039	0.243	0.103	0.090	$1/4$ ②	0.120	2 Rich
	17059492	$11/32$	0.039	0.277	0.129	0.117	$9/32$ ②	0.120	1 Rich
	17059134	$15/32$	38	38	27	—	$1/4$	0.120	1 Lean
	17059136	$15/32$	38	38	27	—	$1/4$	0.120	1 Lean
	17059193	$13/32$	24.5	35	19	17	$1/4$ ②	0.120	2 Rich
	17059194	$11/32$	24.5	35	19	17	$1/4$ ②	0.120	2 Rich
	17059491	$11/32$	24.5	38	23	21	$9/32$ ②	0.120	1 Lean
1980	17080195	$9/32$	24.5	38	19	38	—	0.120	—
	17080197	$9/32$	24.5	38	19	38	—	0.120	—
	17080495	$5/16$	24.5	38	21	30	—	0.120	—
	17080493	$5/16$	24.5	38	21	30	—	0.120	—
	17080150	$3/8$	14	35	38	27	$11/32$ ③	0.120	—
	17080153	$3/8$	14	35	38	27	$11/32$ ③	0.120	—
	17080152	$3/8$	14	35	38	27	$11/32$ ③	0.120	—
	17080496	$5/16$	24.5	38	21	21	$3/8$	0.120	④
	17080498	$5/16$	24.5	38	21	21	$3/8$	0.120	④
	17080490	$5/16$	24.5	38	21	21	$3/8$	0.120	④
	17080492	$5/16$	24.5	38	21	21	$3/8$	0.120	④
	17080491	$5/16$	24.5	38	21	21	$3/8$	0.120	④
	17080190	$9/32$	24.5	38	22	20	$1/4$	0.120	④
	17080191	$11/32$	24.5	38	18	18	$1/4$	0.120	④
	17080195	$9/32$	24.5	38	19	14	$1/4$	0.120	④

2MC, M2MC, M2ME, E2MC, E2ME 2-Barrel Carburetor Specifications (cont.)

Year	Carburetor Identification ①	Float Level (in.)	Fast Idle Cam (Choke Rod) (deg./in.)	Choke Unloader (deg./in.)	Vacuum Break Lean or Front (deg./in.)	Vacuum Break Rich or Rear (deg./in.)	Pump Rod (in.)	Choke Coil Lever (in.)	Automatic Choke (notches)
1980	17080197	$9/32$	24.5	38	19	14	$1/4$	0.120	④
	17080192	$9/32$	24.5	38	22	20	$1/4$	0.120	④
	17080160	$5/16$	14.5	37.5	28.5	33.5	$1/4$	0.120	④
1981	17081191	$5/16$	24.5°	38°	28°	24°	—	0.120	④
	17081192	$3/8$	18°	38°	28°	24°	—	0.120	④
	17081994	$3/8$	18°	38°	28°	24°	—	0.120	④
	17081196	$5/16$	24.5°	38°	28°	24°	—	0.120	④
	17081197	$3/8$	18°	38°	28°	24°	—	0.120	④
	17081198	$3/8$	18°	38°	28°	24°	—	0.120	④
	17081199	$3/8$	18°	38°	28°	24°	—	0.120	④
	17081150	$13/32$	14°	35°	24°	36°	—	0.120	④
	17081152	$13/32$	14°	35°	24°	36°	—	0.120	④
	17080191	$11/32$	24.5°	38°	18°	18°	$1/4$	0.120	④
	17081492	$9/32$	24.5°	38°	17°	19°	$1/4$	0.120	④
	17081493	$9/32$	24.5°	38°	17°	19°	$1/4$	0.120	④
	17081170	$13/32$	20°	38°	25°	—	$1/4$	0.120	④
	17081171	$13/32$	20°	38°	25°	—	$1/4$	0.120	④
	17081174	$9/32$	20°	38°	25°	—	$1/4$	0.120	④
	17081175	$9/32$	20°	38°	25°	—	$1/4$	0.120	④
1982	17082130	$3/8$	20°	38°	27°	—	—	—	—
	17082132	$3/8$	20°	38°	27°	—	—	—	—
	17082138	$3/8$	20°	38°	27°	—	—	—	—
	17082140	$3/8$	20°	38°	27°	—	—	—	—
	17082150	$13/32$	14°	35°	24°	38°	—	—	—
	17082150	$13/32$	14°	35°	24°	40°	—	—	—
	17082182	$5/16$	18°	32°	28°	24°	—	—	—
	17082184	$5/16$	18°	32°	28°	24°	—	—	—
	17082186	$5/16$	18°	27°	21°	19°	—	—	—
	17082192	$5/16$	18°	32°	28°	24°	—	—	—
	17082194	$5/16$	18°	32°	28°	24°	—	—	—
	17082196	$5/16$	18°	27°	21°	19°	—	—	—
1983	17083190	$5/16$	18°	32	28°	24°	—	.1206 ⑤	—
	17083192	$5/16$	18°	32	28°	24°	—	.1206 ⑤	—
	17083193	$5/16$	18°	27	24°	28°	—	.1206 ⑤	—
	17083194	$5/16$	17°	35	27°	25°	—	.1206 ⑤	—
1984	17084191	$5/16$	18°	32°	28°	24°	—	.120 ⑤	—

NOTE: Specifications are not included for 1985 and later years because these carburetors are too complex for do-it-yourself mechanics.
① The carburetor identifications number is stamped on the float bowl, next to the fuel inlet nut.
② Inner hole   ④ Tamper resistant choke
③ Outer hole   ⑤ Use a guage of required dimension

M4MC, M4ME, E4MC, E4ME 4-Barrel Carburetor Specifications

Year	Carburetor Identification ①	Float Level (in.)	Air Valve Spring (turn)	Pump Rod (in.)	Primary Vacuum Break (in. or deg.)	Secondary Vacuum Break (in. or deg.)	Secondary Opening (in. or deg.)	Fast Idle Cam (Choke Rod) (in. or deg.)	Choke Unloader (in. or deg.)	Fast Idle Speed (rpm)
1975	7045183	3/8	1/8	9/32	0.190	0.140	—	0.135	0.235	②
	7045250	3/8	1/2	9/32	0.250	0.180	—	0.170	0.300	②
	7045483	3/8	1/2	9/32	0.275	0.180	—	0.135	0.235	②
	7045550	3/8	1/2	9/32	0.275	0.180	—	0.135	0.235	②
	7045264	17/32	1/2	9/32	0.150	0.260	—	0.130	0.235	②
	7045184	3/8	3/4	9/32	0.190	0.140	—	0.135	0.235	②
	7045185	3/8	3/4	9/32	0.275	0.140	—	0.135	0.235	②
	7045251	3/8	3/4	9/32	0.190	0.140	—	0.135	0.235	②
	7045244	5/16	3/4	15/32	0.130	0.115	Index	0.095	0.240	1800 ③
	7045544	5/16	3/4	15/32	0.145	0.130	Index	0.095	0.240	1800 ③
	7045240	7/16	7/16	9/32	0.135	0.120	Index	0.095	0.240	1800 ③
	7045548	7/16	7/16	9/32	0.135	0.120	Index	0.095	0.240	1800 ③
	7045541	7/16	7/16	9/32	0.135	0.120	Index	0.095	0.240	1800 ③
	7045274	1/2	—	9/32	0.150	0.260	—	0.230	0.230	1800
	7045260	1/2	—	9/32	0.150	0.260	—	0.130	0.230	1800
	7045262	1/2	—	9/32	0.150	0.260	—	0.130	0.230	1800
	7045266	1/2	—	9/32	0.150	0.260	—	0.130	0.230	1800
	7045562	1/2	—	9/32	0.150	0.260	—	0.130	0.230	1800
1976	17056544	5/16	3/4	3/8	0.130	0.130	Index	0.095	0.250	—
	17056244	5/16	3/4	3/8	0.130	0.120	Index	0.095	0.250	—
	17056240	15/32	7/16	9/32	0.135	0.120	Index	0.095	0.250	—
	17056540	15/32	7/16	3/8	0.135	0.120	Index	0.095	0.250	—
	17056250	13/32	1/2	9/32	0.190	0.140	—	0.130	0.230	900 ④
	17056251	13/32	3/4	9/32	0.190	0.140	—	0.130	0.230	900
	17056253	13/32	1/2	9/32	0.190	0.140	—	0.130	0.230	900 ④
	17056255	13/32	3/4	9/32	0.190	0.140	—	0.130	0.230	900
	17056256	13/32	3/4	9/32	0.190	0.140	—	0.130	0.230	900
	17056257	13/32	3/4	9/32	0.190	0.140	—	0.130	0.230	900
	17056550	13/32	1/2	9/32.	0.190	0.140	—	0.130	0.230	1000
	17056551	13/32	3/4	9/32	0.190	0.140	—	0.130	0.230	800
	17056553	13/32	1/2	9/32	0.190	0.140	—	0.130	0.230	1000
1977	17057202	15/32	7/8	9/32	0.160	—	—	0.325	0.280	1600 ⑤
	17057204	15/32	7/8	9/32	0.160	—	—	0.325	0.280	1600 ⑤
	1707250	13/32	1/2	9/32	0.135	0.180	—	0.100	0.220	⑦
	1707253	13/32	1/2	9/32	0.135	0.180	—	0.100	0.220	⑦
	1707255	13/32	1/2	9/32	0.135	0.180	—	0.100	0.220	⑦
	1707256	13/32	1/2	9/32	0.135	0.180	—	0.100	0.220	⑦
	1707258	13/32	1/2	9/32	0.135	0.225	—	0.100	0.220	⑦
	1707550	13/32	1/2	9/32	0.135	0.225	—	0.100	0.220	⑦

M4MC, M4ME, E4MC, E4ME 4-Barrel Carburetor Specifications (cont.)

Year	Carburetor Identification ①	Float Level (in.)	Air Valve Spring (turn)	Pump Rod (in.)	Primary Vacuum Break (in. or deg.)	Secondary Vacuum Break (in. or deg.)	Secondary Opening (in. or deg.)	Fast Idle Cam (Choke Rod) (in. or deg.)	Choke Unloader (in. or deg.)	Fast Idle Speed (rpm)
1977	1707553	$13/32$	$1/2$	$9/32$	0.135	0.225	—	0.100	0.220	⑦
	17057262	$17/32$	$1/2$	$3/8$	0.150	0.240	—	0.130	0.220	⑦
1978	17058253	$13/32$	$1/2$	$9/32$	0.129	0.183	—	0.096	0.220	⑦
	17058250	$13/32$	$1/2$	$9/32$	0.129	0.183	—	0.096	0.220	⑦
	17058258	$13/32$	$1/2$	$9/32$	0.136	0.230	—	0.103	0.220	⑦
	17058553	$13/32$	$1/2$	$9/32$	0.136	0.230	—	0.103	0.220	⑦
	17058272	$15/32$	$5/8$	$3/8$	0.126	0.195	—	0.071	0.227	⑦
	17058241	$5/16$	$3/4$	$3/8$	0.117	0.103	—	0.096	0.243	⑦
	17058274	$17/32$	$1/2$	$3/8$	0.149	0.260	—	0.129	0.220	⑦
	17058264	$17/32$	$1/2$	$3/8$	0.149	0.260	—	0.129	0.220	⑦
1979	17059253	$13/32$	$1/2$	$9/32$	23	30.5	—	18	35	⑦
	17059250	$13/32$	$1/2$	$9/32$	23	30.5	—	18	35	⑦
	17059251	$13/32$	$1/2$	$9/32$	23	30.5	—	—	35	⑦
	17059258	$13/32$	$1/2$	$9/32$	24	32	—	—	35	⑦
	17059256	$13/32$	$1/2$	$9/32$	24	32	—	—	35	⑦
	17059553	$13/32$	$1/2$	$9/32$	24	36.5	—	19	35	⑦
	1709240	$7/32$	$3/4$	$9/32$	21	21	—	14.5	30	⑦
	1709243	$7/32$	$3/4$	$9/32$	21	21	—	14.5	30	⑦
	1709540	$7/32$	$3/4$	$9/32$	21	23	—	14.5	38	⑦
	1709543	$7/32$	$3/4$	$9/32$	21	23	—	14.5	38	⑦
	1709542	$7/32$	$3/4$	$9/32$	13	13	—	14.5	30	⑦
1980	17080253	$13/32$	$1/2$	$9/32$	26	34	—	17	35	⑦
	17080250	$13/32$	$1/2$	$9/32$	26	34	—	17	35	⑦
	17080252	$13/32$	$1/2$	$9/32$	26	34	—	17	35	⑦
	17080251	$13/32$	$1/2$	$9/32$	26	34	—	17	35	⑦
	17080259	$13/32$	$1/2$	$9/32$	26	34	—	17	35	⑦
	17080260	$13/32$	$1/2$	$9/32$	26	34	—	17	35	⑦
	17080553	$15/32$	$1/2$	$9/32$	25	35	—	17	35	⑦
	17080554	$15/32$	$1/2$	$9/32$	25	34	—	17	35	⑦
	17080272	$15/32$	$5/8$	$3/8$	23	29.5	—	14.5	33	⑦
	17080249	$7/16$	$3/4$	$9/32$	23	20.5	—	18	38	⑦
	17080270	$15/32$	$5/8$	$3/8$	26	34	—	14.5	35	⑦
	17080241	$7/16$	$3/4$	$9/32$	23	20.5	—	18	38	⑦
	17080249	$7/16$	$3/4$	$9/32$	23	20.5	—	18	38	⑦
	17080244	$5/16$	$5/8$	$9/32$	18	14	—	24.5	38	⑦
	17080242	$13/32$	$9/16$	$9/32$	15	18	—	14.5	35	⑦
	17080243	$3/16$	$9/16$	$9/32$	16	16	—	14.5	30	⑦
1981	17081248	$3/8$	$5/8$	⑥	28	24	—	24.5	38	⑦
	17081289	$13/32$	$5/8$	⑥	28	24	—	24.5	38	⑦

M4MC, M4ME, E4MC, E4ME 4-Barrel Carburetor Specifications (cont.)

Year	Carburetor Identification ①	Float Level (in.)	Air Valve Spring (turn)	Pump Rod (in.)	Primary Vacuum Break (in. or deg.)	Secondary Vacuum Break (in. or deg.)	Secondary Opening (in. or deg.)	Fast Idle Cam (Choke Rod) (in. or deg.)	Choke Unloader (in. or deg.)	Fast Idle Speed (rpm)
1981	17081253	15/32	1/2	⑥	25	36	—	14	35	⑦
	17081254	15/32	1/2	⑥	25	36	—	14	35	⑦
1982	17082202	11/32	—	⑥	20	20	—	—	—	⑦
	17082204	11/32	—	⑥	20	20	—	—	—	⑦
	17082244	7/16	—	⑥	32	21	16	—	—	⑦
	17082245	3/8	—	⑥	32	26	26	—	—	⑦
	17082246	3/8	—	⑥	32	26	26	—	—	⑦
	17082247	13/32	—	⑥	38	28	24	—	—	⑦
	17082248	13/32	—	⑥	38	28	24	—	—	⑦
1982	17082251	15/32	—	⑥	35	25	45	—	—	⑦
	17082253	15/32	—	⑥	35	25	36	—	—	⑦
	17082264	7/16	—	⑥	32	21	16	—	—	⑦
	17082265	3/8	—	⑥	32	26	26	—	—	⑦
	17082266	3/8	—	⑥	32	26	26	—	—	⑦
1983	17083250	7/16	1/2	⑥	27°	42°	—	14°	35	⑦
	17083253	7/16	1/2	⑥	27°	41°	—	14°	35	⑦
1984	17084205	11/32	7/8	⑥	27°	—	.015	38°	38°	⑦
	17084208	11/32	7/8	⑥	27°	—	.015	20°	38°	⑦
	17084209	11/32	7/8	⑥	27°	—	.015	38°	38°	⑦
	17084210	11/32	7/8	⑥	27°	—	.015	20°	38°	⑦
	17084240	5/16	1	⑥	24°	—	.015	24.5°	32°	⑦
	17084244	5/16	1	⑥	24°	—	.015	24.5°	32°	⑦
	17084246	5/16	1	⑥	22°	—	.015	24.5°	32°	⑦
	17084248	5/16	1	⑥	24°	—	.015	24.5°	32°	⑦
	17084252	7/16	1/2	⑥	27°	—	.015	14°	35°	⑦
	17084254	7/16	1/2	⑥	27°	—	.015	14°	35°	⑦
	17084256	11/32	1/2	⑥	27°	41°	.015	14°	35°	⑦
	17084258	11/32	1/2	⑥	27°	41°	.015	14°	35°	⑦
1985	17084282	11/32	1/2	⑥	25°	43°	.025	14°	35°	⑦
	17085554	14/32	1/2	⑥	27°	41°	.025	14°	35°	⑦
	17085202	11/32	7/8	⑥	27°	—	.025	20°	38°	⑦
	17085203	11/32	7/8	⑥	27°	—	.025	20°	38°	⑦
	17085204	11/32	7/8	⑥	27°	—	.025	20°	38°	⑦
	17085207	11/32	7/8	⑥	27°	—	.025	38°	38°	⑦
	17085218	11/32	7/8	⑥	27°		.025	20°	38°	⑦
	17085502	7/16	7/8	⑥	26°	36°	.025	20°	39°	⑦
	17085503	7/16	7/8	⑥	26°	36°	.025	20°	39°	⑦
	17085506	7/16	1	⑥	27°	36°	.025	20°	36°	⑦
	17085508	7/16	1	⑥	27°	36°	.025	20°	36°	⑦

M4MC, M4ME, E4MC, E4ME 4-Barrel Carburetor Specifications

Year	Carburetor Identification ①	Float Level (in.)	Air Valve Spring (turn)	Pump Rod (in.)	Primary Vacuum Break (in. or deg.)	Secondary Vacuum Break (in. or deg.)	Secondary Opening (in. or deg.)	Fast Idle Cam (Choke Rod) (in. or deg.)	Choke Unloader (in. or deg.)	Fast Idle Speed (rpm)
	17085524	7/16	1	⑥	25°	36°	.025	20°	36°	⑦
	17085526	7/16	1	⑥	25°	36°	.025	20°	36°	⑦
1986	17086008	11/32	1/2	⑥	25°	43°	.025	14°	35°	⑦
	17086077	11/32	1/2	⑥	25°	43°	.025	14°	35°	⑦
1987	17086009	14/32	1/2	⑥	25°	43°	.025	14°	35°	⑦
	17087130	11/32	7/8	⑥	27°	—	.025	20°	38°	⑦
	17087131	11/32	7/8	⑥	27°	—	.025	38°	38°	⑦
	17087133	11/32	7/8	⑥	27°	—	.025	38°	38°	⑦
1988–90	17086008	11/32	1/2	⑥	25°	43°	.025	14°	35°	⑦
	17088115	11/32	1/2	⑥	25°	43°	.025	14°	35°	⑦

① Carburetor identification number is stamped on the float bowl next to the fuel inlet nut
② 900 rpm with fast idle cam follower on lowest step of fast idle cam
③ Trans. in Park with fast idle cam follower on highest step of fast idle cam
④ In Park; 1000 rpm (Park) in California
⑤ In Park
⑥ No pump rod adjustment required on carburetors used with the CCC system
⑦ See underhood decal

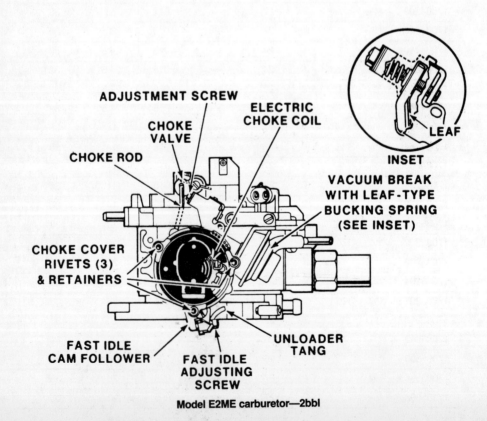

Model E2ME carburetor—2bbl

CHILTON'S
FUEL ECONOMY & TUNE-UP TIPS

Tune-up • Spark Plug Diagnosis • Emission Controls

Fuel System • Cooling System • Tires and Wheels

General Maintenance

CHILTON'S FUEL ECONOMY & TUNE-UP TIPS

Fuel economy is important to everyone, no matter what kind of vehicle you drive. The maintenance-minded motorist can save both money and fuel using these tips and the periodic maintenance and tune-up procedures in this Repair and Tune-Up Guide.

There are more than 130,000,000 cars and trucks registered for private use in the United States. Each travels an average of 10-12,000 miles per year, and, and in total they consume close to 70 billion gallons of fuel each year. This represents nearly ⅔ of the oil imported by the United States each year. The Federal government's goal is to reduce consumption 10% by 1985. A variety of methods are either already in use or under serious consideration, and they all affect you driving and the cars you will drive. In addition to "down-sizing", the auto industry is using or investigating the use of electronic fuel delivery, electronic engine controls and alternative engines for use in smaller and lighter vehicles, among other alternatives to meet the federally mandated Corporate Average Fuel Economy (CAFE) of 27.5 mpg by 1985. The government, for its part, is considering rationing, mandatory driving curtailments and tax increases on motor vehicle fuel in an effort to reduce consumption. The government's goal of a 10% reduction could be realized — and further government regulation avoided — if every private vehicle could use just 1 less gallon of fuel per week.

How Much Can You Save?

Tests have proven that almost anyone can make at least a 10% reduction in fuel consumption through regular maintenance and tune-ups. When a major manufacturer of spark plugs sur-

TUNE-UP

1. Check the cylinder compression to be sure the engine will really benefit from a tune-up and that it is capable of producing good fuel economy. A tune-up will be wasted on an engine in poor mechanical condition.

2. Replace spark plugs regularly. New spark plugs alone can increase fuel economy 3%.

3. Be sure the spark plugs are the correct type (heat range) for your vehicle. See the Tune-Up Specifications.

Heat range refers to the spark plug's ability to conduct heat away from the firing end. It must conduct the heat away in an even pattern to avoid becoming a source of pre-ignition, yet it must also operate hot enough to burn off conductive deposits that could cause misfiring.

The heat range is usually indicated by a number on the spark plug, part of the manufacturer's designation for each individual spark plug. The numbers in bold-face indicate the heat range in each manufacturer's identification system.

Manufacturer	Typical Designation
AC	R **45** TS
Bosch (old)	WA **145** T30
Bosch (new)	HR **8** Y
Champion	RBL **15** Y
Fram/Autolite	**415**
Mopar	P-**62** PR
Motorcraft	BRF-**42**
NGK	BP **5** ES-15
Nippondenso	W **16** EP
Prestolite	14GR **5** 2A

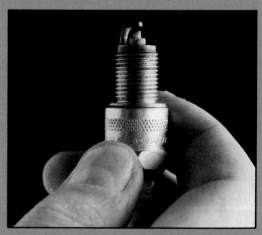

Periodically, check the spark plugs to be sure they are firing efficiently. They are excellent indicators of the internal condition of your engine.

On AC, Bosch (new), Champion, Fram/Autolite, Mopar, Motorcraft and Prestolite, a higher number indicates a hotter plug. On Bosch (old), NGK and Nippondenso, a higher number indicates a colder plug.

4. Make sure the spark plugs are properly gapped. See the Tune-Up Specifications in this book.

5. Be sure the spark plugs are firing efficiently. The illustrations on the next 2 pages show you how to "read" the firing end of the spark plug.

6. Check the ignition timing and set it to specifications. Tests show that almost all cars have incorrect ignition timing by more than 2°.

veyed over 6,000 cars nationwide, they found that a tune-up, on cars that needed one, increased fuel economy over 11%. Replacing worn plugs alone, accounted for a 3% increase. The same test also revealed that 8 out of every 10 vehicles will have some maintenance deficiency that will directly affect fuel economy, emissions or performance. Most of this mileage-robbing neglect could be prevented with regular maintenance.

Modern engines require that all of the functioning systems operate properly for maximum efficiency. A malfunction anywhere wastes fuel. You can keep your vehicle running as efficiently and economically as possible, by being aware of your vehicle's operating and performance characteristics. If your vehicle suddenly develops performance or fuel economy problems it could be due to one or more of the following:

PROBLEM	POSSIBLE CAUSE
Engine Idles Rough	Ignition timing, idle mixture, vacuum leak or something amiss in the emission control system.
Hesitates on Acceleration	Dirty carburetor or fuel filter, improper accelerator pump setting, ignition timing or fouled spark plugs.
Starts Hard or Fails to Start	Worn spark plugs, improperly set automatic choke, ice (or water) in fuel system.
Stalls Frequently	Automatic choke improperly adjusted and possible dirty air filter or fuel filter.
Performs Sluggishly	Worn spark plugs, dirty fuel or air filter, ignition timing or automatic choke out of adjustment.

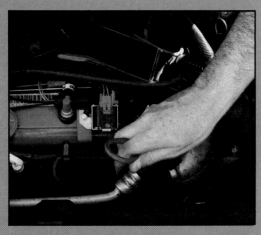

Check spark plug wires on conventional point type ignition for cracks by bending them in a loop around your finger.

Be sure that spark plug wires leading to adjacent cylinders do not run too close together. (Photo courtesy Champion Spark Plug Co.)

7. If your vehicle does not have electronic ignition, check the points, rotor and cap as specified.

8. Check the spark plug wires (used with conventional point-type ignitions) for cracks and burned or broken insulation by bending them in a loop around your finger. Cracked wires decrease fuel efficiency by failing to deliver full voltage to the spark plugs. One misfiring spark plug can cost you as much as 2 mpg.

9. Check the routing of the plug wires. Misfiring can be the result of spark plug leads to adjacent cylinders running parallel to each other and too close together. One wire tends to

pick up voltage from the other causing it to fire "out of time".

10. Check all electrical and ignition circuits for voltage drop and resistance.

11. Check the distributor mechanical and/or vacuum advance mechanisms for proper functioning. The vacuum advance can be checked by twisting the distributor plate in the opposite direction of rotation. It should spring back when released.

12. Check and adjust the valve clearance on engines with mechanical lifters. The clearance should be slightly loose rather than too tight.

SPARK PLUG DIAGNOSIS

Normal

APPEARANCE: This plug is typical of one operating normally. The insulator nose varies from a light tan to grayish color with slight electrode wear. The presence of slight deposits is normal on used plugs and will have no adverse effect on engine performance. The spark plug heat range is correct for the engine and the engine is running normally.

CAUSE: Properly running engine.

RECOMMENDATION: Before reinstalling this plug, the electrodes should be cleaned and filed square. Set the gap to specifications. If the plug has been in service for more than 10-12,000 miles, the entire set should probably be replaced with a fresh set of the same heat range.

Oil Deposits

APPEARANCE: The firing end of the plug is covered with a wet, oily coating.

CAUSE: The problem is poor oil control. On high mileage engines, oil is leaking past the rings or valve guides into the combustion chamber. A common cause is also a plugged PCV valve, and a ruptured fuel pump diaphragm can also cause this condition. Oil fouled plugs such as these are often found in new or recently overhauled engines, before normal oil control is achieved, and can be cleaned and reinstalled.

RECOMMENDATION: A hotter spark plug may temporarily relieve the problem, but the engine is probably in need of work.

Incorrect Heat Range

APPEARANCE: The effects of high temperature on a spark plug are indicated by clean white, often blistered insulator. This can also be accompanied by excessive wear of the electrode, and the absence of deposits.

CAUSE: Check for the correct spark plug heat range. A plug which is too hot for the engine can result in overheating. A car operated mostly at high speeds can require a colder plug. Also check ignition timing, cooling system level, fuel mixture and leaking intake manifold.

RECOMMENDATION: If all ignition and engine adjustments are known to be correct, and no other malfunction exists, install spark plugs one heat range colder.

Carbon Deposits

APPEARANCE: Carbon fouling is easily identified by the presence of dry, soft, black, sooty deposits.

CAUSE: Changing the heat range can often lead to carbon fouling, as can prolonged slow, stop-and-start driving. If the heat range is correct, carbon fouling can be attributed to a rich fuel mixture, sticking choke, clogged air cleaner, worn breaker points, retarded timing or low compression. If only one or two plugs are carbon fouled, check for corroded or cracked wires on the affected plugs. Also look for cracks in the distributor cap between the towers of affected cylinders.

RECOMMENDATION: After the problem is corrected, these plugs can be cleaned and reinstalled if not worn severely.

Photos Courtesy Fram Corporation

MMT Fouled

APPEARANCE: Spark plugs fouled by MMT (Methycyclopentadienyl Maganese Tricarbonyl) have reddish, rusty appearance on the insulator and side electrode.

CAUSE: MMT is an anti-knock additive in gasoline used to replace lead. During the combustion process, the MMT leaves a reddish deposit on the insulator and side electrode.

RECOMMENDATION: No engine malfunction is indicated and the deposits will not affect plug performance any more than lead deposits (see Ash Deposits). MMT fouled plugs can be cleaned, regapped and reinstalled.

High Speed Glazing

APPEARANCE: Glazing appears as shiny coating on the plug, either yellow or tan in color.

CAUSE: During hard, fast acceleration, plug temperatures rise suddenly. Deposits from normal combustion have no chance to fluff-off; instead, they melt on the insulator forming an electrically conductive coating which causes misfiring.

RECOMMENDATION: Glazed plugs are not easily cleaned. They should be replaced with a fresh set of plugs of the correct heat range. If the condition recurs, using plugs with a heat range one step colder may cure the problem.

Ash (Lead) Deposits

APPEARANCE: Ash deposits are characterized by light brown or white colored deposits crusted on the side or center electrodes. In some cases it may give the plug a rusty appearance.

CAUSE: Ash deposits are normally derived from oil or fuel additives burned during normal combustion. Normally they are harmless, though excessive amounts can cause misfiring. If deposits are excessive in short mileage, the valve guides may be worn.

RECOMMENDATION: Ash-fouled plugs can be cleaned, gapped and reinstalled.

Detonation

APPEARANCE: Detonation is usually characterized by a broken plug insulator.

CAUSE: A portion of the fuel charge will begin to burn spontaneously, from the increased heat following ignition. The explosion that results applies extreme pressure to engine components, frequently damaging spark plugs and pistons.

Detonation can result by over-advanced ignition timing, inferior gasoline (low octane) lean air/fuel mixture, poor carburetion, engine lugging or an increase in compression ratio due to combustion chamber deposits or engine modification.

RECOMMENDATION: Replace the plugs after correcting the problem.

Photos Courtesy Champion Spark Plug Co.

EMISSION CONTROLS

13. Be aware of the general condition of the emission control system. It contributes to reduced pollution and should be serviced regularly to maintain efficient engine operation.

14. Check all vacuum lines for dried, cracked or brittle conditions. Something as simple as a leaking vacuum hose can cause poor performance and loss of economy.

15. Avoid tampering with the emission control system. Attempting to improve fuel econ-

FUEL SYSTEM

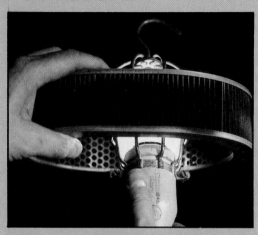

Check the air filter with a light behind it. If you can see light through the filter it can be reused.

Extremely clogged filters should be discarded and replaced with a new one.

18. Replace the air filter regularly. A dirty air filter richens the air/fuel mixture and can increase fuel consumption as much as 10%. Tests show that ⅓ of all vehicles have air filters in need of replacement.

19. Replace the fuel filter at least as often as recommended.

20. Set the idle speed and carburetor mixture to specifications.

21. Check the automatic choke. A sticking or malfunctioning choke wastes gas.

22. During the summer months, adjust the automatic choke for a leaner mixture which will produce faster engine warm-ups.

COOLING SYSTEM

29. Be sure all accessory drive belts are in good condition. Check for cracks or wear.

30. Adjust all accessory drive belts to proper tension.

31. Check all hoses for swollen areas, worn spots, or loose clamps.

32. Check coolant level in the radiator or expansion tank.

33. Be sure the thermostat is operating properly. A stuck thermostat delays engine warm-up and a cold engine uses nearly twice as much fuel as a warm engine.

34. Drain and replace the engine coolant at least as often as recommended. Rust and scale

TIRES & WHEELS

38. Check the tire pressure often with a pencil type gauge. Tests by a major tire manufacturer show that 90% of all vehicles have at least 1 tire improperly inflated. Better mileage can be achieved by over-inflating tires, but never exceed the maximum inflation pressure on the side of the tire.

39. If possible, install radial tires. Radial tires deliver as much as ½ mpg more than bias belted tires.

40. Avoid installing super-wide tires. They only create extra rolling resistance and decrease fuel mileage. Stick to the manufacturer's recommendations.

41. Have the wheels properly balanced.

omy by tampering with emission controls is more likely to worsen fuel economy than improve it. Emission control changes on modern engines are not readily reversible.

16. Clean (or replace) the EGR valve and lines as recommended.

17. Be sure that all vacuum lines and hoses are reconnected properly after working under the hood. An unconnected or misrouted vacuum line can wreak havoc with engine performance.

23. Check for fuel leaks at the carburetor, fuel pump, fuel lines and fuel tank. Be sure all lines and connections are tight.

24. Periodically check the tightness of the carburetor and intake manifold attaching nuts and bolts. These are a common place for vacuum leaks to occur.

25. Clean the carburetor periodically and lubricate the linkage.

26. The condition of the tailpipe can be an excellent indicator of proper engine combustion. After a long drive at highway speeds, the inside of the tailpipe should be a light grey in color. Black or soot on the insides indicates an overly rich mixture.

27. Check the fuel pump pressure. The fuel pump may be supplying more fuel than the engine needs.

28. Use the proper grade of gasoline for your engine. Don't try to compensate for knocking or "pinging" by advancing the ignition timing. This practice will only increase plug temperature and the chances of detonation or pre-ignition with relatively little performance gain.

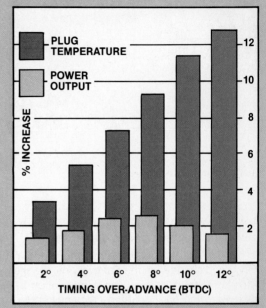

Increasing ignition timing past the specified setting results in a drastic increase in spark plug temperature with increased chance of detonation or preignition. Performance increase is considerably less. (Photo courtesy Champion Spark Plug Co.)

that form in the engine should be flushed out to allow the engine to operate at peak efficiency.

35. Clean the radiator of debris that can decrease cooling efficiency.

36. Install a flex-type or electric cooling fan, if you don't have a clutch type fan. Flex fans use curved plastic blades to push more air at low speeds when more cooling is needed; at high speeds the blades flatten out for less resistance. Electric fans only run when the engine temperature reaches a predetermined level.

37. Check the radiator cap for a worn or cracked gasket. If the cap does not seal properly, the cooling system will not function properly.

42. Be sure the front end is correctly aligned. A misaligned front end actually has wheels going in differed directions. The increased drag can reduce fuel economy by .3 mpg.

43. Correctly adjust the wheel bearings. Wheel bearings that are adjusted too tight increase rolling resistance.

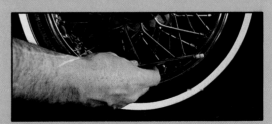

Check tire pressures regularly with a reliable pocket type gauge. Be sure to check the pressure on a cold tire.

GENERAL MAINTENANCE

Check the fluid levels (particularly engine oil) on a regular basis. Be sure to check the oil for grit, water or other contamination.

A vacuum gauge is another excellent indicator of internal engine condition and can also be installed in the dash as a mileage indicator.

44. Periodically check the fluid levels in the engine, power steering pump, master cylinder, automatic transmission and drive axle.

45. Change the oil at the recommended interval and change the filter at every oil change. Dirty oil is thick and causes extra friction between moving parts, cutting efficiency and increasing wear. A worn engine requires more frequent tune-ups and gets progressively worse fuel economy. In general, use the lightest viscosity oil for the driving conditions you will encounter.

46. Use the recommended viscosity fluids in the transmission and axle.

47. Be sure the battery is fully charged for fast starts. A slow starting engine wastes fuel.

48. Be sure battery terminals are clean and tight.

49. Check the battery electrolyte level and add distilled water if necessary.

50. Check the exhaust system for crushed pipes, blockages and leaks.

51. Adjust the brakes. Dragging brakes or brakes that are not releasing create increased drag on the engine.

52. Install a vacuum gauge or miles-per-gallon gauge. These gauges visually indicate engine vacuum in the intake manifold. High vacuum = good mileage and low vacuum = poorer mileage. The gauge can also be an excellent indicator of internal engine conditions.

53. Be sure the clutch is properly adjusted. A slipping clutch wastes fuel.

54. Check and periodically lubricate the heat control valve in the exhaust manifold. A sticking or inoperative valve prevents engine warm-up and wastes gas.

55. Keep accurate records to check fuel economy over a period of time. A sudden drop in fuel economy may signal a need for tune-up or other maintenance.

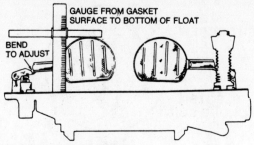

4GC float level adjustment

E2ME Carburetor (1985–87 231 V6)
E4MC Carburetor (1985–87 307 V8)

NOTE: *To make this adjustment, you will need a number of special tools. They are: GM Part Nos. J-34817-1, J-34817-3, J-9789-90, and J-34817-15 or equivalent.*

1. The solenoid plunger, metering rods, and float bowl insert must be removed. Then attach J-34817-1 to the float bowl and place J-34817-3 into it with the contact pin resting on the outer edge of the float lever.

2. Use J-9789-90 to measure the distance from the top of the casting to the top of the float at a point $3/16$ in. (4.7mm) from the large end of the float.

3. If the reading is more than $1/16$ in. (1.6mm) either above or below the specification, use J-34817-15 to bend the lever up or down. Specifications are:

• 1985 E2ME carb numbers 17085192 and 17085194 – $11/32$ in. (8.7mm)

• All other 1985 E2ME and 1986–87 E2ME: $5/16$ in. (7.9mm)

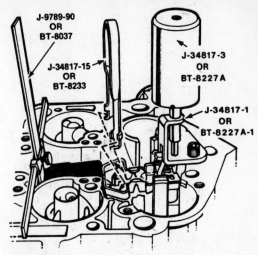

Adjusting float level–E2ME and E4MC

• 1985–90 E4MC: $11/32$ in. (8.7mm).

Remove this tool and remeasure. Repeat the procedure until the specification is met within the tolerance above or in the carburetor specification chart in this chapter.

4-bbl Carburetor (Model M4MC)

1. With the air horn assembly and gasket removed from the carburetor, measure the distance from the air horn gasket surface to the top of the float at the toe.

2. To adjust the float level, bend the float arm by pushing on the pontoon.

3. After the adjustment, check the float alignment.

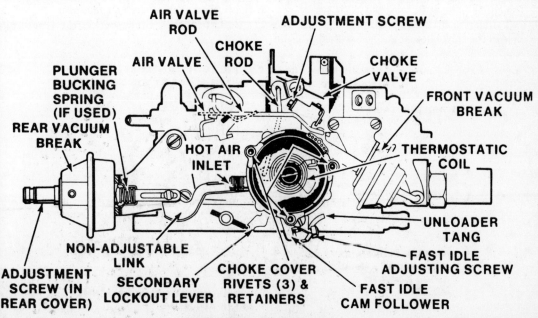

Model E4MC carburetor—4bbl

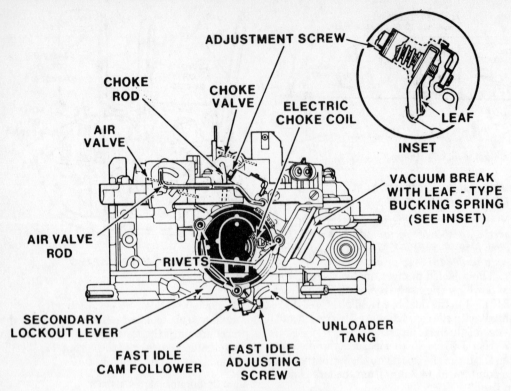

ADJUSTMENT SCREW

CHOKE ROD

CHOKE VALVE

ELECTRIC CHOKE COIL

AIR VALVE

LEAF

INSET

AIR VALVE ROD

VACUUM BREAK WITH LEAF - TYPE BUCKING SPRING (SEE INSET)

RIVETS

SECONDARY LOCKOUT LEVER

UNLOADER TANG

FAST IDLE CAM FOLLOWER

FAST IDLE ADJUSTING SCREW

Model E4ME carburetor—4bbl

CHOKE COIL LEVER ADJUSTMENT

2-bbl Carburetor (2MC, E2MC, E2ME)
4-bbl Carburetor 1975 and Later

1. Remove the choke cover and thermostatic coil from the choke housing.

2. Push the coil tang counterclockwise until the choke plate is fully closed.

3. Insert a 0.120 in. (3mm) gauge into the hole in the choke housing. The lower edge of the choke coil lever should just contact the side of the gauge.

4. Bend the choke rod to adjust, if necessary.

AUTOMATIC CHOKE ADJUSTMENT

2-bbl Carburetor

1. Place the idle speed screw or follower on the highest step of the fast idle cam.

2. Loosen the choke coil cover retaining screws.

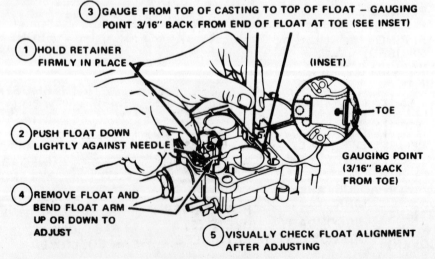

3 GAUGE FROM TOP OF CASTING TO TOP OF FLOAT – GAUGING POINT 3/16" BACK FROM END OF FLOAT AT TOE (SEE INSET)

1 HOLD RETAINER FIRMLY IN PLACE

(INSET)

TOE

2 PUSH FLOAT DOWN LIGHTLY AGAINST NEEDLE

GAUGING POINT (3/16" BACK FROM TOE)

4 REMOVE FLOAT AND BEND FLOAT ARM UP OR DOWN TO ADJUST

5 VISUALLY CHECK FLOAT ALIGNMENT AFTER ADJUSTING

M4MC float adjustment

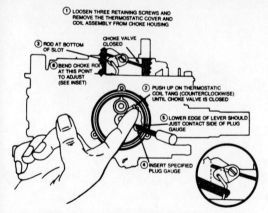

2MC, 4MC choke coil level adjustment

NOTE: *The choke coil may be riveted onto the carburetor housing on most later model vehicles. Drill and remove the rivet head by using a $^5/_{16}$ in. (0.159) drill bit. Punch the remainder of the rivet out of the choke housing. Use the same size rivet for installation.*

3. Rotate the choke cover counterclockwise until the choke plate just closes.

4. Align the index mark on the choke cover with the specified point on the choke housing. Tighten the cover screws or install new rivets.

4-bbl Carburetor

1. Loosen the choke housing cover screws or drill out the rivets using a $^5/_{16}$ in. (0.159) drill bit. Punch the remainder of the rivet out of the choke housing.

2. Place the fast idle cam follower on the highest step of the fast idle cam.

3. Rotate the cover and coil assembly counterclockwise until the choke plate just closes.

4. Align the index mark on the cover with the specified index point on the housing.

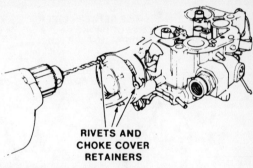

RIVETS AND CHOKE COVER RETAINERS

Removing choke coil retaining rivets

5. Tighten the retaining screws or install new rivets.

UNLOADER ADJUSTMENT

2-bbl Carburetor through 1980

1. Hold the throttle plates wide open.
2. Close the choke plate.
3. Bend the unloader tang to obtain the proper clearance between the upper edge of the choke plate and the airhorn wall.

4-bbl Carburetor through 1980

1. With the choke plate completely closed, hold the throttle plates wide open.
2. Measure the distance between the upper edge of the choke plate and the airhorn wall.
3. Bend the tang on the fast idle lever to adjust.

2- and 4-bbl (E4MC, E4ME) Carburetors 1981 and Later

1. Refer to the illustration in this section. Attach a rubber band to the vacuum break intermediate choke shaft.

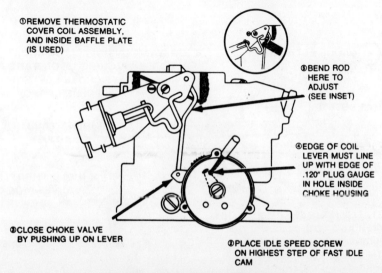

2GC, 2GE choke coil lever adjustment

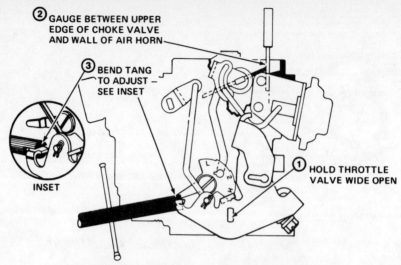

② GAUGE BETWEEN UPPER EDGE OF CHOKE VALVE AND WALL OF AIR HORN

③ BEND TANG TO ADJUST — SEE INSET

INSET

① HOLD THROTTLE VALVE WIDE OPEN

Choke unloader adjustment, 2GE, 2GC carburetors

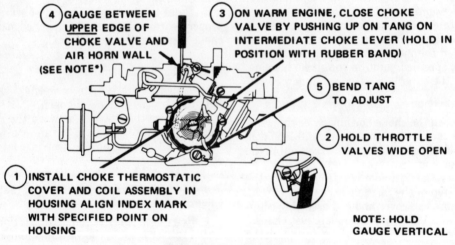

④ GAUGE BETWEEN UPPER EDGE OF CHOKE VALVE AND AIR HORN WALL (SEE NOTE*)

③ ON WARM ENGINE, CLOSE CHOKE VALVE BY PUSHING UP ON TANG ON INTERMEDIATE CHOKE LEVER (HOLD IN POSITION WITH RUBBER BAND)

⑤ BEND TANG TO ADJUST

② HOLD THROTTLE VALVES WIDE OPEN

① INSTALL CHOKE THERMOSTATIC COVER AND COIL ASSEMBLY IN HOUSING ALIGN INDEX MARK WITH SPECIFIED POINT ON HOUSING

NOTE: HOLD GAUGE VERTICAL

2MC unloader adjustment

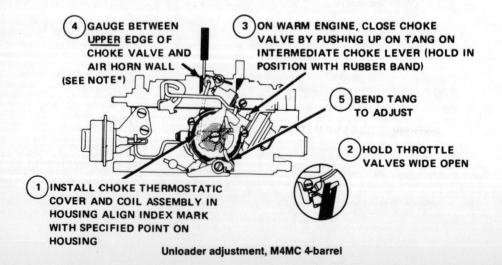

④ GAUGE BETWEEN UPPER EDGE OF CHOKE VALVE AND AIR HORN WALL (SEE NOTE*)

③ ON WARM ENGINE, CLOSE CHOKE VALVE BY PUSHING UP ON TANG ON INTERMEDIATE CHOKE LEVER (HOLD IN POSITION WITH RUBBER BAND)

⑤ BEND TANG TO ADJUST

② HOLD THROTTLE VALVES WIDE OPEN

① INSTALL CHOKE THERMOSTATIC COVER AND COIL ASSEMBLY IN HOUSING ALIGN INDEX MARK WITH SPECIFIED POINT ON HOUSING

Unloader adjustment, M4MC 4-barrel

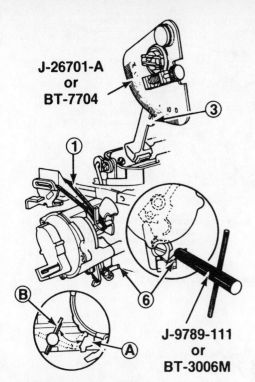

J-26701-A
or
BT-7704

①

③

B

⑥

J-9789-111
or
BT-3006M

Ⓐ

Model E4MC unloader adjustment

2. Open the throttle to allow the choke valve to close.

3. Set the angle gauge J–26701–A or BT–7704 to the angle specification in the specification chart in this chapter.

4. Hold the secondary throttle lockout lever (A) away from the pin (B).

5. Hold the throttle lever in the wide open position.

6. Adjust, if the bubble is not recentered, by bending the fast idle lever using a bending tool J–9789 or B–3006M.

VACUUM BREAK ADJUSTMENT

2-bbl Carburetor Model 2GC

1. Remove the air cleaner. Vehicles equipped with TAC air cleaners should have the sensor's vacuum take-off port plugged.

2. Using an external vacuum source, apply vacuum to the vacuum break diaphragm until the plunger is fully seated. Or, fully seat the plunger and place a piece of tape over the hose fitting.

3. When the plunger is seated, push the choke plate toward the closed position. Place the idle speed screw on the high step of the fast idle cam.

4. Holding the choke plate in the closed position, place the specified size gauge between the upper edge of the choke plate and the air horn wall.

5. If the measurement is not correct, bend the vacuum break rod.

2-bbl Carburetor Model 2MC

1. Place the cam follower on the highest step of the fast idle cam.

2. Seat the vacuum break diaphragm by using an outside vacuum source.

3. Remove the choke cover and coil and push up on the coil lever until the tang on the vacuum break lever contacts the tang on the vacuum break plunger stem. Compress the backing spring for rich adjustment only.

4. With the choke rod in the bottom of the slot in the choke lever, measure the distance between the upper edge of the choke plate and the inside wall of the air horn.

5. Bend the link rod at the vacuum break plunger stem to adjust the lean setting. Bend the link rod at the opposite from the diaphragm to adjust the rich setting.

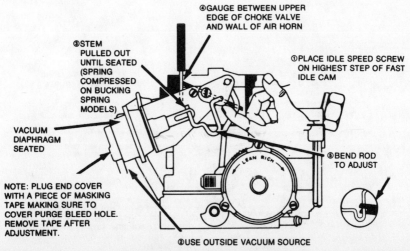

④GAUGE BETWEEN UPPER
EDGE OF CHOKE VALVE
AND WALL OF AIR HORN

②STEM
PULLED OUT
UNTIL SEATED
(SPRING
COMPRESSED
ON BUCKING
SPRING
MODELS)

①PLACE IDLE SPEED SCREW
ON HIGHEST STEP OF FAST
IDLE CAM

VACUUM
DIAPHRAGM
SEATED

⑤BEND ROD
TO ADJUST

LEAN   RICH

NOTE: PLUG END COVER
WITH A PIECE OF MASKING
TAPE MAKING SURE TO
COVER PURGE BLEED HOLE.
REMOVE TAPE AFTER
ADJUSTMENT.

③USE OUTSIDE VACUUM SOURCE

2GC, 2GE vacuum break adjustment

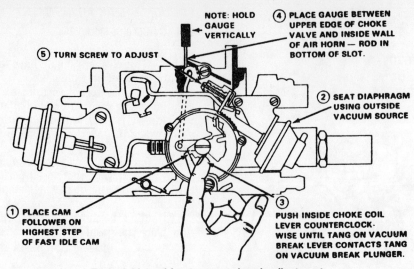

Typical 4-barrel front vacuum break adjustment

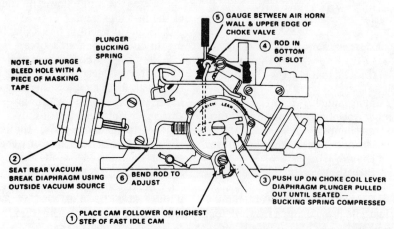

4-barrel rear vacuum break adjustment (without adjusting screw), through 1980

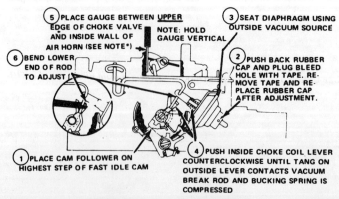

2MC rich vacuum break setting

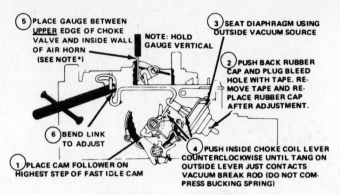

⑤ PLACE GAUGE BETWEEN <u>UPPER</u> EDGE OF CHOKE VALVE AND INSIDE WALL OF AIR HORN (SEE NOTE*)

NOTE: HOLD GAUGE VERTICAL

③ SEAT DIAPHRAGM USING OUTSIDE VACUUM SOURCE

② PUSH BACK RUBBER CAP AND PLUG BLEED HOLE WITH TAPE. REMOVE TAPE AND REPLACE RUBBER CAP AFTER ADJUSTMENT.

⑥ BEND LINK TO ADJUST

① PLACE CAM FOLLOWER ON HIGHEST STEP OF FAST IDLE CAM

④ PUSH INSIDE CHOKE COIL LEVER COUNTERCLOCKWISE UNTIL TANG ON OUTSIDE LEVER JUST CONTACTS VACUUM BREAK ROD (DO NOT COMPRESS BUCKING SPRING)

2MC lean vacuum break setting

4-bbl Carburetor 1975–80

1. Place the cam follower lever on the highest step of the fast idle cam.

2. Remove the choke cover and coil assembly from the choke housing.

3. Seat the front vacuum diaphragm using an outside vacuum source.

4. Push up on the inside choke coil lever until the tang on the vacuum break lever contacts the tang on the vacuum break plunger.

5. Place the proper size gauge between the upper edge of the choke plate and the inside of the air horn wall.

6. To adjust, turn the adjustment screw on the vacuum break plunger lever.

7. To adjust the secondary vacuum break, with the choke cover and coil removed, the cam follower on the highest step of the fast idle cam, tape over the bleed hole in the rear vacuum break diaphragm.

8. Seat the rear diaphragm using an outside vacuum source.

9. Close the choke by pushing up on the choke coil lever inside the choke housing. Make sure the choke rod is in the bottom of the slot in the choke lever.

10. Measure between the upper edge of the choke plate and the air horn wall with a wire type gauge.

11. To adjust, bend the vacuum break rod at the first bend near the diaphragm.

4-bbl Carburetors (E4MC, E4ME) 1981 and Later

FRONT VACUUM BREAK ADJUSTMENT

1. Attach a rubber band to the vacuum break lever of the intermediate choke shaft as shown in the illustration in this section.

2. Open the throttle to allow the choke valve to close.

3. Set up the angle gauge J–26701–A or BT–7704 and set to specifications.

4. Plug the vacuum break plunger. Apply 15 in. Hg (51 k Pa) of vacuum to seat the vacuum break plunger. Seat the bucking spring (A).

J-26701-A or BT-7704

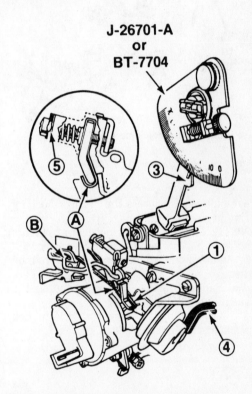

Front vacuum break adjustment—E4MC 4bbl

NOTE: *On some Quadrajets, bend the air valve link (B) to permit full plunger travel.*

5. Adjust if the bubble is not recentered, by turning the screw.

REAR VACUUM BREAK ADJUSTMENT

1. Attach a rubber band to the vacuum break lever of the intermediate choke shaft as shown in the illustration in this section.

2. Open the throttle to allow the choke valve to close.

3. Set up the angle gauge J–26701–A or BT–7704 and set to specifications.

4. Plug the vacuum break plunger. Apply 15 in. Hg (51 k Pa) of vacuum to seat the vacuum

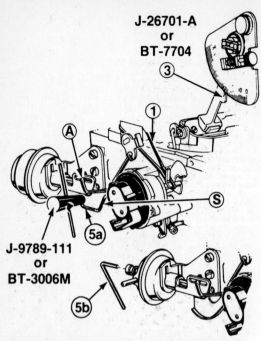

J-26701-A
or
BT-7704

③

①

Ⓐ

Ⓢ

5a

J-9789-111
or
BT-3006M

5b

Rear vacuum break adjustment—E4MC 4bbl

break plunger. Compress the Plunger bucking spring, if so equipped.

NOTE: *On some Quadrajets, bend the air valve link (A) to permit full plunger travel.*

5. Adjust if the bubble is not recentered, by either:

a. Supporting the "S" and bending the vacuum break link.

b. Or, turning the screw with a ⅛ in. hex wrench.

FAST IDLE CAM ADJUSTMENT

2-bbl Carburetor 2GC-2GE

1. Turn the idle speed screw in until it just contacts the lower step of the fast idle cam. Then, turn the screw in one full turn.

2. Place the idle speed screw on the second step of the fast idle cam against the shoulder of the high step.

3. Measure the distance between the upper edge of the choke plate and the air horn wall. Push the choke plate closed first.

4. If adjustment is required, bend the choke lever tang.

2-bbl Carburetor 2MC

1. Adjust the fast idle speed.

2. Place the cam follower lever on the second step of the fast idle cam, holding it firmly against the shoulder of the high step.

3. Close the choke coil lever inside the choke housing.

4. Gauge between the upper edge of the choke plate and the inside of the air horn wall.

5. Bend the tang on the intermediate choke lever to adjust.

4-bbl Carburetor (Before 1980)

1. Adjust the fast idle and place the cam follower on the second step of the fast idle cam.

2. Close the choke plate by pushing counterclockwise on the external choke lever. On 1975–80 models, remove the coil assembly from the choke housing and push on the choke coil lever.

3. Measure between the upper edge of the choke plate and the air horn wall.

4. To adjust, 1975–80 models, bend the tang on the fast idle cam. Be sure that the tang rests against the cam after bending.

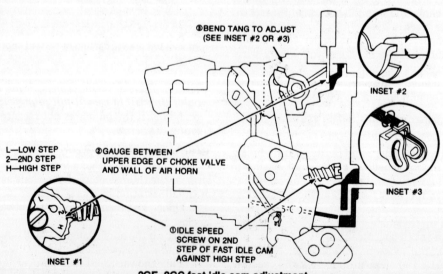

③ BEND TANG TO ADJUST
(SEE INSET #2 OR #3)

INSET #2

INSET #3

L—LOW STEP
2—2ND STEP
H—HIGH STEP

② GAUGE BETWEEN
UPPER EDGE OF CHOKE VALVE
AND WALL OF AIR HORN

① IDLE SPEED
SCREW ON 2ND
STEP OF FAST IDLE CAM
AGAINST HIGH STEP

INSET #1

2GE, 2GC fast idle cam adjustment

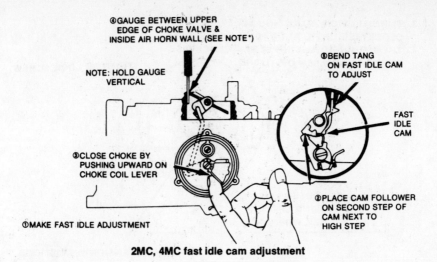

④GAUGE BETWEEN UPPER
EDGE OF CHOKE VALVE &
INSIDE AIR HORN WALL (SEE NOTE*)

⑤BEND TANG
ON FAST IDLE CAM
TO ADJUST

NOTE: HOLD GAUGE
VERTICAL

FAST
IDLE
CAM

③CLOSE CHOKE BY
PUSHING UPWARD ON
CHOKE COIL LEVER

②PLACE CAM FOLLOWER
ON SECOND STEP OF
CAM NEXT TO
HIGH STEP

①MAKE FAST IDLE ADJUSTMENT

2MC, 4MC fast idle cam adjustment

2- and 4-bbl Carburetors 1981 and Later

1. Attach a rubber band to the vacuum break lever of the intermediate choke shaft as shown in the illustration in this section.

2. Open the throttle to allow the choke valve to close.

3. Set up the angle gauge J–26701-A or BT–7704 and set to specifications.

4. Place the fast idle cam (A) on the second step against the cam follower lever (B). With the lever contacting the rise of the high step. If the lever does not contact the cam, turn the fast idle adjusting screw (C) in additional turns.

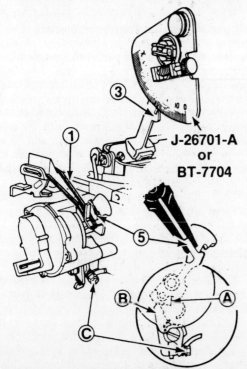

**J-26701-A
or
BT-7704**

Fast idle cam adjustment—E4MC 4bbl

5. Adjust if the bubble is not recentered, by bending the fast idle cam kick lever with pliers.

AIR VALVE LINK (DASHPOT) ADJUSTMENT

4-bbl Carburetor

FRONT

1. Seat the front vacuum break diaphragm by using an outside vacuum source as shown in the air valve link illustrations in this section.

2. The air valves must be closed completely.

3. Measure the clearance between the air valve dashpot and the end of the slot in the air valve lever. The clearance should be 0.050 in. (1.27mm) on models through 1981. Later models use a clearance of 0.025 in. (0.635mm).

4. Bend the air valve link (dashpot) rod, if necessary, to adjust.

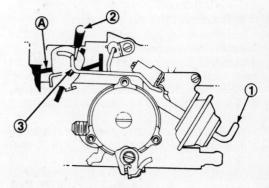

E4MC air valve link adjustment

Carburetor

REMOVAL AND INSTALLATION

Non-Electronic

1. Disconnect the negative (–) battery cable. Remove the air cleaner assembly.

2. Tag and disconnect all vacuum lines, elec-

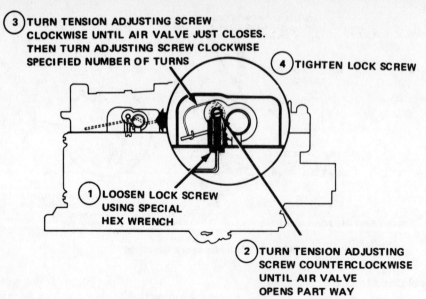

③ TURN TENSION ADJUSTING SCREW
CLOCKWISE UNTIL AIR VALVE JUST CLOSES.
THEN TURN ADJUSTING SCREW CLOCKWISE
SPECIFIED NUMBER OF TURNS

④ TIGHTEN LOCK SCREW

① LOOSEN LOCK SCREW
USING SPECIAL
HEX WRENCH

② TURN TENSION ADJUSTING
SCREW COUNTERCLOCKWISE
UNTIL AIR VALVE
OPENS PART WAY

M4MC air valve spring adjustment

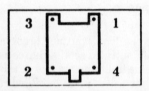

Torque E4MC carburetor mounting bolts to 16 ft. lbs.
in the order shown

tric wires and fuel lines from the carburetor.
Tag and disconnect the throttle linkage and
cruise control (if so equipped).

3. Disconnect the automatic transmission
downshift linkage.

4. Disconnect the idle solenoid wiring.

5. Remove the carburetor attaching nuts or
bolts and remove the carburetor.

To install: Use a new gasket and fill the float
bowl with fuel to ease starting. On late model
vehicles with bolts of two different lengths,
torque the long bolts to 7 ft. lbs. (10 Nm) and
the short bolts to 11 ft. lbs. (14 Nm).

NOTE: *On the E4MC carburetor (1985–90
307 V8), torque the mounting bolts in the pattern shown in the illustration to 16 ft. lbs. (22
Nm). On Oldsmobile 5.0L V8, clear the ECM
memory. To do this, the R terminal of the
ECM must be disconnected from battery voltage for over 10 seconds.*

OVERHAUL

All Types

Efficient carburetion depends greatly on
careful cleaning and inspection during overhaul, since dirt, gum, water, or varnish in or on
the carburetor parts are often responsible for
poor performance.

Overhaul your carburetor in a clean, dust
free area. Carefully disassemble the carburetor,
referring often to the exploded views and directions packaged with the rebuilding kit. Keep all
similar and look-alike parts segregated during
disassembly and cleaning to avoid accidental interchange during assembly. Make a note of all
jet sizes.

When the carburetor is disassembled, wash
all parts (except diaphragms, electric choke
units, pump plunger, and any other plastic,
leather, fiber, or rubber parts) in clean carburetor solvent. Do not leave parts in the solvent
any longer than is necessary to sufficiently loos-
en the deposits. Excessive cleaning may remove
the special finish from the float bowl and choke
valve bodies, leaving these parts unfit for service. Rinse all parts in clean solvent and blow
them dry with compressed air or allow them to
air dry. Wipe clean all cork, plastic, leather, and
fiber parts with a clean, lint-free cloth.

Blow out all passages and jets with compressed air and be sure that there are no restrictions or blockages. Never use wire or similar tools to clean jets, fuel passages, or air
bleeds. *Clean all jets and valves separately to
avoid accidental interchange.*

Check all parts for wear or damage. If wear or
damage is found, replace the defective parts.
Especially check the following:

1. Check the float needle and seat for wear. If
wear is found, replace the complete assembly.

2. Check the float hinge pin for wear and the
float(s) for dents or distortion. Replace the float
if fuel has leaked into it.

3. Check the throttle and choke shaft bores for wear or an out-of-round condition. Damage or wear to the throttle arm, shaft, or shaft bore will often require replacement of the throttle body. These parts require a close tolerance of fit; wear may allow air leakage, which could affect starting and idling.

NOTE: *Throttle shafts and bushings are not included in overhaul kits. They can be purchased separately.*

4. Inspect the idle mixture adjusting needle for burrs or grooves. Any such condition requires replacement of the needle, since you will not be able to obtain a satisfactory idle.

5. Test the accelerator pump check valves. They should pass air one way but not the other. Test for proper seating by blowing and sucking on the valve. Replace the valve as necessary. If

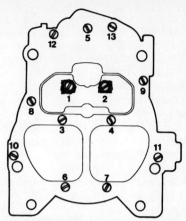

E4ME and E4MC (1983–84) air horn tightening sequence

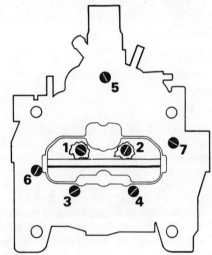

M2MC air horn tightening sequence

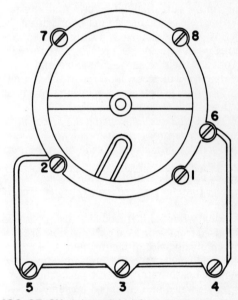

2GC, GE, GV air horn tightening sequence

the valve is satisfactory, wash the valve again to remove breath moisture.

6. Check the bowl cover for warped surfaces with a straightedge.

7. Closely inspect the valves and seats for wear and damage, replacing as necessary.

8. After the carburetor is assembled, check the choke valve for freedom of operation.

Carburetor overhaul kits are recommended for each overhaul. These kits contain all gaskets and new parts to replace those which deteriorate most rapidly. Failure to replace all parts supplied with the kit (especially gaskets) can result in poor performance later.

Some carburetor manufacturers supply overhaul kits of three basic types: minor repair; major repair; and gasket kits. Basically, they contain the following:

Minor Repair Kits:

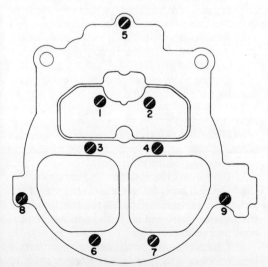

M4MC air horn tightening sequence

- All gaskets
- Float needle valve
- All diaphragms
- Spring for the pump diaphragm

Major Repair Kits
- All jets and gaskets
- All diaphragms
- Float needle valve
- Pump ball valve
- Float
- Complete intermediate rod
- Intermediate pump lever
- Some cover holddown screws and washers

Gasket Kits:
- All gaskets

After cleaning and checking all components, reassemble the carburetor, using new parts and referring to the exploded view. When reassembling, make sure that all screws and jets are tight in their seats, but do not overtighten, as the tips will be distorted. Tighten all screws gradually, in rotation. DO NOT tighten needle valves into their seats; needle valve and valve seat damage will occur, along with uneven jetting. Always use new gaskets. Be sure to adjust the float level when reassembling.

NOTE: *1983 and later model (CCC) carburetors incorporate a mixture solenoid. There are several adjustments that must be performed on this device when the carburetor receives a major rebuild. The adjustments are highly complex and require expensive special tools.*

A quality remanufactured carburetor can be purchased from your local part distributor for a fraction of the price of factory new.

Complete major rebuild and adjustment of late model carburetors is best performed by a properly trained and equipped mechanic.

DIESEL ENGINE FUEL SYSTEM

Injection Lines

REMOVAL AND INSTALLATION

NOTE: *To perform this procedure, you will need screens to cover the intake manifold air inlets and plastic caps to fit the fuel line, nozzle, and pump openings.*

1. Disconnect the negative (−) battery cable.
2. Remove the air cleaner. Remove the oil separator/filters and lines from the valve covers.
3. Remove the air crossover and gaskets from the intake manifold. Install the screen covers onto the manifold to prevent any foreign object from entering it.
4. Remove the line clamps. Note the routing of pump wiring. *With a backup wrench on each*

nozzle body upper (small) hex, loosen the injection line connections at each nozzle. Loosen the connections at the injection pump (you don't need a backup wrench on these connections.
5. Cap off all the openings and remove the lines.

To install:
1. Locate the injection lines in position. Route wiring between the #2 and #3 injection lines. Thread all caps loosely.
2. Torque each connection to 25 ft. lbs. (34 Nm), using a backup wrench on the nozzles as in loosening the connections.
3. Install the line clamps.
4. Remove the screened covers from the manifold, and install the crossover with new gaskets, torquing bolts to 22 ft. lbs. (30 Nm).
5. Reconnect the crankcase ventilation system piping and air cleaner.
6. Connect the negative battery cable, start the engine and check for leaks and proper operation.

Injection Nozzle

REMOVAL AND INSTALLATION

1978–79

LINES REMOVED

1. Disconnect the negative (−) battery cable. Remove the fuel return line from the nozzle as previously outlined.
2 Remove the nozzle holddown clamp and spacer. Then, pull the nozzle out of the cylinder head with tool J–26952 or equivalent.
3. Cap the high pressure line and nozzle tip. WARNING: *The nozzle tip is highly susceptible to damage and must be protected at all times.*

To install:
1. If an old nozzle is to be reinstalled, a new compression seal and carbon stop seal must be installed after removal of the used seals.
2. Remove the caps and install the nozzle, spacer and clamp. Torque to 25 ft. lbs. (34 Nm).
3. Install return line.
4. Connect the negative battery cable, start the engine and check for leaks.

1980 and Later Models

NOTE: *You will need a means to securely cap off fuel nozzles and lines before disconnecting fuel-containing parts.*

1. Disconnect the negative (−) battery cable.
2. Using a back-up wrench on the upper injection nozzle hex, disconnect the fuel line from the nozzle. Then, cap off both openings to prevent fuel contamination.
3. Using a wrench on the lower, larger nozzle hex, unscrew and remove the nozzle. Look to see if the copper gasket installed under the noz-

zle remained on the cylinder head. If so, remove it. Failure to do so will cause engine operating problems!

4. Nozzle testing requires specialized equip-

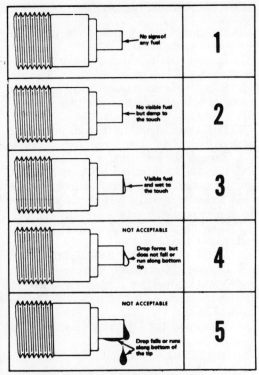

Checking injection nozzle seat tightness

**INLET FITTING TO BODY TORQUE
DIESEL EQUIPMENT — 45 FT. LBS. (60 N·m)
C.A.V. LUCAS — 25 FT. LBS. (34 N·m)**

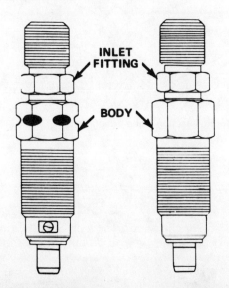

DIESEL EQUIPMENT   C.A.V. LUCAS

Injection nozzles

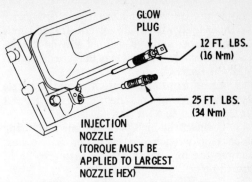

Injection nozzle and glow plug installation

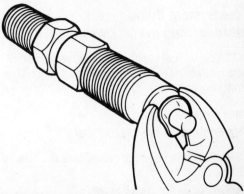

Removing the old sealing washer from 1980 and later injection nozzles

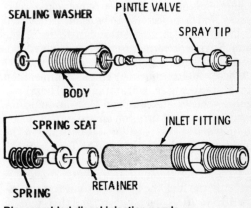

Disassembled diesel injection nozzle

ment, fluids, and training (see illustration). However, it will be cost-effective for you to remove your own nozzles and have them tested and/or repaired at a diesel specialist. If you replace nozzles, make sure they are color coded with a blue band, meaning they are intended for use with the V8.

To install:

1. If the sealing washer remained on the nozzle tip, use diagonal cutters to force it off. Be careful not to squeeze the cutters to the point where they scratch the nozzle tip. Use them

only to pry the washer loose. Clean the nozzle tip thoroughly with a safe solvent. Install a new copper washer and, if it will not stay on the tip, crimp it slightly so it will stay in place as you install the nozzle.

2. Remove protective caps. Install the nozzle by screwing it in, and then, using the largest hex, torque it to 25 ft. lbs. (34 Nm).

3. Connect the high pressure line and, using a back-up wrench on the upper nozzle hex, tighten the high pressure line fitting to 25 ft. lbs. (34 Nm).

4. Connect the negative battery cable, start the engine and check for leaks.

Fuel System Pump

REMOVAL AND INSTALLATION

The diesel fuel supply pump is serviced in the same manner as the fuel pump on the gasoline engines.

Fuel Filter

REMOVAL AND INSTALLATION

See Fuel Filter service procedures in Chapter 1.

WATER IN FUEL (DIESEL)

Water is the worst enemy of the diesel fuel injection system. The injection pump, which is designed and constructed to extremely close tolerances, and the injectors can be easily damaged if enough water is forced through them in the fuel. Engine performance will also be drastically affected, and engine damage can occur.

Diesel fuel is much more susceptible than gasoline to water contamination. Diesel engined vehicles are equipped with an indicator lamp system that turns on an instrument panel lamp if water (1–2½ gallons) is detected in the fuel tank. The lamp will come on for 2 to 5 seconds each time the ignition is turned on, assuring the driver the lamp is working. If there is water in the fuel, the light will come back on after a 15 to 20 second off delay, and then remain on.

PURGING THE FUEL TANK

Vehicles which have a Water in Fuel light may have the water removed from the tank with a siphon pump. The pump hose should be hooked up to the ¼ in. (6mm) fuel return hose (the smaller of the two hoses) above the rear axle or under the hood near the fuel pump. Siphoning should continue until all water is removed from the tank. Use a clear plastic hose or observe the filter bowl on the siphon pump (if equipped) to determine when clear fuel begins to flow. Be sure to remove the cap on the fuel

tank while purging. Replace the cap when finished. Discard the fuel filter and replace with a new filter.

Injection Pump

REMOVAL AND INSTALLATION

1. Disconnect the negative (–) battery cable. Remove the air cleaner.

2. Remove the filters and pipes from the valve covers and air crossover.

3. Remove the air crossover and cap intake manifold with screened covers (tool J–26996–10).

4. Disconnect the throttle rod and return spring.

5. Remove the bellcrank.

6. Remove the throttle and transmission cables from the intake manifold brackets. On 1983 and later models, remove the crankcase depression regulator valve.

7. Disconnect the fuel lines from the filter and remove the filter.

8. Disconnect the fuel inlet line at the pump.

9. Remove the rear A/C compressor brace and remove the fuel line. If equipped with a fuel line heater, remove the fasteners retaining the line and heater.

10. Disconnect the fuel return line from the injection pump.

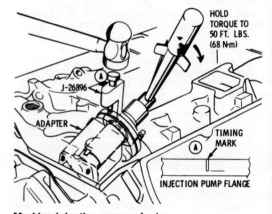

Marking injection pump adapter

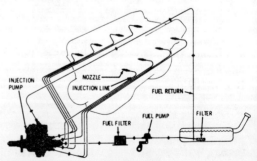

Diesel fuel system circuit

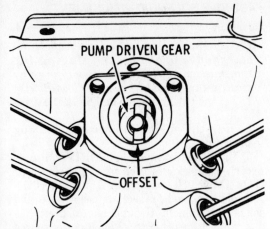

Offset on diesel fuel pump driven gear

On 1982 and earlier models:

11. Remove the clamps and pull the fuel return lines from each injection nozzle.

12. Using two wrenches to avoid putting torque on the nozzles, disconnect the high pressure lines at the nozzles.

On 1983 and later models:

11. Disconnect the injection line clamps.

12. Disconnect the injection lines at the pump and cap all openings. Then, reposition the lines slightly as necessary to gain enough clearance for pump removal.

13. Remove the three injection pump retaining nuts with tool J–26987 or its equivalent.

14. Remove the pump and cap all lines and nozzles. Discard the pump-to-adapter O-ring.

To install:

1. Remove the protective caps.

2. Line up the offset tang on the pump driveshaft with the pump driven gar and install the pump.

3. Install, but do not tighten the pump retaining nuts.

4. On 1982 and earlier models, connect the high pressure lines at the nozzles.

5. Using two wrenches, torque the high pressure line nuts to 25 ft. lbs. (34 Nm) on 1982 and earlier models.

6. Connect the fuel return lines to the nozzles and pump on 1982 and earlier models.

7. Align the timing mark on the injection pump with the line on the timing mark adaptor and torque the mounting nuts to 35 ft. lbs. (47 Nm) on models up to 1979 and 18 ft. lbs. (25 Nm) on models built in 1980 and later years.

NOTE: *A ¾ in. (19mm) open end wrench on the boss at the front of the injection pump will aid in rotating the pump to align the marks.*

On 1983 and later models, remove the protective caps and connect the injection lines to the pump, torquing to 25 ft. lbs. (34 Nm). Then connect the injection lines to the pump, torquing to 25 ft. lbs. (34 Nm). Then connect injection line clamps on these models. Also on these models only, install the fuel filter and bracket, tighten fuel line fittings, and install the fuel line heater clamps (where equipped). Install the crankcase depression regulator.

8. Adjust the throttle rod:

   a. Remove the clip from the cruise control rod and remove the rod from the bellcrank.

   b. Loosen the locknut on the throttle rod a few turns, then shorten the rod several turns.

   c. Rotate the bellcrank to the full throttle stop, then lengthen the throttle rod until the injection pump lever contacts the injection pump full throttle stop, then release the bellcrank.

   d. Tighten the throttle rod locknut.

9. Install the fuel inlet line between the transfer pump and the filter.

10. Install the rear A/C compressor brace.

11. Install the bellcrank and clip.

12. Connect the throttle rod and return spring.

13. Adjust the transmission cable:

   a. Push the snap-lock to the disengaged position.

   b. Rotate the injection pump lever to the full throttle stop and hold it there.

   c. Push in the snap-lock until it is flush.

   d. Release the injection pump lever.

14. Start the engine and check for fuel leaks.

15. Remove the screened covers and install the air crossover.

16. Install the tubes in the air flow control valve in the air crossover and install the ventilation filters in the valve covers.

17. Install the air cleaner.

18. On 1982 and earlier models, use this method to bleed air out of the injection pump: Start the engine and allow it to run for two minutes; stop the engine and allow it to stand for two minutes; then restart the engine.

19. On 1983 and later models, an extremely precise timing meter is used by professional mechanics to set injection timing by replacing the glow plug of No. 3 cylinder with an electronic probe. Since the probe sets timing by measuring crankshaft position when the injected fuel actually ignites, it eliminates a great number of possible kinds of error. Proper injection timing maximizes fuel economy and minimizes all engine stresses. Even though a precise alignment of the injection pump ensures reasonably accurate timing, you should have your timing set professionally to ensure best results.

Also, if you have disturbed the vacuum regulator valve position or replaced the injection pump, this valve should be adjusted professionally. The procedure is very simple, but requires an expensive special tool.

20. Connect the negative battery cable.

21. On all models, adjust the idle speed as described below.

22. Start the engine and check for fuel leaks and proper operation.

SLOW IDLE SPEED ADJUSTMENT

1. Apply the parking brake, put the transmission in Park and block the drive wheels. Check the throttle linkage adjustment and adjust it if necessary.

2. Start the engine and allow it to run until it is warm (about 15 minutes). Then, shut the engine off and remove the air cleaner.

3. Clean off the front cover RPM counter (the probe holder) and the rim of the crankshaft balancer. Install the magnetic pickup probe of the magnetic pickup tachometer fully into the RPM counter. Connect the battery leads (red to positive, black to negative).

4. Disconnect the two lead connector at the generator.

5. Turn off all electrical accessories.

CAUTION: *Block all wheels and apply the emergency brake before placing the transmission in DRIVE. Personal injury may result if this procedure is not followed!*

6. Start the engine and place the transmission in Drive. Read the slow idle speed, making sure the steering wheel and brake pedal are not touched. Reset the idle speed by turning the screw if it does not agree with the figure on the engine compartment sticker. **If the sticker is not present, adjust the idle speed to 600 rpm in DRIVE.** Be sure to put the transmission back in Park, reconnect the generator lead, and reinstall the air cleaner when you have finished.

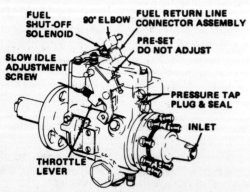

FUEL SHUT-OFF SOLENOID
90° ELBOW
FUEL RETURN LINE CONNECTOR ASSEMBLY
PRE-SET DO NOT ADJUST
SLOW IDLE ADJUSTMENT SCREW
PRESSURE TAP PLUG & SEAL
INLET
THROTTLE LEVER

Roasa-Master diesel injection pump slow idle screw

FAST IDLE SOLENOID ADJUSTMENT
Models up to 1982

CAUTION: *Block all wheels and apply the emergency brake before placing the transmission in DRIVE. Personal injury may result if this procedure is not followed!*

1. Set the parking brake and block the drive wheels.

2. Run the engine to normal operating temperature.

3. Place the transmission in **DRIVE**, disconnect the compressor clutch wire and turn the A/C On. On vehicles without A/C, disconnect the solenoid wire, and connect jumper wires to the solenoid terminals. Ground one of the wires and connect the other to a 12 volt power source to activate the solenoid.

4. Adjust the fast idle solenoid plunger to obtain 650 rpm.

1982 and Later Models

1. Unplug the connector from the EGR-TVS and install a jumper between the connector terminals WITHOUT ALLOWING THE JUMPER TO TOUCH GROUND!

2. Follow Steps 1–5 of the procedure for Slow Idle Speed Adjustment above to prepare the engine. Then, put the transmission in Drive. Check the fast idle speed by reading the magnetic pickup tachometer and compare the reading to the fast idle solenoid speed specified on the engine compartment sticker. **If the sticker is not present, adjust the fast idle to 750 rpm in DRIVE.** Change the setting by turning the solenoid plunger at the flats.

3. Remove the jumper and reconnect the connector. Stop the engine, and then reconnect the generator connector.

4. Remove the tachometer. If the vehicle has cruise control, adjust the servo throttle rod to minimize the slack. Then, install the clip in the first free hole closest to the bellcrank or throttle lever but still within the bail on the servo. Install the air cleaner (make sure to reconnect the EGR hose).

CRUISE CONTROL SERVO RELAY ROD ADJUSTMENT

1. Turn the ignition switch to Off.

2. Adjust the rod to minimum slack then put the clip in the first free hole closest to the bellcrank, but within the servo bail.

INJECTION TIMING ADJUSTMENT
1978–81 Models

For the engine to be properly timed, the lines on the top of the injection pump adapter and the flange of the injection pump must be aligned.

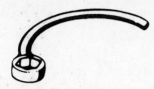

Injection pump wrench J-26987

1. The engine must be off for resetting the timing.

2. Loosen the three pump retaining nuts with tool J-26987, an injection pump intake manifold wrench, or its equivalent.

3. Align the timing marks and torque the pump retaining nuts to 35 ft. lbs. (47 Nm) on 1979 and earlier models and 18 ft. lbs. (25 Nm) on 1980 and later models. On 1982 and later models, timing should be precisely adjusted using the special timing meter discussed in the procedure for injection pump removal and installation.

NOTE: *The use of a ¾ in. (19mm) open end wrench on the boss at the front of the pump will aid in rotating the pump to align the marks.*

4. Adjust the throttle rod. (See Fuel injection Pump Removal and Installation, Step 8.)

Injection Pump Adapter, Adapter Seal, and New Adapter Timing Mark
REMOVAL AND INSTALLATION

1. Remove injection pump and lines as described earlier.

2. Remove the injection pump adapter.

3. Remove the seal from the adapter.

4. File the timing mark from the adapter. Do not file the mark off the pump.

5. Position the engine at TDC of No. 1 cylinder. Align the mark on the balancer with the zero mark on the indicator. The index is offset to the right when No. 1 is at TDC.

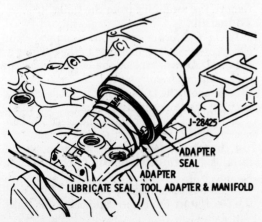

Installing adapter seal

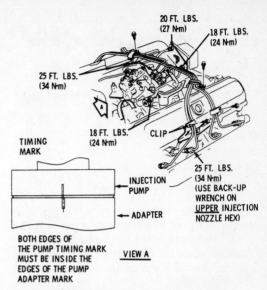

Diesel timing marks and injection pump lines

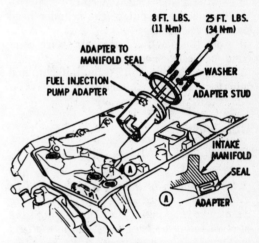

Injection pump adapter bolts

6. Apply a chassis lube to the seal areas. Install, but do not tighten the injection pump.

7. Install the new seal on the adapter using tool J-28425, or its equivalent.

8. Torque the adapter bolts to 25 ft. lbs. (34 Nm).

NOTE: *The procedure below, involving the special timing tool, applies for models built through 1981. For 1982 and later models, set the injection pump at the center of the slots in the pump mounting flange, and then have the pump timed with the special timing device described in the Injection Pump Removal & Installation procedure.*

9. Install timing tool J-26896 into the injection pump adapter. Torque the tool, toward No. 1 cylinder to 50 ft. lbs. (68 Nm). Mark the injection pump adapter. Remove the tool.

10. Install the injection pump.

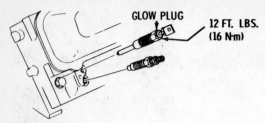

Diesel glow plug

Glow Plug
REMOVAL AND INSTALLATION

NOTE: *A burned out glow plug tip may bulge and then break off and drop into the pre-chamber when the glow plug is removed. If this occurs, the cylinder head must be removed, remove the pre-chamber and remove the broken tip.*

1. Disconnect the negative (−) battery cable and glow plug electrical connector.
2. Turn the plug out of the cylinder head slowly.
3. Coat the new plug with anti-seize compound for electrical components.
4. Torque the plug to 12 ft. lbs. (16 Nm) and connect the electrical connector.

FUEL TANK
DRAINING THE TANK

NOTE: *If the vehicle is to be stored for any extended length of time, the fuel should be drained from the complete system, including carburetor, fuel pump, all fuel lines, and the fuel tank in order to prevent gum formations and poor engine performance.*

1. Have a carbon dioxide fire extinguisher near the work area. Remove the negative battery cable from the battery.
2. Use a hand-operated siphon pump, and follow the manufacturer's instructions for its use. As the fuel tank has a restrictor in the filler neck, connect the drain hose to the main fuel pipe at the fuel pump or at the tank gauge unit. Drain the fuel.
3. Reconnect any removed hoses, lines and cap.

CAUTION: *Never drain or store gasoline in an open container due to the possibility of fire or explosion. Never siphon gasoline by mouth!*

REMOVAL AND INSTALLATION

1. Disconnect the negative (−) battery cable.
2. Drain tank.

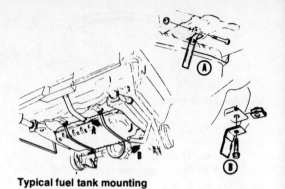

Typical fuel tank mounting

Installing fuel gauge unit into fuel tank—typical

3. Disconnect tank unit wire from connector in rear compartment.
4. Remove the ground wire retaining screw from the underbody.
5. Disconnect the hoses from the tank unit.
6. Support the fuel tank with a suitable jack and disconnect the two fuel tank retaining straps.
7. Remove the tank from the vehicle.
8. Remove the fuel gauge retaining cam, and remove the tank unit from the tank.

To install:
1. On California emissions equipped vehicles, center the fuel filler pipe in the opening as required. Always replace the O-ring when the tank unit has been removed.
2. Support the tank with a suitable jack and position the tank into the vehicle.
3. Connect the fuel hoses and electrical connectors before installing the tank straps.
4. Install the tank strap bolt and nut to 96 inch lbs. (11 Nm) and the bolt-to-body to 26 ft. lbs. (35 Nm).
5. Connect the negative battery cable, refill the tank, start the engine and check for leaks.

Chassis Electrical

6

UNDERSTANDING AND TROUBLESHOOTING ELECTRICAL SYSTEMS

With the rate at which both import and domestic manufacturers are incorporating electronic control systems into their production lines, it won't be long before every new vehicle is equipped with one or more on-board computer. These electronic components (with no moving parts) should theoretically last the life of the vehicle, provided nothing external happens to damage the circuits or memory chips.

While it is true that electronic components should never wear out, in the real world malfunctions do occur. It is also true that any computer-based system is extremely sensitive to electrical voltages and can not tolerate careless or haphazard testing or service procedures. An inexperienced individual can literally do major damage looking for a minor problem by using the wrong kind of test equipment or connecting test leads or connectors with the ignition switch ON. When selecting test equipment, make sure the manufacturers instructions state that the tester is compatible with whatever type of electronic control system is being serviced. Read all instructions carefully and double check all test points before installing probes or making any test connections.

The following section outlines basic diagnosis techniques for dealing with computerized automotive control systems. Along with a general explanation of the various types of test equipment available to aid in servicing modern electronic automotive systems, basic repair techniques for wiring harnesses and connectors is given. Read the basic information before attempting any repairs or testing on any computerized system, to provide the background of information necessary to avoid the most common and obvious mistakes that can cost both time and money. Although the replacement and testing procedures are simple in themselves, the systems are not, and unless one has a thorough understanding of all components and their function within a particular computerized control system, the logical test sequence these systems demand can not be followed. Minor malfunctions can make a big difference, so it is important to know how each component affects the operation of the overall electronic system to find the ultimate cause of a problem without replacing good components unnecessarily. It is not enough to use the correct test equipment; the test equipment must be used correctly.

Safety Precautions

CAUTION: *Whenever working on or around any computer based microprocessor control system, always observe these general precautions to prevent the possibility of personal injury or damage to electronic components.*

• Never install or remove battery cables with the key ON or the engine running. Jumper cables should be connected with the key OFF to avoid power surges that can damage electronic control units. Engines equipped with computer controlled systems should avoid both giving and getting jump starts due to the possibility of serious damage to components from arcing in the engine compartment when connections are made with the ignition ON.

• Always remove the battery cables before charging the battery. Never use a high output charger on an installed battery or attempt to use any type of "hot shot" (24 volt) starting aid.

• Exercise care when inserting test probes into connectors to insure good connections without damaging the connector or spreading the pins. Always probe connectors from the rear (wire) side, NOT the pin side, to avoid accidental shorting of terminals during test procedures.

• Never remove or attach wiring harness

connectors with the ignition switch ON, especially to an electronic control module.

• Do not drop any components during service procedures and never apply 12 volts directly to any component (like a solenoid or relay) unless instructed specifically to do so. Some component electrical windings are designed to safely handle only 4 or 5 volts and can be destroyed in seconds if 12 volts are applied directly to the connector.

• Remove the electronic control module if the vehicle is to be placed in an environment where temperatures exceed approximately 176°F (80°C), such as a paint spray booth or when arc or gas welding near the control unit location in the vehicle.

ORGANIZED TROUBLESHOOTING

When diagnosing a specific problem, organized troubleshooting is a must. The complexity of a modern automobile demands that you approach any problem in a logical, organized manner. There are certain troubleshooting techniques that are standard:

1. Establish when the problem occurs. Does the problem appear only under certain conditions? Were there any noises, odors, or other unusual symptoms?

2. Isolate the problem area. To do this, make some simple tests and observations; then eliminate the systems that are working properly. Check for obvious problems such as broken wires, dirty connections or split or disconnected vacuum hoses. Always check the obvious before assuming something complicated is the cause.

3. Test for problems systematically to determine the cause once the problem area is isolated. Are all the components functioning properly? Is there power going to electrical switches and motors? Is there vacuum at vacuum switches and/or actuators? Is there a mechanical problem such as bent linkage or loose mounting screws? Doing careful, systematic checks will often turn up most causes on the first inspection without wasting time checking components that have little or no relationship to the problem.

4. Test all repairs after the work is done to make sure that the problem is fixed. Some causes can be traced to more than one component, so a careful verification of repair work is important to pick up additional malfunctions that may cause a problem to reappear or a different problem to arise. A blown fuse, for example, is a simple problem that may require more than another fuse to repair. If you don't look for a problem that caused a fuse to blow, for example, a shorted wire may go undetected.

Experience has shown that most problems tend to be the result of a fairly simple and obvious cause, such as loose or corroded connectors or air leaks in the intake system; making careful inspection of components during testing essential to quick and accurate troubleshooting. Special, hand held computerized testers designed specifically for diagnosing the HEI-EST system are available from a variety of aftermarket sources, as well as from the vehicle manufacturer, but care should be taken that any test equipment being used is designed to diagnose that particular computer controlled system accurately without damaging the control module (ECM) or components being tested.

NOTE: *Pinpointing the exact cause of trouble in an electrical system can sometimes only be accomplished by the use of special test equipment. The following describes commonly used test equipment and explains how to put it to best use in diagnosis. In addition to the information covered below, the manufacturer's instructions booklet provided with the tester should be read and clearly understood before attempting any test procedures.*

TEST EQUIPMENT

Jumper Wires

Jumper wires are simple, yet extremely valuable, pieces of test equipment. Jumper wires are merely wires that are used to bypass sections of a circuit. The simplest type of jumper wire is merely a length of multistrand wire with an alligator clip at each end. Jumper wires are usually fabricated from lengths of standard automotive wire and whatever type of connector (alligator clip, spade connector or pin connector) that is required for the particular vehicle being tested. The well equipped tool box will have several different styles of jumper wires in several different lengths. Some jumper wires are made with three or more terminals coming from a common splice for special purpose testing. In cramped, hard-to-reach areas it is advisable to have insulated boots over the jumper wire terminals in order to prevent accidental grounding, sparks, and possible fire, especially when testing fuel system components.

Jumper wires are used primarily to locate open electrical circuits, on either the ground (–) side of the circuit or on the hot (+) side. If an electrical component fails to operate, connect the jumper wire between the component and a good ground. If the component operates only with the jumper installed, the ground circuit is open. If the ground circuit is good, but the component does not operate, the circuit between the power feed and component is open. You can sometimes connect the jumper wire directly from the battery to the hot terminal of the component, but first make sure the component uses 12 volts in operation. Some electrical components, such as fuel injectors, are designed to operate on about 4 volts and running 12 volts directly to the injector terminals can burn out the wiring. By inserting an inline fuseholder between a set of test leads, a fused jumper wire can be used for bypassing open circuits. Use a 5 amp fuse to provide protection against voltage spikes. When in doubt, use a voltmeter to check the voltage input to the component and measure how much voltage is being applied normally. By moving the jumper wire successively back from the lamp toward the power source, you can isolate the area of the circuit where the open is located. When the component stops functioning, or the power is cut off, the open is in the segment of wire between the jumper and the point previously tested.

CAUTION: *Never use jumpers made from wire that is of lighter gauge than used in the circuit under test. If the jumper wire is of too small gauge, it may overheat and possibly melt. Never use jumpers to bypass high resistance loads (such as motors) in a circuit. Bypassing resistances, in effect, creates a short circuit which may, in turn, cause damage and fire. Never use a jumper for anything other than temporary bypassing of components in a circuit.*

12 Volt Test Light

The 12 volt test light is used to check circuits and components while electrical current is flowing through them. It is used for voltage and ground tests. Twelve volt test lights come in different styles but all have three main parts; a ground clip, a probe, and a light. The most commonly used 12 volt test lights have pick-type probes. To use a 12 volt test light, connect the ground clip to a good ground and probe wherever necessary with the pick. The pick should be sharp so that it can penetrate wire insulation to make contact with the wire, without making a large hole in the insulation. The wrap-around light is handy in hard to reach areas or where it is difficult to support a wire to push a probe pick into it. To use the wrap around light, hook the wire to probed with the hook and pull the trigger. A small pick will be forced through the wire insulation into the wire core.

CAUTION: *Do not use a test light to probe electronic ignition spark plug or coil wires. Never use a pick-type test light to probe wiring on computer controlled systems unless specifically instructed to do so. Any wire insulation that is pierced by the test light probe should be taped and sealed with silicone after testing.*

Like the jumper wire, the 12 volt test light is used to isolate opens in circuits. But, whereas the jumper wire is used to bypass the open to operate the load, the 12 volt test light is used to locate the presence of voltage in a circuit. If the test light glows, you know that there is power up to that point; if the 12 volt test light does not glow when its probe is inserted into the wire or connector, you know that there is an open circuit (no power). Move the test light in successive steps back toward the power source until the light in the handle does glow. When it does glow, the open is between the probe and point previously probed.

NOTE: *The test light does not detect that 12 volts (or any particular amount of voltage) is present; it only detects that some voltage is present. It is advisable before using the test light to touch its terminals across the battery posts to make sure the light is operating properly.*

Self-Powered Test Light

The self-powered test light usually contains a 1.5 volt penlight battery. One type of self-powered test light is similar in design to the 12 volt test light. This type has both the battery and the light in the handle and pick-type probe tip. The second type has the light toward the open tip, so that the light illuminates the contact point. The self-powered test light is dual purpose piece of test equipment. It can be used to test for either open or short circuits when power is isolated from the circuit (continuity test). A powered test light should not be used on any computer controlled system or component unless specifically instructed to do so. Many engine sensors can be destroyed by even this small amount of voltage applied directly to the terminals.

Open Circuit Testing

To use the self-powered test light to check for open circuits, first isolate the circuit from the vehicle's 12 volt power source by disconnecting the battery or wiring harness connector. Connect the test light ground clip to a good ground and probe sections of the circuit sequentially with the test light. (start from either end of the circuit). If the light is out, the open is between the probe and the circuit ground. If the light is on, the open is between the probe and end of the circuit toward the power source.

Short Circuit Testing

By isolating the circuit both from power and from ground, and using a self-powered test light, you can check for shorts to ground in the circuit. Isolate the circuit from power and ground. Connect the test light ground clip to a good ground and probe any easy-to-reach test point in the circuit. If the light comes on, there is a short somewhere in the circuit. To isolate the short, probe a test point at either end of the isolated circuit (the light should be on). Leave the test light probe connected and open connectors, switches, remove parts, etc., sequentially, until the light goes out. When the light goes out, the short is between the last circuit component opened and the previous circuit opened.

NOTE: *The 1.5 volt battery in the test light does not provide much current. A weak battery may not provide enough power to illuminate the test light even when a complete circuit is made (especially if there are high resistances in the circuit). Always make sure that the test battery is strong. To check the battery, briefly touch the ground clip to the probe; if the light glows brightly the battery is strong enough for testing. Never use a self-powered test light to perform checks for opens or shorts when power is applied to the electrical system under test. The 12 volt vehicle power will quickly burn out the 1.5 volt light bulb in the test light.*

Voltmeter

A voltmeter is used to measure voltage at any point in a circuit, or to measure the voltage drop across any part of a circuit. It can also be used to check continuity in a wire or circuit by indicating current flow from one end to the other. Voltmeters usually have various scales on the meter dial and a selector switch to allow the selection of different voltages. The voltmeter has a positive and a negative lead. To avoid damage to the meter, always connect the negative lead to the negative ($-$) side of circuit (to ground or nearest the ground side of the circuit) and connect the positive lead to the positive ($+$) side of the circuit (to the power source or the nearest power source). Note that the negative voltmeter lead will always be black and that the positive voltmeter will always be some color other than black (usually red). Depending on how the voltmeter is connected into the circuit, it has several uses.

A voltmeter can be connected either in parallel or in series with a circuit and it has a very high resistance to current flow. When connected in parallel, only a small amount of current will flow through the voltmeter current path; the rest will flow through the normal circuit current path and the circuit will work normally. When the voltmeter is connected in series with a circuit, only a small amount of current can flow through the circuit. The circuit will not work properly, but the voltmeter reading will show if the circuit is complete or not.

Available Voltage Measurement

Set the voltmeter selector switch to the 20V position and connect the meter negative lead to the negative post of the battery. Connect the positive meter lead to the positive post of battery and turn the ignition switch ON to provide a load. Read the voltage on the meter or digital display. A well charged battery should register over 12 volts. If the meter reads below 11.5 volts, the battery power may be insufficient to operate the electrical system properly. This test determines voltage available from the battery and should be the first step in any electrical trouble diagnosis procedure. Many electrical problems, especially on computer controlled systems, can be caused by a low state of charge in the battery. Excessive corrosion at the battery cable terminals can cause a poor contact that will prevent proper charging and full battery current flow.

Normal battery voltage is 12 volts when fully charged. When the battery is supplying current to one or more circuits it is said to be "under load". When everything is off the electrical system is under a "no-load" condition. A fully charged battery may show about 12.5 volts at no load; will drop to 12 volts under medium load; and will drop even lower under heavy load. If the battery is partially discharged the voltage decrease under heavy load may be excessive, even though the battery shows 12 volts or more at no load. When allowed to discharge further, the battery's available voltage under load will decrease more severely. For this reason, it is important that the battery be fully charged during all testing procedures to avoid errors in diagnosis and incorrect test results.

Voltage Drop

When current flows through a resistance, the voltage beyond the resistance is reduced (the larger the current, the greater the reduction in voltage). When no current is flowing, there is no voltage drop because there is no current flow. All points in the circuit which are connected to the power source are at the same voltage as the power source. The total voltage drop always equals the total source voltage. In a long circuit with many connectors, a series of small, unwanted voltage drops due to corrosion at the connectors can add up to a total loss of voltage which impairs the operation of the normal loads in the circuit.

INDIRECT COMPUTATION OF VOLTAGE DROPS

1. Set the voltmeter selector switch to the 20 volt position.
2. Connect the meter negative lead to a good ground.
3. Probe all resistances in the circuit with the positive meter lead.
4. Operate the circuit in all modes and observe the voltage readings.

DIRECT MEASUREMENT OF VOLTAGE DROPS

1. Set the voltmeter switch to the 20 volt position.

2. Connect the voltmeter negative lead to the ground side of the resistance load to be measured.

3. Connect the positive lead to the positive side of the resistance or load to be measured.

4. Read the voltage drop directly on the 20 volt scale.

Too high a voltage indicates too high a resistance. If, for example, a blower motor runs too slowly, you can determine if there is too high a resistance in the resistor pack. By taking voltage drop readings in all parts of the circuit, you can isolate the problem. Too low a voltage drop indicates too low a resistance. If, for example, a blower motor runs too fast in the MED and/or LOW position, the problem can be isolated in the resistor pack by taking voltage drop readings in all parts of the circuit to locate a possibly shorted resistor. The maximum allowable voltage drop under load is critical, especially if there is more than one high resistance problem in a circuit because all voltage drops are cumulative. A small drop is normal due to the resistance of the conductors.

HIGH RESISTANCE TESTING

1. Set the voltmeter selector switch to the 4 volt position.

2. Connect the voltmeter positive lead to the positive post of the battery.

3. Turn on the headlights and heater blower to provide a load.

4. Probe various points in the circuit with the negative voltmeter lead.

5. Read the voltage drop on the 4 volt scale. Some average maximum allowable voltage drops are:

FUSE PANEL – 7 volts
IGNITION SWITCH – 5volts
HEADLIGHT SWITCH – 7 volts
IGNITION COIL (+) – 5 volts
ANY OTHER LOAD – 1.3 volts
NOTE: *Voltage drops are all measured while a load is operating; without current flow, there will be no voltage drop.*

Ohmmeter

The ohmmeter is designed to read resistance (ohms) in a circuit or component. Although there are several different styles of ohmmeters, all will usually have a selector switch which permits the measurement of different ranges of resistance (usually the selector switch allows the multiplication of the meter reading by 10, 100, 1000, and 10,000). A calibration knob allows the meter to be set at zero for accurate measurement. Since all ohmmeters are powered by

an internal battery (usually 9 volts), the ohmmeter can be used as a self-powered test light. When the ohmmeter is connected, current from the ohmmeter flows through the circuit or component being tested. Since the ohmmeter's internal resistance and voltage are known values, the amount of current flow through the meter depends on the resistance of the circuit or component being tested.

The ohmmeter can be used to perform continuity test for opens or shorts (either by observation of the meter needle or as a self-powered test light), and to read actual resistance in a circuit. It should be noted that the ohmmeter is used to check the resistance of a component or wire while there is no voltage applied to the circuit. Current flow from an outside voltage source (such as the vehicle battery) can damage the ohmmeter, so the circuit or component should be isolated from the vehicle electrical system before any testing is done. Since the ohmmeter uses its own voltage source, either lead can be connected to any test point.

NOTE: *When checking diodes or other solid state components, the ohmmeter leads can only be connected one way in order to measure current flow in a single direction. Make sure the positive (+) and negative (–) terminal connections are as described in the test procedures to verify the one-way diode operation.*

In using the meter for making continuity checks, do not be concerned with the actual resistance readings. Zero resistance, or any resistance readings, indicate continuity in the circuit. Infinite resistance indicates an open in the circuit. A high resistance reading where there should be none indicates a problem in the circuit. Checks for short circuits are made in the same manner as checks for open circuits except that the circuit must be isolated from both power and normal ground. Infinite resistance indicates no continuity to ground, while zero resistance indicates a dead short to ground.

RESISTANCE MEASUREMENT

The batteries in an ohmmeter will weaken with age and temperature, so the ohmmeter must be calibrated or "zeroed" before taking measurements. To zero the meter, place the selector switch in its lowest range and touch the two ohmmeter leads together. Turn the calibration knob until the meter needle is exactly on zero.

NOTE: *All analog (needle) type ohmmeters must be zeroed before use, but some digital ohmmeter models are automatically calibrated when the switch is turned on. Self-calibrating digital ohmmeters do not have an adjusting knob, but its a good idea to check for a zero readout before use by touching the leads together. All computer controlled systems require the use of a digital ohmmeter with at least 10 mega-ohms impedance for testing. Before any test procedures are attempted, make sure the ohmmeter used is compatible with the electrical system or damage to the on-board computer could result.*

To measure resistance, first isolate the circuit from the vehicle power source by disconnecting the battery cables or the harness connector. Make sure the key is OFF when disconnecting any components or the battery. Where necessary, also isolate at least one side of the circuit to be checked to avoid reading parallel resistances. Parallel circuit resistances will always give a lower reading than the actual resistance of either of the branches. When measuring the resistance of parallel circuits, the total resistance will always be lower than the smallest resistance in the circuit. Connect the meter leads to both sides of the circuit (wire or component) and read the actual measured ohms on the meter scale. Make sure the selector switch is set to the proper ohm scale for the circuit being tested to avoid misreading the ohmmeter test value.

CAUTION: *Never use an ohmmeter with power applied to the circuit. Like the self-powered test light, the ohmmeter is designed to operate on its own power supply. The normal 12 volt automotive electrical system current could damage the meter.*

Ammeters

An ammeter measures the amount of current flowing through a circuit in units called amperes or amps. Amperes are units of electron flow which indicate how fast the electrons are flowing through the circuit. Since Ohms Law dictates that current flow in a circuit is equal to the circuit voltage divided by the total circuit resistance, increasing voltage also increases the current level (amps). Likewise, any decrease in resistance will increase the amount of amps in a circuit. At normal operating voltage, most circuits have a characteristic amount of amperes, called "current draw" which can be measured using an ammeter. By referring to a specified current draw rating, measuring the amperes, and comparing the two values, one can determine what is happening within the circuit to aid in diagnosis. An open circuit, for example, will not allow any current to flow so the ammeter reading will be zero. More current flows through a heavily loaded circuit or when the charging system is operating.

An ammeter is always connected in series with the circuit being tested. All of the current that normally flows through the circuit must also flow through the ammeter; if there is any other path for the current to follow, the ammeter reading will not be accurate. The ammeter itself has very little resistance to current flow and therefore will not affect the circuit, but it will measure current draw only when the circuit is closed and electricity is flowing. Excessive current draw can blow fuses and drain the battery, while a reduced current draw can cause motors to run slowly, lights to dim and other components to not operate properly. The ammeter can help diagnose these conditions by locating the cause of the high or low reading.

Multimeters

Different combinations of test meters can be built into a single unit designed for specific tests. Some of the more common combination test devices are known as Volt/Amp testers, Tach/Dwell meters, or Digital Multimeters. The Volt/Amp tester is used for charging system, starting system or battery tests and consists of a voltmeter, an ammeter and a variable resistance carbon pile. The voltmeter will usually have at least two ranges for use with 6, 12 and 24 volt systems. The ammeter also has more than one range for testing various levels of battery loads and starter current draw and the carbon pile can be adjusted to offer different amounts of resistance. The Volt/Amp tester has heavy leads to carry large amounts of current and many later models have an inductive ammeter pickup that clamps around the wire to simplify test connections. On some models, the ammeter also has a zero-center scale to allow testing of charging and starting systems without switching leads or polarity. A digital multimeter is a voltmeter, ammeter and ohmmeter combined in an instrument which gives a digital readout. These are often used when testing solid state circuits because of their high input impedance (usually 10 megohms or more).

The tach/dwell meter combines a tachometer and a dwell (cam angle) meter and is a specialized kind of voltmeter. The tachometer scale is marked to show engine speed in rpm and the dwell scale is marked to show degrees of distributor shaft rotation. In most electronic ignition systems, dwell is determined by the control unit, but the dwell meter can also be used to check the duty cycle (operation) of some electronic engine control systems. Some tach/dwell meters are powered by an internal battery, while others take their power from the vehicle battery in use. The battery powered testers usually require calibration much like an ohmmeter before testing.

Special Test Equipment

A variety of diagnostic tools are available to help troubleshoot and repair computerized engine control systems. The most sophisticated of these devices are the console type engine analyzers that usually occupy a garage service bay, but there are several types of aftermarket electronic testers available that will allow quick circuit tests of the engine control system by plugging directly into a special connector located in the engine compartment or under the dashboard. Several tool and equipment manufacturers offer simple, hand held testers that measure various circuit voltage levels on command to check all system components for proper operation. Although these testers usually cost about $300–$500, consider that the average computer control unit (or ECM) can cost just as much and the money saved by not replacing perfectly good sensors or components in an attempt to correct a problem could justify the purchase price of a special diagnostic tester the first time it's used.

These computerized testers can allow quick and easy test measurements while the engine is operating or while the vehicle is being driven. In addition, the on-board computer memory can be read to access any stored trouble codes; in effect allowing the computer to tell you where it hurts and aid trouble diagnosis by pinpointing exactly which circuit or component is malfunctioning. In the same manner, repairs can be tested to make sure the problem has been corrected. The biggest advantage these special testers have is their relatively easy hookups that minimize or eliminate the chances of making the wrong connections and getting false voltage readings or damaging the computer accidentally.

NOTE: *It should be remembered that these testers check voltage levels in circuits; they don't detect mechanical problems or failed components if the circuit voltage falls within the preprogrammed limits stored in the tester PROM unit. Also, most of the hand held testers are designed to work only on one or two systems made by a specific manufacturer.*

A variety of aftermarket testers are available to help diagnose different computerized control systems. Kent-Moore Tool Company 29784 Little Mack Roseville, MI 48066–2298, markets a device which plugs directly into the assembly line diagnostic link (ALDL). The tester makes diagnosis a simple matter of pressing the correct buttons and, by changing the internal PROM or inserting a different diagnosis cartridge, it will work on any model from full size to subcompact, over a wide range of years. An adapter is supplied with the tester to allow connection to all types of ALDL links, regardless of the number of pin terminals used. By inserting an updated PROM into the tester, it can be easily updated to diagnose any new modifications of computerized control systems.

Wiring Harnesses

The average automobile contains about ½ mile of wiring, with hundreds of individual connections. To protect the many wires from damage and to keep them from becoming a confusing tangle, they are organized into bundles, enclosed in plastic or taped together and called wire harnesses. Different wiring harnesses serve different parts of the vehicle. Individual wires are color coded to help trace them through a harness where sections are hidden from view.

A loose or corroded connection or a replacement wire that is too small for the circuit will add extra resistance and an additional voltage drop to the circuit. A ten percent voltage drop can result in slow or erratic motor operation, for example, even though the circuit is complete. Automotive wiring or circuit conductors can be in any one of three forms:

1. Single strand wire
2. Multistrand wire
3. Printed circuitry

Single strand wire has a solid metal core and is usually used inside such components as alternators, motors, relays and other devices. Multistrand wire has a core made of many small strands of wire twisted together into a single conductor. Most of the wiring in an automotive electrical system is made up of multistrand wire, either as a single conductor or grouped together in a harness. All wiring is color coded on the insulator, either as a solid color or as a colored wire with an identification stripe. A printed circuit is a thin film of copper or other conductor that is printed on an insulator backing. Occasionally, a printed circuit is sandwiched between two sheets of plastic for more protection and flexibility. A complete printed circuit, consisting of conductors, insulating material and connectors for lamps or other components is called a printed circuit board. Printed circuitry is used in place of individual wires or harnesses in places where space is limited, such as behind instrument panels.

Wire Gauge

Since computer controlled automotive electrical systems are very sensitive to changes in resistance, the selection of properly sized wires is critical when systems are repaired. The wire gauge number is an expression of the cross section area of the conductor. The most common system for expressing wire size is the American Wire Gauge (AWG) system.

Wire cross section area is measured in circular mils. A mil is $\frac{1}{1000}$ in. (0.001 in.); a circular mil is the area of a circle one mil in diameter. For example, a conductor ¼ in. in diameter is 0.250 in. or 250 mils. The circular mil cross section area of the wire is 250 squared (250^2)or 62,500 circular mils. Imported vehicle models usually use metric wire gauge designations, which is simply the cross section area of the conductor in square millimeters (mm^2).

Gauge numbers are assigned to conductors of various cross section areas. As gauge number increases, area decreases and the conductor becomes smaller. A 5 gauge conductor is smaller than a 1 gauge conductor and a 10 gauge is smaller than a 5 gauge. As the cross section area of a conductor decreases, resistance increases and so does the gauge number. A conductor with a higher gauge number will carry less current than a conductor with a lower gauge number.

NOTE: *Gauge wire size refers to the size of the conductor, not the size of the complete wire. It is possible to have two wires of the same gauge with different diameters because one may have thicker insulation than the other.*

12 volt automotive electrical systems generally use 10, 12, 14, 16 and 18 gauge wire. Main power distribution circuits and larger accessories usually use 10 and 12 gauge wire. Battery cables are usually 4 or 6 gauge, although 1 and 2 gauge wires are occasionally used. Wire length must also be considered when making repairs to a circuit. As conductor length increases, so does resistance. An 18 gauge wire, for example, can carry a 10 amp load for 10 feet without excessive voltage drop; however if a 15 foot wire is required for the same 10 amp load, it must be a 16 gauge wire.

An electrical schematic shows the electrical current paths when a circuit is operating properly. It is essential to understand how a circuit works before trying to figure out why it does not. Schematics break the entire electrical system down into individual circuits and show only one particular circuit. In a schematic, no attempt is made to represent wiring and components as they physically appear on the vehicle; switches and other components are shown as simply as possible. Face views of harness connectors show the cavity or terminal locations in all multi-pin connectors to help locate test points.

If you need to backprobe a connector while it is on the component, the order of the terminals must be mentally reversed. The wire color code can help in this situation, as well as a keyway, lock tab or other reference mark.

NOTE: *Wiring diagrams are not included in this book. As vehicles have become more complex and available with longer option lists, wiring diagrams have grown in size and complexity. It has become almost impossible to provide a readable reproduction of a wiring diagram in a book this size. Information on ordering wiring diagrams from the vehicle manufacturer can be found in the owner's manual.*

WIRING REPAIR

Soldering is a quick, efficient method of joining metals permanently. Everyone who has the occasion to make wiring repairs should know how to solder. Electrical connections that are soldered are far less likely to come apart and will conduct electricity much better than connections that are only "pig-tailed" together. The most popular (and preferred) method of soldering is with an electrical soldering gun. Soldering irons are available in many sizes and wattage ratings. Irons with higher wattage ratings deliver higher temperatures and recover lost heat faster. A small soldering iron rated for no more than 50 watts is recommended, especially on electrical systems where excess heat can damage the components being soldered.

There are three ingredients necessary for successful soldering; proper flux, good solder and sufficient heat. A soldering flux is necessary to clean the metal of tarnish, prepare it for soldering and to enable the solder to spread into tiny crevices. When soldering, always use a resin flux or resin core solder which is non-corrosive and will not attract moisture once the job is finished. Other types of flux (acid core) will leave a residue that will attract moisture and cause the wires to corrode. Tin is a unique metal with a low melting point. In a molten state, it dissolves and alloys easily with many metals. Solder is made by mixing tin with lead. The most common proportions are 40/60, 50/50 and 60/40, with the percentage of tin listed first. Low priced solders usually contain less tin, making them very difficult for a beginner to use because more heat is required to melt the solder. A common solder is 40/60 which is well suited for all-around general use, but 60/40 melts easier, has more tin for a better joint and is preferred for electrical work.

Soldering Techniques

Successful soldering requires that the metals to be joined be heated to a temperature that will melt the solder—usually 360–460°F (182–238°C). Contrary to popular belief, the purpose of the soldering iron is not to melt the solder itself, but to heat the parts being soldered to a temperature high enough to melt the solder when it is touched to the work. Melting flux-cored solder on the soldering iron will usually destroy the effectiveness of the flux.

NOTE: *Soldering tips are made of copper for good heat conductivity, but must be "tinned" regularly for quick transference of heat to the project and to prevent the solder from sticking to the iron. To "tin" the iron, simply heat it and touch the flux-cored solder to the tip; the solder will flow over the hot tip. Wipe the excess off with a clean rag, but be careful as the iron will be hot.*

After some use, the tip may become pitted. If so, simply dress the tip smooth with a smooth file and "tin" the tip again. An old saying holds that "metals well cleaned are half soldered." Flux-cored solder will remove oxides but rust, bits of insulation and oil or grease must be removed with a wire brush or emery cloth. For maximum strength in soldered parts, the joint must start off clean and tight. Weak joints will result in gaps too wide for the solder to bridge.

If a separate soldering flux is used, it should be brushed or swabbed on only those areas that are to be soldered. Most solders contain a core of flux and separate fluxing is unnecessary. Hold the work to be soldered firmly. It is best to solder on a wooden board, because a metal vise will only rob the piece to be soldered of heat and make it difficult to melt the solder. Hold the soldering tip with the broadest face against the work to be soldered. Apply solder under the tip close to the work, using enough solder to give a heavy film between the iron and the piece being soldered, while moving slowly and making sure the solder melts properly. Keep the work level or the solder will run to the lowest part and favor the thicker parts, because these require more heat to melt the solder. If the soldering tip overheats (the solder coating on the face of the tip burns up), it should be retinned. Once the soldering is completed, let the soldered joint stand until cool. Tape and seal all soldered wire splices after the repair has cooled.

Wire Harness and Connectors

The on-board computer (ECM) wire harness electrically connects the control unit to the various solenoids, switches and sensors used by the control system. Most connectors in the engine compartment or otherwise exposed to the elements are protected against moisture and dirt which could create oxidation and deposits on the terminals. This protection is important because of the very low voltage and current levels used by the computer and sensors. All connectors have a lock which secures the male and female terminals together, with a secondary lock

holding the seal and terminal into the connector. Both terminal locks must be released when disconnecting ECM connectors.

These special connectors are weather-proof and all repairs require the use of a special terminal and the tool required to service it. This tool is used to remove the pin and sleeve terminals. If removal is attempted with an ordinary pick, there is a good chance that the terminal will be bent or deformed. Unlike standard blade type terminals, these terminals cannot be straightened once they are bent. Make certain that the connectors are properly seated and all of the sealing rings in place when connecting leads. On some models, a hinge-type flap provides a backup or secondary locking feature for the terminals. Most secondary locks are used to improve the connector reliability by retaining the terminals if the small terminal lock tangs are not positioned properly.

Molded-on connectors require complete replacement of the connection. This means splicing a new connector assembly into the harness. All splices in on-board computer systems should be soldered to insure proper contact. Use care when probing the connections or replacing terminals in them as it is possible to short between opposite terminals. If this happens to the wrong terminal pair, it is possible to damage certain components. Always use jumper wires between connectors for circuit checking and never probe through weatherproof seals.

Open circuits are often difficult to locate by sight because corrosion or terminal misalignment are hidden by the connectors. Merely wiggling a connector on a sensor or in the wiring harness may correct the open circuit condition. This should always be considered when an open circuit or a failed sensor is indicated. Intermittent problems may also be caused by oxidized or loose connections. When using a circuit tester for diagnosis, always probe connections from the wire side. Be careful not to damage sealed connectors with test probes.

All wiring harnesses should be replaced with identical parts, using the same gauge wire and connectors. When signal wires are spliced into a harness, use wire with high temperature insulation only. With the low voltage and current levels found in the system, it is important that the best possible connection at all wire splices be made by soldering the splices together. It is seldom necessary to replace a complete harness. If replacement is necessary, pay close attention to insure proper harness routing. Secure the harness with suitable plastic wire clamps to prevent vibrations from causing the harness to wear in spots or contact any hot components.

NOTE: *Weatherproof connectors cannot be*

replaced with standard connectors. Instructions are provided with replacement connector and terminal packages. Some wire harnesses have mounting indicators (usually pieces of colored tape) to mark where the harness is to be secured.

In making wiring repairs, it's important that you always replace damaged wires with wires that are the same gauge as the wire being replaced. The heavier the wire, the smaller the gauge number. Wires are color-coded to aid in identification and whenever possible the same color coded wire should be used for replacement. A wire stripping and crimping tool is necessary to install solderless terminal connectors. Test all crimps by pulling on the wires; it should not be possible to pull the wires out of a good crimp.

Wires which are open, exposed or otherwise damaged are repaired by simple splicing. Where possible, if the wiring harness is accessible and the damaged place in the wire can be located, it is best to open the harness and check for all possible damage. In an inaccessible harness, the wire must be bypassed with a new insert, usually taped to the outside of the old harness.

When replacing fusible links, be sure to use fusible link wire, NOT ordinary automotive wire. Make sure the fusible segment is of the same gauge and construction as the one being replaced and double the stripped end when crimping the terminal connector for a good contact. The melted (open) fusible link segment of the wiring harness should be cut off as close to the harness as possible, then a new segment spliced in as described. In the case of a damaged fusible link that feeds two harness wires, the harness connections should be replaced with two fusible link wires so that each circuit will have its own separate protection.

NOTE: *Most of the problems caused in the wiring harness are due to bad ground connections. Always check all vehicle ground connections for corrosion or looseness before performing any power feed checks to eliminate the chance of a bad ground affecting the circuit.*

Repairing Hard Shell Connectors

Unlike molded connectors, the terminal contacts in hard shell connectors can be replaced. Weatherproof hard-shell connectors with the leads molded into the shell have non-replaceable terminal ends. Replacement usually involves the use of a special terminal removal tool that depress the locking tangs (barbs) on the connector terminal and allow the connector to be removed from the rear of the shell. The connector shell should be replaced if it shows any evidence of burning, melting, cracks, or breaks.

Replace individual terminals that are burnt, corroded, distorted or loose.

NOTE: *The insulation crimp must be tight to prevent the insulation from sliding back on the wire when the wire is pulled. The insulation must be visibly compressed under the crimp tabs, and the ends of the crimp should be turned in for a firm grip on the insulation.*

The wire crimp must be made with all wire strands inside the crimp. The terminal must be fully compressed on the wire strands with the ends of the crimp tabs turned in to make a firm grip on the wire. Check all connections with an ohmmeter to insure a good contact. There should be no measurable resistance between the wire and the terminal when connected.

Mechanical Test Equipment

Vacuum Gauge

Most gauges are graduated in inches of mercury (in. Hg), although a device called a manometer reads vacuum in inches of water (in. H_2O). The normal vacuum reading usually varies between 18 and 22 in. Hg at sea level. To test engine vacuum, the vacuum gauge must be connected to a source of manifold vacuum. Many engines have a plug in the intake manifold which can be removed and replaced with an adapter fitting. Connect the vacuum gauge to the fitting with a suitable rubber hose or, if no manifold plug is available, connect the vacuum gauge to any device using manifold vacuum, such as EGR valves, etc. The vacuum gauge can be used to determine if enough vacuum is reaching a component to allow its actuation.

Hand Vacuum Pump

Small, hand-held vacuum pumps come in a variety of designs. Most have a built-in vacuum gauge and allow the component to be tested without removing it from the vehicle. Operate the pump lever or plunger to apply the correct amount of vacuum required for the test specified in the diagnosis routines. The level of vacuum in inches of Mercury (in. Hg) is indicated on the pump gauge. For some testing, an additional vacuum gauge may be necessary.

Intake manifold vacuum is used to operate various systems and devices on late model vehicles. To correctly diagnose and solve problems in vacuum control systems, a vacuum source is necessary for testing. In some cases, vacuum can be taken from the intake manifold when the engine is running, but vacuum is normally provided by a hand vacuum pump. These hand vacuum pumps have a built-in vacuum gauge that allow testing while the device is still attached to the component. For some tests, an additional vacuum gauge may be used.

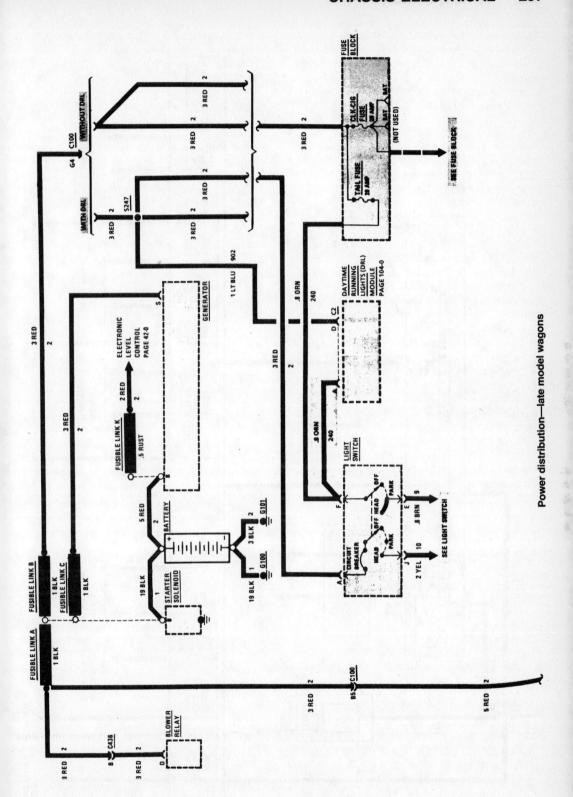

Power distribution—late model wagons

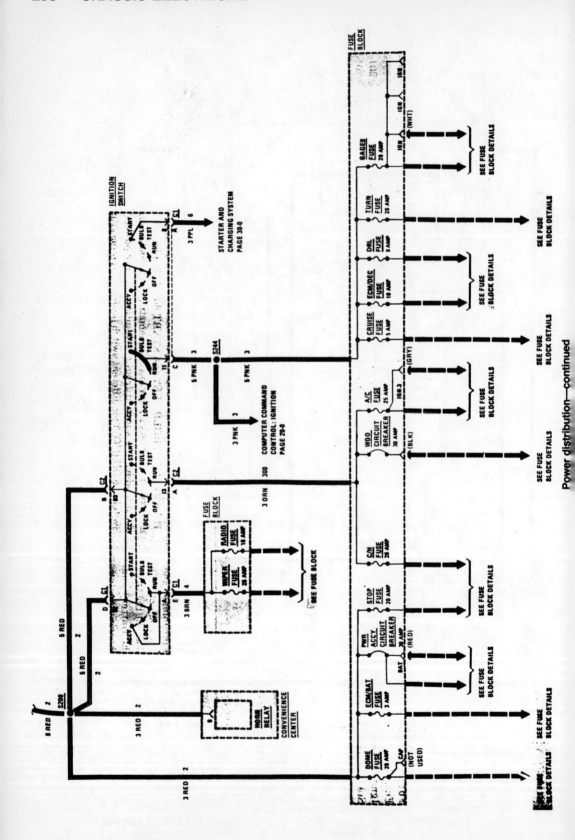

Power distribution—continued

HEATING AND AIR CONDITIONING

Blower Motor
Models without Air Conditioning

REMOVAL AND INSTALLATION

Buick 1975–76

1. Disconnect the negative (−) battery cable. Support the hood and loosen the hood hinge from the extension and plate assembly.

2. Remove the extension and plate assembly.

3. Disconnect the blower motor wire.

4. Remove the blower motor attaching screws and motor.

Oldsmobile and Pontiac 1975–76

1. Raise the front of the vehicle, support with jackstands and remove the right front wheel.

2. Cut an access hole along the stamped outline on the right fender skirt, using an air chisel or electric hand sabre saw.

3. Disconnect the blower power wire.

4. Remove the blower.

To install:

5. Install the blower with the fan, tighten the mounting screws, connect the motor wiring and covering the access hole with a metal plate se-

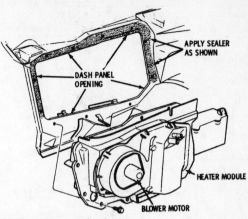

Sealing the heater module

cured with sealer and sheet metal screws if a hole was cut.

6. Connect the negative battery cable and check for proper operation.

All Models 1977 and Later

1. Disconnect the negative (−) battery cable, the blower motor feed wire and the ground wire.

2. Remove the blower motor retaining screws and remove the motor.

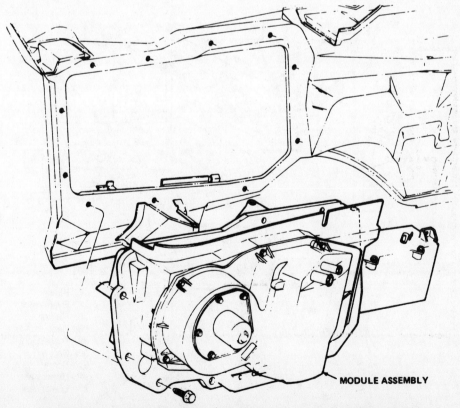

Blower motor and housing, 1977 and later Electra and LeSabre. Others similar

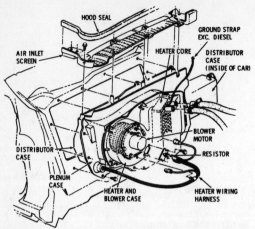

Heater module mounting, 88. Others similar

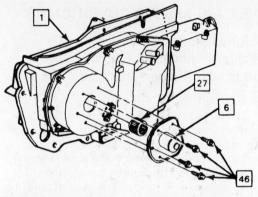

Heater module and blower motor—late model "B" body wagon without A/C

Blower Motor
Models with Air Conditioning
REMOVAL AND INSTALLATION
All Models 1975–76

To install:

3. Use sealer as needed to make a watertight seal, position the motor/fan into the heater module, tighten the mounting screws, connect the motor wiring and negative battery cable and check for proper operation.

This procedure is the same as that for non-air conditioned vehicles.

NOTE: *This procedure does not apply to those models with the A.C.R.S. (air bag) system. For those models with air bags, it is ad-*

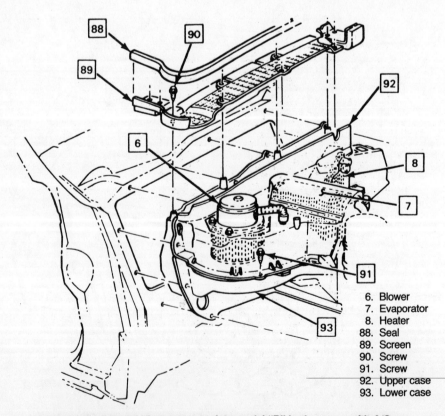

6. Blower
7. Evaporator
8. Heater
88. Seal
89. Screen
90. Screw
91. Screw
92. Upper case
93. Lower case

Heater module and blower motor—late model "B" body wagon with A/C

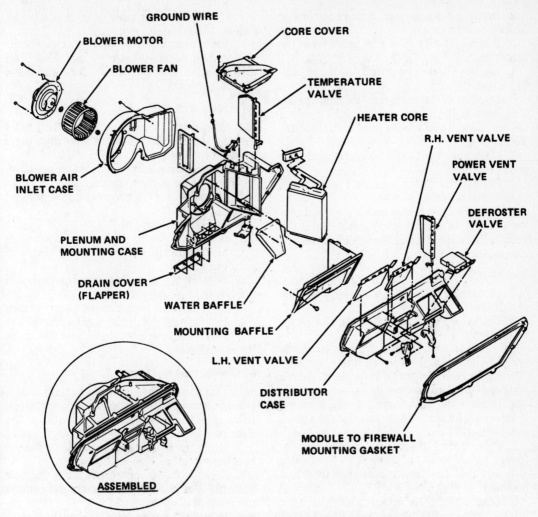

GROUND WIRE

BLOWER MOTOR

CORE COVER

BLOWER FAN

TEMPERATURE
VALVE

HEATER CORE

R.H. VENT VALVE

POWER VENT
VALVE

BLOWER AIR
INLET CASE

DEFROSTER
VALVE

PLENUM AND
MOUNTING CASE

DRAIN COVER
(FLAPPER)

WATER BAFFLE

MOUNTING BAFFLE

L.H. VENT VALVE

DISTRIBUTOR
CASE

MODULE TO FIREWALL
MOUNTING GASKET

ASSEMBLED

1982 Bonneville heater module, exploded view showing heater core

visable to take the vehicle to a dealer for proper servicing.

All Models 1977 and Later

The blower motor is mounted in the upper evaporator and blower case by 6 screws (7 with noise suppressor). Disconnect the electrical connectors and remove the screws. Lift the blower straight up and out.

Heater Core
Models without Air Conditioning
REMOVAL AND INSTALLATION
Buick 1975–76

1. Disconnect the negative (−) battery cable. Drain the radiator and disconnect the heater inlet and outlet hoses at the dash. Be careful not to damage the heater core if the hoses are stuck onto the core.

2. Disconnect the control wires from the de-

froster door and vacuum hose diverter door actuator, and the control cable from the temperature door lever.

3. Remove the 4 nuts securing the heater assembly to the firewall.

4. Remove the screw securing the defroster outlet tab to the heater assembly.

5. Remove the heater from the vehicle.

To install:

6. Make sure the heater assembly seal is in good condition.

7. Position the assembly onto the dash and tighten the retaining screws.

8. Reconnect the heater hoses, electrical connectors and negative battery cable. Refill the engine with coolant, start the vehicle and check for coolant leaks.

Oldsmobile 1975–76

1. Disconnect the negative battery cable and remove the four nuts holding the heater case to the dash panel.

2. Drain the radiator and remove the heater hoses from the case.

3. Disconnect all cables and hoses from the heater case.

4. Remove the defroster duct-to-case attaching screw.

5. Disconnect the lower right side trim panel.

6. Remove the heater case from the inside of the vehicle and remove the core from the case.

To install:

7. Make sure the heater assembly seal is in good condition.

8. Position the assembly onto the dash and tighten the retaining screws.

9. Reconnect the heater hoses, electrical connectors and negative battery cable. Refill the engine with coolant, start the vehicle and check for coolant leaks.

Pontiac 1975–76

1. Disconnect the negative (−) battery cable and drain the radiator.

2. Disconnect the heater hoses at the air inlet assembly.

NOTE: *The water pump hose goes to the right hand heater core pipe, the other hose (from the rear of right cylinder head) goes to the left hand heater core pipe.*

3. Remove the nuts from the core studs on the firewall, under the hood. Remove the glove compartment.

4. From inside the vehicle, remove the defroster nozzle retaining screw from the heater case and pull the heater assembly from the firewall.

5. Disconnect the control cables, vacuum hoses and wires, then remove the heater assembly.

6. Remove the core.

To install:

7. Make sure the heater assembly seal is in good condition.

8. Position the assembly onto the dash and tighten the retaining screws.

9. Reconnect the heater hoses, electrical connectors and negative battery cable. Refill the engine with coolant, start the vehicle and check for coolant leaks.

All Models 1977–81

1. Disconnect the negative (−) battery cable and drain the cooling system.

2. Remove the heater hoses from the core tubes.

3. Disconnect the electrical connections.

4. Remove the front module cover screws, and remove the module assembly.

5. Remove the heater core from the module.

To install:

6. Make sure the heater assembly seal is in good condition.

7. Position the assembly onto the dash and tighten the retaining screws.

8. Reconnect the heater hoses, electrical connectors and negative battery cable. Refill the engine with coolant, start the vehicle and check for coolant leaks.

All Models 1982–83

1. Disconnect the negative (−) battery cable and the Hoses from the core tubes. Plug them to avoid coolant loss.

2. On the engine side of the firewall, remove the heater core cover from the case.

3. Remove the core bracket and ground screw.

4. Lift out the core.

To install:

5. Make sure the heater assembly seal is in good condition.

6. Position the assembly onto the dash and tighten the retaining screws.

7. Reconnect the heater hoses, electrical connectors and negative battery cable. Refill the engine with coolant, start the vehicle and check for coolant leaks.

All Models 1984 and Later

1. Disconnect the negative battery cable, heater blower resistor wires and blower wires. Disconnect the heater core ground strap at the dash panel.

2. Drain the cooling system and then disconnect both heater hoses at the heater.

3. Remove the seven screws attaching the heater/blower case to the plenum and remove the heater/blower base.

4. Remove the four screws from the heater core shroud, and then remove the shroud and core assembly.

5. Separate the core from the shroud by removing the three screws and core mounting clamps and then separating the two.

To install:

6. Using sealer as necessary to prevent leaks at all joints and flanges.

7. Position the assembly onto the dash and tighten the retaining screws.

8. Reconnect the heater hoses, electrical connectors and negative battery cable. Refill the engine with coolant, start the vehicle and check for coolant leaks.

Heater Core
Models with Air Conditioning
REMOVAL AND INSTALLATION
Buick 1975–76

NOTE: *See the above Note concerning vehicles equipped with the air bag system.*

1. Disconnect the negative (−) battery cable,

drain the radiator and disconnect the hoses from the core.

2. Disconnect the wires from the defroster door, diverter door and temperature door.

3. Remove the four nuts securing the core assembly to the dash.

4. Remove the screw securing the defroster outlet tab to the heater assembly.

5. Remove the core assembly.

To install:

6. Using sealer as necessary to prevent leaks at all joints and flanges.

7. Position the assembly onto the dash and tighten the retaining screws.

8. Reconnect the heater hoses, electrical connectors and negative battery cable. Refill the engine with coolant, start the vehicle and check for coolant leaks.

Oldsmobile 1975–76

1. Disconnect the negative (−) battery cable and drain the radiator.

2. Remove the heater case securing nuts. Disconnect the heater hoses.

3. Remove the instrument panel trim pad.

4. Remove the heater case-to-firewall bolts from inside the vehicle.

5. Remove the bottom air duct.

6. Remove the instrument panel crash pad. Unfasten the leads from the clock and glovebox light.

7. Remove the upper right hand trim panel.

8. Separate the air distribution manifold and defroster duct from the heater case.

9. Remove the lower dash trim panel.

10. Lift out the heater case and disconnect the hoses and cables from it.

11. Remove the core from the case.

To install:

1. Install the core into the case.

2. Connect the hoses and cables to the case.

3. Install the lower dash trim panel.

4. Connect the air distribution manifold and defroster duct to the heater case.

5. Install the upper right hand trim panel.

6. Install the instrument panel crash pad. Connect the leads from the clock and glovebox light.

7. Install the bottom air duct.

8. Install the heater case-to-firewall bolts from inside the vehicle.

9. Install the instrument panel trim pad.

10. Install the heater case securing nuts. Connect the heater hoses.

11. Refill the radiator, connect the negative battery cable and check for leaks.

Pontiac 1975–76

1. Disconnect the negative (−) battery cable and drain the coolant.

2. Disconnect the hoses from the heater core. Plug the tubes to prevent damage to the carpeting on removal.

3. Remove the three nuts and one screw holding the core and case assembly in place.

4. Remove the glove box and upper and lower instrument panel trim plates.

5. Remove the radio.

6. Remove the cold air duct.

7. Remove the heater outlet duct.

8. Remove the screw holding the defroster duct to the heater case.

9. Disconnect the vacuum hoses from the diaphragm, and the air conditioner temperature cable at the heater case.

10. Remove the core from the case, after removing the 3 retaining screws.

To install:

1. Install the core into the case and tighten the 3 retaining screws.

2. Connect the vacuum hoses to the diaphragm, and the air conditioner temperature cable to the heater case.

3. Install the screw holding the defroster duct to the heater case.

4. Install the heater outlet duct.

5. Install the cold air duct.

6. Install the radio.

7. Install the glove box and upper and lower instrument panel trim plates.

8. Install the three nuts and one screw holding the core and case assembly in place.

9. Connect the hoses to the heater core.

10. Connect the negative (−) battery cable and refill the coolant.

11. Start the engine and check for leaks.

Buick 1977 and Later

1. Disconnect the battery ground cable. Drain the coolant, and disconnect the heater hoses at the firewall.

2. Disconnect the electrical connections. Remove the diagnostic connector.

3. Remove the thermostatic switch from the heater/air conditioner module cover.

4. Remove the weather seal on top of the module cover.

5. Remove the cowl screen and windshield washer nozzle.

6. Remove the screws and take off the module cover. Remove the core retaining clip, twist the heater core and pull it up and out.

To install:

1. Be sure to reseal the module cover.

2. Install the heater core, core retaining clips and module cover.

3. Install the cowl screen and windshield washer nozzle.

4. Install the weather seal on top of the module cover.

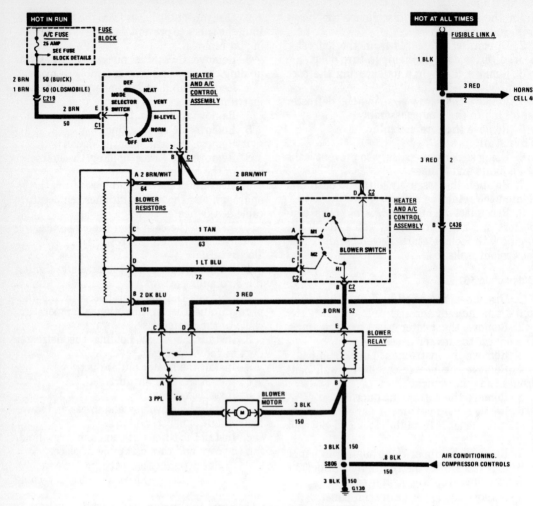

A/C and heater wiring—late model wagons

5. Install the thermostatic switch to the heater/air conditioner module cover.

6. Connect the electrical connections and install the diagnostic connector.

7. Connect the battery ground cable, refill the coolant and connect the heater hoses at the firewall.

8. Start the engine and check for leaks.

Oldsmobile 1977 and Later

1. Disconnect the battery ground. Disconnect the blower wiring.

2. On 1983 and earlier vehicles, remove the thermostatic switch and diagnostic connector.

3. Remove the right end of the hood seal and the air inlet screen screws.

4. Remove the 5 case-to-firewall screws at the top, the 9 upper case-to-lower case screws at the flange and two more at the plenum.

5. Lift the upper case straight up and off. Remove the pipe bracket screws from the case. Disconnect the hoses and position them to prevent spillage.

6. Disconnect and lift out the heater core.

To install:

1. Be sure to reseal the module cover.

2. Install the heater core into the module.

3. Lower the upper case straight down. Install the pipe bracket screws to the case. Connect the hoses.

4. Install and tighten the 5 case-to-firewall screws at the top, the 9 upper case-to-lower case screws at the flange and two more at the plenum.

5. Install the right end of the hood seal and the air inlet screen screws.

6. On 1983 and earlier vehicles, install the thermostatic switch and diagnostic connector.

7. Connect the battery ground and blower wiring.

8. Start the engine and check for leaks.

Pontiac 1977 to 1981

1. Disconnect the negative (−) battery cable and drain the cooling system.

2. Disconnect the heater hoses.

3. Remove the retaining bracket and the ground strap. Disconnect the module rubber seal and module screen.

4. Remove the right windshield wiper arm.

5. Remove the diaphragm connections, the hi/blower relay, the thermal switch mounting screws, and all the electrical connections from the module top.

6. Remove the module top cover and remove the core.

To install:

1. Apply a strip of caulk-type sealer when installing the module top.

2. Install the core and module top cover.

3. Install the diaphragm connections, the hi/blower relay, the thermal switch mounting screws, and all the electrical connections to the module top.

4. Install the right windshield wiper arm.

5. Install the retaining bracket and the ground strap. Connect the module rubber seal and module screen.

6. Connect the heater hoses.

7. Connect the negative (−) battery cable and refill the cooling system.

8. Start the engine and check for coolant and vacuum leaks.

Pontiac 1982 and Later

1. Operate the wipers to the up position.

2. Disconnect the hoses at the core tubes. Remove the sealing material and screens from the cooling modules.

3. Disconnect all wires from the case. Move the lower windshield reverse molding out of the way.

4. Tape a strip of wood to the lower edge of the glass for protection. Remove the module core cover screws.

5. Cut the cover seal with a knife. Pry the cover off from the side, NOT from the top.

6. Lift out the core.

To install:

1. Apply a strip of caulk-type sealer when installing the module top.

2. Position the core into the module.

3. Install the cover and tighten the mounting screws.

4. Connect all wires to the case. Install the lower windshield reverse molding.

5. Connect the hoses to the core tubes. Install the sealing material and screens to the cooling modules.

6. Connect the negative (−) battery cable and refill the cooling system.

7. Start the engine and check for coolant and vacuum leaks.

Control Head

REMOVAL AND INSTALLATION

With or Without Air Conditioning

1. Disconnect the negative battery cable.

2. Remove the center instrument panel trim. On some models, screws for this panel are covered by the left and right panel trims. If screws are hidden, first remove those panels on either side of the center panel; then remove the center panel.

3. Slide all controls all the way to the left.

NOTE: *Mark the routing of each cable to each damper lever. Then, unscrew the cable clip attaching screws from the heater case until the cable housing can be freed and the cable can be unhooked from the damper lever; then, free the cable and unhook the damper.*

4. Remove the screws from the control face. Then, pull the face outward until you can gain access to the electrical and/or vacuum connectors. Disconnect all electrical and vacuum connections. Remove the control head, pulling the cables out through the hole in the dash.

To install:

1. Feed the cables through the hole in the dash and locate the head so the vacuum and electrical connections can be made. Connect vacuum and/or electrical connectors.

2. Install the mounting screws for the head. Then, connect the cables. Adjust each so that its damper is forced all the way closed or open, depending on its position.

3. Install the trim panels and moldings in reverse order of their removal.

Air Conditioner Evaporator Core

REMOVAL AND INSTALLATION

Do NOT service the air conditioning system unless you are equipped with the necessary tools and training. The refrigerant, R-12, is extremely cold when compressed, and when released into the air will instantly freeze any surface it contacts, including your eyes. Although the refrigerant is normally non-toxic, R-12 becomes a deadly poisonous gas in the presence of an open flame. One good whiff of the vapors from burning refrigerant can be fatal.

CAUTION: *The refrigerant gas (R-12) is an extremely cold substance. When exposed to air, it will instantly freeze any surface it comes in contact with, including your eyes. The other hazard relates to fire. Although normally nontoxic, the R-12 gas becomes highly poisonous in the presence of an open flame. One good whiff of the vapor formed by burning R-12 can be fatal. Keep all forms of*

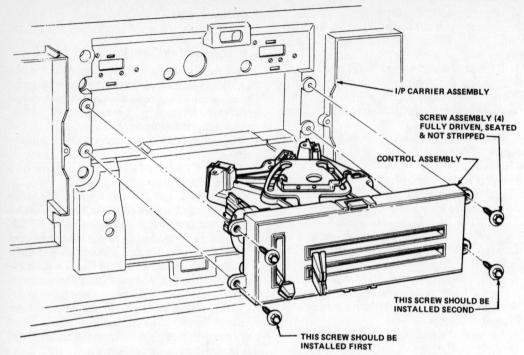

I/P CARRIER ASSEMBLY

SCREW ASSEMBLY (4)
FULLY DRIVEN, SEATED
& NOT STRIPPED

CONTROL ASSEMBLY

THIS SCREW SHOULD BE
INSTALLED SECOND

THIS SCREW SHOULD BE
INSTALLED FIRST

Removal and installation of the heater or heater/A/C control head—typical

A. Retainer clip
B. Pin
2. Control assembly
8. Defroster control
    cable
9. Vent control cable
10. Temperature control cable
16. Blower switch
17. Rear defogger switch
22. Retainer
23. Mode lever
39. Screw
40. Nut

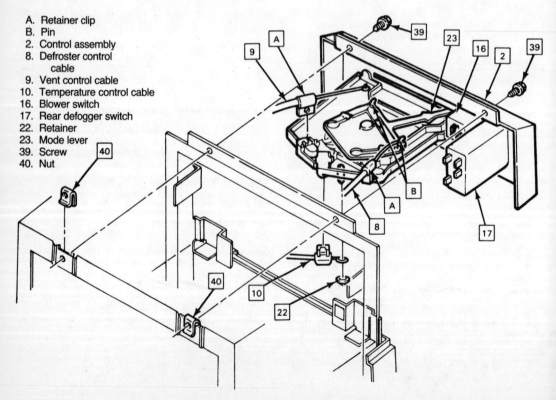

Heater and A/C control cables—typical

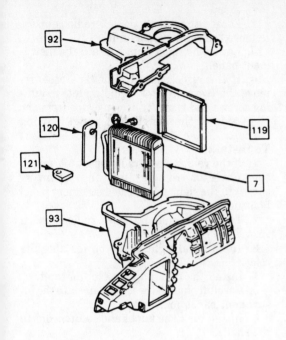

A/C evaporator core—typical

fire (including cigarettes) well clear of the air conditioning system.

1. Disconnect the negative (−) battery cable.

2. Discharge the air conditioning system and recover the refrigerant as outlined in the Air Conditioning section in Chapter 1.

3. Disconnect the evaporator inlet and outlet pipe using a backup and a flare nut wrench. Seal the openings of the accumulator (large aluminum can) and evaporator to prevent moisture and contamination from entering the system.

4. Remove the expansion (orifice) tube from the liquid line of the evaporator as outlined in the "Orifice Tube" section in Chapter 1.

5. Remove the air conditioner module upper case as outlined in this chapter.

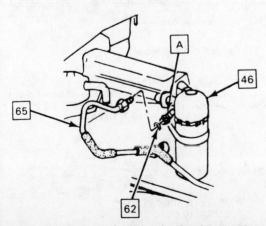

Orifice (expansion) tube location—CCOT systems

6. Remove the evaporator clamp and evaporator by pulling the assembly straight up and out of the module lower case.

To install:

1. Install the evaporator and seals into the lower case. Make sure the seals and evaporator are properly positioned after the evaporator is in place.

2. Install the evaporator clamp.

3. Install the module upper case with a quality sealer.

4. Install the expansion (orifice) tube into the liquid line of the evaporator.

5. Add 3 fluid oz. (90 ml) of 525 viscosity air conditioning oil if a new evaporator is being installed or the oil was removed from the old unit.

6. Install new O-rings and torque the inlet and outlet fittings to the accumulator using a backup and flarenut wrench. Torque steel fittings to 32 ft. lbs. (44 Nm) and aluminum or copper fittings to 24 ft. lbs. (33 Nm).

7. Evacuate and recharge the air conditioning system as outlined in Chapter 1.

8. Connect the negative battery cable and test the system performance.

RADIO

The antenna trim must be adjusted on AM radios when major repair has been done to the unit or the antenna changed. The trimmer screw is located behind the right side knob. Raise the antenna to its full height. Tune to a weak station around 1400 on the dial, and turn the volume down until barely audible. Turn the trimmer screw until the maximum volume is achieved.

REMOVAL AND INSTALLATION

Buick Except with Air Bags 1975–76

1. Disconnect the negative (−) battery cable.

2. Remove the knobs from the radio. If equipped with Trip-Set and/or Speed Alert, remove the cone shaped knobs.

3. Remove the face plate by pulling outward. Disconnect the terminal connector before completely removing the face plate, if equipped with Trip-Set/Speed-Alert.

Adjusting antenna trim

4. Remove the two hex nuts from the control shafts.

5. Remove the ash tray and frame.

6. Disconnect the two connectors behind the dash and unplug the antenna.

7. Unscrew the support bracket nuts and remove the radio to the rear and downward.

To install:

1. Install the radio part way.

2. Connect the two connectors behind the dash and connect the antenna.

3. Tighten the retaining nuts and install the ash tray and frame.

4. Install the two hex nuts to the control shafts.

5. Connect the terminal connector before completely installing the face plate, if equipped with Trip-Set/Speed-Alert. Install the face plate.

6. Install the knobs to the radio. If equipped with Trip-Set and/or Speed Alert, install the cone shaped knobs.

7. Connect the negative (−) battery cable and check operation.

Buick with Air Bags 1975–76

1. Turn the ignition lock to the LOCK position.

2. Disconnect the battery ground cable and tape its end thoroughly to prevent any possibility of a short circuit.

3. Remove both lower instrument panel cover trim plates after prying them out.

4. Disconnect the parking brake release cable and remove the lower left instrument panel cover assembly by removing the 8 retaining screws.

5. Remove:

    a. 2 horizontal screws below the instrument panel.

    b. 4 vertical screws on the upper horizontal instrument panel surface.

    c. 2 screws from the outside of the glove box door hinge.

    d. 1 screw from the right side of the instrument panel cover.

6. Disconnect the radio, speakers, convector (remove unit) connectors, and antenna lead cable from the radio.

7. Release the 4 clips behind the instrument panel by grasping the tongue of the far right side clip, squeezing, and pulling forward.

8. Remove the radio knobs and escutcheons from the shafts.

9. Carefully pull the trim plate off the instrument panel housing.

10. Remove the retaining nuts from the shaft.

11. Unscrew and remove the power antenna relay.

12. Loosen the nut on the left radio support. Remove the right support nut.

13. Lower the radio from beneath the instrument panel.

14. If the vehicle has a radio/tape unit, remove the two convector (remote unit) mounting screws and remove the convector from the right side of the instrument panel housing support.

To install:

1. If the vehicle has a radio/tape unit, install the convector (remote unit) and mounting screws to the right side of the instrument panel housing support.

2. Tighten the nut on the left radio support. Install the right support nut.

3. Install and tighten the power antenna relay.

4. Install the retaining nuts to the shaft.

5. Carefully install the trim plate onto the instrument panel housing.

6. Install the radio knobs and escutcheons to the shafts.

7. Connect the radio, speakers, convector (remove unit) connectors, and antenna lead cable to the radio.

8. Install the screws that were removed in step 5.

9. Connect the parking brake release cable and install the lower left instrument panel cover assembly by installing the 8 retaining screws.

10. Install both lower instrument panel cover trim plates.

11. Connect the negative (−) battery cable.

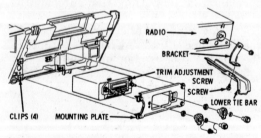

Typical radio installation

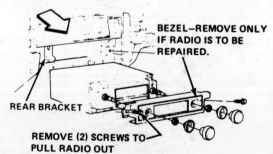

1978 and later Pontiac radio removal

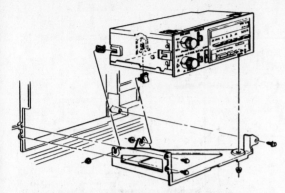

Radio removal & installation—1984–90 Buick

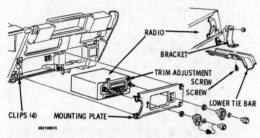

Radio removal & installation—1983–84 Oldsmobile

Turn the ignition lock to the ON position and check operation.

Buick 1977–83

1. Disconnect the battery ground cable.
2. Remove the ashtray and bracket.
3. Pull off the radio knobs and trim washers.
4. Remove the lower left air duct.
5. Remove the two retaining nuts from the control shafts.
6. Unplug the power lead, speaker wire, and antenna lead.
7. Remove the rear radio mounting nut and radio.

NOTE: *On 1981 and later models, remove the headlight switch and place the gear shift lever in the lowest position to remove the left hand instrument panel.*

To install:

1. Install the radio and rear mounting nut.
2. Connect the power lead, speaker wire, and antenna lead.
3. Install the two retaining nuts to the control shafts.
4. Install the lower left air duct.
5. Push on the radio knobs and trim washers.
6. Install the ashtray and bracket.
7. Connect the battery ground cable.

NOTE: *On 1981 and later models, install the headlight switch, place the gear shift lever in the lowest position and install the left hand instrument panel.*

Buick 1984

1. Remove the center trim plate. Remove the three main mounting screws.
2. Pull the radio out far enough to disconnect the three electrical connectors, antenna lead, and clock connector (if equipped). Then, remove the radio.
3. Install in reverse order.

Buick 1985–90

1. Disconnect the negative battery cable. Remove the center trim cover from the dash.
2. Remove the four screws that attach the front panel of the radio to the dash panel. Then, slide the radio out just far enough to gain access to all the connectors.
3. Disconnect the three electrical connectors. Unscrew and disconnect the antenna lead.
4. If the vehicle is equipped with a clock, unscrew and remove the glovebox and disconnect its lead through the glovebox opening.
5. Pull the radio out straight, to avoid snagging any protrusions on the dash panel.

To install:

1. Install the radio in straight, avoid snagging any protrusions on the dash panel.
2. If the vehicle is equipped with a clock, install and screw the glovebox and connect its lead through the glovebox opening.

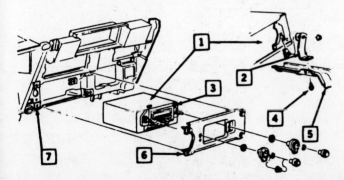

1. Radio unit
2. Mounting bracket
3. Trim adjustment screw
4. Tie bar mounting screw
5. Lower tie bar
6. Mounting plate
7. Mounting plate attaching nuts and bolts

Radio removal & installation—1985–90 Oldsmobile

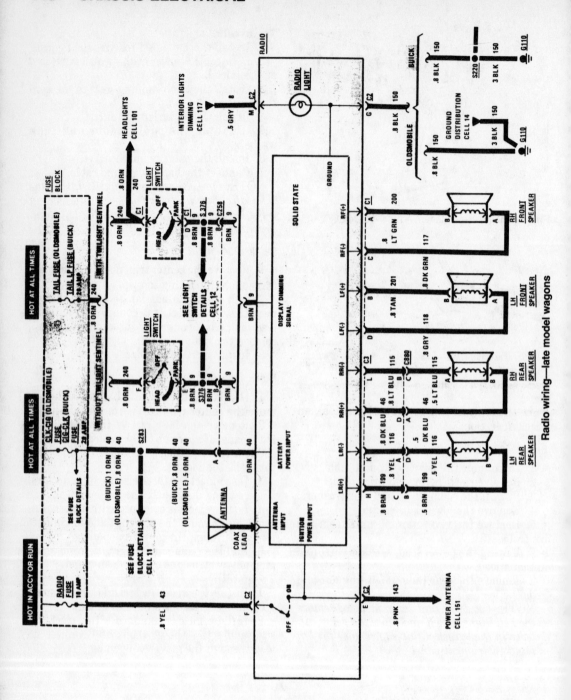

Radio wiring—late model wagons

3. Connect the three electrical connectors and antenna lead.

4. Install the four screws that attach the front panel of the radio to the dash panel.

5. Connect the negative battery cable. Install the center trim cover to the dash.

Oldsmobile 1975–76

1. Disconnect the negative battery cable.

2. Remove the lower trim pad.

3. Disconnect the wiring and the antenna lead.

4. Remove the support bracket-to-tie bar attaching screw.

5. Remove the knobs from the radio. Remove the two radio-to-instrument cluster attaching nuts.

6. Remove the radio from behind the instrument cluster.

To install:

1. Install the radio from behind the instrument cluster.

2. Install the two radio-to-instrument cluster attaching nuts and the knobs onto the radio.

3. Install the support bracket-to-tie bar attaching screw.

4. Connect the wiring and the antenna lead.

5. Install the lower trim pad.

6. Connect the negative battery cable and check operation.

Oldsmobile 1977–82

1. Disconnect the negative battery cable.

2. Remove the knobs from the radio and pull out the cigarette lighter.

3. Remove the two trim cover attaching screws and remove the cover.

4. Remove the radio bracket attaching screw from the lower tie bar.

5. Remove the four mounting plate screws and pull the radio out to obtain access to the electrical connections. Detach the wiring harness and the antenna lead.

6. Remove the mounting plate nuts and remove the radio.

To install:

1. Install the radio and mounting plate nuts.

2. Obtain access to the electrical connections and attach the wiring harness and the antenna lead. Install the four mounting plate screws.

3. Install the radio bracket attaching screw to the lower tie bar.

4. Install the trim cover and attaching screws.

5. Install the knobs onto the radio and push in the cigarette lighter.

6. Connect the negative battery cable and check operation.

1983–84 Oldsmobile

1. Disconnect the negative (–) battery cable.

2. Remove the right side trim panel. Then, remove the four screws and two nuts attaching the mounting plate to the cluster carrier and radio controls. Remove the mounting plate.

3. Remove the ash tray. Remove the left side sound absorber, if so equipped.

4. Remove the screw attaching the lower center air duct to the lower trim panel, and then remove the duct.

5. Remove the nut that attaches the radio support bracket to the radio.

6. Pull the radio to the rear and disconnect all electrical wiring and the antenna lead. Remove the radio.

To install:

1. Install the radio from the rear and connect all electrical wiring and the antenna lead.

2. Install the nut that attaches the radio support bracket to the radio.

3. Install the duct and screw attaching the lower center air duct to the lower trim panel.

4. Install the ash tray. Install the left side sound absorber, if so equipped.

5. Install the right side trim panel and four screws and two nuts attaching the mounting plate to the cluster carrier and radio controls.

6. Connect the negative battery cable and check operation.

1985–87 Oldsmobile

1. Disconnect the negative (–) battery cable. Remove the right hand trim panel.

2. Remove the screws (and nuts on two of them) that attach the mounting plate to the cluster carrier and radio controls. Then, remove the mounting plate.

3. Slide the ashtray out of the dash panel. Remove the sound absorber located on the left side of the dash.

4. Remove the mounting screw for the lower/center air duct and remove the duct.

5. Remove the nut attaching the lower center support bracket to the body of the radio. Then, pull the radio out just far enough to gain access to all wiring.

6. Disconnect the wiring and the antenna lead. Then, remove the radio.

To install:

1. Install the radio and connect the wiring leads.

2. Install the nut attaching the lower center support bracket to the body of the radio.

3. Install the duct and mounting screw for the lower/center air duct.

4. Slide the ashtray into the dash panel. Install the sound absorber located on the left side of the dash.

5. Install the screws (and nuts on two of them) that attach the mounting plate to the cluster carrier and radio controls. Then, Install the mounting plate.

6. Install the right hand trim panel. Connect the negative (–) battery cable and check operation.

Pontiac 1975–76

1. Disconnect the negative battery terminal, then remove the radio knobs and hex nuts.

2. Remove the upper and lower instrument panel trim plates and the lower front radio bracket.

3. Remove the glove box and disconnect the radio connections.

4. Loosen the side brace screw and slide the radio toward the front seat.

5. To install, reverse the removal procedure.

1977–81 Pontiac

1. Disconnect the negative battery terminal.

2. Remove the upper trimplate. Remove the radio trimplate by removing the two top screws, the ashtray assembly, disconnecting the lighter, and removing the ashtray bracket.

3. Remove the two radio screws.

4. Remove the radio through the instrument panel and detach all connectors.

5. Reverse the procedure for installation.

1982–84 Pontiac

1. Disconnect the battery.

2. Remove the radio knobs and bezels.

3. Remove the upper and lower instrument panel trim plates.

4. Remove the four front radio retaining screws.

5. Open the glove box door and lower by releasing the spring clip. Pull the radio out after loosening the rear right side nut. Disconnect all wiring and remove the radio.

6. To install, reverse the removal procedure. If the radio is to be replaced, remove the bushing from the rear of the radio and install it on the replacement radio.

1985–90 Pontiac

1. Disconnect the battery negative cable. Pull the control knobs off the radio shafts.

2. Remove its three mounting screws and then remove the radio trim plate. Remove the two screws and lower mounting nut securing the radio mounting bracket to the instrument panel.

3. Pull the unit out of the dash just far enough to gain access to all connectors. Then, disconnect the electrical connectors and unscrew and disconnect the antenna lead.

4. Remove the radio from the dash with the mounting bracket attached to it. If the radio is being replaced with a new unit, transfer the bracket to it.

To install:

1. Install the radio into the dash with the mounting bracket attached to it and connect the electrical connectors. If the radio is being replaced with a new unit, transfer the bracket to it.

2. Install the three mounting screws and the radio trim plate. Install the two screws and lower mounting nut securing the radio mounting bracket to the instrument panel.

3. Connect the battery negative cable. Push the control knobs onto the radio shafts and check operation.

WINDSHIELD WIPERS

Blade and Arm
REMOVAL AND INSTALLATION

1. On some models, it is necessary to raise the hood to gain access to the arm.

2. To remove the arm, pry underneath the arm with a suitable wiper arm removing tool. Be careful not to scratch the paint.

3. To install, position the arm over the shaft and press down. Make sure you install the arms in the same position on the windshield as they were when they were removed.

4. There are several different types of wiper blades. Most simply slide out of the arm assembly after the release is pressed. See Chapter 1 for wiper blade replacement.

Wiper Motor
REMOVAL AND INSTALLATION

The wiper motor is typically mounted on the driver's side of the cowl, accessible from the engine compartment. Once the hood is opened,

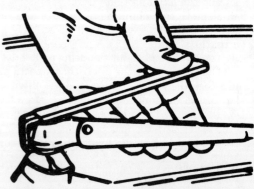

Removing the wiper arm using special wiper arm tool

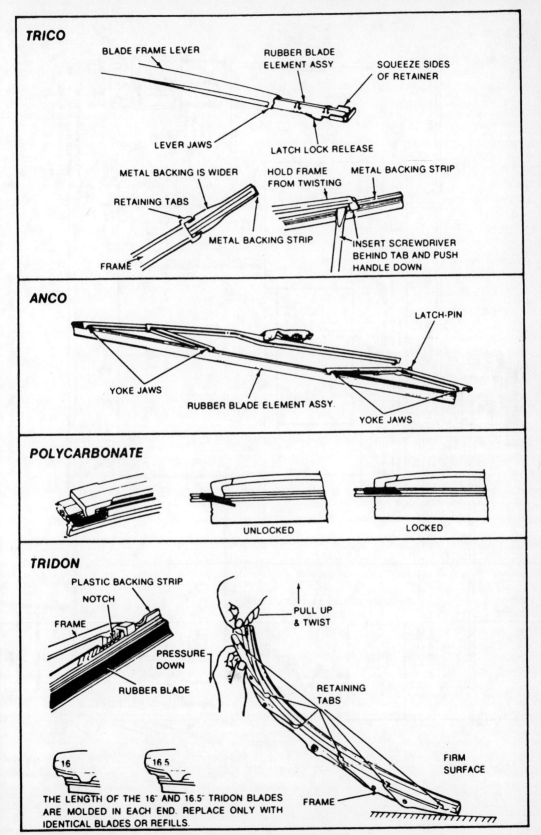

TRICO

BLADE FRAME LEVER

RUBBER BLADE
ELEMENT ASSY

SQUEEZE SIDES
OF RETAINER

LEVER JAWS

LATCH LOCK RELEASE

METAL BACKING IS WIDER

HOLD FRAME
FROM TWISTING

METAL BACKING STRIP

RETAINING TABS

METAL BACKING STRIP

FRAME

INSERT SCREWDRIVER
BEHIND TAB AND PUSH
HANDLE DOWN

ANCO

LATCH-PIN

YOKE JAWS

RUBBER BLADE ELEMENT ASSY.

YOKE JAWS

POLYCARBONATE

UNLOCKED

LOCKED

TRIDON

PLASTIC BACKING STRIP

NOTCH

FRAME

PULL UP
& TWIST

PRESSURE
DOWN

RUBBER BLADE

RETAINING
TABS

16

16.5

THE LENGTH OF THE 16" AND 16.5" TRIDON BLADES
ARE MOLDED IN EACH END. REPLACE ONLY WITH
IDENTICAL BLADES OR REFILLS.

FIRM
SURFACE

FRAME

Wiper insert replacement

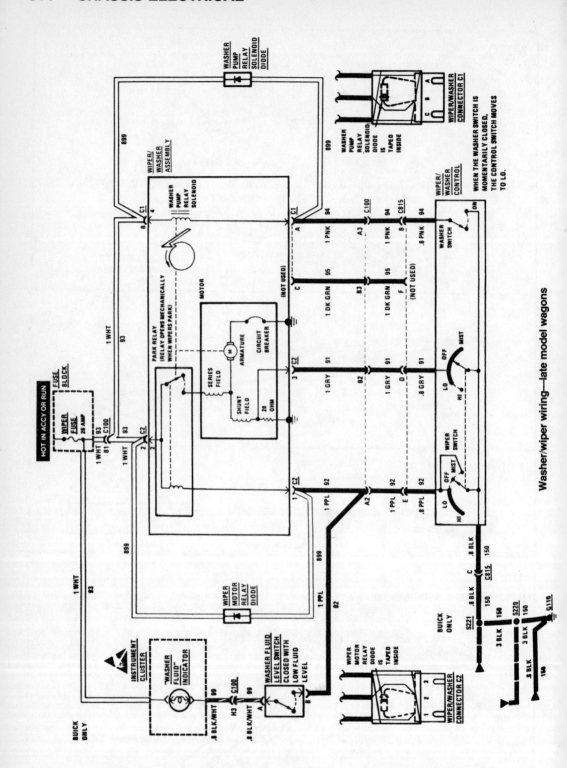

Washer/wiper wiring—late model wagons

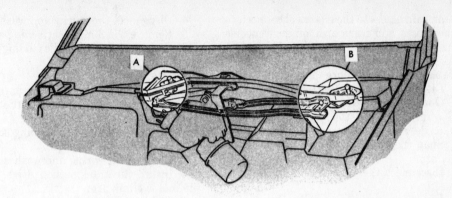

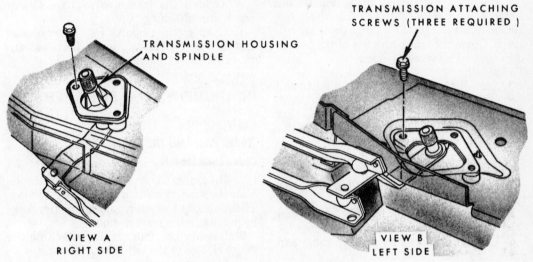

TRANSMISSION HOUSING
AND SPINDLE

TRANSMISSION ATTACHING
SCREWS (THREE REQUIRED)

VIEW A
RIGHT SIDE

VIEW B
LEFT SIDE

Typical wiper transmission installation

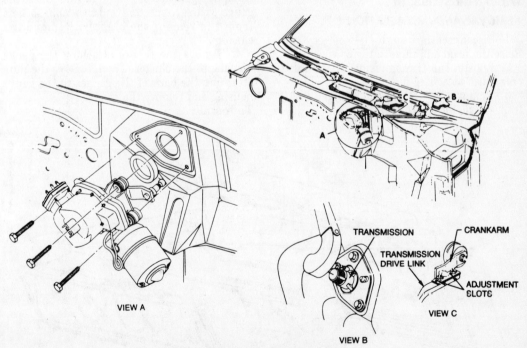

VIEW A

TRANSMISSION

CRANKARM

TRANSMISSION
DRIVE LINK

ADJUSTMENT
SLOTS

VIEW C

VIEW B

Wiper motor installation, typical

you can gain access to the electrical connectors, washer hoses, and crank arm, on most models. On a few models, these items may be located under the cowl screen. If necessary, you can remove this screen easily once the hood is opened.

1. Disconnect the negative (−) battery cable.
2. Open the hood. If necessary, remove the cowl screen. Remove the driver's side wiper arm, as described above.
3. Snap the wiper drive link off the motor crank arm.
4. Disconnect the hoses and the electrical connector.
5. Remove the attaching bolts. Remove the motor, being careful that the rubber bushings remain in the slots of the motor base or are collected. Guide the crank arm out of the hole in the cowl and remove the motor.

To install:

1. Install the motor, attaching bolts and torque to 15 ft. lbs. (20 Nm). Guide the crank arm into the hole in the cowl. Be careful that the rubber bushings remain in the slots of the motor base.
2. Connect the hoses and the electrical connector.
3. Snap the wiper drive link onto the motor crank arm.
4. If removed, install the cowl screen and driver's side wiper arm, as described above.
5. Connect the negative battery cable and check for proper operation.

Wiper Transmission

REMOVAL AND INSTALLATION

1. Disconnect the negative (−) battery cable. Raise the hood and remove the cowl screen.
2. Loosen the transmission drive link to crank arm attaching nuts.
3. Remove the transmission drive link(s) from the motor crank arm.

4. Disconnect the wiring and washer hoses.
5. Remove the 3 motor attaching screws.
6. Remove the motor while guiding the crank arm through the hole.

To install:

1. The motor must be in the park position before assembly the crank arm to the transmission drive link(s).
2. Install the 3 motor attaching screws and torque to 15 ft. lbs. (20 Nm).
3. Connect the wiring and washer hoses.
4. Install the transmission drive link(s) to the motor crank arm.
5. Tighten the transmission drive link to crank arm attaching nuts.
6. Connect the negative (−) battery cable. Install the cowl screen, lower the hood and check for proper operation.

INSTRUMENTS AND SWITCHES

Instrument Cluster

REMOVAL AND INSTALLATION

Oldsmobile Models

1. Disconnect the negative battery cable. Slide the steering column collar up the column. Then, unsnap the steering column trim cover by pulling to the rear. Remove it.
2. Remove the four screws attaching the gauge cluster to the left side trim cover.
3. Pull the gauge cluster rearward just far enough to gain access behind it. Disconnect the gauge wiring connectors and two lamp sockets from the rear of the cluster. Remove the cluster.
4. Remove the screws attaching the gauge housing to the cluster. Then, remove the nuts attaching the back of the gauges to the gauge housing and remove the gauges.

To install:

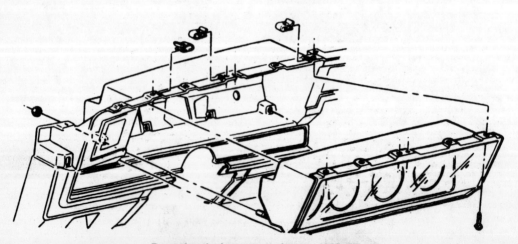

Removing the instrument cluster—1986–87

1. Connect the gauge wiring connectors and two lamp sockets at the rear of the cluster.

2. Install the gauge cluster and nuts attaching the back of the gauges to the gauge housing. Install the screws attaching the gauge housing to the cluster.

3. Install the four screws attaching the gauge cluster to the left side trim cover.

4. Snap the steering column trim cover into place. Connect the negative battery cable and check operation.

Pontiac Safari Wagons and Parisienne

1. Disconnect the negative battery cable. Remove the four screws securing the lower cover to the steering column and then remove the cover.

2. Remove the shift indicator cable from the column.

3. Remove the two mounting bolts attaching the column to the lower side of the dash panel from underneath. Then, lower the column carefully until the steering wheel rests on the seat.

4. Going around the perimeter of the plastic lens, remove the six screws and three snap-in plastic fasteners.

5. Remove the two screws from the upper surface of the gray sheet metal trim plate. Then remove the nuts from the two studs in the lower corner of the cluster.

6. Pull the cluster out just far enough for access to it from the rear. Reach behind the cluster and disconnect the speedometer cable by turning the collar until it unscrews. Then, pull it out of the dash panel.

To install:

1. Push the cluster in just far enough for access to it from the rear. Reach behind the cluster and connect the speedometer cable by turning the collar until it engages.

2. Install the two screws from the upper surface of the gray sheet metal trim plate. Then install the nuts from the two studs in the lower corner of the cluster.

3. Going around the perimeter of the plastic lens, install the six screws and three snap-in plastic fasteners.

4. Install the two mounting bolts attaching the column to the lower side of the dash panel from underneath.

5. Install the shift indicator cable to the column.

6. Remove the four screws securing the lower cover to the steering column and then remove the cover. Connect the negative battery cable and check operation.

Buick Sedans — Analog (Standard) Instrument Cluster

1. Disconnect the battery negative cable. Remove the left side trim cover.

2. Remove the four screws which fasten the cluster carrier to the instrument panel.

3. Look under the vehicle to see if the speedometer cable is of the two-piece design. If it is, disconnect the cable at the transmission end (this will give slack for later work).

4. Remove the steering column trim cover. Disconnect the clip which fastens the shift indicator in place.

5. Remove the two bolts that fasten the steering column to the dash panel and lower it onto the front seat.

6. Pull the cluster far enough out of the dash panel so that you can disconnect the speedometer cable and bulbs at the rear of the cluster.

7. Securely apply the parking brake or block the wheels. Pull the gear selector lever down into low gear. Pull the instrument cluster out far enough to remove the single screw which fastens the Speed Sensor optic head to the speedometer and then remove the cluster.

To install:

1. Securely apply the parking brake or block the wheels. Pull the gear selector lever down into low gear. Push the instrument cluster in far enough to install the single screw which fastens the Speed Sensor optic head to the speedometer.

2. Push the cluster far enough into the dash panel so that you can connect the speedometer cable and bulbs at the rear of the cluster.

3. Install the two bolts that fasten the steering column to the dash panel.

4. Install the steering column trim cover. Connect the clip which fastens the shift indicator in place.

5. Connect the cable at the transmission end, if removed.

6. Install the four screws which fasten the cluster carrier to the instrument panel.

7. Connect the battery negative cable. Install the left side trim cover.

Buick Sedans — Digital Instrument Cluster

1. Disconnect the battery negative cable. Follow all the steps in the procedure above, disconnecting the harness connector in Step 6. Disconnect the ground strap at the back of the instrument carrier and then pull the entire unit out.

2. Unscrew the trip set lever knob. Remove the four screws from the corners of the clear cluster lens. Then, remove the lens and back filler.

3. Remove the spring and needle assembly from the shift indicator.

4. Remove the five screws fastening the tube and circuit board assembly to the cluster carrier. Then, lift the assembly out of the carrier, noting the position of the gasket which covers each of the indicator lights.

5. Hold the speedometer frame against the tube and circuit board face plate and remove the two standard head screws from the face plate. The mechanical odometer may now be removed, as necessary.

To install:

1. Hold the speedometer frame against the tube and circuit board face plate and install the two standard head screws to the face plate. The mechanical odometer may now be installed, as necessary.

2. Install the five screws fastening the tube and circuit board assembly to the cluster carrier.

3. Install the spring and needle assembly to the shift indicator.

4. Install the four screws into the corners of the clear cluster lens. Screw in the trip set lever knob.

5. Connect the battery negative cable and check operation.

Buick Estate Wagons

Instead of an instrument cluster, this dash uses two separate gauge units; a speedometer on the left and a fuel gauge on the right. Removal is similar for the two units. Follow the parts of the procedure specified, depending upon which you need to service.

1. Disconnect the battery negative cable. Remove the left side trim cover.

2. Remove the four screws attaching the gauge unit you want to remove to the dash. If removing the speedometer, disconnect the cable at the transmission or cruise control transducer (under the hood).

3. Pull the unit out far enough to disconnect parts described below.

Speedometer:

a. Two rear light bulb sockets by rotating to release and pulling them out.

b. The speedometer cable by depressing the retaining clip while pulling the cable back.

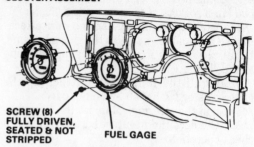

CLUSTER ASSEMBLY

SCREW (8) FULLY DRIVEN, SEATED & NOT STRIPPED

FUEL GAGE

Speedometer and fuel gauge attachments to instrument panel, Buick Estate Wagons

c. The VSS optic head by removing the single screw retaining it in place.

Fuel gauge:

a. Two rear light bulb sockets by rotating to release and pulling them out.

b. The electrical connector.

4. Slide the unit out of the dash.

Late Model Buick, Olds, Pontiac

1. Disconnect the negative (−) battery cable.

2. Remove the left side sound insulator.

3. Remove the steering column trim plate screws and plate.

4. Disconnect the shift indicator cable from the steering column.

5. Remove the left trim plate-to-cluster screws. Remove the steering column-to-panel screws (lower).

6. Remove the screws and snap-in fasteners from the cluster lens.

7. Remove the the gauge housing-to-cluster screws, if so equipped.

8. Remove the nuts and screws from the back of the gauges and upper grey sheet medal trim plate. Remove the cluster from the carrier.

9. Disconnect the speedometer cable, fuel gauge lamp and all electrical connectors.

To install:

1. Position the cluster into the instrument

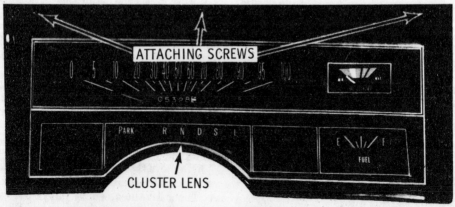

ATTACHING SCREWS

CLUSTER LENS

Instrument cluster lens attachment; mounting varies among years

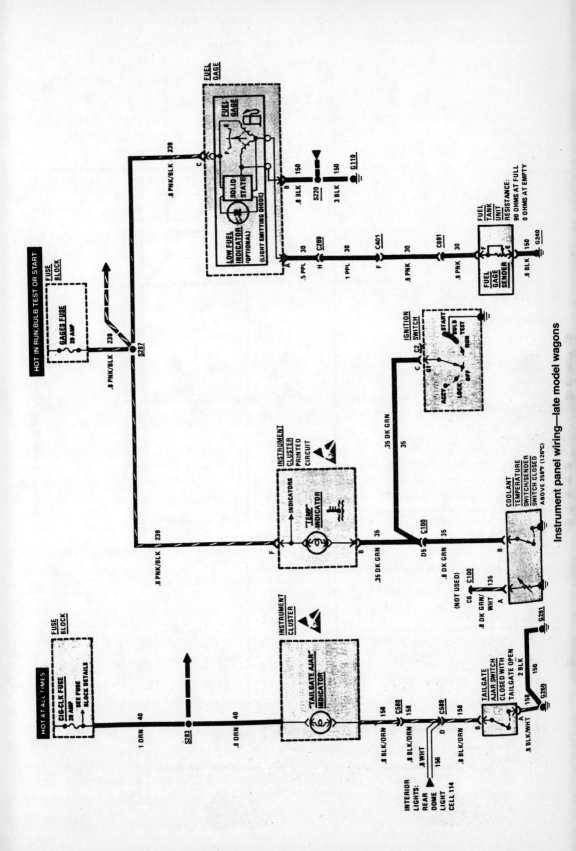

Instrument panel wiring—late model wagons

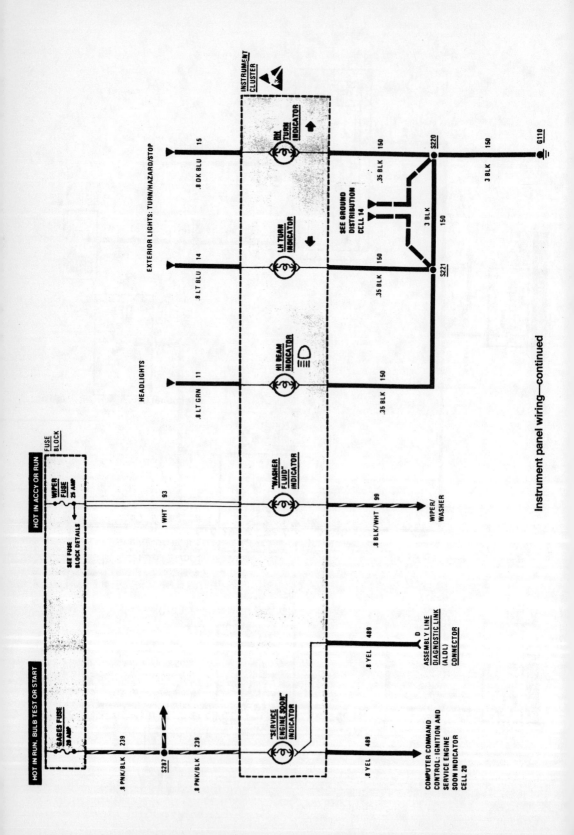

Instrument panel wiring—continued

panel and connect all cable and electrical connections.

2. Install the lower corner nuts, sheet medal trim plate screws and the nuts attaching to the gauges to the gauge housing.

3. Install all remaining screws and nuts.

4. Install the cluster lens, screws and plastic fasteners.

5. Install steering column-to-panel screws, left trim plate and screws.

6. Connect the shift indicator cable and install the sound insulator.

7. Connect the negative battery cable and check for proper operation.

Windshield Wiper Switch
REMOVAL AND INSTALLATION

The windshield wiper switches on all models covered here are removed in the same basic manner. All are mounted on the left side of the instrument panel, and are reached by removing the left side trim panel. Electrical connections must be disconnected at the rear of the switch before removing the switch unit from the dash. Be sure to note how the wires are connected before removing. The switch units are fixed to the instrument panel by two or four screws.

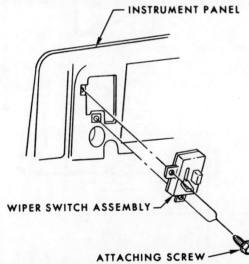

Wiper switch installation, Pontiac, Buick similar

Headlight Switch
REMOVAL AND INSTALLATION

The headlight switch is mounted on the left hand side of the instrument panel on all models covered here. To remove the switch, disconnect the negative battery cable and remove the left instrument panel trim plate. Remove the retaining nut securing the switch, and disconnect the electrical connector from the back of the

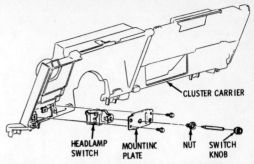

Olds 88 headlight switch, 1981. Others similar

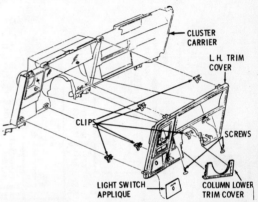

Left side instrument panel trim cover, 1981 Olds 88. Others similar

switch. The switch can now be removed. Reverse the procedure for installation.

Ignition Switch
REMOVAL AND INSTALLATION

Ignition switches found on all Buick, Olds and Pontiac models covered in this guide are mounted on the steering column. Removal and installation procedures are found in Chapter 8.

Speedometer Cable
REPLACEMENT

CAUTION: *If the vehicle is equipped with the air bag system, DO NOT attempt any repair to the instrument panel assembly, or to any part of the electrical system located therein. Repairs to components in this area should be handled by an authorized Buick, Oldsmobile or Pontiac dealer.*

NOTE: *Especially on late model vehicles, be careful to route the cable properly. Any bends in the cable must not have a radius of less than 6 in. (152mm) unless there is a preformed bend in the cable housing. Make sure the cable housing is not routed where it could be pinched or chafed by moving parts or over-*

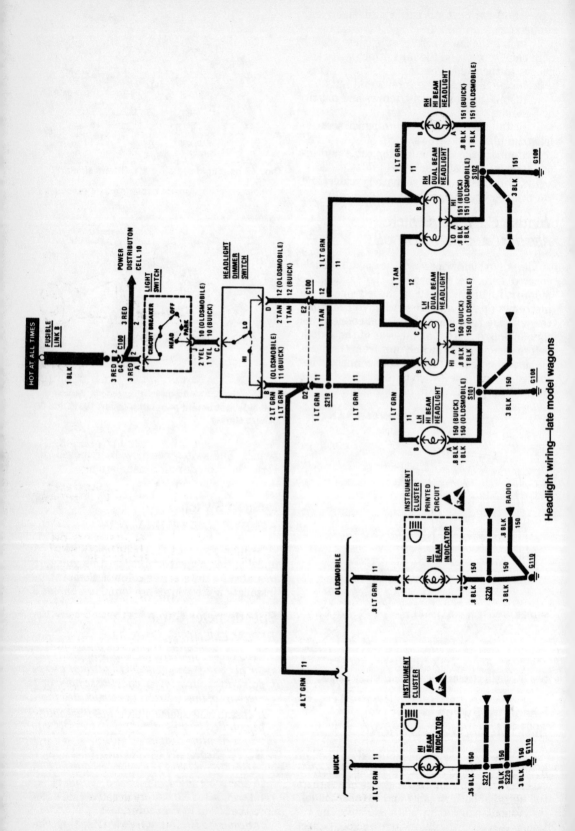

Headlight wiring—late model wagons

heated by an exhaust pipe or the catalytic converter.

1975–87 Buick Sedans

1. Disconnect the negative (–) battery cable. Remove the instrument cluster bezel and lens.

2. Remove the screws and pull the speedometer head assembly out of the cluster housing.

3. Disconnect the speedometer cable from the back of the speedometer. Push down on the spring tab to release.

4. Remove the retainer from the speedometer drive (at rear side of transmission) and remove the cable from the transmission.

5. Remove any retaining clips that attach the cable to the body and carefully pull the cable out of the vehicle. If the cable will not pull out easily, it is still clipped to the vehicle at some point, or it is stuck on other wires or components.

To install:

1. Before installing, grease both ends of the cable with an approved speedometer cable lubricant.

NOTE: *A new type speedometer cable is available as a replacement part for 1981 models only. The new cable is identified by the longer ferrule at the speedometer end. The old style (short ferrule) cable may be used on either the old or new style speedometer head.*

2. Install any retaining clips that attach the cable to the body. If the cable will not install easily, it is may be stuck on other wires or components.

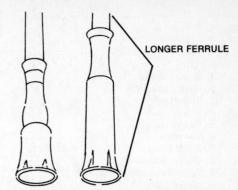

New replacement speedo cable (right), 1981 Buicks only

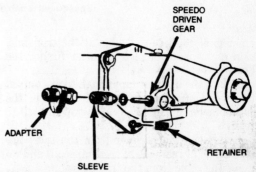

Speedometer cable-to-drive attachment, typical

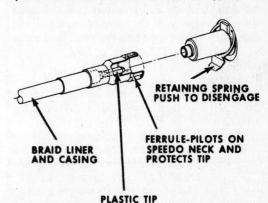

Speedo cable attachment at instrument cluster

3. Install the retainer to the speedometer drive (at rear side of transmission).

4. Connect the speedometer cable to the back of the speedometer. Push down on the spring tab to install.

5. Install the speedometer head assembly and screws.

6. Install the instrument cluster bezel and lens. Connect the negative (–) battery cable.

Buick Estate Wagons

1. Disconnect the battery negative cable. Remove the left side trim cover.

2. Remove the four screws attaching the speedometer to the dash. If removing the speed-

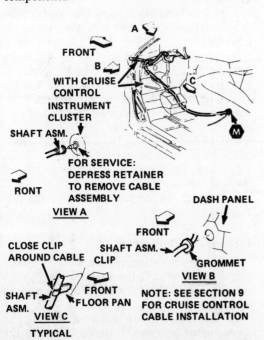

Typical speedo cable routing, 1978 Bonneville shown

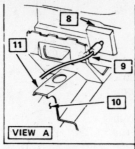
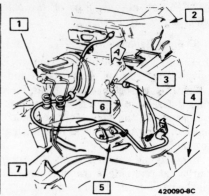

1. Brake cylinder
2. Cluster assembly
3. Transmission
4. Frame
5. Support-dash
6. Grommet
7. Brake pipes
8. Cluster assembly
9. Speedometer shaft assembly
10. Steering column
11. Steering column bracket guide

VIEW A

11—STEERING COLUMN BRACKET GUIDE

420090-8C

Speedometer cable routing—1984 Pontiac

ometer, disconnect the cable at the transmission or cruise control transducer (under the hood).

3. Pull the unit out far enough to disconnect the speedometer cable from the back of the speedometer. Push down on the spring tab to release.

4. Remove the retainer from the speedometer drive (at rear side of transmission) and remove the cable from the transmission.

5. Remove any retaining clips that attach the cable to the body and carefully pull the cable out of the vehicle. If the cable will not pull out easily, it is still clipped to the vehicle at some point, or it is stuck on other wires or components.

To install:

1. Before installing, grease both ends of the cable with an approved speedometer cable lubricant.

NOTE: *A new type speedometer cable is available as a replacement part for 1981 models only. The new cable is identified by the longer ferrule at the speedometer end. The old style (short ferrule) cable may be used on either the old or new style speedometer head.*

2. Install any retaining clips that attach the cable to the body. If the cable will not install easily, it is may be stuck on other wires or components.

3. Install the retainer to the speedometer drive (at rear side of transmission).

4. Connect the speedometer cable to the back of the speedometer. Push down on the spring tab to install.

5. Install the speedometer head assembly and screws.

6. Install the instrument cluster bezel and lens. Connect the negative (−) battery cable.

1975–76 Oldsmobile

1. Disconnect the negative battery cable.

2. Remove the three screws from the top edge of the speedometer lens, then pull out on the top edge of the lens and lift up to disengage the lens tabs at the bottom edge.

3. Remove the four attaching screws, then lift the bezel out of the instrument cluster.

4. Carefully lift the face plate over the shift indicator needle and remove the face plate.

5. Remove the four screws from the face of the speedometer. While holding the speedometer, reach behind the instrument cluster and disconnect the speedometer cable.

6. Remove the retainer from the speedometer drive at the rear side of the transmission, and remove the cable from the transmission.

7. Follow Steps 5 and 6 of the Buick cable procedure for further removal and reassembly.

To install:

1. Before installing, grease both ends of the cable with an approved speedometer cable lubricant.

2. Install the retainer to the speedometer drive at the rear side of the transmission.

3. Install the four screws from the face of the speedometer. While holding the speedometer, reach behind the instrument cluster and connect the speedometer cable.

4. Install the bezel and four attaching screws to the instrument cluster.

5. Install the three screws to the top edge of the speedometer lens.

6. Connect the negative battery cable and check operation.

1977 and later Oldsmobile

1. Remove the steering column trim cover.

2. Remove the left hand trim cover.

3. Remove the trip odometer knob, if equipped.

4. Remove the four screws attaching the speedometer lens to the cluster. Remove the lens.

5. Follow Steps 3 through 7 of the 1975–76

Olds cable procedure for further removal and installation.

1975–87 Pontiac

1. Remove the lower instrument panel trim plates.

2. Reach up and disconnect the speedometer cable casing from the speedometer unit.

3. Slide the old cable out from the upper end of the casing. If the cable is broken, slide it out from both ends of the casing.

4. Remove the cable from the transmission and pull out of vehicle slowly. If the cable binds, make sure the cable clips are disconnected from the body.

5. Take a short piece of speedometer cable with a tip to fit the speedometer and insert it in the speedometer socket. Spin the short cable between your fingers in the direction that a higher speed is indicated on the speedometer dial. Note if there is any tendency for the cable to bind. If there is binding, there is trouble inside the speedometer head.

6. Inspect the cable casing, especially at the transmission end, for sharp breaks and bends. If breaks are noted replace the casing.

To install:

1. To assemble the cable, first wipe it clean with a lint-free cloth. Make sure of the bore of the casing is clean; if not, flush with solvent and blow dry.

2. Place a glob of approved speedometer lube in the palm of your hand. Fed the cable through the lube and into the casing until the lube has been applied to the lower ⅔ of the cable. Do not over-lubricate, and do not apply any lube to the upper third of the cable (this will be lubricated during normal operation, and it is important that all lube is kept away from the speedometer head).

3. Insert the speedometer cable into the back of the speedometer and snap the retainer on the casing. Feed the cable down its proper route, and connect the driven end into the drive on the transmission side.

4. Connect the negative battery cable and check operation.

LIGHTING

Headlights

SEALED BEAM REMOVAL AND INSTALLATION

CAUTION: *Halogen bulbs contain a gas under pressure. Handling a bulb improperly may cause the bulb to shatter into flying glass fragments. To help avoid personal injury, turn headlight switch OFF, allow the bulb to cool, wear eye protection, handle the bulb by*

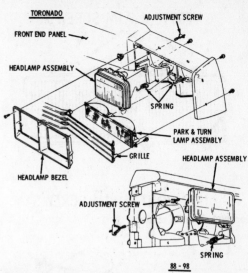

Headlight mounting, 88, 98 Others and round headlight models similar

the base only and do NOT touch the glass part of the bulb.

1. Remove the headlight bezel (outer trim around sealed beam).

2. Remove the sealed beam retainer ring screws and the retainer ring.

3. Lift the sealed beam out and disconnect it from the electrical connector. If the vehicle is equipped with monitor lights, remove the rubber sleeve from the bulb and retain it.

4. To install, connect the sealed beam to the electrical connector, and reinstall the monitor light sleeve if equipped. Hold the sealed beam in place and install the retaining ring and screws. Install the headlight bezel and adjust headlight aim.

HEADLIGHT AIMING

The headlights must be properly aimed to provide the best, safest road illumination. The lights should be checked for proper aim, and adjusted if necessary, after installing a new sealed beam unit or if the front end sheet metal has been replaced. Certain state and local authorities have requirements for headlight aiming and you should check these before adjusting.

NOTE: *The vehicle's fuel tank should be about half full when adjusting the headlights. Tires should be properly inflated, and if a heavy load is carried in the trunk or in the cargo area of station wagons, it should remain there.*

Horizontal and vertical aiming of each sealed beam unit is provided by two adjusting screws, which move the mounting ring in the body against the tension of the coil spring. There is no adjustment for focus; this is done during headlight manufacturing.

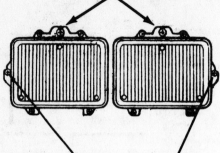

Headlight aiming screws

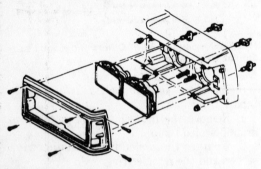

Dual rectangle non-composite headlights

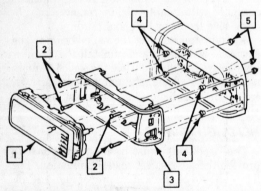

Dual composite headlights

Signal and Marker Lights

REMOVAL AND INSTALLATION

Front Turn Signal and Parking Lights

1. To replace the bulbs, reach in and up behind the front bumper and twist the lamp socket counterclockwise until it can be pulled backward and out.

2. Slightly depress the lamp and turn it counterclockwise to release it. Install in reverse order.

If the entire housing must be replaced:

1. Remove the lamp sockets as described

above. Remove the three screws securing the lamp housing to the bumper and remove it.

2. Remove the three J-nuts from the old housing and install them onto the new one. Install the new housing in reverse order.

Side Marker Lights

1. To replace the bulb, reach up behind the housing and twist the lamp socket counterclockwise until it can be pulled away from the housing and out.

2. Slightly depress the lamp and turn it counterclockwise to release it. Install in reverse order.

If the entire housing must be replaced:

1. Remove the headlight bezel. Remove the two screws that retain the marker light housing from inside the headlamp housing.

2. Remove the marker light housing. Disconnect and remove the bulb and socket as described just above. Unscrew and remove the lens.

3. Install the lens onto the new housing. Install the lamp into the new housing. Install the housing in reverse of removal.

Rear Turn Signal, Brake and Parking Lights

Most rear lenses are fastened in place from inside the luggage compartment. A stud is attached to the lens and passes through the sheet metal at the rear of the body. In many cases, the rear inner wheelhouse panel has to be removed. Remove the attaching nuts from inside the luggage compartment and pull this type of lens off. A few small lenses are attached with screws that are accessible from the rear. To remove these, simply remove the screws and remove the lens.

Once the lens is removed, the bulb can be replaced simply by depressing it, turning it counterclockwise, and removing it. Install in reverse order.

TRAILER WIRING

Wiring the vehicle for towing is fairly easy. There are a number of good wiring kits available and these should be used, rather than trying to design your own. All trailers will need brake lights and turn signals as well as tail lights and side marker lights. Most states require extra marker lights for overly wide trailers. Also, most states have recently required back-up lights for trailers, and most trailer manufacturers have been building trailers with back-up lights for several years.

Additionally, some Class I, most Class II and just about all Class III trailers will have electric brakes.

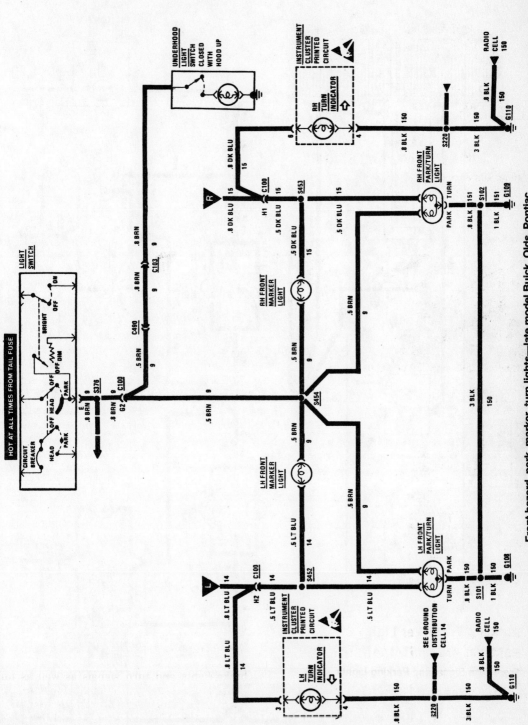

Front hazard, park, marker, turn lights—late model Buick, Olds, Pontiac

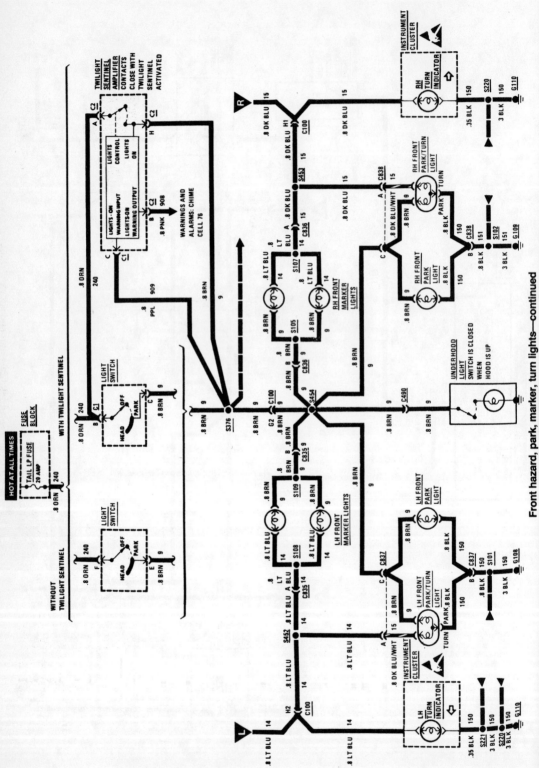

Front hazard, park, marker, turn lights—continued

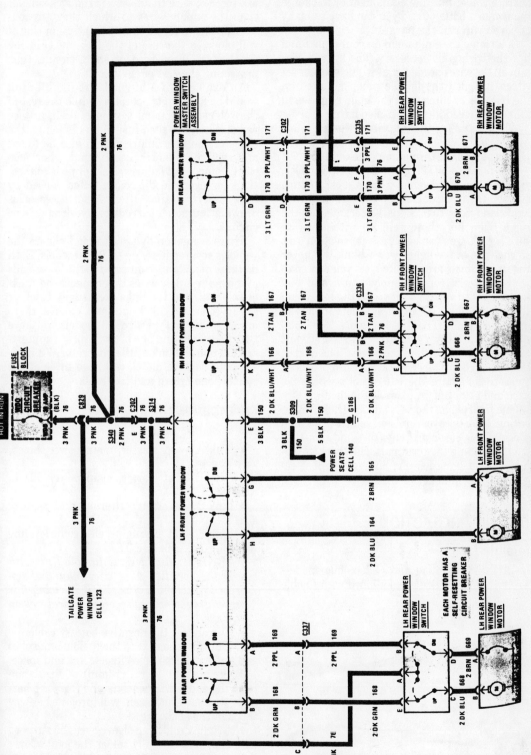

Power window wiring—late model wagons

Add to this number an accessories wire, to operate trailer internal equipment or to charge the trailer's battery, and you can have as many as seven wires in the harness.

Determine the equipment on your trailer and buy the wiring kit necessary. The kit will contain all the wires needed, plus a plug adapter set which included the female plug, mounted on the bumper or hitch, and the male plug, wired into, or plugged into the trailer harness.

When installing the kit, follow the manufacturer's instructions. The color coding of the wires is standard throughout the industry.

One point to NOTE:some domestic vehicles, and most imported vehicles, have separate turn signals. On most domestic vehicles, the brake lights and rear turn signals operate with the same bulb. For those vehicles with separate turn signals, you can purchase an isolation unit so that the brake lights won't blink whenever the turn signals are operated, or, you can go to your local electronics supply house and buy four diodes to wire in series with the brake and turn signal bulbs. Diodes will isolate the brake and turn signals. The choice is yours. The isolation units are simple and quick to install, but far more expensive than the diodes. The diodes, however, require more work to install properly, since they require the cutting of each bulb's wire and soldering in place of the diode.

One final point, the best kits are those with a spring loaded cover on the vehicle mounted socket. This cover prevents dirt and moisture from corroding the terminals. Never let the vehicle socket hang loosely; always mount it securely to the bumper or hitch.

CIRCUIT PROTECTION

Fusible Links

All Buick, Pontiac and Oldsmobile models covered in this guide are equipped with fusible

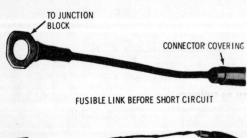

TO JUNCTION BLOCK

CONNECTOR COVERING

FUSIBLE LINK BEFORE SHORT CIRCUIT

CUT WIRE HERE

FUSIBLE LINK AFTER SHORT CIRCUIT

Fusible links before and after a short circuit

links in their electrical systems. The link itself is a piece of wire that is several gauges smaller than the supply wires to which they are connected. The link functions like a fuse in that it will blow (in the case of the link, melt) in the event of an overloaded or short circuit, thus protecting the rest of the circuit.

An example of a burned-out fusible link would be headlights operating while the rest of the vehicle's electrical system is dead, or vice versa. When a melted fusible link is found, the cause of the link failure should also be found and repaired. Some causes include short circuits, component failures, loose or poor connections, or overloaded circuits (often caused by improperly installed aftermarket accessories drawing too much current or overloading one circuit).

There are generally two fusible links on the vehicles covered here, up to 1983 models. Both on these models are connected to the lower ends of the main supply wires that connect the starter solenoid, and the links are usually black or red in color. On 1983 and later models, there are more links. Typically, V6 models will have two black links and one brown link at the starter, and one red link at the generator. V8 models, both gas and diesel, will have three at the starter; one brown and two black.

REPLACEMENT

Late Model "B" Wagons

• Link A — at starter, main power, black, wire size 1

• Link B — at starter, main power, black, wire size 1

• Link C — at starter, alternator, black, wire size 1

• Link K — at alternator, electronic leveling control, rust, wire size 0.5

WARNING: *Replace the fusible link with only the specified wire size, color and approved fusible link wire. NOT following this procedure may cause severe electrical system damage.*

1. Disconnect the negative battery cable.

2. Cut the wire next to the fusible link splice and remove the damaged fusible link and splice.

3. Strip about ½ in. (13mm) of insulation from the end of the new link and from the harness wire so that each will project halfway through the soldering sleeve.

4. Crimp a soldering sleeve over the stripped wire ends and carefully solder the joint. Cover the new joint tightly with a double layer of electrical tape.

5. Install a new link connector eye on the solenoid terminal. Connect the negative battery terminal. To check the new link, simply feel

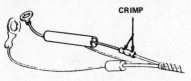

FIGURE 1
REMOVE BATTERY CABLE & FUSIBLE LINK FROM STARTER SOLENOID AND CUT OFF DEFECTIVE WIRE AS SHOWN TWO PLACES.

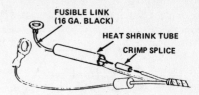

FIGURE 2
STRIP INSULATION FROM WIRE ENDS. PLACE HEAT SHRINK TUBE OVER REPLACEMENT LINK. INSERT WIRE ENDS INTO CRIMP SPLICE AS SHOWN. NOTE: PUSH WIRES IN FAR ENOUGH TO ENGAGE WIRE ENDS.

FIGURE 3
CRIMP SPLICE WITH CRIMPING TOOL TWO PLACES TO BIND BOTH WIRES.

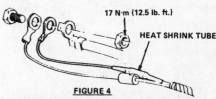

FIGURE 4
SLIDE TUBE OVER SPLICE WITH SPLICE CENTERED IN TUBE. APPLY LOW TEMPERATURE HEAT TO SHRINK TUBE AROUND WIRES & SPLICE. REASSEMBLE LINKS & BATTERY CABLE.

Fusible link repair

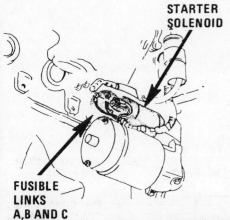

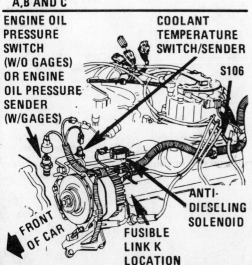

Fusible link location—late model wagons (links A,B,C,K)

and/or gently pull on each link. A good link will be intact and feel solid.

Fuses and Flashers

The fuse block on most of the models covered in this guide is located underneath the far left side of the instrument panel, up towards the floor mat. On a few vehicles, it is located adjacent to the steering column and swings down. Two types of fuses have been used since 1975: the conventional type (cylindrical) fuse, found on 1975 through 1978 vehicles, and the new mini fuses, found on 1978 and later models. The conventional fuses are held in the fuse block by small tangs, and are best removed with a small prybar or awl. The mini fuses are simply pushed into their respective places in the block.

To determine whether either type of fuse is blown, remove the suspect fuse and examine the element in the fuse for a break. If the element (the strip of silver metal inside) is broken, replace the fuse with one of equal amperage. Some fuses have their amperage value molded into the fuse end, and others (and all of the mini fuses) have a color coding system. Color codes are as follows:

Vehicles built in years up to and including 1985:
- 3 amps Violet
- 5 amps Tan
- 7.5 amps Brown
- 10 amps Red
- 20 amps Clear
- 25 amps White

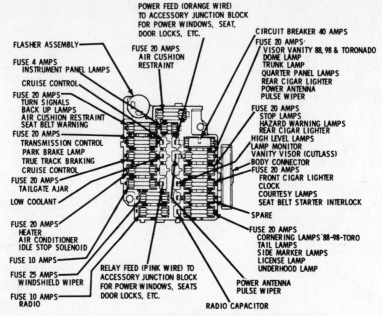

FLASHER ASSEMBLY

FUSE 4 AMPS
  INSTRUMENT PANEL LAMPS

CRUISE CONTROL

FUSE 20 AMPS
  TURN SIGNALS
  BACK UP LAMPS
  AIR CUSHION RESTRAINT
  SEAT BELT WARNING

FUSE 20 AMPS
  TRANSMISSION CONTROL
  PARK BRAKE LAMP
  TRUE TRACK BRAKING
  CRUISE CONTROL

FUSE 20 AMPS
  TAILGATE AJAR

LOW COOLANT

FUSE 20 AMPS
  HEATER
  AIR CONDITIONER
  IDLE STOP SOLENOID

FUSE 10 AMPS

FUSE 25 AMPS
  WINDSHIELD WIPER

FUSE 10 AMPS
  RADIO

POWER FEED (ORANGE WIRE)
TO ACCESSORY JUNCTION BLOCK
FOR POWER WINDOWS, SEAT,
DOOR LOCKS, ETC.

FUSE 20 AMPS
AIR CUSHION
RESTRAINT

RELAY FEED (PINK WIRE) TO
ACCESSORY JUNCTION BLOCK
FOR POWER WINDOWS, SEATS
DOOR LOCKS, ETC.

CIRCUIT BREAKER 40 AMPS

FUSE 20 AMPS·
  VISOR VANITY 88, 98 & TORONADO
  DOME LAMP
  TRUNK LAMP
  QUARTER PANEL LAMPS
  REAR CIGAR LIGHTER
  POWER ANTENNA
  PULSE WIPER

FUSE 20 AMPS
  STOP LAMPS
  HAZARD WARNING LAMPS
  REAR CIGAR LIGHTER
HIGH LEVEL LAMPS
LAMP MONITOR
VANITY VISOR (CUTLASS)
BODY CONNECTOR
FUSE 20 AMPS
  FRONT CIGAR LIGHTER
  CLOCK
  COURTESY LAMPS
  SEAT BELT STARTER INTERLOCK

SPARE

FUSE 20 AMPS
  CORNERING LAMPS 88-98-TORO
  TAIL LAMPS
  SIDE MARKER LAMPS
  LICENSE LAMP
  UNDERHOOD LAMP

POWER ANTENNA
PULSE WIPER

RADIO CAPACITOR

Conventional-type fuses and panel, 1975 Olds shown

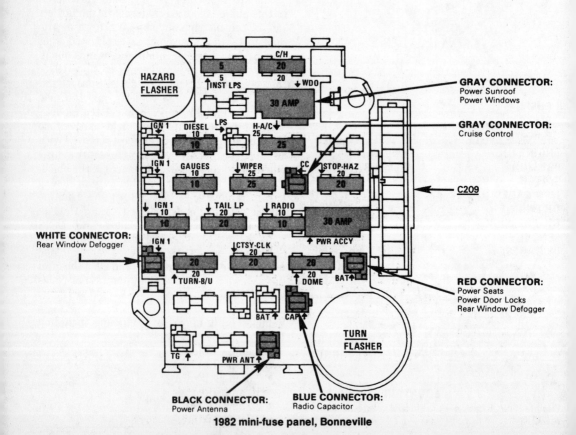

HAZARD FLASHER

GRAY CONNECTOR:
Power Sunroof
Power Windows

GRAY CONNECTOR:
Cruise Control

C209

WHITE CONNECTOR:
Rear Window Defogger

RED CONNECTOR:
Power Seats
Power Door Locks
Rear Window Defogger

TURN FLASHER

BLACK CONNECTOR:
Power Antenna

BLUE CONNECTOR:
Radio Capacitor

1982 mini-fuse panel, Bonneville

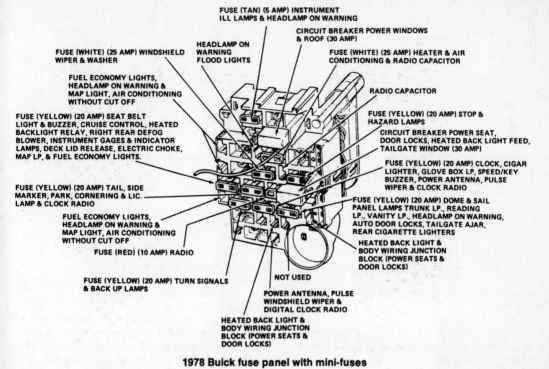

FUSE (TAN) (5 AMP) INSTRUMENT
ILL LAMPS & HEADLAMP ON WARNING

CIRCUIT BREAKER POWER WINDOWS
& ROOF (30 AMP)

HEADLAMP ON
WARNING
FLOOD LIGHTS

FUSE (WHITE) (25 AMP) HEATER & AIR
CONDITIONING & RADIO CAPACITOR

FUSE (WHITE) (25 AMP) WINDSHIELD
WIPER & WASHER

RADIO CAPACITOR

FUEL ECONOMY LIGHTS,
HEADLAMP ON WARNING &
MAP LIGHT, AIR CONDITIONING
WITHOUT CUT OFF

FUSE (YELLOW) (20 AMP) STOP &
HAZARD LAMPS

FUSE (YELLOW) (20 AMP) SEAT BELT
LIGHT & BUZZER, CRUISE CONTROL, HEATED
BACKLIGHT RELAY, RIGHT REAR DEFOG
BLOWER, INSTRUMENT GAGES & INDICATOR
LAMPS, DECK LID RELEASE, ELECTRIC CHOKE,
MAP LP, & FUEL ECONOMY LIGHTS.

CIRCUIT BREAKER POWER SEAT,
DOOR LOCKS, HEATED BACK LIGHT FEED,
TAILGATE WINDOW (30 AMP)

FUSE (YELLOW) (20 AMP) CLOCK, CIGAR
LIGHTER, GLOVE BOX LP, SPEED/KEY
BUZZER, POWER ANTENNA, PULSE
WIPER & CLOCK RADIO

FUSE (YELLOW) (20 AMP) TAIL, SIDE
MARKER, PARK, CORNERING & LIC.
LAMP & CLOCK RADIO

FUSE (YELLOW) (20 AMP) DOME & SAIL
PANEL LAMPS TRUNK LP., READING
LP., VANITY LP., HEADLAMP ON WARNING,
AUTO DOOR LOCKS, TAILGATE AJAR,
REAR CIGARETTE LIGHTERS

FUEL ECONOMY LIGHTS,
HEADLAMP ON WARNING &
MAP LIGHT, AIR CONDITIONING
WITHOUT CUT OFF

FUSE (RED) (10 AMP) RADIO

HEATED BACK LIGHT &
BODY WIRING JUNCTION
BLOCK (POWER SEATS &
DOOR LOCKS)

FUSE (YELLOW) (20 AMP) TURN SIGNALS
& BACK UP LAMPS

NOT USED

POWER ANTENNA, PULSE
WINDSHIELD WIPER &
DIGITAL CLOCK RADIO

HEATED BACK LIGHT &
BODY WIRING JUNCTION
BLOCK (POWER SEATS &
DOOR LOCKS)

1978 Buick fuse panel with mini-fuses

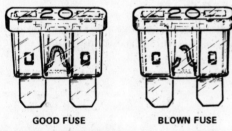

GOOD FUSE   BLOWN FUSE

Mini-fuses, 1978 and later

Vehicles built in 1986 and later years:
- 3 amps Purple
- 5 amps Tan
- 10 amps Red
- 20 amps Yellow
- 25 amps Brown or White
- 30 amps Green

Convenience Center

The convenience center is attached to the left side of the fuse block. The center houses the vehicle speed sensor buffer, turn signal reminder and auto alarm module depending on your vehicle's optional equipment.

Circuit Breakers

The are two circuit breakers located in the fuse block. A 30 amp power sunroof and win-

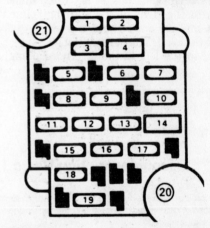

1. (5 amp) Instrument panel illumination
2. (20 amp) Choke heater
3. Spare
4. (30 amp) Circuit breaker
5. Spare
6. (25 amp) Heater and A/C
7. Spare
8. Spare
9. (25 amp) Windshield wiper
10. (20 amp) Stop and hazard lights
11. (10 amp) Instrument panel gauges
12. (20 amp) Tail lights
13. (10 amp) Radio
14. (30 amp) Circuit breaker for power accessory
15. (20 amp) Directional signal and backup lights
16. (20 amp) Clock and Cigar lighter
17. Spare
18. Spare
19. Spare
20. Turn signal flasher
21. Hazard flasher

Fuse panel—late model wagons

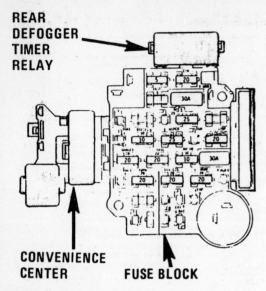

Convenience center located in the fuse block—late model wagons

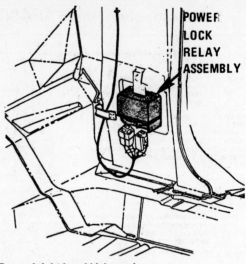

Base of right hand kickpanel

dow breaker is located in spot 4. A 30 amp power accessory breaker is located in the 14 position of the fuse block.

Flashers

The turn signal flasher is located under the dash to the right of the steering column on most models, and is square in shape (as are most flashers). The hazard flasher is under the dash, to the left of the steering column. On 1980 and later models, both the turn signal flasher and the hazard flasher are located at the lower left hand and the upper right hand corners of the fuse block respectively. There is an inline fuse for the underhood spotlamp circuit. The fuse box is marked to indicate fuse size and the circuit(s) protected.

Light Bulbs

Your local automotive parts store has light bulb lists covering your make and model vehicle.

Troubleshooting Basic Turn Signal and Flasher Problems

Most problems in the turn signals or flasher system, can be reduced to defective flashers or bulbs, which are easily replaced. Occasionally, problems in the turn signals are traced to the switch in the steering column, which will require professional service.

F = Front   R = Rear   ● = Lights off   ○ = Lights on

Problem		Solution
Turn signals light, but do not flash		• Replace the flasher
No turn signals light on either side		• Check the fuse. Replace if defective. • Check the flasher by substitution • Check for open circuit, short circuit or poor ground

Troubleshooting Basic Turn Signal and Flasher Problems (cont.)

Problem		Solution
Both turn signals on one side don't work		• Check for bad bulbs • Check for bad ground in both housings
One turn signal light on one side doesn't work		• Check and/or replace bulb • Check for corrosion in socket. Clean contacts. • Check for poor ground at socket
Turn signal flashes too fast or too slow		• Check any bulb on the side flashing too fast. A heavy-duty bulb is probably installed in place of a regular bulb. • Check the bulb flashing too slow. A standard bulb was probably installed in place of a heavy-duty bulb. • Check for loose connections or corrosion at the bulb socket
Indicator lights don't work in either direction		• Check if the turn signals are working • Check the dash indicator lights • Check the flasher by substitution
One indicator light doesn't light		• On systems with 1 dash indicator: See if the lights work on the same side. Often the filaments have been reversed in systems combining stoplights with taillights and turn signals. Check the flasher by substitution • On systems with 2 indicators: Check the bulbs on the same side Check the indicator light bulb Check the flasher by substitution

Troubleshooting Basic Lighting Problems

Problem	Cause	Solution
Lights		
One or more lights don't work, but others do	• Defective bulb(s) • Blown fuse(s) • Dirty fuse clips or light sockets • Poor ground circuit	• Replace bulb(s) • Replace fuse(s) • Clean connections • Run ground wire from light socket housing to car frame
Lights burn out quickly	• Incorrect voltage regulator setting or defective regulator • Poor battery/alternator connections	• Replace voltage regulator • Check battery/alternator connections

Troubleshooting Basic Lighting Problems (cont.)

Problem	Cause	Solution
Lights		
Lights go dim	· Low/discharged battery · Alternator not charging · Corroded sockets or connections · Low voltage output	· Check battery · Check drive belt tension; repair or replace alternator · Clean bulb and socket contacts and connections · Replace voltage regulator
Lights flicker	· Loose connection · Poor ground · Circuit breaker operating (short circuit)	· Tighten all connections · Run ground wire from light housing to car frame · Check connections and look for bare wires
Lights "flare"—Some flare is normal on acceleration—if excessive, see "Lights Burn Out Quickly"	· High voltage setting	· Replace voltage regulator
Lights glare—approaching drivers are blinded	· Lights adjusted too high · Rear springs or shocks sagging · Rear tires soft	· Have headlights aimed · Check rear springs/shocks · Check/correct rear tire pressure
Turn Signals		
Turn signals don't work in either direction	· Blown fuse · Defective flasher · Loose connection	· Replace fuse · Replace flasher · Check/tighten all connections
Right (or left) turn signal only won't work	· Bulb burned out · Right (or left) indicator bulb burned out · Short circuit	· Replace bulb · Check/replace indicator bulb · Check/repair wiring
Flasher rate too slow or too fast	· Incorrect wattage bulb · Incorrect flasher	· Flasher bulb · Replace flasher (use a variable load flasher if you pull a trailer)
Indicator lights do not flash (burn steadily)	· Burned out bulb · Defective flasher	· Replace bulb · Replace flasher
Indicator lights do not light at all	· Burned out indicator bulb · Defective flasher	· Replace indicator bulb · Replace flasher

Troubleshooting Basic Dash Gauge Problems

Problem	Cause	Solution
Coolant Temperature Gauge		
Gauge reads erratically or not at all	· Loose or dirty connections · Defective sending unit · Defective gauge	· Clean/tighten connections · Bi-metal gauge: remove the wire from the sending unit. Ground the wire for an instant. If the gauge registers, replace the sending unit. · Magnetic gauge: disconnect the wire at the sending unit. With ignition ON gauge should register COLD. Ground the wire; gauge should register HOT.
Ammeter Gauge—Turn Headlights ON (do not start engine). Note reaction		
Ammeter shows charge Ammeter shows discharge Ammeter does not move	· Connections reversed on gauge · Ammeter is OK · Loose connections or faulty wiring · Defective gauge	· Reinstall connections · Nothing · Check/correct wiring · Replace gauge
Oil Pressure Gauge		
Gauge does not register or is inaccurate	· On mechanical gauge, Bourdon tube may be bent or kinked	· Check tube for kinks or bends preventing oil from reaching the

Troubleshooting Basic Dash Gauge Problems (cont.)

Problem	Cause	Solution
Oil Pressure Gauge		
		gauge
	• Low oil pressure	• Remove sending unit. Idle the engine briefly. If no oil flows from sending unit hole, problem is in engine.
	• Defective gauge	• Remove the wire from the sending unit and ground it for an instant with the ignition ON. A good gauge will go to the top of the scale.
	• Defective wiring	• Check the wiring to the gauge. If it's OK and the gauge doesn't register when grounded, replace the gauge.
	• Defective sending unit	• If the wiring is OK and the gauge functions when grounded, replace the sending unit
All Gauges		
All gauges do not operate	• Blown fuse	• Replace fuse
	• Defective instrument regulator	• Replace instrument voltage regulator
All gauges read low or erratically	• Defective or dirty instrument voltage regulator	• Clean contacts or replace
All gauges pegged	• Loss of ground between instrument voltage regulator and car	• Check ground
	• Defective instrument regulator	• Replace regulator
Warning Lights		
Light(s) do not come on when ignition is ON, but engine is not started	• Defective bulb	• Replace bulb
	• Defective wire	• Check wire from light to sending unit
	• Defective sending unit	• Disconnect the wire from the sending unit and ground it. Replace the sending unit if the light comes on with the ignition ON.
Light comes on with engine running	• Problem in individual system	• Check system
	• Defective sending unit	• Check sending unit (see above)

Troubleshooting the Heater

Problem	Cause	Solution
Blower motor will not turn at any speed	• Blown fuse	• Replace fuse
	• Loose connection	• Inspect and tighten
	• Defective ground	• Clean and tighten
	• Faulty switch	• Replace switch
	• Faulty motor	• Replace motor
	• Faulty resistor	• Replace resistor
Blower motor turns at one speed only	• Faulty switch	• Replace switch
	• Faulty resistor	• Replace resistor
Blower motor turns but does not circulate air	• Intake blocked	• Clean intake
	• Fan not secured to the motor shaft	• Tighten security
Heater will not heat	• Coolant does not reach proper temperature	• Check and replace thermostat if necessary
	• Heater core blocked internally	• Flush or replace core if necessary
	• Heater core air-bound	• Purge air from core
	• Blend-air door not in proper position	• Adjust cable
Heater will not defrost	• Control cable adjustment incorrect	• Adjust control cable
	• Defroster hose damaged	• Replace defroster hose

Troubleshooting Basic Windshield Wiper Problems

Problem	Cause	Solution
Electric Wipers		

Wipers do not operate—
Wiper motor heats up or hums
	• Internal motor defect
	• Bent or damaged linkage
	• Arms improperly installed on link-
	  ing pivots
		• Replace motor
		• Repair or replace linkage
		• Position linkage in park and rein-
		  stall wiper arms

Wipers do not operate— No current to motor	• Fuse or circuit breaker blown • Loose, open or broken wiring • Defective switch • Defective or corroded terminals • No ground circuit for motor or switch	• Replace fuse or circuit breaker • Repair wiring and connections • Replace switch • Replace or clean terminals • Repair ground circuits
Wipers do not operate— Motor runs	• Linkage disconnected or broken	• Connect wiper linkage or replace broken linkage
Vacuum Wipers		

Wipers do not operate	• Control switch or cable inoperative
	• Loss of engine vacuum to wiper
	  motor (broken hoses, low
	  engine vacuum, defective
	  vacuum/fuel pump)
	• Linkage broken or disconnected
	• Defective wiper motor
		• Repair or replace switch or cable
		• Check vacuum lines, engine
		  vacuum and fuel pump
		
		• Repair linkage
		• Replace wiper motor

Wipers stop on engine acceleration	• Leaking vacuum hoses • Dry windshield • Oversize wiper blades • Defective vacuum/fuel pump	• Repair or replace hoses • Wet windshield with washers • Replace with proper size wiper blades • Replace pump

AUTOMATIC TRANSMISSION

IDENTIFICATION

General Motors Turbo Hydra-Matic automatic transmissions are used in all models covered in this guide. Through the years 1975–83, four basic transmission series have been used, covering four load capacities: the 200, which in-

cludes the 200C and 200-4R; the 250, which includes the 250C; the 350/375B, including the 350C; and the 400.

Starting in 1984, most of the automatics used were in the 200 Series. The 200C offers a lockup clutch; the 2004R offers not only the lockup function, but a 4-speed, overdrive capability. These two transmissions are used through 1990. In addition, in 1984–86 models, there is a

Troubleshooting Basic Automatic Transmission Problems

Problem	Cause	Solution
Fluid leakage	• Defective pan gasket	• Replace gasket or tighten pan bolts
	• Loose filler tube	• Tighten tube nut
	• Loose extension housing to transmission case	• Tighten bolts
	• Converter housing area leakage	• Have transmission checked professionally
Fluid flows out the oil filler tube	• High fluid level	• Check and correct fluid level
	• Breather vent clogged	• Open breather vent
	• Clogged oil filter or screen	• Replace filter or clean screen (change fluid also)
	• Internal fluid leakage	• Have transmission checked professionally
Transmission overheats (this is usually accompanied by a strong burned odor to the fluid)	• Low fluid level	• Check and correct fluid level
	• Fluid cooler lines clogged	• Drain and refill transmission. If this doesn't cure the problem, have cooler lines cleared or replaced.
	• Heavy pulling or hauling with insufficient cooling	• Install a transmission oil cooler
	• Faulty oil pump, internal slippage	• Have transmission checked professionally
Buzzing or whining noise	• Low fluid level	• Check and correct fluid level
	• Defective torque converter, scored gears	• Have transmission checked professionally
No forward or reverse gears or slippage in one or more gears	• Low fluid level	• Check and correct fluid level
	• Defective vacuum or linkage controls, internal clutch or band failure	• Have unit checked professionally
Delayed or erratic shift	• Low fluid level	• Check and correct fluid level
	• Broken vacuum lines	• Repair or replace lines
	• Internal malfunction	• Have transmission checked professionally

Lockup Torque Converter Service Diagnosis

Problem	Cause	Solution

No lockup	• Faulty oil pump
	• Sticking governor valve
	• Valve body malfunction
	   (a) Stuck switch valve
	   (b) Stuck lockup valve
	   (c) Stuck fail-safe valve
	• Failed locking clutch
	• Leaking turbine hub seal
	• Faulty input shaft or seal ring
		• Replace oil pump
		• Repair or replace as necessary
		• Repair or replace valve body or its internal components as necessary
		
		• Replace torque converter
		• Replace torque converter
		• Repair or replace as necessary

Will not unlock	• Sticking governor valve
	• Valve body malfunction
	   (a) Stuck switch valve
	   (b) Stuck lockup valve
	   (c) Stuck fail-safe valve
		• Repair or replace as necessary
		• Repair or replace valve body or its internal components as necessary

Stays locked up at too low a speed in direct	• Sticking governor valve
	• Valve body malfunction
	   (a) Stuck switch valve
	   (b) Stuck lockup valve
	   (c) Stuck fail-safe valve
		• Repair or replace as necessary
		• Repair or replace valve body or its internal components as necessary

Locks up or drags in low or second	• Faulty oil pump
	• Valve body malfunction
	   (a) Stuck switch valve
	   (b) Stuck fail-safe valve
		• Replace oil pump
		• Repair or replace valve body or its internal components as necessary

Sluggish or stalls in reverse	• Faulty oil pump
	• Plugged cooler, cooler lines or fittings
	• Valve body malfunction
	   (a) Stuck switch valve
	   (b) Faulty input shaft or seal ring
		• Replace oil pump as necessary
		• Flush or replace cooler and flush lines and fittings
		• Repair or replace valve body or its internal components as necessary

Loud chatter during lockup engagement (cold)	• Faulty torque converter • Failed locking clutch • Leaking turbine hub seal	• Replace torque converter • Replace torque converter • Replace torque converter
Vibration or shudder during lockup engagement	• Faulty oil pump • Valve body malfunction • Faulty torque converter • Engine needs tune-up	• Repair or replace oil pump as necessary • Repair or replace valve body or its internal components as necessary • Replace torque converter • Tune engine
Vibration after lockup engagement	• Faulty torque converter • Exhaust system strikes underbody • Engine needs tune-up • Throttle linkage misadjusted	• Replace torque converter • Align exhaust system • Tune engine • Adjust throttle linkage
Vibration when revved in neutral Overheating: oil blows out of dip stick tube or pump seal	• Torque converter out of balance • Plugged cooler, cooler lines or fittings • Stuck switch valve	• Replace torque converter • Flush or replace cooler and flush lines and fittings • Repair switch valve in valve body or replace valve body
Shudder after lockup engagement	• Faulty oil pump • Plugged cooler, cooler lines or fittings • Valve body malfunction • Faulty torque converter • Fail locking clutch • Exhaust system strikes underbody • Engine needs tune-up • Throttle linkage misadjusted	• Replace oil pump • Flush or replace cooler and flush lines and fittings • Repair or replace valve body or its internal components as necessary • Replace torque converter • Replace torque converter • Align exhaust system • Tune engine • Adjust throttle linkage

700 Series unit, known as the 700R4. This unit has four speeds with converter lockup.

Transmission Fluid Pan
REMOVAL AND INSTALLATION

The fluid should be changed with the transmission warm. A 20 minute drive at highway speeds should accomplish this.

1. Raise and support the vehicle, preferably in a level attitude.
2. With the Turbo Hydra-Matic 250 or 350, support the transmission and remove the support crossmember.
3. Place a large pan under the transmission pan. Remove all the front and side pan bolts. Loosen the rear bolts about four turns.
4. Pry the pan loose and let it drain.
5. Remove the pan and gasket. Clean the pan

Transmission Fluid Indications

The appearance and odor of the transmission fluid can give valuable clues to the overall condition of the transmission. Always note the appearance of the fluid when you check the fluid level or change the fluid. Rub a small amount of fluid between your fingers to feel for grit and smell the fluid on the dipstick.

If the fluid appears:	It indicates:
Clear and red colored	• Normal operation
Discolored (extremely dark red or brownish) or smells burned	• Band or clutch pack failure, usually caused by an overheated transmission. Hauling very heavy loads with insufficient power or failure to change the fluid, often result in overheating. Do not confuse this appearance with newer fluids that have a darker red color and a strong odor (though not a burned odor).
Foamy or aerated (light in color and full of bubbles)	• The level is too high (gear train is churning oil) • An internal air leak (air is mixing with the fluid). Have the transmission checked professionally.
Solid residue in the fluid	• Defective bands, clutch pack or bearings. Bits of band material or metal abrasives are clinging to the dipstick. Have the transmission checked professionally.
Varnish coating on the dipstick	• The transmission fluid is overheating

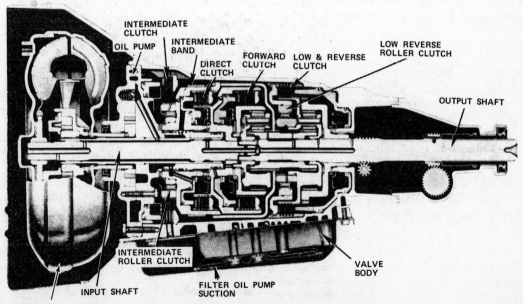

Turbo Hydra-Matic 350 transmission, cutaway view

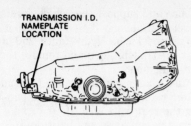

TRANSMISSION I.D.
NAMEPLATE
LOCATION

THM 200-4R TRANSMISSION I.D. NAMEPLATE
THREE RIVERS, MICHIGAN

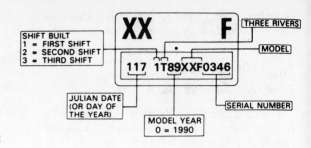

THREE RIVERS

SHIFT BUILT
1 = FIRST SHIFT
2 = SECOND SHIFT
3 = THIRD SHIFT

MODEL

117 1T89XXF0346

JULIAN DATE
(OR DAY OF
THE YEAR)

MODEL YEAR
0 = 1990

SERIAL NUMBER

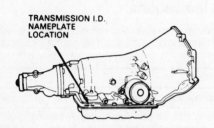

TRANSMISSION I.D.
NAMEPLATE
LOCATION

HYDRA-MATIC 4L60 TRANSMISSION IDENTIFICATION INFORMATION
TOLEDO, OHIO

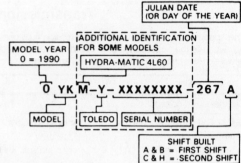

JULIAN DATE
(OR DAY OF THE YEAR)

MODEL YEAR
0 = 1990

ADDITIONAL IDENTIFICATION
FOR SOME MODELS

HYDRA-MATIC 4L60

0 YK M-Y- XXXXXXXX -267 A

MODEL

TOLEDO

SERIAL NUMBER

SHIFT BUILT
A & B = FIRST SHIFT
C & H = SECOND SHIFT

200-4R and 700-4R (4L60) transmission identification

thoroughly with solvent and air dry it. Be very careful not to get any lint from rags in the pan.

NOTE: *It is normal to find a SMALL amount of metal shavings in the pan. An excessive amount of metal shavings indicates transmission damage which must be handled by a professional automatic transmission mechanic.*

6. Remove the strainer-to-valve body screws, the strainer, and the gasket. Most 350 transmissions will have a throw-away filter instead of a strainer. On the 400 transmission, remove

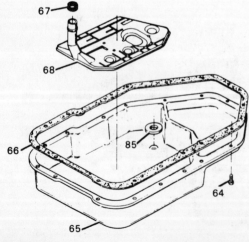

64. Pan bolt
65. Oil pan
66. Pan gasket
67. Filter neck seal
68. Filter assembly
85. Magnet

200-4R fluid pan and filter

the filter retaining bolt, filter, and intake pipe O-ring.

7. If there is a strainer, clean it in solvent and air dry.

8. Install the new filter or cleaned strainer with a new gasket. Tighten the screws to 12 ft. lbs. (16 Nm). On the 400, install a new intake pipe O-ring and a new filter, tightening the retaining bolt to 120 inch. lbs. (14 Nm).

9. Install the pan with a new gasket. Tighten the bolts evenly to:

- 250, 350/375, 400 — 144 inch lbs.
- Powerglide and Torque Drive — 96 inch lbs.
- 200 — 84–120 inch lbs.

10. Lower the vehicle and add the proper amount of DEXRON®II automatic transmission fluid through the dipstick tube.

11. Start the engine in **PARK** and let it idle. Do not race the engine. Shift into each shift lever position, shift back into **PARK**, and check the fluid level on the dipstick. The level should be ¼ in. (6mm) below ADD. Be very careful not to overfill. Recheck the level after the vehicle has been driven long enough to thoroughly warm up the transmission. Add fluid as necessary. The level should then be at **FULL**.

Adjustments

INTERMEDIATE BAND

Turbo Hydra-Matic 250

There are no band adjustments possible or required for the Turbo Hydra-matic 200, 350 or

400 series transmissions. Only the 250 series has an externally adjustable band; the procedure is covered below.

The intermediate band must be adjusted with every required fluid change or whenever there is slippage.

1. Position the shift lever in **NEUTRAL**.

2. Loosen the locknut on the right side of the transmission. Tighten the adjusting screw to 30 inch lbs. (3 Nm).

SHIFT LINKAGE/CABLE

1. Loosen the clamp spring screw on the shift linkage clamp. This is the screw which will slide up and down the rod coming down from the steering column once it is loosened.

2. Set the lever on the transmission into **NEUTRAL** by moving it counterclockwise to the L1 detent, then clockwise the correct number of detent positions to **NEUTRAL**. With three speed automatics, move the lever three positions to **NEUTRAL**; with four speed overdrive units, move it four positions to **NEUTRAL**.

3. Place the transmission selector lever (in the vehicle) in **NEUTRAL** as determined by the stop in the steering column. DO NOT Use the indicator pointer for reference.

4. Hold the clamp (into which the clamp spring screw is threaded) flush against the equalizer shaft lever and then tighten the shift linkage screw just finger tight. You must not exert any force in either direction on the rod or equalizer lever as you tighten the screw. Once the screw is hand tight and its position is fixed, torque it to 21 ft. lbs. (29 Nm).

5. Check that the key cannot be removed and that the steering wheel is not locked with the key in Run and the transmission in **REVERSE**. Check that the key can be removed and the transmission linkage is locked when the key is in Lock and the transmission is in **PARK**. Be sure the vehicle will start only in **PARK** and **NEUTRAL**. If it starts in any gear, the neutral start switch must be adjusted. Start the engine and check for proper shifting in all ranges.

THROTTLE VALVE (TV) CABLE

Late Model "B" Wagons

1. Make sure the ignition switch is off. Depress and hold the metal readjustment tab all the way down. This is located on the engine end of the Throttle Valve cable. Move the slider until it is located directly against the fitting, and then release the adjustment tab.

2. Rotate the throttle lever to give wide open throttle position. Watch the slider as you do this; it must move toward the lever as you rotate the throttle. If the slider works properly, this will complete the adjustment.

NOTE: *After the adjustment, make sure the cable works freely after the engine has warmed to operating temperature.*

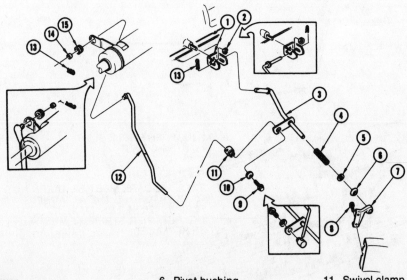

1. Lever
2. Nut (3/8"–16)
3. Equalizer shaft assembly
4. Anti-rattle spring
5. Flat washer
6. Pivot bushing
7. Shaft-to-frame bracket
8. Screw (5/16"–12)
9. Screw (5/16"–18 x 1/2")
10. Washer
11. Swivel clamp
12. Gearshift control rod
13. Retainer
14. Control rod sleeve
15. Bushing

Typical shift linkage; the location of the swivel clamp (11) may differ between models

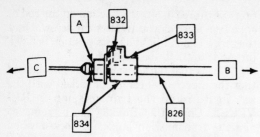

A. Slider against fitting (zero or readjust position)
B. Direction of cable actuating lever
C. Readjusting direction
. 831. Readjustment tab
. 832. Fitting
. 833. Cable
. 834. Slider

Throttle valve cable adjustment—5.0L with 200-4R and 700-4R (4L60) transmissions

NEUTRAL SAFETY SWITCH

NOTE: *1977 and later full size Buick, Olds and Pontiac vehicles do not have a neutral safety switch. Instead, these vehicles have an interlock between the lock and the transmission selector, which is nonadjustable.*

1. Place the shift lever in **NEUTRAL**.

2. Loosen the switch securing screws. Remove the console first if necessary.

3. Move the switch until you can insert a gauge pin, 0.092 in. (2.33mm), for 1975–76,

into the hole in the switch and through to the alignment hole.

4. Tighten the screws and remove the pin.

5. Step on the brake pedal and check to see that the engine will only start in **NEUTRAL** or **PARK**.

DETENT (DOWNSHIFT) SWITCH ADJUSTMENT

Turbo Hydra-Matic 400

All the General Motors divisions covered in this guide use the same detent switch on their THM 400 equipped models. The switch is mounted on the accelerator pedal bracket and is for all intents and purposes, self-adjusting. If a new switch is installed, a preliminary adjustment should be performed according to the accompanying illustration.

1. Perform the adjustment with the engine off.

2. Push the plunger of the downshift switch forward until it is flush with the switch housing.

3. Push the accelerator pedal to the wide open throttle position to set the switch.

DIESEL ENGINE TRANSMISSION LINKAGE ADJUSTMENTS

NOTE: *Before making any linkage adjustments, check the injection timing, and adjust*

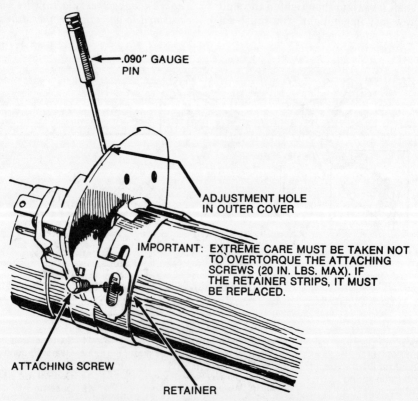

←.090″ GAUGE PIN

ADJUSTMENT HOLE IN OUTER COVER

IMPORTANT: EXTREME CARE MUST BE TAKEN NOT TO OVERTORQUE THE ATTACHING SCREWS (20 IN. LBS. MAX). IF THE RETAINER STRIPS, IT MUST BE REPLACED.

ATTACHING SCREW

RETAINER

Backup, park, neutral safety switch adjustment

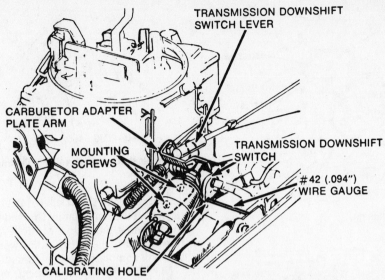

Turbo Hydra-Matic 400 downshift switch adjustment

if necessary. Also note that these adjustments should be performed together. The vacuum valve adjustment (THM350's only) on 1979 and later models requires the use of several special tools. If you do not have these tools at your disposal, refer the adjustment to a qualified, professional technician.

Throttle Rod Adjustment

1. If equipped with cruise control, remove the clip from the control rod, then remove the rod from the bellcrank.

2. Remove the throttle valve cable (THM200) or detent cable (THM350) from the bellcrank.

3. Loosen the locknut on the throttle rod, then shorten the rod several turns.

4. Rotate the bellcrank to the full throttle stop, then lengthen the throttle rod until the injection pump lever contacts the injection pump full throttle stop. Release the bellcrank.

5. Tighten the throttle rod locknut.

6. Connect the throttle valve or detent cable and cruise control rod to the bellcrank. Adjust if necessary.

Throttle Valve (TV) or Detent Cable Adjustment

1979–82 MODELS

1. Make sure the ignition switch is off. Depress and hold the metal readjustment tab all the way down. This is located on the engine end of the Throttle Valve cable. Move the slider until it is located directly against the fitting, and then release the adjustment tab.

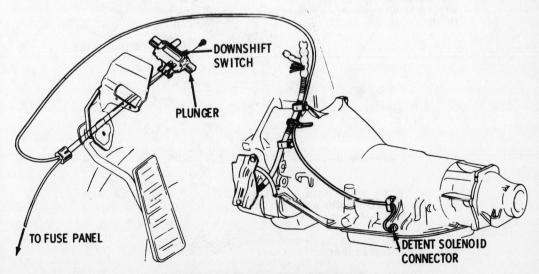

Detent (downshift) switch adjustment

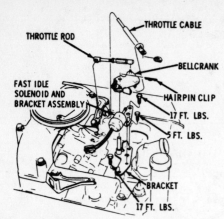

Diesel throttle linkage

THROTTLE CABLE
THROTTLE ROD
BELLCRANK
FAST IDLE SOLENOID AND BRACKET ASSEMBLY
HAIRPIN CLIP
17 FT. LBS.
5 FT. LBS.
BRACKET
17 FT. LBS.

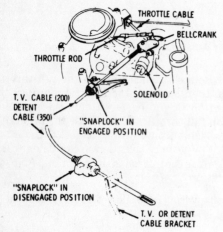

Diesel throttle valve cable adjustment

THROTTLE CABLE
BELLCRANK
THROTTLE ROD
SOLENOID
T.V. CABLE (200) DETENT CABLE (350)
"SNAPLOCK" IN ENGAGED POSITION
"SNAPLOCK" IN DISENGAGED POSITION
T.V. OR DETENT CABLE BRACKET

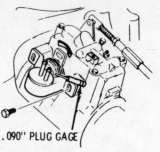

.090" PLUG GAGE

Transmission vacuum valve adjustment, 1978 diesel models

2. Rotate the throttle lever to give wide open throttle position. Watch the slider as you do this; it must move toward the lever as you rotate the throttle. If the slider works properly, this will complete the adjustment.

NOTE: *After the adjustment, make sure the cable works freely after the engine has warmed to operating temperature.*

1983–84 MODELS

1. Disconnect the transmission detent cable from the throttle assembly. If the vehicle has cruise control, disconnect it from the cruise control servo rod as well.

2. Depress and hold the metal lock tab on the upper end of the cable. Move the slider through the fitting away from the bellcrank lever assembly until the slider stops against the metal fitting. Release the metal tab.

3. Install the cruise control serve rod if the vehicle has cruise control. Reconnect the cable.

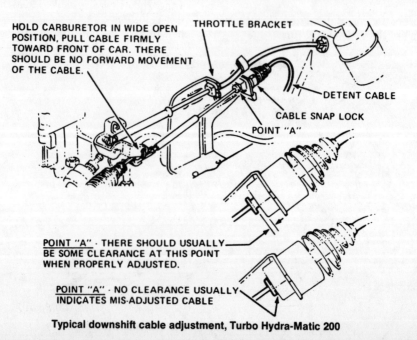

HOLD CARBURETOR IN WIDE OPEN POSITION, PULL CABLE FIRMLY TOWARD FRONT OF CAR. THERE SHOULD BE NO FORWARD MOVEMENT OF THE CABLE.

THROTTLE BRACKET
DETENT CABLE
CABLE SNAP LOCK
POINT "A"

POINT "A" - THERE SHOULD USUALLY BE SOME CLEARANCE AT THIS POINT WHEN PROPERLY ADJUSTED.

POINT "A" - NO CLEARANCE USUALLY INDICATES MIS-ADJUSTED CABLE

Typical downshift cable adjustment, Turbo Hydra-Matic 200

Then, rotate the bellcrank lever assembly until it reaches the full throttle stop and release it.

DIESEL TRANSMISSION VACUUM VALVE ADJUSTMENT

1978 Models

1. Remove the throttle rod from the bellcrank.

2. Loosen the transmission vacuum valve attaching bolts just enough to disengage the valve from the injection pump shaft.

3. Hold the injection pump lever against the full throttle stop.

4. Rotate the valve to the full throttle position, then insert a 0.090 in. (2.28mm) pin to hold the valve in the full throttle position.

5. Rotate the assembly clockwise until the injection pump lever is contacted.

6. While holding the assembly in contact with the lever, tighten the two bolts holding the vacuum valve to the pump, remove the pin and release the lever, and reconnect the throttle rod to the bellcrank.

1979 and Later

1. Remove the air cleaner assembly.

2. Remove the air intake crossover from the intake manifold. Cover the intake manifold passages to prevent foreign material from entering the engine.

3. Disconnect the throttle rod from the injection pump throttle lever.

4. Loosen the transmission vacuum valve-to-injection pump bolts.

5. Mark and disconnect the vacuum lines from the vacuum valve.

6. Attach a carburetor angle gauge adapter (Kent-Moore tool J–26701–15 or its equivalent) to the injection pump throttle lever. Attach an angle gauge (J–26701 or its equivalent) to the gauge adapter.

7. Turn the throttle lever to the wide open throttle position. Set the angle gauge to 0.

8. Center the bubble in the gauge level.

9. Set the angle gauge to one of the following settings, according to the year and type of engine:

Year	Engine	Setting
1979	V8	49°
1980	V8	49–50°
1981	V8—Calif.	49–50°
1981	V8—non-Calif.	58°
1982–84	V8	58°

10. Attach a vacuum gauge to port 2 and a vacuum source (e.g. hand-held vacuum pump) to port 1 of the vacuum valve (as illustrated).

11. Apply 18–22 in. Hg of vacuum to the valve. Slowly rotate the valve until the vacuum reading drops to one of the following values in the vacuum setting charts in this section:

Year	In. Hg.
1979	8½–9
1980	7
1981 Calif.	7–8
1981 non-Calif.	8½–9
1982–84	10½

12. Tighten the vacuum valve retaining bolts.

13. Reconnect the original vacuum lines to the vacuum valve.

14. Remove the angle gauge and adapter.

15. Connect the throttle rod to the throttle lever.

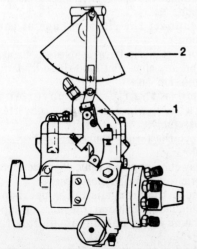
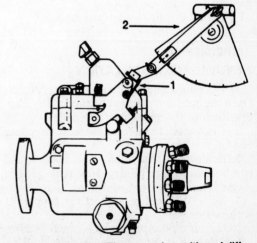

1. Adapter
2. Angle gauge

Angle gauge installation (with adapter) for diesel vacuum valve adjustment. The gauge is positioned differently, depending on the type of throttle lever used.

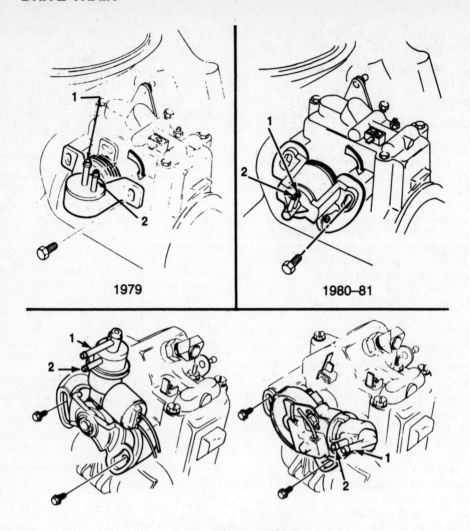

1979   1980–81

1982 AND LATER

1979 and later diesel transmission vacuum valve adjustment

16. Install the air intake crossover, using new gaskets.

17. Install the air cleaner assembly.

Transmission

REMOVAL AND INSTALLATION

1. Disconnect the negative (–) battery cable. Open the hood and place protectors on the fenders. Remove the air cleaner assembly.

2. Disconnect the detent cable at its upper end.

3. Remove the transmission oil dipstick, and the bolt holding the dipstick tube if it is accessible.

4. Raise the vehicle and safety support it with jackstands.

NOTE: *If a floor pan reinforcement is used, remove it if it interferes with driveshaft removal or installation.*

5. Disconnect the speedometer cable at the transmission.

6. Disconnect the shift linkage at the transmission.

7. Disconnect all electrical leads at the transmission and any clips that hold these leads to the transmission case.

8. Remove the flywheel cover and matchmark the flywheel and torque converter for later assembly.

9. Remove the torque converter-to-flywheel bolts and/or nuts.

10. On gasoline engined vehicles, disconnect the catalytic converter support bracket.

11. Remove the transmission support-to-transmission mount bolt and transmission support-to-frame bolts, and any insulators (if used).

12. Position a transmission jack under the transmission and raise it slightly.

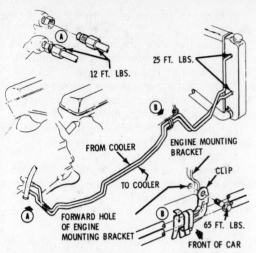

12 FT. LBS.

25 FT. LBS.

FROM COOLER

ENGINE MOUNTING
BRACKET

TO COOLER

CLIP

FORWARD HOLE
OF ENGINE
MOUNTING BRACKET

65 FT. LBS.

FRONT OF CAR

Transmission oil cooler lines

CONVERTER

CONVERTER
HOLDING CLAMP

Torque converter holding fixture. A C-clamp can also
be used.

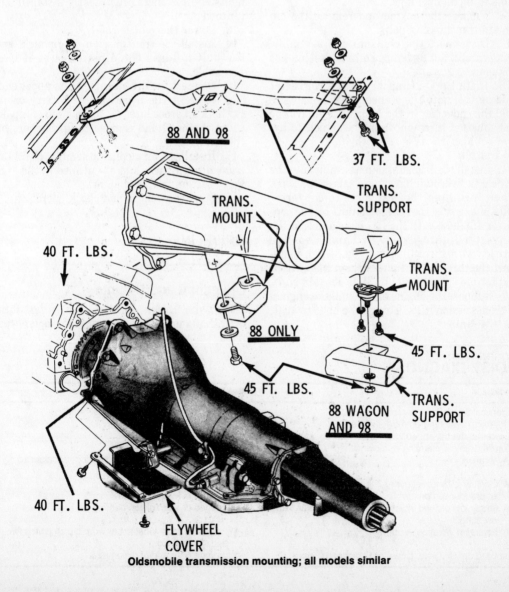

88 AND 98

37 FT. LBS.

TRANS.
SUPPORT

TRANS.
MOUNT

40 FT. LBS.

TRANS.
MOUNT

88 ONLY

45 FT. LBS.

45 FT. LBS.

TRANS.
SUPPORT

88 WAGON
AND 98

40 FT. LBS.

FLYWHEEL
COVER

Oldsmobile transmission mounting; all models similar

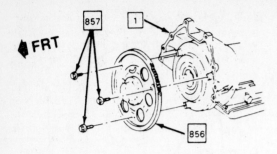

Torque converter-to-flywheel mounting

13. Slide the transmission support rearward.

14. Loosen the transmission enough to gain access to the oil cooler lines and detent cable attachments.

15. Disconnect the oil cooler lines and detent cable. Plug all openings.

16. Support the engine and remove the engine-to-transmission bolts.

17. Disconnect the transmission assembly, being careful not to damage any cables, lines or linkage.

18. Install a C-clamp or torque converter holding tool onto the transmission housing to hold the converter in the housing. Remove the transmission assembly from the vehicle (a hydraulic floor jack is best for this).

To install:

1. Install the transmission assembly into the vehicle (a hydraulic floor jack is best for this). When installing the flex plate-to-converter bolts, make sure that the weld nuts on the converter are flush with the flex plate and that the converter rotates freely by hand. Coat the threads with thread locking compound, hand-start the three bolts, tighten them finger tight and torque them evenly to 35 ft. lbs. (48 Nm).

2. Support the engine and install the engine-to-transmission bolts. Torque the bolts to 40 ft. lbs. (54 Nm).

3. Connect the oil cooler lines and detent cable.

4. Slide the transmission support forward.

5. Position a transmission jack under the transmission and raise it slightly.

6. Install the transmission support-to-transmission mount bolt and transmission support-to-frame bolts, and any insulators (if used).

7. On gasoline engined vehicles, connect the catalytic converter support bracket.

8. Install the flywheel cover.

9. Connect all electrical leads to the transmission and any clips that hold these leads to the transmission case.

10. Connect the shift linkage at the transmission.

11. Connect the speedometer cable at the transmission.

12. Check to see if all under vehicle components and fasteners are properly installed and torqued.

13. Lower the vehicle safely.

14. Install the transmission oil dipstick, and the bolt holding the dipstick tube if it is accessible.

15. Connect the detent cable at its upper end.

16. Connect the negative (−) battery cable. Recheck all procedures for completion of repair. Close the hood and remove the protectors on the fenders.

17. Install the air cleaner assembly. Refill the transmission with fluid as outlined in the "Oil Pan" section in this chapter.

18. Start the vehicle and check operation.

DRIVELINE

Driveshaft and U-joints

Full-size Buick, Pontiac and Oldsmobile driveshafts are of the conventional, open type.

NOISE DIAGNOSIS

The Noise Is	Most Probably Produced By
· Identical under Drive or Coast	· Road surface, tires or front wheel bearings
· Different depending on road surface	· Road surface or tires
· Lower as the car speed is lowered	· Tires
· Similar with car standing or moving	· Engine or transmission
· A vibration	· Unbalanced tires, rear wheel bearing, unbalanced driveshaft or worn U-joint
· A knock or click about every 2 tire revolutions	· Rear wheel bearing
· Most pronounced on turns	· Damaged differential gears
· A steady low-pitched whirring or scraping, starting at low speeds	· Damaged or worn pinion bearing
· A chattering vibration on turns	· Wrong differential lubricant or worn clutch plates (limited slip rear axle)
· Noticed only in Drive, Coast or Float conditions	· Worn ring gear and/or pinion gear

Located at either end of the driveshaft is a U-joint or universal joint, which allows the driveshaft to move up and down to match the motion of the rear axle. The front U-joint connects the driveshaft to a slip-jointed yoke. This yoke is internally splined, and allows the driveshaft to move in and out on the transmission splines. The rear U-joint is clamped or bolted to a companion flange fastened to the rear axle drive pinion. The rear U-joint is secured in the yoke in one of two ways. Dana and Cleveland design driveshafts use a conventional type snapring to hold each bearing cup in the yoke. The snapring fits into a groove located in each yoke end, just on top of the bearing cup. A Saginaw design driveshaft secures the U-joints differently. Nylon material is injected through a small hole in the yoke during manufacture, and flows along a

Troubleshooting Basic Driveshaft and Rear Axle Problems

When abnormal vibrations or noises are detected in the driveshaft area, this chart can be used to help diagnose possible causes. Remember that other components such as wheels, tires, rear axle and suspension can also produce similar conditions.

BASIC DRIVESHAFT PROBLEMS

Problem	Cause	Solution
Shudder as car accelerates from stop or low speed	• Loose U-joint • Defective center bearing	• Replace U-joint • Replace center bearing
Loud clunk in driveshaft when shifting gears	• Worn U-joints	• Replace U-joints
Roughness or vibration at any speed	• Out-of-balance, bent or dented driveshaft • Worn U-joints • U-joint clamp bolts loose	• Balance or replace driveshaft • Replace U-joints • Tighten U-joint clamp bolts
Squeaking noise at low speeds	• Lack of U-joint lubrication	• Lubricate U-joint; if problem persists, replace U-joint
Knock or clicking noise	• U-joint or driveshaft hitting frame tunnel • Worn CV joint	• Correct overloaded condition • Replace CV joint

BASIC REAR AXLE PROBLEMS

First, determine when the noise is most noticeable.

Drive Noise: Produced under vehicle acceleration.

Coast Noise: Produced while the car coasts with a closed throttle.

Float Noise: Occurs while maintaining constant car speed (just enough to keep speed constant) on a level road.

Road Noise

Brick or rough surfaced concrete roads produce noises that seem to come from the rear axle. Road noise is usually identical in Drive or Coast and driving on a different type of road will tell whether the road is the problem.

Tire Noise

Tire noises are often mistaken for rear axle problems. Snow treads or unevenly worn tires produce vibrations seeming to originate elsewhere. **Temporarily** inflating the tires to 40 lbs will significantly alter tire noise, but will have no effect on rear axle noises (which normally cease below about 30 mph).

Engine/Transmission Noise

Determine at what speed the noise is most pronounced, then stop the car in a quiet place. With the transmission in Neutral, run the engine through speeds corresponding to road speeds where the noise was noticed. Noises produced with the car standing still are coming from the engine or transmission.

Front Wheel Bearings

While holding the car speed steady, lightly apply the footbrake; this will often decease bearing noise, as some of the load is taken from the bearing.

Rear Axle Noises

Eliminating other possible sources can narrow the cause to the rear axle, which normally produces noise from worn gears or bearings. Gear noises tend to peak in a narrow speed range, while bearing noises will usually vary in pitch with engine speeds.

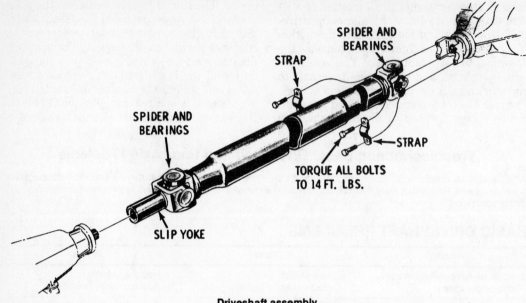

Driveshaft assembly

circular groove between the U-joint and the yoke creating a non-metallic snapring.

There are two methods of attaching the rear U-joint to the rear axle. One method employs a pair of straps, while the other method is a set of bolted flanges. Bad U-joints, requiring replacement, will produce a clunking sound when the vehicle is put into gear and when the transmission shifts from gear to gear. This is due to worn needle bearings or a scored trunnion end possibly caused by improper lubrication during assembly. U-joints require no periodic maintenance and therefore have no lubrication fittings, except replaced U-joints.

Some driveshafts, generally those in heavy duty applications, use a damper as part of the slip joint. This vibration damper cannot be serviced separately from the slip joint. If either component goes bad, the two must be replaced as a unit.

DRIVESHAFT
REMOVAL AND INSTALLATION

1. Disconnect the negative (−) battery cable, raise the vehicle in the air and support it with jackstands.

2. Mark the relationship of the driveshaft to the differential flange so that they can be reassembled in the same position.

3. Disconnect the rear U-joint by removing the U-bolts or retaining straps.

4. To prevent the loss of the needle bearings, tape the bearing caps in place. If you are replacing the U-joint, this is not necessary.

5. Remove the driveshaft from the transmission by sliding it rearward. There will be some oil leakage from the rear of the transmission. It

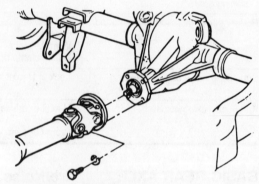

Driveshaft flange attachment

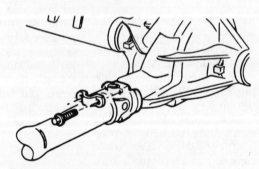

Strap-type retainer on driveshaft

can be contained by placing a small plastic bag over the rear of the transmission and holding it in place with a rubber band.

6. To install the driveshaft, first inspect the outer diameter of the slip yoke to make sure it is not burred, or the transmission seal may be damaged. Apply automatic transmission fluid to all splined driveshaft yokes and then insert the driveshaft into the transmission. Don't

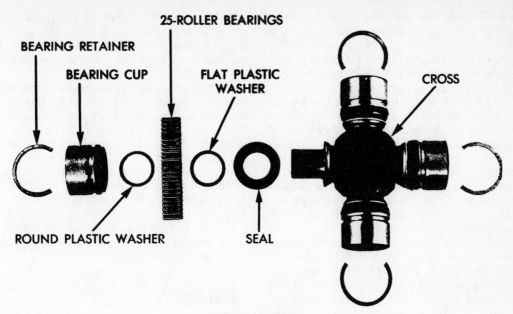

25-ROLLER BEARINGS

BEARING RETAINER

BEARING CUP

FLAT PLASTIC WASHER

CROSS

ROUND PLASTIC WASHER

SEAL

U-joint assembly

force the shaft in. If you seem to be having trouble getting it to slip in, check alignment of the splines. If you're replacing the shaft, check for number and type of splines to make sure they are identical to the shaft you removed.

7. Before making the rear shaft connection, check the mating surfaces of the shaft and flange for nicks and burrs which could prevent proper seating of the shaft to the flange. Then, using the reference marks made earlier, align the driveshaft with the differential flange and secure it with the U-bolts or retaining straps. Make sure the bearings are aligned in the pinion flange yoke before installing bolts or bolts and straps. Torque bolt straps to 16 ft. lbs. (22 Nm).

U-JOINT OVERHAUL

NOTE: *NEVER clamp a driveshaft in a vise, as the tube is easily dented. Always clamp on*

one of the yokes, and support the shaft horizontally.

1. Remove the driveshaft as explained above and remove the snaprings from the ends of the bearing cup.

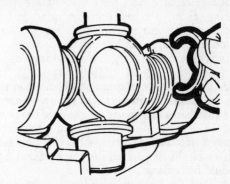

Installing retaining ring

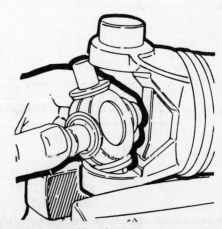

Tapping yoke to seat retaining ring

Partially inserted bearing cap

WARNING: *The driveshaft is easily damaged using improper service methods. Use care not the dent or bend the driveshaft when removing the U-joints. If the bearing caps will not come loose, have a machine shop press them out.*

2. After removing the snaprings, place the driveshaft on the floor and place a large diameter socket under one of the bearing cups. Using a hammer and a drift, tap on the bearing opposite this one. This will push the trunnion through the yoke enough to force the bearing cup out of the yoke and into the socket. Repeat this procedure for the other bearing cups. If a hammer does not loosen the cups, they will have to be pressed out.

NOTE: *A Saginaw design driveshaft secures its U-joints in a different manner than the conventional snaprings of the Dana and Cleveland designs. Nylon material is injected through a small hole in the yoke and flows along a circular groove between the U-joint and the yoke thus creating a synthetic snapring. Disassembly of this Saginaw type U-joint requires that the joint be pressed from the yoke. If a press is not available, it may be carefully hammered out using the same procedure (Step 2) as the Dana design although it may require more force to break the nylon ring. Either method, press or hammer, will damage the bearing cups and destroy the nylon rings. Replacement kits include new bearing cups and conventional metal snaprings to replace the original nylon type rings.*

3. Using solvent, thoroughly clean the entire U-joint assembly. Inspect for excessive wear in the yoke bores and on the four ends of the trunnion. The needle bearings should not be scored, broken, or loose in their cups. Bearing cups may suffer slight distortion during removal and should be replaced.

4. Pack the bearings with chassis lube (lithium base) and completely fill each trunnion end with the same lubricant.

5. Place new dust seals on trunnions with cavity of seal toward end of trunnion. Care must be taken to avoid distortion of the seal. A suitable size socket and a vise can be used to press on the seal.

6. Insert one bearing cup about ¼ of the way into the yoke and place the trunnion into yoke and bearing cup. Install another bearing cup and press both cups in and install the snaprings. Snaprings on the Dana and Cleveland shafts must go on the outside of the yoke while the Saginaw shaft requires that rings go on the inside of the yoke. The gap in the Saginaw ring must face in toward the yoke. Once installed, the trunnion must move freely in yoke.

NOTE: *The Saginaw shaft uses two different size bearing cups (the ones with the groove) fit into the driveshaft yoke.*

REAR AXLE

Identification

The rear axle number is located in the right or left axle tube adjacent to the axle carrier (differential). Limit slip differentials are identified by a tag attached to the lower right section of the axle cover.

Axle Shaft

Two types of axles are used on these models, the C-lock and the non C-lock type. Axle shafts in the C-lock type are retained by C-shaped locks, which fit grooves at the inner end of the shaft. Axle shafts in the non C-lock type are retained by the brake backing plate, which is bolted to the axle housing. Bearings in the C-lock type axle consist of an outer race, bearing rollers, and a roller cage retained by snaprings. The non C-lock type axle uses a unit roller bearing (inner race, rollers, and outer race), which is pressed onto the shaft up to a shoulder. When

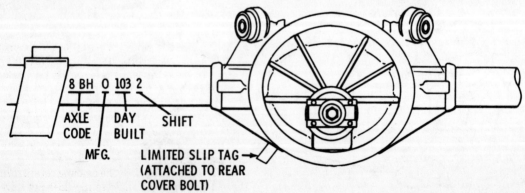

Rear axle identification. Manufacturing codes are: P Pontiac; C Chevrolet-Buffalo; K GM Canada; G Chevrolet-Gear and Axle; O Oldsmobile

servicing C-lock or non C-lock type axles, it is imperative to determine the axle type before attempting any service. Before attempting any service to the drive axle or axle shafts, remove the axle carrier cover and visually determine if the axle shafts are retained by C-shaped locks at the inner end, or by the brake backing plate at the outer end. If the shafts are not retained by C-locks, proceed as follows.

DETERMINING GEAR RATIO

Determining the axle ratio of any given axle can be a very useful tool to the contemporary vehicle owner. Axle ratios are a major factor in a vehicle's fuel mileage, so the vehicle buyer of today should know both what he or she is looking for, and what the salesperson is talking about. Knowledge of axle ratios is also valuable to the owner/mechanic who is shopping through salvage yards for a used axle, who is repairing his or her own rear axle, or who is changing rear axle ratios by changing rear axles.

The rear axle ratio is said to have a certain ratio, say 4.11. It is called a 4.11 rear although the 4.11 actually means 4.11 to 1 (4.11:1). This means that the driveshaft will turn 4.11 times for every turn of the rear wheels. The number 4.11 is determined by dividing the number of teeth on the pinion gear into the number of teeth on the ring gear. In the case of a 4.11 rear, there could be 9 teeth on the pinion and 37 teeth on the ring gear (37 ÷ 9 = 4.11). This provides a sure way, although troublesome, of determining your rear axle's ratio. The axle must be drained and the rear cover removed to do this, and then the teeth counted.

A much easier method is to jack up the vehicle and safely support it with jackstands, so BOTH rear wheels are off the ground. Block the front wheels, set the parking brake and put the transmission in **NEUTRAL**. Make a chalk mark on the rear wheel and the driveshaft. Turn the rear wheel one complete revolution and count the number of turns that the driveshaft makes (having an assistant here to count one or the other is helpful). The number of turns the driveshaft makes in one complete revolution of the rear wheel is an approximation of the rear axle ratio.

Axle Shaft, Bearing and Seal

REMOVAL AND INSTALLATION

CAUTION: *Since the brake shoes will be exposed as you perform this procedure, note that brake shoes contain asbestos, which has been determined to be a cancer causing agent. Never clean the brake surfaces with compressed air! Avoid inhaling any dust from*

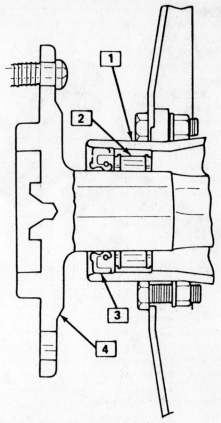

Axleshaft, wheel bearing and seal

any brake surface! If you have to clean in the area of the brake shoes, use a commercially available brake cleaning fluid first to remove remove any brake dust first.

Non C-Lock Type

Design allows for maximum axle shaft endplay of 0.022 in. (0.558mm), which can be measured with a dial indicator. If endplay is found to be excessive, the bearing should be replaced. Shimming the bearing is not recommended as this ignores endplay of the bearing itself and could result in improper seating of the bearing.

1. Remove the wheel, tire and brake drum.
2. Remove the nuts holding the retainer plate to the backing plate. Disconnect the brake line.
3. Remove the retainer and install nuts, fingertight, to prevent the brake backing plate from being dislodged.
4. Pull out the axle shaft and bearing assembly, using a slide hammer.
5. Using a chisel, nick the bearing retainer in three or four places. The retainer does not have to be cut, merely collapsed sufficiently, to allow the bearing retainer to be slid from the shaft.

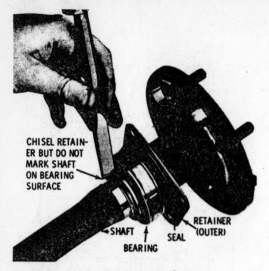

CHISEL RETAIN-
ER BUT DO NOT
MARK SHAFT
ON BEARING
SURFACE

SHAFT — BEARING — SEAL — RETAINER (OUTER)

Cutting the bearing retainer, non C-type

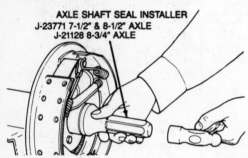

AXLE SHAFT SEAL INSTALLER
J-23771 7-1/2" & 8-1/2" AXLE
J-21128 8-3/4" AXLE

Installing axle seal

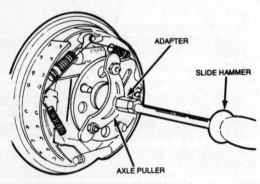

ADAPTER

SLIDE HAMMER

AXLE PULLER

Removing axle shaft

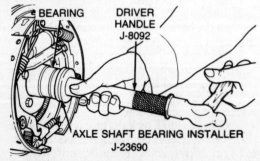

BEARING — DRIVER HANDLE J-8092

AXLE SHAFT BEARING INSTALLER
J-23690

Installing axle bearing

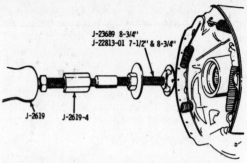

J-23689 8-3/4"
J-22813-01 7-1/2" & 8-3/4"

J-2619   J-2619-4

Removing axle bearing with bearing puller

6. Press off the bearing and install the new one by pressing it into position.

7. Press on the new retainer.

NOTE: *Do not attempt to press the bearing and the retainer on at the same time.*

8. Assemble the shaft and bearing in the housing being sure that the bearing is seated properly in the housing.

9. Install the retainer, drum, wheel and tire. Bleed the brakes.

C-Lock Type

If the axle shafts are retained by C-shaped locks, proceed as follows:

1. Raise the vehicle, support with jackstands and remove the wheels.

2. The differential cover has already been removed (see Caution note). Remove the differential pinion shaft lock-screw and the differential pinion shaft.

3. Push the flanged end of the axle shaft toward the center of the vehicle and remove the C-lock from the end of the shaft.

4. Remove the axle shaft from the housing, being careful not to damage the oil seal.

5. Remove the oil seal by inserting the button end of the axle shaft behind the steel case of the oil seal. Pry the seal loose from the bore.

6. Seat the legs of the bearing puller behind the bearing. Seat a washer against the bearing and hold it in place with a nut. Use a slide hammer to pull the bearing.

7. Pack the cavity between the seal lips with wheel bearing lubricant and lubricate a new wheel bearing with same.

8. Use a suitable driver and install the bearing until it bottoms against the tube. Install the oil seal.

9. Slide the axle shaft into place. Be sure that the splines on the shaft do not damage the oil seal. Make sure that the splines engage the differential side gear.

10. Install the axle shaft C-lock on the inner end of the axle shaft and push the shaft outward so that the C-lock seats in the differential side gear counterbore.

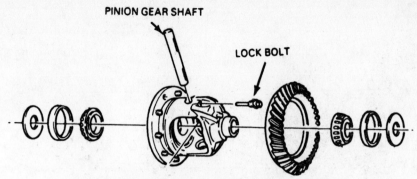

PINION GEAR SHAFT

LOCK BOLT

Removing the pinion gear shaft and lock bolt—C-type axle

11. Position the differential pinion shaft through the case and pinions, aligning the hole in the case with the hole for the lockscrew.

12. Use a new gasket and install the carrier cover. Be sure that the gasket surfaces are clean before installing the gasket and cover. Torque the cover bolts to 22 ft. lbs. (30 Nm).

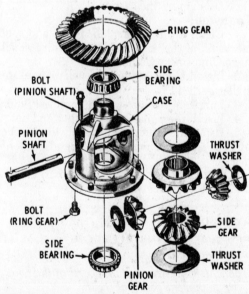

RING GEAR

BOLT
(PINION SHAFT)

SIDE
BEARING

CASE

PINION
SHAFT

BOLT
(RING GEAR)

SIDE
BEARING

THRUST
WASHER

SIDE
GEAR

PINION
GEAR

THRUST
WASHER

Conventional differential case assembly, all models similar

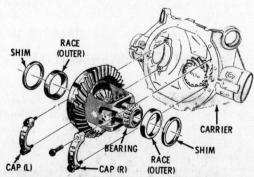

SHIM

RACE
(OUTER)

CARRIER

SHIM

BEARING

RACE
(OUTER)

CAP (L)

CAP (R)

Conventional differential case and bearings

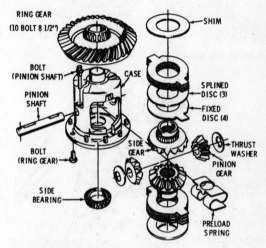

RING GEAR
(10 BOLT 8 1/2")

SHIM

BOLT
(PINION SHAFT)

CASE

PINION
SHAFT

SPLINED
DISC (3)

FIXED
DISC (4)

BOLT
(RING GEAR)

SIDE
GEAR

THRUST
WASHER

PINION
GEAR

SIDE
BEARING

PRELOAD
SPRING

Disc-type limited slip rear axle

13. Fill the axle with lubricant to the bottom of the filler hole.

NOTE: *Special limit slip differential fluid is needed to properly lubricate the limit slip carrier clutches or cones. Standard fluid may cause damage to the rear axle assembly.*

14. Install the brake drum and wheels and lower the vehicle. Check for leaks and road test the vehicle.

Pinion Seal

REMOVAL AND INSTALLATION

1. Raise the vehicle and support with jackstands.

2. Mark the driveshaft and pinion yoke for reinstallation. Remove the driveshaft from the pinion yoke and wire it up to the frame. Tape the U-joint caps in place to prevent dirt from entering the U-joint.

3. Mark the position of the pinion yoke, pinion gear shaft and pinion yoke nut so the proper bearing preload can be maintained.

4. Place a drain pan under the pinion yoke. Remove the pinion nut and washer using a pinion yoke remover J–8614–10 or equivalent.

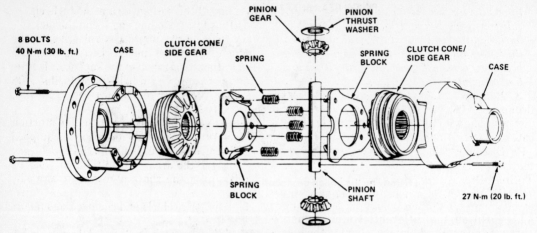

Cone-type limit slip differential

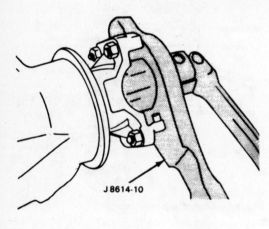

Removing pinion nut and yoke

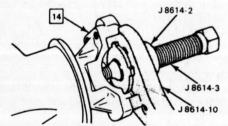

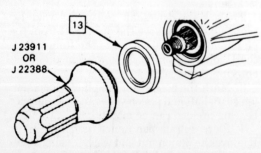

Installing pinion seal

5. Remove the pinion yoke using removing tools J–8614–2, J–8614–3 and J–8614–10.

6. Remove the seal with a slide hammer or by driving it out of the carrier with a blunt chisel. Do NOT damage the carrier.

To install:

1. Clean all dirt, varnish, nicks and tool marks off of the yoke seal carrier with a small file or fine emery cloth.

2. Install a new pinion seal using a seal installer J–23911 or J–22388.

3. Lubricate the seal with differential fluid.

4. Install the pinion yoke, washer and nut.

5. Using the yoke holding tool, torque the nut to $^1/_{16}$ in. (1.6mm) past the alignment marks.

6. Install the drivshaft to the marks positions and lower the vehicle.

Axle Housing

REMOVAL AND INSTALLATION

CAUTION: *The axle housing is a heavy component. Use care when supporting the housing to prevent personal injury.*

1. Disconnect the negative (−) battery cable.

2. Raise the vehicle and support the rear of the vehicle at the frame. A jack must remain under the rear axle housing.

3. Disconnect the shock absorbers from the axle housing.

4. Mark and remove the driveshaft from the rear yoke.

5. Disconnect and plug the brake line from the junction block. Disconnect the height sensor if equipped with Electronic Level Control (ELC).

6. Disconnect the upper control arms from the axle housing.

7. Lower the axle housing using the jack.

CAUTION: *Some brake shoes contain asbes-*

tos, which has been determined to be a cancer causing agent. Never clean the brake surfaces with compressed air! Avoid inhaling any dust from any brake surface! When cleaning brake surfaces, use a commercially available brake cleaning fluid.

8. Remove the springs, rear wheels and drums.

9. Disconnect and remove the parking brake cables from the brake backing plates.

10. Disconnect the lower control arms and remove the axle housing.

To install:

1. Position the axle housing under the vehicle and connect the lower control arms. Only hand tight at this time.

2. Install and connect the parking brake cables to the brake backing plates.

3. Install the springs, drums and wheels.

4. Raise the axle housing using the jack.

5. Connect the upper control arms to the axle housing. Raise the axle housing until the frame starts to raise off of the supports. Torque the upper control arm bolts to 80 ft. lbs. (108 Nm) and the lower control arms to 122 ft. lbs. (165 Nm).

6. Connect the brake line to the junction block. Connect the height sensor if equipped with Electronic Level Control (ELC).

7. Install the driveshaft to the rear yoke.

8. Connect the shock absorbers to the axle housing.

9. Raise the vehicle and remove the support at the frame.

10. Connect the negative (−) battery cable and check operation.

Suspension and Steering

8

FRONT SUSPENSION

The front suspension is designed to allow each wheel to compensate for changes in the road surface level without appreciably affecting the opposite wheel. Each wheel is independently connected to the frame by a steering knuckle, ball joint assemblies, and upper and lower control arms. The control arms are specifically designed and positioned to allow the steering knuckles to move in a prescribed three dimensional arc. The front wheels are held in proper relationship to each other by two tie rods which are connected to steering arms on the knuckles and to an intermediate rod.

Chassis coil springs are mounted between the

Troubleshooting Basic Steering and Suspension Problems

Problem	Cause	Solution
Hard steering (steering wheel is hard to turn)	• Low or uneven tire pressure • Loose power steering pump drive belt • Low or incorrect power steering fluid • Incorrect front end alignment • Defective power steering pump • Bent or poorly lubricated front end parts	• Inflate tires to correct pressure • Adjust belt • Add fluid as necessary • Have front end alignment checked/adjusted • Check pump • Lubricate and/or replace defective parts
Loose steering (too much play in the steering wheel)	• Loose wheel bearings • Loose or worn steering linkage • Faulty shocks • Worn ball joints	• Adjust wheel bearings • Replace worn parts • Replace shocks • Replace ball joints
Car veers or wanders (car pulls to one side with hands off the steering wheel)	• Incorrect tire pressure • Improper front end alignment • Loose wheel bearings • Loose or bent front end components • Faulty shocks	• Inflate tires to correct pressure • Have front end alignment checked/adjusted • Adjust wheel bearings • Replace worn components • Replace shocks
Wheel oscillation or vibration transmitted through steering wheel	• Improper tire pressures • Tires out of balance • Loose wheel bearings • Improper front end alignment • Worn or bent front end components	• Inflate tires to correct pressure • Have tires balanced • Adjust wheel bearings • Have front end alignment checked/adjusted • Replace worn parts
Uneven tire wear	• Incorrect tire pressure • Front end out of alignment • Tires out of balance	• Inflate tires to correct pressure • Have front end alignment checked/adjusted • Have tires balanced

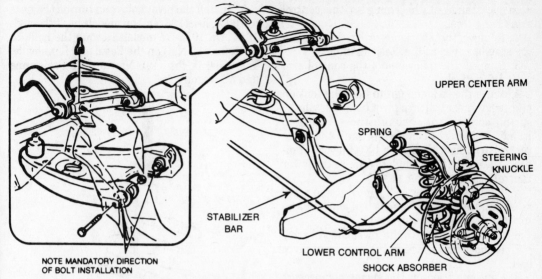

NOTE MANDATORY DIRECTION
OF BOLT INSTALLATION

UPPER CENTER ARM

SPRING

STEERING
KNUCKLE

STABILIZER
BAR

LOWER CONTROL ARM

SHOCK ABSORBER

Front suspension; all models similar design

spring housings on the frame or front end sheet metal and the lower control arms. Ride control is provided by double, direct acting, shock absorbers mounted inside the coil springs and attached to the lower control arms by bolts and nuts. The upper portion of each shock absorber extends through the upper control arm frame bracket and is secured with two grommets, two grommet retainers, and a nut.

Side roll of the front suspension is controlled by a spring steel stabilizer shaft. It is mounted in rubber bushings which are held to the frame side rails by brackets. The ends of the stabilizer are connected to the lower control arms by link bolts isolated by rubber grommets.

The upper control arm is attached to a cross shaft through isolating rubber bushings. The cross shaft, in turn, is bolted to frame brackets.

A ball joint assembly is riveted to the outer end of the upper arm. It is pre-loaded by a rubber spring to insure proper seating of the ball in the socket. The upper ball joint is attached to

the steering knuckle by a torque prevailing nut.

The inner ends of the lower control arm have pressed in bushings. Bolts, passing through the bushings, attach the arm to the frame. The lower ball joint assembly is a press fit in the arm and attaches to the steering knuckle with a torque prevailing nut.

Rubber grease seals are provided at ball socket assemblies to keep dirt and moisture from entering the joint and damaging bearing surfaces.

Coil Springs

REMOVAL AND INSTALLATION

CAUTION: *The coil springs are under a considerable amount of tension. Be extremely careful when removing or installing them; they can exert enough force to cause serious injury. Use only approved spring compressors for suspension servicing.*

1. Raise the front of the vehicle and support

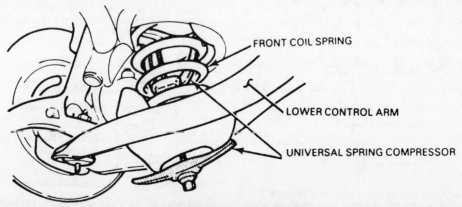

FRONT COIL SPRING

LOWER CONTROL ARM

UNIVERSAL SPRING COMPRESSOR

Compressing the front coil spring

with jackstands at the frame so the control arms hang free.

2. Remove the shock absorber. Disconnect the stabilizer bar at the steering knuckle.

3. Support the inner end of the control arm with a floor jack.

4. Raise the jack enough to take the tension off the lower control arm pivot bolts. Install the spring compressor through the spring and frame. Tighten the compressor until the lower control arm pivots bolts can be removed. Compress the spring far enough to remove the lower control arm and spring.

5. Remove the lower ball joint nut and separate from the knuckle using a ball joint separator tool J–23742 or equivalent.

6. Chain the spring to the lower control arm.

7. Remove first the rear, then the front pivot bolt.

8. Cautiously loosen the spring compressor until all spring tension is released.

9. Note the way in which the spring is installed in relation to the drain holes on the control arm and remove it.

To install:

1. On installation, position the spring to the control arm and raise it into place. On 1985 and later Olds models, note that the spring must be positioned so that the end of the coil covers all or part of one inspection/drain hole in the lower control arm, and the other hole must be only partly covered.

2. Compress the spring far enough to install the front and rear pivot bolts.

3. Install the pivot bolts and torque the nuts to 100 ft. lbs. (136 Nm) on models built through 1984. On 1985–87 models, torque the bolts to 65 ft. lbs. (88 Nm) on the Regal and Bonneville, and to 90 ft. lbs. (122 Nm) on the Parisienne and all wagons.

Spring compressed and ready to install

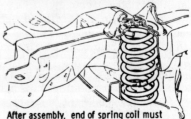

Spring to be installed with tape at lowest position. Bottom of spring is coiled helical, and the top is coiled flat with a gripper notch near end of wire.

After assembly, end of spring coil must cover all or part of one inspection drain hole. The other hole must be partly exposed or completely uncovered.

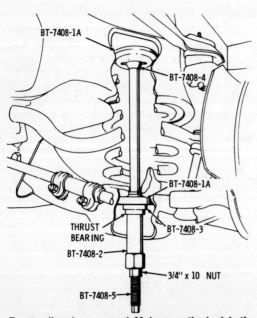

	THRUST BEARING	

BT-7408-1A
BT-7408-4
BT-7408-1A
BT-7408-3
BT-7408-2
3/4" x 10 NUT
BT-7408-5

Front coil spring removal. Make sure the lock in the top of the spring compressor is in position whenever the tool is used.

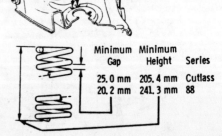

	Minimum Gap	Minimum Height	Series
	25.0 mm	205.4 mm	Cutlass
	20.2 mm	241.3 mm	88

Positioning of front coil springs on 1985–87 Oldsmobiles

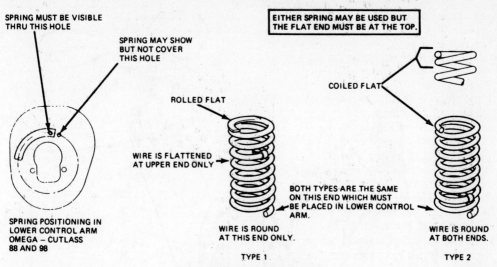

SPRING MUST BE VISIBLE THRU THIS HOLE

SPRING MAY SHOW BUT NOT COVER THIS HOLE

ROLLED FLAT

EITHER SPRING MAY BE USED BUT THE FLAT END MUST BE AT THE TOP.

COILED FLAT

WIRE IS FLATTENED AT UPPER END ONLY

BOTH TYPES ARE THE SAME ON THIS END WHICH MUST BE PLACED IN LOWER CONTROL ARM.

SPRING POSITIONING IN LOWER CONTROL ARM OMEGA – CUTLASS 88 AND 98

WIRE IS ROUND AT THIS END ONLY.

WIRE IS ROUND AT BOTH ENDS.

TYPE 1

TYPE 2

Proper coil spring installation

4. Install the lower ball joint to the knuckle, torque the nut to 85 ft. lbs. (112 Nm) and install a new cotter pin.

5. Replace the shock absorber and stabilizer bar.

Shock Absorbers

REMOVAL AND INSTALLATION

1. Raise the vehicle, and with an open end wrench hold the upper stem of the shock absorber from turning. Remove the upper stem retaining nut, retainer and grommet.

2. Remove the two bolts retaining the lower shock absorber pivot to the lower control arm and then pull the shock out through the bottom of the control arm.

3. With the lower retainer and the rubber

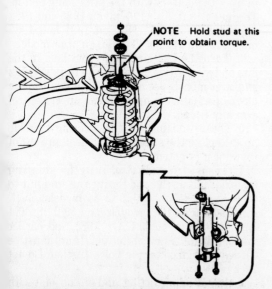

NOTE   Hold stud at this point to obtain torque.

Shock absorber mounting locations

grommet in place over the upper stem, install the shock (fully extended) back through the lower control arm.

4. Install the upper grommet, retainer and nut onto the upper stem.

5. Hold the upper stem from turning with an open end wrench and then tighten the retaining nut.

6. Reinstall the retainers on the lower end of the shock.

TESTING

Visually inspect the shock absorber. If there is evidence of leakage and the shock absorber is covered with oil, the shock has reached the end of its life and should be replaced.

If there is no sign of excessive leakage (a small amount of weeping is normal) bounce the vehicle at one corner by pressing down on the fender or bumper and releasing. When you have the vehicle bouncing as much as you can, release the fender or bumper. The vehicle should stop bouncing after the first rebound. If the bouncing continues past the center point of the bounce more than once, the shock absorbers are worn and should be replaced.

Ball Joints

BALL JOINT INSPECTION

NOTE: *Before performing this inspection, make sure the wheel bearings are adjusted correctly and that the control arm bushings are in good condition. All models covered in this guide are equipped with wear indicators on the lower ball joint. As long as the indicator extends below the ball stud seat, replacement is unnecessary; if only the lower ball joint is bad, however, both upper and lower ball joints should be replaced.*

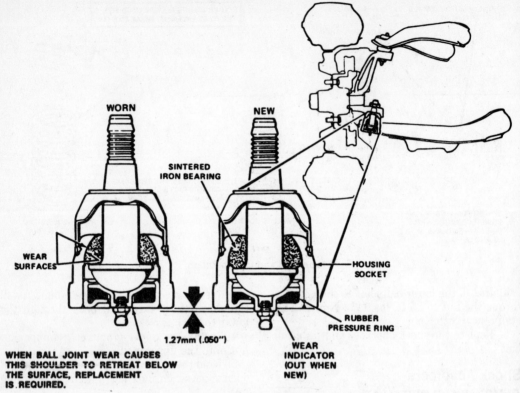

WORN

NEW

SINTERED
IRON BEARING

WEAR
SURFACES

HOUSING
SOCKET

RUBBER
PRESSURE RING

1.27mm (.050")

WEAR
INDICATOR
(OUT WHEN
NEW)

WHEN BALL JOINT WEAR CAUSES
THIS SHOULDER TO RETREAT BELOW
THE SURFACE, REPLACEMENT
IS REQUIRED.

Lower ball joint wear indicator

1. Raise the vehicle by placing the jack under the lower control arm at the spring seat.

2. Raise the vehicle until there is a 1–2 in. (25–51mm) clearance under the wheel.

3. Insert a bar under the wheel and pry upward. If the wheel raises more than 1/8 in. (3mm), the ball joints are worn. Determine whether the upper or lower ball joint is worn by visual inspection while prying on the wheel.

Upper Ball Joints

REMOVAL AND INSTALLATION

1. Raise the vehicle and support securely. Support the lower control arm securely with jackstands. Remove the tire and wheel.

2. Remove the upper ball stud cotter pin and loosen the ball stud nut just one turn.

3. Procure a special tool designed to press out ball joints. These tools are available at most automotive parts stores. Locate the tool between the upper and lower ball joints and press the joints out of the steering knuckle. Remove the tool.

4. Remove the ball joint stud nut, and separate the joint from the steering knuckle. Lift the upper arm up and place a block of wood between the frame and the arm to support it.

5. With the control arm in the raised posi-

tion, drill a hole 1/4 in. (6mm) deep hole into each rivet. Use a 1/8 in. (3mm) drill bit.

6. Use a 1/2 in. drill bit and drill off the heads of each rivet.

7. Punch out the rivets using a small punch and then remove the ball joint.

8. Install the new ball joint using fasteners that meet GM specifications. Bolts should come in from the bottom with the nuts going on top. Torque to 13 ft. lbs. (17 Nm) on 1983 and 1984 models, 8 ft. lbs. (11 Nm) on 1981 and 1982 models, and 10 ft. lbs. (14 Nm) on prior models.

9. Turn the ball stud cotter pin hole to the fore and aft position on models up to 1981. 1982 and later models use no cotter pin. Remove the block of wood from between the upper control arm and frame.

10. Clean and inspect the steering knuckle hole. Replace the steering knuckle if any out of roundness is noted.

11. Insert the ball stud into the steering knuckle, and install and torque the stud nut to 50 ft. lbs. (68 Nm) on 1982–84 models, 55 ft. lbs. (75 Nm) on 1981 models, and 60 ft. lbs. (81 Nm) on earlier models. On 1981 and earlier models, install a new cotter pin. If nut must be turned to align cotter pin holes, further. Do not back off!

12. Install a lube fitting, and fill the joint with fresh grease.

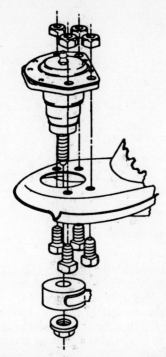

When installing the new upper ball joints, make sure that the nuts are on top

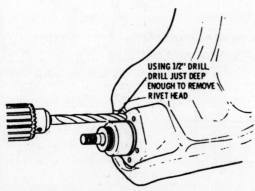

Drill the upper ball joint rivet heads

USING 1/2" DRILL DRILL JUST DEEP ENOUGH TO REMOVE RIVET HEAD

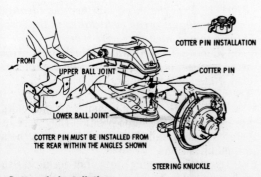

COTTER PIN INSTALLATION

FRONT

UPPER BALL JOINT

COTTER PIN

LOWER BALL JOINT

COTTER PIN MUST BE INSTALLED FROM THE REAR WITHIN THE ANGLES SHOWN

STEERING KNUCKLE

Cotter pin installation

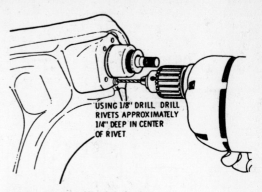

USING 1/8" DRILL DRILL RIVETS APPROXIMATELY 1/4" DEEP IN CENTER OF RIVET

Drill the upper ball joint rivets

13. Remove the lower control arm support (jack, etc.) and lower the vehicle.

Lower Ball Joints
REMOVAL AND INSTALLATION

1. Raise the vehicle and support it securely. Support the lower control arm with a jack or jackstand. Remove the wheel.

2. Remove the lower ball stud cotter pin, and loosen the ball stud nut 2–3 turns.

3. Install a special tool designed for such work between the two ball studs, and press the stud downward in the steering knuckle to free it. Then, remove the stud nut.

4. Guide the lower control arm out of the opening in the splash shield with a putty knife or something similar. Lift up on the upper control arm and place a block of wood between it and the frame. Be careful not to put tension on the brake hose as you do this.

5. Remove the ball joint seal by prying off the retainer with a prybar or driving it off with a chisel.

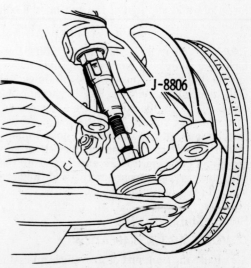

J-8806

Using a ball joint removal tool, disconnect the lower ball joint—always support the lower control arm

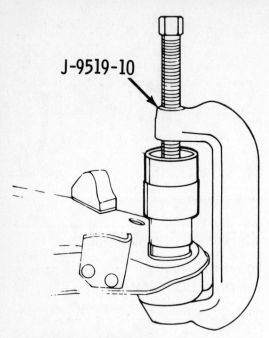

J-9519-10

Pressing out lower ball joint

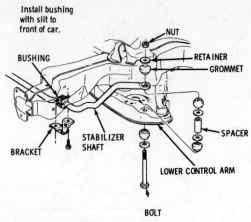

Install bushing with slit to front of car.

NUT

BUSHING

RETAINER

GROMMET

STABILIZER SHAFT

BRACKET

SPACER

LOWER CONTROL ARM

BOLT

Sway bar removal

6. Remove grease fittings and install a tool designed for this purpose and press the ball joint out of the lower control arm. On some models, you may have to disconnect the tie rod at the knuckle to do this.

To install:

1. Position the ball joint in the control arm so that the grease purge on the seal faces inboard. Press the joint in with a tool designed for this purpose until it bottoms on the control arm. Remove the block of wood and then insert the ballstud through the steering knuckle hole on the control arm.

8. Turn the ball stud cotter pin hole so it faces fore and aft. Install the nut on the ball stud and torque it to: 105 ft. lbs. (140 Nm) on 1975–77 vehicles; 83 ft. lbs. (112 Nm) on 1978–79 vehicles; 90 ft. lbs. (122 Nm) on 1980–81 vehicles; 70 ft. lbs. (95 Nm) on 1982–83 models; and 90 ft. lbs. (122 Nm) on 1984–90 Buick and Olds models. On 1984–90 Pontiac, torque the nut to 70 ft. lbs. (95 Nm). Then, as necessary, turn the nut tighter to line up one of the castellations with the cotter pin hole. Finally, install the cotter pin and bend both prongs down and back against the nut. Lubricate the joint until grease appears at the seal. Remove supports and lower the vehicle.

Sway (Stabilizer) Bar

REMOVAL AND INSTALLATION

1. Raise the front end of the vehicle and safely support it with jackstands.

2. Disconnect each side of the sway bar link-age by removing the nut from the link bolt. Pull the bolt from the linkage and remove the retainers, grommets and spacer.

3. Remove the bracket-to-frame or body bolts on both sides of the vehicle and remove the sway bar, rubber bushings and brackets.

To install:

4. Make sure the rubber bushings are installed squarely in the bracket with the slit in the bushings facing the front of the vehicle. Torque the sway bar link nuts to 13 ft. lbs. (18 Nm).

Upper Control Arm

REMOVAL AND INSTALLATION

1. Raise the vehicle and support safely with jackstands.

2. Support the outer end of the lower control arm with a jack.

CAUTION: *Leave the jack in place during removal and installation, in order to keep the spring and control arm positioned.*

3. Remove the wheel.

4. Separate the upper ball joint from the steering knuckle as described above under Upper Ball Joint Replacement.

5. Remove the control arm shaft-to-frame nuts.

NOTE: *Tape the shims together and identify them so that they can be installed in the positions from which they were removed.*

6. Remove the bolts which attach the control arm shaft to the frame and remove the control arm. Note the positions of the bolts.

To install:

1. Make sure that the shaft-to-frame bolts are installed in the same position they were in before removal and that the shims are in their original positions.

2. Use free running nuts (not locknuts) to pull serrated bolts through the frame.

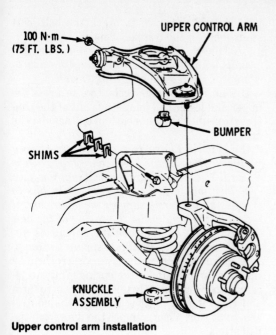

UPPER CONTROL ARM

100 N·m
(75 FT. LBS.)

BUMPER

SHIMS

KNUCKLE
ASSEMBLY

Upper control arm installation

3. Install the locknuts. Tighten the thinner shim pack first.

4. After the vehicle has been lowered to the ground, bounce the front end to center the bushings and then tighten the bushing collar bolts to 45 ft. lbs. (61 Nm). Tighten the shaft-to-frame bolts to 90 ft. lbs. (122 Nm). The control arm shaft nuts are tightened to 75 ft. lbs. (102 Nm) on models through 1982. Use 85 ft. lbs. (120 Nm) on 1983–84 models. On 1985–87 models, torque the bolts to 48 ft. lbs. (65 Nm) on the Regal and Bonneville, and to 70 ft. lbs. (95 Nm) on the Parisienne and all wagons.

Lower Control Arm

REMOVAL AND INSTALLATION

CAUTION: *The coil springs are under a considerable amount of tension. Be extremely careful when removing or installing them; they can exert enough force to cause serious injury. Use only approved spring compressors for suspension servicing.*

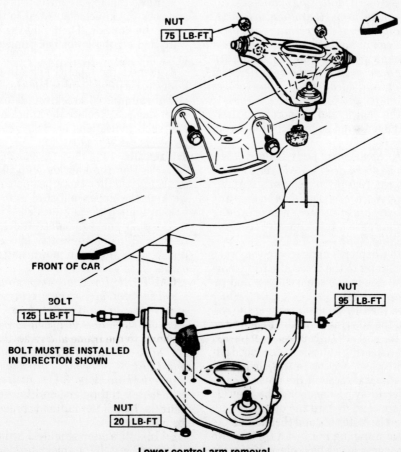

NUT
75 LB-FT

A

FRONT OF CAR

BOLT
125 LB-FT

BOLT MUST BE INSTALLED
IN DIRECTION SHOWN

NUT
95 LB-FT

NUT
20 LB-FT

Lower control arm removal

1. Remove the spring as described earlier.

2. Remove the ball stud from the steering knuckle as described earlier.

3. Remove the control arm pivot bolts and the control arm. On later models, you may have to guide the control arm out of the splash shield, using a putty knife or similar tool to protect parts.

To install:

1. Position the control arm into spring and locate the bushing-to-frame brackets. If any bolts are to be replaced, do so with bolts of equal strength and quality.

2. Install the bolts and nuts loosely. Connect the control arm with the knuckle and torque the nut to 83 ft. lbs. (112 Nm). *Install a new cotter pin.*

3. With a jack supporting the lower control arm, torque the front bolt to 95 ft. lbs. (130 Nm) and the rear bolt to 125 ft. lbs. (168 Nm).

4. Install the shock absorber, sway bar and wheel. Lower the vehicle and check operation.

Knuckle and Spindle

REMOVAL AND INSTALLATION

NOTE: *In order to perform this procedure, you will need a tool for forcing ball joint studs out of the control arms. It would also be helpful to have a tool that will permit you to press the tie rod end out of the steering knuckle. A special tool for seating the tie rod ends when installing them back into the knuckles, GM J–29193 or equivalent, will ensure proper seating.*

1. Raise the vehicle and support it securely under the frame. Do not support the lower control arm yet.

CAUTION: *Some brake pads contain asbestos, which has been determined to be a cancer causing agent. Never clean the brake surfaces with compressed air! Avoid inhaling any dust from any brake surface! When cleaning brake surfaces, use a commercially available brake cleaning fluid.*

2. Refer to Chapter 9 and remove the brake caliper. Then, refer to the procedure for removing the brake disc in the same chapter and remove the disc and hub.

3. Remove the three bolts attaching the water shield to the steering knuckle. Remove the shield and its gasket. Disconnect the tie rod ends from the steering knuckle as described later in the "Steering" section in this chapter.

4. Pry the knuckle seal off the knuckle carefully in order to avoid damaging the knuckle sealing surfaces and discard the old seal.

5. Remove the cotter pin and then loosen the ball joint stud retaining nut just a turn or two on both upper and lower ball joints. You want just enough clearance to break the ball joint studs loose in the control arms.

CAUTION: *The nuts must remain on the studs with plenty of extra threads in order to prevent the release of spring tension.*

Use an appropriate special tool to press the upper and lower ball joint studs out of the control arms until the nuts bottom out against the arms.

CAUTION: *There is tremendous spring pressure forcing the lower control arm downward. You must assure yourself that you have a floor jack or other appropriate means to safely and securely support the lower control arm by the area under the spring in the next step; otherwise, remove the spring as described earlier to eliminate spring tension.*

6. Securely support the lower control arm by the area directly under the spring. You can locate a floor jack directly under the control arm and raise it just until is contacts the control arm to do this. Then, remove the nuts from the ball studs.

7. Remove the tie rod end cotter pin, nut and rod end using a tie rod puller tool J–6627–A. Refer to the "Steering" section in this chapter for assistance.

8. Raise the upper control arm for clearance and rock the knuckle outward so the ball stud clears the knuckle. Then, pull the knuckle upward and off the lower ball joint stud and remove it.

9. Inspect the tapered holes in the steering knuckle, cleaning out dirt and checking for any out-of-roundness, cracking, deformation, or other damage. Replace the knuckle if there are any such indications *or dangerous front end problems could result* .

To install:

1. Position the knuckle onto the lower ball joint stud and then raise the upper control arm, working the upper ball stud into the tapered hole in the top of the knuckle.

2. Install the ball joint stud nuts, torque them, and install the cotter pins as described under "Ball Joint" removal and installation earlier in this chapter.

CAUTION: *It is vitally important that the tie rod end seat fully in the steering knuckle. You may want to use a tool such as GM J–29193 or equivalent to ensure complete seating. This tool is installed over the partly assembled knuckle and tie rod end and its nut is torqued to 15 ft. lbs. (20 Nm) to draw the tie rod end into the knuckle.*

3. Install the tie rod end into the steering knuckle. Install the nut and torque it to 40 ft. lbs. (54 Nm).

4. Install a new shield-to-knuckle splash shield and install the shield, torquing the three

mounting bolts to 120 inch lbs. (14 Nm). Grease its lips with wheel bearing grease and carefully install a new grease seal.

5. Repack the wheel bearings, install the hub and rotor, and readjust the bearings.

6. Install the caliper and remaining parts in reverse order, referring to the "Caliper" removal and installation procedure in chapter 9.

Front End Alignment

NOTE: *The procedure for checking and adjusting front wheel alignment requires specialized equipment and professional skills. The following descriptions and adjustment procedures are for general reference only.*

Front wheel alignment is the position of the front wheels relative to each other and to the vehicle. It is determined, and must be maintained to provide safe, accurate steering with minimum tire wear. Many factors are involved in wheel alignment and adjustments are provided to return those that might change due to normal wear to their original value. The factors which determine wheel alignment are dependent on one another; therefore, when one of the factors is adjusted, the others must be adjusted to compensate. Descriptions of these factors and their affects on the vehicle are provided below.

NOTE: *Do not attempt to check and adjust the front wheel alignment without first making a thorough inspection of the front suspension components.*

CASTER

Caster angle is the number of degrees that a line drawn through the steering knuckle pivots is inclined from the vertical, toward the front or rear of the vehicle. Caster improves directional stability and decreases susceptibility to crosswinds or road surface deviations.

CAMBER

Camber angle is the number of degrees that the centerline of the wheel is inclined from the vertical. Camber reduces loading of the outer

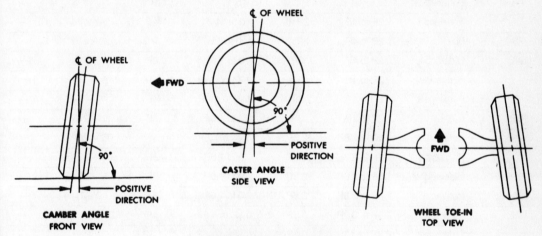

Caster, camber and toe-in

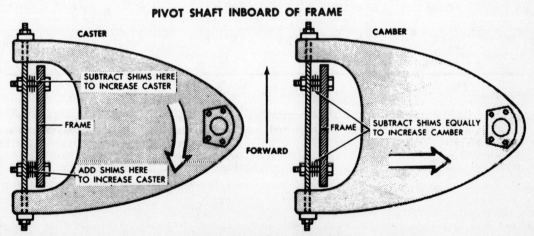

Caster and camber adjustment

Wheel Alignment Specifications

| Year | Make | Caster | | Camber | | Toe-in (in.) | Steering Axle Inclin. (deg.) |
		Range (deg.)	Pref Setting (deg.)	Range (deg.)	Pref Setting (deg.)		
1975–76	Buick	1P to 2P	1½P	½P to 1½P LH / 0–1P RH	1P LH / ½ RH	0 to ⅛	10.5
	Oldsmobile	½P to 2½P	1½P	①	1P LH / ½ RH	0 to ⅛	10.5
	Pontiac	1P to 2P	1½P	½P to 1P LH / 0 to 1P RH	1P / ½P	0 to ⅛	10.3
1977	Buick	2P to 4P	3P	0 to 1½P	¾P	1/16 to 3/16	10.5
	Oldsmobile	2½P to 3½P	3P	¼P to 1¼P	¾P	1/16 to 3/16	10.5
	Pontiac	2½P to 3½P	3P	0 to 1½	¾P	⅛ to ¼	10.3
1978–82	Oldsmobile	2P to 4P	3P	0 to 1⅝P	¾P	0 to ¼	—
	Pontiac	2P to 4P	3P	0 to 1⅔P ②	⅘P ③	1/16 to 3/16 ④	10⅓ ⑤
1978–83	Buick	2P to 4P	3P	0 to 1⅝P	3/16P	1/16 to ¼	—
1983–84	Oldsmobile	2P to 4P	3P	0 to 1⅝P	¾P	1/16 to ¼	—
	Bonneville	3P to 4P ⑥	3P ⑦⑧	⅓N to 1⅓P	½P ⑧	1/16 to ¼	—
	Parisienne	2P to 4P	3P ⑧	0 to 1½P	⅘P	1/16 to ¼	—
1984	Buick	2P to 4P	3P ⑧	0 to 1⅝	¾P ⑧	.1°–.2° ⑨	—
1985	Oldsmobile	2P to 4P	3P	0 to 1.6P	.8P	.1°–.2° ⑨	—
	Bonneville	2P to 4P	3P	⅓P to 1⅓P	½P	1/10–3/16	—
	Parisienne	2P to 4P	3P	⅓P to 1⅓P	⅘P	1/16–3/16	—
1985–87	Buick	2P to 4P	3P	0 to 1.6P	.8P	.1°–.2° ⑨	—
1986	Bonneville	1.8P to 2.8P	2.8P	⅓N to 1⅓P	½P	.05°–.25° ⑨	—
	Parisienne	1.8P to 2.8P	2.8P	0 to 1.6P	.8P	.05°–2.5° ⑨	—
1986–87	Oldsmobile	1.8P to 2.8P	2.8P	0 to 1.6P	.8P	.05°–2.5° ⑨	—
1987	Pontiac	1.8P to 2.8P	2.8P	0 to 1.6P	.8P	0°–2°	—
1988	Buick	2.8P to 3.8P	3.3P	0.8P to 1.6P	1.3P	.05P to .15P	—
	Oldsmobile	2.8P to 3.8P	3.3P	0.8P to 1.6P	1.3P	.05P to .15P ⑨	—
	Pontiac	2.8P to 3.8P	3.3P	0.8P to 1.6P	1.3P	.05P to .15P ⑨	—
1989–90	Buick, Olds, Pontiac	3.0P to 4.0P	3.5P	0.8P to 1.6P	1.3P	.05P to .15P ⑨	—

—Not Specified
P Positive
N Negative
RH Right Hand
LH Left Hand
① ¼P to 1¾P LH
  ¼N to 1¼P RH
② 0 to 1⅝P 1980–83
③ 13/16P 1980–83

④ 1/16 to ¼ 1980–83
⑤ 10 19/32 1980–83
⑥ Manual Steering 1N to 1P
⑦ Manual Steering 1P
⑧ Caster and Camber should not vary more than ½ degree from side to side, and must not vary more than 1 degree from side to side.
⑨ Note that setting is in degrees, not inches.

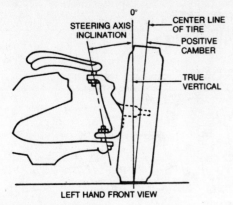

Steering axis inclination

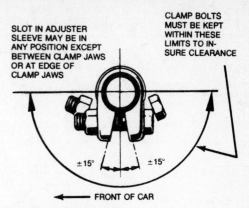

Tie rod clamp positioning

wheel bearing and improves the tire contact patch while cornering.

STEERING AXIS INCLINATION

Steering axis inclination is the number of degrees that a line drawn through the steering knuckle pivots is inclined from the vertical, when viewed from the front of the vehicle. This, in combination with caster, is responsible for directional stability and self-centering of the steering. As the steering knuckle swings from lock to lock, the spindle generates an arc, the high point being the straight-ahead position of the wheel. Due to this arc, as the wheel turns, the front of the vehicle is raised. The weight of the vehicle acts against this lift and attempts to return the spindle to the high point of the arc, resulting in self-centering, when the steering wheel is released, and straight line stability.

TOE-IN

Toe-in is the difference of the distance between the centers of the front and rear of the front wheels. It is most commonly measured in inches, but is occasionally referred to as an angle between the wheels. Toe-in is necessary to compensate for the tendency of the wheels to deflect rearward while in motion. Due to this tendency, the wheels of a vehicle, with properly adjusted toe-in, are traveling straight forward when the vehicle itself is traveling straight forward, resulting in directional stability and minimum tire wear.

NOTE: *The Do-it-Yourself mechanic should not attempt to perform any wheel alignment procedures. Expensive alignment tools are needed and would not be cost efficient to purchase these tools. The wheel alignment should be performed by a certified alignment technician using the proper alignment tools.*

CASTER ADJUSTMENT

1. Loosen the pivot shaft-to-frame nuts on the upper control arm. Keep in mind that the upper arm is supporting the weight of the vehicle. Loosen the nuts only as far as necessary.

2. Caster is adjusted by removing shims from the front bolt and replacing them at the rear bolt, or vice versa.

CAMBER ADJUSTMENT

1. Camber is adjusted at the same time and in the same manner as caster.

2. To adjust the camber, add or subtract shims from both the front and the rear of the shaft at the same time.

TOE-IN ADJUSTMENT

Toe-in is adjusted after the caster and camber adjustments are carried out. Adjust the toe-in by loosening the clamps on the tie rod sleeves, and turning the sleeves an equal amount in the opposite direction, to maintain steering wheel spoke alignment while adjusting toe-in.

REAR SUSPENSION

A four link rear suspension is used on the large-body Buick, Olds and Pontiac models, except 1975–76 station wagons. The axle housing is connected to the frame by two upper and lower control arms with rubber bushings at each end of the arm. The control arms oppose torque reaction on acceleration and braking, and maintain the axle relationship to the frame.

Two coil springs support the weight of the vehicle in the rear. They are retained between seats in the frame and brackets welded to the axle housing. A rubber insulator is used on the upper side. Shock absorbers are mounted on brackets between the axle housing and the frame.

The rear suspension on 1975 and 1976 station wagons is by parallel leaf springs and shock absorbers.

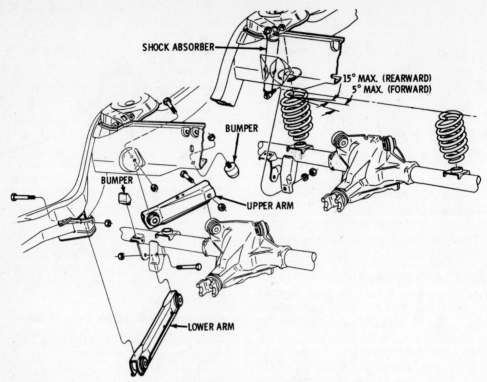

Coil spring rear suspension

A sway bar is optional equipment on coil spring models.

Springs

REMOVAL AND INSTALLATION

All Except 1975–76 Wagons

CAUTION: *When removing the rear coil springs without the aid of a spring compressor, be very careful the spring does not fly out and strike someone. If a spring compressor is available, use it. The following procedure does not use a spring compressor. However, if the axle housing is lowered slowly, the spring should come out without incident.*

1. Raise the rear of the vehicle on the axle housing and support it safely on the frame rails with jackstands. Do not lower the jack yet.

2. Disconnect the brake line at the axle housing.

3. Disconnect the upper control arms at the axle housing.

4. Remove the shock absorber at its lower mount.

5. Lower the jack slowly. Do not allow the rear brake hose to become kinked or stretched.

6. Remove the coil spring.

To install:

7. Mount the coil spring in place.

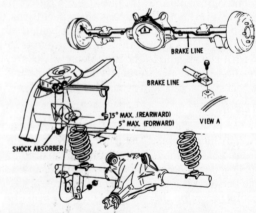

Coil spring mounting

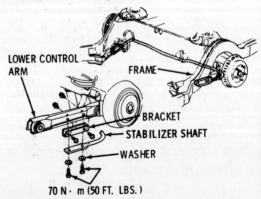

Rear stabilizer bar

8. Jack up the rear axle until you are able to connect the shock at its lower mount.

9. Install the upper control arm bolts at the axle housing and torque to 95 ft. lbs. (128 Nm).

10. Connect the brake line at the axle housing. Bleed the brakes.

11. Remove the jackstands and lower the vehicle.

1975–76 Station Wagons

1. Raise the rear axle housing and safely support the rear end of the vehicle with jackstands placed under the rear frame rails (ahead of the forward rear spring shackles). Do not lower the jack yet.

NOTE: *If removing the right hand spring, loosen the tailpipe and resonator assembly.*

2. Remove the lower shock absorber nut and move the shock out of the bracket. Compress the shock out of the way.

3. Lower the jack until the springs are completely relaxed. The jack must remain underneath the axle housing for support until the spring is completely removed.

NOTE: *Do not stretch the brake hose.*

4. Remove the bolts from the rear spring shackles.

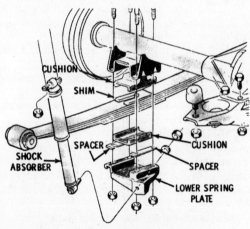

Leaf spring mounting, 1975–76 wagons

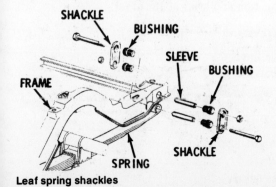

Leaf spring shackles

5. Remove the four U-bolt attaching nuts. Remove the spacers, which will be reused during installation.

6. Remove the NUT ONLY from the front shackle bolt, and while holding the spring up, remove the bolt from the shackle. Remove the spring from the vehicle.

To install:

NOTE: *Before installation, make sure that any parts, including bolts and nuts, that are replaced are replaced with parts of equal strength and quality. Rated nuts and bolts must be replaced with parts of equal rating.*

1. Install the sleeves and bushing halves in the rear shackle (if removed) and loosely install the shackle bolt and nut.

CAUTION: *Do not tighten the shackle nuts until the weight of the vehicle is on the springs.*

2. Place the upper spring cushion pad on the spring so the cushion is indexed on the spring center locating bolt head.

3. Lower the axle housing onto the spring, keeping the jack underneath the housing.

4. Place the lower spring cushion pad on the spring and the shock absorber anchor plate with the dimple on the cushion indexed in the hole in the plate.

5. Position the spring and shock absorber anchor plate to the spring, with the nut of the spring center locating bolt indexed in the dimple of the lower spring cushion pad.

6. Install the lower spring plate, then loosely install the U-bolt nuts.

7. Raise the jack slightly, and install the shim spacers.

8. Lower the axle housing onto the spring, and torque the U-bolt nuts to 50 ft. lbs. (68 Nm). Install the shock absorber lower end stud into the spring plate, and tighten the shock lower end stud nut to 65 ft. lbs. (88 Nm). Make sure the shock stud does not rotate while the nut is tightened.

9. Raise the vehicle so the weight of the vehicle is on the springs. Torque the spring front bolt nut to 60 ft. lbs. (81 Nm), and the rear shackle nut to 105 ft. lbs. (140 Nm).

10. Remove the jack studs and lower the vehicle.

Shock Absorbers

REMOVAL AND INSTALLATION

NOTE: *Examine the shock absorbers following the Testing procedure given for front shocks in this chapter.*

All Models

1. Raise the rear end of the vehicle and support it with jackstands. Support the rear axle

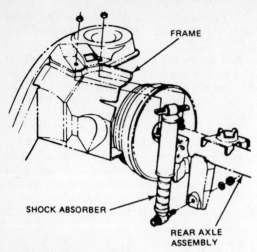

SHOCK ABSORBER

FRAME

REAR AXLE
ASSEMBLY

Shock absorber installation

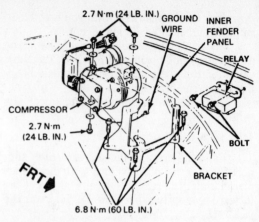

2.7 N·m (24 LB. IN.)   GROUND
WIRE

INNER
FENDER
PANEL

RELAY

COMPRESSOR

2.7 N·m
(24 LB. IN.)

FRT

BOLT

BRACKET

6.8 N·m (60 LB. IN.)

Electronic level control (ELC) pump and relay—late model wagons (optional)

with the hydraulic jack to prevent stretching the brake hose.

2. Remove the nut from the lower end stud of the shock. Tap the shock free from the bracket.

3. Disconnect the shock at the top by removing the bolts, nuts and the lockwashers. Remove the shock from the vehicle.

4. Install the shock and torque the upper bolts to 20 ft. lbs. (27 Nm) and the lower nut to 48 ft. lbs. (65 Nm).

Electronic Level Control (ELC)

The ELC system is an option to the standard rear suspension on late model station wagons. The system adjusts the trim height with varying vehicle loads. The system is activated when weight is added or removed from the rear of the vehicle. A height sensor is mounted to the body and rear suspension to monitor suspension height. As weight is added to the rear of the vehicle the sensor signals the electric air compressor mounted on the right front inner fender to supply air to the rear shocks to raise the vehicle to the proper level. As the weight is removed, the sensor signals the exhaust solenoid to release air from the rear shocks to lower the vehicle.

REMOVAL AND INSTALLATION

Shocks

The ELC shocks are removed the same way as the conventional shocks are removed. The only difference is the air hose has to be disconnected before shock removal

Air Compressor

1. Disconnect the negative (−) battery cable.

2. Disconnect the high pressure hose at the air dryer by rotating the spring clip 90° while holding the connector end and removing the tube assembly.

3. Disconnect the solenoid and motor connections.

4. Remove the support bracket screws, bracket and compressor.

To install:

1. If replacing the compressor, install the dryer and bracket and torque the bolts to 34 inch lbs. (4 Nm). Install the bracket/compressor assembly and torque the screws to 24 inch lbs. (3 Nm).

2. Make all electrical and air connections.

3. Connect the negative battery cable. Cycle the ignition switch and test for system operation and leaks at the dryer.

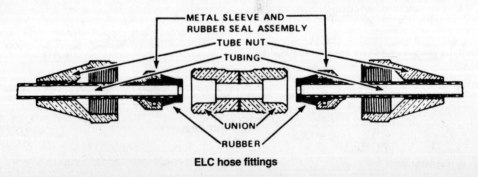

METAL SLEEVE AND
RUBBER SEAL ASSEMBLY

TUBE NUT

TUBING

UNION

RUBBER

ELC hose fittings

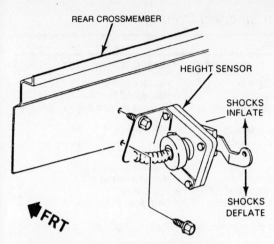

Electronic level control (ELC) height sensor

Height Sensor

The sensor is mounted onto the rear frame crossmember and right control arm.

1. Disconnect the negative (–) battery cable and sensor connection.

2. Remove the link from the control arm, unbolt the sensor bracket and remove the sensor assembly from the vehicle.

To install:

Install the sensor and adjust trim height as follows:

1. Attach the link to the metal arm at the control arm.

2. To increase the vehicle trim height, move the plastic actuator arm upward and tighten the locknut.

3. To decrease the vehicle trim height, move the plastic actuator arm downward and tighten the locknut. **Height sensor adjustment of 1° = ¼ in. at the bumper. Adjustment of 5° total.**

STEERING

Steering Wheel

REMOVAL AND INSTALLATION

All Non-Tilt Wheels

1. Disconnect the negative battery cable.

2. Remove the center pad assembly, either by removing the screws or by gently prying the pad off. Lift up on the pad and disconnect the horn wire by pushing in on the insulator and turning counterclockwise.

3. Remove the steering wheel nut retainer and attaching nut. Using a steering puller, remove the steering wheel.

4. To install, first align the marks on the wheel hub to the marks on the steering shaft.

5. Install the steering wheel, retainer and nut, and torque the nut to 30 ft. lbs. (41 Nm).

NOTE: *When the mark on the steering wheel hub and the steering shaft are lined up, the wheel spokes should be horizontal as the vehicle is driven straight ahead. If they are not horizontal it may be necessary to adjust the tie rod ends until the steering wheel is properly aligned.*

6. Install the horn wire in the cam tower, push in and turn clockwise. Align the pad assembly into position and either press into place or install the screws. Connect the negative battery cable.

Tilt and Telescope Wheels

1. Disconnect the negative battery cable.

2. Remove the pad assembly by either removing the screws or prying the pad off. Disconnect the bayonet-type connector at the horn wire by pushing in and turning counterclockwise.

3. Push the locking lever counterclockwise until the full release position is obtained.

4. Scribe a mark on the plate assembly where the two attaching screws attach the plate assembly to the locking lever. Remove the two screws.

5. Unscrew the plate assembly and remove.

6. Remove the steering wheel nut retainer and nut. Using a puller, remove the wheel.

To install:

1. Install a ⁵⁄₁₆ in. x 18 set screw into the upper shaft at the full extended position and lock.

2. Install the steering wheel, aligning the scribe mark on the hub with the slash mark on the end of the shaft. Make sure that the unattached end of the horn upper contact assembly

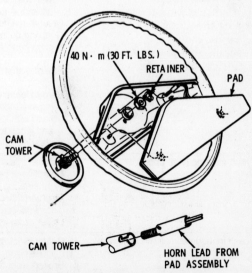

Deluxe steering wheel and pad assembly

Troubleshooting the Steering Column

Problem	Cause	Solution
Will not lock	• Lockbolt spring broken or defective	• Replace lock bolt spring
High effort (required to turn ignition key and lock cylinder)	• Lock cylinder defective	• Replace lock cylinder
	• Ignition switch defective	• Replace ignition switch
	• Rack preload spring broken or deformed	• Replace preload spring
	• Burr on lock sector, lock rack, housing, support or remote rod coupling	• Remove burr
	• Bent sector shaft	• Replace shaft
	• Defective lock rack	• Replace lock rack
	• Remote rod bent, deformed	• Replace rod
	• Ignition switch mounting bracket bent	• Straighten or replace
	• Distorted coupling slot in lock rack (tilt column)	• Replace lock rack
Will stick in "start"	• Remote rod deformed	• Straighten or replace
	• Ignition switch mounting bracket bent	• Straighten or replace
Key cannot be removed in "off-lock"	• Ignition switch is not adjusted correctly	• Adjust switch
	• Defective lock cylinder	• Replace lock cylinder
Lock cylinder can be removed without depressing retainer	• Lock cylinder with defective retainer	• Replace lock cylinder
	• Burr over retainer slot in housing cover or on cylinder retainer	• Remove burr
High effort on lock cylinder between "off" and "off-lock"	• Distorted lock rack	• Replace lock rack
	• Burr on tang of shift gate (automatic column)	• Remove burr
	• Gearshift linkage not adjusted	• Adjust linkage
Noise in column	• One click when in "off-lock" position and the steering wheel is moved (all except automatic column)	• Normal—lock bolt is seating
	• Coupling bolts not tightened	• Tighten pinch bolts
	• Lack of grease on bearings or bearing surfaces	• Lubricate with chassis grease
	• Upper shaft bearing worn or broken	• Replace bearing assembly
	• Lower shaft bearing worn or broken	• Replace bearing. Check shaft and replace if scored.
	• Column not correctly aligned	• Align column
	• Coupling pulled apart	• Replace coupling
	• Broken coupling lower joint	• Repair or replace joint and align column
	• Steering shaft snap ring not seated	• Replace ring. Check for proper seating in groove.
	• Shroud loose on shift bowl. Housing loose on jacket—will be noticed with ignition in "off-lock" and when torque is applied to steering wheel.	• Position shroud over lugs on shift bowl. Tighten mounting screws.
High steering shaft effort	• Column misaligned	• Align column
	• Defective upper or lower bearing	• Replace as required
	• Tight steering shaft universal joint	• Repair or replace
	• Flash on I.D. of shift tube at plastic joint (tilt column only)	• Replace shift tube
	• Upper or lower bearing seized	• Replace bearings
Lash in mounted column assembly	• Column mounting bracket bolts loose	• Tighten bolts
	• Broken weld nuts on column jacket	• Replace column jacket
	• Column capsule bracket sheared	• Replace bracket assembly

Troubleshooting the Steering Column (cont.)

Problem	Cause	Solution
Lash in mounted column assembly (cont.)	• Column bracket to column jacket mounting bolts loose	• Tighten to specified torque
	• Loose lock shoes in housing (tilt column only)	• Replace shoes
	• Loose pivot pins (tilt column only)	• Replace pivot pins and support
	• Loose lock shoe pin (tilt column only)	• Replace pin and housing
	• Loose support screws (tilt column only)	• Tighten screws
Housing loose (tilt column only)	• Excessive clearance between holes in support or housing and pivot pin diameters	• Replace pivot pins and support
	• Housing support-screws loose	• Tighten screws
Steering wheel loose—every other tilt position (tilt column only)	• Loose fit between lock shoe and lock shoe pivot pin	• Replace lock shoes and pivot pin
Steering column not locking in any tilt position (tilt column only)	• Lock shoe seized on pivot pin	• Replace lock shoes and pin
	• Lock shoe grooves have burrs or are filled with foreign material	• Clean or replace lock shoes
	• Lock shoe springs weak or broken	• Replace springs
Noise when tilting column (tilt column only)	• Upper tilt bumpers worn	• Replace tilt bumper
	• Tilt spring rubbing in housing	• Lubricate with chassis grease
One click when in "off-lock" position and the steering wheel is moved	• Seating of lock bolt	• None. Click is normal characteristic sound produced by lock bolt as it seats.
High shift effort (automatic and tilt column only)	• Column not correctly aligned	• Align column
	• Lower bearing not aligned correctly	• Assemble correctly
	• Lack of grease on seal or lower bearing areas	• Lubricate with chassis grease
Improper transmission shifting—automatic and tilt column only	• Sheared shift tube joint	• Replace shift tube
	• Improper transmission gearshift linkage adjustment	• Adjust linkage
	• Loose lower shift lever	• Replace shift tube

Troubleshooting the Ignition Switch

Problem	Cause	Solution
Ignition switch electrically inoperative	• Loose or defective switch connector	• Tighten or replace connector
	• Feed wire open (fusible link)	• Repair or replace
	• Defective ignition switch	• Replace ignition switch
Engine will not crank	• Ignition switch not adjusted properly	• Adjust switch
Ignition switch wil not actuate mechanically	• Defective ignition switch	• Replace switch
	• Defective lock sector	• Replace lock sector
	• Defective remote rod	• Replace remote rod
Ignition switch cannot be adjusted correctly	• Remote rod deformed	• Repair, straighten or replace

Troubleshooting the Turn Signal Switch

Problem	Cause	Solution
Turn signal will not cancel	• Loose switch mounting screws • Switch or anchor bosses broken • Broken, missing or out of position detent, or cancelling spring	• Tighten screws • Replace switch • Reposition springs or replace switch as required
Turn signal difficult to operate	• Turn signal lever loose • Switch yoke broken or distorted • Loose or misplaced springs • Foreign parts and/or materials in switch • Switch mounted loosely	• Tighten mounting screws • Replace switch • Reposition springs or replace switch • Remove foreign parts and/or material • Tighten mounting screws
Turn signal will not indicate lane change	• Broken lane change pressure pad or spring hanger • Broken, missing or misplaced lane change spring • Jammed wires	• Replace switch • Replace or reposition as required • Loosen mounting screws, reposition wires and retighten screws
Turn signal will not stay in turn position	• Foreign material or loose parts impeding movement of switch yoke • Defective switch	• Remove material and/or parts • Replace switch
Hazard switch cannot be pulled out	• Foreign material between hazard support cancelling leg and yoke	• Remove foreign material. No foreign material impeding function of hazard switch—replace turn signal switch.
No turn signal lights	• Inoperative turn signal flasher • Defective or blown fuse • Loose chassis to column harness connector • Disconnect column to chassis connector. Connect new switch to chassis and operate switch by hand. If vehicle lights now operate normally, signal switch is inoperative • If vehicle lights do not operate, check chassis wiring for opens, grounds, etc.	• Replace turn signal flasher • Replace fuse • Connect securely • Replace signal switch • Repair chassis wiring as required
Instrument panel turn indicator lights on but not flashing	• Burned out or damaged front or rear turn signal bulb • If vehicle lights do not operate, check light sockets for high resistance connections, the chassis wiring for opens, grounds, etc. • Inoperative flasher • Loose chassis to column harness connection • Inoperative turn signal switch • To determine if turn signal switch is defective, substitute new switch into circuit and operate switch by hand. If the vehicle's lights operate normally, signal switch is inoperative.	• Replace bulb • Repair chassis wiring as required • Replace flasher • Connect securely • Replace turn signal switch • Replace turn signal switch
Stop light not on when turn indicated	• Loose column to chassis connection • Disconnect column to chassis connector. Connect new switch into system without removing old.	• Connect securely • Replace signal switch

Troubleshooting the Turn Signal Switch (cont.)

Problem	Cause	Solution
Stop light not on when turn indicated (cont.)	Operate switch by hand. If brake lights work with switch in the turn position, signal switch is defective.	
	• If brake lights do not work, check connector to stop light sockets for grounds, opens, etc.	• Repair connector to stop light circuits using service manual as guide
Turn indicator panel lights not flashing	• Burned out bulbs • High resistance to ground at bulb socket	• Replace bulbs • Replace socket
	• Opens, ground in wiring harness from front turn signal bulb socket to indicator lights	• Locate and repair as required
Turn signal lights flash very slowly	• High resistance ground at light sockets • Incorrect capacity turn signal flasher or bulb	• Repair high resistance grounds at light sockets • Replace turn signal flasher or bulb
	• If flashing rate is still extremely slow, check chassis wiring harness from the connector to light sockets for high resistance	• Locate and repair as required
	• Loose chassis to column harness connection	• Connect securely
	• Disconnect column to chassis connector. Connect new switch into system without removing old. Operate switch by hand. If flashing occurs at normal rate, the signal switch is defective.	• Replace turn signal switch
Hazard signal lights will not flash—turn signal functions normally	• Blow fuse • Inoperative hazard warning flasher	• Replace fuse • Replace hazard warning flasher in fuse panel
	• Loose chassis-to-column harness connection	• Conect securely
	• Disconnect column to chassis connector. Connect new switch into system without removing old. Depress the hazard warning lights. If they now work normally, turn signal switch is defective.	• Replace turn signal switch
	• If lights do not flash, check wiring harness "K" lead for open between hazard flasher and connector. If open, fuse block is defective	• Repair or replace brown wire or connector as required

is seated flush against the top of the horn contact assembly.

2. Install the nut on the upper steering shaft, along with the nut retainer. Torque to 30 ft. lbs. (41 Nm).

3. Remove the set screw installed in step 1.

4. Install the plate assembly and tighten finger tight.

5. Position the locking lever in the vertical position and move the lever counterclockwise until the holes in the plate align with the holes in the lever. Install the attaching screws.

6. Align the pad assembly with the holes in the steering wheel and install the retaining screws. Connect the negative battery cable.

Check to see that the locking lever securely locks the wheel travel and that the wheel travel is free in the unlocked position.

Turn Signal Switch
REMOVAL AND INSTALLATION
Models without Tilt and Telescopic Column

1. Disconnect the negative battery cable.

2. Remove the steering wheel as described earlier.

3. Remove the covers from the steering column shaft. The plastic keepers under the cover are not necessary for installation.

Troubleshooting the Manual Steering Gear

Problem	Cause	Solution
Hard or erratic steering	• Incorrect tire pressure	• Inflate tires to recommended pressures
	• Insufficient or incorrect lubrication	• Lubricate as required (refer to Maintenance Section)
	• Suspension, or steering linkage parts damaged or misaligned	• Repair or replace parts as necessary
	• Improper front wheel alignment	• Adjust incorrect wheel alignment angles
	• Incorrect steering gear adjustment	• Adjust steering gear
	• Sagging springs	• Replace springs
Play or looseness in steering	• Steering wheel loose	• Inspect shaft spines and repair as necessary. Tighten attaching nut and stake in place.
	• Steering linkage or attaching parts loose or worn	• Tighten, adjust, or replace faulty components
	• Pitman arm loose	• Inspect shaft splines and repair as necessary. Tighten attaching nut and stake in place
	• Steering gear attaching bolts loose	• Tighten bolts
	• Loose or worn wheel bearings	• Adjust or replace bearings
	• Steering gear adjustment incorrect or parts badly worn	• Adjust gear or replace defective parts
Wheel shimmy or tramp	• Improper tire pressure	• Inflate tires to recommended pressures
	• Wheels, tires, or brake rotors out-of-balance or out-of-round	• Inspect and replace or balance parts
	• Inoperative, worn, or loose shock absorbers or mounting parts	• Repair or replace shocks or mountings
	• Loose or worn steering or suspension parts	• Tighten or replace as necessary
	• Loose or worn wheel bearings	• Adjust or replace bearings
	• Incorrect steering gear adjustments	• Adjust steering gear
	• Incorrect front wheel alignment	• Correct front wheel alignment
Tire wear	• Improper tire pressure	• Inflate tires to recommended pressures
	• Failure to rotate tires	• Rotate tires
	• Brakes grabbing	• Adjust or repair brakes
	• Incorrect front wheel alignment	• Align incorrect angles
	• Broken or damaged steering and suspension parts	• Repair or replace defective parts
	• Wheel runout	• Replace faulty wheel
	• Excessive speed on turns	• Make driver aware of conditions
Vehicle leads to one side	• Improper tire pressures	• Inflate tires to recommended pressures
	• Front tires with uneven tread depth, wear pattern, or different cord design (i.e., one bias ply and one belted or radial tire on front wheels)	• Install tires of same cord construction and reasonably even tread depth, design, and wear pattern
	• Incorrect front wheel alignment	• Align incorrect angles
	• Brakes dragging	• Adjust or repair brakes
	• Pulling due to uneven tire construction	• Replace faulty tire

Troubleshooting the Power Steering Gear

Problem	Cause	Solution
Hissing noise in steering gear	• There is some noise in all power steering systems. One of the most common is a hissing sound most evident at standstill parking. There is no relationship between this noise and performance of the steering. Hiss may be expected when steering wheel is at end of travel or when slowly turning at standstill.	• Slight hiss is normal and in no way affects steering. Do not replace valve unless hiss is extremely objectionable. A replacement valve will also exhibit slight noise and is not always a cure. Investigate clearance around flexible coupling rivets. Be sure steering shaft and gear are aligned so flexible coupling rotates in a flat plane and is not distorted as shaft rotates. Any metal-to-metal contacts through flexible coupling will transmit valve hiss into passenger compartment through the steering column.
Rattle or chuckle noise in steering gear	• Gear loose on frame	• Check gear-to-frame mounting screws. Tighten screws to 88 N·m (65 foot pounds) torque.
	• Steering linkage looseness	• Check linkage pivot points for wear. Replace if necessary.
	• Pressure hose touching other parts of car	• Adjust hose position. Do not bend tubing by hand.
	• Loose pitman shaft over center adjustment **NOTE:** A slight rattle may occur on turns because of increased clearance off the "high point." This is normal and clearance must not be reduced below specified limits to eliminate this slight rattle.	• Adjust to specifications
	• Loose pitman arm	• Tighten pitman arm nut to specifications
Squawk noise in steering gear when turning or recovering from a turn	• Damper O-ring on valve spool cut	• Replace damper O-ring
Poor return of steering wheel to center	• Tires not properly inflated • Lack of lubrication in linkage and ball joints	• Inflate to specified pressure • Lube linkage and ball joints
	• Lower coupling flange rubbing against steering gear adjuster plug	• Loosen pinch bolt and assemble properly
	• Steering gear to column misalignment	• Align steering column
	• Improper front wheel alignment • Steering linkage binding • Ball joints binding • Steering wheel rubbing against housing	• Check and adjust as necessary • Replace pivots • Replace ball joints • Align housing
	• Tight or frozen steering shaft bearings	• Replace bearings
	• Sticking or plugged valve spool	• Remove and clean or replace valve
	• Steering gear adjustments over specifications	• Check adjustment with gear out of car. Adjust as required.
	• Kink in return hose	• Replace hose
Car leads to one side or the other (keep in mind road condition and wind. Test car in both directions on flat road)	• Front end misaligned • Unbalanced steering gear valve **NOTE:** If this is cause, steering effort will be very light in direction of lead and normal or heavier in opposite direction	• Adjust to specifications • Replace valve

Troubleshooting the Power Steering Gear (cont.)

Problem	Cause	Solution
Momentary increase in effort when turning wheel fast to right or left	• Low oil level • Pump belt slipping • High internal leakage	• Add power steering fluid as required • Tighten or replace belt • Check pump pressure. (See pressure test)
Steering wheel surges or jerks when turning with engine running especially during parking	• Low oil level • Loose pump belt • Steering linkage hitting engine oil pan at full turn • Insufficient pump pressure • Pump flow control valve sticking	• Fill as required • Adjust tension to specification • Correct clearance • Check pump pressure. (See pressure test). Replace relief valve if defective. • Inspect for varnish or damage, replace if necessary
Excessive wheel kickback or loose steering	• Air in system • Steering gear loose on frame • Steering linkage joints worn enough to be loose • Worn poppet valve • Loose thrust bearing preload adjustment • Excessive overcenter lash	• Add oil to pump reservoir and bleed by operating steering. Check hose connectors for proper torque and adjust as required. • Tighten attaching screws to specified torque • Replace loose pivots • Replace poppet valve • Adjust to specification with gear out of vehicle • Adjust to specification with gear out of car
Hard steering or lack of assist	• Loose pump belt • Low oil level **NOTE:** Low oil level will also result in excessive pump noise • Steering gear to column misalignment • Lower coupling flange rubbing against steering gear adjuster plug • Tires not properly inflated	• Adjust belt tension to specification • Fill to proper level. If excessively low, check all lines and joints for evidence of external leakage. Tighten loose connectors. • Align steering column • Loosen pinch bolt and assemble properly • Inflate to recommended pressure
Foamy milky power steering fluid, low fluid level and possible low pressure	• Air in the fluid, and loss of fluid due to internal pump leakage causing overflow	• Check for leak and correct. Bleed system. Extremely cold temperatures will cause system aeration should the oil level be low. If oil level is correct and pump still foams, remove pump from vehicle and separate reservoir from housing. Check welsh plug and housing for cracks. If plug is loose or housing is cracked, replace housing.
Low pressure due to steering pump	• Flow control valve stuck or inoperative • Pressure plate not flat against cam ring	• Remove burrs or dirt or replace. Flush system. • Correct
Low pressure due to steering gear	• Pressure loss in cylinder due to worn piston ring or badly worn housing bore • Leakage at valve rings, valve body-to-worm seal	• Remove gear from car for disassembly and inspection of ring and housing bore • Remove gear from car for disassembly and replace seals

Troubleshooting the Power Steering Pump

Problem	Cause	Solution
Chirp noise in steering pump	• Loose belt	• Adjust belt tension to specification
Belt squeal (particularly noticeable at full wheel travel and stand still parking)	• Loose belt	• Adjust belt tension to specification
Growl noise in steering pump	• Excessive back pressure in hoses or steering gear caused by restriction	• Locate restriction and correct. Replace part if necessary.
Growl noise in steering pump (particularly noticeable at stand still parking)	• Scored pressure plates, thrust plate or rotor • Extreme wear of cam ring	• Replace parts and flush system • Replace parts
Groan noise in steering pump	• Low oil level • Air in the oil. Poor pressure hose connection.	• Fill reservoir to proper level • Tighten connector to specified torque. Bleed system by operating steering from right to left— full turn.
Rattle noise in steering pump	• Vanes not installed properly • Vanes sticking in rotor slots	• Install properly • Free up by removing burrs, varnish, or dirt
Swish noise in steering pump	• Defective flow control valve	• Replace part
Whine noise in steering pump	• Pump shaft bearing scored	• Replace housing and shaft. Flush system.
Hard steering or lack of assist	• Loose pump belt • Low oil level in reservoir **NOTE:** Low oil level will also result in excessive pump noise • Steering gear to column misalignment • Lower coupling flange rubbing against steering gear adjuster plug • Tires not properly inflated	• Adjust belt tension to specification • Fill to proper level. If excessively low, check all lines and joints for evidence of external leakage. Tighten loose connectors. • Align steering column • Loosen pinch bolt and assemble properly • Inflate to recommended pressure
Foaming milky power steering fluid, low fluid level and possible low pressure	• Air in the fluid, and loss of fluid due to internal pump leakage causing overflow	• Check for leaks and correct. Bleed system. Extremely cold temperatures will cause system aeration should the oil level be low. If oil level is correct and pump still foams, remove pump from vehicle and separate reservoir from body. Check welsh plug and body for cracks. If plug is loose or body is cracked, replace body.
Low pump pressure	• Flow control valve stuck or inoperative • Pressure plate not flat against cam ring	• Remove burrs or dirt or replace. Flush system. • Correct
Momentary increase in effort when turning wheel fast to right or left	• Low oil level in pump • Pump belt slipping • High internal leakage	• Add power steering fluid as required • Tighten or replace belt • Check pump pressure. (See pressure test)
Steering wheel surges or jerks when turning with engine running especially during parking	• Low oil level • Loose pump belt • Steering linkage hitting engine oil pan at full turn • Insufficient pump pressure	• Fill as required • Adjust tension to specification • Correct clearance • Check pump pressure. (See pressure test). Replace flow control valve if defective.

Troubleshooting the Power Steering Pump (cont.)

Problem	Cause	Solution
Steering wheel surges or jerks when turning with engine running especially during parking (cont.)	• Sticking flow control valve	• Inspect for varnish or damage, replace if necessary
Excessive wheel kickback or loose steering	• Air in system	• Add oil to pump reservoir and bleed by operating steering. Check hose connectors for proper torque and adjust as required.
Low pump pressure	• Extreme wear of cam ring	• Replace parts. Flush system.
	• Scored pressure plate, thrust plate, or rotor	• Replace parts. Flush system.
	• Vanes not installed properly	• Install properly
	• Vanes sticking in rotor slots	• Freeup by removing burrs, varnish, or dirt
	• Cracked or broken thrust or pressure plate	• Replace part

4. Depress the lockplate and remove the snapring from the shaft. Remove the lock-plate and the canceling cam.

5. Remove the upper bearing preload spring.

6. Place the turn signal lever in the right turn position, then remove the turn signal lever attaching screw and the lever. On 1978 and later models with the dimmer switch in the turn signal lever, remove the actuator arm screw and the arm.

7. Push in on the hazard warning knob, then remove the screw and the hazard warning knob.

8. Remove the three turn signal switch attaching screws.

9. Remove the lower trim panel and then disconnect the turn signal connector from the wiring harness. Lift the connector from the mounting bracket on the right side of the jacket.

10. Remove the four bolts which attach the bracket assembly to the jacket.

11. Loosen the screw holding the shift indicator needle and disconnect the clip from the link.

12. Remove the two nuts from the column support bracket while holding the column in position. Remove the bracket assembly and wire protector from the wiring, then loosely install the bracket-to-support column.

13. Tape the turn signal wires at the connec-

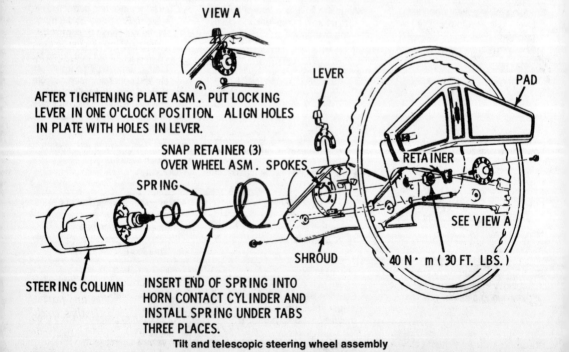

VIEW A

AFTER TIGHTENING PLATE ASM. PUT LOCKING LEVER IN ONE O'CLOCK POSITION. ALIGN HOLES IN PLATE WITH HOLES IN LEVER.

SNAP RETAINER (3) OVER WHEEL ASM. SPOKES

LEVER

PAD

SPRING

RETAINER

SEE VIEW A

STEERING COLUMN

INSERT END OF SPRING INTO HORN CONTACT CYLINDER AND INSTALL SPRING UNDER TABS THREE PLACES.

SHROUD

40 N·m (30 FT. LBS.)

Tilt and telescopic steering wheel assembly

tor, then carefully pull the turn signal switch and wiring from the top end of the column.

To install:

1. Use a new snapring. If the cover screws are to be replaced, make sure the replacement screws are the same size.

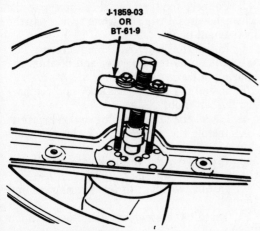

J-1859-03
OR
BT-61-9

Steering wheel puller

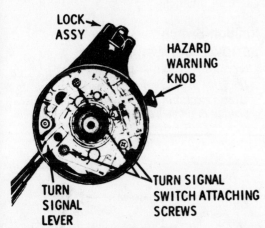

LOCK ASSY

HAZARD WARNING KNOB

TURN SIGNAL LEVER

TURN SIGNAL SWITCH ATTACHING SCREWS

Turn signal switch attachment

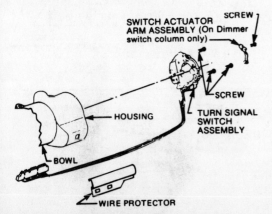

SWITCH ACTUATOR ARM ASSEMBLY (On Dimmer switch column only)

SCREW

HOUSING

SCREW

TURN SIGNAL SWITCH ASSEMBLY

BOWL

WIRE PROTECTOR

Standard column turn signal switch removal

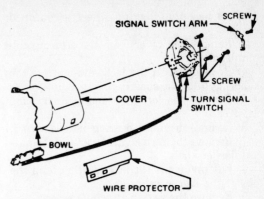

SIGNAL SWITCH ARM

SCREW

COVER

SCREW

TURN SIGNAL SWITCH

BOWL

WIRE PROTECTOR

Tilt column turn signal switch removal

2. Untape the turn signal wires at the connector, then carefully push the turn signal switch and wiring into the top end of the column.

3. Install the two nuts from the column support bracket while holding the column in position. Install the bracket assembly and wire protector to the wiring.

4. Tighten the screw holding the shift indicator needle and connect the clip to the link.

5. Install the four bolts which attach the bracket assembly to the jacket.

6. Install the lower trim panel after connecting the turn signal connector to the wiring harness.

7. Install the three turn signal switch attaching screws.

8. Push in on the hazard warning knob, then install the screw and the hazard warning knob.

9. Place the turn signal lever in the right turn position, then install the turn signal lever attaching screw and the lever. On 1978 and later models with the dimmer switch in the turn signal lever, install the actuator arm screw and the arm.

10. Install the upper bearing preload spring.

11. Install the lock-plate and the canceling cam. Depress the lockplate and install the snapring to the shaft.

12. Install the covers to the steering column shaft. The plastic keepers under the cover are not necessary for installation.

13. Install the steering wheel and torque the nut to 30 ft. lbs. (41 Nm) as described earlier.

14. Connect the negative battery cable and check all functions.

Models with Tilt and Telescopic Column

CAUTION: *All elements of energy-absorbing (telescopic) steering columns are very sensitive to damage. Do not strike any part of the column (nuts, bolts, etc.) as this could ruin the entire assembly.*

1. Disconnect the negative battery cable.

2. Remove the steering wheel as outlined earlier.

3. Remove the cover from the steering column shaft.

4. Press down on the lockplate and pry the snapring from the shaft.

5. Remove the lockplate and the canceling cam.

6. Remove the upper bearing preload spring.

7. Remove the turn signal lever and the hazard flasher knob.

8. Lift up on the tilt lever and position the housing in its central position.

9. Remove the switch attaching screws.

10. Remove the lower trim cap from the instrument panel and disconnect the turn signal connector from the wiring harness.

11. Remove the four bolts which secure the bracket assembly to the jacket.

12. Loosen the screw that holds the shift indicator needle and disconnect the clip from the link.

13. Remove the two nuts from the column support bracket while holding the column in position. Remove the bracket assembly and wire protector from the wiring, then loosely install the support column bracket.

14. Tape the turn signal wires to the connector to keep them fit and parallel.

15. Carefully remove the turn signal switch and wiring from the column.

To install:

1. Carefully install the turn signal switch and wiring into the column.

2. Install the bracket assembly and wire protector to the wiring, then loosely install the support column bracket. Install the two nuts to the column support bracket while holding the column in position.

3. Tighten the screw that holds the shift indicator needle and connect the clip to the link.

4. Install the four bolts which secure the bracket assembly to the jacket.

5. Connect the turn signal connector to the wiring harness. Install the lower trim cap to the instrument panel.

6. Install the switch attaching screws.

7. Lift up on the tilt lever and position the housing in its central position.

8. Install the turn signal lever and the hazard flasher knob.

9. Install the upper bearing preload spring.

10. Install the lockplate and the canceling cam.

11. Press down on the lockplate and install the snapring to the shaft.

12. Install the cover to the steering column shaft.

13. Install the steering wheel as outlined earlier.

14. Connect the negative battery cable and check all functions.

Ignition Switch

REMOVAL AND INSTALLATION

NOTE: *This is an extremely difficult and lengthy procedure. You must remove the steering column from the vehicle and disassemble major portions of it. Because the col-*

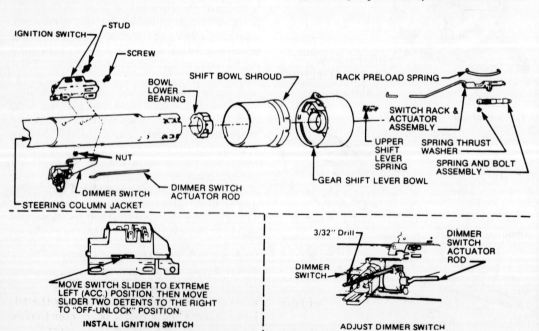

Replacing ignition switch

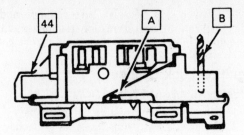

Ignition switch alignment

*umn is collapsible in an accident, it is neces-
sary that it be handled with care to avoid distortion of major parts. It must not be dropped,
hammered on or even leaned on, or vitally important parts may deform. The procedure for
replacing the ignition switch on tilt type columns is not included here because it involves
substantial additional work and the use of
several expensive special tools. Unless you are
rather experienced, we recommend that the
job be left to a competent professional
mechanic.*

1. Disconnect the negative battery cable. Remove the clamp bolt from the steering coupling
at the lower end of the steering column shaft
(located near the steering box, under the hood).

2. Disconnect the shift linkage from the shift
tube lever at the lower end of the column.

3. Remove the steering wheel with a puller,
as described above.

4. Remove the left sound insulator and lower
column cover.

5. Remove the trim cap or lower trim panel
from the instrument panel, depending on
equipment.

6. Remove the steering column cover and
toe-pan attaching screws. Remove the shift indicator needle from the shift bowl.

7. Securely support the column in position
and remove the two nuts attaching the column
to the underside of the instrument panel.

8. Lower the column carefully, being careful
to retain any spacers that may have been used
in order. Disconnect the wiring. Then, carefully
remove the column from the inside of the
vehicle.

9. Begin disassembling the column, removing the lock plate, canceling cam, and turn signal switch. See the "Turn Signal" Removal and
Installation procedure above.

10. Remove the ignition lock and key warning
switch as described below.

11. Remove the spring and bolt assembly, and
the associated thrust washer. Then, remove the
rack preload spring, switch rack, and actuator
assembly.

12. Remove the upper shift lever spring.
Then, remove the gear shift lever bowl.

13. Remove the shift bowl shroud and bowl
lower bearing.

14. Unhook and remove the dimmer switch
actuating rod. Remove the attaching nut and
remove the dimmer switch.

15. Remove the attaching screw and stud and
remove the ignition switch, disassembling the
actuating rod from the hole in the sliding
actuator.

To install:

1. Move the ignition switch sliding actuator
all the way to the left (ACC) position. Then,
move it two detents (OFF-UNLOCK) position
to the right.

2. Then, position the actuating rod hole in
the sliding actuator, and install the ignition
switch, stud, and mounting screw.

3. Install the dimmer switch with its attaching nut tightened only loosely. Then, depress
the switch slightly until you can insert a $3/32$ in.
drill through the hole in the switch housing and
slider. Force the switch upward to remove any
lash and tighten the mounting screw with the
switch in this position.

4. Put the shifter in **NEUTRAL** and install
the shift lever.

5. Install the shift bowl shroud and bowl lower bearing.

6. Install the rack preload spring, switch
rack, and actuator assembly. Install the spring
and bolt assembly, and the associated thrust
washer.

7. Install the ignition lock and key warning
switch as described below.

8. Reinstall the column into the vehicle.
Make sure when assembling the lower and upper dash covers that they can slide on the column. If the bracket which mounts the column
to the dash has been removed, install the bolts
in this order:

    a. Left rear
    b. Left front
    c. Right front
    d. Right rear

Tighten the bolts just snug to avoid distorting
the column.

9. Install the switch connector to the ignition
switch. Then, position the column in the body
and support it there. Install the lockwashers
and nuts for the coupling and tighten them.
Then, loosely assemble the nuts fastening the
mounting bracket for the column to the lower
side of the instrument panel.

10. Position the lower cover to the firewall
and ensure that the cover is lined up by starting
the left lower screw. Then, install and tighten
the right lower screw. Then, tighten the left
lower screw. Finally, install and tighten the two
screws that fit into the top of the cover.

11. Tighten first the screw for the left side of

the cover clamp; then tighten the screw for the right side of the cover clamp. Finally, install and tighten the remaining cover screws.

12. Finally, tighten the nuts fastening the column to the underside of the dash. Reinstall the bolt for the steering coupling clamp.

13. Install the lock plate, canceling cam, and turn signal switch. See the "Turn Signal" Removal and Installation procedure in this chapter.

14. Connect the wiring.

15. Securely support the column in position and install the two nuts attaching the column to the underside of the instrument panel.

16. Install the shift indicator needle from the shift bowl. Install the steering column cover and toe-pan attaching screws.

17. Install the trim cap or lower trim panel to the instrument panel, depending on equipment.

18. Install the left sound insulator and lower column cover.

19. Install the steering wheel, as described above.

20. Connect the shift linkage to the shift tube lever at the lower end of the column.

21. Install the clamp bolt to the steering coupling at the lower end of the steering column shaft (located near the steering box, under the hood).

22. Connect the negative battery cable and check all column operations for free movement and smooth operation.

Ignition Lock Cylinder
REMOVAL AND INSTALLATION

1. Disconnect the negative battery cable.

2. Remove the steering wheel as previously outlined.

3. On models equipped with a tilt and telescope column, pry up the three tabs on the plastic lock cover. On other models, remove the three screws.

4. Depress the steering wheel lock plate and pry the snapring from the shaft.

5. Remove the lock plat, canceling cam, and upper bearing spring.

6. Remove the turn signal lever. Push the hazard warning knob in and unscrew the knob.

7. Remove the turn signal switch screws and pull the switch up out of the way.

8. Turn the ignition key to the **RUN** position.

9. Insert a long thin prybar into the slot in the upper bearing housing and depress the release tab while pulling the cylinder from the column.

To install:

1. Insert a new lock cylinder into the column

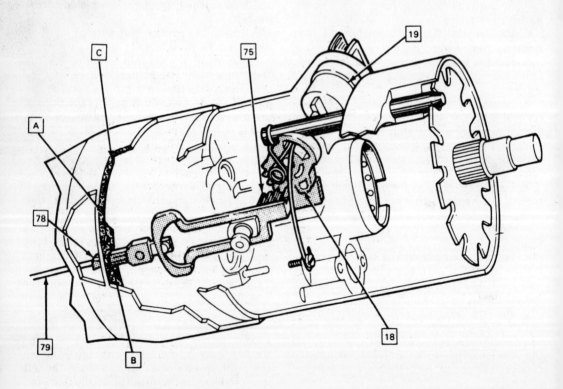

Steering column locking system

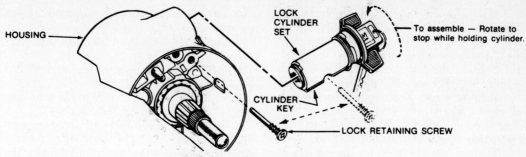

Installing ignition lock, tilt column

after aligning the key on the cylinder with the keyway in the column.

2. Press inward on the cylinder while turning it clockwise.

3. Install the turn signal switch and screws.

4. Install the turn signal lever. Push the hazard warning knob in and install the screw.

5. Install the upper bearing, canceling cam and lock plat.

6. Install the snapring to the shaft.

7. On models equipped with a tilt and telescope column, push down the three tabs on the plastic lock cover. On other models, install the three screws.

8. Install the steering wheel as previously outlined.

9. Connect the negative battery cable and check all column functions.

Steering Column

REMOVAL AND INSTALLATION

NOTE: *This is an extremely difficult and lengthy procedure. You must remove the steering column from the vehicle and disassemble major portions of it. Because the column is collapsible in an accident, it is necessary that it be handled with care to avoid distortion of major parts. It must not be dropped, hammered on or even leaned on, or vitally important parts may deform. The procedure for*

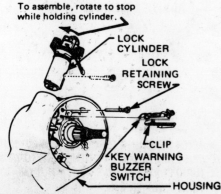

To assemble, rotate to stop while holding cylinder.

LOCK CYLINDER

LOCK RETAINING SCREW

CLIP

KEY WARNING BUZZER SWITCH

HOUSING

Ignition lock removal, standard columns

replacing the ignition switch on tilt type columns is not included here because it involves substantial additional work and the use of several expensive special tools. Unless you are rather experienced, we recommend that the job be left to a competent professional mechanic.

1. Disconnect the negative battery cable. Remove the clamp bolt from the steering coupling at the lower end of the steering column shaft (located near the steering box, under the hood).

2. Disconnect the shift linkage from the shift tube lever at the lower end of the column.

3. Remove the steering wheel with a puller, as described above.

4. Remove the left sound insulator and lower column cover.

5. Remove the trim cap or lower trim panel from the instrument panel, depending on equipment.

6. Remove the steering column cover and toe-pan attaching screws. Remove the shift indicator needle from the shift bowl.

7. Securely support the column in position and remove the two nuts attaching the column to the underside of the instrument panel.

8. Lower the column carefully, being careful to retain any spacers that may have been used in order. Disconnect the wiring. Then, carefully remove the column from the inside of the vehicle.

To install:

9. Position the column in the vehicle. Make sure when assembling the lower and upper dash covers that they can slide on the column. If the bracket which mounts the column to the dash has been removed, install the bolts in this order:

    a. Left rear

    b. Left front

    c. Right front

    d. Right rear

WARNING: *Tighten the bolts just snug to avoid distorting the column!*

10. Install the switch connector to the ignition switch. Then, position the column in the body and support it there. Install the lockwash-

ers and nuts for the coupling and tighten them. Then, loosely assemble the nuts fastening the mounting bracket for the column to the lower side of the instrument panel.

11. Position the lower cover to the firewall and ensure that the cover is lined up by starting the left lower screw. Then, install and tighten the right lower screw. Then, tighten the left lower screw. Finally, install and tighten the two screws that fit into the top of the cover.

12. Tighten first the screw for the left side of the cover clamp; then tighten the screw for the right side of the cover clamp. Finally, install and tighten the remaining cover screws.

13. Finally, tighten the nuts fastening the column to the underside of the dash. Reinstall the bolt for the steering coupling clamp.

14. Install the lock plate, canceling cam, and turn signal switch. See the "Turn Signal" Removal and Installation procedure in this chapter.

15. Connect the wiring.

16. Securely support the column in position and install the two nuts attaching the column to the underside of the instrument panel.

17. Install the shift indicator needle from the shift bowl. Install the steering column cover and toe-pan attaching screws.

18. Install the trim cap or lower trim panel to the instrument panel, depending on equipment.

19. Install the left sound insulator and lower column cover.

20. Install the steering wheel, as described above.

21. Connect the shift linkage to the shift tube lever at the lower end of the column.

22. Install the clamp bolt to the steering coupling at the lower end of the steering column shaft (located near the steering box, under the hood).

23. Connect the negative battery cable and check all column operations for free movement and smooth operation.

Steering Linkage
REMOVAL AND INSTALLATION

Pitman Arm

NOTE: *To perform this procedure, you will need special pullers to pull the center link out of the Pitman arm, and to pull the Pitman arm off the steering box shaft without stressing the bearings in the steering box.*

1. Raise the vehicle and support it with jackstands by the frame rails. Remove the nut from the Pitman arm ballstud.

2. Disconnect the center link at the pitman

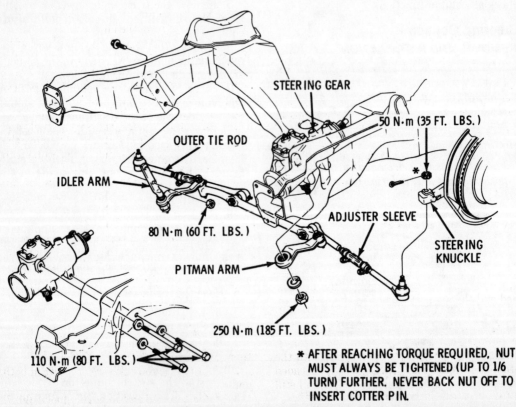

STEERING GEAR

50 N·m (35 FT. LBS.)

OUTER TIE ROD

IDLER ARM

*

80 N·m (60 FT. LBS.)

ADJUSTER SLEEVE

STEERING KNUCKLE

PITMAN ARM

250 N·m (185 FT. LBS.)

110 N·m (80 FT. LBS.)

* AFTER REACHING TORQUE REQUIRED, NUT MUST ALWAYS BE TIGHTENED (UP TO 1/6 TURN) FURTHER. NEVER BACK NUT OFF TO INSERT COTTER PIN.

Steering linkage, all models similar

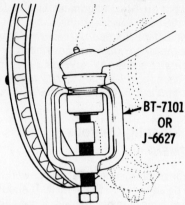

Disconnecting steering linkage using puller or ball joint tool

arm with a puller. Then, pull down on the intermediate rod to remove the stud.

3. Remove the Pitman arm nut and lockwasher from the Pitman shaft. Provide replacement parts and discard them.

4. Mark the relationship between the Pitman arm and the steering box shaft. Then, pull the arm off the shaft. Mark the new arm at the same place as the old one was marked.

To install:

1. Install the new arm on the shaft, aligning the marks. Install the new nut and lockwasher, and torque the nut to 185 ft. lbs. (260 Nm).

2. Put the center link into position onto the Pitman arm, install the attaching nut, and torque it to 40 ft. lbs. (54 Nm).

3. Lower the vehicle and check steering operation before driving.

Idler Arm

NOTE: *You will need a puller suitable for removing the tapered stud on the idler arm from the center link.*

1. Raise the vehicle and support it with jackstands by the frame rails. Remove the nuts, bolts, and washers that attach the idler arm to the frame.

2. Remove the nut that attaches the idler arm to the center link ballstud.

3. Pull the idler arm out of the center link with the puller and remove it.

4. Note that the idler arm has a threaded support. The threaded bushing must be loosened and the support turned in the arm to adjust the distance between the lower bolt hole and the top surface of the arm to $2^{11}/_{32}$ in. (59.5mm). This ensures that, when installed, the idler arm ball socket will be level with the Pitman arm ball socket. Retighten the threaded bushing. Make sure all idler supports will still be fully free to rotate at least 90°.

To install:

1. Position the idler arm support against the frame, lining up the two sets of holes. Install the bolts, washers and nuts, and torque to 60 ft. lbs. (81 Nm).

2. Install the center link to the idler arm by inserting the tapered section on the arm into the link. Make sure the seal is on the stud. Install the nut and torque it to 40 ft. lbs. (54 Nm). On some models, this nut uses a cotter pin. If so, tighten the nut just enough farther to line up holes and then install and secure a new cotter pin. Lower the vehicle.

Center Link

NOTE: *You will need pullers that are suitable for separating the tie rod ends, idler arm, and Pitman arm from the center link. It is ideal to have a tool J–29193 or equivalent to seat the idler arm into the center link.*

1. Raise the vehicle and support it with jackstands by the frame rails. Remove the cotter pins, remove the nuts, and then disconnect the tie rod inner ends at the center link with pullers.

2. Remove the nut from the ballstud on the center link where it attaches to the Pitman arm. Then, use a puller to remove the arm from the ballstud. Shift the linkage to eliminate torque and pull the link away from the Pitman arm.

3. Remove the nut attaching the center link to the idler arm from the idler arm. Use a puller to separate the center link from the idler arm.

To install:

1. Inspect all seals and replace any that are damaged. Make sure all seals that are satisfactory are in place.

2. Install the center link onto the idler arm. If it is available, install the special tool, and torque its nut to 15 ft. lbs. (20 Nm). Remove the tool and install the attaching nut. Torque it to 40 ft. lbs. (54 Nm).

3. Raise the end of the center link and install it onto the Pitman arm. Install the nut and torque it to 40 ft. lbs. (54 Nm).

4. Install the inner tie rod ends into the center link. Install the nuts and torque them to 30 ft. lbs. (41 Nm). Tighten them just enough farther to line up the holes and then install new cotter pins.

5. Have the toe-in set at an alignment shop.

Tie Rod Ends

1. Remove the cotter pins and nuts from the tie rod end studs.

2. Mark the tie rod adjustment sleeve at both ends with tape.

3. Using a tie rod end removing tool J–6627, remove the rod end from the steering knuckle.

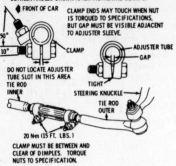

BOLTS MUST BE INSTALLED IN DIRECTION SHOWN. ROTATE BOTH INNER AND OUTER TIE ROD HOUSINGS REARWARD TO THE LIMIT OF BALL JOINT TRAVEL BEFORE TIGHTENING CLAMPS. WITH THIS SAME REARWARD ROTATION ALL BOLT CENTERLINES MUST BE BETWEEN ANGLES SHOWN AFTER TIGHTENING CLAMPS.

FRONT OF CAR

CLAMP ENDS MAY TOUCH WHEN NUT IS TORQUED TO SPECIFICATIONS, BUT GAP MUST BE VISIBLE ADJACENT TO ADJUSTER SLEEVE.

50°

10°

CLAMP

ADJUSTER TUBE

GAP

DO NOT LOCATE ADJUSTER TUBE SLOT IN THIS AREA

TIE ROD INNER

TIGHT

STEERING KNUCKLE

TIE ROD OUTER

20 N·m (15 FT. LBS.)

CLAMP MUST BE BETWEEN AND CLEAR OF DIMPLES. TORQUE NUTS TO SPECIFICATION.

Tie rod clamp and sleeve positioning

4. Remove the inner stud in the same manner as the outer.

5. Loosen the clamp bolts and unscrew the ends if they are being replaced.

To install:

1. Lubricate the tie rod end threads with chassis grease if they were removed. Install each end assembly an equal distance from the sleeve.

2. Ensure that the tie rod end stud threads and nut are clean. Install new seals and install the studs into the steering arms and relay rod.

3. Install the stud nuts. Tighten the inner and outer end nuts to 35 ft. lbs. (41 Nm). Install new cotter pins.

4. Have a qualified alignment mechanic adjust the toe-in to specifications.

NOTE: *Before tightening the sleeve clamps, ensure that the clamps are positioned so that adjusting sleeve slot is covered by the clamp. Never back the nut off to insert cotter pin, always tighten it until the pin can fit through the castellations.*

Power Steering Gearbox

ADJUSTMENT

It is not recommended that the power steering gear be adjusted in the vehicle. It should be adjusted at time of major rebuild. It does not require adjustment as part of periodic maintenance.

REMOVAL AND INSTALLATION

1. Disconnect the negative ($-$) battery cable. Remove the coupling shield from the steering shaft.

2. Disconnect the hoses from the gearbox and cap or plug the hose fittings.

3. Raise the front end of the vehicle and support it with jackstands.

4. Remove the pitman shaft nut, then disconnect the pitman shaft using a special puller (it is a press-fit).

5. Remove the three bolts attaching the gearbox to the frame side rail and remove the gearbox.

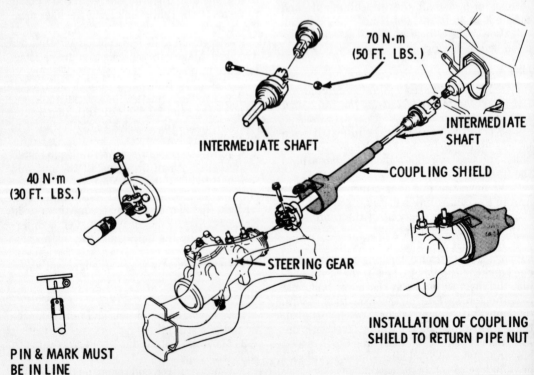

70 N·m (50 FT. LBS.)

INTERMEDIATE SHAFT

INTERMEDIATE SHAFT

COUPLING SHIELD

40 N·m (30 FT. LBS.)

STEERING GEAR

INSTALLATION OF COUPLING SHIELD TO RETURN PIPE NUT

PIN & MARK MUST BE IN LINE

Power steering gearbox, coupling shield and intermediate shaft

To install:

NOTE: *If the mounting threads are stripped, do not repair; replace the housing.*

1. Before installing the gearbox, apply a sodium fiber grease to the gearbox mounting pads to prevent squeaks between the gar housing and the frame. Note that the flat on the gearbox lower shaft must index with the flat in the coupling flange and make sure there is a minimum of 0.040 in. (1mm) clearance between the coupling hub and the steering gearbox upper seal.

2. Before tightening the gearbox-to-frame bolts, shift the gearbox as necessary to place it in the same plane as the steering shaft so that the flexible coupling is not distorted. Torque the gearbox-to-frame bolts to 80 ft. lbs. (108 Nm) and the pitman shaft nut to 185 ft. lbs. (255 Nm).

3. After connecting the hoses to the pump add GM Power Steering Fluid or an equivalent to bring the fluid level to the full COLD mark. Bleed the system by running the engine at idle for 30 seconds then at a fast idle for one minute BEFORE turning the steering wheel. Then, with the engine still running, turn the steering wheel through its full travel two or three times. Recheck the oil level and top up if necessary.

Power Steering Pump

REMOVAL AND INSTALLATION

1. Remove the hoses at the pump and tape the openings shut to prevent leakage.

2. Remove the pump drive belt.

3. Remove the retaining bolts, any braces and the pump.

4. If a new pump is being installed, and the pulley is being transferred, a puller is necessary to remove the pulley.

To install:

1. Torque hose fittings to 20 ft. lbs. (27 Nm). Fill the reservoir with approved power steering fluid and turn the pump backward (counterclockwise as viewed from in front) until bubbles no longer appear in the reservoir.

2. Any time the pump is removed, air must be bled from the system upon reinstallation. Bleed the system as described in the next procedure.

BLEEDING

To bleed the system, proceed as follows:

1. Raise the vehicle in the air and support it with jackstands.

2. Start the engine and let it run at a fast idle.

3. Having made sure the fluid level in the pump is correct, turn the wheels from side to side without hitting the stops.

4. After doing this several times, check the fluid. Fluid with air in it will have a light tan or red appearance.

5. Continue with this procedure until the air is bled from the system. Fill the pump with fluid and road-test the vehicle.

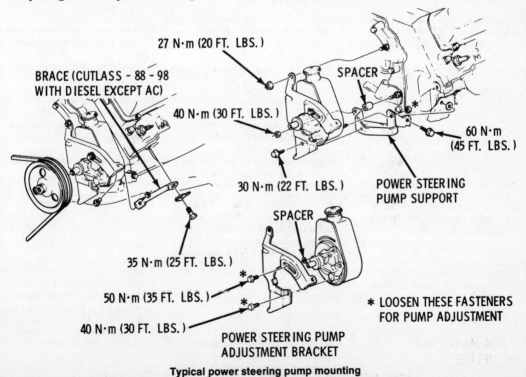

Typical power steering pump mounting

Brakes

Troubleshooting the Brake System

Problem	Cause	Solution
Low brake pedal (excessive pedal travel required for braking action.)	• Excessive clearance between rear linings and drums caused by inoperative automatic adjusters	• Make 10 to 15 alternate forward and reverse brake stops to adjust brakes. If brake pedal does not come up, repair or replace adjuster parts as necessary.
	• Worn rear brakelining	• Inspect and replace lining if worn beyond minimum thickness specification
	• Bent, distorted brakeshoes, front or rear	• Replace brakeshoes in axle sets
	• Air in hydraulic system	• Remove air from system. Refer to Brake Bleeding.
Low brake pedal (pedal may go to floor with steady pressure applied.)	• Fluid leak in hydraulic system	• Fill master cylinder to fill line; have helper apply brakes and check calipers, wheel cylinders, differential valve tubes, hoses and fittings for leaks. Repair or replace as necessary.
	• Air in hydraulic system	• Remove air from system. Refer to Brake Bleeding.
	• Incorrect or non-recommended brake fluid (fluid evaporates at below normal temp).	• Flush hydraulic system with clean brake fluid. Refill with correct-type fluid.
	• Master cylinder piston seals worn, or master cylinder bore is scored, worn or corroded	• Repair or replace master cylinder
Low brake pedal (pedal goes to floor on first application—o.k. on subsequent applications.)	• Disc brake pads sticking on abutment surfaces of anchor plate. Caused by a build-up of dirt, rust, or corrosion on abutment surfaces	• Clean abutment surfaces
Fading brake pedal (pedal height decreases with steady pressure applied.)	• Fluid leak in hydraulic system	• Fill master cylinder reservoirs to fill mark, have helper apply brakes, check calipers, wheel cylinders, differential valve, tubes, hoses, and fittings for fluid leaks. Repair or replace parts as necessary.
	• Master cylinder piston seals worn, or master cylinder bore is scored, worn or corroded	• Repair or replace master cylinder

Troubleshooting the Brake System (cont.)

Problem	Cause	Solution
Decreasing brake pedal travel (pedal travel required for braking action decreases and may be accompanied by a hard pedal.)	• Caliper or wheel cylinder pistons sticking or seized • Master cylinder compensator ports blocked (preventing fluid return to reservoirs) or pistons sticking or seized in master cylinder bore • Power brake unit binding internally	• Repair or replace the calipers, or wheel cylinders • Repair or replace the master cylinder • Test unit according to the following procedure: (a) Shift transmission into neutral and start engine (b) Increase engine speed to 1500 rpm, close throttle and fully depress brake pedal (c) Slow release brake pedal and stop engine (d) Have helper remove vacuum check valve and hose from power unit. Observe for backward movement of brake pedal. (e) If the pedal moves backward, the power unit has an internal bind—replace power unit
Spongy brake pedal (pedal has abnormally soft, springy, spongy feel when depressed.)	• Air in hydraulic system • Brakeshoes bent or distorted • Brakelining not yet seated with drums and rotors • Rear drum brakes not properly adjusted	• Remove air from system. Refer to Brake Bleeding. • Replace brakeshoes • Burnish brakes • Adjust brakes
Hard brake pedal (excessive pedal pressure required to stop vehicle. May be accompanied by brake fade.)	• Loose or leaking power brake unit vacuum hose • Incorrect or poor quality brakelining • Bent, broken, distorted brakeshoes • Calipers binding or dragging on mounting pins. Rear brakeshoes dragging on support plate. • Caliper, wheel cylinder, or master cylinder pistons sticking or seized • Power brake unit vacuum check valve malfunction • Power brake unit has internal bind	• Tighten connections or replace leaking hose • Replace with lining in axle sets • Replace brakeshoes • Replace mounting pins and bushings. Clean rust or burrs from rear brake support plate ledges and lubricate ledges with molydisulfide grease. **NOTE:** If ledges are deeply grooved or scored, do not attempt to sand or grind them smooth—replace support plate. • Repair or replace parts as necessary • Test valve according to the following procedure: (a) Start engine, increase engine speed to 1500 rpm, close throttle and immediately stop engine (b) Wait at least 90 seconds then depress brake pedal (c) If brakes are not vacuum assisted for 2 or more applications, check valve is faulty • Test unit according to the following procedure: (a) With engine stopped, apply brakes several times to exhaust all vacuum in system

Troubleshooting the Brake System (cont.)

Problem	Cause	Solution
Hard brake pedal (excessive pedal pressure required to stop vehicle. May be accompanied by brake fade.)		(b) Shift transmission into neutral, depress brake pedal and start engine (c) If pedal height decreases with foot pressure and less pressure is required to hold pedal in applied position, power unit vacuum system is operating normally. Test power unit. If power unit exhibits a bind condition, replace the power unit.
	• Master cylinder compensator ports (at bottom of reservoirs) blocked by dirt, scale, rust, or have small burrs (blocked ports prevent fluid return to reservoirs). • Brake hoses, tubes, fittings clogged or restricted	• Repair or replace master cylinder **CAUTION:** Do not attempt to clean blocked ports with wire, pencils, or similar implements. Use compressed air only. • Use compressed air to check or unclog parts. Replace any damaged parts.
	• Brake fluid contaminated with improper fluids (motor oil, transmission fluid, causing rubber components to swell and stick in bores • Low engine vacuum	• Replace all rubber components, combination valve and hoses. Flush entire brake system with DOT 3 brake fluid or equivalent. • Adjust or repair engine
Grabbing brakes (severe reaction to brake pedal pressure.)	• Brakelining(s) contaminated by grease or brake fluid	• Determine and correct cause of contamination and replace brakeshoes in axle sets
	• Parking brake cables incorrectly adjusted or seized • Incorrect brakelining or lining loose on brakeshoes • Caliper anchor plate bolts loose • Rear brakeshoes binding on support plate ledges	• Adjust cables. Replace seized cables. • Replace brakeshoes in axle sets • Tighten bolts • Clean and lubricate ledges. Replace support plate(s) if ledges are deeply grooved. Do not attempt to smooth ledges by grinding.
	• Incorrect or missing power brake reaction disc • Rear brake support plates loose	• Install correct disc • Tighten mounting bolts
Dragging brakes (slow or incomplete release of brakes)	• Brake pedal binding at pivot • Power brake unit has internal bind	• Loosen and lubricate • Inspect for internal bind. Replace unit if internal bind exists.
	• Parking brake cables incorrrectly adjusted or seized • Rear brakeshoe return springs weak or broken	• Adjust cables. Replace seized cables. • Replace return springs. Replace brakeshoe if necessary in axle sets.
	• Automatic adjusters malfunctioning	• Repair or replace adjuster parts as required
	• Caliper, wheel cylinder or master cylinder pistons sticking or seized	• Repair or replace parts as necessary
	• Master cylinder compensating ports blocked (fluid does not return to reservoirs).	• Use compressed air to clear ports. Do not use wire, pencils, or similar objects to open blocked ports.
Vehicle moves to one side when brakes are applied	• Incorrect front tire pressure	• Inflate to recommended cold (reduced load) inflation pressure
	• Worn or damaged wheel bearings	• Replace worn or damaged bearings
	• Brakelining on one side contaminated	• Determine and correct cause of contamination and replace brakelining in axle sets

Troubleshooting the Brake System (cont.)

Problem	Cause	Solution
Vehicle moves to one side when brakes are applied	• Brakeshoes on one side bent, distorted, or lining loose on shoe	• Replace brakeshoes in axle sets
	• Support plate bent or loose on one side	• Tighten or replace support plate
	• Brakelining not yet seated with drums or rotors	• Burnish brakelining
	• Caliper anchor plate loose on one side	• Tighten anchor plate bolts
	• Caliper piston sticking or seized	• Repair or replace caliper
	• Brakelinings water soaked	• Drive vehicle with brakes lightly applied to dry linings
	• Loose suspension component attaching or mounting bolts	• Tighten suspension bolts. Replace worn suspension components.
	• Brake combination valve failure	• Replace combination valve
Chatter or shudder when brakes are applied (pedal pulsation and roughness may also occur.)	• Brakeshoes distorted, bent, contaminated, or worn	• Replace brakeshoes in axle sets
	• Caliper anchor plate or support plate loose	• Tighten mounting bolts
	• Excessive thickness variation of rotor(s)	• Refinish or replace rotors in axle sets
Noisy brakes (squealing, clicking, scraping sound when brakes are applied.)	• Bent, broken, distorted brakeshoes	• Replace brakeshoes in axle sets
	• Excessive rust on outer edge of rotor braking surface	• Remove rust
	• Brakelining worn out—shoes contacting drum of rotor	• Replace brakeshoes and lining in axle sets. Refinish or replace drums or rotors.
	• Broken or loose holdown or return springs	• Replace parts as necessary
	• Rough or dry drum brake support plate ledges	• Lubricate support plate ledges
	• Cracked, grooved, or scored rotor(s) or drum(s)	• Replace rotor(s) or drum(s). Replace brakeshoes and lining in axle sets if necessary.
	• Incorrect brakelining and/or shoes (front or rear).	• Install specified shoe and lining assemblies
Pulsating brake pedal	• Out of round drums or excessive lateral runout in disc brake rotor(s)	• Refinish or replace drums, re-index rotors or replace

BRAKE SYSTEM

CAUTION: *Some brake pads contain asbestos, which has been determined to be a cancer causing agent. Never clean the brake surfaces with compressed air! Avoid inhaling any dust from any brake surface! When cleaning brake surfaces, use a commercially available brake cleaning fluid.*

All Buick, Oldsmobile and Pontiac models covered in this guide are equipped with front disc brakes and rear drum brakes as standard equipment. Four wheel disc brakes are optional on some models.

Adjustment
FRONT BRAKES

There is no adjustment provision on hydraulic disc brakes; they are inherently self-adjusting.

REAR DRUM BRAKE SHOES

NOTE: *Drum brakes are self-adjusting, but provision is made for manual adjustment as follows:*

1. Raise the rear of the vehicle and support it with jackstands.

2. The inner sides of the brake backing plates have a lanced area, oblong in shape. Knock this area out with a punch. You will have to remove the brake drum to clean out any metal pieces that will be deposited by the punch, and you will have to purchase rubber plugs at a parts distributor to plug the punched holes now in the backing plates. Many vehicles will already have the holes punched and plugs installed.

3. *Adjustment to tighten*: Insert a brake adjusting spoon into the hole. Turn the star-shaped adjusting screw inside the drum with the spoon, until the wheel has a slight drag. Do this to both wheels until there is equal drag on each wheel. Do NOT overtighten.

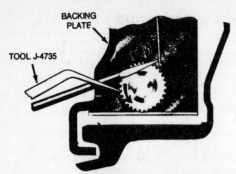

BACKING
PLATE

TOOL J-4735

INSERT SMALL SCREWDRIVER OR AWL
THROUGH BACKING PLATE SLOT AND
HOLD ADJUSTER LEVER AWAY FROM
SPROCKET BEFORE BACKING OFF
BRAKE SHOE ADJUSTMENT

Adjusting rear drum brakes using brake adjusting spoon

4. *Adjustment to loosen and remove the drum*: Insert a brake adjusting spoon and small prybar to hold the adjusting lever away from the sprocket. Back off each adjusting screw until the drum turns freely. If the brake shoes drag with the adjusters backed off all the way, the parking brake cables could be excessively tight.

BRAKE PEDAL

No adjustment of the brake pedal is required on the vehicles covered by this guide. If there are problems of excessive pedal travel, the cause is most likely related to hydraulic leakage or non-functioning automatic adjusters.

Master Cylinder
REMOVAL AND INSTALLATION
Master Cylinders with Vacuum Power Brakes

On vacuum power brake equipped models, the master cylinder can be removed without removing the power vacuum cylinder from the vehicle.

WARNING: *Only use flare nut wrenches when removing the brake lines from any component. Standard wrenches will damage the flare nut and line.*

1. Clean the area around the master cylinder.

2. Disconnect the hydraulic lines at the master cylinder using flare nut wrenches only. Plug or tape the ends of the lines to prevent dirt from entering and to prevent fluid from leaking out.

3. Remove the master cylinder attaching nuts and remove the master cylinder.

4. Drain the master cylinder.

CAUTION: *Be careful to keep brake fluid away from all body paint. The fluid acts like paint remover, and a few drops will quickly bubble any paint with which it comes in contact.*

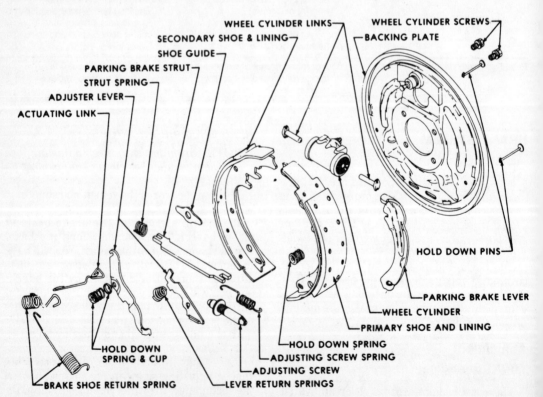

WHEEL CYLINDER LINKS
SECONDARY SHOE & LINING
SHOE GUIDE
PARKING BRAKE STRUT
STRUT SPRING
ADJUSTER LEVER
ACTUATING LINK
WHEEL CYLINDER SCREWS
BACKING PLATE
HOLD DOWN PINS
PARKING BRAKE LEVER
WHEEL CYLINDER
PRIMARY SHOE AND LINING
HOLD DOWN SPRING
ADJUSTING SCREW SPRING
ADJUSTING SCREW
LEVER RETURN SPRINGS
HOLD DOWN SPRING & CUP
BRAKE SHOE RETURN SPRING

Exploded view of a typical drum brake

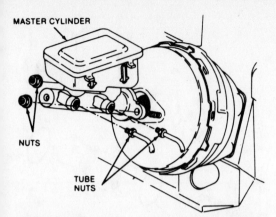

Typical master cylinder mounting for cars equipped with power brakes. Unit is mounted on engine side of the firewall

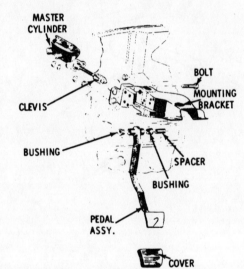

Master cylinder removal, non-power brakes

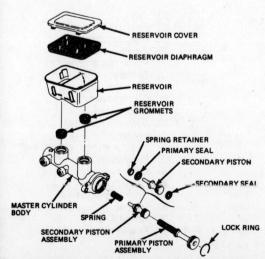

Master cylinder with plastic removable reservoir

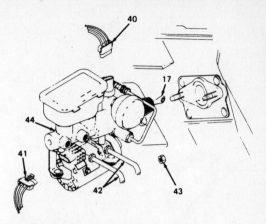

17. Pushrod
40. Pressure switch electrical connector
41. Electro-hydraulic pump electrical connector
42. Brake pipe
43. Mastercylinder and pump unit mounting nut
44. Powermaster® unit

Removing/installing the Powermaster® master cylinder

Powermaster® Hydraulic Power Brakes

This system uses an electrically operated hydraulic pump and an accumulator (pressure storage system) to provide power braking assist.

CAUTION: *Because of the very high pressures used, always follow procedures very carefully, being especially sure to discharge the system prior to disconnecting anything.*

1. Disconnect the negative (−) battery cable. Turn the ignition switch off. Then, discharge all pressure from the system by applying the brake pedal with maximum force (50 lbs. or more) at least 10 full strokes.

2. Disconnect the electrical connector from the pressure switch, located at the rear of the master cylinder on top.

3. Disconnect the electrical connector from the front of the pump, located under the master cylinder.

4. Disconnect the brake and hydraulic pressure pipes at the master cylinder and tape or cap the openings. Use a flarenut wrench only.

5. Remove the two attaching nuts. Pull the clevis pin out of the linkage to the brake pedal. Remove the unit.

To install:

1. Position the unit onto the firewall and torque the mounting nuts to 22–30 ft. lbs. (30–41 Nm) and the brake pipe nuts to 10–13 ft. lbs. (14–17 Nm).

2. Connect the brake and hydraulic pressure pipes at the master cylinder using a flarenut wrench.

3. Connect the electrical connector to the

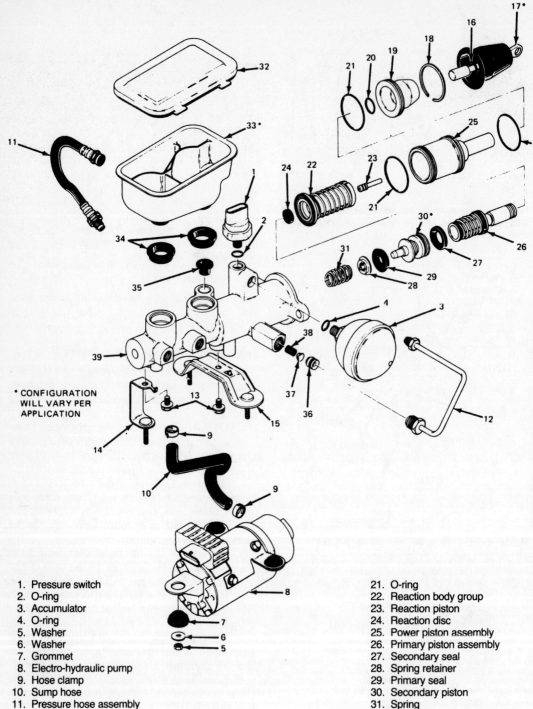

* CONFIGURATION
  WILL VARY PER
  APPLICATION

1. Pressure switch
2. O-ring
3. Accumulator
4. O-ring
5. Washer
6. Washer
7. Grommet
8. Electro-hydraulic pump
9. Hose clamp
10. Sump hose
11. Pressure hose assembly
12. Tube and nut assembly
13. Bolt
14. Electro-hydraulic pump mounting bracket
15. Electro-hydraulic pump mounting bracket
16. Retainer
17. Boot, pushrod, and socket group
18. Retainer
19. Piston guide
20. O-ring

21. O-ring
22. Reaction body group
23. Reaction piston
24. Reaction disc
25. Power piston assembly
26. Primary piston assembly
27. Secondary seal
28. Spring retainer
29. Primary seal
30. Secondary piston
31. Spring
32. Reservoir cover and diaphragm
33. Reservoir
34. Grommet
35. Grommet
36. Valve seat and seal
37. Poppet
38. Spring
39. Powermaster® body

Exploded view of Powermaster® master cylinder

front of the pump, located under the master cylinder.

4. Connect the electrical connector to the pressure switch, located at the rear of the master cylinder on top.

5. Bleed the system as described in the System Bleeding procedures in this section.

OVERHAUL

The models covered in this guide are equipped with either Moraine or Bendix master cylinders. The rebuilding kits may differ slightly, but the procedures are the same. Follow the instructions that come with each particular kit.

NOTE: *Overhaul procedures for power brake master cylinders and manual master cylinders is the same. Note the procedure below for Powermaster® units.*

Disassembly

1. Remove the master cylinder from the vehicle.

2. Remove the mounting gasket and boot, and the main cover, and purge the unit of its fluid.

3. Secure the cylinder in a vise and remove the pushrod retainer and secondary piston stop bolt found inside the forward reservoir (Moraine iron cylinder only).

NOTE: *The plastic composite master cylinder reservoir can be removed by prying against the cylinder and reservoir. Work the reservoir from the rubber grommets using care not to damage either component.*

4. Compress the retaining (lock) ring and extract it along with the primary piston assembly from the end of the bore.

5. Blow compressed air into the piston stop screw hole, if equipped to force the secondary piston, spring, and retainer from the bore of the cylinder. An alternative method is to use hooked wire to snag and extract the secondary piston.

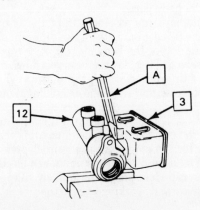

Removing plastic master cylinder reservoir

6. Check the bass tube fitting inserts and if they are damaged, remove them. Leave undamaged inserts in place.

7. If replacement is necessary, thread a $^3/_{16}$ in. × $^5/_8$ in. self-tapping screw into the insert. Hook the end of the screw with a claw hammer and pry the insert free.

8. An alternative way to remove the inserts is to first drill the outlet holes to $^{13}/_{64}$ in. and thread them with a ¼ in.–20 tap. Position a thick washer over the hole to serve as a spacer, and then thread a ¼ in.–20 × ¾ in. hex head bolt into the insert and tighten the bolt until the insert is freed.

9. Use denatured alcohol and compressed air to clean the parts. Slight rust may be removed with crocus cloth. Never use petroleum-based solvents to clan brake parts. Also, a brake hone is helpful in removing varnish and slight rust.

Assembly

1. Replace the brass tube inserts by positioning them in their holes and threading a brake line tube nut into the outlet hole. Turn down the nut until the insert is seated.

2. Check the piston assemblies for correct identification and, when satisfied, position the replacement secondary seals in the twin grooves of the secondary piston.

3. The outside seal is correctly placed when its lips face the flat end of the piston.

4. Slip the primary seal and its protector over the end of the secondary piston opposite the secondary seals. The flat side of this seal should face the piston's compensating hole flange.

5. Replace the primary piston assembly with assembled pieces in the overhaul kit.

6. Moisten the cylinder bore and the secondary piston's inner and outer seals with clean brake fluid. Assemble the secondary piston spring to its retainer and position them over the end of the primary seal.

7. Insert the combined spring and piston assembly into the cylinder and use a small wooden dowel or pencil to seat the spring against the end of the bore.

8. Moisten the primary piston seals with brake fluid and push it, pushrod receptacle end out, into the cylinder.

9. Keep the piston pushed in and snap the retaining (lock) ring into place.

10. Relax the pressure on the pistons and allow them to seek their static positions.

11. Replace the secondary piston stop screw and torque it to 25–40 inch. lbs. (3–4 Nm), if so equipped.

12. Replace the reservoir diaphragm and cover.

13. Install the master cylinder and bleed the entire system.

Powermaster® Units

CAUTION: *The Powermaster® master cylinder unit must be overhauled on a clean bench. Be especially careful that there are no traces of ordinary, mineral type lubricants, as these will ruin the seals.*

DISASSEMBLY

1. Remove the reservoir cover and diaphragm. Drain all brake fluid.

2. Remove:

   a. The pressure switch and O-ring.

   b. Accumulator and O-ring

   c. Electro-hydraulic pump and pressure hose assembly

   d. The sump hose clamps and the sump hose.

   e. The tube and nut assembly that runs from the sump hose to the master cylinder.

   f. Remove the two pump brackets from the master cylinder.

CAUTION: *Do not scratch or deform in any way the outside diameter and sealing surface at the pushrod end of the power piston assembly. Also avoid such damage to the bores of the Powermaster® body.*

3. Remove the retainer (it resembles a piston ring) from the groove in the rear of the unit. The, pull the pushrod to remove the boot, retainer, pushrod and power piston group.

4. Remove the retainer, boot, pushrod, socket group, and piston guide from the power piston assembly.

5. Remove the O-ring from the piston guide. Then, remove the O-rings from the power piston assembly and piston guide.

6. Remove the reaction body group from the power piston assembly.

7. Remove the reaction piston and reaction disc from the reaction body group.

CAUTION: *Do not disassemble the reaction body group or power piston assembly any further! If either are damaged, they must be replaced only as complete assemblies.*

8. Use compressed air cautiously, building pressure slowly, to remove the primary and secondary piston assemblies. Direct the air pressure into the outlet port at the blind end of the master cylinder body. Block the port at the other end of the body.

9. Remove the secondary seal, spring retainer, and primary seal from the secondary piston.

10. Remove the spring from the master cylinder body bore.

11. Mount the master cylinder in a vise with the outboard side upward, *clamping the assembly by the mounting flange located at the rear, and not the body itself*. Then, carefully pry the reservoir off the body with a prybar.

12. Remove the reservoir grommets. Then, gently tap an Easy-Out® type threaded remover tool into the bore of the valve seat. Pull the tool straight out and remove the seat and seal. Discard the seal.

13. Remove the poppet and spring and discard the spring.

ASSEMBLY

1. Clean all parts *except the pressure switch and electro-hydraulic pump* in denatured alcohol. If necessary, wipe external surfaces of the pressure switch and electro-hydraulic pump clean with a cloth dampened slightly in denatured alcohol.

2. Inspect all metal parts for cracks, distortion or other damage. Inspect the primary piston sealing surfaces for scoring, deep scratches, or other damage where the damage could cause leaks. Replace the assembly if any of these defects is noted.

3. Inspect the power piston and master cylinder bores for scoring or corrosion. Replace the assembly if either problem is noted.

CAUTION: *Do not attempt to use an abrasive means to clean up these bores, or dangerous driving conditions could result!*

NOTE: *Use clean, fresh brake fluid to lubricate all parts at sliding surfaces prior to assembly. Lubricate O-rings, grommets, and seals with the same fluid (all should be replaced). Lubricate both the master cylinder and power piston bores with the same fluid prior to installing the piston assemblies into these bores.*

4. Install a new spring and poppet into the body of the Powermaster® unit. Then, install a new valve seat and seal. Bottom these out by threading the nut of the nut and tube assembly into the body port.

5. Remove the assembly from the vise. Install the three grommets (of two different sizes) into the top of the body *making sure they are fully seated*. Then, lay the reservoir down on its upper surface and install the master cylinder onto the reservoir from above, holding it upside down.

6. Install the remaining internal components in reverse order. When installing the retainer for the power piston group, depress the piston guide and power piston. Bench bleed the master cylinder side of the unit by filling the reservoirs and working the pistons back and forth.

7. Install the brackets with the mounting bolts. Install the sump hose, clamps, and hy-

draulic tube. Install the electro-hydraulic pump and pressure hose and clamps.

8. Install the accumulator and O-ring. Install the pressure switch and O-ring.

9. Install the master cylinder in the vehicle and make all connections as described above.

10. Fill both sides of the reservoir with clean, fresh brake fluid meeting the standards shown on the reservoir cover. Then, turn the ignition switch on. Time the running of the pump with your watch. It must not run more than 20 seconds. Have an assistant shut the ignition switch off after 20 seconds if the pump does not cycle off by itself. With the pump running, the fluid level in the booster side of the reservoir should drop. If necessary, add just enough brake fluid to keep the reservoir pump port covered and ensure an adequate supply of air-free fluid to the pump.

11. When the pump stops, check to make sure fluid does not flow back into the reservoir from the booster and check for leaks from the reservoir.

12. Install the reservoir cover securely. Then, pump the brake pedal fully 10 times. Remove the reservoir cover and fill the reservoir to the full line. Again, turn the ignition switch on and time the operation of the pump. It should not run more than 20 seconds. Make sure fluid remains above the level of the reservoir pump port. Again, install the reservoir cover.

13. Turn the ignition switch on and then apply and release the brake pedal to cycle the pump on and off. Count the cycles and repeat the process until the total reaches 15. Make sure the pump does not run more than 20 seconds each cycle (turn the key off if necessary). Recheck the fluid levels and replenish as in Step 11. Check that the pump does not cycle on and off unless you apply the brakes.

14. Install the assembly onto the vehicle and bleed the entire system.

Vacuum Power Booster

REMOVAL AND INSTALLATION

1. Disconnect the negative (−) battery cable. Disconnect the booster pushrod from the brake pedal arm by removing the retaining clip, and sliding the eyelet end of the pushrod off of the pin on the brake arm.

2. Disconnect the master cylinder from the booster.

3. Remove the attaching nuts and remove the booster from the firewall.

To install:

1. Install the booster to the firewall and torque the booster-to-firewall attaching nuts to 22–33 ft. lbs. (29–45 Nm). Reconnect the pushrod at the brake arm.

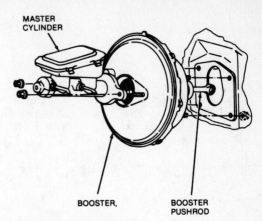

MASTER CYLINDER

BOOSTER,   BOOSTER PUSHROD

Removing power booster

2. Install the master cylinder and bleed the system if the brake lines had to be disconnected.

Hydraulic (Hydro-boost®) Power Booster

REMOVAL AND INSTALLATION

NOTE: *Power steering fluid and brake fluid cannot be mixed; also, power steering fluid damages seals designed for brake fluid, and brake fluid damages power steering type seals.*

1. With the engine off, pump the brake pedal 5 times to deplete fluid stored in the accumulator.

2. Remove the two master cylinder mounting nuts and pull the master cylinder forward and away from the power booster with brake lines attached.

3. Disconnect the three hydraulic lines at the booster. Remove the retainer and washer at the brake pedal, inside the vehicle.

4. Remove the four nuts attaching the booster to the firewall from inside the vehicle and remove it. Remove the gasket.

To install:

1. Position the booster on the dash panel over the gasket and install the four mounting nuts onto the firewall from inside the vehicle. Torque to 15 ft. lbs. (20 Nm). Install the pedal rod washer and retainer.

2. Position the master cylinder to the hydrobooster, install the mounting nuts, and torque to 20 ft. lbs. (27 Nm).

3. Install the three hydraulic lines, torquing the two high pressure lines (which are screwed in) to 20 ft. lbs. (27 Nm).

4. Install power steering fluid into the steering pump until fluid is at the base of the pump reservoir neck.

5. Disconnect the diesel injection pump 12V

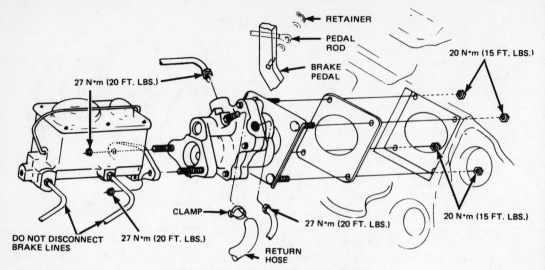

Removing and installing the Hydroboost

wire or the 12V wire to the distributor. THE ENGINE MUST NOT START.

6. Crank the engine for several seconds. Then, check the fluid level and replenish as necessary.

7. Connect wiring and start the engine. Turn the wheel from stop to stop two full times. Then, turn the engine off and depress the brake pedal five times to fully discharge the hydraulic accumulator. Check and if necessary replenish the hydraulic fluid.

8. Again start the engine and turn the wheel from lock to lock two full times. If there is visible foam in the power steering pump reservoir, wait an hour for it to dissipate (engine off). Then, replenish fluid.

Combination Valve

The combination valve used on the large Buicks, Oldsmobiles and Pontiacs is a three-function valve. It serves as a metering valve, balance valve, and brake warning switch. There are two different valves, one manufactured by Bendix and one manufactured by Kelsey-Hayes. Both valves serve the same function and differ only in minor details. In any case, all com-

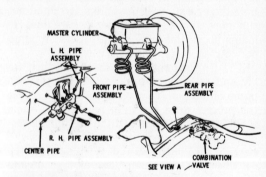

Typical combination valve mounting

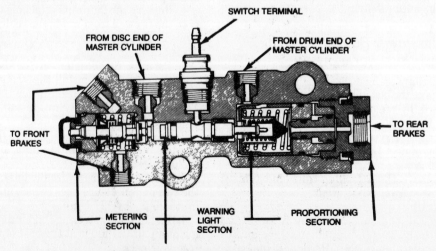

Cutaway of Bendix combination valve

bination valves are non-adjustable and must be replaced if they are found to be defective.

REMOVAL AND INSTALLATION

1. Disconnect all the brake lines at the valve. Plug the lines to prevent contamination and loss of fluid.

2. Disconnect the warning switch wiring connector from the valve switch terminal.

3. Remove the attaching bolts and remove the valve.

4. Install the valve and torque the brake lines to 20 ft. lbs. (27 Nm) using flarenut wrench only.

5. Bleed the entire brake system after valve installation.

Brake Bleeding

The hydraulic brake system must be bled any time one of the lines is disconnected or any time air enters the system. If the brake pedal feels spongy upon application, and goes almost to the floor but regains height when pumped, air has entered the system. It must be bled out. Check for leaks that would have allowed the entry of air and repair them before bleeding the system. The correct bleeding sequence is: right rear wheel cylinder, left rear, right front, and left front. If the master cylinder is equipped with bleeder valves, bleed them first then go to the wheel cylinder nearest the master cylinder (left front) followed by the right front, left rear, and right rear.

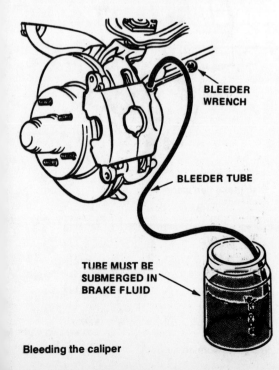

TUBE MUST BE SUBMERGED IN BRAKE FLUID

BLEEDER WRENCH

BLEEDER TUBE

Bleeding the caliper

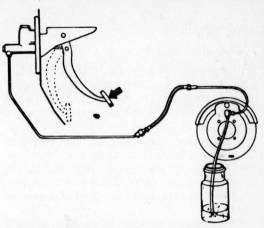

Have an assistant pump the brake pedal while you bleed each wheel

MANUAL BLEEDING

Standard Systems

This method of bleeding requires two people, one to depress the brake pedal and the other to open the bleeder screws.

1. Clean the top of the master cylinder, remove the cover and fill the reservoirs with clean fluid. To prevent squiring fluid, replace the cover.

CAUTION: *On vehicles with front disc brakes, it will be necessary to hold in the metering valve pin during the bleeding procedure. The metering valve is located beneath the master cylinder and the pin is situated under the rubber boot on the end of the combination valve housing. This may be taped in or held by an assistant. Never reuse brake fluid which has been bled from the system.*

2. Fill the master cylinder with brake fluid.

3. Install a box-end wrench on the bleeder screw on the right rear wheel.

4. Attach a length of small diameter, clear vinyl tubing to the bleeder screw. Submerge the other end of the rubber tubing in a glass jar partially filled with clean brake fluid. Make sure the rubber tube fits on the bleeder screw snugly or you may be squirted with brake fluid when the bleeder screw is opened.

5. Have your friend slowly depress the brake pedal. As this is done, open the bleeder screw half a turn and allow the fluid to run through the tube. Close the bleeder screw, then return the brake pedal to its fully released position.

6. Repeat this procedure until no bubbles appear in the jar. Refill the master cylinder.

7. Repeat this procedure on the left rear, right front, and left front wheels, in that order. Periodically refill the master cylinder so it does not run dry.

8. If the brake warning light is on, depress

the brake pedal firmly. If there is no air in the system, the light will go out.

Powermaster® System

1. Pump the brake pedal 10 times with the ignition switched off to remove all power boost effect from the system. Fill the reservoir to the indicated full mark with clean, fresh fluid meeting the specifications shown on the cover.

2. Disconnect the brake line connectors at the master cylinder outlet ports. Allow the fluid to bleed through the system by gravity until it flows out all four ports. Reconnect the brake lines to the ports. Refill the fluid reservoir, if necessary.

3. Tighten the connector closest to the cowl. Then, have an assistant slowly apply the brake pedal fully (50 lbs. pressure). As he holds this position, tighten the forward connector. Then, have him release the pedal. Refill the fluid reservoir, if necessary.

4. Wait five seconds, and then have your assistant re-apply the brake pedal, and hold it down. Open the forward connector ½ turn to purge air. Before the pedal bottoms out, retighten the connector and have your assistant release the pedal again. Repeat the procedure in this step until all air is purged from this port. Refill the fluid reservoir, if necessary.

5. Repeat Steps 3 and 4 to bleed the remaining connectors (the connector closest to the cowl need not be bled). When the bleeding operation has been completed, operate the brakes with the ignition on and system pressure restored. Brake pedal travel should be normal and the brake warning indicator must not light when brakes are applied.

FRONT DISC BRAKES

Disc Brake Pads

CAUTION: *Some brake pads contain asbestos, which has been determined to be a cancer causing agent. Never clean the brake surfaces with compressed air! Avoid inhaling any dust from any brake surface! When cleaning brake surfaces, use a commercially available brake cleaning fluid.*

INSPECTION

Brake pads should be inspected once a year or at 7,500 miles, whichever occurs first. Check both ends of the outboard shoe, looking in at each end of the caliper; then check the lining thickness on the inboard shoe, looking down through the inspection hole. Lining should be more than 0.020 in. (0.5mm) on 1975–82 vehicles; 0.030 in. (0.76mm) on 1983 and later vehi-

cles, thick above the rivet (so that the lining is thicker than the metal backing.). Keep in mind that any applicable state inspection standards that are more stringent take precedence. All

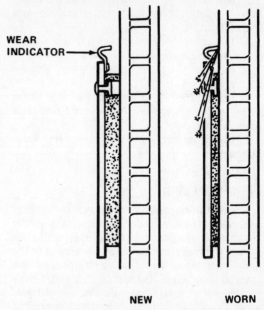

NEW　　　　**WORN**

Front disc brake pad wear indicator—1979 and later

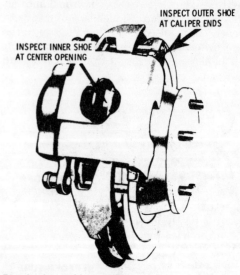

Disc brake pad inspection

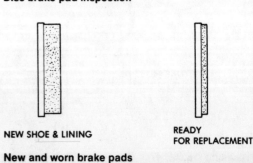

NEW SHOE & LINING　　　READY FOR REPLACEMENT

New and worn brake pads

four pads must be replaced if one shows excessive wear.

NOTE: *All 1979 and later models have a wear indicator that makes a noise when the linings wear to a degree where replacement is necessary. The spring clip is an integral part of the inboard shoe and lining. When the brake pad reaches a certain degree of wear, the clip will contact the rotor and produce a warning noise.*

REMOVAL AND INSTALLATION

1. Siphon off ⅔ of the brake fluid from the master cylinder.

NOTE: *The insertion of the thicker replacement pads will push the caliper piston back into its bore and will cause a full master cylinder to overflow.*

2. Raise the vehicle and support it with jackstands. Remove the wheel(s).

3. Install a C-clamp on the caliper so that the solid side of the clamp rests against the back of the caliper and the screw end rests against the metal part of the outboard pad.

4. Tighten the clamp until the caliper moves enough to bottom the piston in its bore. Remove the clamp.

5. Remove the two allen head caliper mounting bolts enough to allow the caliper to be pulled off the disc.

6. Remove the inboard pad and dislodge the outboard pad. Place the caliper where it won't be supported by the brake hose (hang it by a wire hook from the frame).

7. Remove the pad support spring clip from the piston.

8. Remove the two bolt ear sleeves and the four rubber bushings from the ears.

9. Brake pads should be replaced when they are worn to within ¹⁄₃₂ in. of the rivet heads.

To install:

1. Check the inside of the caliper for leakage and the condition of the piston dust boot.

2. Lubricate the two new sleeves and four bushings with a silicone spray.

3. Install the bushings in each caliper ear. Install the two sleeves in the two inboard ears.

4. Install the pad support spring clip and the old pad into the center of the piston. You will then push this pad down to get the piston flat against the caliper. This part of the job is a hassle and requires an assistant. While the assistant holds the caliper and loosens the bleeder valve to relieve pressure, you get a prybar and try to force the old pad in to make the piston flush with the caliper surface. When it is flush, close the bleeder valve so that no air gets into the system.

NOTE: *On models with wear sensors, make sure the wear sensor is toward the rear of the caliper.*

5. Position the outboard shoe with the ears of the shoes over the caliper ears and the tab at the bottom engaged in the caliper cutout notch.

6. With the two shoes in position, place the caliper over the brake disc and align the holes in the caliper with those of the mounting bracket.

CAUTION: *Make certain that the brake hose is not twisted or kinked.*

7. Install the mounting bracket bolts through the sleeves in the inboard caliper ears and through the mounting bracket, making

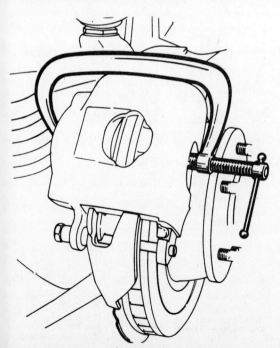

Use a C-clamp to seat the caliper piston

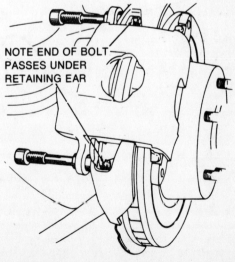

NOTE END OF BOLT PASSES UNDER RETAINING EAR

The Allen head caliper bolts must go under the pad retaining ears

sure that the ends of the bolts pass under the retaining ears on the inboard shoe.

8. Tighten the bolts into the bracket and tighten to 35 ft. lbs. (48 Nm). Bend over the outer pad ears. On 1983 and 1984 vehicles, measure clearance between the caliper and bracket stops. It must be 0.005–0.012 in. (0.127–0.305mm).

9. Install the front wheel and lower the vehicle.

10. Add fluid to the master cylinder reservoirs so that they are ¼ in. (6mm) from the top.

11. Test the brake pedal by pumping it to obtain a hard pedal is obtained. Bleed the brakes if necessary.

Disc Brake Calipers

REMOVAL

1. Perform the removal steps for pad replacement.

2. Disconnect the brake hose and plug the line.

3. Remove the U-shaped retainer from the fitting.

4. Pull the hose from the frame bracket and remove the caliper with the hose attached.

DISASSEMBLY

5. Clean the outside of the caliper with denatured alcohol.

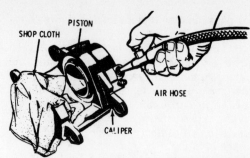

Piston removal using compressed air. Keep fingers out of the way of the piston when the air is applied.

6. Remove the brake hose and discard the copper gasket.

7. Remove the brake fluid from the caliper.

8. Place clean rags or a piece of wood inside the caliper opening to catch the piston when it is released.

CAUTION: *Do not place your fingers in front of the piston in an attempt to catch it while applying compressed air; serious injury could result.*

9. Apply compressed air to the caliper fluid inlet hole and force the piston out of its bore. Do not blow the piston out, but use just enough pressure to ease it out.

10. Use a prybar to pry the boot out of the caliper. Avoid scratching the bore.

11. Remove the piston seal from its groove in

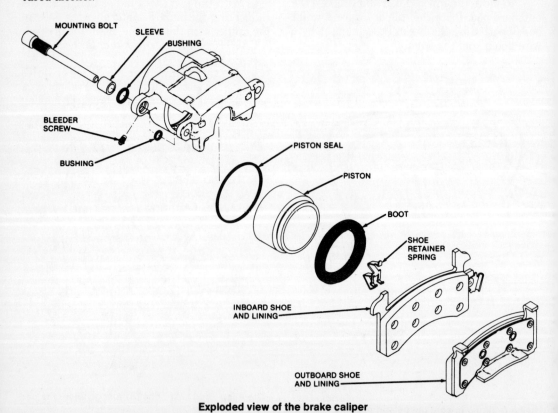

Exploded view of the brake caliper

the caliper bore. Do not use a metal tool of any type for this operation.

ASSEMBLY

12. Blow out all passages in the caliper and bleeder valve. Clean the piston and piston bore with fresh brake fluid.

13. Examine the piston for scoring, scratches or corrosion. If any of these conditions exist the piston must be replaced, as it is plated and cannot be refinished.

14. Examine the bore for the same defects. Light rough spots may be removed by rotating crocus cloth, using finger pressure, in the bore. Do not polish with an in and out motion or use any other abrasive.

15. Lubricate the piston bore and the new rubber parts with fresh brake fluid. Position the seal in the piston bore groove.

16. Lubricate the piston with brake fluid and assemble the boot into the piston groove so that the fold faces the open end of the piston.

17. Insert the piston into the bore, taking care not to unseat the seal.

18. Force the piston to the bottom of the bore. (This will require a force of 50–100 lbs.). Seat the boot lip around the caliper counterbore. Proper seating of the boot is very important for sealing out contaminants.

INSTALLATION

19. Install the brake hose into the caliper using a new copper gasket.

20. Lubricate the new sleeves and rubber

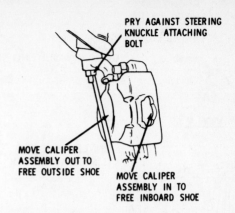

Compressing caliper with pry bar

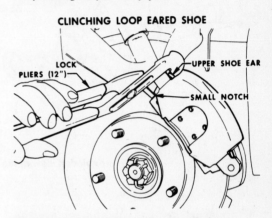

Clinching outboard shoe during installation

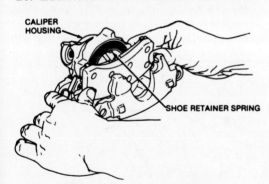

Installing inboard brake shoe and linings

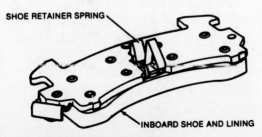

Proper retaining spring installation

bushings. Install the bushings in the caliper ears. Install the sleeves so that the end toward the disc pad is flush with the machined surface.

NOTE: *Lubrication of the sleeves and bushings is essential to ensure the proper operation of the sliding caliper design.*

21. Install the shoe support spring in the piston.

22. Install the disc pads in the caliper and remount the caliper on the hub. See Disc Brake Pad Removal and Installation.

23. Reconnect the brake hose to the steel brake line. Install the retainer clip. Bleed the brakes. See Brake Bleeding.

24. Replace the wheels, check the brake fluid level, check the brake pedal travel, and road-test the vehicle.

Brake Disc (Rotor)

REMOVAL AND INSTALLATION

1. Raise the vehicle, support it with jackstands, and remove the wheel and tire assembly.

2. Remove the brake caliper as previously outlined.

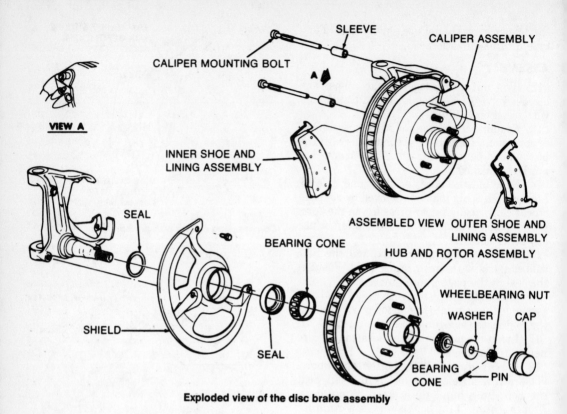

CALIPER MOUNTING BOLT

SLEEVE

CALIPER ASSEMBLY

VIEW A

INNER SHOE AND
LINING ASSEMBLY

SEAL

ASSEMBLED VIEW OUTER SHOE AND
LINING ASSEMBLY

BEARING CONE

HUB AND ROTOR ASSEMBLY

SHIELD

SEAL

WHEELBEARING NUT

WASHER   CAP

BEARING
CONE

PIN

Exploded view of the disc brake assembly

3. Remove the dust cap and remove the wheel bearing nut after removing the cotter pin.

4. Remove the wheel bearing, hub, and disc assembly from the spindle.

5. Install the disc, bearing, washer and nut. Adjust the wheel bearing as follows:

a. Spin the wheel forward by hand. Torque the nut to 12 ft. lbs. to fully seat the bearings.

b. Back off the nut ¼–½ turn until it is just loose, the tighten the nut finger tight.

c. Loosen the nut until either hole in the spindle lines up with a slot in the nut and then insert the cotter pin. This may appear to be too loose, but it is the correct adjustment. The spindle nut should not be even finger tight.

d. Proper adjustment creates a 0.001–0.005 in. (0.025–0.127mm) of end play.

INSPECTION

1. Check the disc for any obvious defects such as excessive rust, chipping, or deep scoring. Light scoring is normal on disc brakes.

2. Make sure there is no wheel bearing play and then check the disc for runout as follows:

3. Install a dial indicator on the caliper so that its feeler will contact the disc about 1 in. below its outer edge.

4. Turn the disc and observe the runout

reading. If the reading exceeds 0.002 in. (0.05mm), the disc should be replaced.

NOTE: *All brake rotors (discs) have a minimum thickness dimension cast into them, on the hub between the lugs. This is the minimum wear dimension and not a refinish dimension. Do not reuse a brake rotor that will not meet specifications. Replace with a new rotor.*

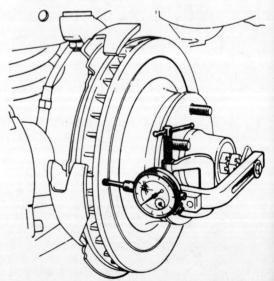

Checking brake disc runout with a dial indicator

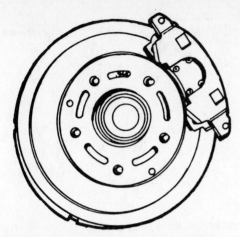

Discard dimension (.965) stamped on disc hub

Refinishing of brake rotors can be handled at machine shops equipped for brake work.

Wheel Bearings

For wheel bearing adjustment, refer to Wheel Bearings, Removal, Installation and Packing in this chapter or chapter 1.

REAR DRUM BRAKES

Brake Drum

REMOVAL AND INSTALLATION

1. Raise and support the vehicle with jackstands.
2. Remove the wheel or wheels.
3. Pull the brake drum off. It may be necessary to gently tap the rear edges of the drum to start it off the studs.
4. If extreme resistance to removal is encountered, it will be necessary to retract the adjusting screw. Knock out the access hole in the brake drum and turn the adjuster to retract the linings away from the drum. If this does not release the drum completely, use a rubber mallet to pound gently all around the outer edge of the drum to loosen it.
5. Install a replacement hole cover before reinstalling drum.
6. Install the drums in the same position on the hub as removed. Adjust front wheel bearings as described in the "Brake Disc" section in this chapter or Chapter 1.

INSPECTION

1. Check the drums for any cracks, scores, grooves, or an out-of-round condition. Replace if cracked. Slight scores can be removed with fine emery cloth while extensive scoring requires turning the drum on a lathe.
2. Never have a drum turned more than 0.060 in. (1.5mm).

Brake Shoes

INSPECTION

To inspect the brake shoes, first remove the drum as described above. Then, measure the thickness of the lining. To do this, you can lay a ruler next to the shoe, perpendicular to the surface, and measure the thickness of the lining alone. If the thickness does not meet or exceed the dimension shown in the specifications chart or state inspection standards in your state *whichever is thicker*, replace the lining. Remember, also, that there must be enough lining left so that the minimum thickness will still exist when you plan to perform your next inspection.

REMOVAL AND INSTALLATION

CAUTION: *Some brake shoes contain asbestos, which has been determined to be a cancer causing agent. Never clean the brake surfaces with compressed air! Avoid inhaling any dust from any brake surface! When cleaning brake surfaces, use a commercially available brake cleaning fluid.*

1. Raise the vehicle and support it on jackstands.
2. Slacken the parking brake cable.
3. Remove the rear wheel and brake drum. The front wheel and drum may be removed as a unit by removing the spindle nut and cotter pin.
4. Free the brake shoe return springs, actuator pull-back spring, holddown pins and springs, and actuator assembly.

NOTE: *Special tools available from auto supply stores will ease removal of the spring and anchor pin, but the job may still be done with common hand tools.*

5. On the rear wheels, disconnect the adjusting mechanism and spring, and remove the primary shoe. The primary shoe has a shorter lin-

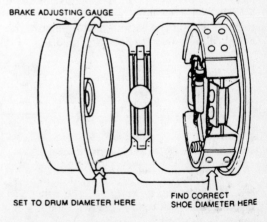

BRAKE ADJUSTING GAUGE

SET TO DRUM DIAMETER HERE   FIND CORRECT SHOE DIAMETER HERE

Measuring brake drum diameter for shoe adjustment

ing than the secondary and is mounted at the front of the wheel.

6. Disconnect the parking brake lever from the secondary shoe and remove the shoe. Rear wheel shoes may be removed together.

To install:

1. Clean and inspect all brake parts.

2. Check the wheel cylinders for seal condition and leaking.

3. Repack wheel bearings and replace the seals.

4. Inspect the replacement shoes for nicks or burrs, lubricate the backing plate contact points, brake cable and levers, and adjusting screws and then assemble.

5. Make sure that the right and left hand adjusting screws are not mixed. You can prevent this by working on one side at a time. This will also provide you with a reference for reassembly. The star wheel should be nearest to the secondary shoe when correctly installed.

6. When completed, make an initial adjustment as previously described.

NOTE: *Maintenance procedures for the metallic lining option are the same as those for standard linings. Do not substitute these linings in standard drums, unless they have been honed to a 20 micro-inch finish and equipped with special heat resistant springs.*

Wheel Cylinders

REMOVAL AND INSTALLATION

1. Raise the vehicle and support with jackstands. Remove the wheels and brake drum as described above.

2. Clean all dirt away from around the brake line connection, and disconnect the brake line.

3. The wheel cylinders are retained by two types of fasteners. One type uses a round retainer with locking clips, which attaches to the wheel cylinder on the back side of the brake backing plate. Use two awls to release the two locking clips. The other type simply uses two bolts, which screw into the wheel cylinder from the back side of the backing plate. Remove the wheel cylinder from the backing plate.

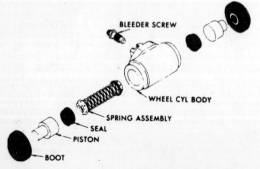

Exploded view of a typical wheel cylinder

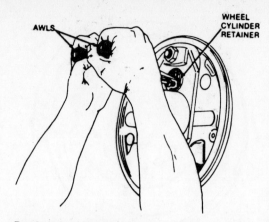

Bend retainer stubs using awls

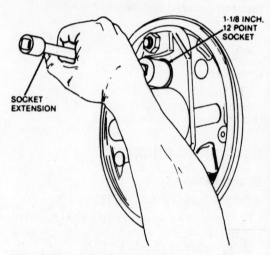

Use a socket and extension to seat the new retainer

To install:

1. Install the wheel cylinder onto the backing plate. Using a 1⅛ in. socket and extension, press the locking clip onto the wheel cylinder. Torque the retaining bolts to 15 ft. lbs. (20 Nm) for the other type.

2. Connect the brake pipe. Torque the connection to 100 inch lbs. (12 Nm).

3. Install brake shoes, drum, and wheel, and flush and bleed brakes.

REAR DISC BRAKES

CAUTION: *Brake shoes contain asbestos, which has been determined to be a cancer causing agent. Never clean the brake surfaces with compressed air! Avoid inhaling any dust from any brake surface! When cleaning brake surfaces, use a commercially available brake cleaning fluid.*

The brakes are almost identical in design and operation to the front disc brakes, with the ex-

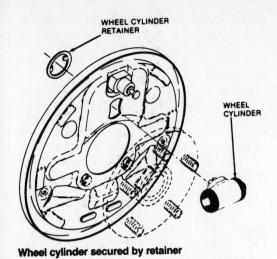

Wheel cylinder secured by retainer

WHEEL CYLINDER
RETAINER

WHEEL
CYLINDER

WHEEL CYLINDER BOLT

CYLINDER
LINKS

WHEEL
CYLINDER

Bolt-type wheel cylinder

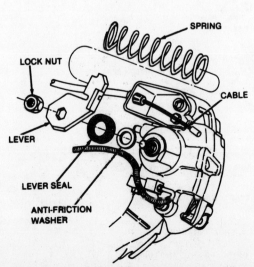

SPRING

LOCK NUT

CABLE

LEVER

LEVER SEAL

ANTI-FRICTION
WASHER

Parking brake mounting on rear disc brake caliper

ception of the parking brake mechanism that is built into the rear brake calipers. When the parking brake is applied, the lever turns the actuator screw which is threaded into a nut in the piston assembly. This causes the piston to move outward and the caliper to slide inward mechanically, forcing the linings against the brake disc. The piston assembly contains a self-adjusting mechanism for the parking brake.

Disc Brake Pads
REMOVAL AND INSTALLATION

1. Siphon off ⅔ of the brake fluid from the master cylinder.
   NOTE: *The insertion of the thicker replacement pads will push the caliper piston back into its bore and will cause a full master cylinder to overflow.*
2. Raise the rear of the vehicle and support it with safety stands. Remove the wheel and tire assembly.
3. Remove the caliper as detailed later in this section.
4. Remove the outboard brake shoe and lining by unsnapping the shoe springs from the caliper holes.
5. From the inside of the caliper, press on the edge of the inboard brake shoe and tilt it outward so that it is released from the shoe retainer.
6. Remove the flexible two way check valve from the end of the piston assembly with a small screwdriver.
   NOTE: *If new shoes and linings are to be installed, remove the parking brake lever and bottom the piston in the caliper bore as shown in the accompanying illustration.*
7. To install, lubricate a new two way check valve with silicone fluid and press it into the end of the piston.
8. Install the inboard brake shoe. Make sure that the shoe retainer and the piston are positioned as shown in the illustration. The tabs on the retainer are different; rotate the retainer into position if necessary. The buttons on the backing of the shoe must engage the larger, D-shaped notches in the piston. The piston will be properly aligned when the larger notches are aligned with the caliper mounting bolt holes as shown. Engage the inboard edge of the shoe with the straight tabs on the retainer, press downward and snap the shoe under the S-shaped tabs.
9. Install the outboard brake shoe. The shoe is properly installed when the wear sensor is at the trailing edge of the shoe during forward rotation.
10. Be sure to snap both shoe springs into the

caliper holes so that the back of the shoe is flat against the caliper.

11. Install the caliper.

12. Bleed the brakes, install the wheels and lower the vehicle.

Disc Brake Caliper

REMOVAL AND INSTALLATION

1. Siphon off ⅔ of the brake fluid from the master cylinder.

NOTE: *The insertion of the thicker replacement pads will push the caliper piston back into its bore and will cause a full master cylinder to overflow.*

2. Raise the rear of the vehicle and support it with safety stands. Remove the wheel and tire assembly.

3. Reinstall two lug nuts to keep the rotor from turning.

4. Remove the retaining clip from the parking brake actuator lever.

5. Disconnect the parking brake cable and spring from the lever.

6. While holding the parking brake lever in place, remove the lock nut. Remove the lever, lever seal and the anti-friction washer.

7. If the caliper is to be overhauled or re-placed, remove the bolt attaching the brake line inlet fitting.

8. Remove the caliper mounting bolts and then remove the caliper from the rotor and mounting bracket.

9. Check the lever seal and the anti-friction washer for wear and replace if worn.

10. Check the mounting bolts for any wear or damage, replace if necessary. Check the bolt boots, support bushings and caliper piston boot for any wear, cracking or other damage, replace as necessary.

11. Replace the insulators.

12. To install, coat the entire shaft of the caliper mounting bolts with a thin film of silicone grease.

13. Slide the caliper over the rotor and into the mounting bracket. Make sure that the new insulators are in position. Tighten the mounting bolts to 63 ft. lbs. (85 Nm).

14. If you disconnected the inlet fitting, install it and tighten to 32 ft. lbs. (44 Nm). Use two NEW copper washers.

15. Lubricate the parking brake lever seal with silicone grease and then install it and the anti-friction washer.

16. Install the lever onto the actuator screw hex so that it is pointing as shown in the illus-

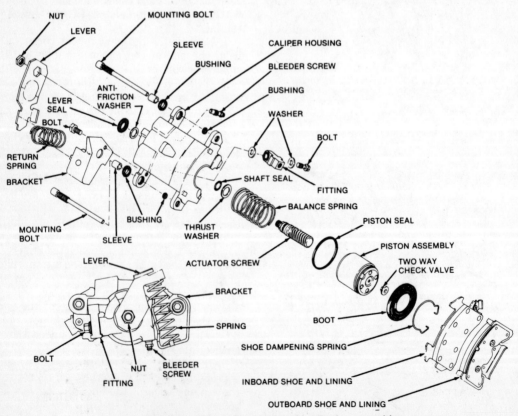

Rear disc brake caliper and parking brake assembly

tration. Tighten the nut to 35 ft. lbs. (48 Nm) while holding the lever in position and then rotate the lever back against the stop on the caliper.

17. Install the spring with the damper and then connect the parking brake cable.

18. Install the retaining clip onto the lever so that it prevents the parking brake cable from sliding out of the slot in the lever.

19. Adjust the parking brake cable by tightening the cable at the adjuster until the lever begins to move off the stop on the caliper. Loosen the adjustment just enough so that the lever moves back against the stop. Apply and release the parking brake three times to verify proper adjustment.

20. Remove the two lug nuts and then replace the wheels. Lower the vehicle.

21. Bleed the brake system and recheck the fluid level.

PARKING BRAKE

All models are equipped with a foot operated ratchet type parking brake. A cable assembly connects this pedal to an intermediate cable by means of an equalizer. Adjustment is made at the equalizer. The intermediate cable connects with two rear cables and each of these cables enters a rear wheel.

Cables
REMOVAL AND INSTALLATION

Front cable

1. Raise the vehicle and support it securely by the frame. Loosen the adjusting nut and disconnect the front cable at the connector. Compress the fingers of the cable retainer and disconnect it at the frame.

2. Lower the vehicle to the ground. Then, remove the lower rear bolt from the wheelhouse panel and then pull the panel outward to gain access to the front cable. Disconnect the cable at the parking brake pedal assembly by compressing the fingers of the retainer and pulling it out.

3. Install a new cable in reverse order, checking carefully that it is properly routed and securely retained. Adjust the parking brake.

Left Rear Cable
DRUM BRAKES

1. Raise the vehicle and support it securely by the frame. Loosen the adjusting nut and compress the retainer fingers at the equalizer lever to loosen the cable.

2. Disconnect the cable at the connector and then remove it from the equalizer.

3. Mark the relationship between the wheel

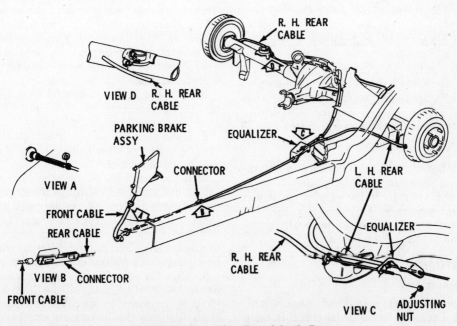

Parking brake cable, all models similar

and axle flange and remove the wheel. Remove the brake drum as described above.

4. Using an appropriate tool, disconnect and remove the primary shoe return spring and parking brake strut.

5. Compress the retainer fingers and loosen the cable housing at the backing plate. Then, disconnect the cable from the parking brake lever and remove it.

6. Install a new cable in reverse order, checking carefully that it is properly routed and securely retained. Adjust the parking brake.

Right Rear Cable

DRUM BRAKES

1. Raise the vehicle and support it securely by the frame. Remove the adjusting nut at the equalizer lever. Compress the fingers of the retainers and then loosen the cable housing from the retainers at the frame and at the axle housing retaining clip.

2. Mark the relationship between the wheel and axle flange and then remove the wheel. Remove the brake drum as described above.

3. Using an appropriate tool, disconnect and remove the primary shoe return spring and parking brake strut. Remove the secondary brake shoe holddown spring.

4. Compress the retainer fingers and loosen the cable housing at the backing plate. Then, disconnect the cable from the parking brake lever and remove it.

5. Install a new cable in reverse order, checking carefully that it is properly routed and securely retained. Adjust the parking brake.

Rear Cables

DISC BRAKES

1. Raise the vehicle and support it on safety stands.

2. Loosen the cable at the adjuster.

3. Disconnect all cables at the equalizer.

4. Disengage the cable housing retainer from the rear suspension crossmember assembly.

5. Remove the cable from the caliper assembly as detailed earlier in this section and then remove the cable.

6. To install, position the cables in the retainers as shown in the illustration.

7. Install the cable in the caliper assembly as described previously.

8. Reconnect all cables at the equalizer.

9. Adjust the parking brake.

ADJUSTMENT

Rear Drum Brakes

The need for parking brake adjustment is indicated if parking brake pedal travel is more than 15 clicks under heavy foot pressure.

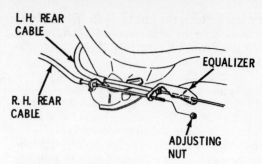

Parking brake adjustment

1. Depress the parking brake pedal exactly two ratchet clicks.

2. Raise the vehicle and safely support it with jackstands.

3. Tighten the adjusting nut until the left rear wheel can just be turned rearward using two hands, but is locked when forward rotation is attempted.

4. With the mechanism totally disengaged, the rear wheels should turn freely in either direction with no brake drag.

NOTE: *It is very important that the parking brake cables are not adjusted too tightly causing brake drag.*

5. Remove the jackstands and lower the vehicle.

Rear Disc Brakes

1. Lubricate the parking brake cables at the underbody rub points and at the equalizer hooks. Make sure there is free movement at all cables, and that the parking brake pedal is in the fully released position.

2. Raise the rear of the vehicle and support it with jackstands.

3. Hold the brake cable stud from turning and tighten the equalizer nut until all cable slack is removed.

4. Make sure the caliper levers are against the stops on the caliper housings after tightening the equalizer nut.

5. If the levers are off the stops, loosen the cable until the levers return to the stops.

6. Operate the parking brake pedal several times to check the adjustment. When the cable is properly adjusted, the parking brake pedal should travel 4–5½ in. (102–140mm) with approximately 125 pounds of force on the pedal.

7. After the adjustment, the levers must be on the caliper stops. Back off the brake adjustment if necessary to keep the levers on the stops. Remove the jackstands and lower the vehicle.

Brake Specifications
All measurements given are (in.) unless noted

Year	Model	Lug Nut Torque (ft. lbs.)	Master Cylinder Bore	Brake Disc		Brake Drum		Minimum Lining Thickness	
				Minimum Thickness	Maximum Run-Out	Max Machine O/S	Max Wear Limit	Front	Rear
1975	Cpe., Snd.	100 ①	1.125 ②	1.215	.004	11.060	11.090	.125	③
	Wagons	100 ①	1.125 ②	1.215	.004	12.060	12.090	.125	③
1976	Cpe., Sdns.	100 ①	1.125	1.215	.005	11.060	11.090	④	③
	Wagons	100 ①	1.125	1.215	.005	12.060	12.090	④	③
1977	Cpe., Sdns.	100 ①	1.125	.965	.005	11.060	11.090	④	③
	Wagons	100 ①	1.125	.965	.005	11.060	11.090	④	③
1978	Cpe., Sdns.	100	1.125	.965	.004	11.060	11.090	④	③
	Wagons	100	1.125	.965	.005	11.060	11.090	④	③
1979	Cpe., Sdns.	100	1.125	.965	.004	11.060	11.090	④	③
	Wagons	100	1.125	.965	.005	11.060	11.090	④	③
1980	Cpe., Sdns.	100	1.125	.965	.004	11.060	11.090	④	③
	Wagons	100	1.125	.965	.005	11.060	11.090	④	③
1981	Cpe., Sdns.	100	1.125	.965	.004	11.060	11.090	④	③
	Wagons	100	1.125	.965	.005	11.060	11.090	④	③
1982	All	100	1.125	.965	.005	11.060	11.090	④	③
1983–84	B Series	100 ⑥	1.125 ⑦	.980 ⑧	.004 ⑨	11.06 ⑨	—	⑩	⑩
	C-D Series	100 ⑥	1.125 ⑦	.980 ⑧	.004 ⑨	11.09 ⑨	—	⑩	⑩
1985–87	All	100 ⑪	1.125	.965 ⑫	.004	11.060 ⑫	11.090	⑩	⑩
1988–90	Wagons	100 ①	1.125	.965 ⑫	.004	11.060 ⑫	11.090	⑩	⑩

① 90 ft. lbs. w/cast aluminum wheels
② 1.000 in. w/manual brakes
③ ⅓ in. above rivets
④ To within .020 in. of rivets
⑤ B Cars are Olds 88, Buick Le Sabre, and Pontiac Parisienne
　C Cars are Olds 98, models built in 1983
　D Cars are Olds 98, Buick Electra, and Pontiac Bonneville
⑥ 90 ft. lbs. with cast aluminum wheels, 80 ft. lbs. with steel wheels and 7/16″ studs.
⑦ With Hydroboost—1.1875
⑧ All Olds 1983 Models, and Olds 88 built in 1984—1.02
⑨ With 9.5″ drums, figures are 9.56 and 9.59
⑩ To within .030 in. of rivets
⑪ With 7/16-20 wheels—80
⑫ Discard thickness

Body and Trim

![Chapter 10 icon depicting a car door]

EXTERIOR

Doors

REMOVAL AND INSTALLATION

CAUTION: *Removing a door is a simple operation, but it requires careful handling of a heavy object that is awkward to handle. You must have a helper who will hold the door and ensure that it does not get out of control, which could hurt someone or strip the threads of the mounting bolts. Put a floor jack or other adjustable means of holding the door underneath before starting, so that the helper*

must only keep the door from tipping as you remove the fasteners.

The easiest and best way to remove the door is to remove the bolts that fasten the door assembly to the hinges, rather than attempting to remove the bolts fastening the hinges to the body. This is true because it is much easier to gain access to these bolts.

1. If the vehicle has power operated components in the doors (electric windows or motor operated mirrors), disconnect the negative ($-$) battery cable, remove the trim panel (see the appropriate procedure later in this chapter), and lift the watershield out far enough to reach the electrical connectors. Then, disconnect these connectors. Detach the rubber wire conduit and pull the harness coming from the body out of the door.

2. Very precisely use a sharp scribe to mark the relationship between the door and the door hinges so that you can remount it without the need to adjust it.

3. Open the door all the way and, with the help of another person and using a floor jack or other means, support the door.

4. Remove both the upper and lower bolts attaching the door to the outer portions of the hinges. Remove the door.

To install:

1. Install the mounting bolts and turn them in until they are nearly ready to clamp the hinge to the door.

2. Position the door carefully so that the matchmarks line up.

3. Tighten the bolts alternately top and bottom until the door is tightly held in position. Torque the bolts to 15–21 ft. lbs. (20–28 Nm).

4. Install and connect all disconnected wiring and battery cable.

ADJUSTMENT

Doors are adjustable by using floating plates inside both the doors and hinge pillars. Always

40. Upper hinge-to-body bolt
41. Upper hinge-to-door bolt
42. Rubber conduit
43. Lower hinge-to-door bolt
44. Lower hinge-to-body bolt
57. Spring
172. Upper hinge
173. Lower hinge

Door hinge bolt locations

mark locations of bolts before loosening them and beginning adjustment. It is best to remove the door lock striker to permit the door to hang free and then close the door so you can observe exactly how it fits onto the body.

Front Doors

1. If the door requires for and aft or up or down adjustment, loosen the body hinge pillar adjustments. Shift the position of the door with the help of an assistant and a floor jack. Then, tighten the bolts. When the position fore and aft and up and down is correct, torque the bolts to 15–21 ft. lbs. (20–28 Nm). If you have to move the door to the rear, replace the door jamb light switch.

2. If the door must be adjusted in or out, loosen the bolts attaching the door at the hinge pillar attachments. Shift the position of the door with the help of an assistant and a floor jack. Then, tighten the bolts. When the position in or out is correct, torque the bolts to 15–21 ft. lbs. (20–28 Nm).

Rear Doors

1. If the door requires in or out or significant up or down adjustment, loosen the door side hinge attaching screws. Shift the position of the door with the help of an assistant and a floor jack. Then, tighten the bolts. When the position in or out and up and down is correct, torque the bolts to 15–21 ft. lbs. (20–28 Nm).

2. If the door requires fore or aft or a slight up or down adjustment, loosen the body side, center pillar hinge adjusting bolts. Shift the position of the door with the help of an assistant and a floor jack. Then, tighten the bolts. When the position is correct, torque the bolts to 15–21 ft. lbs. (20–28 Nm). If you have to move the door to the rear, replace the door jamb light switch.

Hood

REMOVAL AND INSTALLATION

1. Raise the hood. Cover the fenders with protective pads. This is necessary to protect the paint because the hood will often contact these areas during removal or installation procedures. Place masking tape on the fender and hood covers and edges.

2. On models equipped with an underhood light disconnect the lamp wiring.

3. Very precisely use a sharp scribe to mark the relationship between the hood and the hood hinges so that you can remount it without the need to adjust it.

4. Support the hood, especially at the front, in a secure manner. Remove the bolts on either side that fasten the tops of the hinges to the un-

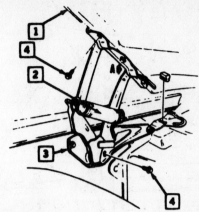

1. Hood assembly
2. Balance spring
3. Hood hinge
4. Hood mounting bolts. Torque to 20 ft. lbs.

Removing the hood. Remove the bolts shown. At installation, torque to the figure shown.

derside of the hood. Remove the bolts starting at the front and moving toward the rear to help avoid placing stress on the assembly. Make sure the hood is securely supported to help prevent bending of it as you work.

5. When all the bolts are removed, lift the rear of the hood off the hinges and then lift the unit off the vehicle.

To install:

1. Carry the hood from either side and position it over the engine compartment in its normal position. Raise the front and position it at the right angle to the upper surfaces of the hinges. Pass all the bolts through the upper hinges and start them into the lower side of the hood. Do not tighten them, but leave plenty of clearance to adjust the position of the hood on the hinges.

2. Carefully shift the hood on both hinges simultaneously to align the matchmarks. Then, tighten the mounting bolts, torquing to 20 ft. lbs. (27 Nm). Close the hood and check its fit in the body and the alignment of the hood latch. If necessary, readjust the hood alignment as described below. Reconnect the underhood light wiring, if the vehicle is so equipped.

ALIGNMENT

1. Close the hood and check its fit in the body and the alignment of the hood latch. If necessary, loosen *all* the mounting bolts just slightly and shift the adjustment in the correct direction.

2. Repeat this procedure until the hood latches smoothly and securely and all gaps between the hood and body are of equal width. Torque the mounting bolts to 20 ft. lbs. (27 Nm).

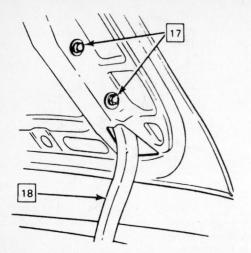

Removing the trunk lid. It is easiest to remove the attaching bolts shown, leaving the trunk lid hinges in place on the body

Trunk Lid
REMOVAL AND INSTALLATION

1. Raise the trunk lid. Cover the fenders with some sort of protective pads. This is necessary to protect the paint because the trunk lid will often contact these areas during removal or installation procedures.

2. On models equipped with an underhood light disconnect the lamp wiring.

3. Very precisely use a sharp scribe to mark the relationship between the trunk lid and the hinges so that you can remount it without the need to adjust it.

4. Support the trunk lid, especially at the rear, in a secure manner. Remove the bolts on either side that fasten the sides of the hinges to the underside of the trunk lid. Remove the bolts starting at the rear and moving toward the front to help avoid placing stress on the assembly. Make sure the trunk lid is securely supported to help prevent bending of it as you work.

5. When all the bolts are removed, lift the rear of the trunk lid off the hinges and then lift the unit off the vehicle.

To install:

1. Carry the trunk lid from either side and position it over the luggage compartment in its normal position. Raise the rear and position it at the right angle to the upper surfaces of the hinges. Pass all the bolts through the trunk lid and start them into the side of the upper hinges. Do not tighten them, but leave plenty of clearance to adjust the position of the trunk lid on the hinges.

2. Carefully shift the trunk lid on both hinges simultaneously to align the matchmarks. Then, tighten the mounting

bolts, torquing to 20 ft. lbs. (27 Nm). Close the trunk lid and check its fit in the body and the alignment of the trunk lid latch. If necessary, readjust the alignment. Reconnect the underhood light wiring, if the vehicle is so equipped.

ADJUSTMENT

All adjustments (fore and aft and up and down) are made by loosening the hinge strap-to-lid attaching bolts. Loosen *all* the bolts before adjusting the position of the lid to avoid springing it and to make adjustment easier. Slide the hood back and forth, locating both sides as required; then tighten the bolts. No side-to-side adjustment is provided.

If the hood has adjustable rear bumpers and it does not sit level, loosen the locknuts and turn the bumper screws up or down as necessary. Retighten the locknuts. You may find it helpful to close the trunk lid and measure the gap between the hood and body with a finely calibrated ruler.

Station Wagon Tailgate
REMOVAL AND INSTALLATION

NOTE: *To perform this procedure, you will need a length of rod $^3/_{16}$ in. (5mm) in diameter and 12 in. (305mm) long. You will also need new, service hinge pins and retaining rings.*

1. First, rotate the tailgate up and down until the torque rod tension has been eliminated. This occurs at a point near the vertical position of the gate, when spring tension is not required to keep the gate under control. You should be able to feel the point at which there is no longer significant weight to be supported as you raise the gate, and stop there.

CAUTION: *Proceed carefully with the next step in case there is still some tension on the torque rod.*

2. Mark the position of the torque rod assist link on the rear body pillar, and then remove it.

3. Open the tailgate and support it in the horizontal position. When the gate is securely supported, disconnect the support cables at the sides of the gate.

4. Place the length of rod against the point of one of the hinge pins. Strike the rod hard with a hammer to force the pin out of the hinge. You have to shear the retaining ring tabs to do this. Repeat this on the hinge on the other side. Then, remove the tailgate.

To install:

1. Install new retaining rings in the grooves in the new hinge pins, positioning the rings so the tabs point toward the heads of the pins. To

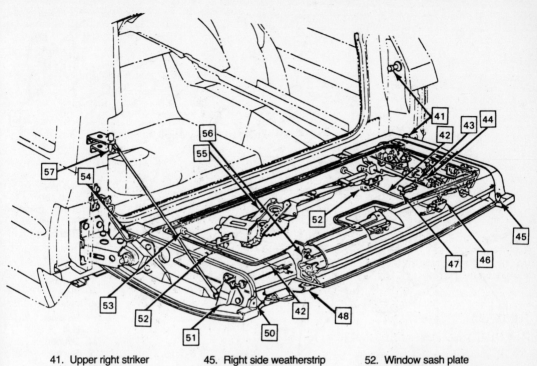

41. Upper right striker assembly
42. Window guide tube
43. Lock rod
44. Electric lock actuator rod
45. Right side weatherstrip
46. Outside handle
47. Lock cylinder
48. Sealing strip
50. Left side weatherstrip
51. Upper left hinge lock
52. Window sash plate
53. Window down bumper
54. Grommet
55. Regulator
56. Retainer
57. Upper left striker

Station wagon tailgate components

install, first align the gate to the body and so the hinge halves fit together properly. Then, tap the new hinge pins into position in the same direction in which the original pins were installed. Reverse the remaining procedures, installing the torque rod assist link in the same position, according to the markings made earlier.

ALIGNMENT

Adjust the tailgate horizontally by loosening all the hinge-to-body bolts, repositioning the gate, and then retightening the bolts. Make sure to retain all the shims in position, unless the gate is too close to or too far from the body.

If it is necessary to move the tailgate bottom in or out, loosen the hinge bolts and add or subtract shims between the hinge and body.

Bumpers

REMOVAL AND INSTALLATION

Front

1. Raise the vehicle and support with jackstands.
2. Disconnect the parking lamp connectors.
3. With the aid of an assistant, remove the eight bumper reinforcement-to-energy absorber nuts and remove the bumper. Note the size and position of the shims if used.

To install:

1. With an assistant, install the bumper shims and nuts only hand tight.
2. Move the bumper from side to side to gain sideward adjustment. Add or subtract shims to gain in or out adjustment. Torque the retaining nuts to 18 ft. lbs. (24 Nm).
3. Connect the parking lamp wires and lower the vehicle.

Rear

1. Raise the vehicle and support with jackstands.
2. Disconnect the license plate lamp connectors.
3. With the aid of an assistant, remove the eight bumper reinforcement-to-energy absorber nuts and remove the bumper. Note the size and position of the shims if used.

To install:

1. With an assistant, install the bumper shims and nuts only hand tight.
2. Move the bumper from side to side to gain sideward adjustment. Add or subtract shims to

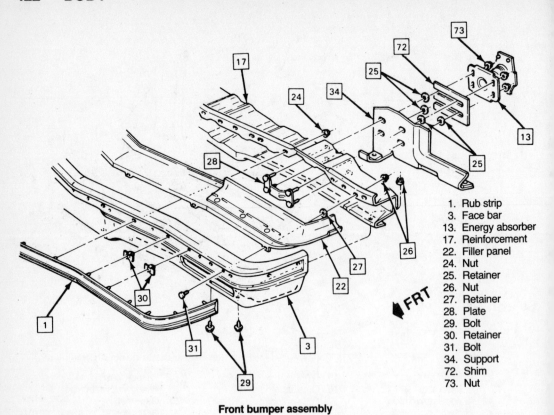

1. Rub strip
3. Face bar
13. Energy absorber
17. Reinforcement
22. Filler panel
24. Nut
25. Retainer
26. Nut
27. Retainer
28. Plate
29. Bolt
30. Retainer
31. Bolt
34. Support
72. Shim
73. Nut

Front bumper assembly

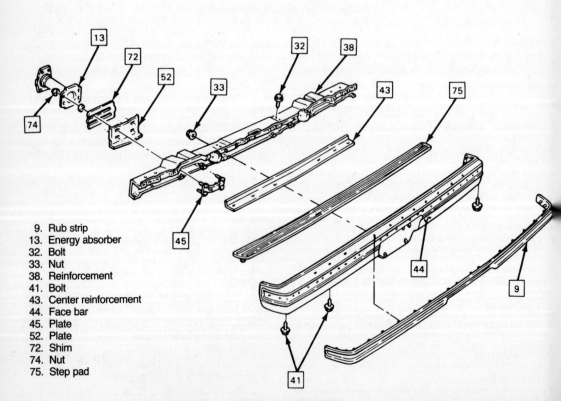

9. Rub strip
13. Energy absorber
32. Bolt
33. Nut
38. Reinforcement
41. Bolt
43. Center reinforcement
44. Face bar
45. Plate
52. Plate
72. Shim
74. Nut
75. Step pad

Rear bumper assembly

gain in or out adjustment. Torque the retaining nuts to 18 ft. lbs. (24 Nm).

3. Connect the license plate lamp wires and lower the vehicle.

Grille

REMOVAL AND INSTALLATION

Buick

1. Remove the two grille return springs, radiator grille nuts and grille.

2. Install the grille, torque the nuts to 97 inch lbs. (11 Nm) and install the return springs.

Oldsmobile and Pontiac

1. Remove the radiator grille bolts, grille and baffle if equipped.

2. Install the grille, baffle and bolts. Torque the bolts to 13 inch lbs. (1.5 Nm).

Windshield

REMOVAL AND INSTALLATION

NOTE: *To install a new windshield, you will have to use an adhesive service kit. The GM part No. is 9636067 or you can shop for an equivalent. You will also need: an alcohol base solvent; an adhesive dispensing gun GM part No. J–24811 or equivalent; a commercial type of razor knife; a hot knife; black weatherstrip adhesive; two side support spacers; if the windshield has an embedded antenna, a butyl strip; lower support spacers; masking tape. The area in which you work must be at room temperature to ensure timely curing of adhesive.*

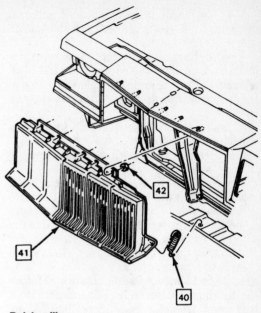

Buick grille

1. Place protective coverings around the areas of the body around the glass.

2. Remove the trim moldings around the windshield. These are retained by wire clips. You can carefully pry these moldings out until the clip ends are visible. The ends can be pried away from retaining grooves in the body to free them and permit removal of the moldings.

3. Remove the windshield wiper arms as described in Chapter 6. If it looks like lower glass stops will interfere with removal of the windshield, remove them too.

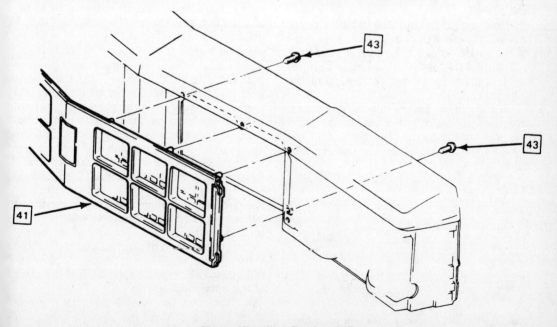

Oldsmobile grille—Pontiac similar

4. If the vehicle has an embedded antenna, disconnect the wiring connector at the bottom center of the windshield.

5. With the razor knife, cut the adhesive material built up along the edge of the windshield all around. Run the knife right along the edge of the windshield to do this, cutting as close as possible.

6. Install the foam sealing strip to the new windshield, as follows:

   a. Remove the backing paper from the sticky side of the strip.

   b. Apply the strip to the windshield, using the original windshield as a guide. Check to make sure that the new strip will not obscure the view of the serial number mounted to the top of the dash.

   c. Trim the strip as necessary with a sharp knife to remove excess.

7. Inspect all the retaining clips which fasten the moldings to the body. Clips must not be bent away from the body more than $1/16$ in. (1.6mm). If possible, bend the clips back into the proper configuration; otherwise, replace them.

8. Locate the lower support spacers for the glass as shown in the illustration. Then, carefully position the new glass on these spacers, resting on the original adhesive. See Step 15 for pointers on getting the glass safely into the right position. Check the relationship between the glass and adhesive mounting material on the pinchweld flange. Mark these areas so that later, when you apply additional adhesive, you can fill in any gaps and ensure proper mounting and sealing of the glass. Gaps must not exceed $1/8$ in. (3mm).

9. Now, apply masking tape to both sides of the windshield with the inside edge on the glass and the outside edge on the adjacent body pillar. Then, slit the tape with the knife. (This will provide a guide for proper positioning of the windshield later).

10. If the vehicle has an imbedded antenna, mark the location of either end of the butyl strip, mark the location of either end of the strip with the masking tape. On vehicles with this type antenna only, after the glass is removed in the next step, replace the butyl strip originally used to fill the gap between the windshield and body in this area. It should be approximately 8 in. (203mm) long.

11. Now, remove the glass from the opening. Apply masking tape to the inside of the glass $1/4$ in. (6mm) inboard from the edge of the glass, across the top and down both sides. This will make clean up easier. Make sure not to apply the tape farther in than this to keep it from being visible after installation.

12. Clean the glass around the edge of the inside surface by wiping it with a clean cloth dampened with the alcohol. Make sure the glass dries without application of heat before installation.

13. Apply the *clear* primer as follows, depending on the type of antenna used:

   a. Normal antenna: Apply the primer around the entire periphery of the glass edge *and* $1/4$ in. (6mm) inboard on the inner surface. Allow the primer to dry five minutes.

   b. Embedded antenna: Apply the clear primer just as for the plain windshield; around the entire periphery of the glass edge *and* $1/4$ in. (6mm) inboard on the inner surface. But, avoid getting any of the primer at all into the area marked by the tape in Step 10. Allow the primer to dry five minutes.

14. Apply a smooth bead of adhesive material over the entire *inside edge only* of the glass where the primer was applied in the step above. Make sure the bead is continuous and smooth.

15. Make sure the front windows/windwings are open. Now, with a helper, carry the glass over to the vehicle. Put one hand on the inside of the glass and one on the outside. Tilt the glass until it is horizontal. One person at a time can hold one hand to support the inside of the glass while reaching around the body pillar to grab the glass with the other. Once the glass is held with both hands (one inside the pillar and the other outside), tilt the glass into position, position the glass on the lower supports and, using the tape markers made above, line the glass up in the right position and then drop it straight into place. Press the glass down firmly to squeeze the adhesive material slightly. Avoid too much squeeze-out, as this will cause an ugly appearance. Paddle on additional adhesive, if necessary, to ensure a full and effective seal, utilizing marks made in Step 8 and inspecting for any other areas of poor seal, as well. If the vehicle has an embedded antenna, one place additional material must be applied is at the edges of the butyl sealing strip.

16. Watertest the windshield with a *gentle* spray from a garden hose. *A hard spray will disturb adhesive.* Use warm water, if you can (it

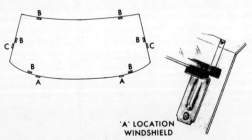

'A' LOCATION
WINDSHIELD

Locate the support spacers for the new windshield as shown

finds leaks more readily). Paddle extra adhesive in to seal any areas that leak and then retest them.

17. Once all leaks have been stopped, cement a rubber spacer between both the right and left sides of the windshield and the body metal to retain the windshield tightly in its present position as the adhesive cures.

18. Install the moldings. Remove clean-up masking tape from the inner surface of the glass and install/connect any remaining parts. Make sure the vehicle sits for six hours at room temperature before moving it so that the adhesive is properly cured.

Rear Window Glass

Since the glass is bonded and sealed in the same manner with the same adhesives, proceed exactly as described above, with one exception. On many rear window installations, you cannot reach around inside the vehicle with one hand in order to support and handle the glass. In these cases, you will have to use special suction cup devices to handle the glass. Be careful to ensure adequate seal of the cups for safe handling.

Outside Mirrors

REMOVAL AND INSTALLATION

1. Disconnect the negative (−) battery cable.
2. Remove the door trim panel, sound deflector and peel back the water shield as outlined in this chapter.
3. Remove the remote mirror control and cable from the instrument panel. If power mirrors, disconnect the electrical connector.
4. Disconnect the control cable guide clips from inside the door.
5. The window has to be down. Remove the two mirror-to-door retaining nuts and mirror.
To install:

1. Thread the control cable or wire through the access hole, install the mirror and insulator.
2. Reconnect the control cable or wiring to the retaining clips.
3. Install the water deflector, sound insulator and trim panel.
4. Install the remote control to the instrument panel.

MIRROR FACE REPLACEMENT

CAUTION: *To minimize the chance of personal injury, wear gloves and safety glasses when removing the broken mirror glass.*
1. Place protective covers over the painted surface of the door.
2. Place masking tape over the mirror face.
3. Break the mirror face and remove the broken pieces.
To install:
1. Remove the paper backing to expose the adhesive.
2. Press the face firmly onto the center of the mirror frame.

Antenna

REMOVAL AND INSTALLATION

Fixed

1. Remove the steel antenna out of the base and masking tape the front edge of the right door.
2. Using a antenna bezel socket, loosen the bezel nut at the top of the fender.

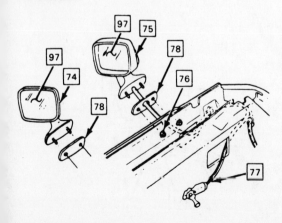

Outside mirror removal

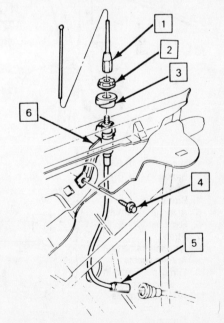

Fixed mast antenna

3. Remove the side mounting bolt and disconnect the antenna lead at the junction.

4. Raise the vehicle and support with jackstands.

5. Remove the lower fender-to-body bolt and rocker panel molding screws.

6. Remove the inner fender and block.

7. Remove the bezel and the antenna base assembly.

To install:

1. Install the antenna assembly and loosely tighten the bezel nut.

2. Install the inner fender screws, rocker panel molding screws and lower fender-to-body bolt.

3. Lower the vehicle.

4. Connect the antenna leads and tighten the bezel nut using the bezel socket J–28641 or equivalent. Install the side mounting bolt.

Power

1. Disconnect the negative (–) battery cable.

2. Protect the door with masking tape and remove the five outer-to-inner fender panel screws.

3. Remove the lower fender-to-body bolt and rocker panel molding screws.

4. Remove the three fender-to-inner fender screws along the rear half of the wheel opening.

5. Remove the antenna bezel nut using a bezel nut socket tool J–28641 and disconnect the electrical wiring.

6. Block the lower edge of the fender out, remove the antenna bracket screw and remove the antenna assembly.

To install:

1. Install the antenna, gasket and bezel nut. Do NOT tighten at this time.

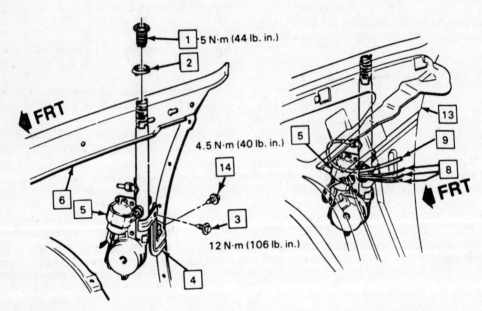

1. Nut
2. Bezel
3. Screw
4. Bracket
5. Antenna assembly
6. Right fender
7. Strap
8. Antenna harness
9. Antenna cable
10. Firmly push lead-in wires together
11. Antenna harness connector
12. Grommet
13. Inner fender panel
14. Screw

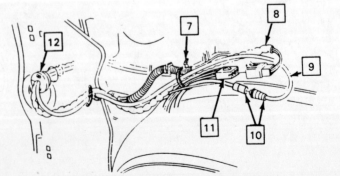

Power antenna and wiring

2. Install the mounting bolts. Do NOT tighten at this time.

3. Torque the bezel using the bezel socket and the lower mounting bolts.

4. Connect all antenna leads.

5. Install the fender bolts and screws.

6. Connect the negative battery cable and check operation.

INTERIOR

Door Panels

REMOVAL AND INSTALLATION

NOTE: *You can use a special tool GM Part No. BT-7323 or equivalent to disengage the clips fastening the inner panel to the door on front, rear, and lower edges. You'll also need a rubber mallet.*

1. Disconnect the negative (–) battery cable. Remove the inside handles by removing the two attaching screws. These are usually Phillips® head screws and accessible from underneath via recesses.

2. Unscrew and remove the inside door locking knob. If the vehicle is equipped with a strap type door pull handle, pull the escutcheons out of the centers of the strap mounts on either end to reveal the mounting screws. Since these screws pass through the door panel and into the metal shell of the door behind, remove them.

3. If the vehicle has a remote control mirror, remove the remote mirror escutcheon and then disengage the end of the mirror control cable from the escutcheon.

4. If the vehicle has a switch cover plate in the armrest, remove the screws securing the cover plate and disconnect the switch connec-

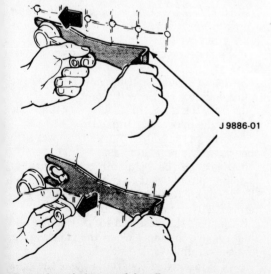

J 9886-01

Removing window crank handle

tors and, if the vehicle has one, the cigar lighter connectors from the wiring harness.

5. If the vehicle has remote control cover plates, remove the attaching screws and remove the cover plates. Then, remove the screws (which were under the cover plate) which secure the cover plate to the inner panel.

6. If the vehicle has integral armrests, remove the screws inserted through the pull cup and into the armrest hanger support.

7. If the vehicle has electric switches located in the door trim panel, disconnect the wiring harness at the switch. If the vehicle has courtesy or reading lamps in the panel, disconnect the wiring harness at the lamp.

8. Use a special tool or flat bladed prybar to carefully pry the panel out from the door, going around the periphery to release all the clips from the inner door.

9. To remove the panel, first push it slightly downward and then pull it outward to release it from the inner door at the beltline. Then, lift the panel upward to release it at the top of the door, where it hangs over.

To install:

1. First check that all trim retainers are securely installed and are undamaged. If any require replacement:

   a. Start the retainer with a ¼ in. (6mm) cutout into the attachment hole in the trim panel.

   b. Rotate the retainer until the flange that has the ¼ in. (6mm) cutout is inside the attachment hole.

2. Connect all electrical connectors.

3. Pull the inside door handle inward and position the inner panel near the door, passing the handle through the handle hole in the panel. Then, lift the panel slightly and install the retainers over the top of the inner door.

4. Position the inner panel so all retainers line up with the holes in the inner door. Start one into the retainer hole to ensure alignment and hold. Then, use a rubber mallet to tap all the retainers into the corresponding holes in the inner door.

5. Install all trim and handle screws, window crank and connect the negative battery cable.

Door Locks

REMOVAL AND INSTALLATION

1. Make sure the window is up all the way. Then, remove both the upper and lower portions of the trim panel as outlined in this chapter.

2. Going in through the largest access hole, disengage the rod connecting the remote control to the lock as follows:

   a. Use a flat-bladed prybar to slide the

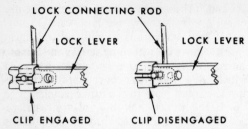

To disengage the spring clips attaching the lockrod to the door lock levers, slide them along the rod as shown until the ends of the clip are no longer engaged with the grooved end of the rod

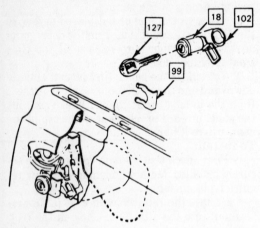

Door lock cylinder

spring clip out of engagement. The clip must be slid on the lock lever until the ends of the clip no longer engage with the grooved section of the end of the lock rod. You don't need to remove the clip from the lock lever. There is a slot in the rear side of the clip so it can shift on the lock lever even though the lockrod passes right through it.

b. Pull the lock rod out of the lock lever.

3. If the vehicle has electric locks, remove the solenoid.

4. Remove the three screws mounting the lock onto the door lock pillar section of the door and remove the lock. On some models, it may be necessary to remove the inside remote handle and then remove the lock and its connecting rod together. On four door models, it will be necessary to remove the lock, then separate the lockrod from the lock on a workbench, and install the rod onto the new lock.

5. Install in exact reverse order. Torque the lock mounting screws to 84–144 inch lbs. (10–15 Nm).

Door Glass and Window Regulator

The glass and related regulator parts (the glass guide) are removed as an assembly and the glass is then separated from the regulator

and rebonded on a bench. The regulator itself works through a metal tape, and is removed separately from the window and guide parts.

REGULATOR
REMOVAL AND INSTALLATION

NOTE: *To perform this operation, you will need a ¼ in. drill and a rivet tool such as GM J–29022 or equivalent and aluminum ¼ in. x ½ in. peel type rivets. You will also need a soft adhesive to reseal the water deflector, a center punch and cloth-backed tape.*

1. Disconnect the negative (–) battery cable. Remove the door inner panel as described above.

2. Remove the trim panel and peel the water deflector off the soft sealer.

3. With the glass up all the way, tape the glass to the upper door frame.

4. Remove the lower sash channel bolts.

5. Use the punch to drive out the centers of the regulator mounting rivets. Then, drill the remaining portions of the rivets out with the ¼ in. drill.

6. If the vehicle has electric windows, disconnect it from the wiring harness at the connector.

7. Pull the window regulator out through the access hole in the inner panel.

To install:

1. Position the new regulator in the door in reverse of the removal procedure.

2. Install the rivets with the rivet tool. Bolt and nut sets with thread locking compound may be used. Connect the negative battery cable.

WINDOW GLASS
REMOVAL AND INSTALLATION

CAUTION: *If the glass is being removed because of breakage or a crack, wear gloves and eye protection as you handle it to protect yourself from cuts.*

1. Remove the door inner panel as described above.

2. Remove the door trim panel and peel the water deflector off the soft sealer.

3. With the glass up all the way, tape the glass to the upper door frame.

4. Remove the bolts that hold the lower sash channel to the regulator sash.

5. Reattach the regulator handle without fastening it and use it to run the regulator all the way down. Remove the regulator sash by rotating it 90° and pulling it out.

6. Support the glass in a secure manner and then remove the tape. When the glass is free, lower it carefully all the way.

7. Now, disengage the front edge of the glass from the front glass run channel. Slide the glass

CHILTON'S
AUTO BODY
REPAIR TIPS

**Tools and Materials • Step-by-Step Illustrated Procedures
How To Repair Dents, Scratches and Rust Holes
Spray Painting and Refinishing Tips**

With a little practice, basic body repair procedures can be mastered by any do-it-yourself mechanic. The step-by-step repairs shown here can be applied to almost any type of auto body repair.

TOOLS & MATERIALS

You may already have basic tools, such as hammers and electric drills. Other tools unique to body repair — body hammers, grinding attachments, sanding blocks, dent puller, half-round plastic file and plastic spreaders — are relatively inexpensive and can be obtained wherever auto parts or auto body repair parts are sold. Portable air compressors and paint spray guns can be purchased or rented.

Auto Body Repair Kits

The best and most often used products are available to the do-it-yourselfer in kit form, from major manufacturers of auto body repair products. The same manufacturers also merchandise the individual products for use by pros.

Kits are available to make a wide variety of repairs, including holes, dents and scratches and fiberglass, and offer the advantage of buying the materials you'll need for the job. There is little waste or chance of materials going bad from not being used. Many kits may also contain basic body-working tools such as body files, sanding blocks and spreaders. Check the contents of the kit before buying your tools.

BODY REPAIR TIPS

Safety

Many of the products associated with auto body repair and refinishing contain toxic chemicals. Read all labels before opening containers and store them in a safe place and manner.

• Wear eye protection (safety goggles) when using power tools or when performing any operation that involves the removal of any type of material.

• Wear lung protection (disposable mask or respirator) when grinding, sanding or painting.

Sanding

1 Sand off paint before using a dent puller. When using a non-adhesive sanding disc, cover the back of the disc with an overlapping layer or two of masking tape and trim the edges. The disc will last considerably longer.

2 Use the circular motion of the sanding disc to grind *into* the edge of the repair. Grinding or sanding away from the jagged edge will only tear the sandpaper.

3 Use the palm of your hand flat on the panel to detect high and low spots. Do not use your fingertips. Slide your hand slowly back and forth.

WORKING WITH BODY FILLER

Mixing The Filler

Cleanliness and proper mixing and application are extremely important. Use a clean piece of plastic or glass or a disposable artist's palette to mix body filler.

1 Allow plenty of time and follow directions. No useful purpose will be served by adding more hardener to make it cure (set-up) faster. Less hardener means more curing time, but the mixture dries harder; more hardener means less curing time but a softer mixture.

2 Both the hardener and the filler should be thoroughly kneaded or stirred before mixing. Hardener should be a solid paste and dispense like thin toothpaste. Body filler should be smooth, and free of lumps or thick spots.

Getting the proper amount of hardener in the filler is the trickiest part of preparing the filler. Use the same amount of hardener in cold or warm weather. For contour filler (thick coats), a bead of hardener twice the diameter of the filler is about right. There's about a 15% margin on either side, but, if in doubt use less hardener.

3 Mix the body filler and hardener by wiping across the mixing surface, picking the mixture up and wiping it again. Colder weather requires longer mixing times. Do not mix in a circular motion; this will trap air bubbles which will become holes in the cured filler.

Applying The Filler

1 For best results, filler should not be applied over 1/4" thick.

Apply the filler in several coats. Build it up to above the level of the repair surface so that it can be sanded or grated down.

The first coat of filler must be pressed on with a firm wiping motion.

Apply the filler in one direction only. Working the filler back and forth will either pull it off the metal or trap air bubbles.

REPAIRING DENTS

Before you start, take a few minutes to study the damaged area. Try to visualize the shape of the panel before it was damaged. If the damage is on the left fender, look at the right fender and use it as a guide. If there is access to the panel from behind, you can reshape it with a body hammer. If not, you'll have to use a dent puller. Go slowly and work the metal a little at a time. Get the panel as straight as possible before applying filler.

1 This dent is typical of one that can be pulled out or hammered out from behind. Remove the headlight cover, headlight assembly and turn signal housing.

2 Drill a series of holes ½ the size of the end of the dent puller along the stress line. Make some trial pulls and assess the results. If necessary, drill more holes and try again. Do not hurry.

3 If possible, use a body hammer and block to shape the metal back to its original contours. Get the metal back as close to its original shape as possible. Don't depend on body filler to fill dents.

4 Using an 80-grit grinding disc on an electric drill, grind the paint from the surrounding area down to bare metal. Use a new grinding pad to prevent heat buildup that will warp metal.

5 The area should look like this when you're finished grinding. Knock the drill holes in and tape over small openings to keep plastic filler out.

6 Mix the body filler (see Body Repair Tips). Spread the body filler evenly over the entire area (see Body Repair Tips). Be sure to cover the area completely.

7 Let the body filler dry until the surface can just be scratched with your fingernail. Knock the high spots from the body filler with a body file ("Cheesegrater"). Check frequently with the palm of your hand for high and low spots.

8 Check to be sure that trim pieces that will be installed later will fit exactly. Sand the area with 40-grit paper.

9 If you wind up with low spots, you may have to apply another layer of filler.

10 Knock the high spots off with 40-grit paper. When you are satisfied with the contours of the repair, apply a thin coat of filler to cover pin holes and scratches.

11 Block sand the area with 40-grit paper to a smooth finish. Pay particular attention to body lines and ridges that must be well-defined.

12 Sand the area with 400 paper and then finish with a scuff pad. The finished repair is ready for priming and painting (see Painting Tips).

Materials and photos courtesy of Ritt Jones Auto Body, Prospect Park, PA.

REPAIRING RUST HOLES

There are many ways to repair rust holes. The fiberglass cloth kit shown here is one of the most cost efficient for the owner because it provides a strong repair that resists cracking and moisture and is relatively easy to use. It can be used on large and small holes (with or without backing) and can be applied over contoured areas. Remember, however, that short of replacing an entire panel, no repair is a guarantee that the rust will not return.

1 Remove any trim that will be in the way. Clean away all loose debris. Cut away all the rusted metal. But be sure to leave enough metal to retain the contour or body shape.

2 Grind away all traces of rust with a 24-grit grinding disc. Be sure to grind back 3-4 inches from the edge of the hole down to bare metal and be sure all traces of paint, primer and rust are removed.

3 Block sand the area with 80 or 100 grit sandpaper to get a clear, shiny surface and feathered paint edge. Tap the edges of the hole inward with a ball peen hammer.

4 If you are going to use release film, cut a piece about 2-3″ larger than the area you have sanded. Place the film over the repair and mark the sanded area on the film. Avoid any unnecessary wrinkling of the film.

5 Cut 2 pieces of fiberglass matte to match the shape of the repair. One piece should be about 1″ smaller than the sanded area and the second piece should be 1″ smaller than the first. Mix enough filler and hardener to saturate the fiberglass material (see Body Repair Tips).

6 Lay the release sheet on a flat surface and spread an even layer of filler, large enough to cover the repair. Lay the smaller piece of fiberglass cloth in the center of the sheet and spread another layer of filler over the fiberglass cloth. Repeat the operation for the larger piece of cloth.

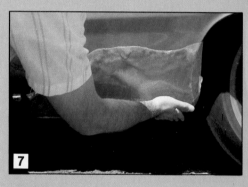

7 Place the repair material over the repair area, with the release film facing outward. Use a spreader and work from the center outward to smooth the material, following the body contours. Be sure to remove all air bubbles.

8 Wait until the repair has dried tack-free and peel off the release sheet. The ideal working temperature is 60°-90° F. Cooler or warmer temperatures or high humidity may require additional curing time. Wait longer, if in doubt.

9 Sand and feather-edge the entire area. The initial sanding can be done with a sanding disc on an electric drill if care is used. Finish the sanding with a block sander. Low spots can be filled with body filler; this may require several applications.

10 When the filler can just be scratched with a fingernail, knock the high spots down with a body file and smooth the entire area with 80-grit. Feather the filled areas into the surrounding areas.

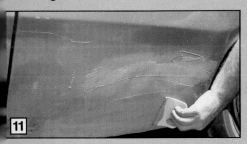

11 When the area is sanded smooth, mix some topcoat and hardener and apply it directly with a spreader. This will give a smooth finish and prevent the glass matte from showing through the paint.

12 Block sand the topcoat smooth with finishing sandpaper (200 grit), and 400 grit. The repair is ready for masking, priming and painting (see Painting Tips).

Materials and photos courtesy Marson Corporation, Chelsea, Massachusetts

PAINTING TIPS

Preparation

1 SANDING — Use a 400 or 600 grit wet or dry sandpaper. Wet-sand the area with a 1/4 sheet of sandpaper soaked in clean water. Keep the paper wet while sanding. Sand the area until the repaired area tapers into the original finish.

2 CLEANING — Wash the area to be painted thoroughly with water and a clean rag. Rinse it thoroughly and wipe the surface dry until you're sure it's completely free of dirt, dust, fingerprints, wax, detergent or other foreign matter.

3 MASKING — Protect any areas you don't want to overspray by covering them with masking tape and newspaper. Be careful not get fingerprints on the area to be painted.

4 PRIMING — All exposed metal should be primed before painting. Primer protects the metal and provides an excellent surface for paint adhesion. When the primer is dry, wet-sand the area again with 600 grit wet-sandpaper. Clean the area again after sanding.

Painting Techniques

P aint applied from either a spray gun or a spray can (for small areas) will provide good results. Experiment on an old piece of metal to get the right combination before you begin painting.

SPRAYING VISCOSITY (SPRAY GUN ONLY) — Paint should be thinned to spraying viscosity according to the directions on the can. Use only the recommended thinner or reducer and the same amount of reduction regardless of temperature.

AIR PRESSURE (SPRAY GUN ONLY) — This is extremely important. Be sure you are using the proper recommended pressure.

TEMPERATURE — The surface to be painted should be approximately the same temperature as the surrounding air. Applying warm paint to a cold surface, or vice versa, will completely upset the paint characteristics.

THICKNESS — Spray with smooth strokes. In general, the thicker the coat of paint, the longer the drying time. Apply several thin coats about 30 seconds apart. The paint should remain wet long enough to flow out and no longer; heavier coats will only produce sags or wrinkles. Spray a light (fog) coat, followed by heavier color coats.

DISTANCE — The ideal spraying distance is 8"-12" from the gun or can to the surface. Shorter distances will produce ripples, while greater distances will result in orange peel, dry film and poor color match and loss of material due to overspray.

OVERLAPPING — The gun or can should be kept at right angles to the surface at all times. Work to a wet edge at an even speed, using a 50% overlap and direct the center of the spray at the lower or nearest edge of the previous stroke.

RUBBING OUT (BLENDING) FRESH PAINT — Let the paint dry thoroughly. Runs or imperfections can be sanded out, primed and repainted.

Don't be in too big a hurry to remove the masking. This only produces paint ridges. When the finish has dried for at least a week, apply a small amount of fine grade rubbing compound with a clean, wet cloth. Use lots of water and blend the new paint with the surrounding area.

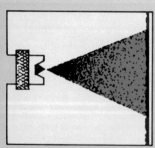

WRONG

Thin coat. Stroke too fast, not enough overlap, gun too far away.

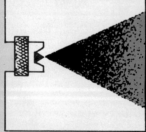

CORRECT

Medium coat. Proper distance, good stroke, proper overlap.

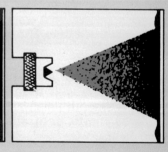

WRONG

Heavy coat. Stroke too slow, too much overlap, gun too close.

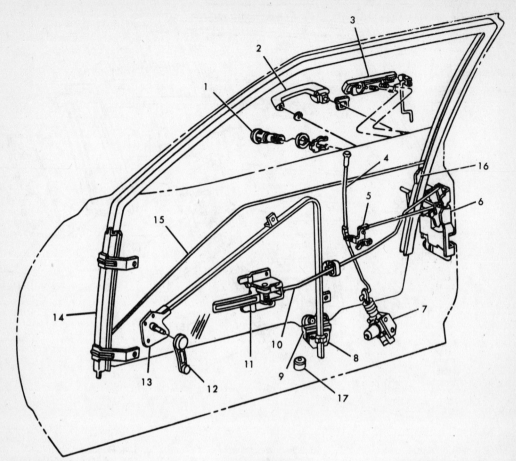

1. Lock cylinder
2. Outside door handle (push button type)
3. Outside door handle (lift bar type)
4. Inside locking rod
5. Locking rod bell crank
6. Door lock
7. Lock actuator
8. Lower sash channel
9. Regulator sash
10. Inside handle connecting rod
11. Inside remote handle
12. Window regulator handle
13. Window regulator
14. Front glass run channel
15. Door glass
16. Plastic guide clip
17. Rubber down stop

Front door glass operating hardware—typical

forward, tilt it slightly, and remove the guide from the retainer in the run channel located in the rear leg of the door frame.

8. Now, tilt the glass forward and remove it from the door.

To install:

1. On a workbench, unbolt the lower sash channel from the glass and bolt it onto the new glass.

2. Use the following method to install the guide retainer:

   a. Install the glass and raise it about half way.

   b. Supporting the glass with one hand on the lower edge, rotate it rearward to snap the guide into the retainer.

Electric Window Motor
REMOVAL AND INSTALLATION

NOTE: *To perform this operation, you will need a drill and $3/16$ in. drill bit, $3/16$ in. rivets.*

1. Disconnect the negative ($-$) battery cable. Remove the door trim panel as described above.

2. Remove the interior pad and peel the water deflector off the soft sealer.

3. With the glass up all the way, tape the glass to the upper door frame.

4. Remove the regulator and glass as described above.

5. Disconnect the electrical connector. Drill out the rivets that attach the motor to the door and then remove it.

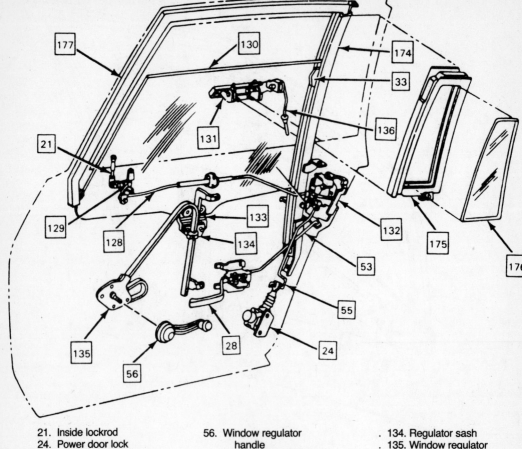

21. Inside lockrod	56. Window regulator	. 134. Regulator sash
24. Power door lock	handle	. 135. Window regulator
actuator	. 128. Lock cylinder rod	. 136. Outside lockrod
28. Inside remote handle	. 129. Bellcrank	. 174. Vent division
33. Window glass upper	. 130. Door glass	channel
guide	. 131. Outside handle	. 175. Vent glass channel
53. Inside handle rod	. 132. Door lock	. 176. Vent window glass
55. Lock actuator rod	. 133. Window sash	. 177. Glass run channel

Rear door glass operating hardware

To install:

1. Install the motor, and then mount it with the new rivets. Reconnect the electrical connector.

2. Install the window and regulator as described above.

Inside Rear View Mirror

REPLACEMENT

The rearview mirror is attached to a support which is secured to the windshield glass. A service replacement windshield glass has the support bonded to the glass assembly. To install a detached mirror support or install a new part, use the following procedures to complete the service.

1. Locate the support position at the center of the glass 22 in. (557mm) from the bottom of the glass to the bottom of the support.

2. Circle the location on the outside of the glass with a wax pencil or crayon. Draw a large circle around the support circle.

3. Clean the area within the circle with household cleaner and dry with a clean towel. Repeat the procedures using rubbing alcohol.

4. Sand the bonding surface of the support with fine grit (320-360) emery cloth or sandpaper. If the original support is being used, remove the old adhesive with rubbing alcohol and a clean towel.

5. Apply the adhesive as outlined in the kit instructions.

6. Position the support to the marked location with the rounded end UP.

7. Press the support to the glass for 30–60 seconds. Excessive adhesive can be removed after five minutes with rubbing alcohol.

CAUTION: *Do NOT apply excessive pressure to the windshield glass. The glass may break, causing personal injury.*

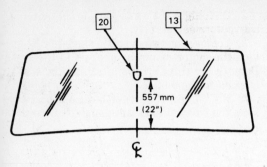

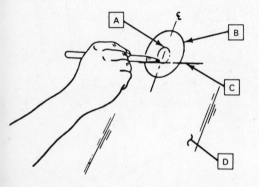

Inside rearview mirror installation

Seats

REMOVAL AND INSTALLATION

Front

1. Disconnect the negative (−) battery cable.
2. Operate the front seat to the full forward position.
3. Remove the screws, rear support covers and adjuster hold down nuts.
4. Remove the seat belt cover.
5. Operate the seat to the full rearward position.
6. Remove the screws, front support covers and adjuster hold down nuts.
7. Remove the seat belt anchor bolt using a Torx® socket J–29843–9.
8. Disconnect and electrical connections to the seat.
9. Before removing the seat, place paint protection over the trim to prevent damage.
10. With an assistant, remove the seat assembly with adjusters attached.
To install:
1. With an assistant, install the seat assembly onto the mounting studs.
2. Connect all electrical connections and seat belts. Torque the seat belt anchor to 31 ft. lbs. (42 Nm).
3. Install and torque the front nuts to 22 ft. lbs. (30 Nm). Install the support covers.

4. Move the seat to the full forward position.
5. Install the seat belt cover, rear nuts and torque to 22 ft. lbs. (30 Nm).
6. Install the support covers, connect the negative battery cable and check operation.

Rear

SEAT BOTTOM

1. The seatbottom is held in place by dome stops located on the floor pan. The dome stops hook over the frame wires on the seatbottom.
2. To disengage, push the lower front edge of the seatbottom rearward, lift up and pull forward to disengage the dome stops.
To install: Slide the bottom rearward, press down and pull forward. The frame wire in the bottom should slide into the dome stops.

SEATBACK – SEDAN

1. Remove the two retaining bolts in the lower corners.
2. Lift the rear seatback off the hooks on the seat panel.
3. Hang the seatback over the hooks on the panel and install the two bolts.

SEATBACK – WAGON

1. Lower the second seat and remove the bolts from each side of the seatback.
2. Remove the screws from the bottom edge of the seat.
3. Raise the seat enough to pull the lower edge forward.
4. Lift upward to release the upper edge of the seat from the hooks on the seat panel and remove the seatback.
To install:
1. Hang the seatback over the hooks on the seat panel.
2. Install the screws and bolts.
3. Raise the seat and check operation.

Power Seat Motor

REMOVAL AND INSTALLATION

Two-Way Power Seats

1. If the seat will move, shift it to a position near the middle of it travel.
2. Remove the nuts that attach the seat adjuster to the floor and then tilt the seat forward for access.
3. On the full width seat, disconnect both power cables at the motor.
4. Disconnect the wiring harness at the motor.
5. Remove the screws that secure the motor support to the seat frame. Remove the motor with the support attached. Then, remove the screws that attach the motor to the support bracket and remove the motor from the bracket.

6. Installation is the reverse of removal. Make sure you test the motor for proper operation to the extremes of travel in both directions.

Six-Way Power Seat Permanent Magnet Motor

1. Unbolt the seat from the floor of the vehicle. Place it upside down in a location where the upholstery is protected from dirt.

2. Disconnect the wires going to the motor at the motor control relay.

3. Remove the two mounting screws that attach the motor mounting support to the seat. Remove the three screws attaching the transmission to the motor.

4. Now, move the motor outboard or away from the transmission far enough to disengage

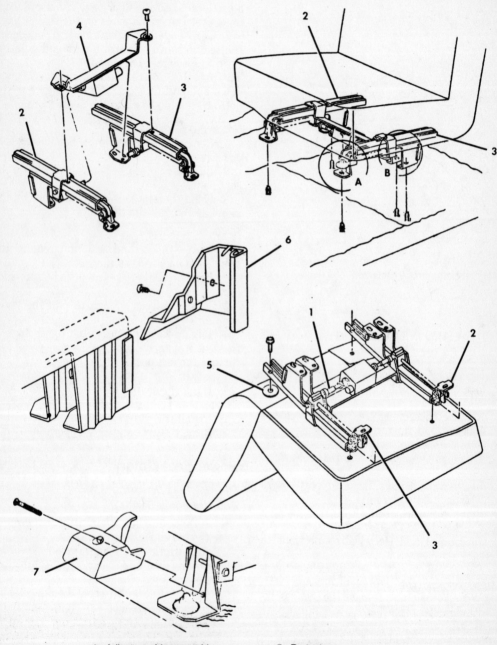

1. Adjuster cable assembly
2. Inner seat adjuster
3. Outer seat adjuster
4. Motor and support assembly
5. Protector
6. Outer rear track cover
7. Adjuster front track cover

Two-way seat adjuster and covers—typical

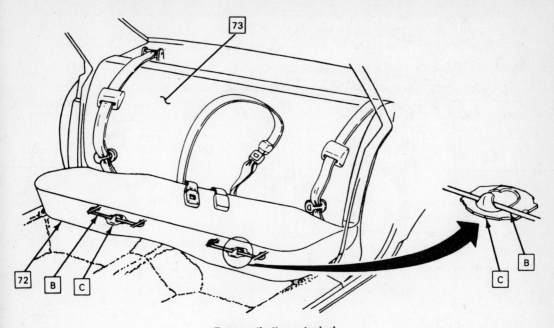

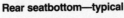

Rear seatbottom—typical

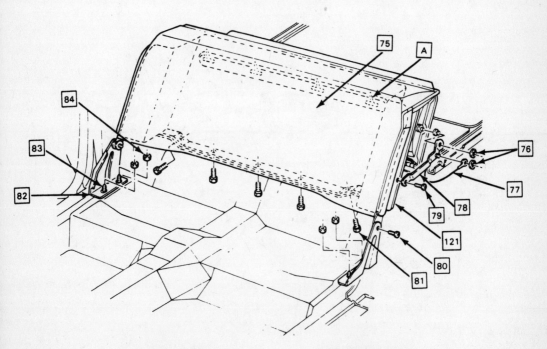

A. Hook
75. Second seatback
76. Retaining ring
77. Cable
78. Filler panel link
79. Bolt
80. Support screw
81. Screw
82. Pivot support
83. Stud
84. Nut
. 121. Seatback panel

Rear seatback—station wagon

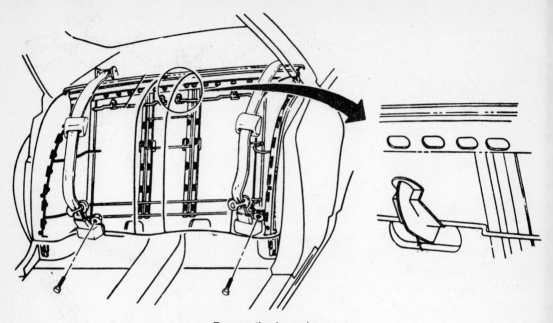

Rear seatback—sedan

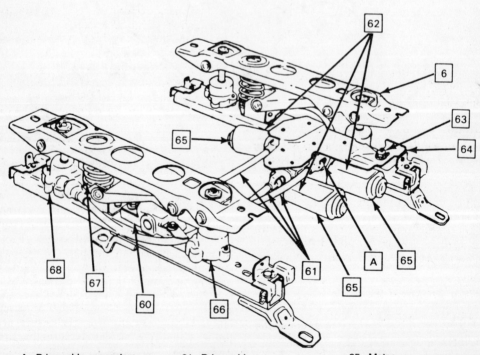

A. Drive cable connectors	61. Drive cable	65. Motor
6. Adjuster	62. Electrical connector	66. Front vertical gearnut
60. Adjuster horizontal actuator	63. Nut	67. Vertical assist spring
	64. Motor support bracket	68. Rear vertical gearnut

Power seat actuator assembly

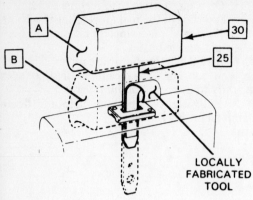

LOCALLY
FABRICATED
TOOL

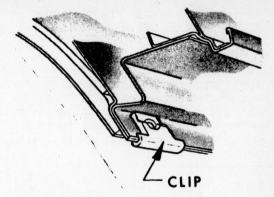

One type of headliner attaching clip

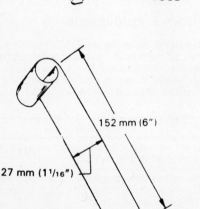

152 mm (6")

27 mm (1 1/16")

10 mm (3/8")

16 mm (5/8")

Headrest removal

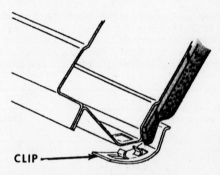

A second type of headliner attaching clip

it from the rubber coupling that connects it to the transmission, and remove it.

5. Installation is the reverse of removal.

Headliner

Vehicles with deluxe trim use a formed type of headliner that, as a replacement part, comes in two pieces. The headliner cover must be glued to the foundation. This is an extremely difficult operation requiring the use of a number of special tools. It would best be left to a competent automotive upholstery shop. Only the procedure for the standard headliner, which is relatively straightforward, are included here.

REMOVAL AND INSTALLATION

NOTE: *On wagons, you will need a special tool J-2772 or equivalent to remove the headliner.*

1. Remove the following items from the roof of the vehicle:

  a. Courtesy lamps.
  b. Sunshade supports.
  c. Coat hooks.
  d. Upper quarter trim finishing panels.
  e. Side roof rail moldings.
  f. Windshield and back window garnish moldings.
  g. Shoulder strap retainers.
  h. Windshield side garnish molding.
  i. Roof mounted assist straps.
  j. Sun roof trim finishing lace (if the vehicle has a sunroof).
  k. Twin lift-off panel roof garnish moldings (if so-equipped).

2. Disengage tabs or clips on each side of the headlining from the attaching slots. On wagons, use the tool J-2772 at one end of the molding and pry the molding loose from the retainer.

3. Then, on sedans move the entire assembly far enough rearward to provide clearance for its front to be pulled out through the front door opening, and remove it. On wagons, remove the headlining through the body rear opening.

If the replacement lining does not have an insulator cemented to the upper surface, carefully remove the insulator from the original headlining. Then, spot cement the insulator to the replacement headlining to hold it in position during installation.

CAUTION: *Load the assembly into the vehicle very carefully and excessive flexing can cause permanent deformation.*

4. On all sedans, install the rear portion of the headlining through the right front door opening, holding it diagonally. On wagons, put it in through the tailgate opening.

5. Engage the headlining at the tabs to retain it temporarily to the roof. Install the side roof rail attaching clips.

6. Align the headlining so that the cutouts for the sunshades and dome lamp line up. Install these two types of accessories, but do not fully tighten the mounting screws.

7. On wagons, align the finishing molding at the centerline of the roof and engage it with its retainer. Install the complete molding on both the right and left sides.

8. Install all other hardware removed in Step 1. You can shift the headliner in that area slightly to fit each item into place.

9. Fully tighten the sunshade and dome lamp mounting screws.

How to Remove Stains from Fabric Interior

For rest results, spots and stains should be removed as soon as possible. Never use gasoline, lacquer thinner, acetone, nail polish remover or bleach. Use a 3′ x 3″ piece of cheesecloth. Squeeze most of the liquid from the fabric and wipe the stained fabric from the outside of the stain toward the center with a lifting motion. Turn the cheesecloth as soon as one side becomes soiled. When using water to remove a stain, be sure to wash the entire section after the spot has been removed to avoid water stains. Encrusted spots can be broken up with a dull knife and vacuumed before removing the stain.

Type of Stain	How to Remove It
Surface spots	Brush the spots out with a small hand brush or use a commercial preparation such as K2R to lift the stain.
Mildew	Clean around the mildew with warm suds. Rinse in cold water and soak the mildew area in a solution of 1 part table salt and 2 parts water. Wash with upholstery cleaner.
Water stains	Water stains in fabric materials can be removed with a solution made from 1 cup of table salt dissolved in 1 quart of water. Vigorously scrub the solution into the stain and rinse with clear water. Water stains in nylon or other synthetic fabrics should be removed with a commercial type spot remover.
Chewing gum, tar, crayons, shoe polish (greasy stains)	Do not use a cleaner that will soften gum or tar. Harden the deposit with an ice cube and scrape away as much as possible with a dull knife. Moisten the remainder with cleaning fluid and scrub clean.
Ice cream, candy	Most candy has a sugar base and can be removed with a cloth wrung out in warm water. Oily candy, after cleaning with warm water, should be cleaned with upholstery cleaner. Rinse with warm water and clean the remainder with cleaning fluid.
Wine, alcohol, egg, milk, soft drink (non-greasy stains)	Do not use soap. Scrub the stain with a cloth wrung out in warm water. Remove the remainder with cleaning fluid.
Grease, oil, lipstick, butter and related stains	Use a spot remover to avoid leaving a ring. Work from the outisde of the stain to the center and dry with a clean cloth when the spot is gone.
Headliners (cloth)	Mix a solution of warm water and foam upholstery cleaner to give thick suds. Use only foam—liquid may streak or spot. Clean the entire headliner in one operation using a circular motion with a natural sponge.
Headliner (vinyl)	Use a vinyl cleaner with a sponge and wipe clean with a dry cloth.
Seats and door panels	Mix 1 pint upholstery cleaner in 1 gallon of water. Do not soak the fabric around the buttons.
Leather or vinyl fabric	Use a multi-purpose cleaner full strength and a stiff brush. Let stand 2 minutes and scrub thoroughly. Wipe with a clean, soft rag.
Nylon or synthetic fabrics	For normal stains, use the same procedures you would for washing cloth upholstery. If the fabric is extremely dirty, use a multi-purpose cleaner full strength with a stiff scrub brush. Scrub thoroughly in all directions and wipe with a cotton towel or soft rag.

Mechanic's Data

General Conversion Table

Multiply By	To Convert	To	
LENGTH			
2.54	Inches	Centimeters	.3937
25.4	Inches	Millimeters	.03937
30.48	Feet	Centimeters	.0328
.304	Feet	Meters	3.28
.914	Yards	Meters	1.094
1.609	Miles	Kilometers	621
VOLUME			
.473	Pints	Liters	2.11
.946	Quarts	Liters	1.06
3.785	Gallons	Liters	.264
.016	Cubic inches	Liters	61.02
16.39	Cubic inches	Cubic cms.	.061
28.3	Cubic feet	Liters	.0353
MASS (Weight)			
28.35	Ounces	Grams	.035
.4536	Pounds	Kilograms	2.20
—	To obtain	From	Multiply by

Multiply By	To Convert	To	
AREA			
.645	Square inches	Square cms.	.155
.836	Square yds.	Square meters	1.196
FORCE			
4.448	Pounds	Newtons	.225
.138	Ft./lbs.	Kilogram/meters	7.23
1.36	Ft./lbs.	Newton-meters	.737
.112	In./lbs.	Newton-meters	8.844
PRESSURE			
.068	Psi	Atmospheres	14.7
6.89	Psi	Kilopascals	.145
OTHER			
1.104	Horsepower (DIN)	Horsepower (SAE)	.9861
.746	Horsepower (SAE)	Kilowatts (KW)	1.34
1.60	Mph	Km/h	.625
.425	Mpg	Km/1	2.35
—	To obtain	From	Multiply by

Tap Drill Sizes

National Coarse or U.S.S.

Screw & Tap Size	Threads Per Inch	Use Drill Number
No. 5	40	.39
No. 6	32	.36
No. 8	32	.29
No. 10	24	.25
No. 12	24	.17
$1/4$	20	8
$5/16$	18	F
$3/8$	16	$5/16$
$7/16$	14	U
$1/2$	13	$27/64$
$9/16$	12	$31/64$
$5/8$	11	$17/32$
$3/4$	10	$21/32$
$7/8$	9	$49/64$

National Coarse or U.S.S.

Screw & Tap Size	Threads Per Inch	Use Drill Number
1	8	$7/8$
$1\frac{1}{8}$	7	$63/64$
$1\frac{1}{4}$	7	$1^7/64$
$1\frac{1}{2}$	6	$1^{11}/32$

National Fine or S.A.E.

Screw & Tap Size	Threads Per Inch	Use Drill Number
No. 5	44	.37
No. 6	40	.33
No. 8	36	.29
No. 10	32	.21

National Fine or S.A.E.

Screw & Tap Size	Threads Per Inch	Use Drill Number
No. 12	28	15
$1/4$	28	3
$6/16$	24	1
$3/8$	24	Q
$7/16$	20	W
$1/2$	20	$29/64$
$9/16$	18	$33/64$
$5/8$	18	$37/64$
$3/4$	16	$11/16$
$7/8$	14	$13/16$
$1\frac{1}{8}$	12	$1^3/64$
$1\frac{1}{4}$	12	$1^{11}/64$
$1\frac{1}{2}$	12	$1^{27}/64$

Drill Sizes In Decimal Equivalents

Inch	Decimal	Wire	mm	Inch	Decimal	Wire	mm	Inch	Decimal	Wire & Letter	mm	Inch	Decimal	Letter	mm	Inch	Decimal	mm
1/64	.0156		.39		.0730	49			.1614		4.1		.2717		6.9		.4331	11.0
	.0157		.4		.0748		1.9		.1654		4.2		.2720	I		7/16	.4375	11.11
	.0160	78			.0760	48			.1660	19			.2756		7.0		.4528	11.5
	.0165		.42		.0768		1.95		.1673		4.25		.2770	J		29/64	.4531	11.51
	.0173		.44	5/64	.0781		1.98		.1693		4.3		.2795		7.1	15/32	.4688	11.90
	.0177		.45		.0785	47			.1695	18			.2810	K			.4724	12.0
	.0180	77			.0787		2.0	11/64	.1719		4.36	9/32	.2812		7.14	31/64	.4844	12.30
	.0181		.46		.0807		2.05		.1730	17			.2835		7.2		.4921	12.5
	.0189		.48		.0810	46			.1732		4.4		.2854		7.25	1/2	.5000	12.70
	.0197		.5		.0820	45			.1770	16			.2874		7.3		.5118	13.0
	.0200	76			.0827		2.1		.1772		4.5		.2900	L		33/64	.5156	13.09
	.0210	75			.0846		2.15		.1800	15			.2913		7.4	17/32	.5312	13.49
	.0217		.55		.0860	44			.1811		4.6		.2950	M			.5315	13.5
	.0225	74			.0866		2.2		.1820	14			.2953		7.5	35/64	.5469	13.89
	.0236		.6		.0886		2.25		.1850	13		19/64	.2969		7.54		.5512	14.0
	.0240	73			.0890	43			.1850		4.7		.2992		7.6	9/16	.5625	14.28
	.0250	72			.0906		2.3		.1870		4.75		.3020	N			.5709	14.5
	.0256		.65		.0925		2.35	3/16	.1875		4.76		.3031		7.7	37/64	.5781	14.68
	.0260	71			.0935	42			.1890		4.8		.3051		7.75		.5906	15.0
	.0276		.7	3/32	.0938		2.38		.1890	12			.3071		7.8	19/32	.5938	15.08
	.0280	70			.0945		2.4		.1910	11			.3110		7.9	39/64	.6094	15.47
	.0292	69			.0960	41			.1929		4.9	5/16	.3125		7.93		.6102	15.5
	.0295		.75		.0965		2.45		.1935	10			.3150		8.0	5/8	.6250	15.87
	.0310	68			.0980	40			.1960	9			.3160	O			.6299	16.0
1/32	.0312		.79		.0981		2.5		.1969		5.0		.3189		8.1	41/64	.6406	16.27
	.0315		.8		.0995	39			.1990	8			.3228		8.2		.6496	16.5
	.0320	67			.1015	38			.2008		5.1		.3230	P		21/32	.6562	16.66
	.0330	66			.1024		2.6		.2010	7			.3248		8.25		.6693	17.0
	.0335		.85		.1040	37		13/64	.2031		5.16		.3268		8.3	43/64	.6719	17.06
	.0350	65			.1063		2.7		.2040	6		21/64	.3281		8.33	11/16	.6875	17.46
	.0354		.9		.1065	36			.2047		5.2		.3307		8.4		.6890	17.5
	.0360	64			.1083		2.75		.2055	5			.3320	Q		45/64	.7031	17.85
	.0370	63		7/64	.1094		2.77		.2067		5.25		.3346		8.5		.7087	18.0
	.0374		.95		.1100	35			.2087		5.3		.3386		8.6	23/32	.7188	18.25
	.0380	62			.1102		2.8		.2090	4			.3390	R			.7283	18.5
	.0390	61			.1110	34			.2126		5.4		.3425		8.7	47/64	.7344	18.65
	.0394		1.0		.1130	33			.2130	3		11/32	.3438		8.73		.7480	19.0
	.0400	60			.1142		2.9		.2165		5.5		.3445		8.75	3/4	.7500	19.05
	.0410	59			.1160	32		7/32	2188		5.55		.3465		8.8	49/64	.7656	19.44
	.0413		1.05		.1181		3.0		.2205		5.6		.3480	S			.7677	19.5
	.0420	58			.1200	31			.2210	2			.3504		8.9	25/32	.7812	19.84
	.0430	57			.1220		3.1		.2244		5.7		.3543		9.0		.7874	20.0
	.0433		1.1	1/8	.1250		3.17		.2264		5.75		.3580	T		51/64	.7969	20.24
	.0453		1.15		.1260		3.2		.2280	1			.3583		9.1		.8071	20.5
	.0465	56			.1280		3.25		.2283		5.8	23/64	.3594		9.12	13/16	.8125	20.63
3/64	.0469		1.19		.1285	30			.2323		5.9		.3622		9.2		.8268	21.0
	.0472		1.2		.1299		3.3		.2340	A			.3642		9.25	53/64	.8281	21.03
	.0492		1.25		.1339		3.4	15/64	.2344		5.95		.3661		9.3	27/32	.8438	21.43
	.0512		1.3		.1360	29			.2362		6.0		.3680	U			.8465	21.5
	.0520	55			.1378		3.5		.2380	B			.3701		9.4	55/64	.8594	21.82
	.0531		1.35		.1405	28			.2402		6.1		.3740		9.5		.8661	22.0
	.0550	54		9/64	.1406		3.57		.2420	C		3/8	.3750		9.52	7/8	.8750	22.22
	.0551		1.4		.1417		3.6		.2441		6.2		.3770	V			.8858	22.5
	.0571		1.45		.1440	27			.2460	D			.3780		9.6	57/64	.8906	22.62
	.0591		1.5		.1457		3.7		.2461		6.25		.3819		9.7		.9055	23.0
	.0595	53			.1470	26			.2480		6.3		.3839		9.75	29/32	.9062	23.01
	.0610		1.55		.1476		3.75	1/4	.2500	E	6.35		.3858		9.8	59/64	.9219	23.41
1/16	.0625		1.59		.1495	25			.2520		6.		.3860	W			.9252	23.5
	.0630		1.6		.1496		3.8		.2559		6.5		.3898		9.9	15/16	.9375	23.81
	.0635	52			.1520	24			.2570	F		25/64	.3906		9.92		.9449	24.0
	.0650		1.65		.1535		3.9		.2598		6.6		.3937		10.0	61/64	.9531	24.2
	.0669		1.7		.1540	23			.2610	G			.3970	X			.9646	24.5
	.0670	51		5/32	.1562		3.96		.2638		6.7		.4040	Y		31/32	.9688	24.6
	.0689		1.75		.1570	22		17/64	.2656		6.74	13/32	.4062		10.31		.9843	25.0
	.0700	50			.1575		4.0		.2657		6.75		.4130	Z		63/64	.9844	25.0
	.0709		1.8		.1590	21			.2660	H			.4134		10.5	1	1.0000	25.4
	.0728		1.85		.1610	20			.2677		6.8	27/64	.4219		10.71			

AIR/FUEL RATIO: The ratio of air to gasoline by weight in the fuel mixture drawn into the engine.

AIR INJECTION: One method of reducing harmful exhaust emissions by injecting air into each of the exhaust ports of an engine. The fresh air entering the hot exhaust manifold causes any remaining fuel to be burned before it can exit the tailpipe.

ALTERNATOR: A device used for converting mechanical energy into electrical energy.

AMMETER: An instrument, calibrated in amperes, used to measure the flow of an electrical current in a circuit. Ammeters are always connected in series with the circuit being tested.

AMPERE: The rate of flow of electrical current present when one volt of electrical pressure is applied against one ohm of electrical resistance.

ANALOG COMPUTER: Any microprocessor that uses similar (analogous) electrical signals to make its calculations.

ARMATURE: A laminated, soft iron core wrapped by a wire that converts electrical energy to mechanical energy as in a motor or relay. When rotated in a magnetic field, it changes mechanical energy into electrical energy as in a generator.

ATMOSPHERIC PRESSURE: The pressure on the Earth's surface caused by the weight of the air in the atmosphere. At sea level, this pressure is 14.7 psi at 32°F (101 kPa at 0°C).

ATOMIZATION: The breaking down of a liquid into a fine mist that can be suspended in air.

AXIAL PLAY: Movement parallel to a shaft or bearing bore.

BACKFIRE: The sudden combustion of gases in the intake or exhaust system that results in a loud explosion.

BACKLASH: The clearance or play between two parts, such as meshed gears.

BACKPRESSURE: Restrictions in the exhaust system that slow the exit of exhaust gases from the combustion chamber.

BAKELITE: A heat resistant, plastic insulator material commonly used in printed circuit boards and transistorized components.

BALL BEARING: A bearing made up of hardened inner and outer races between which hardened steel ball roll.

BALLAST RESISTOR: A resistor in the primary ignition circuit that lowers voltage after the engine is started to reduce wear on ignition components.

BEARING: A friction reducing, supportive device usually located between a stationary part and a moving part.

BIMETAL TEMPERATURE SENSOR: Any sensor or switch made of two dissimilar types of metal that bend when heated or cooled due to the different expansion rates of the alloys. These types of sensors usually function as an on/off switch.

BLOWBY: Combustion gases, composed of water vapor and unburned fuel, that leak past the piston rings into the crankcase during normal engine operation. These gases are removed by the PCV system to prevent the build-up of harmful acids in the crankcase.

BRAKE PAD: A brake shoe and lining assembly used with disc brakes.

BRAKE SHOE: The backing for the brake lining. The term is, however, usually applied to the assembly of the brake backing and lining.

BUSHING: A liner, usually removable, for a bearing; an anti-friction liner used in place of a bearing.

BYPASS: System used to bypass ballast resistor during engine cranking to increase voltage supplied to the coil.

CALIPER: A hydraulically activated device in a disc brake system, which is mounted straddling the brake rotor (disc). The caliper contains at least one piston and two brake pads. Hydraulic pressure on the piston(s) forces the pads against the rotor.

CAMSHAFT: A shaft in the engine on which are the lobes (cams) which operate the valves. The camshaft is driven by the crankshaft, via a belt, chain or gears, at one half the crankshaft speed.

CAPACITOR: A device which stores an electrical charge.

CARBON MONOXIDE (CO): a colorless, odorless gas given off as a normal byproduct of combustion. It is poisonous and extremely dangerous in confined areas, building up slowly to toxic levels without warning if adequate ventilation is not available.

CARBURETOR: A device, usually mounted on the intake manifold of an engine, which mixes the air and fuel in the proper proportion to allow even combustion.

CATALYTIC CONVERTER: A device installed in the exhaust system, like a muffler, that converts harmful byproducts of combustion into carbon dioxide and water vapor by means of a heat-producing chemical reaction.

CENTRIFUGAL ADVANCE: A mechanical method of advancing the spark timing by using flyweights in the distributor that react to centrifugal force generated by the distributor shaft rotation.

CHECK VALVE: Any one-way valve installed to permit the flow of air, fuel or vacuum in one direction only.

CHOKE: A device, usually a moveable valve, placed in the intake path of a carburetor to restrict the flow of air.

CIRCUIT: Any unbroken path through which an electrical current can flow. Also used to describe fuel flow in some instances.

CIRCUIT BREAKER: A switch which protects an electrical circuit from overload by opening the circuit when the current flow exceeds a predetermined level. Some circuit breakers must be reset manually, while other reset automatically

COIL (IGNITION): A transformer in the ignition circuit which steps of the voltage provided to the spark plugs.

COMBINATION MANIFOLD: An assembly which includes both the intake and exhaust manifolds in one casting.

COMBINATION VALVE: A device used in some fuel systems that routes fuel vapors to a charcoal storage canister instead of venting them into the atmosphere. The valve relieves fuel tank pressure and allows fresh air into the tank as fuel level drops to prevent a vapor lock situation.

COMPRESSION RATIO: The comparison of the total volume of the cylinder and combustion chamber with the piston at BDC and the piston at TDC.

CONDENSER: 1. An electrical device which acts to store an electrical charge, preventing voltage surges.
2. A radiator-like device in the air conditioning system in which refrigerant gas condenses into a liquid, giving off heat.

CONDUCTOR: Any material through which an electrical current can be transmitted easily.

CONTINUITY: Continuous or complete circuit. Can be checked with an ohmmeter.

COUNTERSHAFT: An intermediate shaft which is rotated by a mainshaft and transmits, in turn, that rotation to a working part.

CRANKCASE: The lower part of an engine in which the crankshaft and related parts operate.

CRANKSHAFT: The main driving shaft of an engine which receives reciprocating motion from the pistons and converts it to rotary motion.

CYLINDER: In an engine, the round hole in the engine block in which the piston(s) ride

CYLINDER BLOCK: The main structural member of an engine in which is found the cylinders, crankshaft and other principal parts.

CYLINDER HEAD: The detachable portion of the engine, fastened, usually, to the top of the cylinder block, containing all or most of the combustion chambers. On overhead valve engines, it contains the valves and their operating parts. On overhead cam engines, it contains the camshaft as well.

DEAD CENTER: The extreme top or bottom of the piston stroke.

DETONATION: An unwanted explosion of the air fuel mixture in the combustion chamber caused by excess heat and compression, advanced timing, or an overly lean mixture. Also referred to as "ping".

DIAPHRAGM: A thin, flexible wall separating two cavities, such as in a vacuum advance unit.

DIESELING: A condition in which hot spots in the combustion chamber cause the engine to run on after the key is turned off.

DIFFERENTIAL: A geared assembly which allows the transmission of motion between drive axles, giving one axle the ability to turn faster than the other.

DIODE: An electrical device that will allow current to flow in one direction only.

DISC BRAKE: A hydraulic braking assembly consisting of a brake disc, or rotor, mounted on an axle, and a caliper assembly containing, usually two brake pads which are activated by hydraulic pressure. The pads are forced against the sides of the disc, creating friction which slows the vehicle.

DISTRIBUTOR: A mechanically driven device on an engine which is responsible for electrically firing the spark plug at a predetermined point of the piston stroke.

DOWEL PIN: A pin, inserted in mating holes in two different parts allowing those parts to maintain a fixed relationship.

DRUM BRAKE: A braking system which consists of two brake shoes and one or two wheel cylinders, mounted on a fixed backing plate, and a brake drum, mounted on an axle, which revolves around the assembly. Hydraulic action applied to the wheel cylinders forces the shoes outward against the drum, creating friction and slowing the vehicle.

DWELL: The rate, measured in degrees of shaft rotation, at which an electrical circuit cycles on and off.

ELECTRONIC CONTROL UNIT (ECU): Ignition module, module, amplifier or igniter. See Module for definition.

ELECTRONIC IGNITION: A system in which the timing and firing of the spark plugs is controlled by an electronic control unit, usually called a module. These systems have not points or condenser.

ENDPLAY: The measured amount of axial movement in a shaft.

ENGINE: A device that converts heat into mechanical energy.

EXHAUST MANIFOLD: A set of cast passages or pipes which conduct exhaust gases from the engine.

FEELER GAUGE: A blade, usually metal, of precisely predetermined thickness, used to measure the clearance between two parts. These blades usually are available in sets of assorted thicknesses.

F-Head: An engine configuration in which the intake valves are in the cylinder head, while the camshaft and exhaust valves are located in the cylinder block. The camshaft operates the intake valves via lifters and pushrods, while it operates the exhaust valves directly.

FIRING ORDER: The order in which combustion occurs in the cylinders of an engine. Also the order in which spark is distributed to the plugs by the distributor.

FLATHEAD: An engine configuration in which the camshaft and all the valves are located in the cylinder block.

FLOODING: The presence of too much fuel in the intake manifold and combustion chamber which prevents the air/fuel mixture from firing, thereby causing a no-start situation.

FLYWHEEL: A disc shaped part bolted to the rear end of the crankshaft. Around the outer perimeter is affixed the ring gear. The starter drive engages the ring gear, turning the flywheel, which rotates the crankshaft, imparting the initial starting motion to the engine.

FOOT POUND (ft.lb. or sometimes, ft. lbs.): The amount of energy or work needed to raise an item weighing one pound, a distance of one foot.

FUSE: A protective device in a circuit which prevents circuit overload by breaking the circuit when a specific amperage is present. The device is constructed around a strip or wire of a lower amperage rating than the circuit it is designed to protect. When an amperage higher than that stamped on the fuse is present in the circuit, the strip or wire melts, opening the circuit.

GEAR RATIO: The ratio between the number of teeth on meshing gears.

GENERATOR: A device which converts mechanical energy into electrical energy.

HEAT RANGE: The measure of a spark plug's ability to dissipate heat from its firing end. The higher the heat range, the hotter the plug fires.

HUB: The center part of a wheel or gear.

HYDROCARBON (HC): Any chemical compound made up of hydrogen and carbon. A major pollutant formed by the engine as a byproduct of combustion.

HYDROMETER: An instrument used to measure the specific gravity of a solution.

INCH POUND (in.lb. or sometimes, in. lbs.): One twelfth of a foot pound.

INDUCTION: A means of transferring electrical energy in the form of a magnetic field. Principle used in the ignition coil to increase voltage.

INJECTION PUMP: A device, usually mechanically operated, which meters and delivers fuel under pressure to the fuel injector.

INJECTOR: A device which receives metered fuel under relatively low pressure and is activated to inject the fuel into the engine under relatively high pressure at a predetermined time.

INPUT SHAFT: The shaft to which torque is applied, usually carrying the driving gear or gears.

INTAKE MANIFOLD: A casting of passages or pipes used to conduct air or a fuel/air mixture to the cylinders.

JOURNAL: The bearing surface within which a shaft operates.

KEY: A small block usually fitted in a notch between a shaft and a hub to prevent slippage of the two parts.

MANIFOLD: A casting of passages or set of pipes which connect the cylinders to an inlet or outlet source.

MANIFOLD VACUUM: Low pressure in an engine intake manifold formed just below the throttle plates. Manifold vacuum is highest at idle and drops under acceleration.

MASTER CYLINDER: The primary fluid pressurizing device in a hydraulic system. In automotive use, it is found in brake and hydraulic clutch systems and is pedal activated, either directly or, in a power brake system, through the power booster.

MODULE: Electronic control unit, amplifier or igniter of solid state or integrated design which controls the current flow in the ignition primary circuit based on input from the pickup coil. When the module opens the primary circuit, the high secondary voltage is induced in the coil.

NEEDLE BEARING: A bearing which consists of a number (usually a large number) of long, thin rollers.

OHM: (Ω) The unit used to measure the resistance of conductor to electrical flow. One ohm is the amount of resistance that limits current flow to one ampere in a circuit with one volt of pressure.

OHMMETER: An instrument used for measuring the resistance, in ohms, in an electrical circuit.

OUTPUT SHAFT: The shaft which transmits torque from a device, such as a transmission.

OVERDRIVE: A gear assembly which produces more shaft revolutions than that transmitted to it.

OVERHEAD CAMSHAFT (OHC): An engine configuration in which the camshaft is mounted on top of the cylinder head and operates the valve either directly or by means of rocker arms.

OVERHEAD VALVE (OHV): An engine configuration in which all of the valves are located in the cylinder head and the camshaft is located in the cylinder block. The camshaft operates the valves via lifters and pushrods.

OXIDES OF NITROGEN (NOx): Chemical compounds of nitrogen produced as a byproduct of combustion. They combine with hydrocarbons to produce smog.

OXYGEN SENSOR: Used with the feedback system to sense the presence of oxygen in the exhaust gas and signal the computer which can reference the voltage signal to an air/fuel ratio.

PINION: The smaller of two meshing gears.

PISTON RING: An open ended ring which fits into a groove on the outer diameter of the piston. Its chief function is to form a seal between the piston and cylinder wall. Most automotive pistons have three rings: two for compression sealing; one for oil sealing.

PRELOAD: A predetermined load placed on a bearing during assembly or by adjustment.

PRIMARY CIRCUIT: Is the low voltage side of the ignition system which consists of the ignition switch, ballast resistor or resistance wire, bypass, coil, electronic control unit and pick-up coil as well as the connecting wires and harnesses.

PRESS FIT: The mating of two parts under pressure, due to the inner diameter of one being smaller than the outer diameter of the other, or vice versa; an interference fit.

RACE: The surface on the inner or outer ring of a bearing on which the balls, needles or rollers move.

REGULATOR: A device which maintains the amperage and/or voltage levels of a circuit at predetermined values.

RELAY: A switch which automatically opens and/or closes a circuit.

RESISTANCE: The opposition to the flow of current through a circuit or electrical device, and is measured in ohms. Resistance is equal to the voltage divided by the amperage.

RESISTOR: A device, usually made of wire, which offers a preset amount of resistance in an electrical circuit.

RING GEAR: The name given to a ring-shaped gear attached to a differential case, or affixed to a flywheel or as part a planetary gear set.

ROLLER BEARING: A bearing made up of hardened inner and outer races between which hardened steel rollers move.

ROTOR: 1. The disc-shaped part of a disc brake assembly, upon which the brake pads bear; also called, brake disc.
2. The device mounted atop the distributor shaft, which passes current to the distributor cap tower contacts.

SECONDARY CIRCUIT: The high voltage side of the ignition system, usually above 20,000 volts. The secondary includes the ignition coil, coil wire, distributor cap and rotor, spark plug wires and spark plugs.

SENDING UNIT: A mechanical, electrical, hydraulic or electromagnetic device which transmits information to a gauge.

SENSOR: Any device designed to measure engine operating conditions or ambient pressures and temperatures. Usually electronic in nature and designed to send a voltage signal to an on-board computer, some sensors may operate as a simple on/off switch or they may provide a variable voltage signal (like a potentiometer) as conditions or measured parameters change.

SHIM: Spacers of precise, predetermined thickness used between parts to establish a proper working relationship.

SLAVE CYLINDER: In automotive use, a device in the hydraulic clutch system which is activated by hydraulic force, disengaging the clutch.

SOLENOID: A coil used to produce a magnetic field, the effect of which is produce work.

SPARK PLUG: A device screwed into the combustion chamber of a spark ignition engine. The basic construction is a conductive core inside of a ceramic insulator, mounted in an outer conductive base. An electrical charge from the spark plug wire travels along the conductive core and jumps a preset air gap to a grounding point or points at the end of the conductive base. The resultant spark ignites the fuel/air mixture in the combustion chamber.

SPLINES: Ridges machined or cast onto the outer diameter of a shaft or inner diameter of a bore to enable parts to mate without rotation.

TACHOMETER: A device used to measure the rotary speed of an engine, shaft, gear, etc., usually in rotations per minute.

THERMOSTAT: A valve, located in the cooling system of an engine, which is closed when cold and opens gradually in response to engine heating, controlling the temperature of the coolant and rate of coolant flow.

TOP DEAD CENTER (TDC): The point at which the piston reaches the top of its travel on the compression stroke.

TORQUE: The twisting force applied to an object.

TORQUE CONVERTER: A turbine used to transmit power from a driving member to a driven member via hydraulic action, providing changes in drive ratio and torque. In automotive use, it links the driveplate at the rear of the engine to the automatic transmission.

TRANSDUCER: A device used to change a force into an electrical signal.

TRANSISTOR: A semi-conductor component which can be actuated by a small voltage to perform an electrical switching function.

TUNE-UP: A regular maintenance function, usually associated with the replacement and adjustment of parts and components in the electrical and fuel systems of a vehicle for the purpose of attaining optimum performance.

TURBOCHARGER: An exhaust driven pump which compresses intake air and forces it into the combustion chambers at higher than atmospheric pressures. The increased air pressure allows more fuel to be burned and results in increased horsepower being produced.

VACUUM ADVANCE: A device which advances the ignition timing in response to increased engine vacuum.

VACUUM GAUGE: An instrument used to measure the presence of vacuum in a chamber.

VALVE: A device which control the pressure, direction of flow or rate of flow of a liquid or gas.

VALVE CLEARANCE: The measured gap between the end of the valve stem and the rocker arm, cam lobe or follower that activates the valve.

VISCOSITY: The rating of a liquid's internal resistance to flow.

VOLTMETER: An instrument used for measuring electrical force in units called volts. Voltmeters are always connected parallel with the circuit being tested.

WHEEL CYLINDER: Found in the automotive drum brake assembly, it is a device, actuated by hydraulic pressure, which, through internal pistons, pushes the brake shoes outward against the drums.

ABBREVIATIONS AND SYMBOLS

A: Ampere

AC: Alternating current

A/C: Air conditioning

A-h: Ampere hour

AT: Automatic transmission

ATDC: After top dead center

μA: Microampere

bbl: Barrel

BDC: Bottom dead center

bhp: Brake horsepower

BTDC: Before top dead center

BTU: British thermal unit

C: Celsius (Centigrade)

CCA: Cold cranking amps

cd: Candela

cm^2: Square centimeter

cm^3, cc: Cubic centimeter

CO: Carbon monoxide

CO_2: Carbon dioxide

cu.in., in^3: Cubic inch

CV: Constant velocity

Cyl.: Cylinder

DC: Direct current

ECM: Electronic control module

EFE: Early fuel evaporation

EFI: Electronic fuel injection

EGR: Exhaust gas recirculation

Exh.: Exhaust

F: Fahrenheit

F: Farad

pF: Picofarad

μF: Microfarad

FI: Fuel injection

ft.lb., ft. lb., ft. lbs.: foot pound(s)

gal: Gallon

g: Gram

HC: Hydrocarbon

HEI: High energy ignition

HO: High output

hp: Horsepower

Hyd.: Hydraulic

Hz: Hertz

ID: Inside diameter

in.lb.; in. lb.; in. lbs: inch pound(s)

Int.: Intake

K: Kelvin

kg: Kilogram

kHz: Kilohertz

km: Kilometer

km/h: Kilometers per hour

kΩ: Kilohm

kPa: Kilopascal

kV: Kilovolt

kW: Kilowatt

l: Liter

l/s: Liters per second

m: Meter

mA: Milliampere

mg: Milligram

mHz: Megahertz

mm: Millimeter

mm^2: Square millimeter

m^3: Cubic meter

$M\Omega$: Megohm

m/s: Meters per second

MT: Manual transmission

mV: Millivolt

μm: Micrometer

N: Newton

N-m: Newton meter

NOx: Nitrous oxide

OD: Outside diameter

OHC: Over head camshaft

OHV: Over head valve

Ω: Ohm

PCV: Positive crankcase ventilation

psi: Pounds per square inch

pts: Pints

qts: Quarts

rpm: Rotations per minute

rps: Rotations per second

R-12: A refrigerant gas (Freon)

SAE: Society of Automotive Engineers

SO_2: Sulfur dioxide

T: Ton

t: Megagram

TBI: Throttle Body Injection

TPS: Throttle Position Sensor

V: 1. Volt; 2. Venturi

μV: Microvolt

W: Watt

∞: Infinity

<: Less than

>: Greater than

Index

Part No.	Model	Repair Manual Title	Part No.	Model	Repair Manual Title
6980	Accord	Honda 1973-88	6739	Cherokee 1974-83	Jeep Wagoneer, Commando, Cherokee, Truck 1957-86
7747	Aerostar	Ford Aerostar 1986-90	7939	Cherokee 1984-89	Jeep Wagoneer, Comanche, Cherokee 1984-89
7165	Alliance	Renault 1975-85			
7199	AMX	AMC 1975-86	6840	Chevelle	Chevrolet Mid-Size 1964-88
7163	Aries	Chrysler Front Wheel Drive 1981-88	6836	Chevette	Chevette/T-1000 1976-88
7041	Arrow	Champ/Arrow/Sapporo 1978-83	6841	Chevy II	Chevy II/Nova 1962-79
7032	Arrow Pick-Ups	D-50/Arrow Pick-Up 1979-81	7309	Ciera	Celebrity, Century, Ciera, 6000 1982-88
6637	Aspen	Aspen/Volare 1976-80			
6935	Astre	GM Subcompact 1971-80	7059	Cimarron	Cavalier, Skyhawk, Cimarron, 2000 1982-88
7750	Astro	Chevrolet Astro/GMC Safari 1985-90			
6934	A100, 200, 300	Dodge/Plymouth Vans 1967-88	7049	Citation	GM X-Body 1980-85
5807	Barracuda	Barracuda/Challenger 1965-72	6980	Civic	Honda 1973-88
6844	Bavaria	BMW 1970-88	6817	CJ-2A, 3A, 3B, 5, 6, 7	Jeep 1945-87
5796	Beetle	Volkswagen 1949-71			
6837	Beetle	Volkswagen 1970-81	8034	CJ-5, 6, 7	Jeep 1971-90
7135	Bel Air	Chevrolet 1968-88	6842	Colony Park	Ford/Mercury/Lincoln 1968-88
5821	Belvedere	Roadrunner/Satellite/Belvedere/GTX 1968-73	7037	Colt	Colt/Challenger/Vista/Conquest 1971-88
7849	Beretta	Chevrolet Corsica and Beretta 1988	6634	Comet	Maverick/Comet 1971-77
7317	Berlinetta	Camaro 1982-88	7939	Comanche	Jeep Wagoneer, Comanche, Cherokee 1984-89
7135	Biscayne	Chevrolet 1968-88			
6931	Blazer	Blazer/Jimmy 1969-82	6739	Commando	Jeep Wagoneer, Commando, Cherokee, Truck 1957-86
7383	Blazer	Chevy S-10 Blazer/GMC S-15 Jimmy 1982-87			
			6842	Commuter	Ford/Mercury/Lincoln 1968-88
7027	Bobcat	Pinto/Bobcat 1971-80	7199	Concord	AMC 1975-86
7308	Bonneville	Buick/Olds/Pontiac 1975-87	7037	Conquest	Colt/Challenger/Vista/Conquest 1971-88
6982	BRAT	Subaru 1970-88			
7042	Brava	Fiat 1969-81	6696	Continental 1982-85	Ford/Mercury/Lincoln Mid-Size 1971-85
7140	Bronco	Ford Bronco 1966-86			
7829	Bronco	Ford Pick-Ups and Bronco 1987-88	7814	Continental 1982-87	Thunderbird, Cougar, Continental 1980-87
7408	Bronco II	Ford Ranger/Bronco II 1983-88			
7135	Brookwood	Chevrolet 1968-88	7830	Continental 1988-89	Taurus/Sable/Continental 1986-89
6326	Brougham 1975-75	Valiant/Duster 1968-76	7583	Cordia	Mitsubishi 1983-89
6934	B100, 150, 200, 250, 300, 350	Dodge/Plymouth Vans 1967-88	5795	Corolla 1968-70	Toyota 1966-70
			7036	Corolla	Toyota Corolla/Carina/Tercel/Starlet 1970-87
7197	B210	Datsun 1200/210/Nissan Sentra 1973-88			
			5795	Corona	Toyota 1966-70
7659	B1600, 1800, 2000, 2200, 2600	Mazda Trucks 1971-89	7004	Corona	Toyota Corona/Crown/Cressida/Mk.II/Van 1970-87
6840	Caballero	Chevrolet Mid-Size 1964-88	6962	Corrado	VW Front Wheel Drive 1974-90
7657	Calais	Calais, Grand Am, Skylark, Somerset 1985-86	7849	Corsica	Chevrolet Corsica and Beretta 1988
			6576	Corvette	Corvette 1953-62
6735	Camaro	Camaro 1967-81	6843	Corvette	Corvette 1963-86
7317	Camaro	Camaro 1982-88	6542	Cougar	Mustang/Cougar 1965-73
7740	Camry	Toyota Camry 1983-88	6696	Cougar	Ford/Mercury/Lincoln Mid-Size 1971-85
6695	Capri, Capri II	Capri 1970-77			
6963	Capri	Mustang/Capri/Merkur 1979-88	7814	Cougar	Thunderbird, Cougar, Continental 1980-87
7135	Caprice	Chevrolet 1968-88			
7482	Caravan	Dodge Caravan/Plymouth Voyager 1984-89	6842	Country Sedan	Ford/Mercury/Lincoln 1968-88
			6842	Country Squire	Ford/Mercury/Lincoln 1968-88
7163	Caravelle	Chrysler Front Wheel Drive 1981-88	6983	Courier	Ford Courier 1972-82
7036	Carina	Toyota Corolla/Carina/Tercel/Starlet 1970-87	7004	Cressida	Toyota Corona/Crown/Cressida/Mk.II/Van 1970-87
			5795	Crown	Toyota 1966-70
7308	Catalina	Buick/Olds/Pontiac 1975-90	7004	Crown	Toyota Corona/Crown/Cressida/Mk.II/Van 1970-87
7059	Cavalier	Cavalier, Skyhawk, Cimarron, 2000 1982-88			
			6842	Crown Victoria	Ford/Mercury/Lincoln 1968-88
7309	Celebrity	Celebrity, Century, Ciera, 6000 1982-88	6980	CRX	Honda 1973-88
			6842	Custom	Ford/Mercury/Lincoln 1968-88
7043	Celica	Toyota Celica/Supra 1971-87	6326	Custom	Valiant/Duster 1968-76
8058	Celica	Toyota Celica/Supra 1986-90	6842	Custom 500	Ford/Mercury/Lincoln 1968-88
7309	Century FWD	Celebrity, Century, Ciera, 6000 1982-88	7950	Cutlass FWD	Lumina/Grand Prix/Cutlass/Regal 1988-90
7307	Century RWD	Century/Regal 1975-87	6933	Cutlass RWD	Cutlass 1970-87
5807	Challenger 1965-72	Barracuda/Challenger 1965-72	7309	Cutlass Ciera	Celebrity, Century, Ciera, 6000 1982-88
7037	Challenger 1977-83	Colt/Challenger/Vista/Conquest 1971-88			
			6936	C-10, 20, 30	Chevrolet/GMC Pick-Ups & Suburban 1970-87
7041	Champ	Champ/Arrow/Sapporo 1978-83			
6486	Charger	Dodge Charger 1967-70			
6845	Charger 2.2	Omni/Horizon/Rampage 1978-88			

Chilton's Repair Manuals are available at your local retailer or by mailing a check or money order for **$15.95** per book plus **$3.50** for 1st book and **$.50** for each additional book to cover postage and handling to:

Chilton Book Company
Dept. DM
Radnor, PA 19089

NOTE: When ordering be sure to include your name & address, book part No. & title.

CHILTON'S REPAIR MANUAL MODEL INDEX
Car and truck model names are listed in alphabetical and numerical order

Part No.	Model	Repair Manual Title
8055	C-15, 25, 35	Chevrolet/GMC Pick-Ups & Suburban 1988-90
6324	Dart	Dart/Demon 1968-76
6962	Dasher	VW Front Wheel Drive 1974-90
5790	Datsun Pickups	Datsun 1961-72
6816	Datsun Pickups	Datsun Pick-Ups and Pathfinder 1970-89
7163	Daytona	Chrysler Front Wheel Drive 1981-88
6486	Daytona Charger	Dodge Charger 1967-70
6324	Demon	Dart/Demon 1968-76
7462	deVille	Cadillac 1967-89
7587	deVille	GM C-Body 1985
6817	DJ-3B	Jeep 1945-87
7040	DL	Volvo 1970-88
6326	Duster	Valiant/Duster 1968-76
7032	D-50	D-50/Arrow Pick-Ups 1979-81
7459	D100, 150, 200, 250, 300, 350	Dodge/Plymouth Trucks 1967-88
7199	Eagle	AMC 1975-86
7163	E-Class	Chrysler Front Wheel Drive 1981-88
6840	El Camino	Chevrolet Mid-Size 1964-88
7462	Eldorado	Cadillac 1967-89
7308	Electra	Buick/Olds/Pontiac 1975-90
7587	Electra	GM C-Body 1985
6696	Elite	Ford/Mercury/Lincoln Mid-Size 1971-85
7165	Encore	Renault 1975-85
7055	Escort	Ford/Mercury Front Wheel Drive 1981-87
7059	Eurosport	Cavalier, Skyhawk, Cimarron, 2000 1982-88
7760	Excel	Hyundai 1986-90
7163	Executive Sedan	Chrysler Front Wheel Drive 1981-88
7055	EXP	Ford/Mercury Front Wheel Drive 1981-87
6849	E-100, 150, 200, 250, 300, 350	Ford Vans 1961-88
6320	Fairlane	Fairlane/Torino 1962-75
6965	Fairmont	Fairmont/Zephyr 1978-83
5796	Fastback	Volkswagen 1949-71
6837	Fastback	Volkswagen 1970-81
6739	FC-150, 170	Jeep Wagoneer, Commando, Cherokee, Truck 1957-86
6982	FF-1	Subaru 1970-88
7571	Fiero	Pontiac Fiero 1984-88
6846	Fiesta	Fiesta 1978-80
5996	Firebird	Firebird 1967-81
7345	Firebird	Firebird 1982-90
7059	Firenza	Cavalier, Skyhawk, Cimarron, 2000 1982-88
7462	Fleetwood	Cadillac 1967-89
7587	Fleetwood	GM C-Body 1985
7829	F-Super Duty	Ford Pick-Ups and Bronco 1987-88
7165	Fuego	Renault 1975-85
6552	Fury	Plymouth 1968-76
7196	F-10	Datsun/Nissan F-10, 310, Stanza, Pulsar 1976-88
6933	F-85	Cutlass 1970-87
6913	F-100, 150, 200, 250, 300, 350	Ford Pick-Ups 1965-86
7829	F-150, 250, 350	Ford Pick-Ups and Bronco 1987-88
7583	Galant	Mitsubishi 1983-89
6842	Galaxie	Ford/Mercury/Lincoln 1968-88
7040	GL	Volvo 1970-88
6739	Gladiator	Jeep Wagoneer, Commando, Cherokee, Truck 1962-86
6981	GLC	Mazda 1978-89
7040	GLE	Volvo 1970-88
7040	GLT	Volvo 1970-88
7593	Golf	VW Front Wheel Drive 1974-90
7165	Gordini	Renault 1975-85
6937	Granada	Granada/Monarch 1975-82
6552	Gran Coupe	Plymouth 1968-76
6552	Gran Fury	Plymouth 1968-76
6842	Gran Marquis	Ford/Mercury/Lincoln 1968-88
6552	Gran Sedan	Plymouth 1968-76
6696	Gran Torino	Ford/Mercury/Lincoln Mid-Size 1971-85
	1972-76	
7346	Grand Am	Pontiac Mid-Size 1974-83
7657	Grand Am	Calais, Grand Am, Skylark, Somerset 1985-86
7346	Grand LeMans	Pontiac Mid-Size 1974-83
7346	Grand Prix	Pontiac Mid-Size 1974-83
7950	Grand Prix FWD	Lumina/Grand Prix/Cutlass/Regal 1988-90
7308	Grand Safari	Buick/Olds/Pontiac 1975-87
7308	Grand Ville	Buick/Olds/Pontiac 1975-87
6739	Grand Wagoneer	Jeep Wagoneer, Commando, Cherokee, Truck 1957-86
7199	Gremlin	AMC 1975-86
6575	GT	Opel 1971-75
7593	GTI	VW Front Wheel Drive 1974-90
5905	GTO 1968-73	Tempest/GTO/LeMans 1968-73
7346	GTO 1974	Pontiac Mid-Size 1974-83
5821	GTX	Roadrunner/Satellite/Belvedere/GTX 1968-73
5910	GT6	Triumph 1969-73
6542	G.T.350, 500	Mustang/Cougar 1965-73
6930	G-10, 20, 30	Chevy/GMC Vans 1967-86
6930	G-1500, 2500, 3500	Chevy/GMC Vans 1967-86
8040	G-10, 20, 30	Chevy/GMC Vans 1987-90
8040	G-1500, 2500, 3500	Chevy/GMC Vans 1987-90
5795	Hi-Lux	Toyota 1966-70
6845	Horizon	Omni/Horizon/Rampage 1978-88
7199	Hornet	AMC 1975-86
7135	Impala	Chevrolet 1968-88
7317	IROC-Z	Camaro 1982-88
6739	Jeepster	Jeep Wagoneer, Commando, Cherokee, Truck 1957-86
7593	Jetta	VW Front Wheel Drive 1974-90
6931	Jimmy	Blazer/Jimmy 1969-82
7383	Jimmy	Chevy S-10 Blazer/GMC S-15 Jimmy 1982-87
6739	J-10, 20	Jeep Wagoneer, Commando, Cherokee, Truck 1957-86
6739	J-100, 200, 300	Jeep Wagoneer, Commando, Cherokee, Truck 1957-86
6575	Kadett	Opel 1971-75
7199	Kammback	AMC 1975-86
5796	Karmann Ghia	Volkswagen 1949-71
6837	Karmann Ghia	Volkswagen 1970-81
7135	Kingswood	Chevrolet 1968-88
6931	K-5	Blazer/Jimmy 1969-82
6936	K-10, 20, 30	Chevy/GMC Pick-Ups & Suburban 1970-87
6936	K-1500, 2500, 3500	Chevy/GMC Pick-Ups & Suburban 1970-87
8055	K-10, 20, 30	Chevy/GMC Pick-Ups & Suburban 1988-90
8055	K-1500, 2500, 3500	Chevy/GMC Pick-Ups & Suburban 1988-90
6840	Laguna	Chevrolet Mid-Size 1964-88
7041	Lancer	Champ/Arrow/Sapporo 1977-83
5795	Land Cruiser	Toyota 1966-70
7035	Land Cruiser	Toyota Trucks 1970-88
7163	Laser	Chrysler Front Wheel Drive 1981-88
7163	LeBaron	Chrysler Front Wheel Drive 1981-88
7165	LeCar	Renault 1975-85

Chilton's Repair Manuals are available at your local retailer or by mailing a check or money order for **$15.95** per book plus **$3.50** for 1st book and **$.50** for each additional book to cover postage and handling to:

Chilton Book Company
Dept. DM
Radnor, PA 19089

NOTE: When ordering be sure to include your name & address, book part No. & title.

CHILTON'S REPAIR MANUAL MODEL INDEX
Car and truck model names are listed in alphabetical and numerical order

Part No.	Model	Repair Manual Title
6817	4 × 4-63	Jeep 1981-87
6817	4-73	Jeep 1981-87
6817	4 × 4-73	Jeep 1981-87
6817	4-75	Jeep 1981-87
7035	4Runner	Toyota Trucks 1970-88
6982	4wd Wagon	Subaru 1970-88
6982	4wd Coupe	Subaru 1970-88
6933	4-4-2 1970-80	Cutlass 1970-87
6817	6-63	Jeep 1981-87
6809	6.9	Mercedes-Benz 1974-84
7308	88	Buick/Olds/Pontiac 1975-90
7308	98	Buick/Olds/Pontiac 1975-90
7587	98 Regency	GM C-Body 1985
5902	100LS, 100GL	Audi 1970-73
6529	122, 122S	Volvo 1956-69
7042	124	Fiat 1969-81
7042	128	Fiat 1969-81
7042	131	Fiat 1969-81
6529	142	Volvo 1956-69
7040	142	Volvo 1970-88
6529	144	Volvo 1956-69
7040	144	Volvo 1970-88
6529	145	Volvo 1956-69
7040	145	Volvo 1970-88
6529	164	Volvo 1956-69
7040	164	Volvo 1970-88
6065	190C	Mercedes-Benz 1959-70
6809	190D	Mercedes-Benz 1974-84
6065	190DC	Mercedes-Benz 1959-70
6809	190E	Mercedes-Benz 1974-84
6065	200, 200D	Mercedes-Benz 1959-70
7170	200SX	Nissan 200SX, 240SX, 510, 610, 710, 810, Maxima 1973-88
7197	210	Datsun 1200, 210, Nissan Sentra 1971-88
6065	220B, 220D, 220Sb, 220SEb	Mercedes-Benz 1959-70
5907	220/8 1968-73	Mercedes-Benz 1968-73
6809	230 1974-78	Mercedes-Benz 1974-84
6065	230S, 230SL	Mercedes-Benz 1959-70
5907	230/8	Mercedes-Benz 1968-73
6809	240D	Mercedes-Benz 1974-84
7170	240SX	Nissan 200SX, 240SX, 510, 610, 710, 810, Maxima 1973-88
6932	240Z	Datsun Z & ZX 1970-87
7040	242, 244, 245	Volvo 1970-88
5907	250C	Mercedes-Benz 1968-73
6065	250S, 250SE, 250SL	Mercedes-Benz 1959-70
5907	250/8	Mercedes-Benz 1968-73
6932	260Z	Datsun Z & ZX 1970-87
7040	262, 264, 265	Volvo 1970-88
5907	280	Mercedes-Benz 1968-73
6809	280	Mercedes-Benz 1974-84
5907	280C	Mercedes-Benz 1968-73
6809	280C, 280CE, 280E	Mercedes-Benz 1974-84
6065	280S, 280SE	Mercedes-Benz 1959-70
5907	280SE, 280S/8, 280SE/8	Mercedes-Benz 1968-73
6809	280SEL, 280SEL/8, 280SL	Mercedes-Benz 1974-84
6932	280Z, 280ZX	Datsun Z & ZX 1970-87
6065	300CD, 300D, 300SD, 300SE	Mercedes-Benz 1959-70
5907	300SEL 3.5, 300SEL 4.5	Mercedes-Benz 1968-73
5907	300SEL 6.3, 300SEL/8	Mercedes-Benz 1968-73
6809	300TD	Mercedes-Benz 1974-84
6932	300ZX	Datsun Z & ZX 1970-87
5982	304	Peugeot 1970-74
5790	310	Datsun 1961-72
7196	310	Datsun/Nissan F-10, 310, Stanza, Pulsar 1977-88
5790	311	Datsun 1961-72
6844	318i, 320i	BMW 1970-88
6981	323	Mazda 1978-89
6844	325E, 325ES, 325i, 325iS, 325iX	BMW 1970-88
6809	380SEC, 380SEL, 380SL, 380SLC	Mercedes-Benz 1974-84
5907	350SL	Mercedes-Benz 1968-73
7163	400	Chrysler Front Wheel Drive 1981-88
5790	410	Datsun 1961-72
5790	411	Datsun 1961-72
7081	411, 412	Volkswagen 1970-81
6809	450SE, 450SEL, 450 SEL 6.9	Mercedes-Benz 1974-84
6809	450SL, 450SLC	Mercedes-Benz 1974-84
5907	450SLC	Mercedes-Benz 1968-73
6809	500SEC, 500SEL	Mercedes-Benz 1974-84
5982	504	Peugeot 1970-74
5790	510	Datsun 1961-72
7170	510	Nissan 200SX, 240SX, 510, 610, 710, 810, Maxima 1973-88
6816	520	Datsun/Nissan Pick-Ups and Pathfinder 1970-89
6844	524TD	BMW 1970-88
6844	525i	BMW 1970-88
6844	528e	BMW 1970-88
6844	528i	BMW 1970-88
6844	530i	BMW 1970-88
6844	533i	BMW 1970-88
6844	535i, 535iS	BMW 1970-88
6980	600	Honda 1973-88
7163	600	Chrysler Front Wheel Drive 1981-88
7170	610	Nissan 200SX, 240SX, 510, 610, 710, 810, Maxima 1973-88
6816	620	Datsun/Nissan Pick-Ups and Pathfinder 1970-89
6981	626	Mazda 1978-89
6844	630 CSi	BMW 1970-88
6844	633 CSi	BMW 1970-88
6844	635CSi	BMW 1970-88
7170	710	Nissan 200SX, 240SX, 510, 610, 710, 810, Maxima 1973-88
6816	720	Datsun/Nissan Pick-Ups and Pathfinder 1970-89
6844	733i	BMW 1970-88
6844	735i	BMW 1970-88
7040	760, 760GLE	Volvo 1970-88
7040	780	Volvo 1970-88
6981	808	Mazda 1978-89
7170	810	Nissan 200SX, 240SX, 510, 610, 710, 810, Maxima 1973-88
7042	850	Fiat 1969-81
7572	900, 900 Turbo	SAAB 900 1976-85
7048	924	Porsche 924/928 1976-81
7048	928	Porsche 924/928 1976-81
6981	929	Mazda 1978-89
6836	1000	Chevette/1000 1976-88
6780	1100	MG 1961-81
5790	1200	Datsun 1961-72
7197	1200	Datsun 1200, 210, Nissan Sentra 1973-88
6982	1400GL, 1400DL, 1400GF	Subaru 1970-88
5790	1500	Datsun 1961-72

Chilton's Repair Manuals are available at your local retailer or by mailing a check or money order for **$15.95** per book plus **$3.50** for 1st book and **$.50** for each additional book to cover postage and handling to:

Chilton Book Company
Dept. DM
Radnor, PA 19089

NOTE: When ordering be sure to include your name & address, book part No. & title.

CHILTON'S REPAIR MANUAL MODEL INDEX
Car and truck model names are listed in alphabetical and numerical order

Part No.	Model	Repair Manual Title
5905	LeMans	Tempest/GTO/LeMans 1968-73
7346	LeMans	Pontiac Mid-Size 1974-83
7308	LeSabre	Buick/Olds/Pontiac 1975-87
6842	Lincoln	Ford/Mercury/Lincoln 1968-88
7055	LN-7	Ford/Mercury Front Wheel Drive 1981-87
6842	LTD	Ford/Mercury/Lincoln 1968-88
6696	LTD II	Ford/Mercury/Lincoln Mid-Size 1971-85
7950	Lumina	Lumina/Grand Prix/Cutlass/Regal 1988-90
6815	LUV	Chevrolet LUV 1972-81
6575	Luxus	Opel 1971-75
7055	Lynx	Ford/Mercury Front Wheel Drive 1981-87
6844	L6	BMW 1970-88
6344	L7	BMW 1970-88
6542	Mach I	Mustang/Cougar 1965-73
6812	Mach I Ghia	Mustang II 1974-78
6840	Malibu	Chevrolet Mid-Size 1964-88
6575	Manta	Opel 1971-75
6696	Mark IV, V, VI, VII	Ford/Mercury/Lincoln Mid-Size 1971-85
7814	Mark VII	Thunderbird, Cougar, Continental 1980-87
6842	Marquis	Ford/Mercury/Lincoln 1968-88
6696	Marquis	Ford/Mercury/Lincoln Mid-Size 1971-85
7199	Matador	AMC 1975-86
6634	Maverick	Maverick/Comet 1970-77
6817	Maverick	Jeep 1945-87
7170	Maxima	Nissan 200SX, 240SX, 510, 610, 710, 810, Maxima 1973-88
6842	Mercury	Ford/Mercury/Lincoln 1968-88
6963	Merkur	Mustang/Capri/Merkur 1979-88
6780	MGB, MGB-GT, MGC-GT	MG 1961-81
6780	Midget	MG 1961-81
7583	Mighty Max	Mitsubishi 1983-89
7583	Mirage	Mitsubishi 1983-89
5795	Mk.II 1969-70	Toyota 1966-70
7004	Mk.II 1970-76	Toyota Corona/Crown/Cressida/Mk.II/Van 1970-87
6554	Monaco	Dodge 1968-77
6937	Monarch	Granada/Monarch 1975-82
6840	Monte Carlo	Chevrolet Mid-Size 1964-88
6696	Montego	Ford/Mercury/Lincoln Mid-Size 1971-85
6842	Monterey	Ford/Mercury/Lincoln 1968-88
7583	Montero	Mitsubishi 1983-89
6935	Monza 1975-80	GM Subcompact 1971-80
6981	MPV	Mazda 1978-89
6542	Mustang	Mustang/Cougar 1965-73
6963	Mustang	Mustang/Capri/Merkur 1979-88
6812	Mustang II	Mustang II 1974-78
6981	MX6	Mazda 1978-89
6844	M3, M6	BMW 1970-88
7163	New Yorker	Chrysler Front Wheel Drive 1981-88
6841	Nova	Chevy II/Nova 1962-79
7658	Nova	Chevrolet Nova/GEO Prizm 1985-89
7049	Omega	GM X-Body 1980-85
6845	Omni	Omni/Horizon/Rampage 1978-88
6575	Opel	Opel 1971-75
7199	Pacer	AMC 1975-86
7587	Park Avenue	GM C-Body 1985
6842	Park Lane	Ford/Mercury/Lincoln 1968-88
6962	Passat	VW Front Wheel Drive 1974-90
6816	Pathfinder	Datsun/Nissan Pick-Ups and Pathfinder 1970-89
5790	Patrol	Datsun 1961-72
6934	PB100, 150, 200, 250, 300, 350	Dodge/Plymouth Vans 1967-88
5982	Peugeot	Peugeot 1970-74
7049	Phoenix	GM X-Body 1980-85
7027	Pinto	Pinto/Bobcat 1971-80
6554	Polara	Dodge 1968-77
7583	Precis	Mitsubishi 1983-89
6980	Prelude	Honda 1973-88
7658	Prizm	Chevrolet Nova/GEO Prizm 1985-89
8012	Probe	Ford Probe 1989
7660	Pulsar	Datsun/Nissan F-10, 310, Stanza, Pulsar 1976-88
6529	PV-444	Volvo 1956-69
6529	PV-544	Volvo 1956-69
6529	P-1800	Volvo 1956-69
7593	Quantum	VW Front Wheel Drive 1974-87
7593	Rabbit	VW Front Wheel Drive 1974-87
7593	Rabbit Pickup	VW Front Wheel Drive 1974-87
6575	Rallye	Opel 1971-75
7459	Ramcharger	Dodge/Plymouth Trucks 1967-88
6845	Rampage	Omni/Horizon/Rampage 1978-88
6320	Ranchero	Fairlane/Torino 1962-70
6696	Ranchero	Ford/Mercury/Lincoln Mid-Size 1971-85
6842	Ranch Wagon	Ford/Mercury/Lincoln 1968-88
7338	Ranger Pickup	Ford Ranger/Bronco II 1983-88
7307	Regal RWD	Century/Regal 1975-87
7950	Regal FWD 1988-90	Lumina/Grand Prix/Cutlass/Regal 1988-90
7163	Reliant	Chrysler Front Wheel Drive 1981-88
5821	Roadrunner	Roadrunner/Satellite/Belvedere/GTX 1968-73
7659	Rotary Pick-Up	Mazda Trucks 1971-89
6981	RX-7	Mazda 1978-89
7165	R-12, 15, 17, 18, 18i	Renault 1975-85
7830	Sable	Taurus/Sable/Continental 1986-89
7750	Safari	Chevrolet Astro/GMC Safari 1985-90
7041	Sapporo	Champ/Arrow/Sapporo 1978-83
5821	Satellite	Roadrunner/Satellite/Belvedere/GTX 1968-73
6326	Scamp	Valiant/Duster 1968-76
6845	Scamp	Omni/Horizon/Rampage 1978-88
6962	Scirocco	VW Front Wheel Drive 1974-90
6936	Scottsdale	Chevrolet/GMC Pick-Ups & Suburban 1970-87
8055	Scottsdale	Chevrolet/GMC Pick-Ups & Suburban 1988-90
5912	Scout	International Scout 1967-73
8034	Scrambler	Jeep 1971-90
7197	Sentra	Datsun 1200, 210, Nissan Sentra 1973-88
7462	Seville	Cadillac 1967-89
7163	Shadow	Chrysler Front Wheel Drive 1981-88
6936	Siera	Chevrolet/GMC Pick-Ups & Suburban 1970-87
8055	Siera	Chevrolet/GMC Pick-Ups & Suburban 1988-90
7583	Sigma	Mitsubishi 1983-89
6326	Signet	Valiant/Duster 1968-76
6936	Silverado	Chevrolet/GMC Pick-Ups & Suburban 1970-87
8055	Silverado	Chevrolet/GMC Pick-Ups & Suburban 1988-90
6935	Skyhawk	GM Subcompact 1971-80
7059	Skyhawk	Cavalier, Skyhawk, Cimarron, 2000 1982-88
7049	Skylark	GM X-Body 1980-85

Chilton's Repair Manuals are available at your local retailer or by mailing a check or money order for **$15.95** per book plus **$3.50** for 1st book and **$.50** for each additional book to cover postage and handling to:

**Chilton Book Company
Dept. DM
Radnor, PA 19089**

NOTE: When ordering be sure to include your name & address, book part No. & title.

Part No.	Model	Repair Manual Title	Part No.	Model	Repair Manual Title
75	Skylark	Calais, Grand Am, Skylark, Somerset 1985-86	7040	Turbo	Volvo 1970-88
57	Somerset	Calais, Grand Am, Skylark, Somerset 1985-86	5796	Type 1 Sedan 1949-71	Volkswagen 1949-71
42	Spider 2000	Fiat 1969-81	6837	Type 1 Sedan 1970-80	Volkswagen 1970-81
99	Spirit	AMC 1975-86	5796	Type 1 Karmann Ghia 1960-71	Volkswagen 1949-71
52	Sport Fury	Plymouth 1968–76	6837	Type 1 Karmann Ghia 1970-74	Volkswagen 1970-81
65	Sport Wagon	Renault 1975-85	5796	Type 1 Convertible 1964-71	Volkswagen 1949-71
96	Squareback	Volkswagen 1949-71	6837	Type 1 Convertible 1970-80	Volkswagen 1970-81
37	Squareback	Volkswagen 1970-81	5796	Type 1 Super Beetle 1971	Volkswagen 1949-71
96	Stanza	Datsun/Nissan F-10, 310, Stanza, Pulsar 1976-88	6837	Type 1 Super Beetle 1971-75	Volkswagen 1970-81
35	Starfire	GM Subcompact 1971-80	5796	Type 2 Bus 1953-71	Volkswagen 1949-71
83	Starion	Mitsubishi 1983-89	6837	Type 2 Bus 1970-80	Volkswagen 1970-81
36	Starlet	Toyota Corolla/Carina/Tercel/Starlet 1970-87	5796	Type 2 Kombi 1954-71	Volkswagen 1949-71
59	STE	Cavalier, Skyhawk, Cimarron, 2000 1982-88	6837	Type 2 Kombi 1970-73	Volkswagen 1970-81
95	Stout	Toyota 1966-70	6837	Type 2 Vanagon 1981	Volkswagen 1970-81
42	Strada	Fiat 1969-81	5796	Type 3 Fastback & Squareback 1961-71	Volkswagen 1949-71
52	Suburban	Plymouth 1968-76	7081	Type 3 Fastback & Squareback 1970-73	Volkswagen 1970-70
36	Suburban	Chevy/GMC Pick-Ups & Suburban 1970-87	5796	Type 4 411 1971	Volkswagen 1949-71
55	Suburban	Chevy/GMC Pick-Ups & Suburban 1988-90	6837	Type 4 411 1971-72	Volkswagen 1970-81
35	Sunbird	GM Subcompact 1971-80	5796	Type 4 412 1971	Volkswagen 1949-71
59	Sunbird	Cavalier, Skyhawk, Cimarron, 2000 1982-88	6845	Turismo	Omni/Horizon/Rampage 1978-88
63	Sundance	Chrysler Front Wheel Drive 1981-88	5905	T-37	Tempest/GTO/LeMans 1968-73
43	Supra	Toyota Celica/Supra 1971-87	6836	T-1000	Chevette/T-1000 1976-88
58	Supra	Toyota Celica/Supra 1986-90	6935	Vega	GM Subcompact 1971-80
37	Super Beetle	Volkswagen 1970-81	7346	Ventura	Pontiac Mid-Size 1974-83
99	SX-4	AMC 1975-86	6696	Versailles	Ford/Mercury/Lincoln Mid-Size 1971-85
83	S-10 Blazer	Chevy S-10 Blazer/GMC S-15 Jimmy 1982-87	6552	VIP	Plymouth 1968-76
10	S-10 Pick-Up	Chevy S-10/GMC S-15 Pick-Ups 1982-87	7037	Vista	Colt/Challenger/Vista/Conquest 1971-88
83	S-15 Jimmy	Chevy S-10 Blazer/GMC S-15 Jimmy 1982-87	6933	Vista Cruiser	Cutlass 1970-87
10	S-15 Pick-Up	Chevy S-10/GMC S-15 Pick-Ups 1982-87	6637	Volare	Aspen/Volare 1976-80
30	Taurus	Taurus/Sable/Continental 1986-89	7482	Voyager	Dodge Caravan/Plymouth Voyager 1984-88
45	TC-3	Omni/Horizon/Rampage 1978-88	6326	V-100	Valiant/Duster 1968-76
05	Tempest	Tempest/GTO/LeMans 1968-73	6739	Wagoneer 1962-83	Jeep Wagoneer, Commando, Cherokee, Truck 1957-86
55	Tempo	Ford/Mercury Front Wheel Drive 1981-87	7939	Wagoneer 1984-89	Jeep Wagoneer, Comanche, Cherokee 1984-89
36	Tercel	Toyota Corolla/Carina/Tercel/Starlet 1970-87	8034	Wrangler	Jeep 1971-90
81	Thing	Volkswagen 1970-81	7459	W100, 150, 200, 250, 300, 350	Dodge/Plymouth Trucks 1967-88
96	Thunderbird	Ford/Mercury/Lincoln Mid-Size 1971-85	7459	WM300	Dodge/Plymouth Trucks 1967-88
14	Thunderbird	Thunderbird, Cougar, Continental 1980-87	6842	XL	Ford/Mercury/Lincoln 1968-88
55	Topaz	Ford/Mercury Front Wheel Drive 1981-87	6963	XR4Ti	Mustang/Capri/Merkur 1979-88
20	Torino	Fairlane/Torino 1962-75	6696	XR-7	Ford/Mercury/Lincoln Mid-Size 1971-85
96	Torino	Ford/Mercury/Lincoln Mid-Size 1971-85	6982	XT Coupe	Subaru 1970-88
63	Town & Country	Chrysler Front Wheel Drive 1981-88	7042	X1/9	Fiat 1969-81
42	Town Car	Ford/Mercury/Lincoln 1968-88	6965	Zephyr	Fairmont/Zephyr 1978-83
35	Townsman	Chevrolet 1968-88	7059	Z-24	Cavalier, Skyhawk, Cimarron, 2000 1982-88
95	Toyota Pickups	Toyota 1966-70	6735	Z-28	Camaro 1967-81
35	Toyota Pickups	Toyota Trucks 1970-88	7318	Z-28	Camaro 1982-88
04	Toyota Van	Toyota Corona/Crown/Cressida/Mk.II/Van 1970-87	6845	024	Omni/Horizon/Rampage 1978-88
59	Trail Duster	Dodge/Plymouth Trucks 1967-88	6844	3.0S, 3.0Si, 3.0CS	BMW 1970-88
46	Trans Am	Firebird 1967-81	6817	4-63	Jeep 1981-87
45	Trans Am	Firebird 1982-90			
83	Tredia	Mitsubishi 1983-89			

CHILTON'S REPAIR MANUAL MODEL INDEX
Car and truck model names are listed in alphabetical and numerical order

Part No.	Model	Repair Manual Title	Part No.	Model	Repair Manual Title
6844	1500	DMW 1970-88	6844	2000	BMW 1970-88
6936	1500	Chevy/GMC Pick-Ups & Suburban 1970-87	6844	2002, 2002Ti, 2002Tii	BMW 1970-88
8055	1500	Chevy/GMC Pick-Ups & Suburban 1988-90	6936	2500	Chevy/GMC Pick-Ups & Suburban 1970-87
6844	1600	BMW 1970-88	8055	2500	Chevy/GMC Pick-Ups & Suburban 1988-90
5790	1600	Datsun 1961-72			
6982	1600DL, 1600GL, 1600GLF	Subaru 1970-88	6844	2500	BMW 1970-88
6844	1600-2	BMW 1970-88	6844	2800	BMW 1970-88
6844	1800	BMW 1970-88	6936	3500	Chevy/GMC Pick-Ups & Suburban 1970-87
6982	1800DL, 1800GL, 1800GLF	Subaru 1970-88	8055	3500	Chevy/GMC Pick-Ups & Suburban 1988-90
6529	1800, 1800S	Volvo 1956-69	7028	4000	Audi 4000/5000 1978-81
7040	1800E, 1800ES	Volvo 1970-88	7028	5000	Audi 4000/5000 1978-81
5790	2000	Datsun 1961-72	7309	6000	Celebrity, Century, Ciera, 6000 1982-88
7059	2000	Cavalier, Skyhawk, Cimarron, 2000 1982-88			

Chilton's Repair Manuals are available at your local retailer or by mailing a check or money order for **$15.95** per book plus **$3.50** for 1st book and **$.50** for each additional book to cover postage and handling to:

Chilton Book Company
Dept. DM
Radnor, PA 19089

NOTE: When ordering be sure to include your name & address, book part No. & title.